HE MADE IT SAFE TO MURDER

THE LIFE OF MOMAN PRUIETT

HOWARD K. BERRY

HE MADE IT SAFE to murder

BY HOWARD K. BERRY

RESEARCH EDITOR: RICHARD E. JONES

OKLAHOMA HERITAGE ASSOCIATION

OKLAHOMA CITY

OKLAHOMA TRACKMAKER SERIES

Printed in the United States of America

ISBN 1-885596-19-7

LC Number 2001089959

Designed by Carol Haralson

OKLAHOMA HERITAGE ASSOCIATION
201 NORTHWEST FOURTEENTH STREET
OKLAHOMA CITY, OKLAHOMA 73103

B
PRUIETT,
MOMAN

THE
LIFE OF
MOMAN
PRUIETT

THIS BOOK IS DEDICATED

To the memory of my mother,
Elsie Ellen (Tratchel) Berry;

To the memory of my wife,
Virginia (Gochenour) Berry,
who worked overtime raising our small
children while I was writing this book; and,

In respect for the wishes of my friend and
colleague, Moman Pruiett, I further dedicate
this book to his memory of his mother,
Elizabeth Louise "Betty"
Laws-Moorman-Pruiett.

CONTENTS

Please be not hasty in judging my story. Profane...? Coarse...? Vulgar...? Those are harsh words to apply to an account which contains nothing save proof-supplied reproductions of fact. Harsh words—yes—but indispensable in the language of a Nation which was born and lived, and thrived and grew, on the efforts of men who were necessarily rough and coarse and profane.

There is mud in the mortar which holds the stones of the temple together. Washington held slaves, and as unabridged history teaches us, he treated and used them as slaves. Brutality was a necessary ingredient in the make-up of the great men of our early periods—else they would not have been able to survive and be great. American development was a series of brutal periods and the history best describing it is written in a frank and brutal manner. Was Jackson in Louisiana, or Florida, renowned for his gentility? Was Grant's victory at Vicksburg bloodless? Was Lincoln's imperious resistance against secession without brutality? Can true accounts of these events be given without the utility of coarse, harsh words and phrases?

There came a time in the growth of our country—its voice had changed, fuzz was sprouting on its lip and it was leaving a turbulent adolescence behind—when its ambitious populace was gripped with fortune frenzy. It was not so young, then, that its potential wealth and power was an uncertain quantity. Astor had founded an unbelievable fortune—and had obtained the power that went with it—on raw furs. The Vanderbilts had launched their steamships at the right time, and expanding commerce had laid an enormous fortune—with its power—in their wool-draped laps. The big railroad fortunes were built. The new fields—the virgin fields for exploitation were running out. The furs were gone. The Atlantic was connected with the Pacific by bands of steel, and the early-grabbers had the commerce at the seaports in a safe monopoly.

"Where are we going now for our wealth?" the fortune-hungry populace demanded. "We have idled with plenty about us, and seen our wiser brethren gather up that which we want and need, and now the resources are gone. Where shall we go? Whither shall we turn? What shall we do?"

Industrial expansion in the east was doubling the values of real estate each day and night. There would be no limit to the ultimate value of Astor real estate in New York. Immense fortunes were growing in the Ohio valley and on the Great Lakes, merely from holding land and letting western expansion catapult its values. That was the answer. Land! Get land and hold it. The national boom of the land of the free and the home of the brave would do the rest. Grab land before it's too late. Where is it? Get it and hold it.

The fortune conscious population of the period turned its eyes toward the hitherto inexhaustible source of cheap land—the buffeted, booze-besotted American Indian. The remnants of what had once been proud races were huddled, under government supervision, in nature's last garden outpost east of the great American Desert. The Five Civilized Tribes had their Indian Nations, and they went through the motions of governing themselves while white speculators, nestors or intermarried citizens, winked and grinned and made sharp bargains with them.

The vast alluvial plain, drained by the Neosho, the Grand, the Verdigris, the Arkansas, the Illinois, the Cimarron, the North Canadian and the South Canadian, the Washita, and the various forks of the Red, was divided into two territories. The northernmost was Oklahoma Territory, south of it, bounded by Red River and big Texas, was the Indian Territory. The soil of the territories was rich. The climate was temperate and natural resources were abundant. There were limitless acres of land to be had—not for the asking—but for the fighting and taking. You couldn't get it without strength. You couldn't hold it without strength.

So, the fortune conscious army converged upon the Territories. They saw that settlement and expansion would bring statehood. They knew that values would increase with the expansion, as it had on the Atlantic, and as it had on the shores of the Great Lakes and down through the valleys of the Ohio and the Missouri. They were late fortune seekers. They hungered for wealth and they lamented the loss of opportunity which they had let slip from their grasp in the developed sections from whence they came. They were rough, and strong and determined. They were hardy, and coarse and profane.

Weaklings could not survive. Strong men fell while they vulgarly displayed their prodigious strength. There were no new fields to invade if they failed here. It was the last frontier. Realization of the fact contributed to the air of vicious determination—desperation—which influenced the conduct of men who strove for fortune and greatness while their shoulder blades were pressed close against the rock wall.

So if the content hereof seems coarse and cruel, please recall that being true, it is necessarily so, and that there is no other way for coarse, cruel fact to be presented.

Moman Pruiett strode into the midst of the fortune frenzy with a chip on both shoulders and an unconcealed contempt for law and order. He was essentially radical, being fresh from the shanty of the grumbling under-privileged. The wrath of the law had visited itself upon him, he resented it, and he was never inclined to forgive or forget. His courage was the kind that made him ill at ease when out of trouble and danger. He sought difficulties, he shouldered his way into battles already lost, because he loved to fight.

The lightning of genius had singed the top-most branches of his family tree. With his profound mind and memory, with his powerful eloquence, and with his utter lack of fear, he wrote his own chapter into the history of the last frontier. There was not another before—nor shall there be another to come—like Moman Pruiett. He came at the time of shaping municipal development when there was a place for him and his peculiar kind of genius. In the generation before, there was not enough of law on the frontier to permit his development and growth, in the generation afterward, there was too much of advance, and of refinement, to allow it.

He was a lawyer who would heed no law. What was right and wrong was the rule for measuring the conduct of others—but not Pruiett. His was to do as he damned well pleased. When he saw the rough veneer of the territorial government scaling from the structure which supported him at the top, he was wise enough to know that he had to work up with the government, which was supplanting it, or fall with it into decay. He tossed off his rough exterior and wrapped a new one—slick and smooth to outward observation—about the callous core of his true being. The hard center, breaking through the fictitious outside refinement in times of stress, made Pruiett the dread of every enforcement officer and prosecutor in the West and Southwest. The rough territory became a rich State, cross-road hamlets became great cities. Their phenomenal development was the result of the contentious nature of their fortune-hungry, ambitious inhabitants. Pruiett paced along. He was the rough territorial lawyer; he became the polished, urbane barrister.

This new world has produced some notable lawyers—lawyers whose achievements we recall as great and worthy of note. The questions involved in their trials are now settled and moot. Their eloquent voices have been silenced by the blanket of stillness which spreads from the gloom of the caverns of time. The records of their accomplishments are webbed and crumbling with age. What made them great? What made them and their exploits noteworthy? What counts with posterity? Not so much the way they tried their cases, as it was the ultimate outcome which they obtained. Victory! That is the answer—Victory!

Pruiett defended more murderers in murder cases than any other lawyer to cry into a jury's ear since the settlement of the Americas. Time and territory is being included in that declaration, yet conscientious research justifies it. He vouched for persons charged with fiendish crimes when the evidence of their guilt was overwhelming, yet never did one of his clients go to death on the order of law or law enforcement. Clients to be convicted, on compromise verdicts and sentences, which were flagrantly apologetic and slight in comparison to the crimes, were astonishingly numerous. Those to be turned free—to walk smilingly into liberty from the very shadow of death, made up a sizable, though none too loyal and appreciative, army.

The story of his means, his conduct and his methods, go to make up a material section of that great crazy-quilt which we call Americana. The liberties of our form of government permit the development of rare personalities—we call them freaks, sometimes—who form as important a part of our national identity as do the true greats of song and poetry and politics. Truth is stranger than fiction, as the hackneyed phrase constantly reminds us. Your credibility stands to be tested by this account—taken chiefly from preserved public records and documents—of what a humble butcher's boy, without funds or friends but with a stout heart and brilliant mind, accomplished for himself in the short span of a lifetime.

HOWARD K. BERRY, SR.
1940

Moman Pruiett, ca. 1920 Courtesy *The Daily Oklahoman*

FOREWORD

Judge Roy Bean, the creature of popular myth about the lawlessness of the Wild American West, is said to have claimed, "I know the Law... for I have spent the majority of my life in its vast disregard." Moman Pruiett was anything but mythical, and both his disregard for the law and his success in the practice of it stand unparalleled in American history: Three hundred forty-three murder trials, three hundred three acquittals, and the only client to face execution spared by presidential clemency. I know of no lawyer in fact or fiction that can equal Pruiett's record—not Clarence Darrow or Daniel Webster, not F. Lee Bailey or Gerry Spence, not even Perry Mason or Tony Lord. This record will never be repeated. It can only be hoped that the methods he used to obtain these results, some fully told in this edition for the first time, will also never be repeated.

Sixty years ago Pruiett published, with the factual "modifications" that characterized his career, *Moman Pruiett: Criminal Lawyer*, a highly expurgated version of Howard K. Berry, Sr.'s original Pruiett biography. While it may be true that no man is a hero to his valet, biographical valets often come to admire their subject and occasionally varnish the scratches. But young Berry's original unadmiring but frank work, entitled *He Made It Safe to Murder*, was not just varnished by Pruiett's piracy—it was decoupaged.

Yet even in its Pruiettized plastic form, *Moman Pruiett: Criminal Lawyer* became a collector's classic—a must-have for those colorful individuals known as trial lawyers, always looking for new techniques—and a handbook for historians and readers of Western Americana. It made clear the fact that the West was wilder for longer than often thought. The book was first distributed by the increasingly inebriated Pruiett to judges and lawyers who felt sorry for the decaying Demosthenes. But its potentially libelous stories about the remarkable crooks and characters of Oklahoma's often sordid early history gave it added appeal—in today's terms, it was perhaps something like a combination of Zane Grey, Stephen King, Gore Vidal, and *The National Inquirer*.

Besides, people seemed to be into violent entertainment in those days, too, and Pruiett was just as liable to punctuate a point with a bullet as an epigram. As one late contemporary, Albert McRill, wrote in his exposé, *And Satan Came Also,* "They hit the floor when Moman reached for his hip," and some of the people that dived either to hide or avoid the ricochets of shots fired on their behalf included: Temple Houston, the son of the Founder of Texas and no mean lawyer and marksman himself; Senator Thomas Pryor Gore, Oklahoma's legendary blind United States Senator, whom Pruiett defended in an early sexual harassment case that had national implications (See Chapter 14); Governor Alfalfa Bill Murray, whom Pruiett challenged to a duel in order to achieve "the last expiring hiss of a bruised and dying serpent"; and Governor Charles Haskell, Oklahoma's "corruptible" first Governor, who described Pruiett as "an ex-convict and a moral and mental pervert."

This book is both a republication and a correction of *Moman Pruiett: Criminal Lawyer,* which Pruiett acquired from Berry, altered, and had a local press publish. The original blue-covered tome is all but impossible to acquire, bringing prices of $300 to $1000, depending upon the condition and previous owners. In addition to being chock-full of the incredible controversy that was Pruiett's life and Oklahoma's history, the book itself was a matter of controversy, finally requiring the Oklahoma State Supreme Court to decide that the true author should be able to recover control of his altered manuscript. This edition tells even more than Pruiett's pirated one. It is more of a "warts and all" story of this man, whom Dr. J. G. Hervey, Dean of the School of Law, described as "the most resourceful criminal lawyer ever to rise out of the Southwest," and perhaps the most successful criminal lawyer in history. How the original book came into existence is not so widely known....

In 1934, young Howard K. Berry, Sr., began a new career. His background in journalism at the University of Missouri, and his early job as a "beat patrolman" with the Oklahoma City Police Department, certainly helped prepare him for his career as an attorney. Associating himself with the O. A. Cargill lawfirm, Berry began a career that would culminate with his being recognized as one of the finest and most ethical lawyers Oklahoma would ever produce. Cargill would later come under considerable ethical attack, but in those days, he attracted capable talent such as Berry. And Berry's law firm in later years would likewise attract exceptional personalities: the young Alma Wilson, later Oklahoma's first female Supreme Court Justice, and Charles Nesbitt, later Corporation Commissioner and Attorney General.

But in the early years, Berry had to acquire a reputation. He was sent by his firm to Madill, in southern Oklahoma, to represent clients involved in an estate dispute. Evidently, the old farmer, who had died, had acquired land with lots of oil. He had also acquired three or four wives along the way without the bothersome task of obtaining a divorce from any of them, resulting in fifteen or twenty children with varying legal status and claims to the estate. Dying without a will, he created a legal gusher. Recently, Berry told me, "I don't know—that case may still be going on."

Moman Pruiett, then past his prime and well into the cups, heard about the young lawyer from the Cargill firm who was going to Madill and called to see if he could hitch a ride. Berry grew up in Oklahoma City and thus knew a lot about Pruiett—who couldn't know about "the Black Stud of the Washita" from reading the papers that frequently featured his courtroom accomplishments and antics? Partly out of curiosity, partly out of professional courtesy, Berry agreed to drive the old barrister. On that trip, and several others later, Pruiett began recalling tales of his life and indicated that he had some contact with the *Saturday Evening Post,* which wanted to serialize some of his story.

The *Post,* and Doubleday (which Pruiett also said was interested in his biography) probably weren't that interested, but Berry was. These stories were sensational—"everything was sensational with Pruiett"—and some of them were even true. Thus began a labor not of love but of curiosity, and Berry spent hundreds of hours comparing Pruiett's recollections with the fossil record—old newspapers, court records, and interviews. Working evenings and nights, often from a rented hotel room where his research was kept, Berry's labor was remarkable. While holding, indeed prospering in, his day job, he dedicated all the hours he could away from work to compiling the story that follows this introduction. He wrote the manuscript in long hand, and his younger brother, James W. Bill Berry, recently schooled in high-school typing, typed it.

When the manuscript first went to the publisher, Thomas B. Costain of Doubleday, Doran and Company of New York, in July of 1940, Costain advised Berry that they couldn't print it in its presently submitted form because "there is too much dynamite in it—the probability of libel suits. When a man is pronounced 'not guilty' by a jury, he becomes innocent of the crime in the eyes of the law. In most of these cases, you have treated the prisoners as though they were guilty of murder in the full legal sense, and as though only jury-swaying eloquence or trickery could have brought them through. We feel it would be necessary to take a quite different approach on nearly all the cases, letting the facts speak for themselves and not convicting the defendants in a sort of ethical post-trial."

Berry attempted to alleviate some of the publisher's concerns about being sued. He wrote to Costain saying, "With reference to the dynamite, which identical term I had often employed myself in referring to this story, I wish to remind you that causes of action based upon libel and slander abate with the death of the party aggrieved, in most jurisdictions, and that the right to protest in most of the Pruiett episodes have [sic] long since been buried. In a majority of [the] instances [mentioned in the book], the actual homicide was established, or at least never denied by the accused. Pruiett usually admitted the misconduct of his client, but managed to clothe it with some technical justification which enabled him to procure their acquittal." Costain suggested changing the names. "A real story makes a good plot for a novel," Berry laughingly told me. "The names would be changed to protect the guilty."

But when Pruiett discovered that the manuscript, which he hadn't had the opportunity to read, told more of the truth about him than he wanted the public to know, he began to run interference. He wrote to Costain, imploring him "not to enter into any contract for purchasing or publishing of the manuscript without his personal signature." Eventually, his confusing efforts helped to deep six the project. In September of the following year, Pruiett asked Berry for the manuscript to see if he could get some action going on the project. Berry allowed Pruiett to take his (Berry's) manuscript with the following caveat. "I have explicit confidence in your integrity and ability where our contract is concerned; and, I am glad to give you this letter granting you full and unrestricted authority to make any kind of an assignment, obligation or sale you care to. I would indeed be glad to have the copy placed in the hands of a competent re-write man, and to see the story, which is a great one in text if not in execution, placed in print."

Pruiett, with the assistance of a wholly incompetent, self-styled editor from Springfield, Illinois, greatly revised the text, keeping his favorite hero in mind, and unevenly removing passages from it, while cleverly keeping much of the organization. Pruiett switched several chapters and added a chapter towards the end that merely consisted of some of his early-day "law and order" speeches to various civic groups. And in a final attempt to completely disguise this work from Berry's original manuscript, he discarded the twenty or thirty pages of "Notes and Sources"—references that Berry had accumulated to document this rather bizarre and unbelievable story. "Its sole effect was to necessitate Berry's reconstruction of mutilated parts of the manuscript after much trouble in securing its return. Berry was called to the Army in March 1944. Thereafter on June 21, 1944, Pruiett made a contract with the Harlow Publishing Company of Oklahoma City for publication of a number of copies of the book" patterned from a pirated copy of the "mutilated" manuscript.

Now, sixty years later, and after the Oklahoma State Supreme Court has ruled in Case No. 33200, *Preston v. Berry* (234 P.2d 417), that Berry is the true author and owner of the manuscript and book, the correct, original version has at last been published.

As I discussed this matter recently with the author, I thought of some further ironies in this story. In Berry we have one of the most highly respected lawyers in this state's history. The Patriarch of a distinguished family of barristers, he was selected by the Supreme Court to be the very first prosecutor of the Oklahoma Court on the Judiciary—the court that prosecutes cases against judges charged with violating their offices. He served on the Judicial Nominating Commission and received Distinguished Service Awards from the Oklahoma Bar Association and the *Journal Record.* He is a Fellow in the American College of Trial Lawyers, the most distinguished organization of trial attorneys in the world. The honors and commendations go on and on.

What was it that caused Berry, a paragon of principle, to write about one of the most unprincipled advocates to ever take to the bar? How could this distinguished "lawyer's lawyer," a man whom the Bar and the Supreme Court would choose to represent themselves, take it upon himself to write about Pruiett, a man who would create and destroy evidence, suborn perjury, scream at a jury, pull a gun on jurors, lie down on the floor and play dead, and prosecute the prosecutor with anti-Semitic tirades?

Berry told me some of the reasons: "It's kind of comical. Initially, I didn't know what I was getting into—didn't know what kind of a man I was going to be in the middle of. . . .You could learn from experiences like Moman Pruiett's. I was compensated in education, exposure to tricks of the game, but not in dollars and cents. You could learn a lot about practical law—indirectly, I learned how to cross-examine a witness correctly from buying beers for ol' Moman. His closing arguments were often masterpieces. But I also learned things not to do if you're going to build up a clientele. I would never contemplate doing many of the things Moman regularly did."

"It seems to me that there was a fatalism to Moman Pruiett. He was drawn to his own demise. You can get a lot more done for people in the law by means other than being drunk and getting rude. His was a wasted talent."

I don't think I would have liked Pruiett. I marvel at his record; I admire his rhetorical skill; I rejoice in some of the mercy if not justice he achieved. But Pruiett certainly abused his skills as well. He fought duels, beat up on decent witnesses, pushed the envelope, managed to get disbarred in his later years by the Oklahoma Supreme Court, which later reduced the penalty upon appeal to a one-year suspension from the practice of law. This story is not Rumpole for the defense; it is not the tale of one who believes in a good system and makes it work. It is largely one of an abuser of the law, who also abused his uncommon gift.

Indeed, everything about Pruiett was controversial. Perhaps the fact that he was himself a felon—a person who would not be allowed to practice law today—led to his desire to defend the down-and-out crowd. Perhaps his own gunfights caused him to defend other gunslingers. Maybe his own inability to avoid fisticuffs gave him the natural inclination to defend other pugilists. Possibly, his own alcoholism caused him to sympathize with others who likewise suffered with problems of addiction. Maybe in Pruiett's case it did "take one to know one."

But this remarkable tale is more than just Pruiett's story. It is also a story of the rough and tumble frontier that bred men like Pruiett, that indeed, as the book argues, probably required men like Pruiett. Had Pruiett lived thirty years earlier, there would not have been enough law to have lawyers; had he lived thirty years later, there would have been too much law to have his kind of lawyer. This is a story that every student of the frontier, every student of Oklahoma history, and every trial attorney could learn from. It is also a story of interest to those who reflect on human nature and hope for a way to improve its shortcomings. Perhaps most tragically, it is a story of the abject squandering of great raw talent—a talent that surrendered to bigotry, charlatanism, jealousy, and alcohol. It is a story of how the law can be bent to sordid purposes even as it struggles and strives to civilize a new state.

JUDGE ROBERT HENRY
2001

EDITOR'S NOTE— The following is the original manuscript of Moman Pruiett's biography as written by Howard K. Berry, Sr., in 1939-1940. Only grammatical errors have been corrected and names and other clarifications have been added to the original manuscript to aid the reader in the identification of people and locations and to correct government titles and positions. The reader should bear in mind that literature reflects the mores of the era in which it is written. This manuscript was prepared three-quarters of a century ago when language and use of derogatory terms that are unacceptable today were common. Pruiett often took unpopular cases and was known for defending minorities in what was then an all-white court system. It was Pruiett who defended Will Robinson, a black man accused of starting the Tulsa race riot of 1921. Roscoe Dunjee, the state's premier civil rights spokesman of the era, praised Pruiett for his defense of penniless blacks and other minorities.

HOWARD K. BERRY, SR., CA. 1945, AUTHOR OF *HE MADE IT SAFE TO MURDER.*
COURTESY RICHARD JONES.

ACKNOWLEDGMENTS

First and foremost, a tip of the hat to Moman Pruiett, whose life spawned this story and whose willingness to open up his life to me provided the material for it. Next, I acknowledge the efforts of my younger siblings, James W. "Bill" Berry and Dorothy (Berry) Drane, who assisted the typing process, leaving to me the creative part of the effort. Then, I'd like to acknowledge the efforts of the attorneys who assisted me in getting this property judicially declared to be of my authorship by the Oklahoma Supreme Court.

I would like to acknowledge my grandson, Howard K. Berry III, and Richard Jones of Oklahoma City, who shepherded the manuscript from its 1940s status into New Millennium form, aided by a wonderful group of researchers.

Thanks to the Oklahoma Historical Society and its staff, including Scott Dowell, Delbert Amen, Chester Cowen, Fred "Butch" Standley, Nancy Laub, Laura Martin, Jean Miller, Bryan Bashore, the late Mary Moran, the late Linda Fanslau, Francie Helm, Mary Logsdon. The Western History Collection and the Carl Albert Center at the University of Oklahoma, the Pauls Valley Historical Society, and Linda Lynn, Mary Phillips, Melissa Hayer, Robin Davison, and Billie Harry at *The Daily Oklahoman* were instrumental in locating photographs.

I also want to thank Hugh and Shannon Smith, Sue Hodges, Candice Blaylock, Dan Sprouse, Caroline Hanneman, Adrienne Grimmett, Joann Schnorrenberg, Louise A. Deaton, Dale Talkington, Ron Owens, Ken Butler, Diana Jones, and Frank Parman for their contributions.

Finally, I would like to thank the Oklahoma Heritage Association and its Chairman of the Board Lee Allan Smith, President Paul F. Lambert, Director of Education Kenny A. Franks, and Managing Editor Gini Moore Campbell for taking on the project and adding it to the popular Oklahoma Trackmaker Series.

HOWARD K. BERRY, SR.
2001

After his client Charlie Bias, a black man charged with murder, was convicted in 1899 Pruiett was determined to obtain a presidential commutation so Bias could cheat the gallows. Declaring that if he ever lost a client to the hangman, he would never try another murder case, Pruiett mortgaged all that he owned to finance the trip and hurried to Washington, D. C., to plead his case before President William McKinley. Courtesy Hugh and Shannon SMith.

CHAPTER ONE

Wherein a country lawyer goes to Washington, and meets, under circumstances vastly dissimilar, a man who had known and befriended him in a day not so prodigal. And how he offends the Attorney General of the United States, but captures the fancy and good will of the Senators—the President—by his quick wit, his sharp tongue and bluff manner, to make himself the savior of a convict condemned to die and the subject of some flattering comment in the Capitol press.

Charles Allen Culberson of Texas and Albert Jeremiah Beveridge of Indiana lounged in the Senate offices of the latter. Their short conversation had dealt with such ponderous topics as the prospect for prosperity in Nineteen Hundred, the Century whose recent beginning was revealed across the face of a brass-plated calendar pad on the senator's desk, and how long the steady fall of snow, as discernible through the slightly sooty windows, might continue. Senator Culberson's original intention of a brief visit, evidenced by his failure to have removed his long black coat, was further indicated by a slow ascension from the deep chair he had been occupying, and a cautious sidewise movement toward the corridor exit.

"I promised Silas Hare I'd meet him in the Court for opening," he said. "I want to be there when he moves the admission of one of my former—er—constituents, a young lawyer from the Indian Territory. He used to live in Texas."

Culberson was gazing beyond the one he addressed and out into the cloud of falling white. He was reminiscing—and on a subject not unpleasant—as he pondered for a moment in the selection of words to employ.

"We've got too many lawyers in this country, already," Beveridge replied. "Where's the business coming from to keep 'em going? I had a letter today from some law school in Kansas City, where they want me to speak at their graduation exercises. At the rate they are being turned out we'll have such a damned surplus soon. . . . "

Culberson laughed as he interrupted. "I'd like to have your formula for gettin' expense-paid commencement invitations," he said. "It's the best graft in Washington. But, if you've got time before the train, I'd like for you to meet this youngster. He even claims a branch connection with Indiana—besides Kentucky and Texas. Unless I'm badly mistaken, you'll agree that the business won't be overcrowded with his kind."

Beveridge refilled the two short glasses on the corner of the desk, corked the bottle, and locked it in a desk drawer.

"All right," he replied. "I was goin' out anyway. I'll drop in with you and see what you and Hare can produce from this place you call Texas and bring it to Washington without even offering an apology."

Court was opening and the justices were filing to their places as the two senators entered the Supreme Court chambers. Taking seats they waited, hats in hand, until that item of business was called which excited the idle curiosity of one, but a strange, half-mournful and half-pleasant glance into retrospection, for the other.

Silas Hare, former member of Congress from the Lone Star State—and who had relinquished his seat there only after a close contest to the inimitable Joseph Weldon Bailey—was addressing the court. Hare, a lawyer, maintained offices in the National Capitol.

"With your Honors' pleasure," he said as soon as Motions for Admissions were allowed, "I move the admission of Mr. Moman Pruiett, licensed attorney of Texas and the Indian Territory—now residing in the territory—to practice before the Supreme Court."

After the routine observation and inquiry, Chief Justice Edward D. White directed the clerk to administer the oath. When the young man who had been sitting quietly behind Hare arose and took the oath, the senator from Texas nudged his Indiana colleague.

"That's the one," he said in a hoarse whisper. A stronger emotion than the one prompted in professional pride was evident in his tone and expression.

The object of his attention and concern was a young man of not more than 27 or 28 years, and obviously from that rapidly vanishing sector called the frontier. His suit was neat and well pressed, but of a cut that suggested an origin different from that of the Washington, D.C., tailored array of Hare. He was of but average height. Heavy square shoulders and a robust brown neck lent him the appearance of physical strength and endurance, while the color of his hands and face, as brown and leathery as his neck, marked him at once as a man more than casually acquainted with the outdoors.

An amazing crop of coal-black hair extended backward and about his close-set ears to a point immediately above his coat collar. There, by the ingenuity of a territorial barber, it ended abruptly and proceeded neckward in a solid wall of the severed ends of black wire strands. The bulk, the glow and the faultless array of the remarkable growth was matched by black brows, unnaturally shaggy and prominent. The coarse bronze texture of the skin over the countenance underneath caused the head to appear to be much too large for the body, and to give it an aura of animal-like power and strength.

Beveridge and Culberson waited in the hall for Hare and his companion. Pruiett was aware of Culberson's presence, and he was looking about for him as he came out. He proceeded directly to the senator and connected with a powerful handclasp. Then they stood apart—without speaking—gazing intently into each other's faces. The gentleman from Indiana was not certain, on subsequent reflection, whether it was a tear he saw on Culberson's cheek as he brushed it with the back of his hand, or but a trick of his own imagination, as produced by the uncanny tenseness of the atmosphere.

"Beveridge," the taller and older of the two said, "this is Moorman Pruiett, whom I first knew in Texas. I have quite an interest in his future—and his success. I guess I don't need to tell you again that I'm very proud of him."

"I have long anticipated the pleasure of your acquaintance, Senator Beveridge," Pruiett responded, in a deep, well-modulated voice. The oratorical flourish, of both the language and delivery, was not forced or out of place, "to have made it through Senator Culberson is doubly agreeable."

Culberson interrupted, but the interruption was not made to place the younger man at his ease. That indefinable quality of charm and personality radiated from the young lawyer as spontaneously as the gleam of the corridor lights reflected from the shiny blackness of his hair. As an office associate was to say of him later, "there was that something about him—he could get a total stranger to do more for him, than I could get my best friend to do for me."

"If you remember, Bailey was talking about the fellow who raised so much hell with Attorney General John W. Griggs?" Culberson was saying, "Well, this is the one..."

Beveridge whistled a surprised interruption. Then he laughed. "Young man," he said, "It's bad business to offend Griggs, even when

TEXAS GOVERNOR, AND LATER UNITED STATES SENATOR CHARLES A. CULBERSON, PAROLED MOORMAN PRUIETT FROM THE TEXAS STATE PRISON AT RUSK, TEXAS, IN 1895. THREE YEARS PREVIOUSLY PRUIETT HAD BEEN CONVICTED OF ROBBERY AND SENTENCED TO FIVE YEARS IN PRISON. CULBERSON'S BELIEF THAT PRUIETT HAD REFORMED WAS JUSTIFIED IN 1900 WHEN HE WITNESSED MOMAN PRUIETT TAKING THE OATH GRANTING HIM THE RIGHT TO PRACTICE BEFORE THE UNITED STATES SUPREME COURT. COURTESY WESTERN HISTORY COLLECTIONS, UNIVERSITY OF OKLAHOMA LIBRARIES.

you have no business with him. I'm surprised, after what Joe Bailey told me about that deal, that your motion for admission here wasn't refused. That Attorney General's as tough as hell—an' he'll even fix the Supreme Court on you if you don't watch him."

Pruiett exhibited his good taste and judgment by saying nothing—and smiling agreeably. The other members of the group were laughing. He didn't have to be told that his advisor was not inclined to censor him for the scrape he had had with Griggs, the cabinet member, a whispered report of which had been traveling about the Capitol. With Hare's approach to the group and a renewed exchange of greetings, Pruiett shook hands with the senators again, and departed. As he and Hare walked out of hearing down the hallway, Beveridge turned to Culberson.

"That's a fine boy," he said, warmly. "Nice appearance. Nice manners—an' smart as hell. Got regular senatorial polish an' culture. What school's he from—an' what's the story behind all the feelin' between you an' him? He's not some orphan kin-folks, who's struggled through college, or somethin' like that, is he?"

Culberson was silent for a moment. He held searching eyes full into those of the friend he knew he could trust.

"On your Indiana honor, Beveridge, don't repeat this," he said. "I shouldn't say it, and don't misunderstand me when I do, but this thing here this morning has torn me up, and by god, I got to tell somebody what I know. Six years ago, on June 18, 1895, while I was governor of Texas, I pardoned that kid from the state penitentiary at Rusk. He's had no schooling, an' I'll be damned if he hadn't served a term in Arkansas, before gettin' in trouble in Texas. He had three years left, out of a five year sentence, when I turned him over to his mother—an' she was one of the most persistent and devoted women I ever saw. That Pruiett is a genius—just a natural born genius. Maybe a little on the crooked side, understand, a little shifty, but he's got a head full of the damnedest brain I ever came in contact with, an' a belly plumb full of guts. No education, a'tall, but you just watch him. He's learned his lesson the hard way, an' he'll stay out of trouble from now on. You'll see him at the top—an' in damn short order."

The *Washington Post* made note of the more formal part of the proceeding in a casual item. "Hon. Bryan Houston, of New York, formerly of San Antonio and Wichita Falls, was here today for the purpose of extending to Representative Bailey an invitation to speak before the Harlem Democratic Club on the 17th of March. Mr. Bailey was compelled to decline the invitation for the reason that his engagements in Texas will begin long before that date. Mr. Bailey expects to spend nearly three months on the stump in Texas during the time of the holding of the Democratic primaries. Mr. Houston was admitted to practice before the Supreme Court yesterday, as was Norman [sic] Pruiett of Pauls Valley, I.T., formerly of Paris, Texas."

Pruiett's admission to practice before the Supreme Court was but incidental to his real business in Washington—as in the case of the Honorable Houston. Charlie Bias, a stoic negro, was in the Federal Prison at Ardmore, Indian Territory, sentenced to be hanged. The scaffold was built and the inhabitants of the countryside, white, black, and Indian alike, were straining the accommodations of the settlement's hotels and rooms as they came to town for the execution.

"People of the Indian Territory," announced the *Daily Ardmoreite,* "should not fail to be at Ardmore on the 19th [January, 1900], for there the great government of the United States, represented by [deputy United States Marshal John] Hammer, will provide a festival which will bring to the mind tender suggestions of ancient Israel and Rome. Take your children with you and wait with them, exposed to the elements, as the people of Jerusalem were wont to wait outside the gates for the coming of their victims. Of course, the sport will be less exciting than in the days of Moses, when everybody who could throw a stone was allowed to take part in the execution, or in Nero's time when the victims of the law were torn by wild beasts 'to make a Roman Holiday', or in the later days of our own Anglo-Saxon race, when ignorant negroes were artistically tortured to death by refined and civilized men."

Bias and a young African named Gus Wright differed over the respective rights of each to a community wench. They were freedmen descendants, a strain which began as half Indian–half negro, as the male Indian owner impregnated his female negro slave, but which rapidly graduated toward a black predominance as the half-caste get was taken up by the black slave associates. According to custom, the young bucks rode their poor ponies to the weedy flats of Wild Horse Creek to fight it out—fist and skull. Bias, a battered and bruised victor, had started to remount and ride away when Wright, with enough of the vengeful red-man's blood

Appointed in 1898 as United States Attorney for the Southern District of Indian Territory, William B. Johnson prosecuted and obtained a death sentence for Moman Pruiett's client, Charlie Bias, a sentence that was commuted to life in prison by President William McKinley. Courtesy *Chronicles of Oklahoma.*

Attorney Andrew Cavitt "A. C." Cruce, a prominent Ardmore attorney, was a friend and confidante to Moman Pruiett. Their friendship dated from Pruiett's arrival in Pauls Valley in 1897 and during the next two decades, Cruce and Pruiett often found themselves either sharing the defense table or as opposing counsel in murder trials. Cruce was the brother of future Oklahoma Governor Lee Cruce. Courtesy *Men of Affairs.*

under his black hide to make his lacing doubly distasteful, violated the rules by grabbing a knife and reopening the fracas. Bias killed him.

"I've always been an optimist, Bill, but I ain't got no idea I can clear Charlie Bias," Pruiett said. "An' I didn't ask that damned old carpetbagger court to appoint me to defend him. I'll plead him guilty an' take twenty-five years."

"I might consider life for the bastard if you want'a make a trade, but that's all," the prosecutor replied. It was William B. "Bill" Johnson, the government's hob-nailed vice-destroyer on the last frontier. Officially, he was District Attorney for the Southern District of the Indian Territory. "The evidence in this case is goin' to shock even the roughest element of this little old community. I ain't never heard of a murder so brutal, an' I heard about this one from the guy that done it. I got a full confession out of him, an' it's witnessed."

"That's my best talkin' point," Pruiett answered. "He's so utterly ignorant an' brutal that we shouldn't measure him by our law, that makes hangin' or life in the pen the punishment for murder. Charlie wouldn't kill a rabbit unless it hurt him first—but after he got started he'd just as soon kill a dozen men as one rabbit. He ain't mean—he's just ignorant. He won't never learn no better."

"I'll recommend life, but I don't think Judge Hosea Townsend'll let Charlie have it," Johnson persisted. "This is a' awful bad case."

Pruiett reflected. "I hate to do it—but I think I'd better," he said. "Tell Townsend that all the case I got's based on the nigger's savage ignorance. He's never been near a school—never seen a railroad train, an' the Santa Fe to Fort Worth runs sixteen miles from their shack. His folks are awful poor an' awful ignorant. Tell him we'll take life an' save the government the cost of tryin' him. That's all a jury will give him, anyway."

But the Bias case came on for trial before a jury. Hosea Townsend had refused to accept the guilty plea. Self-defense refused to fit the vicious conduct exhibited by the evidence, but Pruiett put the dull negro on the stand, and turned him over to Johnson for cross-examination.

"So you say he rushed up behind your back with this weepun in his hand?" Johnson bellowed, as he began.

"Uh-huh," Charlie replied. His languid gaze enveloped vista of green-budding cottonwoods through the open window.

"An' you took this chunk and knocked him down with it?"

"Uh-huh."

"He was layin' there at your feet, unconscious, was he?"

"Uh-huh."

"So you took his knife from his hand and stuck it into his heart, like this?" Johnson roared, as he flourished the death-knife through the air and brought it up sharply as though he had a body before him on the floor.

"Uh-huh."

"An' you took him by the hair, an' pulled his head this a-way, and cut his throat on this side?" "Uh-huh." "An' then you pulled his head over this a-way and cut his throat on the other side?" "Uh-huh." "Then you stabbed him in the right eye, did you?" he inquired. "Uh-huh." "An' then you stuck the knife in to the handle in his left eye?" "Uh-huh."

"You can stand aside." Johnson mopped the perspiration produced through the horror of his own device from his brow and head, as he walked slowly to his chair.

The government won the case. The jury convicted Bias and sentenced him to hang, but Pruiett hadn't been a pushover. No agency or individual, opposing Pruiett in a jury trial, had an instant's peace from the time the case was called until the last word was said and the courtroom as cleared. He charged Johnson with using the walls of the temple of justice for a canvas, and the blood of an underprivileged chattel for oils, while he painted a gory picture of hate and vengeance to obstruct the jurors' view of the right. He roared and tore, he emulated black Charlie, on Wild Horse, but it was wasted effort. The evidence was decidedly unfavorable—and he didn't have a single friend on the jury.

The condemned negro, a pauper, had the same kind of representation at South McAlester, where the Territorial Court of Criminal Appeals was in session. Pruiett duplicated, even embellished, the fierce forensics of the trial court, but the result was the same. He was drooped and dejected when he returned to the valley. Charlie's death sentence was affirmed; the date of the hanging was fixed.

Pruiett was telling his troubles to the Cruce brothers, Andrew Cavit or A. C. and Will, two attorneys at Ardmore. "I ain't goin' to let that nigger hang," he said, doggedly. "It's just like torturin' a cat, or dog.

He's just a plain animal—he don't know anything about civilized conduct—or the laws we got to regulate conduct."

"What you aim to do about it?" A. C. Cruce inquired.

"I don't know," Pruiett answered. "What have I got left to do?"

"Make yourself a little trip to Washington, an' talk Bill McKinley out of a reprieve, or a commutation of sentence," Will Cruce suggested, a trifle sarcastically. "It won't cost you much, an' he can't do no more than sic the White House dog on you. Be sure you have the cow-dung off your heel before they lead you in."

Pruiett reflected. "I'd like to go to Washington," he said. "How much would it cost?"

"It ain't what it costs to go that counts," Will Cruce said. "It's what it takes to get along while you're there, an' what it costs to check out. What them pauper niggers of yours could raise wouldn't get you to Wichita."

Pruiett continued to reflect. "Suppose you was goin' to Washington—to get a sentence commuted. What would you do the first thing?"

"Get me a lot of pull," A. C. answered. "A few senators—an' a few representatives, to put the pressure on. Big time politics ain't much different from backwoods politics. It's the pull and the fix that gets the results."

"Know any big guns up there?" Pruiett inquired, innocently.

The Cruces laughed in unison. "There's an old man up there from Kentucky—we're from Kentucky, you know—that's a senator and Bill McKinley's right hand man. Senator William Joseph DeBoe, they call him." A. C. Cruce was still laughing. "He was the doctor with my mother when I was born, an' when all the Cruce kids were born. We know him pretty well."

"Would he help a friend of yours, if you asked him to?"

"I ain't sure," Cruce replied, "but I think Old Doc would do anything on earth he could for us. If he won't help, I ain't got a friend in the world."

"I know a senator, too." Pruiett said.

"Which one do you know?" Will Cruce inquired.

"Culberson, from Texas," Pruiett answered.

The Cruce brows arched, with a suggestion of a little more respect. "I forgot you was from Texas," A. C. said. "Do you know him very well? Ever have any business with him?"

"Yeah—I had a little business with him," Pruiett said, slowly. "An' I believe he'd help me. I may call on him—but I don't guess it's any use to figure that far ahead. Bill Johnson told me he was conscientiously opposed to capital punishment, an' that if the Department of Justice asked for it, he'd tell them so, and agree that my application for commutation be allowed. I think he'll take care of ever'thing for me."

"Did Bill Johnson tell you that?" Will Cruce asked, showing his surprise. "Did he—really?"

"Hell, yes, he did." Pruiett showed his complacence with his answer.

"Let me tell you something," Will said earnestly. "He's offered to do that before—lots of times—but they keep wearin' out the ropes over at the hangin' pen. He wants you to rest on that written application to the department. When they write him, he turns it down, an' then it's too late to do anything else. They hang your nigger before you can catch a train out of town."

"You mean that?"

"Hell yes, I mean it. Ever'body around here knows it. You ought to, by this time."

"Write me a letter of introduction to DeBoe, will you?" Pruiett asked. "An' ask him to do his best for me with the President. I'm goin' to the valley, an' catch me a train to the capitol. I always wanted to go up there, anyway."

"Who's goin' to pay your expenses?"

"Old man Grant at the Pauls Valley bank," Pruiett laughed.

"You ain't goin' to borrow money an' make such an expensive trip—for a pauper nigger, are you, Pruiett?" A. C. Cruce inquired.

"I'm goin' to save that nigger's life, or I'll never try another lawsuit as long as I live," Pruiett said. "I didn't ask for this case—but I got it—an' I'm stayin' with it. That nigger is not goin' to swing."

Pruiett left the valley on the day after Christmas, 1899. He made the Oxford Hotel, at 14th Street and New York Avenue, his stopping place in Washington, and set out to get his work done.

"I got a letter from the Cruce brothers, in the Indian Territory, Senator," he grinned at the tall Kentuckian. "They said to tell you 'hello', an' to try to get you interested. Do you remember 'em?"

"I caught 'em," DeBoe said. "Ever' damn one of the Cruce kids, an' ever' damn one is a good one. Good stock—good timber. Waited on 'em while they was children, sick, an' watched 'em grow up. The Cruces were genuine Kentucky."

"My people was from Kentucky," Pruiett suggested, hopefully.

DeBoe was a man of some fifty years, with a tall brow that extended, uninterrupted, into an expanse of oily baldness. He stopped the conversation to read the letter from the Cruce boys.

"It says here," DeBoe observed, "that you're up here on your own expense; got a pauper client. How can you do that?"

"I can't," Pruiett answered with a doleful look. DeBoe laughed.

"Have you got your application filed with the Department of Justice?" he asked.

"I sent that in by mail," Pruiett said.

"John Griggs is a good friend of mine," DeBoe said. "He's the Attorney General. Do you want a personal hearin'?"

"I want ever'thing that it takes to get a nigger a reprieve," Pruiett answered. "The Attorney General, the Supreme Court, the President of the United States. Are you goin' to help me?"

DeBoe laughed again. "I ain't nothin' but a senator," he said. "But if you got the guts to make it up here at your own cost, son, I sure can't afford to turn you down. When do we go to see Griggs?"

"How about right now?"

"Maybe I ought to make an appointment," DeBoe said. "Let's make it tomorrow. Where are you stayin'?"

"At the Oxford. It's not so fancy, but...."

"It's a good place," DeBoe interrupted. "Senator George Gilmore Gilbert, from Kentucky, stays there. Get acquainted with him as soon as you can. An' old ex-senator John Edward Kenna from West Virginia lives there, too. Work on 'em. Make friends, 'cause I can see it's easy for you, an' you may need all the help on this thing you can get, before you're through."

DeBoe went for the Pruiett personality. "He got stuck on me," Pruiett explained it, later. The Kentucky Senator made him acquainted with the best people in Washington. He gave him a big send-off with the Attorney General, who promised to send for the records of the case and to give them a hearing. Pruiett told him that Bill Johnson would agree, if solicited, that the death penalty be commuted to life imprisonment. He thought of what the Cruces had told him, and wished that he hadn't said it, before the words were out of his mouth.

The delay connected with the production of the letters and records from the Washita was neither noted nor despaired of by Pruiett. DeBoe took him around; the Charlie Bias cause gained a few converts. There was Congressman John Levi Sheppard, of Texas, and his colleague, Texas Congressman Reese Calhoun DeGraffenreid. Pruiett tried to enlist Joe Bailey.

"The trouble is," Bailey declared, "you won't be able to get any one to believe you're up here at your own expense—that you ain't tryin' to make a fee out of it." It was obvious from his tone and manner that he doubted it himself.

When Pruiett reappeared before Griggs, accompanied by DeBoe, the hope and cheerfulness he had carried with him since DeBoe's welcome was chilled by a hostile face and manner. Without a greeting or an introductory declaration, Griggs lifted a paper from his desk and threw it across at Pruiett.

"I was sorry to find that you are not worthy of confidence," he said. "I admit I was favorably impressed by you—and the nature of your business—but I see now that you have deliberately mis-stated the facts, in an effort to deceive me."

Pruiett was pale, but without retort as he read the letter. It was from Bill Johnson. "Replying to your inquiry of Jan. 3rd," it said, "regarding Chas. S. Bias, awaiting execution here after murder conviction, I must advise that I have no recommendation to make. The trial disclosed the most atrocious murder recorded in territorial criminal history. The record is without apparent justification or extenuating circumstances of any kind. This is the one case, in my experience, which requires the infliction of the death penalty."

Johnson's treachery, and Grigg's abuse, were ringing in his head as he turned.

"If you mean to say I deliberately mis-state facts you're a god damned liar," he roared, as he hurled the letter into the face of the astonished Attorney General. Griggs had presumed that his official rank would insure him against such an outburst. "You're just a god damned liar, an' Bill Johnson's a god damned liar, an' the records of this case will prove it," Pruiett howled. "Show me the record—let me show you the record. Show me some facts, not a letter from a god damned lyin' hypocrite..."

"Get out of here," Griggs shouted, keeping the desk between himself and Pruiett. "Get out—an' don't let me see you in my office again."

"You played hell, now," DeBoe exploded, as they stalked through the slushy snow. "Jesus Christ! That's the Attorney General you're talkin' to. You've got us both in a fix."

"I guess so," Pruiett growled, "but you can't afford to let 'em get started with that kind of language, where I have to make my livin'. I should have broke his dirty neck."

"You just the same as broke your nigger's neck," DeBoe corrected him.

"Yeah, I guess I did," he agreed. "I made a mistake in mentionin' Bill Johnson. Cruce told me he wasn't to be trusted. I sure hate to see 'em murder that ignorant nigger, but I've done about all I can do. Let's have a drink."

"Griggs isn't really such a bad sort," DeBoe said. "He lost his temper, like you did, an' said some things he didn't mean, or expect to say. But he told me, before I came out, to tell you that you had an appeal direct to the President—this being a capital case—and that he was forwarding his unfavorable report to him this afternoon."

Pruiett's manner brightened. "Will you help me arrange...?"

"I can't be responsible for you before the President," DeBoe said, dubiously. "It's a miracle you got by with what you did before Griggs. He may decide to give you some trouble over it yet, after he thinks about it a bit. Talk to some of the other boys, an' see if they can't work something out for you."

Pruiett had dinner that evening at the Metropolitan Hotel, with Congressman Sheppard and Mrs. Sheppard. It was both pleasant and profitable.

"And," he wound up the narrative of the day's events, "he threw me out of his office an' told me not to come back. They'll hang that nigger, and they hadn't ought to do it—an' I've sworn to quit practicing law if he swings. How's that?"

The Sheppards were concerned. "It's a pity," Mrs. Sheppard opined.

"It's a damned outrage," the congressman said. "What's your next move? What have you got in your mind for me to do?"

"Well," said Pruiett, "DeBoe is scared off—a little. I know how he

A MEMBER OF THE CONGRESS FROM ILLINOIS, WILLIAM M. SPRINGER LED THE FIGHT FOR THE ORGANIZATION OF OKLAHOMA TERRITORY. IN 1895, PRESIDENT GROVER CLEVELAND APPOINTED SPRINGER UNITED STATES JUDGE FOR THE NORTHERN DISTRICT OF INDIAN TERRITORY. HE EVENTUALLY BECAME CHIEF JUSTICE OF THE CRIMINAL COURT OF APPEALS, INDIAN TERRITORY. ALTHOUGH SPRINGER'S COURT CONFIRMED THE DEATH SENTENCE ON CHARLIE BIAS, PRUIETT CONVINCED HIM TO WRITE A FAVORABLE LETTER TO THE DEPARTMENT OF JUSTICE RECOMMENDING LENIENCY. COURTESY ARCHIVES & MANUSCRIPTS DIVISION OF THE OKLAHOMA HISTORICAL SOCIETY.

feels. I'd be embarrassed myself if some one I was sponsorin' blew up in my face, like I did this morning. What I want—I want to get this before the President."

"I can do that for you. I can get you in," Sheppard said, "but you ought to have DeBoe, too. He's strong with McKinley. The President thinks a lot of the old boy. Can you get DeBoe to come back?"

"I think I can—if you'll go with me," Pruiett said.

"I'll meet you in the lobby of the Riggs Hotel in the morning, an' we'll go up to his room. We'll make him go along with us."

Pruiett, without question or interruption, retold the Charlie Bias case to the President. DeBoe and Sheppard sat quietly—apprehensively—as if in dread of what might occur. Perhaps it was the congenital kindliness of the executive, and not the charm of the young lawyer who was telling the long story. It may have been that the peculiar nature of the facts involved held his interest.

"Your Excellency," Pruiett concluded dramatically, "this has become a question now, of veracity. I want mine tested. I said there are extenuating circumstances in that record, circumstances which justify, and require a commutation of sentence. Johnson has told the Attorney General that there are none. The official record will show which of us have told the truth."

President McKinley was impressed and called George B. Cortelyou, his personal secretary. "Cortelyou," he said to the secretary who answered his ring, "Get me the file in this case of the government against Charles Bias. It's in the Department of Justice."

"I have them here," Cortelyou said. "They came from the Attorney General today. There is a recommendation that no action be taken, attached."

"Griggs is mad," Pruiett interrupted. "He's sore. The only way you can find out about this is to study the official record, yourself."

"Have the Department forward the official record," the President said, "and leave it with the file, on my desk."

Pruiett interrupted again. "By the record, I mean the transcript of the testimony in the case," he said, "and it's never been sent to Washington. Griggs wants to dispose of this case on the correspondence of interested parties in the Indian Territory. That's no way to get information."

"Where is this record?" McKinley inquired, showing signs of impatience.

"Where we tried the appeal," Pruiett said, "at South McAlester, in the territory."

The President studied. "Direct the Department of Justice to send for it, Cortelyou," he said, "and write Mr. Griggs to the effect that Mr. Pruiett is to have another hearing on this matter, ON THE OFFICIAL RECORD, as soon as it reaches Washington."

The Indian Territory was bone dry, but on the Arkansas River, and in Texas, liquor was abundant. As a boy, and as a young man, the saloons and joints in the fringe of the states had never interested Pruiett. He had, innately, an insatiable yen to see another card, or to watch the wheel spin. The bulk of his contact with alcoholic liquors, prior to his first eastern trip, had been in the occasional drink that went along with his visits to the gambling hall bars.

But it was different in Washington. There was a brilliance about the gaudy interiors of the cafes and lounges, with their gay and smart talking patrons, which captivated him. On the wings of the stimulated eloquence of Culberson and Beveridge, of DeBoe, Sheppard and DeGraffenreid, Pruiett suffered a fascination for the refined conviviality's which went with the stimulation of the cafe liquor. The slightest suggestion of a cause or excuse, in his later and more profitable years, was all that was necessary to cause him to pack and start for what he invariably called "business in Washington."

"The Attorney-General desires to give you a hearing at 2:30 today." The terse communication, reaching Pruiett on January 12, was signed by J. S. Easby Smith, Pardon Attorney. Pruiett attempted to apologize to Griggs—DeBoe had insisted—but the cabinet member was cold.

"We must be brief, gentlemen," he said. Turning on Pruiett he thrust the voluminous transcript of the Territorial Court proceeding at him, in the same manner as he had previously tendered Johnson's letter. "This is the official record. I have read most of it, and fail to find anything to substantiate your position. Where, if you please, is there a suggestion of evidence to support your contention that there are circumstances either mitigating or extenuating?"

Pruiett was game. Thumbing the pages, he stopped long enough to extract an old envelope from his coat pocket and insert it between the pages for a bookmark, as he turned on to find substance for argument. He had repeated those movements some four or five times, when an orderly entered the room. It was a welcome interruption, for the silence, unbroken save for the slight rustling of the pages in Pruiett's hands, was more than painful. The messenger handed a yellow slip—a telegram or cable—to the Attorney General, who casually directed his cold gaze into it.

"My God," he exclaimed with feeling which Pruiett would have sworn he lacked, "she's dead." Griggs gazed beyond his audience and into the intricate grain design of the handsome hall door of his chamber. Rising, he walked around his desk, took the record from Pruiett, and handed it to the still silent pardon attorney.

"I'll be unable to continue with the hearing of this matter," he said. "Please transmit the entire proceedings to Solicitor General J. K. Richards, with the suggestion that he hear it and make a recommendation to the President, for the department."

"This is indeed fortunate for you," Easby Smith said to Pruiett as they moved down the corridor toward the Solicitor General's offices. "Mr. Richards is a very considerate gentleman, and directly opposed to capital punishment."

"But who's dead? To whom am I indebted for this good fortune?" Pruiett's inquiry was in a tone of ripe sarcasm.

"Mrs. Griggs's mother has been very low for several days," Smith explained. "I rather believe that the telegram was the advice of her death."

"God bless her," Pruiett said. "I hope she's in heaven, although I'd be burdened to say as much for her son-in-law. The Lord giveth and He taketh away. The old lady's death may mean that my nigger can live a little longer. That's the compensation of nature, for you."

The strange caprices of fate that dogged the career of Pruiett, to attach an almost uncanny glamor to his successes or defeats, were already beginning to appear. Scarcely had the act of good fortune that removed the hostile Griggs from the problem been assimilated, then another appeared. Easby Smith told him that Federal Judge William M. Springer of the Northern District of the territory, one of the members of the appellate body that heard the territorial appeal of Bias, was in town. Pruiett determined to see him, in an attempt to get a favorable recommendation for his application, at least more favorable than the one he had acquired from the District Attorney at home.

He called on Judge Springer on the following morning. "Have you been able to make any one believe you are here on your own expense?" he inquired.

"Joe Bailey wouldn't believe it, an' he said that nobody else would," Pruiett replied. "But men like Senator DeBoe and Senator Culberson have been very kind to me. President McKinley was very considerate."

"What did Johnson do about it?" Springer inquired.

"He turned me down, and after he had—." Pruiett launched into the details of the Johnson letter and the episode in the Attorney General's office. It was highly amusing to his listener.

"Johnson doesn't want to disappoint the crowd," the Judge laughed, as he scratched his chin through a sparse gray beard. "They're all set to have a big time at the Charlie Bias party. But, did you know that Johnson told me the same thing at McAlester, after that sentence was affirmed? I mean all that about his having conscientious scruples and stuff."

Pruiett admitted that he hadn't known of it.

"And did you know that I thought the penalty too stiff at the review, and told old John R. Thomas and William H. H. Clayton so, at the time. I felt that you were right about him bein' too ignorant and savage to have a real murderous intent. I couldn't convince the others, an' I was in the minority, so I had to keep quiet."

The gleam in Pruiett's eye was indicative of the new impetus being added to his rapidly ascending hope. "Could you say now that there were circumstances in that record which might be considered as extenuating?" he asked.

"Well—yes," the judge said, slowly. "I consider the proof of the crime, in connection with the evidence of his utter lack of intelligence and contact with the outside world, sufficient to establish that he should not be measured by the same standard as that employed in the measuring of a civilized man's conduct."

"Will you give me a letter to the Department of Justice to that effect?" Pruiett almost whispered.

"I'll be glad to, my boy," Springer said. "It's refreshing to find an occasional person with a noble motive and the courage to stand up and fight for it. Don't build your hopes too high, because the men here who have the say don't pay much attention to an old judge from the territory, and I may not do you and Charlie much good."

Execution time was drawing unpleasantly close. The greater part of January 17, 1900, Pruiett spent in the waiting room of Solicitor General Richards' office, or in pacing the corridor, outside. No information was being put out. On the same date and under the forbidding black head of "Death Watch Set" the *Daily Ardmoreite,* back in the territory, carried related Pruiett news.

"This forenoon the negro Chas. Bias was taken from among his fellow-prisoners in the United States Jail and furnished more comfortable quarters wherein to spend the few remaining days of his existence. During his removal today Marshal Hammer notified the prisoner of the nearness of death, and advised him to employ his time in making peace with his Maker. He partakes heartily of his food, and when informed that he could get anything he desired to order in the way of food, replied that he was getting all he wanted and had no desire for anything else. In his cell Bias seems perfectly content, has nothing to say, and seems wholly indifferent to the fate which awaits him, on next Friday, when he will hang by the neck until he is dead, unless perchance the President's clemency intervenes."

At four the next day the Solicitor General, acting as Attorney General in charge of the Bias case, completed and forwarded his report to the President. Pruiett, with his senatorial connections, couldn't get the grapevine on its content. The *Times-Herald,* in a special article in the late edition, made public the text of the report.

"A remarkable fight to save a human life ended successfully this evening when Attorney General Griggs, through Solicitor General Richards, to whom the matter had been referred, decided to recommend commutation of sentence for a colored boy named Chas. S. Bias. Bias is incarcerated at Ardmore, I. T., and was to have been hanged for murder next Friday. Only the efforts of his attorney, Moman Pruiett of Ardmore, will give the prisoner commutation of sentence from hanging to life imprisonment. Pruiett sought many senators and they became interested, chiefly because his mission was purely charitable and because they were told the boy had really killed Wright in a fair fight and in self-defense. Great pressure was brought to bear, and the Attorney General undoubtedly gave exceptional attention to the case."

The full column front gave the gory details of the affray, the conviction and sentence, and the names of all the participants. The Washington press was taking out a charter membership certificate in the national organization that was to engage in plastering Pruiett on the front page for more than a quarter century.

"Pruiett is 27 years old and has defended men in twenty murder cases in the country, and has acquitted all but Bias, and now has saved that boy's neck by almost a miracle. Pruiett himself is a typical southerner—slouch hat, top boots all there. But his heart is as full of charity as his head is full of brains. Many of the notables of Washington, who have become interested in his case, were congratulating the young lawyer tonight."

The bottle was off the shelf. The notables were before the bar at the Metropolitan Hotel, and the congratulations were prolix and verbose. Sheppard and DeGraffenreid, Easby Smith and DeBoe, were vying with each other, and all with Pruiett, for the coinage of an oratorical expression sublime enough to fit the occasion. Pruiett was learning to like his liquor, and to hear the boys talk about Pruiett.

The *Daily Ardmoreite,* the sheet that had previously decried the contemplated hanging and Roman holiday, was more descriptive than exultant. "Seated in the death cell, with his two guards, never speaking one word and evidently suffering no mental anguish, when informed last evening that the President had commuted his sentence to life imprisonment and that he would not be hanged, with muscles unmoved and without any apparent effort from gladness or joy, his only answer was 'all right'."

The *Chickasaw Weekly Enterprise,* a Pauls Valley paper, tried to emulate its more established and influential kin-organs. "Word was received in Ardmore Monday from Washington that the sentence of Chas. Bias had been commuted to life imprisonment. Bias would have been hanged tomorrow. Attorney Moman Pruiett of this city has been in Washington the last two weeks working on this case."

CHAPTER TWO

WHEREIN A HASTY GLANCE INTO RETROSPECT IS TAKEN, AND AFTER THE PRUIETT PROGENITORS ARE GIVEN CASUAL GLANCE, THE ACCOUNT OF HOW A DEADHEAD BEING HAULED ABOARD A RIVER PACKET, IS MADE. AND HOW THE SCENES SHIFT FROM THE OHIO RIVER TO THE ARKANSAS RIVER, AND FROM RIVERBOATS TO RAILROAD TRAINS, BUT THE TRANSIENT CHARACTERISTICS OF THE PRUIETT FAMILY REMAIN UNCHANGED. AND HOW A MOTHER'S DREAM OF A PRE-NATAL GIFT IS CONFIDED IN HER OFFSPRING, AS SHE CHARGES HIM WITH THE RESPONSIBILITY OF WINNING ACCLAIM FOR HIMSELF IN THE COURTROOMS, BUT HOW SHE SORROWFULLY SEES HIM THERE, NOT THE ACCLAIMED, AS SHE HAD DREAMED, BUT AS THE LOWLY CULPRIT, PAUSING IN THE PARADE TO THE PEN.

Captain Warren Legrande Pruiett had been a Confederate, but it was the Union Army that mustered him out. When the war was over, and the luckless inmates of the federal prisoner of war camp at Elmira, New York, were released, he was starting his fifteenth month as a captive of the North. It was a long way to Leitchfield, Kentucky, and Captain Pruiett was sick of body and heart. He skulked and begged his way out of the hated territory and back into Kentucky, with little spirit or hope. It was well for him he despaired, for it served to prepare him. Martha Harris Pruiett, his wife, had been dead for almost a year. Oscar, Albert, and Anna, the happy kids he had left behind, were gaunt, backward starvelings.

The Moormans, near Elizabethtown, in Hardin County, Kentucky, had suffered the complete reduction that accompanied Confederate defeat. The elegance of the plantation, flourishing when old Colonel William Moorman exhibited Elizabeth Louisa, the new grandchild, in 1850, and still maintained by slave cultured tobacco wealth in '62, had become a sad memory. In cheerless December, of the year of '68, the grandchild stood above a fresh mound on the plantation grounds, beside a group of older stones. Grandpa Moorman was dead. Little Betty Moorman's heart would break, if her violent sobbing was an indicator, before the crumbling columns of the old balcony fell.

Betty Moorman had been born Elizabeth Louisa Laws. When Mary, the Colonel's only child, married Thomas Laws, no objections were made. The Laws were aristocrats, and southern Ohio wasn't so far north as to amount to a complete disqualification. Black-haired and black-eyed Betty, when she came, made up for her father's various minor shortcomings. After her pudgy hand had given the Colonel's black beard a single jerk, Tommy Laws had a permanent home. But, when he went home with the coming of the war, and thence to a Yankee regiment, he committed the unpardonable sin. The seldom invoked Hardin County divorcement act was brought forth, and with the stern Colonel Moorman guiding her, Mary Laws insisted that despite her matronly status and pig-tailed Betty, she be divorced, and restored to the name of Moorman.

A Tennessee slug put an end to Tommy Laws and the speculation on what his attitude toward Mary's maneuvers would be, on returning. Elizabeth Louisa Laws moved into adolescence as Betty Moorman.

No one knew, no one was concerned, in fact, how elderly Captain Pruiett and the dejected orphan of the Moormans came together. Pasts weren't important, with presents so difficult to maintain and futures so hard to predict. Men were scarce after the war. Niggers and white trash terrified unescorted women. A man with three sick and hungry kids had to have a mother for them, whether a dowry went with the deal or not. There was no magnolia scented romance on the columned veranda of the manor house, at least not the Moorman manor house, for the official county records for 1869 revealed that the long delinquent mortgage on it had been canceled in foreclosure during the summer of the preceding year. The records said that Warren Legrande Pruiett and Elizabeth Louisa Moorman were united in Elizabethtown, on March 23, 1869. She was 19; he was 42.

The *Gray Eagle,* a steamship operated by the Louisville and Evansville Packet Company, on the Ohio River between Louisville, Kentucky, and Cincinnati, Ohio, was showering cinders and soot through the Kentucky side of the soft spring atmosphere.

"That's Looeyville, ain't it?" A young woman, with a pretty face, was asking the question of the man beside her, a man much taller, and older than she. It was Betty Pruiett, and the former Captain of the Confederacy. As they looked down the river they each cast quick and constant glances toward two ponderously bundled infants sitting back to back on the rough-planked deck beside them.

"That's her," the man said. He was leaning against the rail of the upper deck and staring at a black smudge visible above the bending green of the riverbank. "That's old Looeyville, an' we'll be dockin' in less than an hour. I ain't seen her since I was through on my way home—after the war." There was a touch of sadness, and bitterness, with the addition of the phrase.

They stood together, watching the smudge in the sky, the verdant shore and the foaming muddy water. "You better set down," he cautioned. The attempted style in the cut of her homemade coat didn't conceal her abnormal contour. She was advanced with child. "It ain't good to ride on these rough boats, nohow, the way you are. Let's set."

As he led her toward a wooden bench on the deck, near the babies, she clung to a small imitation-leather accessory bag. "I just had to come with you, even if we did have to bring the babies," she said. "It's kinda like a vacation, gettin' back in this part of Kentucky—just for a day. I'm glad the lawyers an' creditors for Bruner Brothers decided to have a meetin'. I couldn't 'ave stood that Indiana winter much longer, without a little rest."

"It ain't been no worse at Alton, Indiana, than it's been at Looeyville, or Leitchfield, Kentucky, this winter," he said. "You've been homesick, an' run down with takin' care of these twins, Lois and Jessie, an' gettin' ready to have another one, maybe more, so soon."

"We've done perty good at Alton," she agreed. "Makin' our own expenses an' gettin' all this cash out of an' old bankrupt store stock. You done real good, to do that, Warren."

"There's $3,000 in greenbacks in that old didy satchel," he grinned. "Three thousand dollars, an' that's about all anybody could milk out of the old junk. It won't surprise me a damn bit if they don't close her up an' turn me loose, when they take this money an' examine my accounts. Then we're outa work again. What the hell we goin' t' do?"

"You'll find somethin'," she said. "Maybe the tobacco price'll be better, or...."

"Maybe I can get me another butcher shop an' go back to cuttin' meat—'til I go broke. It's funny I can make money out of a worn-out stock someone else has gone busted in, but if it's for me, I can't get over."

Moman Pruiett's mother, Elizabeth Louise Laws Moorman Pruiett, was his most dedicated, loyal, and staunch supporter. Called Betty by her family, she saw him through years of poverty and deprivation and his time in prison, but she never gave up on her dream of him becoming a famous lawyer. She divorced her first husband, Thomas Laws, when he joined the Union Army at the outbreak of the Civil war. Courtesy *Moman Pruiett: Criminal Lawyer.*

Betty looked sad. "Bad luck," she said. "Bad luck. That's all I've seen since the war came. There's Grandpa Moorman—with his big house an' his money, an' mother an' me havin' ever'thing we need. Then he loses his money an' the niggers, then his property, an' finally dyin'. I remember that, an' me an' mother bein' left in that big house, until they took it away from us an' moved us out. It's just one misfortune after another, 'til you came to Elizabethtown, an' we met...."

"Misfortune was what brought us together," the Captain said. "Hard luck—misfortune—was what done it, an' it looks like the two of us together have been gettin' a double dose ever' since. You was just a kid when the war came, just a girl when it was over. Why, I was grown, had a good business an' was makin' good money, classin' tobacco there in Leitchfield, raisin' three kids. I thought I was gettin' some place. Two years in the army—one year in the god-damn Elmira, sick to death all the time in the filthy prison camp, an' what do I find when the war's over an' I get home? Wife dead, kids sick an' half starved. Business blowed. The wife's folks helpin' to push the god-damn niggers in so the poor devils like me'll be sure to finish our starvin' to death. I ain't never come out of it—an' I'm gettin' to be a' old man."

"I ain't goin' to let you get discouraged," Betty said. "We was on starvation when we married. You remember, we agreed to join forces an' fight it out, because it seemed ever' one an' ever'thing was against us? It was my fault you quit the tobacco business in Brandenburg an' went into that meat market. If times hadn't been so unnatural tough you'd a' made money, instead of losin'. An' just remember, Oscar an' Albert are gettin' big enough, almost, to get a little job here an' there, an' Anna's a heap of help to me about the house. The...."

"Them poor kids," he lamented. "They're perty near like you, only you had a little better care when you was little. They've had sadness to live on since they was born. They ain't had no chance an' it looks...."

They each held a pudgy year-old twin on their laps. "No," Betty objected, "it don't, neither. We're goin' to do better, an' these kids of ours is goin' to know a little happiness, an' have a little education. I'm goin' to see to that."

"Let's quit croakin' an' watch her dock," he interrupted. The green fringe of the west bank had disappeared. In its place was an expanse of churned water with dingy house-boats and coal barges. Beyond and above them were smoking stacks, dirty windows and the streaked sides of flat industrial buildings.

"Listen to her blow." The *Gray Eagle* was letting it out. Her hoarse, grunting whistle was blowing almost constantly. Holding a child apiece in their arms—Betty holding tight to the diaper bag—they moved to the rail to watch the noon-day bustle of the river traffic. "Ain't I glad to see old Looeyville," Betty said.

"Say," said the Captain. "Lois's wet. She's got to have a dry napkin afore we get off'en this boat. She feels like she fell overboard."

"Ain't she a dandy, now," Betty said. "Jessie's a lady; she's dry, an' clean, too. Here—let's trade, an' I'll change her. We'll be gettin' off in a minute. I'll take a didy an' go inside with her, an' you hang onto this bag."

She placed the flat bottom of the bag on the flat rail of the boat, and holding the handle with her left hand, the hand and arm supporting the baby, she flipped the spring and opened the bag.

"I'm goin' to put two of 'em on this young lady, for the city," she laughed, as she jerked the white cloths out of the bag. A worn leather wallet, the one containing Bruner Brothers' greenbacks, leaped out with a white fold, and balanced for an instant on the lip of the satchel.

"Good god," gasped the Captain, with a wild lunge forward. He caught it after it started its fall toward the muddy water. "I got it, by god. Say, what the hell?"

Betty and Lois were flat on the deck. Lois was making protest with frantic screams, but the mother lay quite still.

"Drive us up to the Gault House."

"We shouldn't go to such an expensive place, Warren," Betty protested from the interior of the hack. "Let's go some place that ain't so high."

"This is a kind of a vacation for us, an' I'll try to get by with it on my expense account," he said. "An' besides, if them pains keep up you'll need a doctor. The Cap'in of the boat says they got a house man at the Gault."

"I feel awful silly, faintin' like a plumb ninny, but I never was so scared in all my life. I saw that money start to fall, an' it seems like an eternity I was froze there. I couldn't move, an' I couldn't scream. All I could see was both of us goin' to prison for stealin' it. Nobody would've ever believed we lost it, if we did. Are you sure you caught it?"

"I showed it to you a dozen times now," he laughed. "I'll take it out an' count it if it'll make you feel better. Ain't them pains goin' away any?"

"They are—some," she said. "But, if they got a doctor, an' it don't cost extra, why let's have him look at me. They go away—an' then they come back, an' I feel awful weak."

"It's just what I told you," the Captain said, as he came into their rooms at the Gault House that evening. "The court says to close her out. We'll auction off what's left when we get back. I get half o'what she brings for my commission, an' old Bruner Brothers is buttoned up. How you feelin'? Has the doctor been back?"

"The doctor's been here, an' he says I'm havin' early labor pains. He says the scare I got, an' the fall, almost brought the baby. It ain't hardly seven months yet, neither."

"I knew it wasn't right, ridin' that rough boat an' all," he said. "I'm supposed to get right back, an' the *Gray Eagle* goes at noon tomorrow. How you goin' to make the trip?"

"I'll be all right," she said. "The doctor said to stay still tonight; that's a fine vacation, ain't it? I can get up all right in the mornin' . You go out somewhere tonight, an' see how old Looeyville looks, an' then tell me about it in the morning."

"Nope, I'll stay in an' rest, an' try to make some plans with you. What we goin' to do after I wind up this liquidatin' job I got now?"

"What you goin' to have when you get through?"

"The stockholders was tickled to death with the report I made 'em, an' with that $3,000. They hadn't thought anybody could do it, an' they admitted it. I got 10 percent, $300, out of it. They said I could have half of what the sale of the balance brought, an' I know it'll do for $1,500. That'll make us better than a $1,000 an' our expenses, out'a this job."

"Why, that's a good year, after all." Betty's face was glowing. "With $1,000, you can go in business. You can get a good start with that."

"There's somethin' I been thinkin' about for quite awhile," the Captain said slowly. "I been thinkin', with business so bad around here—me failin' in ever'thing I try, well—maybe we ought to move plumb out an' start over fresh somewhere. Out..."

"Go ahead, Warren," she urged. "Don't be afraid to talk to me. What you been thinkin'?"

"Well," he repeated, "I was in the West once—it was with Major General Earl Van Dorn. They transferred me to a Tennessee outfit, an' moved us into Missouri, an' south from there into Arkansas. We fought at a place called Elk Horn Tavern, also called the Battle of Pea Ridge, an' got whipped, of course, an' scattered all over that Ozark hill country. I hid out in the woods and caves for a couple of months. It's a lot like east Kentucky, lots of little fast-runnin' streams, rough, hilly as hell, an' the soil's shallow an' rocky. There's lots of it, an' its awful cheap. I got the idea right then that it would raise tobacco, same as Kentucky soil, an' that the bird to start it would get richer'n hell."

"If it was good for tobacco, they'd be raisin' it out there," Betty observed. "They wouldn't be crowdin' up an' wearin' these pore old hills out, if there was all that good land to work on."

"Maybe nobody ain't thought of it," he said, doggedly.

One of the twins fretted in the adjoining room. "We got little babies, an' goin' to have more, Warren," she said. "It'd be awful hard on me, goin' to a strange country, an' a wild one, with the babies. I think we better think about investin' in a little business, an' startin' over again around here. We get awful homesick, both of us, when we get out of Kentucky."

The soot sifted over the river docks. The black laborers cursed the white ones, and the white laborers cursed the black ones. Cursing truckers beat big-footed horses as the huge wagons were backed into unloading position at the *Gray Eagle*'s side. Passengers with luggage were climbing from horse-drawn hacks and scrambling up the plank runway.

"Be careful," Betty said, as the Captain helped her from the step of the hack. "I'm awful sore. I'm still havin' a touch of them pains."

"I don't think you'd better try it, makin' this trip," he told her. "I can arrange for you to stay with some one here. I'll go up and hold this sale, an' get the other kids, an' come back here. We was plannin' to come anyway."

"Just let me lay down in the cabin, an' ever'things all right," she said. "You ain't leavin' me here by myself. You got your hands full of kids now you can't hardly help me up the boards. What'd we do? You take Lois an' Jessie, or leave 'em with me, sick? Let's get in where I can lay down, an' get home."

The *Gray Eagle* cleared the docks at two o'clock, an hour late. At six, with her side wheels churning the flood-stage muddy current, she was well above Louisville, vibrating in every joint and timber as she struggled to make way against the current's pull. Betty Pruiett, trying to smile through the anguish-stamped lines of her face, shivered as a helpful passenger held a wet cloth to her forehead. Captain Pruiett, with bloody wrists and cuffs, stood awkwardly beside her. She lay in the bunk of their cabin. He held a squirming infant in his hands. It was swaddled in a boat towel.

"Ain't he got the god-awfulest head of hair you ever seen?" he said, "an' just a seven monther, too."

"Just like Grandpa Moorman," Betty was able to whisper.

"What we goin' to call him?" he inquired.

"I'd like to name him for Grandpa Moorman," she said.

"That's good for me," the Captain agreed. "His name's Moorman. Moorman Pruiett. That's name enough for anybody, I guess."

"God bless his little soul," the mother whispered, as she looked at the ugly infant. The wide mouth that was partly covered by the long ropes of birth-wet black hair, stringing down from its head and about its face, flew open, and a lusty wail arose. "God bless his soul," she whispered again.

Hovering genius swung low and clipped the ear of the infant with a mark, reserving him to her as her own. While the big mouth was open and the tiny pointed tongue protruded between the toothless gums, the muse of eloquence dropped down to touch it with his magic wand. The deity of all the paradoxes stopped long enough, as gliding by on the cool river mists, she endowed the scrawny being with the strangest mixture of impulse and motive ever assembled under a single section of human flesh and skin.

The soft light of a heavenly presence illuminated the dusky ripples of the muddy water in its beam, and over the dark waves, emissaries from above and below met to touch the squalling, squirming body at the same instant. When he was laid in the improvised crib, furnished by gaping passengers, there rested the best and the worst, the most kind and the most brutal, the most considerate, and the roughest and toughest, of all the curiosities ever assembled in human form.

Five years of assorted failures—Pruiett luck was gaining momentum as it rolled from bad to worse—was enough to convince Betty. She followed the Captain on his long considered experiment into the southwestern hills. Her brood, with increases and losses, remained the same in number. Lois and Jessie had died; they had been buried side by side at Alton, Indiana. The stepchildren, the war-stunted get of the Captain's first marriage, were plodding through adolescence, still awkward and stunned by the tragedies of their infancy. The boy with "the godawful" hair was thriving. Another boy, named White, was born before the Kentucky exodus began.

The Captain tried his tobacco in '80, and followed it in '81 and '82. "She just won't work," he complained, disconsolately. "The climate's about the same, the rainfall's about the same, an' the ground's just like Hardin County ground, all but the smell, but she sure as hell won't sprout tobacco. I've worked my god damn head off, an' here I am. Rented farm with no rent paid, no crop out, a house full of kids an' no money. I'm at the end of my row."

"Oh, no, you ain't," Betty argued. "This here's a great country. It's good for the kids, an' our health's better since we come out. We'll sell this furniture, an' these tools, an' move up to Fort Smith, Arkansas. I seen that was a good town the minute I got in it. We'll just quit the farm, an' you an' Oscar an' Albert can get jobs."

"Whose team's that?" the Captain interrupted, peering through the window. A wagon had stopped in the road in front of the house.

"It's old man Silas Sykes" she answered.

"Wants his rent, I guess," the Captain growled. "Well, I'll just have to owe him, or he can..."

Betty showed Sykes into the kitchen, where they had been talking. It was Silas Sykes, the owner of the farm they had worked for three years. Silas and his brother Wade Sykes founded the town of Rogers, Arkansas, and gave the land for the original townsite.

"I guess you won't be wantin' the farm any more, Pruiett," he said. "I ain't goin' to have the whole thing to let, now."

"That won't be botherin' us, I reckon," Pruiett replied. "We was..."

"We're broke," Betty cut in, bluntly. "We was goin' to give you notice. We're goin' to move to Fort Smith."

"It ain't my affair, but you're goin' at the wrong time," Sykes said.

WARREN LEGRAND "THE CAPTAIN" PRUIETT, MOMAN PRUIETT'S FATHER. WHILE SERVING IN THE CONFEDERATE ARMY DURING THE CIVIL WAR, WARREN PRUIETT WAS CAPTURED AND SENT TO A PRISONER OF WAR CAMP. RELEASED FOLLOWING THE END OF THE FIGHTING, THE ELDER PRUIETT RETURNED TO FIND A HOMELAND DESTROYED BY THE WAR AND HIS FIRST WIFE, MARTHA HARRIS PRUIETT, DEAD. HE HAD TWO SONS, OSCAR AND ALBERT, AND A DAUGHTER, ANNA, BY HIS FIRST WIFE. ON MARCH 23, 1869, HE MARRIED ELIZABETH LOUISE LAWS MOORMAN. SHE WAS 19; HE WAS 42. COURTESY *MOMAN PRUIETT: CRIMINAL LAWYER.*

"I'm givin' up a lot of my farm to get things opened around here, you're workin' your heads off an' goin' broke, an' then when she's ready to hum, you get up an' get. But, it ain't my business."

"Ain't you said you was sellin' part of the farm?" Betty inquired.

"Nope, I ain't sellin' her; I'm givin' her away. Just deedin' forty acres away, an' a strip two rods wide through another forty. Just deedin' her away, free."

"You mean you got that god damn railroad survey turned this way, after all?" guessed the Captain.

"The St. Louis and San Francisco Railroad's cuttin' right through the north eighty, an' I'm deedin' forty to the townsite company to go to make a town. You're goin' to see a city right on the Sykes farm, what I'm tellin' you."

"I'm glad for you, Mr. Sykes," Betty said. "You worked hard to get these farms, an' to keep 'em. I know that. You worked hard, an' you're entitled to get your values up with the railroad. I'm mighty glad for you."

"I'm glad too, Sykes," the Captain said. "Some guys get all the luck—all the good luck. I get all the tough. I hope it makes you double rich, Sykes."

"Are you bound to make this move to Fort Smith?"

"Well," answered the Captain, looking doubtfully toward Betty, "we ain't got much choice. It's like Betty just said, we're busted. We're down to the bottom of the pan, an' we got to try a new trick."

"You got a little choice," Sykes said. "I knew you was broke. I watched you work this farm, an' seen how hard you tried to make tobacco grow on it, an' I hated to see you fail time after time. But I seen you was a good worker, an' good to your family, an' it ain't ever'body that's got that much to his credit. I came over to make you a little proposition."

"It'll have to be a little one for me to consider it," the Captain said. Betty smiled.

"You told me you was in the meat business, a time or two?"

"I cut meat all over Kentucky, an' never made a god damn cent out of it," agreed the Captain.

"Was it grocery-store meat business—retail business?"

"Yep. Just little business, but I never could make it go. Went broke ever' time."

"These railroad contractors have to have a hell of a lot of fresh meat," Sykes explained. "Bridge gangs, steel gangs, flocks of laborers. Live beef's cheap an' easy to get, but killed meat ain't, an' won't be. The man that gets the beef contracts with that construction is goin' to make a lot of money."

"We got a milk cow an' a calf, an' we can butcher in the bedroom," the Captain said, dolefully. "I'm afraid I ain't got nothin' to start on."

"We're goin' to have a town," Sykes said, "an' these new towns are cracker-jacks. An' this one, right here in this good country, this farmin' country, an' with the minerals an' timber we got, is goin' to be a big one. You'll have to have a shop, an' do it right."

"What they goin' to call the town?" Betty inquired. "Sykesville?"

"I wanted 'em to, but the townsite company wouldn't hear of it. They're callin' it 'Rogers'."

"What the hell for?" asked the Captain.

"Some muckety-muck in the Frisco," said Sykes. "A big stockholder, or somethin'."

"You really think it'll make a big settlement?"

"Hell yes, Pruiett. The promoters come in an' promote each other, an' some of the natives'll fall for it, but the smart guy'll get some holdin's an' let'em go up in value. Property values'll sky rocket."

"I wisht we could stay for it an' make some money, but I guess it ain't for me," said the Captain. "We ain't got nothin' to start on."

"You ain't never let me make my proposition," Sykes said. "I gave'm the forty for the townsite. They gave me back my pick of some of the choice town lots. I got some good ones facin' the depot an' the right-of-way. I'm goin' to build a two-story frame on the best ones, with store-room downstairs an' rentin' rooms upstairs. You an' the missus is good workers, an' you ought to have first shot, seein' as the town starts right on your farm—anyway, the one you been farmin' for three years. Put in a butcher shop, with a roomin' an' boardin' house. I'll help you get started, an' we'll go after them railroad meat contracts. Missus Pruiett can feed the promoters an' the new one's that come to town. We'll clean up."

The transit-born Pruiett child, the *Gray Eagle*'s unbooked passenger, was eleven. He was average in size, but odd of act and appearance. He had a glittering, gimlet-like dark eye, and a crowning mop of crow-black hair. The Captain cut it and Betty cut it, the neighbors cut it, and he hacked at it himself, until the shears were dulled, but the black flag continued to wave defiantly. It was of prodigious thickness.

Moorman was Mawman in Betty's Kentucky accent. He moved with the Captain and Betty to a large new house with rooms upstairs. He had watched it grow from the stacks of yellow lumber dumped about from the six- and eight-horse wagon-freighters. He saw men with soft hats and laced leather boots come and go on their horses, and in wagons and buggies, and he heard them talk to his father, and to Sykes, about depots, and streets and sidewalks. He played in the shavings, when he could get away from minding the ever-troublesome White, and walked the rafters of the line of new one-story buildings, which the men, who were becoming more numerous about the farm, were building.

And then one day he saw the square yellow ties being swung and dropped along the fresh ridge of earth in front of the new buildings, and he saw sweating, straining men, with queer clamp-like tools, carrying heavy steel rails and laying them, with cursing and swearing, across the picket line of the square ties.

The new house was full of the strange men who shoveled the dirt and carried the rails, or who carried great rolls of blue paper with white and red lines upon it, and who sat around the house at night, smoking pipes and uttering unnecessary oaths as they talked about the railroad. Anna was helping Betty with the work, and it was good that she could. He knew that. Betty didn't stop to pet him, and run her hands through his hair, and tell him how nice it was. He was glad. He hated to be coddled. She didn't have the time—he knew that, too—for the big sign hanging out over the muddy street in front, unpainted, like the house, brought constant crowds to eat the food which Betty and Anna took from their great iron stove.

The line of the St. Louis and San Francisco Railway was pressing out of southern Missouri toward Fort Smith, with north Texas its ultimate objective. The peaceful beauty of the hills, cut by the foaming lines of spring-fed streams, was being revealed to the increasing tide of settlers and speculators who followed the extension of the rails. Settlements strove to get the survey to head their way. They tempted the road with land grants. Where the trains went, increased values and prosperity followed. Towns were established by an executive's pen dot upon a blue diagram. What had been a wooded tract or a cultivated field became a bustling camp.

Captain Pruiett had the best thing in Rogers. The name of the new town was painted with black letters on the boxed-ends of the dung-colored depot. A downstairs stall of Pruiett's boarding house was his butcher shop. The men, who toiled on the fills and in the cuts, had to have red meat, and he worked at night, trimming bones and stuffing guts for the morning wagon load to the camp. He whistled and counted his money. Sure, he went broke cuttin' meat at Hawesville, Kentucky—but, what the hell? Sure he flunked trying to make tobacco grow in Benton County. What about now? Them railroad contractors have got plenty of money, an' you can buy fat calves for whatever you want to pay.

Rogers became a town overnight. Within a year it had a staid and established appearance, with the unpainted houses and buildings near the depot adopting a duller shade of dung than that of the railroad station. The yellow pine walls and roofs faded and blended. They appeared to be as indigenous to the landscape as the small oaks and granite boulders. Professor James Woolsey came to take charge of classes in the new school, and Betty Pruiett smiled one of her rare smiles. Mawman would get him some book learnin'.

"Don't coddle me, Ma. Keep your hands to your self."

A plain woman, with a slightly pained expression, sat beside a scowling boy. They were in a plain room, on the side of a red-quilted iron bed.

"Don't resent your mother, son, she loves you," she said. "You're not too big for mother to touch you, even if you are thirteen."

She attempted to run her hands through his hair. It was coal black, bulky and uncut, but shiningly smooth and sleek. He recoiled from her again. "I wish't you wouldn't do that all the time, Ma."

"Paw says you fought with the teacher today, hit him with the water bucket and cut his head. That's what I called you in here to talk about."

"Old Woolsey ain't fit to be a teacher. He ought t'be a muleskinner—the bully. I wish I'd a-killed him."

"Don't say things like that, Mawman," the woman said. "It's sinful to say it—even think it. The Bible says 'thou shalt not kill'. It's been hard, draggin' about from place to place, not hardly settled long enough to get you into school, but I've tried..."

"It ain't your fault, Ma, but I just can't get along in school. It's no use."

"Why?" she asked, wearily. "The other boys ain't always in trouble, comin' home with their clothes torn and bloody, with their faces all scratched up. Fightin'. Always fightin'. An' now its the teacher, so you can't ever go back to this school."

"Mutton-chops," he answered laconically. "Mutton-chops. They call me that 'cause paw's a meat-cutter, an' I don't like it. I said I'd whip ever' one that call me that, an' I done it—all but a few girls. I hate schools."

"But why the teacher? Why did you have to hit the professor with the water bucket, and..."

"He called me white-trash," the boy said, still defiant, "called me white-trash, an' all the time he's floggin' me. I can lick him—even if he is growed. He squawled like an ol' girl when I swung that bucket."

"You've got to get yourself educated, son," the mother persisted. "Let me tell you a story. I've wanted to tell you for a long time, but I just never could get up to it. We was livin' up at Alton, in Indiana, just before you was born, an' I had a dream. It was just about the time for you to come to us—your paw an' me—an' I hadn't been feelin' so well. There was a big case bein' tried at the courthouse. Congressman Daniel Wolsey Voorhees was on one side, and Judge Clement Vallandingham of Ohio was on the other. Missus Shellenbarger got me to go down to the courthouse with her, just to sit an' listen to the case, to listen to the big lawyers that was tryin' it."

A beautiful light shone in her tired eyes, and a work-worn hand moved to the child's shoulder. He nestled to her, unconsciously. "I won't never forget it," she went on. "It was Judge Voorhees, they called him 'The Tall Sycamore of the Wabash', that interested me. He was seven foot tall, it seemed, with a long frock coat on, and long cut hair. An' how he could talk, low, an' real confidential like, at times, an' then he'd stand up to his full height, an' roar like the thunder. He'd been to college, an' been to congress, an' he was smart. He had educated his self. An' there he was, a leader, a leader of men, with his hands full of wonderful power. I closed my eyes, right there while he was cryin' out with his great voice, an' prayed that my baby would be a boy, an' that I'd be able to get him educated, for a great lawyer like Judge Voorhees."

"An' that night I dreamed," she said, her face glowing and the dirty urchin held close to her bosom, "that I was in the same courtroom, an' that my son, my own flesh an' blood, was standin' before the jury makin' the rafters sing with his great voice—an' makin' the people think with his great learnin'. It was just about two days later, son, that you was born to me. I thought it had been a sign, a vision I was havin', an' that it would be a part of you, an' you'd help to make it come true. I've dreamed an' prayed that it would; but, son, you've got to have schoolin'. You got to have educatin' to be a great lawyer."

He jerked away defiantly. "I ain't goin' to no more school, an' I ain't in for bein' no lawyer. I can work on the railroad when I'm a little bigger. I'll..."

"But you got to learn," she interrupted. "You can't lay naked in White River all summer, with the gang of no 'count town boys, an' loaf with the old man on the sidewalks all winter, or ride with your paw on that meat wagon. You're growin', an' you got to improve yourself."

Moorman stood up and stretched. "I'm leavin' home," he said. "I'm goin' to the city an' get me a job."

"I'll thrash you myself, if I ever think you're serious about leavin' me, an' goin' to Fort Smith..."

" 'Tain't Fort Smith, it's Fayetteville, Arkansas" he said. "Big mills an' fine buildings, an' swell people with lots of money. I guess I could get along all right—other boys have done it. I ain't a baby no more. I'll show 'em whos' the Mutton-chops."

After a despondent shake of her head, the mother laughed. "Don't think, Mister Smarty, that 'cause you can whip the professor, you can run me. I'll cut me a hickory, an' whip you ever' step of the way home, just you try it."

Fayetteville, the Arkansas Athens and the home of the University of Arkansas, hung like a weird, smoky painting on the maple covered drops of the Boston Mountains. On two slopes, and in a portion of one gully, the old buildings of the state university covered easily-accessible learning. The living-places, built before the war, scaled their paint in sullen defiance behind huge lawn trees. Bright colors, and bright lights and sounds, proceeded from the smaller and more modern homes, which rested amongst smaller trees, fresh set along neat, narrow streets. Carriages and carts and freight-wagons rolled regularly around the well-kept central square. The business buildings facing the square enjoyed brisk patronage.

Business was good. The pine and hard-timber from Fayetteville's adjoining hillsides was being hurried to market. Coal was being dug and stripped in every direction from the square, and new steel of the various railroads was literally strapping the countryside. Money was easy to get; every one seemed to have it. Crops were good; provender was plentiful; fish from the flashing mountain streams and game from the brush along their banks made high living commonplace.

Colonel Peter Van Winkle, one of the leading merchants in Fayetteville, owned the War Eagle Mills on old War Eagle. Riverboat owner, mine promoter and capitalist, general man of ease, he had graded the lumber at his big mill on the mountain creek with a purpose. The best of the piles, plank and siding he held unto himself. The Van Winkle House, something special in Boston Mountains extravagance, was being built just west of the public square in Fayetteville. "She ain't got a knot in her," the Colonel boasted. He was dreaming dreams of hospitality a la Memphis or Nashville, Tennessee.

Wire nails and metal bolts took the place of wooden pegs. Mill-turned columns of ornate complexity supported the roof of the two-sided veranda. Gingerbread, as the natives called it, spiraled and curly-cued about the veranda rails, the shutters and the cornices. The Colonel christened it 'The Van Winkle House—the Pride of the South'. Its massive outline encompassed three full stories with ceilings eighteen feet tall in every room on every floor. Southern food served southern style contributed to the fame of the Van Winkle. It became the mingling place of the society that flourished with Fayetteville's new prosperity, and the base for the operation of the drummers and speculators, who had business with the industrial developers of the wild territory to the south and west.

"How much y' make to-day?" Ed Graves, owner of the Fayetteville Livery Barn was addressing a serious-faced boy.

"Forty cents," come a prompt, proud answer. "Thirty for shines and a dime for holdin' the horses. Them folks at the Van Winkle are some sports."

"I could take a shinin' box and rag an' make it better than I can with this damn barn," Graves grumbled. "Guess I'll have to take to chargin' you for sleepin' in that hay loft. I didn't spose you'd get wealthy so fast."

The boy grinned. "It is pretty good, now, ain't it?" he inquired.

"It's damn good," Graves admitted. "Say, there's a half a san'wich an' a hunk of cake in that bucket of mine. The old lady put in too much. You can have it, if you want."

"Thank you, Mr. Graves, you're awful nice; but, you don't need to leave me nothin' out of your dinner bucket. You know what? I'm goin' back tonight an' wash dishes in the kitchen, and get a dinin' room dinner when I get through."

"At the Van Winkle?" the amazed Graves gasped.

"Yep, an' I don't want to ruin my belly with no san'wich. I get a whiff out of that dinin' room once in a while when I'm shinin' on the veranda, an' I see them swells—through the window—in there eatin'. They carried a little pig, cooked whole, with a' apple in his mouth, right out where I could see it. An' you should've smelled that pork." He rubbed his lank mid-section in anticipation. "I'm goin' to eat so much pork tonight..."

"Look out for them teams," Graves shouted, yanking him aside. A rumbling freighter, pulled by four lathering black mules, rolled through the wide doorway.

"Hi, Mawman, how you makin' out?" the dirty driver sung out from the high seat.

"I'm all right, Lane," the boy chirped. "How you makin' out?"

"I saw your maw an' paw," the driver replied, ignoring the inquiry. "They was out to see me when I pulled in Rogers, this trip."

"Were they hot?"

"Nope," the driver said.

"Worried?"

"Nope. Jest ask a few questions and walk off. Not hot an' not worried. I guess they know old Mawman's a man. A growed man."

Young Pruiett swelled with importance. "Well—what did they say?" Man or not, he had to have a word from home.

"Well," came the reply, "your maw comes up—I've got the bits out, waterin' the mules—an' she says, 'Lane Robberson' she says, 'my boy Mawman's been gone for six days, an' he left the same day as you was through here last. I want to know if you know where he's at?' I says—you know me, Mawman, I don't tell nobody no lies—an' I says, 'Missus Pruiett, Mawman is up to Fayetteville, livin' at Ed Graves' place, an' makin' his livin' a'shinin' shoes.' That's what I says. She says 'what do you mean, haulin' my boy off on your ole rickety freight wagon—gettin' his tail all skinned up with pine splinters? You helpin' a little boy run away from home?' An' I says... say, Mawman, want a chaw?"

Pruiett took a lusty bite of twist. Lane Robberson spat on the wagon spokes before he resumed the narrative. "The Captain comes up about that time, an' your maw tells him I said you was down here. 'Why hell, yes,' the Captain says, 'I told you where he was. The boys at the wagon yard told me he rode off with Lane. He ain't no baby no more. He's able to take keer of hisself.' That's what the old man says. He ain't worried a bit."

"Are they a'comin' after me?" the boy inquired.

"Nope," said Lane. "They says to tell you if you get to makin' more money than you need, offen these pine-lumber swells around here, not to forgit 'em. The Captain says his business ain't none too good. An' your maw says," he lowered his voice, as if to keep a privileged communication from Graves, who had the mules in stalls and was hanging up the last of the harness, "she says if you need a little cash, for me to give it to you, an' she'll pay me back when I come in next trip."

The boy beamed. "You tell 'em I got a good place to stay, an' that I'm makin' money. I made three an' a half in five days, an' I got a job at the Hotel now, washin' dishes for my supper. I guess I won't need no help from nobody."

"I'll tell 'em I seen you, kid," Robberson waved as he swung off toward a saloon on the square. "An' you can ride back with me any time you want."

"I ain't goin' home," the boy shouted. "I ain't goin' home—not for a hell of a time."

"That's pretty strong language for a kid," Graves observed from a mule stall.

"I'm goin' on fourteen," Pruiett said.

"Excuse me," said Graves.

"When I get rich," he said, "I'm goin' to have me a room at the Van Winkle, an' eat three meals a day in the dinin' room. I'll keep my buggy an' team here with you, Mr. Graves, an' I'll have a derby an' patent leathers. Say, Mr. Graves, who's the old coot at the hotel that keeps the fancy team up the street—an' wears such flashy clothes?"

"The one with the mustaches an' the loud band on his sailor?"

"Yeah, the city dude."

"His name's F. L. Van Zant," Graves answered. "He's from Pennsylvania. Ain't he a dandy?"

"I shined him three times today, an' a different pair of kicks ever' time. He changed his suit before dinner, an' had on a fresh one this evenin' when I started down here. He must be awful rich."

"He is," said Graves. "Some one died an' left it to him. He's investin' it in timberland an' coal mines. He's goin' to live in Fayetteville an' take care of his property from here. He's got a few farms an' some railroad stock besides."

"He's got the handsomest vests an' the biggest watch chain I ever seen," the boy said. "An' I'll bet ya that I get the regular job of holdin' his horses, 'fore very long."

The summer sun was half out of sight behind the wood-covered slopes west of town when Pruiett trudged up to the side veranda of the Van Winkle House. His strap was over his shoulder and his box hung at his side. Ed Graves had reminded him that he might pick up some shine money after supper. The elegant Van Zant, with a straight cheroot slanting down from his mustaches, was leaving the hotel by the side steps.

"Hi, sonny," Van Zant said. "Hit 'em a few licks for me."

Pruiett looked at his boots. "Ain't I just shined 'em for you?" he asked.

"They got dusty awful quick in this dry weather," Van Zant answered. "Shine 'em up."

The boy was already on his knees, lifting a boot to the footrest on the box. "When you'r comin' by the hotel, an' have your buggy out, I'd like to hold your horses," he said. "I like horses awful well, an' always get along easy with 'em. I sleep in a livery stable."

"I'll see about it," said the easterner. He was smiling at the boy's frankness. "Hurry up with that shine."

"Yes sir. Pull up your pants-leg a little—up off'a your boots, an' I can go faster." Van Zant complied, exposing a dazzling expanse of pure white sock. The flying paste-brush was covering the leather with happy strokes.

"I'll keep your boots shined, an' your buggy wheels, too, Mister," the boy smiled, looking up enraptured. I'll take..."

"Look what you're doin'," Van Zant cried. The unwatched brush had traced an ugly trail across the white of the sock. "You little fool. What's the matter with you?"

The boy continued to kneel before him, a perfect pose for the penitence and pain, which showed in the expression of his face. "I'm awful sorry, Mister, I'm just terrible sorry."

Van Zant scowled blackly. He would damn himself for a spot of soup dribbled on a cravat. He might overlook a foul name; but, he would fight for the continued beauty of his fine raiment. He lashed out with his open hand, not to strike, but in a gesture of his extreme annoyance. He slapped at the flopping brim of the shoe-shiner's nickel straw hat.

"You've hurt me," came a loud wail, as the kneeling shiner doubled up in a Hindu bend. "You put my eye out. Call the doctor..."

"Shut up, you little whelp, or I'll stomp your head off," Van Zant grated, looking about to see if he was being made into a spectacle. There was no one on the veranda. "Shut up—an' get out of here."

"Oh! Oh, my eye. I'm goin' blind! You've hurt me bad." A flake of pressed straw from the brittle brim of the hat had been driven into his eye. The sudden pain, with the humiliation that went with blacking a customer's sock, was bringing out some hitherto undisclosed dramatic talent in the boy Pruiett. "Call the Doctor," he moaned, "Call the Doctor."

Van Zant dropped a dime in the gravel of the path. "I'll get you a doctor, you dirty little bastard," he said. "You'd better shut that god damn clack..." Looking about, and still being unable to see any one about, he aimed a kick at the upturned rump. "There's your doctor." The kick turned him over. Van Zant ran up the steps and into the side door of the hotel.

It was ten o'clock at night. Ed Graves rapped cautiously at the door of Van Zant's room in the Van Winkle House. "I thought I'd better tell you, sir, about the kid," he mumbled, apologetically. "He's perty bad off. He's sick. Maybe he ought to have a doctor."

"What kid?" Van Zant demanded.

"The boot-black," Graves persisted. "I saw it—well—I saw you out there this evenin'—well, when you kicked him. I seen it. I had to carry him back to the stable, an' he ain't gettin' over it too quick. I think he's hurt bad."

"Jesus Christ," Van Zant gritted. "I might 'ave killed him. What's the matter with me? Them drinks I had with supper must've made me crazy. Where is he?"

Graves led the way to the canvas covered straw bed in the loft of the livery barn. "I'm awful sorry about them white socks," the boy whimpered as they came in. "An' I'm sorry about this—too. I know you didn't mean to, an'..."

"That boy's hurt," Van Zant said, with one look at his streaked, suffering countenance. "Get a doctor, an' have him come to my room at the hotel. I'll carry the kid over there an' put him to bed."

"Am I really goin' to sleep in the Van Winkle?" Pruiett inquired, as Van Zant was carrying him up the hotel stairs. "In your room at the Van Winkle House?" The affirmative answer he received relieved the bruised and sprained rump more than did the arnica and tape which the doctor applied.

Betty and the Captain arrived from Rogers two days later.

"This here $12, I'm givin' you," Van Zant said, "is for damages, damages for the injury I done to your fine boy. Of course, it was an accident; but, I want to do what's right, an'..."

"It seems like an awful lot, Mr. Van Zant," Betty demurred.

"Not a'tall," Van Zant flourished. "An' I want you to sign this little paper sayin' that it's all right, an' that you don't expect me to pay no more. My lawyer fixed it up. You sign the paper and take the money. Then I got it all fixed for the hotel bus to haul you home."

"You mean—you mean we're goin' plumb to Rogers in the Van Winkle bus?" Young Pruiett had risen to two elbows in the big bed, and was staring incredulously.

" 'Tain't no sense in such extravagance, with such good train connections," the Captain opined. "You're spoilen us."

"One seat's just right for a bed for the kid," Van Zant explained. "You have plenty of room for yourselves, an' for takin' care of him."

"Good God," the boy sighed, falling backward. "Plumb to Rogers—in the bus."

The conveyance consisted of four fancy horses, a surplus of brass-trapped harness, four rubber-tired wheels to a veneer covered and varnished box, and an enclosure upholstered with real leather. "She's stuffed with horse-hair," Moorman observed as they bounced over the gravel toward Rogers.

"Mr. Van Zant's a fine gentleman," Betty said.

"The folks'll set up an' take notice when they see us rollin' up in this trap," the Captain said. "We ought to have a carriage ourselves. They don't cost so much, an' horses ain't expensive to keep, but it just seems ever' time I get about ready, why somethin' has to happen. Right now, we ain't makin' expenses. The construction has run too far from us, an' that's all there is to my meat business. If it wasn't for your boardin' house, we'd be in a hell..."

"I know," Betty nodded. "I been seein' it in your eyes for a long spell. Them pastures across the valley are lookin' greener. I guess it's about time to get movin' again."

"Well," he said, defensively, "the Frisco's done fifty miles southwest, an' them paddies is eatin' beef down there just the same as they was when they was buildin' through these hills. Ever' one says that the goin' is slowin' down while they make them mountains through the Indian Territory. The rougher it gets, the better prices the supply men will get for their stuff. So..."

"I seen that look on your face at Elizabethtown, an' at Brandenburg, an' Alton. I can tell when you get to thinkin' about how much better you could do if you was just some place else. I know."

"I ain't no quitter," he replied. "But, there ain't no sense in lettin' a mistake starve you to death. I thought tobacco would do good in this country, but I was wrong. I thought sellin' meat to the damn railroad would make us rich, an' it did make us a good livin', but it didn't last. I can't get a contract an' ship the stuff down on the supply trains. They want it fresh, killed an' delivered right on the job. We got to move with the road, or get into somethin' else."

"Yes," Betty agreed, listlessly. "There's more people than ever on them trains, but they ain't none of 'em stoppin'. They just go right on through, an' my rooms stay empty. We ain't doin' no good where we are. Where we headed?"

The Captain grinned. "Hackett City's a comer," he said, jerking his head for emphasis. "Four miles from the territory boundary, good timber all around, coal mines openin' up all around it, an' the Frisco headed right for her big middle. I'll get the meat contract back. We'll put the kids all in school, an' we'll save up some money. We're gettin' old."

Betty looked at the sleeping boy on the seat of the hack. The bouncing had shaken a black lock from his bulky crown, and it lay carelessly across his handsome features. Her expression softened.

"Then Mawman can go back to school. He can't go back to that old Woolsey. He's just got to get some learnin'."

"School, hell," said the Captain. "You won't never keep that boy in school. He's too tough. Always fightin'. Always got to have his own way. In trouble all the time. He's most big enough to put on the section. We'll get him to work, an' help him save his pay. Educatin' ain't goin' to do a kid like him no good."

Betty's eyes flashed. "He'll have educatin' if I have to pick on the section myself," she said. "He's smart. Just eleven months, that's all the schoolin' he's had in his whole life, an' it's done him more good than all the years the other children has got. He's got a good brain; he don't forget nothin'. He can repeat ever' word the professor says, just as fancy as he says it himself, if he wants to. He remembers, an' he imitates. He could draw a better paper right now than Mr. Van Zant's lawyer had us sign—only he wanted to. He just thinks it's sissy to be smart, so he hides his smartness. I'm goin' to make a lawyer out of Mawman."

"You'll play hell makin' a lawyer out of that one," the Captain laughed. "He's just another woods colt. He comes in slick in the springtime, an' runs perty fast around the barn lot, but put him upside a real racehorse an' he'll fall down. If you don't get such high an' mighty ideas, you won't get such hefty disappointments. Mawman'll always be just like he is right now. He'll fight like hell just for the right to be sulky an' stupid."

The law firm of Phillip Doddridge Brewer and Jap Hale, with offices above Preslie B. Cole's Hardware Store, contained the cream of the Hackett City bar. A pot-bellied stove, surrounded by tin spit-buckets, ash boxes and straight backed chairs, stood in the center of the principal room. Phillip Brewer's big desk set in a corner near the windows.

"Would you tell me, please, what the requirements for bein' a successful lawyer are?" An awkward boy, with fuzz and pimples, was speaking an obviously rehearsed speech to Brewer. Brewer stared in amazement.

"Hey, Jap," he bawled, "Come 'ere. Come 'ere quick."

Jap Hale appeared in the frame of the open doorway into his adjoining room. "What's the trouble?" he inquired.

"I been practicin' law for near to twenty years," Brewer said. "I had some tough questions put to me, an' if I do say so myself, I ain't never had one I couldn't answer, 'til right now. Mawman's asked me one that beats me."

Hale feigned interest. "I can't imagine," he said.

"Mawman walks in an' asks me, right out of a clear sky, 'what's the requisites of a successful lawyer?' I hadn't never thought of it."

"I'll be god-damned," Hale acknowledged. "Now there's one that ain't in the book. It never occurred to me, neither. Set down, Mawman, an' we'll worry over it together." He pulled up a straight chair and sat down beside Brewer.

"Abe Lincoln got ahead by bein' honest, an' chargin' his clients starvation fees," Brewer ruminated.

"An' he'd a starved to death as a lawyer, if he'd a stayed with it long enough," Hale objected. "That's part of the background for a successful politician, not a lawyer. That's out."

"My maw says I'd make a good lawyer," Pruiett said, complacently. "But she says that lawyers has got to have a lot of education—if they're successful."

"Well," said Hale, "mothers are most usually right."

"I can't remember ever seein' a successful lawyer," Brewer interrupted. "About the time you get it all learned, why some damn fool up an' changes the law, or somethin' happens to ruin you. There was one that was almost successful, one time. He came down to Fort Smith, from back east, an' he hadn't never lost a case; but, when he got through tryin' his case before old Isaac Parker, the federal judge for the Western District of Arkansas, he was so turned around he had to hire a nigger to lead him from the courthouse back to his hotel. They hung his client the next day, an' by god, they'd a hung him, too, if he hadn't a got out of town on the night train. This success business is just awful hard to figger."

"There was an' old Texas lawyer through this country one time," Jap Hale recalled, "who had some damn good idears on the subject. He said 'if the evidence was agin' you to raise hell with the law, an' if the law was agin' you to raise hell with the evidence. 'An' ,' he says, 'if the law an' the evidence is both agin' you, raise hell with the lawyer on the other side of the case.' Well—he won his case all right, but he raised so much hell he made the other lawyer sore, an' he shot him dead on the steps as he was walkin' out of the courthouse."

Pruiett joined with Brewer in a laugh. "Have you read all them books?" he inquired, pointing toward the crowded wall-shelves.

A native of Hackett City, Arkansas, Oklahoma City attorney Philip Doddridge Brewer was the first to introduce Moman Pruiett to the legal profession by allowing the teenaged Pruiett to sweep the floors, empty the spitoons, and stock the firebox with wood in his law office. Once Pruiett's daily chores were completed, Brewer allowed him to read the writings of Sir William Blackstone and Mansfield's Digest in his books on law. Courtesy *Men of Affairs.*

Brewer and Hale laughed again. "Hell, no," said Hale. "You don't need to read 'em. You get in an' get started—you wait till you get a problem, an' then you look it up in the books. You got to start tryin' cases before you learn anything about law."

"Then I don't see why you need to spend so much time studyin'," the boy said. "All you need is a few books, an' to know enough to know where to look. Is that it?"

"That's almost it," Brewer agreed. "You see, I ain't had a lot of education, an' neither has Jap. We just got enough to get by with. But we can see now, with the opportunity gone, how much it'd help if we just had it. Good grammar, knowledge of how to make correct sentences, an' paragraphs. That helps when you go to drawin' your pleadings, an' gettin' ready to try your case. An' history, an' literature, an' the classics. You can spot a' educated lawyer in court by the material like that he has to draw on when he's makin' his speeches. But the little feller, that just knows how to look it up, an' make a dry, ignorant argument on a measly state of facts, like me an' Jap, they ain't successful. We ain't jokin', right now, Mawman. We ain't qualified to answer your question."

"I see what you mean," the boy answered. "My maw told me the same thing, but I didn't think she knew what she was talkin' about. I see it, the way you put it. But I don't get along good in school. I could learn all right, but I hate the kids. Always foolin'—always teasin'. The boys is worse than the girls, an' they don't teach no law at the Hackett City school. Where am I goin' to learn?"

"What's your main trouble?" Hale inquired.

"They call me Mutton-chops, cause paw's a butcher, an' they holler, 'get yore hair cut or pay yore dog-tax'. It ain't my fault about this hair, or paw bein' a butcher, neither."

"Knock it down their throats," Hale grinned, "that's easy..."

"I've licked ever' kid in school," he interrupted, "an' I thought I had things where I could go ahead about my learnin'. I told the teacher I'd speak a piece at the exercises last night—I like to do that kind of stuff—an' so I got up before the school, an' started. 'No more shall smoke curl from the teepee of the lowly American Indian,' I says, an' that's as far as I get. Ever' kid in the room yells, 'shut up, Mutton-chops! Go pay your dog-tax,' an' they keep it up, throwin' chalk an' paper wads, 'til the teacher makes me set down. I ain't never goin' back to that school."

"The boys are just jealous, about the hair cuts," Brewer observed, "but I believe I would cut more of it off if I was you. You got more damn hair on your head than any boy I ever saw."

"I took Gay Forbes home from the exercises," Pruiett went on. "When we got up to the front gate, she told me that Doc Forbes says for her to stop walkin' home from school with me, that he didn't want his girl runnin' around town with a butcher's boy. She said..."

Brewer laughed. "You been a hell of a time gettin' around to the point," he said. "There's a woman in the case. I might'a known that any one with his hair brushed that oily would have a gal. I never seen a crow with blacker an' shinier feathers. You want to show ol' Doctor Joseph H. Forbes that you can get rich, an' successful, in a hurry, an' make him sorry for what he said about you."

"Well," he hesitated a little embarrassed, "my maw has told me of how bad she wanted me to be a lawyer. I just wisht I knew how to get started."

"William J. Blackstone, who authored *Commentaries on the Laws of England,* was supposed to know somethin' about law, an' he wrote that big book right there in the corner of the shelf," Hale said. "Start out by readin' it—come up any time you want—an' when I got time I'll go over some of these indexes with you, an' show you how to look up cases. An' hang around court—watchin'. That's the way to get started."

"I'll come up an' read ever' day," the boy agreed, "but I got to do somethin' for the trouble I'll be. I'm a good worker. What can I do?"

Brewer looked at Hale before he answered. "You can take charge of the heatin' department," he said, pointing toward the pot-bellied item in the room's center. "Empty the cat-boxes an' spittoons, an' sweep the floor down once in awhile. We'll try you out as a new member, for that much work."

"I'll do 'er," he said. "An' them buckets is damn near full, right now."

John Sebastian Little, with full speed on toward the Arkansas governorship, was District Judge for Sebastian County. The courthouse was at Greenwood. It was January 6, 1888. "In the case of *State vs. Pruiett,* the parties will please come forward," he said.

Four persons moved into position before his rough bench. One was C. B. Neal, lawyer, who had previously held the position then occupied by Little. One was a bushy-headed boy in his 'teens. The real sufferers, whose sad-eyed misery was unconcealed, were the parents of the youth, Betty and the stooped Captain.

"How old are you, young man?" the court inquired.

"I'm sixteen, sir." There was no quaver in the stout voice.

"You've been convicted by a jury composed of citizens of this county—they've found you guilty of the crime of forgery—an' recommended that you be sentenced to two years in the penitentiary. It is my unpleasant duty to pass sentence on you, and if you've got anything to say—got any reasons for me not doin' my duty—I want to hear about it. You got anything to say?"

The convicted boy looked toward his counsel; contempt was unconcealed in his face as the painful silence continued. A woman's voice was heard.

"Mawman ain't guilty, judge, your honor," Betty said. "Even if the jury says so, he ain't. He's a good boy, he's always worked hard an' always obedient. An' he's so young. Why, he's only sixteen. Penitentiaries ain't built for little boys—they're meant for criminals—an Mawman ain't no criminal."

The court leaned back and reflected. "The proof in this case showed that your boy was workin' for a Mr. Patterson, that he was the station agent for the railroad spur line, an' it showed that he was drivin' the express wagon, makin' freight and express deliveries from the depot, an' collectin' the freight an' express bills on the stuff delivered."

"He wasn't workin' for Patterson," Betty interrupted. The defendant shot another contempt-laden look at his lawyer, who stood in stupid silence, while the miserable woman begged. "He owned the wagon an' the mule too, hisself. Just a boy, an' doin' a man's work. Why—in just a year he's bought the outfit an' paid for it, helped me an' his paw, an' managed to save money for hisself. An' all the time he's readin' law, an' workin' in the lawyers' office, tryin' to learn law just to please me."

"Why ain't he been in school?" the judge asked.

"Just because we...." Betty was interrupted by the boy, who pushed her aside.

"Don't beg 'em no more," he directed. Then he turned to the court. "I can do all the time you got for me," he said. "I ain't no baby. I told you I wasn't guilty in the first place, an' this thing you called a trial wasn't nothin' but a farce. If I got to go to Little Rock, Arkansas, to the state penitentiary let's get it over with, only don't mistreat my maw. She ain't done nothin'."

"The evidence showed that you were kitin' freight bills; that you made threes look like eights, an' ones look like nines, an' was holdin' out the exorbitant amounts you collected on these raised bills. That is a serious offense, an' it continued over a considerable time. You were takin' advantage of the confidence that your friends an' neighbors put in you, when they hired you to do their haulin'."

"Nobody saw Mawman do it," Betty pleaded. "Maybe Mr. Patterson done it. Maybe some of the other railroad men done it. An' Mawman's just a child. Ain't the law big enough to give a little child another chance?"

"The special agents for the Frisco had convincin' evidence. I can see how the jury was able to agree on your boy's bein' guilty. I was satisfied he was guilty, by their evidence." The court was leaning across the bench with an unfriendly light in his eye.

"The other boys Mawman's age is walkin' across the platform at the Hackett City school today—gettin' their diplomas—just startin' out in life, the right way. It ain't fair to send my boy away, for such a little thing; mark him for life, even if he was guilty. Please don't make a criminal out of my boy." Betty was pleading; great tears were streaming down her careworn face.

"Let's have it over with, judge," the defendant said, gruffly, as he pushed her aside again. He looked toward his still silent, obviously confused attorney. He thought of what Phil Brewer and Jap Hale had told him. 'The little feller, that just knows how to look it up, an' make a dry, ignorant argument on a measly state of facts, he ain't successful.' "I ain't guilty, yer honor, but you can't hurt me. Let's have it over."

"I sentence you to confinement in the state penitentiary at Little Rock, for a period of two years. The proof in the case, an' your attitude here, don't warrant my suspendin' the sentence. The Sheriff is directed to deliver you to the warden, an' the sentence begins to run with your delivery." Little set his sharp chin. Betty sobbed, miserable, uncontrollable sobs.

The kids at Hackett, with unintelligible giggles, took their graduation certificates and shuffled from the platform. Mutton-chops, manfully defiant, walked erect from the presence of the stern court and his distressed parents, with the Sheriff. He had protested his guilt, and his plea had been spurned. The State had its judgment to execute.

CHAPTER THREE

WHEREIN CURRENT EVENTS, AS INDICATED BY THE NOTICES OF THE NATIONAL PRESS, ARE CONTRASTED WITH THOSE OF A DAY WHEN PRUIETT, AN ADOLESCENT YOUTH, RETURNS FROM PRISON TO A MOTHER STILL DETERMINED TO PUSH HIM INTO THE LAW. AND HOW HE HAS HIS FIRST VIEW OF JUDGE VOORHEES, KNOWN AS THE "TALL SYCAMORE OF THE WABASH," IN ACTION IN A CELEBRATED INDIAN MURDER CASE. AND HOW HIS CONNECTION WITH THE RAILROAD LABORING CREW TAKES HIM, WITH THE WANDERING PRUIETTS, TO NORTH TEXAS, AND, WHEREIN, HE EXPRESSES HIS DOUBTS AND FEARS CONCERNING THE EFFECT OF THE FELON'S BRAND HE CARRIES. HOW IT FORTHWITH CONFRONTS HIM, TO CARRY HIM DOWN FOR THE SECOND TIME UNDER A FELONY CONVICTION, AND HOW THE BOY WHO WENT TO PRISON IS A MAN WHEN HE RETURNS, AND HOW HARD WORK, THICK SKIN AND THE GENEROSITY OF A FEDERAL JUDGE COMBINE TO MAKE A NEW LAWYER IN TEXAS.

"The men of the southwest were living wide-open lives in the days when Pruiett, by the sheer force of his appeals to the emotions of his juries, was setting out to unlock the doors for prisoners who faced the hangman's noose." In New York City, the *New York Sun,* three and a half decades after the professional beginning of the strange career, was reproducing a part of the legend which had sprung up about the man Pruiett.

Thirty-six hundred miles away in California, the *Long Beach Sun,* impressed by the news value of the same subject observed "then began the career which has stamped Pruiett a genius at defending criminals before the bar. In 36 years, he defended 342 men accused of murder. Of this number, 304 went free. Thirty-eight were found guilty and were given sentences ranging from four years to life. Not a single sentence of death in 342 cases!" (A correction, please, Mr. Reporter. One death sentence, but no execution of it. President McKinley saved him his record.) "He often boasted that he would quit whenever the death sentence was passed on one of his clients."

Where is the lawyer in America—in the universe—who has defied the dark angel's retribution and walked arm in arm through the valley of the shadow with so many accused murderers? Let him who knows stand and proclaim the fame of the advocate who has gained half the number of acquittals, for faith, he is entitled to it. The *Suns* on Long Island's smelly sound and the Pacific's sunny slope, could have truthfully charged that Pruiett's deliverances were gained over the undeniable, and often times, obvious guilt of his clients. Brutal murder—single, triple, five at a time, with poison, axe and firearm, he could clothe it with the white robe of justification and procure, in some manner, the acquittal of his clients.

"It needed no unusual reportorial perspicacity to spot him as the best story on the courthouse beat," Wesley Stout, the western cub who rose to the editorship of the *Saturday Evening Post,* once observed in a letter in retrospect on Pruiett. "I worked in Oklahoma City only a little more than three months, but in that brief time Moman defended and acquitted four or five men whose guilt was as obvious as the clock in the tower. Once I thought he was stuck. He feared so, too, and tried a move of desperation. It worked. The assistant prosecuting attorney was a Jew, named Saul. I had not even been conscious that he was a Jew. I never had encountered anti-Jewish feeling. When he took the jury, Moman launched into a savage Jew-baiting harangue and soon had the twelve good men and true eager to lynch Saul for the betrayal of Jesus Christ."

Lemuel F. Parton, publicizing the Tammany Hall corruption trial, which banished boss Hines to Sing Sing Prison in New York and moved the ambitious and trust-busting Thomas Dewey a notch nearer to the White House, couldn't keep the old Washita campaigner out of his mind—or copy. Commenting upon the able but unsuccessful efforts of Lloyd Paul Stryker, Hines's counsel, Parton said, "Old-timers around here tell me that only Morton Rutherford and Moman Pruiett, of Oklahoma, have ever topped him in courtroom decibels, metaphors, similes and all-around tear jerking."

But back to Gotham's reverie on Pruiett. "In the forward of her novel *Cimarron* Edna Ferber wrote: 'There was no Yancy Cravat—he is a blending of a number of dashing Oklahoma figures of a past and present day'. In that forward, she had explained, too, that 'only the more fantastic and improbable events' contained in her book were true. But in the pen picture of the various characters who figure in the book Oklahomans who have lived through any of the fantastic or improbable incidents which form its structure have no difficulty in identifying many of its personalities."

"Oklahoma Territorial juries first came under Pruiett's spell thirty-six years ago. He was graduated from the school of the streets of Fort Smith as a bootblack and took to books. He admits that the culture of the frontier was deeply ingrained in him. Men were being put to death daily at the Federal hanging pen for crimes they might not have committed. 'I studied backwoods psychology,' he once said, 'by watching juries and noting the reaction of the lawyers' arguments. The Government had all the best of them. The defendants for the most part were so poor or so ignorant they didn't hire lawyers, and those who were hired made their appeals on dry facts, alone. The jury would go to sleep and the bailiff would have to wake them up. Sometimes they'd bring in a verdict without leaving their seats. I made up my mind that I'd be a lawyer and that no jury would ever go to sleep on me'."

"Possibly that process of applied jury psychology has something to do with the record of this remarkable lawyer, who during his career at the bar has defended 342 persons accused of murder, 304 of whom have been acquitted."

"Moman Pruiett is the last of his type. The swashbuckler, with his turgid appeal to the frail sentiments of the prairie folks, is vanishing along the lines that once marked the frontier. In his best days, he (Yancy Cravat, of course) was only a feeble imitator of Moman Pruiett, or Temple Houston, 'scion of a nobler forbear who made his word into law', or Morton Rutherford, the Virginia Aristocrat, who carried respect for law into the Indian Territory at the end of his six-shooter. From the Arkansas to the Panhandle, from the Strip to Red River, no man, qualified to venture an opinion, will deny that these three stood at the head of the Southwest's list of criminal lawyers."

Pruiett methods, with the story of his prowess and success, were woven into the fabric of legend which lived and grew after age and adversity had pulled him from active conflict. A Pruiett conducted trial was a continuing chord of climaxes. What the promoter did to keep the jury, and an invariably packed courtroom, laughing, wondering, and crying, was of some benefit to the accused culprit, of course, but Pruiett's clients always had the proof.

"During the last decade of his career, Pruiett and his ability to win acquittals have made him the subject of many legends accounting his ability and his readiness to act on the spur of the moment. One, which he denies but delights in recounting, tells of a telegram he received from a man in a distant state which read like this: 'I am charged with murder. Have $5000. Will you defend me?' Pruiett's reply, according to the story, was: 'Am leaving on next train with three eye witnesses'."

And, not all of the tons of newsprint and barrels of printers' ink used on the Pruiett process was turned into favorable or flattering comment. His capacity for making bitter enemies was as great as was his acumen for winning lasting friendships. Criminal law was his bower; politics was his hobby. Such a strange compound was emblematic of the extremes of his nature.

"Last week was a strenuous one in the big political circus; big guns, little guns, and some we would be inclined to call sons-of-guns, appeared on the horizon, shed their little lights and disappeared, probably never to be seen again. As we might be prejudiced in our views, however, we will content ourselves with giving a brief description of some of the animals and leave their classifications to a candid world."

"In the latter class may be mentioned Moman Pruiett of Oklahoma City, who denounced Socialism as the 'red-handed enemy of the government', and in the next breath damned the federal government. If a Socialist had used the language he did in his condemnation of the government, he would probably have been run in by the police."

"Moman is a curiosity. He has some admirable qualities, such as energy and courage, but on the whole the animal so predominates in him that he is repellent to those of more kindly and humane natures. Of medium height, a shock of coal black hair extending far down towards the nose over a narrow forehead, glittering, deep set eyes, and a stooping, crouching gesture, he makes you feel that he is the embodiment of animal cunning and ferocity. He prides himself on his reputation as a criminal lawyer, and he is probably deserving of the reputation to a greater extent than even he realizes."

"We might drop the last word, lawyer, and get a clearer idea of the situation. His reputation is such that criminals seek his services for safety and deliverances. The man who protects a criminal is worse, as a rule, than the criminal himself, because, he is usually more intelligent and therefor more dangerous. In this view of the case, Moman would probably be the greatest criminal in the state and being a lawyer better enables him to protect crime."

"Of course, this is all done under the form of law and the theory that right and justice prevails, but how sadly untrue that is, attested by the universal suspicion of the courts, and the common remark that there is no justice in law. Thus it is that such a man would not only become the greatest criminal, but the very essence and incarnation of anarchy, breeding contempt for all law."

"Suppose we stood in that lofty temple of jurisprudence," old Wendell Phillips had howled at his prompt-to-cheer Boston audience. "On either side of us the statues of the great lawyers of every age and clime—and let us see what part New England—Puritan, educated, free New England—would bear in the pageant. Rome points to a colossal figure and says, 'This is Papinian, who, when the Emperor Caracalla murdered his own brother, and ordered the lawyer to defend the deed, went cheerfully to death rather than sully his lips with the atrocious plea'."

"And France stretches forth her grateful hands, crying, 'This is D'Aguesseau, worthy, when he went to face an enraged king, of the farewell his wife addressed him: "Go! Forget that you have a wife and children to ruin, and remember only that you have France to save'." England says, 'That is Coke, who flung the laurels of eighty years in the face of the first Stuart, in defense of the people. This is Selden, on every book of whose library you saw written the motto of which he lived worthy, "Before everything, LIBERTY!" That is Mansfield, silver-tongued, who proclaimed, 'Slaves cannot live in England; if their lungs receive our air, that moment they are free.' 'This is Romilly, who spent life trying to make law synonymous with justice, and succeeded in making life and property safer in every city of the Empire. And that is Erskine, whose eloquence, spite of Lord Eldon and George III, made it safe to speak and print."

"Then New England shouts, 'This is Choate, WHO MADE IT SAFE TO MURDER; and of whose health thieves asked before they began to steal.'"

But Rufus Choate's ventures into the field of the criminal law were comparatively slight, and only casually noteworthy. The abolitionist's flattering finger of scorn, although he knew it not, was pointed across a half century of turbulent American development toward the untutored son of an itinerant butcher, who vowed, while he lock-stepped with the condemned in southwestern prisons, that he would make it safe to murder, and possible to steal in peace.

"The Governor pardoned Morman [sic] Pruiett, convicted December term, '87 of the Sebastian County Court and sentenced to two years in penitentiary. He is but 16 years old, has served 7 months of his sentence, and his pardon was asked by the Judge, Pros. Atty., and many good citizens of Sebastian County." So spake the *Executive Register* at Little Rock.

"Mawman's comin' home tomorrow." Betty tried to keep elation out of her tone. Her hands were in a steaming washtub full of dirty dishes. She spoke to the Captain, who smoked and rocked in an old chair beside the kitchen stove.

"I'll be glad to see the colt," he said. "Been a long time since he went away."

"Ain't been much over six months, but it seems a heap longer. It seems like a year, almost, just between visits I been makin'."

"How many times you been up there?"

"I been up there ever' month, six times, an' you haven't been a single time. You oughta have gone with me."

"Hell," he said, "I'm gettin' old. Too old to be goin' that far to see anybody. An' anyway, some one's got to run that damn meat wagon out ever' day. It's pore enough with it runnin' regular. Between it an' the boardin' house we ain't hardly makin' it."

"I managed to lay enough away ever' month to get up on it, an' it's a good thing Anna's so much help, an' knows how to run things around here. I just had to see Mawman, an' I had to see that Governor."

"I'll bet that Governor got a belly full of your clack."

"Governor Simon P. Hughes is a gentleman," Betty retorted. "He's awful stern, an' awful stubborn, all right, but he's honest an' fair. I knowed I'd be able to make him see the right, if I went after it long enough."

"It took him a hell of a long time to make up his mind," said the Captain.

"He started out by sayin' he'd have to serve his term. After three or four months, an' me comin' in ever' month, an' just settin' 'til I got to talk to him, he got to askin' questions—about where I was tryin' to get with Mawman, an' who was payin' all the cost it took for me to make the trips up there. Then he visited the prison an' had them bring Mawman in to see him. That was what got the pardon. He saw that Mawman wasn't really nothin' but a child, an' that he was awful sick."

"It just don't sound like Mawman—bein' sick."

"He can't stand bein' shut up," she said. "He's like a wild animal, a woods colt, like you said. He started wastin' and fadin' from the day they locked him up, just turnin' yeller an' gettin' thin. An' then his knees an' ankles started swellin', an' they had to put him in the hospital. It ain't natural for a kid to be havin' inflammatory rheumatism, so I tell's the Governor that the cold and damp of them cells is what is causin' it, an' he just can't get better unless he can get back with me for nursin'."

"Have you thought any about what we was goin' to do with him, after we get him home?" There was a doleful look on the Captain's face. "You know how he is, an' if he'd fight the whole county 'cause they called him mutton-chops, what's he goin' to do when some bastard calls him a' ex-convict?"

"I'll cure him up an' get him well before I go to worryin' about such stuff as that," she answered. "I guess we can manage. For one thing, that big Cornelius Boudinot murder case is comin' up at Fort Smith, an' Senator Voorhees is goin' to be there. I'm goin' to see that Mawman gets to see him—an' hear him."

"Who's Voorhees?" inquired the Captain.

"He's the finest lawyer that ever banged a table," she said. "He's the Tall Sycamore of the Wabash. I heard him at Alton, an' it seems I been hearin' him ever' since. Them rich Boudinots is payin' $5,000 for him to come from the United States Senate, just to defend that wild Cornelius. I read all about it in a Fort Smith Sunday paper. Voorhees says that Federal Judge Isaac 'Ike' Parker at Fort Smith ain't goin' to get to sentence this Indian to hang."

"You still got them law notions in your head?"

"You bet I have, an' I ain't gettin' 'em out, neither. That Mawman has got a brain for a lawyer, an' don't you forget it."

"Gettin' jailin' for schoolin' ain't goin' to help his lawin' none," observed the Captain. "If I can get him on one of them crews in the territory, he'd better take it an' get to makin' some money. That cut an' trestle work they're doin' in the Windin' Stair Mountain is goin' to last a long time. It's a hell of a job, with floods an' cave-ins an' slides. They need men, an' if Mawman's in any kind of shape at all, I can get him on."

"Sure, he can help us by workin' when he's able, but first he goes to Fort Smith. Phil Brewer told me he could go right back to his law readin', as soon as he got back an' got able, an' workin' on the road won't last forever. They've almost run away from our boardin' house an' meat market again, an' it won't be long now before we got to move, or think about doin' somethin' else."

The Captain removed his pipe from his mouth and pointed it at her. "Now," he said, "you're talkin'. You took the words right outa my mouth. When they get through them hills in the Injun country an' hit the Texas flats, they's goin' to be some fast track layin'. Old Hackett's blowed up. We gotta go to Texas."

"I guess we gotta keep movin'," Betty sighed. "I wisht we could get a nice little thing somewhere where we could get the kids in school, so's they could learn to be somethin', but the line keeps movin', an' all we got is a workin' interest in it. When they get through the hills, I guess we'll be movin' on south."

The gang camps on the banks of Kiamichi River and Black Fork River were embracing the virgin fastness of the Choctaw Nation, preparatory to making the first violation of its maidenliness. The fox-squirrels that darted and chattered in the treetops and invaded the grounds of the camps for scraps of food were no less commonplace than the spotted deer that would not give up their watering place to the noisy white men. They came back in large droves, to sniff statuesquely of the aroma of the shacks and tents, and to drink long and freely before scampering back into the wooded oblivion of the hillsides.

A wood fire reflected red and yellow upon a variety of faces in the ring about it. The bushy-headed Pruiett kid, with sun-color back in his skin and with his great black eyes outflashing the gleam of the fire, had the floor.

"You should have heard it, and seen it," he said. "He had iron gray hair, an' a long, square chin. He paced up an' down in front of that jury like a tiger in a cage, talkin' to 'em all the time, low, an' soothin' like—an' then all of a sudden he would throw back his arms, wide, like Jesus on the cross, an' beller like a bull in a wrecked box-car. He was a great big feller, tall an' slim, an' with the clearest voice you ever hear. Had a high collar an' a Prince Albert coat, an' wore a white carnation in his button-hole. When he says that it'll be a prostitution of justice if they hang that Cherokee, an' how purity would be dragged through the muck an' mire, he walks over to the ash box beside the stove, an' he takes the white carnation out of his coat button. Then he winds up like he was goin' to throw a fast curve, an' he throws the flower down in the ash box with all his might. The dust flew up an' drifted around in the room, an' he just walks over to the table an' sits down, with his arms folded an' a superior look on his mug. He looks just like he don't give a damn."

"You got a good way of rememberin' it, an' tellin' it," a bearded listener observed, with a spew of tobacco. "How you remember all that fancy langridge?"

"I been to school a few days, I guess," came the answer.

"An' a damn few," came from the half-lighted circle. There were more youngsters than Pruiett working with the railroad crew.

"Mawman's got a right to be excited over Dan'l Voorhees," one of the old men opined. "They ain't kept him in the Senate all these years for bein' a damn fool. Mawman's right—if it ain't for him they'd hung that Injun."

"What was all the ruckus about in the first place?" came an inquiry from the fringe. "I ain't never heered of it before."

"It was murder," said Pruiett, carelessly. "Old Elias Boudinot, who's the uncle of Cornelius, is way up there in the Cherokee Council, an' been to Washington a lot of times on Indian business. That's how he knows who to pick, an' he picks Voorhees. This Cornelius is a wild Indian that's about half smart, an' double-tough. He was runnin' a little newspaper up to Tahlequah an' he gets in a fuss with another Indian, named B. H. Stone, the editor of the *Tahlequah Telephone* newspaper. He shoots hell out of him and kills him an' the marshals move him up to Fort Smith an' toss him in the cooler. Ever'body says old 'Ike' Parker'll hang hell out of him, so the rich Indians jar aloose. They hire Voorhees."

"How much?" some one inquired.

"Five thousand bucks is what they said around the courthouse, an' if one Indian's worth $5,000, they got their money's worth. Oscar Miles and old man Sandels, that was prosecutin' for the government ain't no green hands, an' they wasn't pullin' punches. The Boudinots have got lawyers in the family, an' they was there worryin' an' workin', an' they had old Circuit Judge Robert B. Rutherford in the case, an' old Blair from Kansas City. But, they're all scrub timber up to the side of Voorhees. He pulled their biscuits out of the fire. They call him the Tall Sycamore of the Wabash, up in the east."

"Where you getting' all this crap?" a listener inquired.

"Anyone that knows how to wipe hisself knows about Voorhees," he scoffed. "Why, hell, I was there. I rode up on a lumber wagon, an' I'll tell you that courtroom was packed to the rafters ever'day. Half the people didn't get in that tried to, but I had a good seat. Old Voorhees, when he was windin' her up, stood up real straight, an' it looked like he was as tall as a windmill. He stuck his hands up in the air an' just stood there, an' it got still in the room just like it does in that cut before the fuse gets up to the dynamite."

Pruiett, carried away by his own unconscious eloquence, jumped up and stood in the center of the circle, with a clenched fist above his head, and a wild flame dancing in his eyes.

"I spurn the charge on assault! I spurn the charge on manslaughter! Better, it would be, to end the life of this noble red man on the scaffold, than to grind his spirit out with his life—to wring his liberty-loving life out by degrees in a felon's dungeon. I defy you to sentence him to the rope. If you lack the courage required to do your duty, to acquit him, then hang him and be done with it.' He says it so loud it's like a hunerd an' fifty pound charge goin' off in the granite. Then he says, 'Let the great God of the universe, the keeper of men's souls and consciences, be your guide, an' I shall have no fear'. It came in like an echo, kinda like the pines an' little rocks slidin' down the mountainside after the blast. God, but he had the power!"

"It musta been ketchin', to get you to goin' like that over it, Mawman," the old man said. "Air you goin' in for law now?"

The boy slid back into his place, abashed. "I can if I want, or I can do somethin' else. It's just what I damn please. Jap Hale says I got a good head for lawin', an' I done quite a bit of readin' in his office, but maw says it takes a lot of schoolin', an' I ain't got too much of that."

"If you can carry all that fancy langridge back, just after hearin' it once, you don't need no educatin'. Just loaf in the courthouse awhile, an' listen to the big windy ones, an' then go to chargin' for the spoutin' yourself. I ain't heered much better speeches anywhere, afore, than that one you just put on."

"I guess bein' a powder monkey's better pay, between it an' the kind of a lawyer I'd make. But at that, I could beat some I've heard right now, an' not half try." A hard look tightened about his dark eyes, and they bored into the smoky fire. "I'm goin' to keep on readin', when I get the chance, 'cause it may come in handy in some other kind of business. Maw says she always dreamed I'd get to lawin', an' it'd suit her, but I ain't sure about it. I'm goin' to do some lookin' before I say whether I will or not."

South of the swamps of the southeastern Indian Territory, below the ever-changing sweep of Red River, Paris, Texas, was the terminus of the Frisco's extension. Pruiett's boarding house, in the eastern part of the sprawling prairie town, was one of the new enterprises to come in with the new railroad. Paris had grown from a depot on the Texas and Pacific Railroad into a robust town. It wouldn't let another line inflate it. Like a new chew, the Frisco and its followers were maneuvered into a handy place in the cheek, and Paris browsed casually along.

"Did you get a job, Mawman?"

"Not just exactly, Ma, I didn't. I got all the work I want to do cleanin' a law office, but there ain't no pay in it. Just the right to hang around and read."

"Jesus," the Captain came in, "don't lawyers ever put out anything? What's wrong with a lawyer payin' for service he gets, like any one else?"

"I ain't never seen one that had a quarter," Moorman said. "I was with Brewer an' Hale for most a year an' all I ever saw pass over the counter for fees was butter an' vegetables an' cured meats. Ma hollers about gettin' to be a lawyer, an' then you'll be somethin', but the lawyers is the brokest bunch I ever saw."

"You ain't been in with the right kind, that's all," Betty retorted. "You just work an' learn for me, an' the pay'll take care of itself."

"Who you goin' to work for?" the Captain inquired.

"Colonel Jake C. Hodges of Paris, Texas," he answered.

"There's a lawyer that ain't broke," the elder Pruiett replied. "What he can't make tryin' murder an' cow thief cases, he can make playin' poker. I've heard of him ever since the railroad got across White River. He's the best lawyer in this part of Texas."

"That's what I heard, an' if full gabboons is any evidence of office business, he's got all he can handle. It's the filthiest place I ever seen, up there."

"How'd you happen to get in with him, Mawman?" Betty inquired.

"He's got a brother that's just my age, an' I ran into him down at the Peterson Hotel in Paris, where I been tryin' to get a job. He got to braggin' as how his brother was the best lawyer in Paris. I told him I cleaned offices for lawyers back in Hackett, an' that as soon as I got lined up I was goin' to get back into it, an' do some more law readin'. He took me up to the office, an' there's a big poker game goin' on. The spittoons an' buckets are so full they're runnin' over, an' the whole bunch is spittin' out the windows an' on the floor. Bob Hodges, that's the Colonel's brother, says 'Jake, here's a friend of mine from Arkansas that read some law with Jap Hale, up at Hackett City', an' Colonel Jake looks up from his hand for just a minute, an' he says, 'tell him to take off his wig an' make hisself at home.' The bunch started to laugh, an' I says, 'ever' country son-of-a-bitch in Arkansas has pulled that one on me. If you want to get up to date, ask me if I got my dog-tax paid.' They all gave Jake the horse laugh, an' I started to walk out. 'I was joshin',' Jake called. 'Hang around here with Bob 'til I get this hand down. I want to talk to you.' "

"It don't sound just like the right kind of a place, to me," Betty observed.

"Jake Hodges is a good man, Maw. He's rough, an' don't take nobody's backwater, but he's on the level. He talked to me awhile, an' asked about my plans, real polite like, an' then he tells me to clean'er up, so's he can see what I can do. When I got through, in about two hours, he says its the best the offices have looked for thirteen years. He gives me a bucket an' some money, an' sends me to the Peterson bar for beer for the bunch. When I get back he gives me a key an' a quarter, an' he tells me I'm a member. I got the run of the office an' it's got plenty of books. All I got to do is keep her clean."

"I wisht he had a good payin' job, an' had these law ideas out of his head," the Captain said. "Hard work is what pays in the long run. An' look at me, gettin' too old to cut meat or chop ties, an' nothin' but a broke lawyer as prospects for support."

"You keep out'a this, paw," Betty said. "Mawman don't need to work as long as I can cook an' scrub floors. My slavin' an' prayin' ain't goin' to waste. You read in Colonel Hodges' office, an' apply yourself 'til you get to know the law. Then you can take care of your maw an' pay her back."

She ran her hand through his black brush and caressed him. He didn't pull away from her. "Ever' time I ask for a job, an' I get turned down, it just feels like some one is lookin' down my windpipe," he said. "I get to wonderin' if they know about that stretch I had to do at Little Rock."

"One reason I was so glad to come out here, when your paw got to talkin' about it, was to get away from that," Betty answered. "Just you forget about it. You're young, an' you ain't got the hard look that goes with that awful experience you had. Keep your head up an' keep lookin' ahead; think about what there is to be done, an' how easy it's goin' to be for a boy with a clear head like yourn to do it. That's been a bad dream, somethin' that ain't true, an' look at it that way. Nobody knows about it out here."

"There was an old duck in Little Rock that was oldern paw, an' he'd spent the biggest part of his life there, or in some one else's jug. He said he was doin' his ninth stretch. He said he got homesick if he was aloose very long."

"I said for you to forget about that, son," Betty persisted.

"The old man didn't care much about bein' inside, like I did, most of the time. He just set around, an' didn't care what day of the week it was, an' he was always glad when the Salvation Army church was over on Sunday. But once in a while they slipped a little dope in to him—morphine—an' after he'd had his shot, he seemed to come to life, an' really worry an' hurt. One time, when he was high on the needle an'

Moman Pruiett, third from right, and his parents, Warren and Betty Pruiett, far right, stand with tenants on the porch of their boarding house in Paris, Texas, in the 1890s. Courtesy Howard K. Berry Photo Collection.

cryin' soft to hisself, we was together in the cell block, an' I ask him how in Christ's name he stood it, bein' locked up an' pushed around all his life. He said—"

"Please, Mawman, let's don't keep talkin' about such things."

"I been thinkin' about this, lately, an' I want to tell you an' paw," he persisted. "This old codger, he grew up an' got old in solitary, he told me one time, he says, 'son, I used to be chock full of hope like you are, an' while I was that a'way, it hurt me somethin' awful. I made a mistake, an' I paid for it. I done my full stretch, an' they turned me out, but I was just a god damned con. Ever' place I went, it got out that I'd done a rap, that I was a one-time loser. I'd get a job, maybe, but couldn't keep it. I left the serpent's trail behind me, an' no matter where I went, the god damned blue-noses would dig it up on me. When that snake's track's behind you, you don't need to do nothin' to get in trouble. If somethin's missin', you stole it, 'cause you're a ex-con. Somebody's house burns down, an' you're the son-of-a-bitch whether you got matches in your pocket or not. They held me in jail investigatin' me for murder one time, 'cause a drunk stumbled in front of a freight train, an' I had done two stretches in the penitentiary before, an' I happened to be in their damn town. Ain't that a fine system?' he says. The pore old man cried like a baby, an' when I tells him to cheer up, that maybe it won't be so tough on him next time he says, 'Jesus Christ, I ain't worryin' about that. I'm upset about you. You got the trail of the serpent behind you, an' just as sure as hell, you'll keep comin' back to the joints as long as you live. I got mine most done, but hell, you're just sixteen, an' you got a lot of misery ahead of you'."

"I told you to hush, Mawman," Betty said, crying softly. "The prison hurt your knees an' made them swell up, an' almost crippled you, but it didn't do nothin' to you inside. It's different in your case, 'cause you wasn't bad in the first place. You went for somethin' you didn't do."

"Is that goin' to make any difference if some one finds out about it, an' there's somethin' goin' on that looks bad for somebody?"

"I ain't goin' to argue. I don't want to hear no more about it, an' that's final with me. Now you hush."

"Mawman, will you run down to DeShong's Saloon an' get me a quart of whiskey before you go home?" Jake Hodges was calling from his private office. Pruiett was reading under the gas light in the vestibule.

"I hope you'll excuse me, Colonel, but I couldn't help overhearing your discussion," Pruiett answered, coming to the door. "I believe I can find you some cases that will help you."

"Meet Judge Stillwell H. Russell from Dallas," Hodges said, carelessly.

"How are you, son," Russell inquired with gravity, rising and shaking hands."

"I just happened to read some cases on the same subject a week or so ago," Pruiett repeated, half in apology.

"Well," Hodges grinned, "me an' the judge is right about it, ain't we?"

"No sir, you're not," came the frank answer. "You're wrong. That's why I thought I'd better butt in an' tell you about these cases I read."

"This is Stillwell H. Russell, you're talkin' to," Hodges suggested, with a mock politeness. "He's supposed to know a little law, hisself."

"It's a pretty fine point, an' an easy one to go wrong on. You don't want no error in your record if you can keep it out, I'm sure," Pruiett persisted.

"You're absolutely right, young man," Russell agreed. "Now, look here—maybe we don't understand each other. Do you know what our question is?"

"I think I do," Pruiett replied. "You're here as special prosecutor in the Buck Williams murder case. Buck Williams is pleadin' self-defense; that he killed a man named Mitchell after Mitchell tried to slug him in the head with a bar off a binder. You say, now that Williams has said Mitchell jumped him, that Mitchell's reputation has been put in issue, an' that the state's entitled to prove Mitchell's reputation for bein' quiet an' peaceable, an' so forth. Ain't that it?"

"That's it, just exactly," Russell acknowledged. "An' Colonel Jake says, and I quite agree, that when Williams testified that Mitchell attacked him, that he opened up the gate. He assaulted Mitchell's character—his reputation—and now we can prove that Mitchell was a man with a reputation for being peaceable and law abiding, and not usually expected to act like Williams said he did on this occasion."

"It's reversible error if you do it," Pruiett said, with finality. "You

Stillwell H. Russell was one of the most highly respected criminal lawyers in northern Texas. Although he had offices in Gainesville and Dallas, he met Moman Pruiett in the Paris, Texas, office of Jake Hodges. Russell became Pruiett's closest friend, as well as his mentor. Russell helped Pruiett gain experience by letting him sit in as his co-counselor on several high profile cases. Pruiett named one of his children after Russell. Russell, who gave the eulogy at Lilly Pruiett's funeral, became the first District Judge of the Southern District of Oklahoma after statehood. He was serving on the Oklahoma Supreme Court when he died in 1914. Courtesy Archives & Manuscripts Division of the Oklahoma Historical Society.

just got to suggest an' assault in a self-defense plea, an' that alone don't put reputations in issue. I can remember the book numbers, an' I think I can remember the page. Want to see 'em?"

"I want a drink of whiskey," Hodges interrupted. "That's what I called you about. What do you say?"

"I'll be back in a jiffy," Pruiett answered from the doorway.

"Who's the squirt?" Stillwell Russell asked.

"Just a pore folks kid. Good worker, though, an' tryin' hard. He's a little too fresh, an' talks back a little too quick. That's the worst thing I see in him."

"It's not a fault, if it's handled right," Russell said. "How old is he?"

"He's only seventeen or eighteen, but he looks older. I'm watchin' him pretty close here lately. I heard he done a stretch in Arkansas on a forgery. Maybe that's what makes him look older than he actually is."

"It's that heavy black hair, for one thing, and that agate eye. I'm a fair judge of men an' horses, an' I'd say a kid with a cold eye like that—when a kid eye can bore you like a gimlet—is either plumb good or plumb bad. And it takes a lot of guts to tell your elders they're wrong, right to their face, even if you don't know what you're talkin about."

"It's just like I was tellin' you," Hodges answered. "He keeps these offices shined, an' reads law in spurts. I think the eye's bad. He's been makin' the joints a lot with that wild kid brother of mine, an' he's had a helluva fight or two. He most beat a guy from Arkansas to death in the Peterson Hotel's bar—bigger'n older'n him—an' its talked about that the guy was mouthin' about this Arkansas conviction. I ain't passin' no judgment; I'm just watchin'. If he'll keep the place clean, an' his nose clean, too, we'll be able to get along all right together."

Pruiett banged a big bottle on the desk, smiled and went out.

"He's got a nice appearance, an' a likable manner," Russell observed.

"Yeah, he's got personality. Makes friends quick, an' gets along with ever' body. If he'd justa gone to school, an' prepared himself, I mighta been able to make a lawyer outa him."

"Here's a Texas case that illustrates my position," Pruiett said, walking between them and laying a volume on the desk. "An' here are two more, from other states, that follow the same rule. They reversed this case and sent it back for a new trial, just because the court let the prosecution prove exactly what you want to prove about Mitchell, against Williams."

"I'll be god damned," Hodges grunted, without looking up from the pages.

"With Pruiett and the Supreme Court against us, we are in an ineffective minority, Colonel," Russell said. "As little as I like to do it, I am going to confess error, and apologize to your assistant."

"I think I'll run along, Colonel," Pruiett said. "It's gettin' pretty late, an I ought..."

"You ought to go home, not to that Peterson saloon an' gamblin' room," Hodges interrupted. "An' quit keepin' Bob out so god damn late. He can't drink beer an' shoot craps all night, an' wake up daisy fresh in the mornin' like you can."

With a wave and an infectious grin, the black-haired boy was away.

"That kid keeps facts in his head better than you or I," Russell said. "It didn't take him a minute to apply the rule in this case, just overhearin' our conversation, an' he knew exactly where to go for the case. Was it an accident, or is he that good?"

"I really don't know," Hodges confessed. "This makes me think. He's slipped up on me a time or two, with material suggestions, on things I was overlookin'. An' its always memory stuff. He don't seem to forget nothin'. Maybe he's got somethin'."

Killings, and murder trials, were like cotton-picking and beef-shipping time, in Paris. Liquor and easy money made the stock raisers and speculators hot headed and quick to shoot. The Indian Territory north of Red River was dry, and visitors from across that line were usually saloon bound. The United States District Court, with jurisdiction over the territory, met and tried cases at Paris, to add variety to the local brand of felony displays. In the northern extremity of the territory, in the 'no man's land' sector of the Texas-Oklahoma panhandle, the Hay Meadow Massacre in which six men were killed as part of the Woodsdale and Hugoton county seat feud, of southern Kansas, had erred in extinguishing Sheriff John Cross and his posse on land under federal jurisdiction. And, they had made one slight additional error. One of the dead victims, perforated with Winchester slugs and buckshot, got well. Their victory, in the light of his testimony from the witness stand, was sour and hollow.

With the venue of the crimes in the Federal Court's jurisdiction in the territory, the cases were heard at Paris. Colonel Jake Hodges, acknowledged best of the criminal lawyers of the section, was counsel for the defendants. The Colonel was a typical frontier type. His voice was deep and booming; his identifying gesture was a big-fisted slap on the back, accompanied by a roaring laugh. He had memorized all of the Henry Woodfin Grady orations on the old south, the Constitution of the United States and the Declaration of Independence. His jury arguments in criminal cases were hybrid composites of these three sources, embellished with the homely delivery he had acquired with his years of experience. With a huge gold chain draped across his portly paunch, and with his wrinkled, freckled neck flushed with effort, he waved the bloody shirt in front of the cow-man jury.

The six defendants, Charles Edward Cook and his brother, Oran Cook, and John J. Chamberlain, Cyrus Fields, John Jackson and Jack Lawrence, were convicted of murder in spite of the Colonel's lusty bawling, and were sentenced to hang. Young Pruiett heard every syllable of the evidence, the court's charge and the arguments of counsel. He had correctly predicted the outcome before the jury returned its verdict.

"The Colonel didn't have much chance to win those cases." He and Bob Hodges were having beer at the far end of the Peterson Hotel's bar.

"They was guilty, wasn't they?" Hodges inquired. "Why the hell shouldn't they have been stuck?"

"Well, now," Pruiett mused. "If you're convicted when you're guilty, an' acquitted when you ain't—why have lawyers, a'tall? Why have courts? Just call a guy in an' ask him 'are you guilty or ain't you?' and then lock him up or turn him aloose. Is that your idea of how to work it?"

"It's all the same to me, lawyers or no lawyers," Bob answered. "They're all grafters, anyway. That cheap brother of mine is a crook, an' he don't split none of the dough he makes with me. He's tryin' to starve me to death, so I don't give a damn whether he goes good or not."

"I wisht I could get it straight in my head, just once," Pruiett said. "There's times when I get in heat over the prospects, an' then times when just thinkin' about tryin' a lawsuit makes me sick. Have you got any idea how hard a job it is, to get up an' vouch for a bunch of dirty bastards like Colonel Jake did today, knowin' all the time they're guilty? Do you think it's easy to stand up an' beg an' argue for acquittal, when you can see conviction in ever' expression in ever' juror's face? You got to be an actor, an' you got to be a hypocrite, an' you got to be a faker, to be a good lawyer. An' if you ain't goin' to be a good one, then you ain't got no business bein' one at all, 'cause then you double your clients an' take pay for something you can't deliver—an' in the long run—a party to spreadin' misery, an' sufferin' an' distress. Did you know that?"

"I don't know nothin' about it, an' I don't care. I do know that old Jake'll raise a lot of hell with me for bein' out so late. It's past midnight. We better go."

"I'm ready," Pruiett said, and they started toward the exit. As they walked by the bar, the tender motioned for them to stop.

"I got a drunk over there that ought to be put to bed, an' I ain't got no one here to look after the place while I do it," he said, indicating a limp figure bending over a small table. "It's old Pat Riley from Bonham, an' I been tryin' to send him to his room all evenin'. Couldn't you boys help him up the stairs an' into bed?"

"I've poured plenty of drunks into bed," Bob Hodges answered. "Grab an arm, Mawman, an' we'll hist him up. Let's go!"

Riley was an old tailor who had sold his business in Bonham, Texas. preparatory to opening a shop in Paris. "You boys is awful nice to old Pat," he mumbled, as they half-carried him up the stairway.

"Maybe you can do as much for us sometime, when we get in the same fix," Moorman suggested.

"You boys is too nice to drink old nasty licker," Pat said. "You are good little boys. I'm goin' to pay you a nice reward for helpin' me to bed. I got plenty of dough."

"You'd better keep your mouth shut about it 'til you sober up a little," one of the boys suggested. They unlocked the door to his room, lighted the lamp on the dresser, and started unbuttoning his shoes. He began to kick.

"Let's all go back an' have just one more drink," he suggested.

"You ain't goin' nowhere but to bed," Hodges said.

"One of you good boys go down an' get ol' Pat a bottle of whiskey, then," he said. "I'll need a drink for sure in the mornin'."

"We ain't gettin' you nothin'." Pruiett was holding his shoulders off the bed while Hodges peeled off his coat.

Riley managed to drag a bulging wallet from the inside pocket of the coat. Spreading its frayed jaws apart, he exhibited its contents, with pride. "I got plenty of money, an' I want to pay you nice boys a reward. An' I want you to buy me a bottle of whiskey. Just help yourself."

Hodges and Pruiett looked at each other in amazement. The case was crowded with $100 bills.

"Where do you suppose the old son-of-a-bitch got all that jack?" Hodges whispered.

"It's a wonder he ain't been rolled, drunk as he is. I guess nobody thought he had the price of another drink," Pruiett answered, in the same tone. "Should we take any of it? He's offerin' to give it to us, ain't he?"

"Now ain't you the hell of a' amateur lawyer?" Hodges gritted, with disgust. "This old bastard is dog drunk. He don't know what he's a'-doin'. If we let him give us a big bill, he wouldn't remember about it in the mornin', an' he'd start a squawk at the desk about bein' robbed. Well? Who put him to bed? Who was the last ones with him? Bob Hodges and Moorman Pruiett. We say he gave it to us. He says he didn't, an' what kind of a fix are we in? Ever'body'll say we hooked it."

"You ain't wrong about that, Bob," Pruiett agreed. "Let's chuck him in an' get goin'. But say—suppose he gets up an' wanders back downstairs for that drink—or, some one comes in here an' rolls him on the quiet? We still might git our tit in the wringer."

"I don't want you nice boys to run out an' leave me," Riley whimpered. "I got the shakes comin' on, an' I have 'em awful bad once they start. They's snakes an' wildcats an' ever'thing gets after me."

"Maybe we ought to stay an' kinda watch out for him," Hodges suggested. "But, I'd never make Jake believe me, tellin' him what I was doin'."

"We'd do pretty good, three in one bed, an' one limber drunk, now, wouldn't we?" Pruiett inquired.

"You could stay an' look out for him, Mawman," said Hodges. "Your folks don't know when you get in, anyway, they don't know whether it's you or some of the roomers, an' the two of you could make out all right on that big bed. Do you think so?"

"I guess I could, if it's necessary," Pruiett agreed. "What do you say?"

"I say take good care of Uncle Pat an' get him sober, an' then if he wants to pay off a little, in appreciation, it'll be all right to take it. I'll see you tomorrow." Hodges waved and disappeared into the darkness of the hallway.

It was visitors' day at the jail. Betty Pruiett was there to see her Mawman.

"Colonel Jake says he won't defend you, honey," she said, through the bars. "I begged him, an' offered to pay him good, too, but he just said no. He said the deal kind of involved Bob, an' that Bob would have to be a witness. He said he just couldn't afford to take it at all."

"There ain't much use to fight it," the boy said. "You remember what I told you—the trail of the serpent? The old codger was just exactly right. When somethin' happens, the first one they jump on is the guy with snake's tracks behind him."

"I got H. B. Birmingham of Paris, Texas, hired," she said. "An' there's plenty of use to fight it, if you're innocent. Tell me the truth, Mawman, what happened? What was you doin' in the old man's room?"

"I told you once, Maw, an' you got to believe me whether any one else does or not. Bob an' me helped him upstairs an' we put him to bed. He had about $3,000 in $100 bills, an' he was dog-drunk an' talkin' about goin' after some more whiskey. We decided I'd better stay all night in the room an' watch him an' take care of him. I put the wallet with the money under his pillow, an' turned the lamp down real low, an' went to bed with him. He was asleep when I dozed off, an' the next thing I knew they was throwin' water in my face in the Peterson Hotel lobby, an' the place was full of smoke. I ran upstairs to the room an' it was burnt up inside. The lamp must have exploded while I was asleep an' set the bed on fire. The mattress, an' the bed clothes an' the curtains all burned up, an' the smoke must have knocked me out. I was unconscious when they pulled me downstairs, an' I don't know nothin' about his money. They didn't find none of it on me, did they?"

"No, but that room clerk at the Peterson Hotel says he got kinda worried about the old man, an' went up an' looked in the room about two o'clock. He says the lamp was lit an' the door was open a little, an' he saw you sittin' on the side of the bed countin' bills, an' that in about fifteen minutes he saw the smoke, an' ran up an' found you an' the old man in bed together. He says he doesn't think you were really unconscious when he hauled you out."

"There's a guy I'll kill if I ever get out of jail," Pruiett gritted. "Why, he's the son-of-a-bitch that stole Riley's money. He's the one that done it, an' he's cooked up that tale to cover up his own stealin'. Nobody would believe it was me, though, if it wasn't for the bum deal I got in Arkansas."

"The money might have burned up in the bed," Betty suggested.

"If that thievin' clerk hadn't a-lied on me, I'd a-thought the same thing," he said. "There was no way on god a'mighty's earth to tell, the shape that room was in. The bedding, and the curtains, was solid char; just black an' gray flakes all over the room. The old wallet an' the bills might have been there, burned to flakes, but so long as they got a ex-convict around, why not send him back to hell? Why not make the serpent's trail a little heavier behind him, so's that he won't never have no chance to do nothin' but bust back into the big joint?"

"Don't get bitter, Mawman," she said, wiping her eyes. "Your paw an' I'll be behind you, an' Mr. Birmingham will be over to see you right away, about the trial. Just you tell the truth, an' I'll pray. There's got to be some justice left in the world somewhere, for us."

"It's damn scarce, the kind you're lookin' for," he told her, as she turned to leave. "But there's another kind, the kind you make for yourself, like that lyin' room clerk did. The home-made kind might work pretty good in place of the real thing, if you just can't get anything else."

The prosecuting attorney toyed with a one-page document in his hand and smiled, tolerantly. A sad faced boy with piercing eyes and shining black hair was telling his story of the fire in Riley's room at the Peterson. The paper was proof of a conviction in Arkansas; it was a certified copy of the Sebastian County District Court record. It would soon be time to cross-examine. He glanced at the record and smiled like a miser counting his money.

Birmingham, the defense attorney, had a listless sincerity and perseverance which barely kept him in practice. "You may cross-examine," he mumbled, when Pruiett had concluded his account.

"May I inquire," the prosecutor drawled, rising to his feet, "have you ever been convicted of a felony?"

The witnesses' eyes flashed. "Well, it was like this... "

"That calls for a 'yes' or 'no' answer, your honor," the prosecutor interrupted.

"That's right," agreed the court. "No self-serving declarations, Mr. Pruiett. Just answer 'yes' or 'no'."

"Yes," came the crisp answer. There was a dangerous glint of defiance in the dark eyes, and his lips were set in a hard, straight line.

Betty cried and the bailiff had to take the Captain out of the courtroom. His caustic comment, when state's witnesses were on the stand interrupted the process of justice. The jurors slept or pondered over their own personal problems after the defendant acknowledged the prior conviction. If he'd been convicted once, what more was to be said? Write him a ticket to the state prison at Rusk, Texas, and save the state the expense of trying him.

"We find the defendant, Moorman Pruiett, guilty of robbery, as charged, and fix his punishment at imprisonment in the state Penitentiary at Rusk, for a period of five years," droned the court clerk, reading the verdict while the jurors looked indifferently at the opposite wall of the courtroom. Betty continued to cry. The defendant leaped to his feet.

"You'll all regret this," he cried, shaking a clenched fist in the jury's face. "Ever' damned one of you'll regret it. You never would have arrested me in this case if I hadn't a-had that term in Arkansas, an' you never would have convicted me, neither, if it hadn't a-been for that. It's the trail of the serpent, follerin' me from Little Rock, an' takin' me back to prison. You think you can break me with it, but by God, you can't. As sure as I live, I'll make you sorry. I'll empty your damned jails an' I'll turn the murderers an' thieves a'loose in your midst. I'll... "

A deputy grabbed him and pulled him from the courtroom. There was a look of fiendish hatred on his face as he passed from his sobbing mother's sight.

Pruiett did two years of the five-year term. Charles A. Culberson, who was Governor of Texas, had been receiving visits from Betty Pruiett, periodically, during the time he stayed in confinement.

Betty had changed. The bloom of her blue grass beauty had been washed away by the stream of sweat in her years of transient toil. Her once proud shoulders, graceful and square, emulated old Sugar Loaf, the mountain which had separated the burst of the summer sunrise at Hackett City. The shapely things that had propelled her through the throngs at Elizabethtown, and carried with them glances of unconcealed admiration, mingled obesely with the bulk which obscured the smooth, flat abdomen of yesterday.

She had grown old and unlovely, but there was an intangible beauty about her year-seamed face and labor-bent body. Her eyes were like those of a crusader. The dream of the future for the confined son had lost none of its reality; her prayers for his development were as fervent each night as they had been while he writhed within her womb.

"I'm sorry that I wasn't able to see you yesterday," Culberson was saying. "I noticed you in the waiting room, and I thought... "

"You thought I might get tired and go away?" she interrupted.

"Frankly—yes, Mrs. Pruiett. I'm thoroughly familiar with the nature of your business, and it's impossible for me to help you."

Betty gave him a wan smile. "When you're that familiar with it, Governor, you'll turn him aloose," she said.

"How many times have we gone over this application, Mrs. Pruiett?" the Governor inquired.

She smiled again. "I don't remember," she said, "but we'll have to do it again. I was going to come back tomorrow if you didn't let me in today. It's too far down here, from where we live, for me to come an' then get chicken-hearted."

"Yes, I knew that, and I felt bad about it at home last night. I thought of you waiting there, as I slipped out the side door and went away. You come from Paris to Austin, Texas—from the Red River to the Colorado River. It's almost like travel between foreign countries. Who pays for it?"

"I do," she said simply. "I start savin' as soon as I get back, for the next trip to visit him. I go to Rusk first; then, I come on down to Austin to see you. We're poor, an' the boardin' house doesn't make a lot, but we've cut down on our livin' since Mawman got in this trouble."

"You spoil him," the Governor said. "Look here—if you hadn't prevailed on Simon Hughes, and I know you worked on him just like you're working on me right now, and had just let him serve that two years he got, then maybe he'd a-learned his lesson. Maybe he wouldn't be back in now. If he thinks the law can be trifled with, an' that he won't have to pay for his violations of it, he'll be more apt to take chances, and do things that he knows shouldn't be done."

"You've told me that before, Governor," she said, "but I say if he hadn't been mistreated the first time, an' sent up for somethin' he didn't do, that he never would have been suspected in this case. Why, they never did prove that a crime had been committed, much less that Mawman done it. That room was full of waste an' char, an' the burned money might have been there all the time, an' the officers never would have knowed it."

Culberson shook his head. "We always come right back to the place where we started," he said. "I had my own attorney make an investigation of this case, and ask for recommendations, but we couldn't get them. The judge that tried the case says his conduct was brazen, and hardened, both when the jury convicted him and later when sentence was passed. The warden says that he's not made a good prisoner, that he's an agitator, an' makes speeches in the prison yard that disturbs the other prisoners. My man, that went down and talked to him, said that he was a little off. All he would say, in answer to questions, was something about the serpent's trail, and to ask another question. To ever' question they asked him, he answers the same.... 'If an innocent man can be convicted, then why can't a guilty man be acquitted?' You see, Mrs. Pruiett, that there's really not much that I can do."

"He's not makin' speeches in the prison yard any more," Betty answered, daubing a soiled handkerchief to her eyes. "He's in the hospital, an' his knees are swold up as big as his head, an' his ankles are so swole it looks like he hasn't got any feet—just big chunks of flesh at the end of his legs. He didn't hardly know me, his fever was so high, an' he's talkin' about the trail of the serpent, all right, but there ain't many around to hear. It was the same way after they kept him caged up at Little Rock. You got to turn him loose, or you got to bury him, an' I know your great big state ain't meanin' to sentence a little boy to death for somethin' he didn't do."

Culberson drummed his desk and looked out the big windows. "I heard he was sick, too, but I can't turn 'em out as fast as they get sick. That's an old gag to get out of the work routine."

"It's a long way to Rusk, Governor, but it ain't too far a piece to go for findin' the truth," she said. "I'll leave it up to you. You're fair, an' honest, an' tryin' to do the right thing. I know that. You go down an' talk to him. See how sick he is, an' what them old damp cells is doin' to that inflammatory rheumatism, an' then you look him in the eye an' ask him to tell you what happened up at the Peterson Hotel that night. If you think he's lyin' about it, an' if you think he ain't goin' to die if he stays in your pen, then you just tell me. If you say no after seein' him an' talkin' to him, I promise I won't bother you any more. I'll just make my visits to Rusk, as long as he lasts—an' I got some one there to visit."

She was laboring to speak without breaking. Culberson patted her shoulder. "All right," he said. "I'll go to Rusk, and I'll see your boy. If he's the flesh and blood of suffering soul like you, there must be something in him worth saving. I'll go down and take a look."

Summer of 1894 was burning its Texas best. The mistress of the Pruiett Boarding House rocked listlessly on the porch as she read a pencil-written letter she had just taken from the postman. Her wayward son, more mature of face but less robust of physique, sat on the rough planks of the porch floor. Shaggier brows matched the still abundant raven growth which adorned his bare head, and shone in the dust-laden heat of the early afternoon. His feet, which he permitted to rest below the floor level on the crust of the grassless yard, were covered with shoes not conforming to the style of the place and period. He was consciously holding them there, so they would be out of the mother's vision. They were prison cut.

"What's the trouble, Maw?" He thought he had seen her brush a tear away.

"Nothing," she said. "Nothing at all." She folded the letter, and after placing it in her apron pocket, walked over to where he was sitting. With her characteristic gesture of indulgence, she ran her rough hands through his thick hair before she stooped and kissed him. He had not been mistaken. Tears were in her eyes and on her cheek.

When he heard her busy in the kitchen, he went to the place where he knew she would place the letter. He took it, and after locking himself in the outhouse on the rear of the lot, sat down to read. The quivering hand suggested the great age of the writer. It was from Aunt Millie Huff of Kentucky, the sister of the long departed Colonel Moorman.

"My dear Betty:" it said. "We have all heard about Moorman being in trouble again. I know how you must feel with your flesh and blood turning out bad, an' causing you so much expense and trouble. It is the first time that the good name of Moorman has ever been connected with shame and disgrace, and Lucy and I were saying that we wish you had named your boy something else. It makes me sick to think of what your good mother, and her father would say, if they heard... "

The letter went quietly back to its place, and the subject quietly about his business. Then the regular mail brought Betty another letter,

Although Moman Pruiett had served two sentences in state penal institutions and had less than ten months of formal education, Federal Judge David E. Bryant admitted Pruiett to practice law on his own motion. Courtesy *Moman Pruiett: Criminal Lawyer.*

addressed in a familiar hand. "My Dear Mother," she read. "Please try to excuse the liberty I took in reading Aunt Millie's letter to you. She expressed some of the same sentiments that I have felt, along those lines, for a long time. I would gladly abandon the name of Moorman, and even Pruiett, if I could get away from the hardships that seem to go with the disgrace I have brought it."

The formal discourse was in a well formed scroll. He was drawing upon his remarkable memory and capacity for imitation in presenting the words and phrases. "I feel that I have no right to carry the name of the Moormans further, and you may so advise Aunt Millie and the meddling Lucy. Every tub must stand on its own bottom, and I am convinced that the time is come for me to get along without your constant support, and to make a name for myself. I am, and will continue to be, your devoted son, MOMAN Pruiett."

The United States District Court for the Eastern District of Texas held an occasional term at Paris. David E. Bryant of Sherman, Texas, was the judge. During the court session at Paris, he stopped at the Hotel Lamar; and, on the warm evenings of Spring and Fall, he would pull his chair from the lobby to the sidewalk in front, drummer fashion. In the way that a good man of position knows of the little man of misfortune, Judge Bryant knew of the reborn Moman.

"Moman," he called. "Come here. Got time to stop a minute an' talk?"

The boy, hurrying in the September twilight, hesitated before he stopped or turned. Had something happened? Were the snakes tracks behind ready to involve him again? He walked back, slowly.

"I'm Judge Bryant, of Sherman," the judge said. "I been in town holdin' a term of court."

Pruiett accepted his cordial handshake with suspicion. "I know you well enough, Judge Bryant. My name's Pruiett... Moman Pruiett."

"Sure it is," agreed the judge. "I know you, an' I know about you. First time I heard of you was through Stillwell Russell. I been talkin' to Jake Hodges about you since I been in town this trip. Ain't you got time to set down here, an' talk to me for a little while?"

"I got plenty of time," he said, dropping into a wooden rocker. "An' I'm right proud to talk to a judge."

"Stillwell Russell was tellin' me about you showin' him an' Colonel Jake some law when he was down here tryin' a murder case a couple of years ago—an' then a little later he told me about your tough luck, an' about you gettin' sent away. Russell said the whole thing sounded like a big mistake, an' Stillwell Russell is one of the best lawyers, and one of the best all 'round men, we got in Texas. Do you know that?"

"He was very kind to me, and I heard him try the Williams case; that was all I heard him try. I'd say he was a fine lawyer."

Bryant laughed. "You got a nice way of expressin' yourself, Moman, an' of lettin' the praise kind of glance off. It ain't ever' kid readin' law in a country law office that Stillwell Russell remembers to talk about, after he gets away from 'em."

Pruiett smiled and said nothing.

"Jake Hodges brought it up in a little session we was havin' in chambers this afternoon. He says that it looks kind of funny, nobody never findin' that money the old Irishman lost, an' then the room clerk quittin' his job an' leavin' town all of a sudden, when the word gets out that Culberson's givin' you a pardon an' sendin' you home. He..."

"I was goin' to kill him," Pruiett interrupted to explain.

Bryant laughed again. "An' Jake says if you surprised Stillwell Russell with how you could remember citations an' opinions two years ago, he ought to come back an' try you now. He says you ain't made a joint since you came home, an' that you've read about ever' book in his whole library."

"I made up my mind I was goin' to make up for lost time," Pruiett answered.

"How you gettin' along? I mean, what you doin' to make your livin'? Does this conviction make it hard on you that way?"

"Well," he answered slowly. "I had a pretty hard time, an' I'd a'either had to leave town or really go to stealin' if it wasn't for old man Ambrose Long. He runs the Lamar County, Texas, Warehouse, you know, an' I finally told him right out that nobody in town would hire me 'cause I was a convict. He says, 'well, I don't really need help at the warehouse; but, if that's the way these bastards around here are, I'll just put you to work.' I'm wrasslin' cotton bales an' goods boxes for Long, an' makin' $30 a month. I read law ever' night, an' keep busy all the time. I don't think they'll be able to hang anything on me, no matter what happens around here. But I ain't sure."

"Did you ever try a law suit?" Bryant inquired.

"Not to really try one," he answered. "I fronted for a farmer one time in a horse-deal squabble up to Hackett. Just a scrap before a country squire, but I read 'em some law an' made a little speech. I was just a kid."

"Do you actually want to be a lawyer?" the judge asked. "I mean, if you got to be one, would you work at it, an' try to make something out of yourself?"

"It's serious business with me, judge," he said. There was a dangerous glint in his eye which Bryant could not see there in the half-darkness. "I'm goin' to learn how to try cases an' I'm goin' to learn to try 'em right. You watch me an' see."

"How you fixed for clothes?" was the next question.

"These overalls is the best I got right now, but I got a pay day comin' so's I can get me a suit. But while I ain't goin' no place, I don't need no clothes, much."

There was silence between them for several minutes. Then Judge Bryant pressed something into the boy's hand and arose from his chair.

"Fix yourself up, an' spend a day in my court before the session's over," he said. "Tell old man Long I said to give you a day off."

"This here's a twenty, judge," Pruiett said, peering at it in the light from the hotel window.

"I know it, son," he answered. "Some one ought to try to make up for the way these bastards around here been usin' you. I want to help that much. Get you a suit, an' spend a day in court with me. That's all I want you to do for the twenty."

So, Pruiett went to court. Before adjournment at noon, Judge Bryant looked uncertainly at him, and then, after pointing his finger, crooked it in a beckoning gesture.

"Come up here, Moman," he said, loudly.

When the boy reached the space in front of his desk, the judge extended his hand for a handshake, and then turned to the surprised clerk.

"Swear Moman in, an' place his name on the rolls, as a lawyer, an' as an officer of my court. See that it shows that it's done on the court's own motion."

Thus did Moorman Pruiett become Moman Pruiett, and thus did Moman Pruiett become a lawyer. Twenty-three years had fled since his unscheduled arrival on the old *Gray Eagle.* Ten months he had spent in institutions of learning. Thrice as many months had he spent in institutions of correction. The hopes and prayers of a sacrificing mother, and the invisible touch of pure genius made up his stock in trade. A smoldering hatred for the system which had wrongfully taken away his liberty, a tongue of unsurpassed, although untried, eloquence, a psychological flair for the dramatic and unexpected, were some of the intangible attributes of his unorthodox personality. Without fear; without scruples, if the straits of his client were difficult enough, he was to become the most formidable obstacle in the path of organizations which would attempt to assert and maintain order on the last frontier.

CHAPTER FOUR

Wherein rumblings from the dungeon of Rusk and Little Rock begin to reverberate, as Pruiett's plan for courtroom procedure is discussed and put into operation. How he tries his first case and wins—and tries a murder case and wins—and tries for the hand of a maiden and is likewise successful. And how his aptitude attracts the attention of a pair of powers from the dark and wild territory, and how he goes, on their invitation, recommendation, and capital, to try it as a proving ground for his long-nourished and anti-social experiment.

Jake Hodges shook his cigar ashes into the air and spit into the corner. "Now that you got to be an attorney, Mawman, I guess I got to get me a new spittoon cleaner."

"Nope," Pruiett disagreed. "In the first place, I ain't no attorney. I'm a lawyer. In the second place, I don't want to lose my office space in this waitin' room, 'cause if I did I wouldn't have no office a'tall. I go on workin' for you for my keep, an' I get to interview my clients, if I can get 'em, right up here."

"If that suits you it tickles me to death," Hodges said. "And maybe I can cut you in, with some briefin' or investigation, so's that you can make a fee out of me once in a while. What you goin' to do about your job?"

"I've quit 'er," Pruiett answered. "I've been talkin' about lightin' out for myself for a long time, an' sayin' a tub has got to set on its own bottom, an' I know I ain't goin' to get started any younger. I say if some of the guys I've seen an' heard tryin' lawsuits can make a livin', then there ain't nothin' to keep me from gettin' rich. From now on I'm a lawyer, with a capital L."

"I got a murder case set for next week," Hodges said.

"I know it," said Pruiett. "It's the Tissy Hotema case. I'm goin' to watch you try it."

"How'd you like to watch it from the counsel table?"

In 1891, when the Pruiett family moved from Hackett City, Arkansas, to Paris, Texas, Colonel Jacob Calvin "Jake" Hodges was the most prominent criminal lawyer in Lamar County, Texas. Moman Pruiett's first priority upon arrival was to get a job—any job—in a good law office so that he could continue his study of the law. At the same time Hodges needed a custodian and hired Pruiett. The two men formed a long-lasting professional and personal relationship. Courtesy Sue Hodges.

"First rate."

"It's you an' me then, bud," Hodges laughed. "It ain't much of a case; that is, it ain't much of a case to defend."

"Why, he killed three or four people up there in the territory, didn't he?"

"Yeah, three, but that ain't many for a Choctaw to kill if he gets on a bloody drunk. An' old Tissy could have got away with it, if he hadn't talked so much. After he got through choppin' 'em up, he threw the bloody axe in the well an' set fire to the shanty. Ever'body thinks its a' accidental fire 'til Tissy pops off, an' then he puts his X on a written confession in the marshal's office. He's been makin' marks on the inside wall of a cell ever since."

"How you goin' to try him?"

"Plead insanity an' try to make it stick," Hodges answered. "I'd bet my fee he hangs."

"If you can fool the jury, you can clear him," Pruiett suggested, "an' it ain't so awful hard to fool one. I say, if they can be made to find a' innocent man guilty, that there's ways of makin' 'em turn a guilty one loose."

"That ain't sound logic," Hodges said.

"Why ain't it?"

"It just ain't, that's all."

"Tell the jury that Tissy ain't guilty just because he ain't, an' he'll get hung, all right. I haven't got the formula for it right now, but I'm workin' on it, an' maybe some day I'll be able to prove I'm right. I'm goin' to specialize in murder."

"If you was tryin' Tissy, how'd you go about it?" asked the Colonel.

"I'd cook me up an alibi. There ain't no eye witnesses, so's I'd have a chance of clearin' him; gettin' him clear out."

"What about the statement they got, that Tissy made in front of witnesses?"

"I'd repudiate hell out of her," Pruiett replied, promptly. "An' I'd prove by somebody, if it wasn't nobody by Tissy, that he was framed, or brow-beat, into signin' it. That's what I'd do."

"An' the court an' the district attorney an' the marshals would all be lookin' right into your hand. They'd know you was hittin' below the table."

"If they're my witnesses, the prosecutin' attorney or nobody else ain't goin' to prove nothin'. What they think don't cut no ice with me.

Do they care what I think about them, the corner-cuttin' bastards, for fudgin' me into five years of hell at the bloody Rusk? Ain't you got the guts to look 'em in the eye an' shoot the proof to 'em?"

"I ain't tryin' lawsuits that way," Hodges answered.

"I'm tryin' 'em to win 'em," said Pruiett. "They ain't nothin' but lyin' contests, an' the biggest liar naturally wins. If it takes proof to win, an' you can get it but don't, you ought to give your fee back to your client. Why you goin' to be so sanctimonious? The trial judge's got curvature of the spine from leanin' over to help his pal, the prosecutin' attorney. The jury swears to uphold the Constitution, an' give the prisoner a fair an' a Constitutional trial, an' then one whispers to the other, 'if the dirty bastard ain't guilty, then what they got that deputy settin' over there guardin' him for?' An' the other ones wink an' laugh, an' they say 'let's hurry up an' get this one over with so's that we can get at another one.' I say the system is so damn rotten an' so damn crooked that the gate's wide open. Put on the proof it takes to wake 'em up and acquit, an' nobody's got a right to cheep."

"That line ain't new an' it ain't novel," Hodges said. "I've heard it before, an' from some pretty wise little lawyers. I even thought about it myself, once, but it don't work. Cat-tail witnesses are hard to find, an' shady jurors are hard to approach. How do you know the witness ain't goin' to flunk—blow right up under cross-examination—an' ruin you an' your case too? What if you make a pass at a juror an' he high-tails it for the judge's chambers to squawk? All you've worked for is gone with one puff. All you got to work for in the future is gone. Let me tell you, son, that tryin' lawsuits is just like ridin' a' outlaw horse or walkin' a tight rope. The guy in the saddle or holdin' the umbrella has got a snap, the way it looks, but boy, when you get in his britches, she don't look the same at all. These courts of ours didn't just happen. They grew. An' the courts an' the procedure that goes with 'em are the result of long years of trial and error, elimination an' substitution. The witness chair is the hottest place on earth for a liar to park his butt, an' the guy that fixed him has got just as much load to carry as the witness. Those are things that just take care of themselves. Experience just naturally eliminates 'em, an' when you get into it, you'll find out, an' remember old Colonel Jake."

"Maybe so, but I'm goin' to fight, an' I ain't goin' to use no feather-duster when a crooked prosecutor goes to blastin' a double-barrel shotgun at me an' my clients."

"I don't mean to say you can't doctor the facts up a little," Hodges replied. "I don't say walk in an' plead guilty just because you're technically guilty. Hell, I fight, don't I? I been fightin' for thirty years. It's all right to prove the chump was reachin' for a knife or a gun, when all he had in his jeans was a tobacco pouch or a bunch of cigarette papers. That's self-defense, an' that's number one for the lawyer's book that's going to try murder cases. Number two is the unwritten law. If there's a little daughter's virtue violated, or the holy bed of matrimony defiled, you can raise a lot of hell an' quote a lot of scriptures. Next comes insanity, either temporary, or the kind like I'm tryin' to put in for Tissy, the kind that gets your client in the asylum instead of the prison buryin' grounds."

"What about the alibi?"

"Alibis look phoney to me, even when they're genuine. I hate to touch 'em. They're like playin' with dynamite."

"I think they've got possibilities," Pruiett grinned. "The right kind, I mean."

"The case against Sam C. Thrasher, who was arrested some weeks ago, charged with the robbery of an intoxicated stranger in a restaurant on the east side of the square in Paris, Texas, and which since then has attracted a great deal of interest, was tried yesterday, and resulted in a speedy acquittal of the accused. The defense was by Moman Pruiett, and it was most brilliantly conducted under most unpromising circumstances. He displayed superb skill at every juncture, and made one of the most forcible and eloquent speeches heard in the courthouse here in a long time."

Pruiett stood on the walk in front of the Lynch Building, reading his notice in the *Paris Daily Advocate.*

"That was a nice job of work you did in the Thrasher case," a man said, walking up and stopping beside him. It was Enoch Fagan, of the local law firm of Brants and Fagan in Paris. "That guy was generally considered as guilty. I didn't have any idea he'd come clear."

"Thanks," Pruiett responded, indifferently. "What you're generally considered, an' what you are, is two different things. If you'd a asked me, I'd a told you he was comin' out all right."

"I guess you knew it all the time," Fagan suggested, with a touch of sarcasm.

"I ain't braggin', I'm just makin' conversation. I tried him to acquit him, not to stick him."

"That was pretty neat, all right, takin' that little baby off his wife's lap, there when you was arguin' to the jury, an' holdin' it in your arms all the time you was makin' your speech. Did Jake Hodges put you wise to that?"

"Jake Hodges told me to plead him guilty."

"Who wrote that speech for you?" Fagan persisted.

"Nobody," Pruiett answered. "I wrote a speech for that jury, all right, but I didn't use it. I changed my mind at the last minute, and let'em have just what came to me. I heard a good lawyer try a case at Fort Smith when I was a kid, an' I was just apin' him, mostly."

Fagan took on a confused look. He didn't know whether the black-eyed boy was making fun, or in earnest.

"Brants and I got plenty of room in our offices, an' if you want to use the library any time, or meet a client up there, you're welcome. We want to see you get along."

"Much obliged," Pruiett said. "I'm partners with Colonel Jake. He makes the noise an' collects the fees. I brief the cases an' dump the spittoons. The charity cases, like the Thrasher's, are all mine."

He was trying to be indifferent when he walked into the boarding house that evening. He knew Betty would be elated, and that she would probably make an embarrassing scene in her elation. "I'm awful glad you won your case, Mawman," was all she said. "I knew you could do it."

"Thanks, maw," he replied. "I really don't see nothin' to it. Ever' trick I had figured worked just right. I was givin' the jury somethin' to keep 'em awake, an' to keep 'em from thinkin' about that guy Thrasher. I took that month-old kid, an' I helt it in my arms, wrapped in its blanket, an' I says, 'could you hold a precious bundle like this to your heart an' utter an untruth?' I says 'could you lie to the Savior with an angel sittin' on your knee? When that little woman, with this little baby in her arms, testified that its daddy was home all evenin' that evenin', she was tellin' the truth like God loves it. Straight an' untarnished. The men that says they saw Thrasher hangin' around the front of the restaurant that night are mistaken, or. .', I says, 'or they got a guilty motive for bein' so positive it was him.' I poured it on the deputies that arrested him, an' I poured it on old Taliaferro an' Frank Lee, the prosecutors.

Old Frank twisted an' the jurors grinned. They like it, so I kept goin'. They smiled when I ate the sheriff up, an' they cried when I pulled the flap back an' showed 'em that baby's face. The jury wasn't out fifteen minutes, an' they says Thrasher's not guilty."

"You're pretty proud, ain't you, son?" she asked.

"It's a start for me," he said. "A little start on a big job I got to do. Tissy Hoteme might as well of got off, as gettin' life, is what I still say."

"A good lawyer's got a wonderful power," she said. "All I've been through with ain't shaken my faith in my vision. I knew it was goin' to be, ever since I heard Dan'l Voorhees make that wonderful speech at Alton, before you was born. You was born to be a lawyer, an' nothin' could keep you from it, not even your serpent's trail, as you call it."

"Keep me from it?" he whispered, with a black look. "Keep me from it? Why, maw, that's what's pulled me into it. You know that. I ain't goin' to fool you."

She kissed him and ran her fingers through his black mane. "That's good enough for an excuse, if you need one; but, when you soften up, you'll find you was the one that was fooled, yourself. It's your gift, not this foolish hate you got, that's pullin' you on."

"Let's not talk about it," he smiled. "I wouldn't even have said that much to any one else."

"How'd you like to have a murder case? Maybe two of 'em?"

"I'll land one, an' when I do I'll show that swelled-up Jake Hodges how to try it," he said. "I'll—."

"I think I got you one."

"What?"

"I think I got you one. There's two women from the territory rented the back room this mornin', an' they're here for court. There's two men in the Federal jail charged with murder, one's a wife, an' the other's the sister, of these two. I told 'em there was a lawyer in the house, an' they seemed interested. I'll call an' tell 'em that you're home."

"Just a minute, Maw," he said. "There's something else I want to talk to you about first. You know it's important with me if I'd let a chance at a real murder case wait, don't you?"

"There's not any trouble comin' from tryin' this Thrasher case, is there? You ain't in trouble again?"

He smiled and hesitated, awkwardly. "Not the kind of trouble that worries you," he answered. "I got female trouble."

"Why, all boys your age has got that," Betty laughed, relieved. "But, if it's serious, I want you to tell me about it right now."

"Well," he said, "you know this Sam Thrasher I been defendin'? He ain't much good. He's always in some kind of a jam, an' he ain't good to his wife an' kids an' things like that, but just the same, he's cut of good stock. You know that. The Thrashers are good people, all but Sam."

"That's right," she agreed. "There's nothin wrong with the Thrashers, all but Sam."

"You know Lilly Belle Thrasher, don't you?"

"She's a sweet girl," Betty said.

"Did you ever notice that her hair was really red, instead of black, like it usually looks?"

"Why, no, I hadn't," Betty laughed. "But I never looked very close to see. Do you mean to tell me that it's actually dark red?"

"It really is," he said, earnestly, "an' her skin's so thin that you can see right through it. You can see the bottom side of those little freckles on the side of her nose, if you look real close, an' the pink flesh of her face, underneath." His dark eyes and hair sparkled with his complete animation.

"I noticed her clear skin, all right," Betty agreed. "She's a lovely girl, but she's awful young. She ain't more than fifteen, now, is she?"

"She's almost eighteen," he answered. "I've been goin' over to their place in the evenin's, an' she an' her mother have been like real folks with me. They ain't got the old poker in their back like a lot of these hypocrites around here have ever' time they see me a'comin. I think I'll ask Lilly Belle to marry me, if you think it'd be all right."

"If it'd make you happy, son, it's goin' to be all right with me," she said. "It's nice of you to tell me about it, an' I'm glad you trust me an' tell me things like that, but I really ain't got any right to say. You're a grown man now, an' you do what you know's the best for you."

"You ain't exactly old, maw, but you ain't young, neither, an' pa—he's gettin' old. He's countin' a lot on me, even if he does think I'm makin' a big mistake in tryin' to be a lawyer. You ain't done nothin' since I was born but worry with me an' about me, an' try to keep me out of scrapes. I won't have nothin' in my life that ain't yours, an' havin' a wife an' home ain't goin' to interfere with that. If she'll have me, it'll be subject to my takin' care of you an' tryin' to make things comfortable for you in the future. I'll have that out, the first thing."

"Don't you worry about me," Betty smiled at him. "If she's what you want, just take her, don't ask nobody about it. The girl that get's married to you is never goin' to regret it, bein' married to the best lawyer in the country."

"Run your murder case in here," he cried, "while I got the big-head from your braggin'. I'll mak'em think they're talkin' to Stillwell Russell."

"I'm John Evans's sister, an' this is Missus Richards. She's Doc Richards' wife."

"I've heard about them cases," Pruiett answered, with professional gravity. "They're charged with killin' Armon V. Beatty up in the Indian territory, ain't they?"

"That's right," the prospects agreed. Pruiett was interviewing them in the parlor of the boarding house.

"I thought they had lawyers defendin' 'em," he said. "They're set for trial ahead of the John Stevenson case who was charged with murdering Deputy Marshal Joe Gaines, an' that's on the docket for week after next."

"They ain't been able to raise no money," the Evans woman said. "We had some lawyers at Fort Worth that was goin' to try 'em, but when we didn't raise the money, they got awful busy an' wrote us that they couldn't make it over here for the trial."

"Don't you have no money at all?" he inquired.

The women shook their heads despondently.

"Bein' in jail charged with murder in that kind of a case is bad, an' bein' broke makes it worse," Pruiett observed. No one disagreed, so he continued. "I ain't takin' no murder cases under false pretenses; there's too much involved. I've just been practicin' less than a year, an' I ain't had a lot of experience in court. I'd like to help you, but I want you to know that before we say any more."

"Your ma showed us what they said about you in the papers down here, an' besides, I can see you're a lawyer, a good lawyer, just to look at you an' listen to you. If I had plenty of money, I'd still hire you." Richards' simple wife was frank in her praise.

"I'll do the best I can for 'em, if you say take it," he said.

"I want you to represent Doc," she said.

"An' if John says it's all right, I say take 'em both together," her companion agreed. "All we come down here for was to learn the hangin' date, anyway, so's we could tell the folks back home. We don't expect a lot."

Pruiett ignored her unintentional cut. "There ought to be a little expense money advanced for me to work on," he said.

"We can give you $10, an' that's all we got over our two weeks room an' board," Mrs. Richards told him. "We'll put that up if it'll do you any good, but that's the best we can do."

"I want a note, signed by all four of you, for a $100," he said, trying to look unconcerned with the mention of notes and amounts. "I'll take the ten an' the note, an' see what I can do with the cases. Now, I want to know all about the facts; so, just tell me all you can about it."

"Well," John Evans's sister began, "Armon Beatty was killed at John's house up near Emet in the Chickasaw country. John an' Clara, his wife, had been havin' trouble almost ever since John brought Beatty home an' gave him a job on the ranch as a hired man. Clara an' Armon was cheatin' on John for a long time, an' ever' body knew it, it seemed like, but John. But, finally, him an' Clara has a fallin' out, an' John goes to drinkin' an' stayin' away from home while he runs around with Doc Richards. About daylight, one mornin' last summer, two men walk up in the yard with a shotgun, an' Armon's sleepin' out, it's so hot, you know, he's got his mattress on a wagon-box in the yard. Well, someone blows Armon's head plumb off with a shotgun. That's about all there is to tell."

"Is there any witnesses, or is it a circumstantial case?" Pruiett almost fumbled the high sounding final phrase of the question.

"There's two witnesses, Clara an' Clarence. Clara's his wife, an' Clarence is a nine year old orphan nephew of Clara's they was a'raisin'. They both claim they seen it, an' that it was John an' Doc that walked up in the yard. They say John did the shootin'."

"Clara can't testify. She's his wife, an' a wife can't testify against a husband in a criminal prosecution," Pruiett said. "That's cuttin' it down to Clarence. Is he smart?"

"He's a pretty smart kid."

"Is he friendly or unfriendly?"

"He'd be friendly, if it wasn't for Clara, but she's seein' that he stays plenty mad at his uncle John. They're goin' to prove that he was awake when the two of 'em walked up, an' that when John pulled the trigger, Clarence jumped up an' says, 'Why, Uncle John, what did you want to do that for?' Clara wants to see 'em hang, an' she won't let Clarence cool off."

"A jury won't never hang two men on the testimony of a kid like that," Pruiett observed. "A kid's too changeable; he's too likely to be excited, an' mistaken. He'd admit in a minute, on cross-examination, that the light was bad an' he was sleepy, an' that he could have been mistaken about who it was. I wouldn't be afraid of him so much. What else they got?"

"They're goin' to prove that John an' Doc were in that neighborhood the night Armon was killed, by John's horse. He had a big stallion, a big roan, an' it's a easy horse to remember. Well, Clara's neighbors are goin' to testify that their mares were cuttin' up an' restless, between midnight and dawn, like there was a stud around the lot somewhere. The marshals found a tree on the creek a quarter mile from the place where Beatty was shot, where some horses had been tied with short lines that night. One was rubbed up an' the bark was full of roan hair. The shoe prints all around it was big, like stud prints. The marshals saved a lot of that hair, an' they took some samples from John's horse after they arrested him, an' they say they match up perfect."

"That's pretty smart prosecutin'," Pruiett admitted. "It's damn clever, an' that'll hurt the case worse than little Clarence. That's somethin' a cow-man jury will understand. Is that all they got, now?"

"Well," she pondered, "Doc's place, up on Pennington Creek, is about forty miles north of John's place at Emet. There was a couple of ranch hands camped about half way between, an' along after sun up, accordin' to their story, John an' Doc rode through the brush an' helped them drink their can of coffee. They say the roan an' the black was showin' signs of awful hard ridin', an' the marshals say that the trail, from the creek back of the house where Armon was shot, up to this camp, was clear, an' especially of the big horse. Them cowboys are government witnesses."

"Is that all?" he persisted.

"Yes," they agreed, "that's all, unless John an' Doc can think of somethin'."

"I'm goin' down to the jail to see 'em an' tell'em I'm hired in the case, an' I may not be back 'til kind of late," Pruiett said. "Would you please tell Maw at supper that I won't be home to eat?"

The *Paris Tribune* made official note of the only interruption permitted in the preparation of the John Evans and Doc Richards murder case. "Merrily the wedding bells pealed at the Congregational Church last night, May 3, 1896, when at 8 o'clock Mr. Mormon [sic] Pruiett led to the altar Miss Lillie Belle Thrasher, where, in the impressive silence which followed the strains of the wedding march, Rev. Luther Reese read the service which made the happy young couple man and wife. Both are well known in the city, and their friends join the *Tribune* in wishing them a long, happy and prosperous journey down the rugged pathway of life."

"How many recesses has Pruiett had to have in this case, judge?" Jake Hodges was showing unmistakable signs of peevishness.

"I've lost track, a long time ago," Judge David E. Bryant answered. "But, I feel like I got to give him all the time he wants. This is a capital case, an' that Pruiett kid is makin' a hell of a record on me. They'll sentence Evans an' Richards to hang as sure as the world, an' he'll be just as sure to take an' appeal on it. I don't want no error in the darn record."

"We got fifty witnesses here for that Stevenson case; had 'em here for two days, an' it's costin' like the devil," Hodges complained. "It's..."

"I don't mind the waitin', so long as it's so edifyin'," Stillwell Russell interrupted. "I'd rather watch that bushy-headed devil work than listen to Bob Ingersoll. If we'd a had him in the Stevenson case the last time we tried it, we might have got better than a hangin' sentence out of it for our client."

"Yeah, an' if I'd a'been as careful with the record then as I'm bein' in this one, the Circuit Court wouldn't have reversed it, an' John Stevenson would'a been dead, like he ought'a be, instead of back here runnin' up the government's cost bill," the judge said.

"That janitor of Jake's is nobody's damn fool," Russell continued. "I don't agree when you say his men will get death."

"They ain't got a chance in a million," Bryant scoffed.

"What about that old man Washington, the old white-haired stockman?" Russell reminded. "How's the jury goin' to discount his testimony?"

"Hell," Hodges said. "He was fixed. There ain't nobody goin' to believe that kind of crap."

"He sounded good to me," Russell persisted. "He said he was over to Richards at sunup the mornin' of the killin', an' that Evans an' Richards was there, an' helped him have his mare served by John's stud. Them old stock owners keep records of their breedin' dates, ever' one of 'em does, an' there's eight or ten stockmen on that jury. When the old man pulled that record book, with the date in it in John Evans' handwritin', an' the receipt for the stud fee, I thought old Taliaferro was goin' to drop his uppers."

"It's all cooked up," Bryant snorted. "Ever' damned bit perjury, an' that jury knows it."

"I notice you ain't letting none of your ideas on that subject get in the record, like you did on Stevenson," Russell laughed. "An' if it's perjury, it's a long ways ahead of the type you'd normally expect this section of the country to produce. I think it's the truth, an' the government ain't got a sign of a case."

"I guess you believed that damned old blacksmith?" Jake Hodges put in.

"Why not?" countered Russell. "He's got no more motive for lyin' than them deputy marshals that are testifyin' to ever' thing the government wants 'em to. The marshals claim they followed the killer's trail up toward the Pennington Creek country, an' that he was ridin' a big horse, with heavy calks on his shoes. The old blacksmith swears that he put the shoes on Evans' stud four days after Beatty got his head blowed off, an' that he could tell from the hooves that there never had been a nail in 'em before he put his in. If that ain't competent, an' credible proof, I ain't learned nothin' about lawsuits in these years I been tryin' 'em."

"It'd be good if it wasn't so obviously hand-tooled," Bryant said.

"Who tooled it?" Russell demanded. "These boys have been in jail for almost a year. They got a green country kid that's tryin' his first murder case defendin' 'em, an' ever'body on the jury knows it. Just on the surface, I'd say the government was in for a trimmin'."

"I know who tooled it," Jake Hodges interrupted.

"You ain't been on the stand yet, an' what's more, you ain't goin'," Russell retorted.

"It doesn't make a damn bit of difference to me how she goes," Bryant began. "I'm just the trial judge..."

Russell interrupted again. "When Pruiett asked that old white haired codger if John's stud was shod the mornin' he stood his mare to him, an' he swelled up an' said 'hell no, there ain't no shod stallion goin' to claw up my mare's flanks,' the jury caught it. I saw Pruiett had made a point, an' I think Taliaferro an' Lee did too. It's things like that that wins or loses cases."

"Like I said, it don't make a damn to me," Bryant said. "You know how I feel about Moman. He's my baby, whether he makes a go or not. He's practicin' law on my own motion, an' old Judge McClelland, in the state court, hated like hell to give him a license down there. Why, McClelland tried him for robbery, an' sentenced him to five years at Rusk. When I admitted him here, Mac said he felt like he almost had to send him down there, so he gave him a temporary license. I think he'll make good, an' I ain't apologizin' to nobody for what I did."

"He ain't human, in some respects," Jake Hodges said. "He's got a filin' cabinet for a head an' ice water in his veins instead of blood. When he's in the courtroom you'd swear he was graduated out of Harvard or Princeton, an' down at the office or at the DeShong's saloon, you'd think he was a gutter-monkey. An' another thing, he carries a grudge. I think he's a killer."

"I been wonderin' about that fine courtroom manner of his," Bryant said. "I know he ain't educated. I've heard he hadn't had a full year's schoolin' in his life. Where does that come in?"

"It's imitation; nothin' but imitation," Hodges stated. "Ask Russell about how he can remember things. He reads a case, an' he notices a citation, an' he sticks it in that filin' case with all the wild hair on it, and he keeps it there 'til he needs it. Then, he yanks it out. I've had him around me for better'n three years, off an' on, an' I tell you he's a bear on memory. He stood up in the office one time, an' he made my speech back to me, the one I made in the Tissy Hoteme case, an' I swear to Christ it was word for word, an' with ever' gesture. I asked him how he kept it in his mind so long, an' he took a drink out of my bottle an' started recitin' another speech, an' I recognized it right off as the one I made in them Hay Meadow Massacre cases. He told me once that if he just had a little chance to follow Dan Voorhees, an' watch him try a few cases, that he'd show the boys around Lamar County how lawsuits ought to be tried."

"That's right," Russell agreed. "He's a kind of genius that way. He don't forget nothin', an' even when you think he's asleep, he's watchin' out of them slit eyes an' storin' stuff up for use in the future. He's goin to make an' awful good trial man, if I'm any judge of lawyers at all."

"I wish to Christ he'd hurry this case up," Hodges sighed. "This witness expense is eatin' me up."

Pruiett's technique, as it was subsequently perfected and nationally recognized, was marked by a slow gathering attack in the opening period, a well calculated stall through the intervening rounds, and an annihilating final attack. He would take more time to qualify a jury than the average lawyer took to try an entire case. He studied prospective jurors with a cold and deliberate eye; he boasted that he could tell a bad eye from a good one, by the way it reflected his own cold stare. He took enough time with the individual juror to place him, at least partially, under the spell of the personality which seemed to make people feel that they would like to do something for him.

Court baiting, although occasionally indulged in, was not practiced to the same extent as counsel baiting. He quickly acquired a capacity for exciting and haranguing a prosecutor which was unsurpassed. He liked to have the stage exactly right for the particular brand of final eloquence he intended to deliver up to the jury. The final appeal was the master's touch. He stood to win or lose, in most of his cases, on the blistering heat of his closing plea.

The Evans-Richards alibi didn't afford a footing for his subsequently developed flights into eloquence. He had to have some unwritten law, or self-defense, for that. His stock and stencil from the scriptures and the classics were not employed; he gave the jury a cold, logical analysis of the conflicting—or coinciding—facts in evidence.

Frank Lee, the assistant to the district attorney, was closing the case. He assembled the breeding books, the stud receipts and the blacksmith's receipt before him on the counsel table, and began to soliloquize.

"We can discern here," he said, "the alibi for two murderers, penned in a fine Italian hand. No novice drew this device. No amateur laid this trap to ensnare the feet of stumbling justice. The cunning brain of a man who would see murder go unpunished, the smooth tongue of a man who would prostitute truth has brought this perjury before you. Justice cannot be deceived by this cunning Italian hand."

Frank Lee was in error, in at least one respect. Justice aborted. Evans and Richards were found guiltless by the jury.

"Moman, I want'a introduce you to a couple friends of mine," Colonel Jake condescended. "This here's Samuel Johnson Garvin, an' Calvin J. Grant. They're from Pauls Valley, in the Chickasaw Nation."

"I'm right glad to meet'cha." Pruiett said, shaking hands.

"I heered you try that murder case, son," Garvin said, "An' I want to tell you right now that you done it right. You was sure entitled to win it."

"I'm feelin' good about it," he said. "It was my first murder case, an' I was worried sick 'til the jury came in. When they says 'not guilty,' I bet I felt more relieved than Evans an' Richards did."

"You mean that's the first murder case you tried?" Calvin Grant's question was accompanied by a look of surprise.

"He's been in plenty of 'em with me," Hodges interrupted, "but that's the first one he took over all by hisself."

"That's right," Pruiett agreed. If Hodges wanted to take a little credit for what he had just accomplished, it was all right with him. He wasn't going to tell that Hodges had done his best to keep him out of the case, because 'there wasn't a chance in a million to get anything but a pulled neck.'

"You ought to get in a few with him," Grant suggested, flatly. Garvin laughed and Hodges grinned weakly. Pruiett said nothing. "We wouldn't a'had to be back here for another trial if you'd a put a little life in that last one we had."

"You got a lawsuit?" Pruiett inquired.

"We're witnesses in the John Stevenson case," Garvin said. "That's where he killed Joe Gaines, up at the valley."

"What you doin' down at the office tonight?" Colonel Jake asked.

"I been so excited this evenin' over that verdict I couldn't set still," Pruiett answered. "An' I thought about a question or two that come up during the trial that I wanted to look up. I didn't expect to run into a crowd up here, though."

"I'm goin' to be workin' with witnesses," Hodges replied. "I got some people in the private office. Garvin an' Grant is just killin' time, waitin' for this case to get over with so's they can go home. Tell 'em about what's been goin' on 'til I get through, will you?"

Pruiett dropped into a chair and threw his feet to a table top. "What kind of business you gen'lemen in?" he inquired, carelessly. All the time he was making a slit-eyed survey.

"Mister Grant here, he's the banker at the valley," Garvin said. "I'm

Samuel J. "Sam" Garvin. Pruiett once said of Garvin County's namesake, "I love the old boy like he was my paw." Courtesy Archives & Manuscript Division of the Oklahoma Historical Society.

CALVIN J. GRANT, LEANING ON THE COUNTER OF THE FIRST NATIONAL BANK OF PAULS VALLEY. AFTER WITNESSING MOMAN PRUIETT IN THE COURTROOM, GRANT TOLD THE YOUNG ATTORNEY "BY THE TIME YOU GET GROWED, YOU OUGHT TO BE SOMETHIN' OF A LAWYER." COURTESY PAULS VALLEY HISTORICAL SOCIETY.

in the cattle business, I guess you'd call it. Land and cattle. How old are you, son?"

"I'm twenty-three," Pruiett answered.

"God Almighty," Grant said. "By the time you get growed, you ought to be somethin' of a lawyer. I ain't foolin'. You got the world by the tail an' she's scramblin' on a slick hillside. If I could make a speech like you, I'd stay up all night, just talkin' an' listenin' to myself."

"There's a bill through Congress an' about ready to go into effect, givin' us courts of our own up in the territory," Garvin said. "They's goin' to be one hell of a lot of litigatin' up there, an' a hell of a lot of money for good lawyers to make. Now, if I was young like you, an' with your ability, I'd..."

"What kind of a country you got up there?" Pruiett interrupted. "I made a trip or two across the river workin' on this murder case; but, I didn't see much."

Garvin was a huge man, with a bulging belly and fat face. He started a process of pride-expansion before he started to speak in reply.

"You ain't seen no country 'til you get in the Washita River bottoms," he beamed, rubbing his fat hands over the tight-stretched trousers on his thighs. "That little old river is as crooked as a pan of hog guts; she bends an' doubles back on herself like she's afraid somebody is goin' to slip a little upland in on her. Six cuttin's of alfalfa for feed a season an' the last one makes a whale of a seed harvest. A bale an' a half of cotton to the acre; corn that beats Iowa all holler, that's what she does. The main line of the Santa Fe Railroad from Wichita, Kansas to Fort Worth splits her right down the middle, an' when the cattle is ready to ship, the god damn buyers come in from both ends an' fight on the depot platform to see who gets to pay the most for beef. There's..."

"Lay off, Sam, for Christ's sake," Grant chuckled. "Don't..."

"What about this valley you talk about?" asked Pruiett. "What's that?"

"It's our town," Grant explained. "It's on the Santa Fe, in one of them bends of the Washita. Some calls it Smith Paul's, an' some calls it Pauls's Valley, but us old timers are cuttin' it down to just the valley."

"Smith Paul was a' old Englishman that settled there in the early day; married a Chickasaw an' grabbed off a choice batch of land," Garvin interrupted. "Ain't nothin' wrong with that. I married a Choctaw myself, an' I wouldn't trade her for a European duchess. Paul

PRUIETT BECAME A FAMILIAR FIGURE IN THE GARVIN COUNTY COURTHOUSE IN PAULS VALLEY. HE ALLOWED HIS WAVY BLACK HAIR TO GROW LONG AND WORE BAT-WING CELLULOID COLLARS, BULGING HARD CUFFS, AND SILK SHOESTRING TIES. IN COURT HE SWAGGERED AND DIRECTED BITING, SARCASTIC REMARKS AGAINST OPPOSING ATTORNEYS AND THE BENCH AS HE SMOKED THE BIGGEST AND SMELLIEST CIGARS HE COULD BUY WHENEVER A JUDGE ALLOWED IT. AT OTHER TIMES HE CHEWED TOBACCO AND SPAT ITS JUICE THROUGHOUT COURT HEARINGS. COURTESY PAULS VALLEY PUBLIC LIBRARY.

puts in a tradin' post an' store, an' starts gettin' well. The Chickasaws let their inter-married citizens have all the ground they can fence an' keep away from the nesters. The post growed an' settlers started to buildin' around, especially after they got the railroad through. It's the finest little old town right now, you ever saw."

"You got a town with a bank?" He inquired, looking at Grant.

"You're damn right, an' I just wisht my customers didn't pay their notes so prompt," Grant said. "I'd like to take over a little land on the mortgages, but they won't let me. That land's sure hard to grab."

"You live in town?"

"I do, but Sam don't," Grant said. "He's up west in the Washita River valley, calls his place White Bead Hill. Just to tell the truth about

FEDERAL MARSHALS OF THE SOUTHERN DISTRICT OF INDIAN TERRITORY, OFTEN CALLED THE SANDY LAND COURT. LEFT TO RIGHT, MARSHAL GROSVENOR A. PORTER; JOHN HAMMER, OFFICE DEPUTY; JIM HAVENS, FIELD DEPUTY; J. P. IRBY, FIELD DEPUTY; AND JAMES NORVELL, FIELD DEPUTY. IT WAS THEIR PRISONERS WHO TURNED TO PRUIETT FOR HELP AFTER BEING ARRESTED. COURTESY *MOMAN PRUIETT: CRIMINAL LAWYER.*

it, he had a store an' tradin' post an' was about to run Smith Paul out of business, 'til the Santa Fe lit where she did. When Smith Paul's got the depot, Sam gave up. All he's got is a nice start toward a little town that he calls his ranch. White Bead is perty complete."

"My folks has always been movers," said Pruiett. "They came to this town in easy hitches. Just followed the Frisco as she came out of southern Missouri, across Arkansas, an' right into Texas. I don't like it none too well here, an' I'm lookin' for a place where I can settle an' work, an' make some jack."

"You married? Got'a family?" Garvin inquired.

"Yeah," he answered. "I got a wife. Ain't no kids—yet."

"You'd be just as at home in the valley as a cottonwood sprout," Grant said. "An' I'm tellin' the truth when I say that the folks up there has put off their suin' a long time, just 'cause courts is so inconvenient an' far away. Hell, comin' to Texas, or Arkansas or Kansas, just to law with some bastard, ain't worth it. But, if they get that territorial court started, an' go to tryin' cases up an' down that Washita bottom, just look out. It'll be the place for a smart lawyer to get well. I mean plumb recovered."

The United States District Court for the Oklahoma and Indian Territories was established by the Congressional Act of March 1895, and authorized the division of Indian Territory into three judicial districts; the Northern, the Central and Southern. Known familiarly as 'The Sandy Land' Court, it invoked and attempted to enforce, as the law, the statutes of the State of Arkansas. (Mansfield's *Arkansas Digest* was the Sandy Land Bible.) For a limited period it held concurrent jurisdiction with the Federal Courts of the Eastern District of Texas—Judge Bryant's court—and with the Western District of Arkansas, the domain of hanging Ike Parker. President Grover Cleveland appointed Constantine Buckley "Buck" Kilgore, of northeast Texas, as judge over the southern division of the new court. This division included the Chickasaw country, or the territory west of Fort Smith and north of Paris.

Pruiett took the Texas and Pacific Railroad from Paris to Gainesville, Texas, and the Santa Fe north to Smith Pauls. Calvin Grant and Sam Garvin were together in Grant's bank when he sauntered in.

"It's Jake Hodges's spittoon cleaner that tries lawsuits in his spare time," Grant greeted, rising and grinning.

"I'll be god damned if it ain't," the ponderous Garvin agreed. "Hi, son! Is there anybody with you? You got some law business up here?"

"Nope," Pruiett answered. "I come up at your invitation. Ever since you been down there, talkin' about your valley garden, I been restless. I got to strike out for myself in a place that's growin'. Paris is about as big as it's goin' to get, an' just as long as the old timers like Colonel Jake, an' Enoch Fagan, an' old man Brants keep livin', they'll get the choice business. Competition's too strong for me. I'm prospectin' an' if this place is half what you say it is, I'm goin' to hang out my shingle."

Garvin shook his hand the second time. "Son," he said, "the last time I'm talkin' to you I says you are a real lawyer, one with real ability an' a future. Well, I had just seen you try a tough case an' win it, an' that's the test that decides, more'n any other, whether a lawyer's got the stuff or not. Right after that I seen Jake Hodges try one, not any tougher, neither, an' Jake's got a reputation for bein' a smooth trial lawyer. He got a hung jury an' thought he was doin' perty good. You got Jake skinned a mile in a comparison, an' I'll promise you right now that, if you stay in the valley, you got one client, an' that's old Sam Garvin."

"That's mighty nice of you, to say that, Colonel Garvin," he said.

"An' if there's a lawyer in town that I know's got the guts to fight an' head enough to do it right, then I'm through runnin' plumb to Ardmore to hire my law work done," Grant smiled. "An' ever onct in a while the banker gets to recommend his lawyer to folks that ain't just sure which one's the best in town."

"I like that kind of talk whether you mean it or not," Pruiett said. "But, there's things I got to think about, an' decide on, before I take up anybody's proposition. Is this place goin' to last, an' is she goin' to keep good business, or is she goin' to stall an' stagger an' wind up with a bunch of hungry bums playin' against each other, an' none of 'em got enough to get out an' move to the next place on? How much is it goin' to take to start, an' to hold on 'til the money season comes around?"

"You mean 'til they hold a term of court here?" Grant inquired.

"Yeah, an' 'til some stealin' an' shootin' starts? Fightin' fence rows an' suin' on notes is goin' to be all right, on the side, but I'm goin' in for criminal law. How's the field for that?"

"This has been the longest quiet spell we had in years, just since we been talkin' here," Garvin said. "Shootin's an' killin's is ever'day stuff on Paul Avenue. The hills up off the bottom are chock full of horse thieves an' cattle thieves, mostly crossed between Indians an' their old nigger slaves. If you're lookin' for that kind of stuff, you shore don't need to go no farther. Didn't John Stevenson take a Winchester to Joe Gaines right in front of this buildin', an' Joe a Deputy United States Marshal, too?'

"I ain't got enough cash to start on," Pruiett said, frankly. "How'm I goin' to get credit around here for a little while, a stranger to ever'body but you?"

"I'll hire you for my lawyer, an' I'll stake you in the business," Garvin agreed. "If I ain't got enough, I'll sign your note an' let my bankin' friend here spend a little of his money. I'd take the risk just to get to hear you defend some wild Chickasaw half-breed when the travelin' court comes to town."

"I ain't jokin', Colonel Garvin," Pruiett insisted. "I mean..."

"An' I ain't either," Garvin interrupted. "You see that little box shack with the big window in front, across there an' down the street a little?"

"The shoe shop?"

"Yeah. Where the shoe-shop sign is. It ain't no shoe shop no more, on account of the cobbler that was runnin' it got lickered up one night, an' got in a scrape in one of these damn Uno joints. He didn't have enough change on his body to start to pay the back rent."

"What's a Uno joint?"

"Uno stands for one; one percent alcohol, that's all the kick the government let's 'em put in beer in the territory. It's mostly Longhorn brand, shipped in here from Fort Worth, an' some of the Chickasaws say Longhorn, an' others just plain Uno. A Uno joint is a beer joint where they sell beer that won't make nobody drunk, but where you find ever' son of a bitch on the inside dog-drunk."

"Well," Pruiett encouraged, "what about the shoe shop?"

"They killed this damn cobbler in the fight, is what I'm tellin' you, an' he didn't have enough on him to pay up the rent. I own the damn buildin', that's what I'm gettin' at, an' I'll put a table an' some chairs in it; you can paint your lawyer sign over that shoe shop sign, an' you'll have one of the best damned locations for startin' in this here town."

"If you're on the level, I'm takin' you up. The rent is to be charged."

"I'm right square on the level, an' the rent's to be charged. She's $10 a month, an' the chairs an' table'll be in there in the mornin'. What you goin' to do about your wife?"

"She's carryin' a baby," Pruiett explained, a little embarrassed. "I'll have to go back to her in a month or six weeks. In the meantime, I'll batch up here an' see how things are goin' to go. After she's up again, if I think I'll be able to make it, I'll have her up here with me."

"MOMAN PRUIETT—LAWYER". Pruiett was admitted to the bar in Indian Territory on February 22, 1897. Indian Smear paint made from lamp-black mixed with kerosene and painted roughly on a tan pine board, announced the willingness of the box-building's inmate to be of service. Rusting bailing wire, nailed to the plank siding, kept the sign from swinging too far about in a gusty morning wind.

"How you makin' out, son?" Two pairs of muddy boots covered the table top and Sam Garvin was speaking. An iron cot, with a rough quilt neatly arranged, stretched across the back wall. The shoe shop had become a combination law-office and dwelling.

"It's perty good," Pruiett replied. "I ain't made no money, but I got it on the book, an' just as soon as a term of court hits town, I'm goin' to settle up a little of it an' collect some fees."

"When you goin' back to Paris?"

"Wont be but a day or two. Lilly Belle's bound to be comin' around perty soon, an' I want to be sure an' be there with her."

"Are you comin' back?"

"You mean to the valley?"

"Yeah."

"Why hell, yes, Colonel. What you think I am? Think I'm goin' to get down there owin' you an' Grant, an' a bunch of others, an' not come back to settle?"

"I ain't even thinkin' about that," Garvin growled. "What I'm tryin' to ask you, do you think this here valley's got a future for your kind of business? You been awful quiet the last couple of weeks, an' you ain't looked exactly contented. I just wanted to know."

"I can do more learnin' when I keep my mouth shut," Pruiett said. "I wanted to learn as much as I could as quick as I could, in decidin' whether to bring my wife and kid up here to live. That's..."

"Well, if you been learnin', let me in on it. What you picked up since you been here?"

A great drove of spotted steers pushed and slid past the front of the office, hoof deep in the mire of Paul Avenue. Men on horseback whooped and swore and banged their big hats on their horses' flanks, hurrying them on. A drunk farmer ambled slowly past the front window.

"I learned that they got this country named wrong," Pruiett observed. "It ain't the Indian Territory; it's the white man's territory."

"Ain't that the god damn truth," Garvin agreed.

"I've found out why all the old lawyers that used to come to the boardin' house at Paris, when they was there for court, carried a big pistol in their carpet bag. These birds around here can't see the lawyer in a disinterested position. They get as mad at their adversary's lawyer as they do at their adversary."

"She's tough as a boot," Garvin acknowledged.

"I found out that this government whiskey regulation is a lot of bull. It's as easy to get liquor here as it is at Fort Smith, an' this white lightnin' they still off in the hills, an' the alky they run in from Texas, makes a god damn Indian crazy instead of plain drunk."

"You ain't missed yet," said Garvin.

In a 1900 speech to a group of Garvin County citizens at an Old Settler Reunion Moman Pruiett compared their beautiful Washita River with the great romantic rivers of history and the world. He said "the sinuous Washita winds itself like a silver thread, far and away the crown jewel of all the lands of which I have ever read and been blessed with a vision." However among friends he referred to the river as "that little ol' river that is as crooked as a pan of hog guts." Here a group is boating on the Washita beneath a wooden bridge. Behind the bridge a pipeline is suspended over the waterway. Courtesy Howard K. Berry Photo Collection.

"They're fallin' off these Santa Fe trains an' drivin' in on wagon gangs so fast, an' nestin' around on this black land, that the damned old Indian's goin' to have to fight or move on again. I say the government's goin' to have to make a better arrangement for 'em than they got now."

"I'd a said the same thing, if you'd a ask me."

"An' another thing that occurs to me," Pruiett continued, "is that this territorial court is a temporary move, just to fill in a gap until somethin' permanent is worked out. I'm talkin' about statehood."

Garvin smiled and nodded.

"I found out that my luck ain't all bad," Pruiett mused. "I fell into the hottest little spot left in the West, an' got adopted by two of the biggest men in the place. I learned that you an' Grant ain't hot air, like a lot of the bunch I been thrown in with, an' that when a man like you say somethin', that I can depend on it bein' so."

"Have you discovered the why for that?" Garvin inquired. "That you got an exceptional way about you, your face, an' your eyes, an' a voice an' manner that excites attention, an' makes friends. Have you found that out?"

"You an' Grant have woke me up, in a way," he admitted. "I got more self-confidence now than I ever did have."

"Have you discovered that the main thing it's goin' to take in the next few years, with the territorial government runnin', an' with things gradually workin' around to statehood, is guts? Do you understand that the guy with brains an' guts together is goin' to be the one to get on top in this mess?"

"I was gettin' ready to tell you that, Colonel," he laughed. "The guy that can get the toughest, an' is luckiest, is the one that's goin' to get along. I say lucky, 'cause it's goin' to take more than brains. It's goin' to take plain luck, to dodge all the stray lead that's goin' to be flyin' around this here valley in the next few years."

CHAPTER FIVE

Wherein lawyer Pruiett makes definite location in the Indian Territory, and begins, forthwith, to keep apace with the so-called rougher element of the section. And how he goes back to Texas to try a murder case, and, after having jailed himself for his lack of respect for the local court, frees himself and wrests a verdict of acquittal from the jury. And, wherein, he lets the territory's light of promise blind him against an attractive offer of partnership from a distinguished Dallas attorney, and he goes back to the valley to find a surplus of assorted criminal business awaiting. And how begins an offensive against the serpent's trail, and he receives commendations from the friendly jury for having cracked a skull in the fray.

Late April had the Washita River Valley in its spring finest when he brought Lilly and the baby there for trial inspection. The inhabitants, even the Indians, were abustle with the promise of plenty in the atmosphere. The sprouting corn in the fertile bottoms was racing to overtake the dark bulk of the alfalfa and clover in adjoining fields. Sleek, well-fed beef moved restlessly in the unpainted pens along the railroad tracks, as if impatient to be off and away to market. The crated poultry, stacked high on four-wheeled trucks, cackled a dual hello and good-bye as it rattled over the rough brick of the platform toward the forward portion of the freight train on the passing track.

The Garvins, Colonel Sam and Sue Mouncrief Garvin, his Choctaw princess, as he called her, were waiting at the depot with a buggy.

"Let me see the shaver," Garvin said, as Lilly pulled the blanket back. "Perty good. Is it a boy or girl?"

"It's a boy," Pruiett said.

"What you name him?" Garvin inquired.

"Hayden Warren. The Hayden's for Lilly's grand-dad; my father's name is Warren," Pruiett explained.

"I got a house vacant for you to take over," Garvin said.

"We ain't got no furniture—yet," Lilly Belle reminded.

"Well, this place ain't furnished, but you got to have furniture sooner or later. I'll help you make arrangements to buy some." Sam Garvin was willing to help in any way at any time.

"Thanks, Colonel," Pruiett said, "but I made a deal with Kate Scrivener before I left, to take some of her light-housekeepin' rooms. They'll do us for a while, 'til I can get straightened up a little."

"Court opens here in ten days, an' things are goin' to hum," Garvin said. "An' I got you some more business while you was gone. The marshal's arrested Sam Willingham an' Cole Collins for breakin' enclosures, an' I signed their bonds. I wouldn't go for 'em, 'til they agreed to hire you to defend 'em. An' old Uncle Henry Gordon's been askin' when you'd be back. One of his boys is in jail at Ardmore, charged with stealin' cattle."

"That's the kind of friends I got here in the valley," Pruiett beamed, aside to Lilly Belle. "How's a guy goin' to keep from gettin' along with that kind of backin'?"

Fortune, long indifferent, began to bear a faint semblance of a smile. As the Judge, court clerk, and lawyers began to gather for the first local session of the territorial court, he was able to collect on the J. C. Harmon note, the subject of one of his first valley cases. He got the full $50 reserved on its face for legal services. Vancie Wyatt, who had employed him to sue E. J., her husband, decided to abandon her suit for divorce and incidental relief, and to take him back regardless of his shortcomings. She paid Pruiett $20 to dismiss the case she had on file. Rose and Jack Goodwin, who lived above the valley on the South Canadian River, agreed to disagree, and divided $35 from the proceeds of the sale of a load of beef with Pruiett, for taking care of the technical points of unhitching them. Willingham and Collins, up for trial for violating government fence rules, paid $25 apiece, in advance, for his services.

He bought a stock of furniture and moved into Garvin's box house on a side street, three blocks from the office. He took a shaggy saddle pony for services in adjusting a difference over shares of crops for farm rent, and kept it in a three-sided shed behind the house. Uncle Henry brought a bushel of pecans and a burlap bag of apples as part payment of the fee for defending his cow-stealing son. Bill Tucker owed him $20 for the replevin of a span of mules; Pruiett rode the pony eight miles east to Bill's place and took a red milk cow in full payment. He took

UNCLE HENRY GORDON, LEFT, WAS A FORMER SLAVE FROM VIRGINIA. MOMAN PRUIETT DEFENDED FOUR OF UNCLE HENRY'S SONS WHO HAD BEEN CHARGED WITH MURDER AND LATER SPOKE AT GORDON'S FUNERAL. GORDON WAS THE SOURCE FOR THE FOLKTALE "WHAT THE SCREECH OWL'S CALL MEANS." COURTESY HOWARD K. BERRY PHOTO COLLECTION.

half the night riding back; the cow had such a bulging udder that she lagged and held the pony back. Lilly Belle wasn't giving milk like she should, and Hayden Warren wouldn't make modification of his constant demand upon her.

"When Pruiett located at Pauls Valley that village was just a little wilder, a little woollier, a little rougher and a little tougher than any stomping ground in the Chickasaw Nation or any other nation. It was in the period of municipal career in the frontier west when a six-shooter acted as the town clock and the sexton of the cemetery was the most important officer. The saloons, or rather, the 'Uno Joints,' never closed, and the merry clink of the festive liquor glass and the rattle of the festive poker chip blended together into a weird music that only those who have known the early days in Oklahoma appreciated as music."

Sam Paul, surviving eldest son of old Smith Paul, the settlement's founder and heaviest land-holder, kept the John Stevenson standard aloft by shooting and wounding his own son, Joe, in a muddy Paul Avenue Uno joint. Joe was able to recover, and as soon as he was about, he shot Sam (his father), in December of 1891, in the same den where his own assassination had been attempted. Sam died. Jennison McClure, white and Chickasaw cousin of the Pauls, shot Joe Paul to death with a six shooter in April of 1895. Bill Paul, Joe's boy, who was attending boarding school at Sherman, Texas, was sent word of Joe's demise with advice not to come home to the funeral.

Pruiett was playing blackjack at the upstairs Odd Fellows hall. Claude Weaver, who went to Congress from the Fifth Oklahoma District, and Dave Langdon and Scott Jones, were holding hands. The half-breed McClure was there, and it was late—or early.

"It's damn near mornin'," Pruiett reminded them.

"Ain't no use to quit now, before breakfast time," Weaver said.

"Keep dealin'," Jones said. "Who's comin' up? Somebody's wife think he's stayin' out too late, an' comin' after him?"

The door to the outside-stair approach opened and a squatty half-breed sidled in. He stood beside the table for several minutes, watching the play indifferently, before he spoke. "Bill Paul in town. I just seen him."

The players exchanged significant glances and continued their play. When the hand was finished, Jennison McClure pushed his stack to-

Claude Weaver arrived in Pauls Valley from Gainesville, Texas, in 1895 and practiced law until about 1908 when he moved to Oklahoma City. Whenever Moman Pruiett needed a personal lawyer he called on Weaver. From 1913 to 1915 Weaver served as Congressman from Oklahoma's Fifth District and from 1915 to 1923 he was Oklahoma City's Postmaster.Courtesy Archives & Manuscripts Division of the Oklahoma Historical Society.

ward Weaver, who was banking, and arched his black eyebrows.

"You quittin'?"

"I go home now," he said.

"It's almost daylight, Mac," Pruiett suggested. "Hadn't you better play a couple more before you leave?"

"I go home now," he repeated.

"Look here, now, Jennison," Weaver said. "It ain't hardly safe to be runnin' aound here in the dark, without knowin' where he is. Why don't you stick around a little longer. You know damn well he ain't comin' up here."

"I go home now," McClure said, without changing tone or expression.

"Pay him off," said Pruiett. "He says he go home."

The squatty informer was already dozing in a chair. New hands were dealt and McClure walked carelessly out the side door.

"It's gettin' light, now, as sure as hell," Pruiett observed. "Let's go an' get some breakfast after this hand. How long's Jennison been gone?"

"Listen!"

"That was a shot!" Pruiett whispered.

There was a short silence, then two more shots. The players glanced toward the little Indian, who slouched low in his chair with his dirty hands folded peacefully across his pot belly. His eyes had opened wide and understandingly. With a significant shrug of his shoulders, he closed them again and began to nod.

"God damn it," Pruiett gritted. "I'm out. If you guys can play any more it's all right, but I'm quittin'. What the hell's that?" He jumped and started.

"You're all upset," Weaver laughed. "It's just a train whistle. It's the mornin' Santa Fe. I'm out, too."

"Come on, Shorty, coffee." Pruiett called to the little Indian. He was close at the heels of the quartet as it reached the bottom of the staircase which ran up the side of the stone building. A woman hurried up Paul Avenue from the east, from the direction of the Santa Fe depot.

"Is Doc Young up here?" she inquired breathlessly. James Archibald Young was the town's principal doctor.

"No, he ain't," one of the men said. "What's wrong?"

"The mornin' train just ran over a man," she said.

"You want Doc for professional service, or official service?" Pruiett asked. Young also was the mayor and chief magistrate.

DURING THE EARLY 1900S THE GALLOWS IN THE YARD AT THE FEDERAL JAIL IN ARDMORE WORKED OVERTIME. DEPUTY UNITED STATES MARSHALS SUCH AS WILLIAM "BILL" TILGHMAN, CHRIS MADSEN, AND HECK THOMAS SCOURED THE COUNTRYSIDE FOR OUTLAWS AND BROUGHT THEM TO COURT WHERE THE FEDERAL PROSECUTOR WIL-LIAM B. JOHNSON WAS ASSIGNED THE TASK OF TRYING THE ACCUSED. COURTESY *MOMAN PRUIETT: CRIMINAL LAWYER.*

"It ain't for treatment," she answered. "He's mince meat. We just want him there for the identification, an' to watch the pickin' up."

The four looked understandingly at each other, and then at the Indian. He shrugged his shoulders again.

"I'll give you three guesses an' the first two don't count." Pruiett said. They were walking toward the railroad property.

"Perty bloody mess," Weaver observed.

"Somebody ought to have a basket ready for Doc to use when he gets here," Pruiett suggested.

"Anybody know who it was?" some one asked. The curious were arriving from every direction. "Was it a bum? Did he fall under gettin' off?"

Pruiett picked up a blood colored fragment of coarse cloth. He held it in front of the short Indian.

"Jennison?" he asked.

"Jennison home now," was the answer. The Indian was gazing placidly up the tracks toward the north. The rails were beginning to glimmer with the rising light in the east.

"If we was to look, we might find some little round holes in them biggest pieces, holes that a Santa Fe engine couldn't make," Pruiett said.

"An' if we keep our god damn noses out of other people's business, we ain't liable to catch a stink that turns our stomach," Weaver replied.

Langdon laughed and said, "You'll learn somethin' worthwhile ever' day, if you keep your eyes open. Claude's taught you a damn good lesson, already this mornin', Moman. I'm gettin' some eggs an' ham. What do you guys say?"

The government met the recklessness of its territorial populace by meting out, measure for measure, the same heedless and heartless conduct. The gallows in the yard of the Federal jail at Ardmore worked over time. The color of the neck being pulled until it popped was of no consequence to the hangman. White ones, red ones and black ones, and occasionally one of foreign stripe, were stretched with indifference. The swinging tactics of Arkansas Ike Parker were adopted. William B. Johnson; a vigorous and vicious prosecutor, was assigned to try the outlaws and murderers as such enforcement officers as U. S. Deputy Marshals Bill Tilghman, Chris Madsen, and Heck Thomas were able to apprehend. The fact that murder and robbery was rife didn't mean that it went unwhipped or uncensored. If you killed your man but missed the getaway, you were a better than even bet to drop through a Federal gallows trap.

As the *Cherokee Republican* reported "Pruiett hung out his shingle with the determination to be just as bad as any 'real bad man' the village contained. He started in by whipping a dozen or so of the bad men of the place, and then, to save further effort along those lines, he declared himself to be the official bad man of Pauls Valley, and maintained the position until civilization came and robbed the Indian Territory municipalities of this important dignitary."

Success in the valley put the slow-blossoming Pruiett into full bloom. He was naturally fearless, non-conforming, and tough. The opportunity, the desire, and the necessity to be tougher suited him. The contempt which he had previously expressed for courts and the administration of justice had grown within him. His hatred for the system which had wronged him had climbed and spread like the poison ivy on the river cottonwoods.

He developed into a definite type. His appearance was something to distinguish him, to make him stand out, in the gatherings of the wild community. He permitted his black hair to grow a bushy, unwieldy bulk; he brushed and groomed it until it outshone the dress of the crows that circled and roosted on the river through the valley. He was quick to fight or shoot; to curse and swear and be consumed by fits of useless rage. For the frontier, his dress was the finest. He shaved twice daily. He wore bat-wing celluloid collars and bulging hard cuffs, and he changed so often that they were usually spotlessly white. He went in debt for store clothes, fancy alpacas and broadcloths, and his shoestring tie wasn't real shoestring, it was tight-stitched genuine silk.

But all his finery didn't conceal the hostility he had for the law. He swaggered in the courtroom. He made baiting, sarcastic remarks when matters of serious court business were being considered. He laughed at the efforts of the locals to have law, and to have order, so that they might prosper and progress in peace. He smoked cigars, the biggest and smelliest he could buy, when the courts would permit him. He chewed tobacco and squirted its juice at random all of the time he was in court.

"He's like a mutilated Madonna, a Raphael or an Angelo that the alley kids have slung mud an' rotten eggs all over," a press commentator remarked in mentioning his later acquired success. He came into court with his custom-tailored suit and shining high-collar in faultless fashion. In an hour he was roaring and ranting from a surrounding circle of ashes and stubs and brown expectoration.

Pruiett and his eatin' tobacco were legendary before his prowess for holding hard liquor was proven. "*Quid Pro Quo!*" was the title of a hastily concocted courtroom sonnet, printed in the *Tulsa World* on September 28, 1913, typifying Pruiett engrossed in the practice of his life work—helping justice to miscarry—twisting facts and circumstances so that a guilty murderer might come clear.

Mister Moman Pruiett,
We've watched you as you do it;
Watched you closely as you stack
Away tobacco by the sack;
Seems so easy for you, too—
Double handful for a chew;
Gives you so much pleasure,
Oh
Commensurate with measure,
That we very often rue
That we cannot do it too.
Oh, Mister Moman Pruiett,
Please tell us how you chew it.

MOMAN PRUIETT "RAISING A LITTLE CANE" IN THE WASHITA BOTTOMS OF INDIAN TERRITORY. THIS PHOTOGRAPH WAS ORIGINALLY TO BE INCLUDED IN THE FIRST EDITION OF *MOMAN PRUIETT: CRIMINAL LAWYER,* BUT WAS LEFT OUT OF THE BOOK. ITS ORIGINAL CAPTION READ "PRUIETT HUNG OUT HIS SHINGLE WITH THE DETERMINATION TO BE JUST AS BAD AS ANY 'REAL BAD MAN' THE VILLAGE CONTAINED." COURTESY HOWARD K. BERRY PHOTO COLLECTION.

"This here's a perty good party, you're havin', Moman," John Stevenson, the marshal killer, pulled his face from a mug of Choctaw beer to compliment his host.

"Christmas don't come but onct a year," Pruiett replied.

"It's all right to play poker an' drink Choc, but don't make so much noise," Lilly Belle complained. "You'll have the baby awake again if you keep on."

Sam Garvin gathered her to his bulging belly in a fatherly embrace. "It ain't just a Christmas party, don't forget. It's a farewell party, too. Ain't your old man leavin' for Texas tomorrow to try a big murder case?"

"I guess I'll be goin' back for trial again before long," John Stevenson said. "An' I'm gettin' awful tired of that case. Sentenced to hang once, an' gettin' a hung jury after the conviction was reversed. I got ever' thing I own mortgaged to pay costs, an' bills an' lawyers, an' it looks like I'm just ruined for nothin'."

"Ever' since I went to Paris with you the second time, I been tellin' you you ought to reorganize your defense. Stillwell Russell an' Jake Hodges ain't effective like my lawyer. If you'd a had Pruiett to that last jury, you'd a come clear."

"Don't be slanderin' Stillwell Russell," Lilly Belle said. "He's my favorite lawyer, that is, all but one." She caressed her young husband.

"You're just like poor old Betty," Pruiett laughed. "Can't keep your paws out of my wool. Always runnin' your fingers through it an' mussin' it up."

"Russell's all right, he's a damn good lawyer, an' Jake Hodges is too," Garvin said. "I didn't have nobody representin' me for a long time but them, but ain't I been doin' better since Moman came to the valley?"

"It seems like just one murder after another, to me," Lilly Belle observed. "I see'em, an' I hear about'em 'til I dream about'em. I'm scared all the time."

"How many you had since you been here, Moman, an' how long you been here?" Stevenson asked two questions at once.

"I come in February, an' then I went back for Lilly an' the baby. Let's see, it was April, '96, an' this Christmas, '98, makes it most three years." He mused and sipped his drink. "It don't seem that long to me; but, I tried Bud Nolen and Jake Henson at Ardmore, an' old Pink Bruner here, an' Charlie Bias..."

"Time gets away when you're busy," Garvin explained. "I had a little trouble weanin' these bastards that was mixed up serious with the law away from old Circuit Judge Henry B. Furman, an' them Cruce brothers, at Ardmore—an' from old Stillwell Russell, but they done took care of that for me now. Since you won that Clarence B. Douglas case for'em, you'll get their criminal business—all of it."

"Maybe not," Pruiett grinned, complacently.

"They had old man Walter A. Ledbetter an' C. L. Potter in there too, didn't they?" Stevenson asked.

"Yeah, they damn near had too many lawyers," Garvin answered. "I heard an old cuss up there at Purcell sayin' 'it looks to me like Douglas is guilty, or he wouldn't have so many lawyers to try to prove he ain't'. They hired you last, didn't they, Moman?"

"I didn't hardly have time to get ready," Pruiett said.

"How come they try it at Purcell, when he killed Williams at Ardmore," Stevenson interrupted.

"Cruces took care of that, a change of venue," Pruiett answered. "There was some prejudice down there, an' here in the valley, too. We took it up on the South Canadian, right to the boundary of the Chickasaw nation, so's that we'd be as far away as we could get."

"Self defense'll work for anybody but me," lamented Stevenson. "That was as thin as hell, what you put over for Douglas. A pencil lookin' like a knife? Hell's fire!"

"What did he really want to kill him for, Moman?" Garvin inquired.

"That defense was on the level," Pruiett answered. "I saw a case

Clarence B. Douglas, seated center, was a Muskogee newspaper editor who shot and killed a rival editor on the streets of Ardmore. After the first two murder trials ended with hung juries, the defense team asked Moman Pruiett, front row, second from right, to join the counsel of A. C. Cruce, front row, second from left, for the third trial. As a result of Pruiett's wild theatrics Douglas was cleared of all charges. Courtesy Howard K. Berry Photo Collection.

tried before Ike Parker, at Fort Smith, that was damn near a ringer for this one. Boudinot killed Stone up at Tahlequah, an' they was editors of rival papers. Jimmy Williams was runnin' the *Ardmore Chronicle,* an' Douglas was writin' for some other sheet when this happened. Williams says in a' editorial that Douglas considered himself eligible for service cleanin' spittoons in a Uno joint or as a member of the Dawes Commission. That started feelin' between'em, an' they was both on edge, watchin' for the other to make a move. If Douglas made a mistake in killin' him—in bein' too hasty—it was a' honest mistake. He really thought Jimmy was pullin' a knife."

"Apologizin' for them kind of mistakes don't help much," Garvin grunted.

"You ought to see what the *Purcell Register* says about Moman," Lilly Belle said. "Not Guilty: The Verdict at Last Reached in the Douglas Case".

"I cut it out an' I'm goin' to save it."

"I saw the real thing," Garvin laughed, "an' it was good enough to write up. Old Ledbetter an' Potter had been mumblin' around for the defense, an' old James E. Humphrey, the assistant U. S. Attorney, had been stumblin' around for the government, 'til they had that farmer jury dozin' off about right. Moman had told me what he was goin' to do, an' I was watchin' for it. He had a pencil, exactly like the defense had introduced in evidence, in his pocket. It was one of them bullet-lookin' affairs that you pull in two in the middle an' reverse ends, for carryin' around in your pocket. It was made out of metal, alright, an' it was perty big. Well—that jury was restin' an' wishin' they was at home lookin' after the cattle, an' Moman just kept a talkin', low an' smooth, about that pencil he had in his hand. That was the real pencil. Then he tossed it right into the middle of the table, an' left it there where ever'-body could see it, an' he went on talkin' real careless like about somethin' else. Then, Jesus Christ, he lets out a squall like a steer-hooked nigger, an' he jumps right straight up in the air. When he hits the floor, his hair's down in his eyes an' he looks like a maniac, an' he grabs a juror, right in the middle of the front row, by the throat. All the time he's doin' his yellin' an' jumpin', he's haulin' out this other pencil he's got, the one that the jury don't know about, an' he raises that up over his head like he's goin' to stab the juror with it. You should've seen them bastards scramble."

Garvin paused to laugh and slap his fat thighs. Pruiett cut in.

"I ain't never goin' to do the right thing in court again," he said. "Them wild antics is what gets results. The guys that come to the courthouse for jury service, they're just farmers an' clerks out of grocery stores an' things like that, they want to see somethin'. When a stockman goes to Kansas City with a load of beef, he don't go out to the packin' plant to see what the best way of killin' an' dressin' is. He gets him a jug an' goes to a leg show. Jury service is just somethin' the boys have to endure, an' if you'll liven things up for 'em, they'll show their appreciation for it. Have a fit, or shoot off a blank cartridge, or carry the baby. Anything to relieve the monotony that guys like Potter an' Humphrey hang onto a case."

"Moman either entertained 'em out of the verdict, or he scared 'em out of it," Garvin laughed. "He says 'why gen'lemen, don't be a'scared. I ain't got no dangerous weepun; I just got a little pencil. Its just a little pencil exactly like the one that Jimmy Williams was carryin', an' that you knew was a'layin' there on the table. But, you thought it was a knife, an' that I was a'goin' to slash your throats. Don't deny me that, 'cause it's evident in your faces', he says, an' by god, it was. They was scared out of their chairs. 'It wasn't so much what I had in my hand, as they way I handled it, an' the expression I had on my face while I was a'doin' it. Unless you are able to conclude beyond all reasonable doubt that Douglas was not justifiably scared, that he was not frightened for his life an' safety, then it's your duty to acquit him—to turn him a'loose.' That was all Moman said. His whole speech didn't last ten minutes."

"I'm goin' to read a part of this clippin' on it," Lilly Belle insisted. " 'About four o'clock on Thursday afternoon the jury in the case against Clarence B. Douglas, charged with the murder of James Williams, was brought into court, and when asked by the judge if they arrived at a verdict stated that they had, and the foreman, C. W. Henry handed in same, which was read as follows: We find the defendant, C. B. Douglas, not guilty as charged in the indictment.

The case was stated to the jury last Friday night, after which the jurors were put in charge of the bailiffs. On Saturday morning, witnesses were examined. Court was resumed at 3 o'clock Monday afternoon, the train from the south being late.The arguments by the attorneys began Tuesday afternoon, Assistant Prosecuting Attorney Jas. E. Humphrey, of this place, opening for the government, presenting the case in a forceful manner. He was followed by C. L. Potter, of Ardmore, who spoke for an hour, very ably presenting his side of the defense. At the evening, W. A. Ledbetter took up the entire time with an eloquent address for the defense. At the morning session Wednesday Mr. J. F. Sharp gave a succinct and lucid exposition of the government's position. He was followed by Messrs. W. I. Cruce of Ardmore, and Moman Pruiett of Pauls Valley, who spoke very briefly for the defense. Mr. Pruiett's speech was especially complimented, members of the jury stating at the close of the case that it had a very strong effect in determining the verdict."

"It had ever'thin' to do with it," Garvin said.

"I didn't know a hell of a lot about the evidence in that case," Pruiett said. "I was hired to do two things, empanel the jury an' make one of the arguments. I wasn't to examine no witnesses. When I got the jury in the box, I had to come home. Lilly Belle was havin' the baby, an' I was here a couple of days. I just got back in time to have Cruce tell me what had took place, an' to figure out that little stunt for my speech."

"Is Cruce still joshin' you about namin' the kid?" Stevenson inquired.

"Hell yes, an' I guess he will from now on," Pruiett smiled. "But, I don't give a damn. We ain't changin' it."

"He named that baby after a high-hat nome de ploom," Stevenson explained, seriously. "He'd been readin' a couple of them new books by a dame that signed her name Gail Hamilton. Moman like'em so well he wanted the girl kid to have a big name like hers; so, he named her Gail Hamilton Pruiett. Perty soon he found out that the books was by Jim Blaine's sister-in-law, an' that her real name was Mary Abigail Dodge. Moman's got one named after nobody."

"I don't give a damn," Pruiett persisted. "Her name's Gail, an' that what its stayin'."

"This is a perty tough case you got at Wichita Falls, ain't it, Moman?" Stevenson inquired.

"Why hell, no," John Webb put in. Webb was a quiet fellow who liked to listen. He was head ranch hand for the Garvin properties. His judgment in livestock matters, especially in horses, was considered infallible. "Old Dorsey Wilson just shot a deputy sheriff in two with a shotgun. It ain't very tough, killin' deputy sheriffs in Texas."

"Did he have any good reason for doin' it?" Stevenson asked. "I had a little experience in that kind of a case. Maybe there was some excuse—or maybe he thought he had some excuse—for doin' it."

"The only reason I see for it is that the deputy was cuttin' in on his whore," Webb replied. "I guess Moman, now, ain't goin' to let it go to the jury just that a'way, but that's the way I heard it."

"Dorsey 'Doll' Wilson's sister an' brother-in-law rents one of my places on the river," Garvin explained to Stevenson. "I heard about it so many times from them that I know it by heart. The gal's name was Maude Crumpacker. She was a fat wench around town there in Wichita Falls that the boys just kind of took turn about with. Doll got stuck on her an' wanted to marry her, but she didn't want to be limited so much. She'd tried marryin' a time or two before. She an' Doll was kind of livin' together—Doll says he considered her the same as his wife, that it was a common law marriage—an' one night he comes home an' sees Sam Abbot Mosely, the deputy, sneakin' out the side door. Doll just happened to have a twelve gauge in his hands, wasn't figgerin' on doin' no killin', an' he asks Sam real polite like where he's been an' what he's been a'-doin'. Sam give him a cussin' an' starts to pull a hog leg outa its holster, an' Doll shoots the shotgun from his hip."

"Now, that sounds like Moman Pruiett," Webb grinned. "Has he got the explanation for carryin' the shotgun around with him all the time worked out?"

"That parts a little more difficult," Pruiett supplied. "The shotgun belonged to Billy Dees, a guy that runs a saloon where Doll hung out, an' he says he don't know what Doll was doin' with it. Billy says he kept it leanin' in the corner just inside the back room, an' that he didn't give it to Doll. Doll ain't explained it, not even to me, yet."

"What you goin' down so early for?" Stevenson asked.

"Just on a writ," Pruiett answered. "Garvin an' Grant an' a lot of people around Wichita'll sign his bond if the court'll allow it. We got to get him out of jail an' out of town for awhile. The way feelin' is around there right now, they'd vote to hang him in a minute."

"You ought to try him somewhere away from Wichita Falls," Garvin said.

"How the hell you goin' to arrange for that?" Pruiett inquired.

"You're the lawyer, not me," Garvin said. "But, if you think it oughta be done, then you'll think of a way of doin' it. You win that case an' these local bastards 'll wake up. It's too bad you got to go clear to Texas to try murder cases, when we got some of the best ones in the country right here at home."

"I got to go to St. Joseph, Missouri, as soon as I get back," Pruiett said. "I got to go up there an' try Wade Hampton..."

"Wade Hampton, hell," Garvin exploded. "What the hell you want to get mixed up with that cow thief for?"

" 'Cause he's got the money to pay a damn good fee, principally," Pruiett answered.

"He's as guilty as hell," Garvin insisted.

"It's my business to prove he ain't," Pruiett laughed.

"Wade Hampton was a southern gen'leman, an' a great soldier," John Webb interrupted. "What right's this cow thief got to be usin' his name?"

Pruiett laughed again. "That ain't none of my business," he said. "It may be yours, but it ain't mine. I did mention it to him, an' he says they made it so hot for him he had to run off an' leave his real name, an' that Wade Hampton was dead an' the name was a good one; so, he just adopted it for himself. He said people that was born with big names had life a lot easier, an' so long as he had to have a new one, he was just goin' to snatch a good one while he was at it. It sounded perty smart to me."

"He stole them cattle in the first place, an' he stole the feed he half-fattened 'em on. He mortgaged 'em for more than they was worth, an' then he sold 'em to them Saint Joe packers for twict as much as they was worth. Well, when that Kansas City Livestock Association gets after somebody, they're blowed up."

"He's got a right to trial by jury, whether a big outfit like the K. C. is tryin' to railroad him, or not. That's all he's askin' for, an' if they can convict him, I guess Wade can do the time they give him."

"Wade hell," Garvin fumed.

There was a distinct odor of hostility in the Texas atmosphere when Pruiett, accompanied by John R. Flood, an attorney he had engaged to assist him, presented his writ to habeas corpus in an attempt to compel the court to permit bail for Wilson. George Miller, judge of the district court, made no effort to conceal the disapprobation he contained for any one who appeared in behalf of the killer of his friend, Sam Mosely. Pruiett arose as an officer led the prisoner into the room.

"We have invoked this right on a strict proceedings to have bond fixed," he said, quietly.

"Our laws don't permit bond in capital cases, an' I understand this is one." Miller looked calmly and defiantly over his thick lensed glasses.

"Your honor is familiar with the way that section has been construed by the Supreme Court," Pruiett replied, still low and respectful. "We are in a position to show that this case comes within that rule."

"No man is in a position to show this court something he knows is not true," Miller cried, rising from his chair with the color that mounted from his collar. "Before you take any more of our time, make a statement as to what you expect to offer."

Pruiett's color was rising, too. He looked to Flood for some kind of assistance, but Flood was engaged in tracing a pattern on the linoleum of the courtroom floor with the toe of his boot.

"We expect to show that the proof of the defendant's guilt is not evident, nor the presumption of his guilt great," he said. "Our courts have stated that in such cases..."

An angry court interrupted him. "That might be your law up in the Injun Territory where murderers and horse thieves go unwhipped of justice," he roared. "But, it ain't the law in Texas. If that's all you've got, the writ is denied."

Miller expected his listener to fold up his scant collection of papers and retire, as Flood or the local advocates, more familiar with his style, would have done. Instead, Pruiett advanced and stood defiant in the vacant space between the plain counsel tables and the bench.

"I am a member of the Texas bar and I know that the laws of Texas are as fair and just as those of the Injun Land, as you call it, or any other state or territory in the union. The trouble is that Texas has to have an occasional judge who lacks the mental and judicial capacity to understand and interpret the law. I'll file this writ in the court of criminal appeals, and, and..."

Miller had resumed the pose which his act had required that he temporarily abandon. He eyed the attorney coolly.

"Your remarks are deliberately contemptuous, Mr. Pruiett," he said. "You may withdraw them, or it will be the Court's duty to levy punishment against you."

"My remarks are for the record of this hearing," Pruiett replied. "The record will reflect that they were invited and provoked by the unwarranted statements of the court; I have nothing to withdraw, or say further."

"Very well, young man." The court was now painfully deliberate.

"You are sentenced to confinement in the jail of this county, until you have purged yourself of contempt by paying a $25 fine, and withdrawing your contemptuous remarks."

Flood watched with dismay as Pruiett followed the sheriff from the courthouse and into the square red-brick jail behind the building. When he went to talk to him, through the rusty bars, he found him jubilant and radiant, instead of crestfallen and discouraged. As soon as the jailer was out of hearing, Pruiett grasped his lapels and pulled him close.

"File a motion for a change of venue and set up prejudice on the court's part, in connection with this contempt," he whispered. "As soon as you have it filed, I'll apologize to the old son-of-a-bitch, an' pay the fine. He'll either have to change it or disqualify, an' in either case we'll be ahead. I believe he'll change the venue rather than see some one else assigned here to try the case in his court."

Flood whistled in frank admiration and amazement.

"Did you do that on purpose? Did you have it figured this way before you went in there?"

"Hell no," Pruiett replied. "When I saw how tough he wanted to get about it, I knew somethin' had to be done. When I saw the opening, I just pushed my little stack of white chips in. Go on, now, get started."

The kid lawyer defending the Dorsey Wilson murder case to be tried in late January of 1899 was attracting considerable notice and attention at Decatur, Texas, in Wise County.

"Ain't that Pruiett awful young to be tryin' this kind of a case?"

"Watch him an' see. He don't act like no school boy, does he?"

"He's the one that old Miller put in the can at Wichita Falls, Texas, for contempt. That's why they're tryin' it out here, 'cause Miller lost his temper an' was goin' to have to disqualify."

"I've heard how Pruiett done that on purpose. He knew that Mosely's friends was so strong at Wichita Falls that Wilson didn't stand a show, so he just made old Miller disqualify."

"Well, Pruiett's tried murder cases before. He beat a couple tough ones in Lamar County, they tell me."

"He might be good an' he might be smart, but he's a long way from winnin' this case. Killin' a deputy sheriff ain't no safer in Wise County than it is up at Wichita Falls. 'Honest Pat' an' these old nesters they got on this jury panel ain't no cinch for any killer."

Judge J. W. Patterson, Honest Pat, was the trial judge. Pruiett was working on the *voir dire* examination of prospective jurors. He was tying up progress with his customary detailed questioning of each juror.

"Some one ought to tell the kid about old Baldy, that bastard he's examinin' now," one courtroom lounger whispered to another. "He's a sticker."

"Let him handle his own troubles," came the answer. "Let Baldy stick 'em."

The bald-headed prospect was from nearby Paradise, Texas. His name was Baldy Conner. He was tall and gaunt and bald, with a sharp and eagle-like countenance.

"What is your native state, Mr. Conner?" Pruiett inquired, never looking for so much as an instant from the prospect's glassy grey optics.

"Kentucky," was the passive, cold reply, as the level stare was returned.

"Have you had previous jury service?"

"Yes sir."

"Have you served on the jury in a capital case?"

"Yes sir."

"And what was the jury's judgment in it?" Pruiett continued.

"The state objects," the prosecutor said. "It's improper examination of the juror."

"Sustained." Honest Pat made the ruling with finality.

But, Pruiett had more than one way of getting at the subject. He thanked the court and put another question.

"Do you know whether or not the defendant in that case is living at this time?" he inquired.

The state's attorney objected again.

"Overruled," Pat stated. "You may answer the question."

The venireman had never taken his cold gaze from his examiner's face. "He is dead." He said evenly. "I saw him die."

The heavy silence which followed was broken only by the sound of an uncomfortable spectator in the crowded courtroom, shifting his boots over the rough pine floor.

"Is that the only capital case you've been in?" Pruiett was being painfully deliberate. A local lawyer near the door whispered to another standing against him. He said that Pruiett was unwise in pursuing such an examination, for it prejudiced his client with the other jurors. He was assuming that Conner would unquestionably be challenged by the defense.

"No," was the barely communicative reply he received.

"Do you know whether the second defendant you tried is alive or dead?" Pruiett was being careful to draw his inquiries so as to comply with the previously expressed ideas of the trial court.

"He's dead," the reply came in the same words and tones. "I saw him die, too. I went to the hangin'."

Pruiett was as persistent in his examination as he was in his gaze. As they stared at each other, he said, "Were those the only capital cases you have heard?"

"No." It was the same cold response.

"Is the third one living or dead?" "He's living, so far as I know. We only gave him life."

He was forced to smile with this declaration, and the tension of the room was broken. A wave of relieved laughter swept over it. Pruiett proceeded to questioning the prospect seated next to Conner.

It was growing late in the day, and the early darkness of western January, 1899, was enveloping the corridors of the old court building; but, the spectators and interested parties in case of the State of Texas against Dorsey Wilson remained each in their places in the courtroom. The day had been consumed in selecting a jury, and each side, state and defendant, still had a lone peremptory challenge to assert. Baldy Conner of Paradise was still sitting defiantly in the box.

Pruiett was conferring with his client, preparatory to excusing his last man.

"Baldy has got a damn good eye," he whispered. "I never saw a better one in a man's head. I hate to excuse him, but you know what he is by what he said here in court. Ever'body in the courthouse has warned me against him and told me to take him off, but I like him. What do you say?"

"I'd as soon hang as stay in their lousy jail any longer," Wilson replied. "It makes no difference to me. If you like him let him stay; if not, kick him off."

The answer left Pruiett in a difficult position; he tried Conner with one more question.

"Mr. Conner," he inquired, "do you believe in the old sayin' 'it's a long lane that has no turning'?"

The prosecutor's objection was overruled. Judge Patterson was too tired to interfere. "Answer the question if you can, Mr. Juror," he said wearily.

Conner gazed long and unwaveringly at Pruiett, as if pondering over a weighty problem. "Why, sure," he said, slowly, as he gazed for a moment out the window and over the tops of the trees of the square. "It'd have to be a' awful long one that never did turn."

"The defendant will waive his last peremptory challenge," Pruiett announced, rising to address the court. "The defendant will accept the jurors as they are in the box."

It was on the fourth day after the trial began that Pruiett began to pace the floor in the delivery of his final argument. His defense of Doll had been home-spun and simple, like that of Evan and Richards. A mutual friend of Billy Dees, and of the accused, swore that he had removed the gun, on the license of his friendship with Billy, for use in a bird hunt, and that he had asked Wilson to carry it home for him. There was no suggestion of pre-meditation of murder in the handy possession of the shotgun. Mosely had made the fatal hip-pocket pass. He had commenced the assault by grabbing for the iron. What red-blooded American citizen would have done less than long-suffering Doll Wilson?

Pruiett called down the wrath of the Texas gods, to plague and destroy all those who had lost their fundamental sense of justice and fair play. The peace and tranquillity of the placid Ohio, and of his early days in the Kentucky hills, he recalled and called back, and shed a tear for them. He talked of love, and of peace, and of hate and fear. He reminded his hearers of Texas' resplendent past and its encouraging future. He talked about everything but his case; of everything but the guilt or innocence of Doll Wilson.

Four hours, hours that slipped away like minutes, were engaged and filled with a brand of eloquence and oratory that had theretofore been unheard by the western court fans. Not in the Thrasher case, as with a crying child, he enlisted the attention and sympathy of his listeners, and drew their interest from the only issue of the case; not in the Evans and Richards trial, for his activity there was encumbered by the burdensome weight of an unsavory past, and a realization that his listeners knew of it.

He was a free spirit, safe from the narrowing confines of boyhood weaknesses and adolescent indiscretions. He was trying a man for his life, charged with murder, and he had a jury to work on. Like the true genius, first realizing the power of his gift, he gained poise and power with each prompt response which he received from the untried brain and voice box. He shamed the court and jury and made them cry; then, he sat down. He even knew the time and place to quit.

A Mamie Taylor cocktail was the proper and stylish thing to order in west Texas saloons in 1899. Pruiett was proper and in style until the bar on the corner closed at midnight. Then the poker players moved down the street to an available hotel room. As they walked past the square, Pruiett saw the light burning in the upstairs room of the courthouse. The jury was still deliberating.

There was no sleep for him that night. At ten the next morning, the report went about that the jury was coming in. The trial of another case was interrupted as the twelve bedraggled jurors, one with a bruised face and black eye, stood in line in front of the bench.

Pruiett heard a whisper. "Old Baldy beat hell out of that Dutchman," someone said.

The bailiff had passed the verdict to the clerk and the clerk had transmitted it to the judge.

The state's attorney arose, cautiously. "If the court pleases," he said, "the defendant isn't in the courtroom. He hasn't been brought from the jail, yet."

Honest Pat was staring at the verdict, the jury, and the state's attorney, all at the same time. "It ain't necessary for him to be here," he said in loud tones. "The jury has done turned him a'loose."

Stillwell H. Russell, the Dallas lawyer, had had business on the Wise County docket. He had been in the courtroom throughout the trial of the Dorsey "Doll" Wilson case, and had followed Pruiett's process of handling it with more than casual concern. He and Pruiett were riding the train together, as far as Fort Worth, where Pruiett changed to take the cars north to the territory.

Doll Wilson was going back with Pruiett, 'to pay his respects to his sister and thank her for giving him a hand,' as he called it. Pruiett's private, although unexpressed, opinion was that he was going back to make a touch. They were sitting side by side in the chair car, neither speaking, when Russell came through and spoke to them. Pruiett nudged Wilson and whispered something; Wilson got up and walked away. Pruiett shook hands with Russell and invited him to take the newly vacated chair beside him. Russell accepted.

"You handled the Wilson case very capably," Russell said. "I could see a touch or two of Colonel Jake's handiwork in it. However, I don't believe he would have ever had the nerve to leave Conner on."

Pruiett smiled as he thanked him. "Colonel Hodges was very kind to me. I'll always owe him a debt of gratitude for his kindness." That was all of his reply. He chose to ignore the reference to his success.

Russell persisted. "You won Conner completely," he said. "He stood for acquittal from the beginning, and he had a fight with one of the jurors over you. I talked to the bailiff."

"Is that so?" He asked, registering mild surprise. "I hadn't heard of it. I was so glad to win that I scarcely thought to thank them for the verdict. I didn't have much time to make the train, either."

"He said that a Dutchman that was for conviction said something unbecoming of you, something about that trouble you had in Paris, and that Conner swung on him. He did such a good job that the Dutchman and another fellow that had been stayin' came over and signed the verdict. We all thought that Conner was a sticker; he's hung a few in his time."

Pruiett was meditating. Even that far from Paris, and so long afterward, the serpent's track was still discernible in the dry soil. He continued to look out the window as he answered.

"He had a' awful good eye," he said. "I never saw such a keen eye in a man's head before. He had a' awful good eye."

"That long lane stuff was pretty good. At first, I thought it was too deep for him; but, it was all right. It showed him what a narrow viewpoint he was goin' to have if he kept lookin' in the same knot-hole all the time. It was a good way to wake him up."

Pruiett was looking far out into the moving prairie, and saying nothing. Russell was not sure that he was listening.

"Would you be interested in movin' to Dallas, and making an association with me?"

"I beg your pardon, sir, but I was studyin' for a moment. What did you say?"

"I asked if you would be interested in comin' to Dallas, into my office. I could offer you an association where you could make $4,000 a year, possibly more."

Pruiett shook his head. "No sir, but thank you," he said. "I'm honored, and hardly know what to say, except—I have other plans, and I just can't. I just simply can't."

Russell, with his carefully developed poise and control, was unable to conceal all of the surprise he felt at receiving so prompt a rejection. While he was not inclined to be self-admiring, he knew of Pruiett's background and previous circumstances. He knew that the same offer would have been relished by many a more successful and accomplished lawyer. It was his turn to gaze away, and to ponder.

"I've got my plans worked out quite a' ways ahead," Pruiett said, doggedly. "I've got a little start up in the valley where my family is, and some friends that are helpin' me along. I don't think I'd like it back in Texas.

"But you'll have friends wherever you go," Russell said assuringly. "Dallas is a good town, and it's growing. You can make more money there in the next year than you can in five in the Sandy Land Courts. There's money for you in Dallas."

"I'm thinkin' about statehood," Pruiett replied. "At the rate the whites are takin' up land and crowdin' the Indians out, it won't be long before the government'll see the futility of tryin' to protect 'em and their property. I look for the government to settle with the tribes, an' open all the unassigned land to settlers. If they do, it means there'll be another state in the union."

"We've pushed the Indians as far as we're goin' to be able to," Russell replied. "What you get in the territory will be temporary, like the nesters that marry the squaws for a good place to lay down, or the traders that run those dinky little stores. The marshals'll get tired of the squaw-robbers an' bootleggers some of these days, and run every damned white person out of there. Then they'll disband that funny little court, and you and all the other lawyers will have to come back to Texas, or take a chance on Arkansas."

Pruiett smiled at him, conscious of a feeling of superiority, and shook his head. Was it possible that the great Russell, with his experience and wisdom, could have such a narrow and warped idea of what

A YOUNG MOMAN PRUIETT SHORTLY AFTER THE BEGINNING OF THE 20TH CENTURY. COURTESY GARVIN COUNTY BAR ASSOCIATION.

Moman Pruiett poses holding his driver and smoking a cigar. Pruiett was fond of fashionable clothing that was, like this golfing attire, appropriately suited to the activity he was engaged in. Courtesy *The Daily Oklahoman*

was goin' to come? If he did, he would have to continue to labor under it, for he was too big a man to be informed or corrected by a "Sandy Land" practitioner. He smiled again, but made no spoken reply.

Pruiett climbed into Garvin's waiting buggy beside the depot. "It was grapes," he laughed. "I took after the toughest hand they had on the jury, an' started sellin' him stock. He brought the verdict in just like I thought he would."

"I got the wire," Garvin said, "an' I sure was proud of you. You got to get down to Ardmore. There's..."

"I got to go to Saint Joe," he interrupted. "Hell, I told you that. How's Lilly Belle an' the kid?"

"They're fine, but ain't you interested in this Ardmore business I got you? It's murder."

"What?"

"You're damn right. Murder, right here on the home diamond. You know Frank Henderson and his boy, the boy's name's Mike? The tall ganglin' boy? They're bein' held by the Federals, goin' to be indicted for murder. They killed Charley Anderson an' Fred Stevens from up around Paoli, an' it's a hell of a case."

"You mean they killed 'em both?"

"Yes sir, I sure as hell do," Garvin said. His excitement was obvious. "Soon as anybody gets in trouble around here they come high-tailin' to me for a bond. I told their folks right to their faces that if Furman or Cruce or any of that bunch got the cases ahead of you, that I don't schedule a foot of ground. They promised to give it to you."

"What's the dope?" Pruiett asked. "What brought it up?"

"Frank's got a girl named Virginia, it's his baby girl." Garvin explained. "Maybe you don't know her, she's a' overgrowed wench about sixteen that looks like she's twenty, an' she's been runnin' around. Frank an' Mike caught her out with both of these boys, an' in a hell of a fix. She did about all she could do, under the circumstances, bein' caught by her paw an' brother. She started to bawl an' said that Charley an' Fred used force on her. They shot 'em both dead."

"The unwritten law," Pruiett whispered. "The unwritten law..."

"Don't it sound good to you?" Garvin inquired.

"Hell yes, it does," he answered. "I'll make this trip with you an' get 'em released on bond, if the commissioner'll allow it. I suppose we won't have no trouble on that? Then, I'll have to hustle up to Missouri."

"He's indicated to their folks that under the circumstances, he's willin' to set bail, but it'll have to be kinda high."

"Has these folks got any money?" Pruiett asked. "Do they expect to lay out a perty fair fee?"

"They're able to pay," Garvin grinned. "When you learn to fix fees as well as you can try cases, then you are goin' to be a genuine lawyer."

"You know more about law business for bein' a cattle breeder, than anybody else I ever saw," Pruiett laughed. "You should have been a lawyer, yourself."

"Did you want to see me, Moman?" Claude Weaver, Pruiett's poker playing colleague, walked into the converted shoe-shop. "Thought you was out of town 'til John Webb saw me on the street an' said you was lookin' for me."

"I got in on the night train," Pruiett explained.

"How'd you get along with your case?"

"I won it," he answered, shortly.

"What?" Weaver demanded. "You don't mean you got an acquittal for Wade Hampton?" He smiled with his use of the alias.

"Hell yes, I did. The jury turned him loose. He rode back as far as Guthrie with me on the train."

"How in the hell did you do it?" Weaver asked.

"I don't know, exactly, how I did do it," he answered. "You probably wouldn't believe me if I was to tell you. I found a long lost uncle on the jury, for one thing, an' Buchanan County's the home of Fightin' Joe Shelby. Wade Hampton stood ace high with the Shelby gang; but, that ain't what I want to talk about right now. With the help I'd give you, could you clear me of murder?"

"What do you mean?"

"I mean I'm goin' to kill a son-of-a-bitch, right here on Paul Avenue," he muttered. "I've done decided to kill him. I'm just studyin' now on how to go about it."

"If you cleared that cow thief, you ain't justified in bein' mad at anybody," Weaver observed. "An' if its murder, count me out. I ain't encouragin' none of that, not even for my friends."

"Would you consider assault and battery?" Pruiett inquired.

"I might stay with you if you was just goin' to beat hell out of somebody, but this killin' is out with me. I don't believe in it."

"Here's the layout," Pruiett said. "I gets up to Saint Joe an' they got Louis C. Boyle, the former Attorney General of Kansas, there to prosecute. The Livestock Association hired him special. He's one gentleman. Well, he's havin' some wires back an' forth with the lawyers here that investigated Wade an' the case. You know who that is—Leonida C. 'L. C.' Andrews, a lawyer in Pauls Valley. Boyle gets stuck on me an' we go out together for a few drinks, an' the trial of the case is rockin' along all right, 'til Boyle gets another wire. It says that Pruiett is a two-time loser from Arkansas an' Texas, an' to bring it out an' the defense will be blowed up. Can you believe it? He wires'em I'm a' ex-convict."

"Well," Weaver waited. "What happened? Did it get you in any trouble?"

"Old man Boyle brought it to me an' he was so mad he was purple. He didn't wait, an' he didn't take it to anybody else. He brought it right to me. He says 'Look what some scoundrel down in the territory says about you. It's an' outrage. I'll notify my company, an' see that his services are discontinued at once.' I looked at it for a minute, an' I hands it back to Boyle an' I says, 'it's true, judge, as far as it goes,' an' the old man just got madder, an' he tore the telegram up into little pieces an' says, 'I disagree with you, sir. It's a' sufferable lie, an' I shall demand that Mr. Andrews make a retraction. You are a gentleman an' a worthy member of the bar—an' my friend.' Well—that's the way it was. The old man was friendlier than ever, an' I really think he was pullin' punches after that. He helped me to win the case."

"You ain't hurt much then," Weaver said. "But, I didn't think old L. C. was built that away."

"That misfortune ain't goin to follow me around, an' keep draggin' down at me," Pruiett declared. "My friends know how it's hurt me. They won't talk it an' don't like to hear me mention it. The others, the enemies or the ones that think they can get wise, have got to learn that it ain't healthy. I'm goin' to kill ever' bastard that repeats it."

"You can do a sight more good by cripplin' 'em," Weaver observed.

"Who's that comin' down the walk?" Pruiett asked.

"It's old L. C.," Weaver answered.

"Here's where we settle," Pruiett grated. He opened the drawer of his table and pulled out a blue-barreled pistol.

Leonidas C. "L. C." Andrews, a Pauls Valley attorney who was a contemporary of Moman Pruiett. Andrews called Pruiett an "ex-convict," and Pruiett clubbed him on the side of the head with a pistol. Pruiett was charged with assault and battery in the attack. He was later acquitted by a jury of his poker-playing buddies. Courtesy Garvin County Bar Association.

"Don't do no murder," Weaver cautioned. Pruiett slid the gun into a coat pocket and started up the board walk.

"I read that telegram you sent to Saint Joe about me," Pruiett said as he began fishing out the weapon. Andrews was a big man, powerful of mind and body, but he turned to flee. Pruiett clubbed him in the back of the head with the barrel and cylinder. The first blow dropped him like a beef. He fell to his knees and elbows, but he scrambled up; blood was spurting from a great gash above his neck. Pruiett was in front of him as he regained his feet, with the big gun high above his head. He brought it crashing down between Andrew's eyes, and Andrews went down again.

The second blow—the combination of blows—should have disabled the victim; but, Andrews was big and strong, and he was conscious enough to know that he was in a precarious predicament. If he lay still, he stood to be stomped or beaten to death. With an unnatural effort, he lurched to his feet, charged into Thomas L. Kendall's grocery on his right and raced for its back door. Pruiett was in close pursuit, sliding in the blood that gushed from Andrew's battered head. Proprietor Kendall grabbed the pursuer and struggled with him; the pursued found painful safety behind the locked door of Doctor J. A. Young's office—the office of the combination doctor and mayor. Pruiett was rounded up in a Uno joint by the City Marshal, and charged with an assault and battery.

The trial of the case of the Town of Pauls Valley versus Moman Pruiett was representative of the Pruiett theory. Four of the six men on the jury owed him money. The other two played poker with him and with Weaver, his lawyer. Pruiett leered and spat as the prosecution's witnesses testified; he took the stand and grinned as he repeatedly said that he couldn't remember. He hooked his thumbs in the armholes of his vest and nodded in satisfaction as the jury foreman winked at him and announced that they had found the defendant 'not guilty'.

"I ain't satisfied with that verdict," Mayor Young stormed. "It's agin' the clear weight of the evidence, an' it's a reflection on the peaceful natur' of this here community."

"I object," Weaver howled. Pruiett made the rim of the tin can, being used for a cuspidor, sing with an accurately aimed squirt.

"This town ain't goin' to be made a joke of, this a'way," Young insisted. "Call another jury an' let's try 'er again."

Pruiett grinned as he pulled Weaver close and whispered into his ear.

"I object," Weaver repeated. "It's agin' the Constitution of the United States. No man can be put in jeopardy twict for the same offense. I can show it to you in Mansfield's *Arkansas Digest.*"

"I reckon that's right," Young ruminated, scratching his chin. "but, there ain't nothin' wrong with tryin' him agin' on somethin' else. Where's the City Marshal?"

"I'm here," the officer called from his seat in the window.

"Put Moman under arrest an' charge him with carryin' concealed weapons. Charge him as on the date of this assault on L. C., an' his bond will be fixed at $250." Young slammed his table with a book, for emphasis.

Sam Garvin signed the bond and the same witnesses were called back when the case was reset. Pruiett kept up the insolent grin. Weaver reappeared as the attorney for the defense, and the routine of the trial was put on. The prosecution introduced the pistol and Pruiett acknowledged that it was his; but, he just couldn't remember about carrying it. The jury, all under obligation to the defendant this time, found him 'not guilty'. Mayor Young despaired and gave up.

But life in the valley wasn't all glitter.

"Friday morning, after an illness of two weeks, little Hayden Warren Pruiett, son of Mr. and Mrs. Moman Pruiett, departed this life. Mrs. Pruiett was nearly crazed by the death of her babe, and were it not for the efficient ministration of Dr. Young and Dr. A. E. Davenport it might have been our sad duty to chronicle two deaths instead of one. Saturday morning all that was earthly of the little one was taken to Paris, Texas, accompanied by the father and mother and Dr. Davenport."

The reunion with Betty and the Captain, the first in almost two years, was a sorrowful one.

"Things ain't lookin' good around here," Pruiett observed, bluntly.

"The money you been sendin' from time to time has come in handy, alright," Betty answered, with a wan, wrinkled smile.

"The Captain's just too old to be any help to you at all, ain't he?"

"He's almost like a child," Betty confessed. "He gets around all right, but he's forgetful, an' I have to watch out for him. He starts the garden in the spring but he usually forgets about it, or gets tired of it, before long, an' I have to either mind it for him or let the weeds have it. My eatin' customers has just about all quit me, by now."

"You an' the old boy'll have to go back with us, up to the valley."

"I ain't aimin' to get in your way, son," she said. "We can..."

"You can do what I say," he interrupted. "I own a good house with six or eight lots, about a block an' a half away from our new house. I took it for a fee in a murder case, an' it ain't rentin' for hardly nothin'. You see the fix Lilly's in. If losin' this one don't kill 'er, she's goin' to have another one in days or weeks, an' you can help her durin' the bedfast period. Don't argue with me, now. Just get ready to go back with us. When the old man turns over a spadeful of that valley ground for his garden, he won't walk off an' leave it. You won't be able to run him off."

There was a letter for the Pruietts when they returned. It was from Luther Reese, the preacher who had married them at Paris. "My dear Brother and Sister in Christ," he began. "I was shocked when Mrs. Reese handed me, on my return from South Louisiana, the telegram containing the sad news that your dear little babe had fallen asleep. Was so sorry that I did not get to see you and especially was I sorry that I was away when the message came. I could not have done any good, but I did long for fellowship with you in your deep sorrow. In it all, it is blessed to know that the sweet babe is with the Lord, 'Safe in the arms of Jesus', which Paul, by the Holy Spirit says, 'is far better'. I am on my way to Cleveland, Ohio, where I am to speak at the annual meeting of the Congregational Home Missionary Society in behalf of our work in Texas and Louisiana. Pray for me—both of you. Praying that you may receive this affliction from your Father as one of the 'all things that work together for the good of His children,' I am, Yours in Christ Jesus —The Reverend Luther Reese."

CHAPTER SIX

WHEREIN PRUIETT CLEARS A DOUBLE MURDERER IN A SINGLE TRIAL, AND ALTHOUGH HE OFFENDS HIS BEST FRIEND AND BENEFACTOR, HE EARNS A CASH FEE WHICH RELIEVES HIS SLIGHTLY DAMAGED CONSCIENCE. AND WITH HIS ACHIEVEMENT HE DEMONSTRATES THAT STERN MASCULINITY WILL TURN ITS BACK UPON SWORN PUBLIC DUTY WHEN A COMELY WENCH WILLS IT, THAT A FIXED JURY CAN BE UN-FIXED AND RE-FIXED, AND THAT THE BENT SAPLING NOT ONLY GROWS WITH THE CROOK IN IT, BUT THAT IT GROWS, AND GROWS AND GROWS.

Sam Ashton, in the Federal jail at Ardmore, was charged with shooting Charley Dismukes and his aged father to death. The double killing occurred in the Dismukes's country store and post-office at Hickory, Indian Territory, on July 12, 1900. The one redeeming feature, if any, of the bloody fracas, rested in the existence of two wealthy uncles and a willingness on their part to spend some money to keep Sam from being hung.

Pruiett, back from Washington, D. C., and enjoying a profitable run of business from the attention attracted by his successful efforts in the Bias case, swore profusely as he saw old Uncle Hugh Forehand, from Lexington on the South Canadian River, and Uncle Matt or Mat Wolfe of the valley, pass him up and go on to Ardmore. They employed Henry Furman and A. C. Cruce to defend their murderous nephew.

The case was about ready for trial, and Sam's attorneys came to town ahead of schedule to argue a motion for a change of venue. "There's a lot of feelin' against old Sam, for one thing," A. C. Cruce told Pruiett as the two of them stood near the entrance of the court building. "And for another..."

"That's hell, now, ain't it?" mocked Pruiett. "Old Sam just goes out to Dismukes' country post-office, shoots Charley down in cold blood, and plugs his daddy in the back because he's runnin' away, and they get some feelin' up about it. Ain't it funny how people are?"

"Old man Garvin's too bitter," Cruce continued, ignoring the interruption. "He's agitated opinion around here, knockin' Sam and boostin' the Dismukes, 'til we haven't got a chance for a fair trial, at all."

"The Colonel was awful fond of Charley Dismukes," Pruiett agreed, "an' he hates Sam's guts. Just between me and you, he says he'll pull up and leave the valley if Sam don't hang, an' I believe he means it. You know me. I don't like the prosecution side of the table a bit; but, they're makin' it look mighty interestin'. The Colonel's puttin' up some of his own money."

"You mean—Garvin is tryin' to hire you?"

"That's just what I mean."

"Listen, Moman," Cruce hastened. "Henry Furman and I been talkin' about local counsel—about you. If we don't get this motion for a change of scenery over, we want you to help us and we'll make old Uncle Matt pay you a fee. He's tight as hell, but we can work him. Leave that to me."

"Old man Garvin would run me out of town," Pruiett said.

"Forehand and Wolfe will pay you more than Garvin, an' you don't want to get in with the prosecution. You'd be all out of place, tryin' to send a man to the gallows."

Pruiett studied. The look of hybrid anguish and hatred, which had faded somewhat with the years since Rusk, passed across his face. "How come I ain't been consulted about this before? What's the reason that nothin's been said?"

"You know how old Matt Wolfe and Sam Garvin hate each other," Cruce said. "That's why Garvin is persecutin' Ashton, and why Wolfe is willin' to spend money. Garvin says he'll hang him, mainly because he hates old Matt so much. Wolfe says he'll save him, just to spite old man Garvin. I told Matt, an' old Forehand, too, what we ought to get you in this case, but Matt says you're Garvin's man; that you'd work to get him stuck, even if he paid you. You know how it is; but, if we got to try it here, I'll get you in or get out myself."

"Suppose I get in, what you got to work with?" Pruiett was being practical and matter-of-fact. "Here's the way I get it. Sam Ashton goes on Charley Dismukes' bond, when Charley gets charged with assault an' attempt to kill. Then Charley gets drunk again an' tried to kill somebody else, an' they get another warrant out for him, so Sam thinks his bond's in trouble—that Charley's liable to jump. He gets a certified copy of the bond and goes out to arrest Charley; he's got the right to do that, just take him in and surrender him, but he don't get any authority like a regular officer, to use force, an' kill if he meets resistance. He didn't have no right to kill Charley."

"No, he didn't have no right to kill him, just to get off his bond," Cruce agreed, "but it shows you Sam was properly motivated when he went out there. That's our best point. When Sam told him what he wanted, Charley got tough. They got in an argument and Charley reaches for his gun. Sam shot him in self defense."

"What did he shoot the old man in the back for, as he ran out the front door?" Pruiett inquired, casually. "He wasn't on his bond, too, was he?"

"Well...", Cruce began, "well... let's cross that bridge when we come to it. Sam don't have to stand trial in but one case at a time, and the one for killin' Charley is set first. Maybe killin' the old man makes it bad, in the long run, but right now, just remember he was the only witness, an' he can't testify through them clods piled up in his face."

"You don't know much about your case," Pruiett observed. "Charley's wife saw the whole thing, and so did her sister. They're goin' to say that the guns were in the back, where they lived, an' that there wasn't any guns up in the front part of the store."

"Do you know what you're talkin' about?" Cruce demanded.

"You're damn right, I do," Pruiett answered.

"You stick close to your office this afternoon, and tomorrow morning," Cruce said. "You are goin' to get a visit from Mr. Wolfe and Mr. Forehand, and if you don't take care of yourself on the fee, it's your own fault. Don't make any deals with Garvin 'til you talk to them."

Pruiett smiled softly, midway of the following morning, as he saw two men in a buckboard stop in the shade outside the window of his office. It was Wolfe and Forehand. He planted his muddy shoes amongst the papers on his desk with professional indifference as he saw them alight and move toward his door.

Forehand introduced himself. "An' this is Mr. Wolfe—Mr. Matt Wolfe," he said, stepping to one side so that Pruiett could reach him for the hand shake. Forehand acted as spokesman, and was to the point, according to his nature, in an instant.

"Would you be able to take employment in the Sam Ashton case, next week?" he blurted.

Pruiett was deliberate and studious. "I'm afraid it would be embarrassin' for me to go into that case," he said, watching his callers closely.

"While I ain't employed, I've been talked to. Colonel Garvin said the Dismukes wanted to hire me as a special prosecutor."

Matt Wolfe uttered a grunt that was near to a groan.

"We been sent here by A. C. Cruce. He said he had worked with you before in cases." Forehand was trying to speak lightly and persuasively at the same time. "He said that you would give us a consideration on his account, that is, if you could."

"I would've been glad to, with a little more notice," Pruiett said, carelessly, "but I wouldn't have time to prepare for trial—that is—on the defense. No, gentlemen, I'm afraid I can't be of any service to you."

Neither of the callers was inclined to abandon their purpose so early. Wolfe finally spoke: "Now, if it's a matter of money, Mr. Pruiett, I think Mr. Forehand and I can interest you. Maybe you can get a continuance, so as to be able to get ready. We'll pay a fee, just for a continuance of the trial."

Pruiett was well acquainted with the unsuccessful efforts already made to continue the case, and knew why they had failed. He knew that a continuance of the case for the term was out of the question.

"No," he said. "My friend Garvin would be sore if I went into it. I heard him say that Ashton was guilty as hell, an' what he thought the punishment ought to be. I couldn't afford to get myself in such a position."

"We'll pay you $500 to sit in the case with Cruce and Furman," Wolfe said, desperately.

"Yes," said Forehand.

"No," said Pruiett. "I wouldn't be interested. I'm sorry but I'm just not interested."

"We'll pay you a $1,000 to try the case," said Wolfe, with real pain and desperation in his coarse face. "A thousand dollars."

That was money. That was money for the territorial days, or any other days, and Pruiett had to look again. Turning squarely upon his callers, he studied them for a moment before he spoke.

"I'll try him for $2,500. I'll go in for $2,500—cash."

The gleam in Pruiett's eye indicated a quiet enjoyment of the discomfort he beheld. Forehand looked at Wolfe and Wolfe looked at Forehand.

"It's plum out of reason," Wolfe exploded. "Why, we only paid Furman and Cruce $1,500. Why, why,..."

Forehand, giving Wolfe a dark look for disclosing the terms of their previous contract for legal services, interrupted him. "Mr. Cruce told us you would be reasonable, at least," he said. "That kind of fee is ridiculous. It's impossible." He and Wolfe arose to go.

In a last and final effort, Wolfe turned. "I'll still pay the $1,000. That's cash. A thousand bucks."

Pruiett wanted that $1,000. He was beginning to believe he was carrying the fee fixing bluff a little too far; so, he changed his tactics. "Do you want Sam Ashton acquitted," he inquired patronizingly, "or do you just want to save him from swingin'?"

"Acquitted," the two uncles answered in chorus. "We want him turned a'loose."

"Well, sit down. Maybe I can make you a different proposition," Pruiett suggested. "Maybe I can make a deal with you where you don't pay unless you get what you want."

Wolfe and Forehand resumed their seats, a little more cheerful and hopeful. "Mr. Cruce told us you would be reasonable." That was all Forehand could think of, so he said it again.

"I'll tell you, now," Pruiett began, "I can take this case for the $1,000, and try to get it continued. If I do, or if I don't, I sit in it with A. C. an' Furman, and help try it when it comes up. If Sam's acquitted, you pay me $4,000 more. If he ain't, you don't pay me any more."

The plan didn't appeal to Forehand, but it did to Wolfe. He turned to his companion. "We should've made a deal something like that with the other lawyers," he said. "It would've been cheaper, an' then they would have worked harder."

"It's too much. Five thousand is too much money. A thousand ought to be enough." Forehand was yanking his short whiskers as he jerked out the short sentences.

"I couldn't afford to have old man Garvin on me for the $1,000," Pruiett explained. "I'd take my chances with him if you made it that interestin'. Pay me the $1,000 an' I start to work, an' if your man doesn't come clear, you don't owe me another cent. I can get the $1,000 out of the Dismukes."

Wolfe winced with the mention of the Dismukes. Having to try the case in the valley, with Garvin hostile, was all that he could stand. His hatred for the proprietor of White Bead, as much as interest in his kin by marriage, had prompted his activity in the case thus far. He spoke hastily, "Could we have a word in private, Mr. Forehand and I? Just a word or two, to talk it over?"

Pruiett ushered them into a small room adjoining the office. A few old books and papers, a rack and a chair, were discernible in the scant light admitted by a small, high window. When they had closed the door behind them, he resumed his chair behind the table, which served as a desk, the principal piece of furniture of the room, and placed his feet back amid the litter of papers on its top. Gazing through the open door and up the unobstructed street, he could see the olive coaches of the Santa Fe's regular train from the north, passing as it pulled into the valley station.

Forehand and Wolfe came out slowly. Forehand was still attempting to serve as spokesman. "We can agree to $2,500," he said. "The $1,000 in cash, an' if you clear him, you get $1,500 more, just as soon as Sam comes clear."

"Hell, no!" Pruiett exploded. "Hell, no! I won't represent you at all." He was finally and genuinely mad. "Just tell Cruce and Furman that, if I'm in the Ashton case, I'll be with Johnson, on the other side of the table."

As the two stockmen went out, Pruiett looked over their heads and up the street again. He was vaguely conscious of the dark railroad cars, which had been blocking the street, slowly moving again, as the train's brief stop ended and it resumed its journey southward into the territory and Texas. He had let a good fee get away, and at a time when he could have used it; but, by god, he wasn't going to be prostituted by a pair of misers. He had made them a fair proposition, and they had made light of it. After all, he could tell Sam Garvin he had turned down a $2,500 fee in the case, and it would put him in there more solidly than ever. He might cause Garvin to get the Dismukes up a little, after this, and..."

His musings were cut short. Forehand and his friend were standing in the open door. They had gone as far as the hitching rail under the tree, conferred further on the matter, and retraced their steps to his office.

"We decided it was a deal." Forehand said. "We pay you $1,000, an' you get in the case with Furman an' Cruce. If Sam comes out free, we pay $4,000 more. If he doesn't..."

"If he don't, you don't pay me another dime," Pruiett supplied for the somewhat deliberate speaker. "Not another damned dime."

A brief memorandum of the agreement was drawn up in Pruiett's long-hand, and signed by the visitors. Forehand gave a check on the Lexington bank for $1,000. Pruiett, with his feet back on the table had hardly time to contemplate what, if anything, could be done to make good for the $4,000, when the door was opened again. He glanced up, half provoked, expecting to see Wolfe and Forehand back again. He looked, instead, into the inquiring face of an unusually attractive woman.

She was a stranger in the town. He knew by her dress and manner. She had just arrived on the train he had seen pass through, he surmised, as his gaze traveled slowly down past a shapely mid-structure to the hand at her side, which held a small leather traveling bag. Pruiett arose, stuffing the check into his pocket, and rendered his most charming of bows and smiles.

"This is Mr. Pruiett," she said, not inquiringly, but with finality. "Mr. Moman Pruiett, the criminal lawyer."

Pruiett's chest swelled, and the black foliage atop his handsome head sparkled as though charged with an electric current.

"Yes. Yes, this is Mr. Pruiett. I am at your service."

He dusted off one of the straight-back chairs before offering it to her, and after she had daintily deposited the rhythmically shifting hips upon it, he stood in the middle of the floor and stared at her.

"I'm strange in this part of the country," she said. "I'm from Colorado."

"I've never seen that part of the country," Pruiett replied. "I've just got back from a trip east. I..."

"Yes, I know of that," she interrupted. "I read of it in the papers at Denver. That's what brought me to your office, reading of the things you did for that poor, unfortunate negro. I think it was wonderful of you to do that, Mr. Pruiett. Just simply wonderful."

She was throwing a lot of feeling in with her flattery and Pruiett was catching it all. He could scarcely stammer a word or two about it 'being nothing at all'. His ability to do the right thing under pressure, as in court and pressed for a maneuver before the judge or jury, didn't include a situation such as this. Here was a creature in his own little office, with a face as faultless and with hair as fluffy as Lillian Russell's, whom he had seen on the stage in the East. The eyes which beamed her undisguised admiration upon him were inviting and compelling.

"I'm here to see if I could interest you in the defense of Sam Ashton," she said. "Sam Ashton, the man who's to be tried for killing two men. I came down here to help him, if I could.

"You mean," he inquired, "that you want to hire me to defend Sam?"

"Why, yes," she said. "That is, I..."

"I know quite a bit about that case," he said. "He looks as guilty as hell to me, an' ever'one's bettin' he gets the rope, on one trial."

Pruiett's temporary confusion was gone. He was in full control. She didn't expect to pay him—in money, at least, and he didn't want her to. He relished the look of anguish that passed across her handsome face as he baited her.

"Please don't say that," she whimpered.

"What you got in mind for me to do?" he demanded, gruffly.

"I'm looking for some money by mail, in a few days," she said, lamely, "and I could pay you something on the fee then. I read in the papers about you bein' such a wonderful lawyer, and..."

"What's Sam Ashton to you?" Pruiett asked.

She hesitated. "He's my half brother," she answered.

Pruiett whistled. "Is that a stall, or is..."

"He's my half-brother," she insisted.

"Does anybody in town know you," he inquired.

"They don't know me, or they don't know about me, either," she said. "I don't think..."

"I'll take the case for you," Pruiett announced. "How far'll you go to get Sam acquitted?" His agile brain was wheeling.

"As far as it's necessary to go," she replied, coolly.

"Any limits?"

"No limits."

"You just came in on that Santa Fe, didn't you?" Pruiett inquired.

She nodded.

"When that rattler left here yesterday, it hauled a whole car load of prisoners south, for hangin' an' for jail at Ardmore, an' for keeps at Atlanta, Georgia. They been havin' a term of court here that's rough as hell. Springin' Sam ain't goin' to be no cinch."

"What can I do to help?" she asked.

"They got a bird on this panel named Tom Adkins. They call him

Squire Adkins. He's a body-boss an' he's the foreman of ever' jury he gets on. He'd vote for life for chicken-stealin', an' he's high on himself. He's a' old bachelor, an' I think he'd fall for a twist. Get it?"

She nodded again.

"That's the Hampton House across there," Pruiett said, pointing toward the town's principal hotel. "The squire stays there, an' that's where you're to stay. We got three days. Can you build into him in that time?"

"I think so," she smiled.

"I think so, too," Pruiett grinned, as he appraised her with a frank stare. "Now, listen. I want to be able to keep that old bastard on Sam's jury, without no danger whatever of gettin' stuck. You understand what I mean? I want him fixed for sure."

"I'll take care of him," she said, simply.

"Better show me you know how," Pruiett suggested. "I'm representin' him for you, an' we'll have to talk about the fee later." Pruiett and his newest client were understanding spirits when she departed.

Stillwell H. Russell sauntered into Pruiett's office. "Hello, Judge," Pruiett grinned. "I been expectin' you to come to town."

"I didn't send any word in advance, that I was coming," Russell answered, shaking hands with him.

"When I told old man Garvin I had got into the Sam Ashton case, he damn near came unwell. When he couldn't bribe or bully me out of it, he took out for the telegraph office. I figured he was wirin' for you to come an' help him."

"You wasn't wrong," Russell agreed. "I'm hired as special prosecutor, to help Bill Johnson."

"You can thank me for a nice fee," Pruiett said. "If I hadn't a' crossed the old man, he wouldn't have come across."

"Much obliged," Russell acknowledged.

"How's things in Texas?" Pruiett inquired.

"Not so good," Russell answered. "I was over to Paris a couple of weeks ago and saw Colonel Jake. We was talkin' about the Doll Wilson case, and about you. Jake told me to watch you, if I ever got in a case against you. He said you'd fix a jury, with the other side lookin' right at you."

"I didn't fix no jury in the Doll Wilson case, did I?" Pruiett laughed. "How's Jake's poker?"

"He's gradually givin' up his law for it," Russell replied. "I had to go over to the Peterson Hotel to see him, when I was in town. He was layin' out of the office, and when I went over to the hotel, there he was, in a game."

"You knew I lost one of my babies, didn't you?"

"Yeah, and I'm sorry," Russell answered. "How's Lilly?"

"She's not well at all, an' she's carryin' another. We're all worried about her. She can't pick up a bit."

"I got to be sure an' see her before I leave town," Russell said.

"Let's go out for supper," Pruiett suggested.

"I got to see Sam Garvin," Russell said. "I was supposed to see my principal first, I guess, instead of my adversary; but, you was the handiest. What about this Ashton case the old man's so worked up about?"

"The Colonel's gettin' childish," Pruiett laughed.

"Is it tough for you, or me?" Russell demanded.

"For you, I'm sorry to say," Pruiett said, indulgently. "Sam's innocent."

"Do I rely on you, or Garvin?" Russell inquired. "There seems to be quite a conflict in the reports that come to me."

"Take my word for it," Pruiett said. "The old man's biased. If he wasn't payin' good, I'd advise you to let this case alone. I'm goin' to win it."

"Come on over to the Hampton with me, an' lets visit with Garvin," Russell suggested. "I don't guess it'll make him mad for me to bring you along."

"He gets sore easy; but, he gets over it easy," Pruiett said. "If you think it's safe, I'll go along with you."

"Come on. We'll all eat supper together," Russell agreed. "If the Colonel won't pay for it, I will. We can outline the prosecution, and the defense, at the same time."

So, the three of them grabbed their viands, served up the family-style way, at the Hampton. Pruiett could see that Garvin's attention, and Russell's, too, was being attracted by a handsome woman seated at a long table opposite them.

"Who's the flashy lookin' dame?" Pruiett inquired.

"Don't know," grunted Garvin.

"The squire's wife?" he persisted.

"You know damn well the squire ain't never been married."

"He's got ideas in his mind then," answered Pruiett. "The old boy keeps pilin' them potatoes on her plate like he thought she was starvin'."

"A damn fool, if I know anything about it," growled Garvin. "Just a damned old fool."

"If I know anything about it," Russell interrupted, "he's a pretty smart man. That girl's got some class."

"No good looker like that would make eyes at an old fool like Adkins, except for one thing. It's his money. She'll take some of it away from him, if he don't watch out."

"Do you reckon that's what it is?" Pruiett inquired, innocently.

"Hell yes," Garvin said, as he watched the squire and his shapely companion leave the table. They walked onto the veranda, arm in arm.

"It was Rudyard Kipling, wasn't it," Pruiett inquired, "who said 'when the devil can't get a man any other way, he sends a woman'. Wasn't that it?"

"What the devil's that got to do with it?" Garvin demanded.

"Maybe it ain't," Pruiett grinned. "You ain't feelin' so well these days, Colonel. You better watch your indigestion."

Pruiett asked the court for a continuance because asking for a continuance was part of his contract with Wolfe and Forehand. He knew he wouldn't get it, and he didn't want it, for word from his ally at the Hampton House was in. If they call Squire Adkins, keep him. He's mama's baby. He'll whip the boys into line.

"What we goin' to do about John Webb?" Cruce whispered.

"He's one of the best friends I got on earth," Pruiett answered.

"He's Garvin's ranch overseer, an' he's been workin' for him for ten years. What about that?"

"John comes as near to bein' a' honest man as I ever want to see," Pruiett persisted.

"Can you trust him to be right?"

"I think I can trust him to be fair," Pruiett answered.

"I said right," Cruce hissed. "Who gives a damn about a man's fairness when he's on the jury. If he's fair, he'll vote for hangin'."

"I couldn't fix him, I know that; so, I don't think Garvin could, not even with him drawin' his pay from him. I may be wrong; but, I say leave him on." Pruiett reflected. "If they don't kick him off, we can afford to keep him on."

"I heard old Stillwell Russell whisper to Johnson, to take Adkins off," Cruce said. "What you think of that?"

"He's suspicious 'cause we ain't knocked him off already," Pruiett answered. "That Russell's got horse sense. He knows the Squire's a convictor, an' he knows I know it. What did Johnson say?"

"He told him he was a god damn fool."

Pruiett smiled, understandingly. "Russell's settin' on more brains than Bill could rake up above his shoulders countin' ears and dandruff," he said. "Don't worry. Johnson won't let'em take Adkins off, an' if he stays, we're settin' pretty."

The clerk swore John Webb and Squire Adkins, and ten others, to try the issues to be submitted to them in *Territory vs Samuel Ashton.* Cruce moved the court for a short recess. Pruiett crammed a huge cut of tobacco into his jaw and moved a rusty coffee can into convenient range.

"If at first you don't succeed, try, try again," he observed, as he tested his aim on the nearest can. "If you can't make it the first time, maybe your luck'll be better next time."

"What do you mean by that," Johnson inquired from across the board. "What you drivin' at?"

"Oh, just that other charge you got against Sam, for pluggin' the old man," Pruiett grinned, insolently. "If you don't fool this jury, maybe you will the next one. Too bad you ain't got three or four."

"You're as crazy as hell," Johnson cried. "That second one's a case the government'll waste. You can't hang a man but once, or we'd just try Mr. Sam twict. We'd like to drop him through the trap, stiff and dead."

"You ain't got a chance to convict this time, an' you know it," Pruiett persisted. "If Sam ever gets as much as five years, it'll be because the law of averages lets you win a case once in a while. Why don't you admit it? What you got a special assistant for?"

Johnson's face was livid. "It ain't cause I want a special prosecutor, or need one, either, that I got one. I ain't got nothin' to say about what these god damned relatives, an' others, do about hirin' some one. I just..."

"I know," Pruiett interrupted. "You got a' alibi for this case, an' then you'll show 'em how good you are by winnin' the next one single-handed. Why, everybody knows the case for shootin' the old man is the worst case."

Johnson shook his head in rage, unable to trust himself to reply.

"I got a good notion to waive my rights and stand trial on both indictments, just to take your grandstand play away from you," Pruiett continued, grinning insolently. "I know how to turn up your bottom ace."

"You mean," stammered Johnson, "that you'll agree in the record to dispose of both cases at once? Let the government make proof on both killin's?"

"You mean you got the guts to try'em that way, if I would agree?"

"Hell, yes," Johnson howled.

Pruiett feigned confusion. "I guess I better talk to my client, an' his folks," he said. "Let me talk to them, an I'll let you know."

While Pruiett was whispering with Sam, his uncles and the other members of the counsel, Stillwell Russell called Johnson aside. "You better go easy," he said, "there's something fishy in this business, as sure as hell. I know that boy better'n you, an' he's too smart to leave Squire Adkins on a jury, when he's got challenges, if he didn't know somethin'. An' what he's offerin' to do now is foolhardy, or awful smart, an' Pruiett ain't a fool. Don't be afraid to back up. If he offers to stipulate that the verdict in this case goes in both—if he accepts to go in jeopardy on both of 'em at once—don't do it. It ain't natural, and somethin's wrong."

"He's swell-head crazy, that's all," Johnson growled. "He won a case or two, an' it went to his head. This case is a cinch as it is; throw in the evidence on shootin' the old man in the back, an' it'll be worse than the murders at Hickory. I just hope he falls for it."

Pruiett fell. "The defendant will stipulate," he announced to the astonished judge, when court and reconvened, "that the government may present both of its indictments at this trial, and that the verdict in this case may be considered as the verdict in each of them."

Pruiett in the Sam Ashton case was Pruiett, the frontier lawyer, at his best. Progress, which was to lift the frontier into the field of more decorous manner and appearance of refinement, was to carry him with it and see him keep pace. But here, tanned and animal-like, with the bristling bulk of his bushy black hair creating a veritable shaft of light for him to shine in—with the fresh notices of the Washington press to require his utmost—with a hitherto unheard of fee in his grasp, he was the romantic representative of a vanishing era.

His heavy lapeled coat and waistcoat, buttoned so high in the front as to almost conceal the black shoe string which encircled the white celluloid collar, gave him a disproportionate massiveness and breadth of upper trunk. This effect was accentuated by the narrowness of the pant legs which extended but slightly past his boot tops. As he grasped classic utterances from the rank aromas of the crowded room and decorated them with polished gestures, he was as impressive as Dan Voorhees had been, there at the Boudinot trial in Fort Smith, when he had torn the white carnation from the lapel of his satin trimmed Prince Albert and had hurled it, for emphasis, into the waste of the ash box.

And old P. Watt Hardin had never been more subtle, crouching in the faces of the jurors, and whispering, instead of shouting, to make a point. But, when Pruiett shouted, his voice and its eloquence was amplified by an immobile trance or mechanical frenzy, as he stood or paraded. He shook the rafters with the reverberations of his great voice.

And he had the witnesses. The four days that had seen the trial drag out, before the final arguments began, had seen a great number of witnesses, for both sides. Sam was relying on self-defense, and he had to have a corroborating witness to that theory of justification. It was said of Pruiett, in his later, and generally accepted, greater success, that he quoted two prices to a client when fixing a fee, one if he furnished the witnesses with the defense of the case, and the other, and lesser, if the accused himself furnished the witnesses. Pruiett called them 'swamp foxes,' or 'cat tail' witnesses. Eye ball witnesses, or fixed witnesses, others called them. But, if they were fixed, they had been fixed by a master, whose charm of assurance could induce them to assume that uninviting and uncomfortable position on a witness stand, under relentless cross examination, and whose anticipation of detail had them so well prepared that they never slipped, or they never broke. Pruiett had the evidence of unimpeached testimony to refer to and analyze as he delivered his blazing final argument.

The jury acquitted Sam Ashton. Squire Adkins was its foreman, and led a two day fight for the verdict which it finally reached. John Webb was the last to sign it. It had been Webb's lone vote from the beginning that had kept them out. Colonel Garvin was a member of the crowd which gathered—it was Sunday evening—when word of the jury's report was circulated about. He was purple and shaking with rage as he stalked out, and there was a perplexed, confused expression on the face of John Webb as he filed slowly out into the dusk with the other jurors. John Robert Thomas, the trial judge in the Sam Aston case, had berated them for the effrontery of their verdict, as he directed his clerk to see that none of them were summoned for jury duty in his court again.

Garvin and Webb met in the wagon yard around the corner from the court building. Murder was written in every seam of Garvin's tanned countenance.

"You double-crossin' coward," he choked. "After all I've done for you, and you turn me down. Get your pay and get your stuff out of my house, and don't let me see you on one of my places again as long as I live."

"But Sam," the perplexed Webb managed to say, "I got your note and I only did what you said. I wouldn't go against you for anything in the..."

"Don't lie," Garvin cried. "Don't lie to me. You sold me out to that young pup, and by god..."

He caught himself and lowered his voice. He realized that he was in no position to make public the details of his plan and plot, even if they did miscarry.

"You told me not to hold out any longer, it was in writin', or I'd have been there yet, Sam." Webb's manner and tone was impressive.

"What the hell are you talkin' about?" Garvin demanded.

"The note the bailiff slipped me this evenin'. It was from you, and I did just what you said in it."

"Who gave it to you?"

"The bailiff, Jim Mays..."

"And who signed it?"

"You did. It was your writin', an' signed S. J. G."

"And what did it say?" Garvin was near the exploding point again.

"It said, 'don't hold out any longer—turn the poor devil loose'."

"Let me see it," Garvin demanded.

"But I couldn't keep a thing like that, Sam. I couldn't do that. I was protectin' you, an' I tore it up and chewed it up. I wasn't goin' to have anything like that around."

Webb was speaking both wisely and truthfully, and Garvin could doubt it no longer.

"I'll have the son-of-a-bitch in jail by mornin'," he groaned, "just as soon as I can get this to Johnson. An' you're fired, Webb, don't forget that. You're dumb as a nigger Indian, an' you're fired.

Garvin and Bill Johnson were waiting in front of Pruiett's office when he drove up in his new Phaeton automobile. He was stopping by, to pick up the Forehand-Wolfe agreement before the drive up to Lexington, seventeen miles north, for collection. And he was going to pick up a buxom little widow at the Hampton House.

His smile of complacency was not affected by the blackness of the cloud over the faces of his two visitors. The storm broke as soon as the three were inside the office and the door was securely closed.

"Did you write that god-damn note?" Johnson thundered.

"Hell yes, I did. What about it?" Pruiett was unruffled.

"I'll tell you what about it," Johnson continued in the same loud tone. "I'm goin' to have you indicted, and prosecute you myself, and by god, we won't stop until we run you out of this country. By god..."

"By god? Who do you mean we?" Pruiett was perfectly serene as he asked him.

"Me, that's who," Garvin chimed in. He could stand the suffocating pain of the situation no longer. "Me, the man who befriended you, and got you started. I'm in on it, an' I won't stop 'til I see it done."

Pruiett continued to beam. "You got to have a witness," he said, soothingly. "You got to have a witness. You can't do all that on just plain talk, you know."

"We got John Webb," Garvin screamed. "Webb, an' what he told me already. We'll get you, and besides, when it comes out, Thomas will set that verdict aside, and we'll try Sam Ashton again."

It might have been that the reference to an attack upon his victory offended him, or that he was tired of the interview and wanted to be away to the more pleasant pursuits of the widow and the brakes above the valley. Pruiett turned off the smile.

"It'd be awful damn smart to get John to tell the folks he was your sinker on the jury, Colonel. It'd do you a lot of good to let the court know that, when John qualified, he was a directed delegate from your camp, on to convict or hang the jury. It would sure look good when it came out that he changed his vote just because he thought you wanted him to, and that he wouldn't have done it if he thought you hadn't. You hired Russell, an' I know it. Russell knew you had Webb fixed against me, an' he told Johnson so, or Johnson never would have let him stay. If you put Russell on the stand, you know he'll tell the truth. Now, both of you get out of here and let me alone. You might scare off a sucker."

It was evolution... It was development... It was progress. The boy of the neglected and misspent youth was a man with power, and he was using it as he had told his elders he would use it, when they inflicted upon him the punishment of their doctrines. It was the fine Italian hand, writing with a stroke more bold. The message could not be misunderstood.

CHAPTER SEVEN

WHEREIN PRUIETT PROMINENCE AND PROSPERITY HAS TO BE NOTED, AND PRUIETT EXCELLENCE CANNOT BE IGNORED, AS THE MURDERERS AND THIEVES ARE BROUGHT UP, TRIED, AND LIBERATED THROUGH HIS POWER. HOW TRAGEDY RETURNS TO DETRACT FROM THE CONTENTMENT OF THE NEW HOME IN THE PECAN ORCHARD, AND SENDS HIM ON A BUSINESS HOLIDAY IN QUEST OF FORGETFULNESS, BACK TO WASHINGTON. AND HOW THE SAME UNWELCOME VISITOR CALLS HIM BACK TO THE VALLEY, AND HE PIGEON-HOLES HIS GRIEF TO PLUNGE INTO BLOODY MURDER WHICH IS CLAMORING FOR ATTENTION ON HIS DOCKET. AND WHEREIN A PRUIETT CLIENT IS CONVICTED, AND HE CONGRATULATES HIMSELF AND FEELS FULL WELL, AS THE JURY SENTENCES HIM TO CONFINEMENT FOR THE BALANCE OF HIS LIFE.

"The fellows who only stole chickens were soon turned away from the office of Pruiett, counselor of criminal law, and nothing but murderers and horse thieves were accepted."

Victory in the Douglas and Wilson cases, and the delivery of Sam Ashton, made Pruiett. The little incident of a conviction and death sentence in between them, for black Charlie Bias, didn't detract from his popularity. Charges for services went up. L. J. Roberson, charged with the killing of Tom Vick at Hickory, had to deed him a quarter section of valley land before he'd front for him. Stillwell Russell, employed by George Hancock, who was charged with taking the Winchester to Charles Liddell, the marshal at Thackerville, early in 1901 split his fat fee with Pruiett to get him to come into the case. Frank Hunt, delinquent son of a wealthy family west of the valley, was charged with armed robbery, and Pruiett was retained to defend him. Dave Putty, territorial whiskey runner and horse thief, shot Deputy United States Marshal Ed Thurlow to death. Pruiett took $1,000 cash, and agreed to defend him in the Federal Court back at Paris, where he had been charged.

"Moman Pruiett received a fine office safe of the Baum make,

IN THE SUMMER OF 1901, MOMAN PRUIETT RELOCATED HIS PAULS VALLEY LAW OFFICE TO THE UPPER FLOOR OF A TWO-STORY BRICK BUILDING THAT HE HAD CONSTRUCTED ON THE NORTHWEST CORNER OF PAUL AVENUE AND WILLOW STREET. PRUIETT WORKED BEHIND THE DESK WHILE HIS CLIENTS WERE SEATED IN THE CHAIRS. A WOOD-BURNING STOVE, A 5,000-POUND SAFE, AND BOOKCASES FILLED OUT THE OFFICE. PRUIETT'S LAW LIBRARY WAS ONE OF THE MOST EXTENSIVE IN THE TERRITORY. THE MAN SEATED ON THE RIGHT IS VICTOR SNIGGS, PRUIETT'S JUNIOR LAW PARTNER. PRUIETT'S SECOND WIFE WAS LEDA SNIGGS, VICTOR'S SISTER. THE MAN ON THE LEFT IS UNIDENTIFIED. COURTESY HUGH AND SHANNON SMITH.

which weighs about 5000 pounds. This, with other new furniture which Mr. Pruiett has been getting, makes his office more than ordinary, and is far above the average in point of elegance and convenience." The big publisher of the weekly *Chickasaw Enterprise* was noting, on March 3, 1904, Pruiett prosperity, the inevitable accompanist of accomplishment.

Pruiett expansion extended in another direction. In an angle made by the intersection of Paul Avenue with Rush Creek, in the western extremity of the town, the Pruietts built their new home. Native young pecans shaded the Bermuda grass lawn behind a white picket fence. A mortgage at Calvin Grant's bank shadowed the entire premises.

"Frank an' Mike Henderson owe me a $1,000. Frank Hunt'll have to raise more than that for me before trial. Why hell, I got plenty o' money; I just can't collect it right now, an' that trip to Washington, D.C., for the nigger cost me a lot." Pruiett was closing a loan with his banker.

"I ain't objectin' to loanin' you the money," Grant insisted. "You can have twict as much if you want to sign up for it. I'm just tellin' you, in a friendly sort of way, that there ain't no sense a man that's made the money you have in the last year havin' to borrow. You ought to be loanin' it out, on interest."

"I never was much for chargin' interest," Pruiett grinned. "I ain't hardly got the heart to ask 'em to pay me when they're overdue, much less charge 'em for the use of it."

"I got them $600 worth of checks you wrote at Madill charged against you. You was a damn fool for makin' me pay."

"I'm twenty-one years old an' I'm supposed to know what I'm doin'," Pruiett answered, "but I ought to have a guardian. I went over there an' collected $1,750 that I made fair an' square, clearin' Jeff Aiken of murder, an' what do I do with it? Lose it ever damn cent in a crooked poker game; write six checks for $100 apiece an' drop them in the game, an' then come home an' borrow $2,000 to finish payin' for my new house."

"All you had to do was to follow my advice an' stop payment on the checks, an' you could've save $600. They never could collect 'em against you."

"I ain't no welsher," Pruiett answered. "I wrote 'em an' I want to pay 'em. I'll straighten the account up in a few weeks."

"That's a classy house you built," Grant said. "Where'd you get the idea of that cupola and the curvin' porch all the way around the side, that way?"

"The lumber company furnished the plans," Pruiett said. "Lilly picked 'em out. It ain't near as big as that place of yours, an' it ain't got all the outbuildings an' ground that Sam Garvin's got with his place; but, it's goin' to be damn nice for us an' the kids."

"Speakin' of Sam Garvin, it's about time for you an' him to make up. He's cooled off on that Sam Ashton deal." Grant was hurt by the hostility between his friends.

"He sure got his fire hot all of a sudden," Pruiett grinned.

"Look him up an' talk to him," Grant suggested. "He'll shake hands and start over—that is, if you want to."

"I love the old boy like he was my paw," Pruiett said, earnestly. "He looks at things from my perch, usually, an' I couldn't understand how he could get so set on gettin' a conviction against Sam. But, hell, I'll crawl on my hands an' knees if he'll pay me a little attention."

"He'll do it," said Grant. "He was just sayin', the last time I talked to him, that that was the fastest screwin' he ever got, an' that nobody but a mental freak like you could've ever done it to him."

Pruiett laughed. "Me an' the old man feels the same way about those kind of things. He wants to help the dog under the heap, that's why he took me under his wing. I wouldn't have gone against him in any case but that one, but it was a lot for me an' a little for him. I had fee, an' principal, an' a good chance to make some more reputation for myself. All he had up was the grudge he's been carryin' against Sam Ashton. You see the difference, don't you, Mr. Grant?"

"I been seein' it all the time, an' don't think I'm carin' about you gettin' Sam off. I was damn proud to see it. An' I think that now, seein' that the sting's goin' out of the beatin', old man Garvin sees it too. You apologize to him, an' I'll bet he says he was the one that was in the wrong, an' apologize to you. I'd like to have a three-handed, windjamin' session in here again, like we used to have."

"I'll look him up today," Pruiett promised. "You an' the missus drive by an' see the new shanty."

"We'll do it Sunday," Grant said. "Say, how many lightnin' rods you got on that place, anyway?"

Pruiett ignored Grant's flattery. "You remember," he mused, "when I pulled in, an' opened up the office in the shoe shop? You an' the missus loaned me an' iron cot, an' I batched in the same room."

"You've done damn good," Grant agreed. "Them new offices upstairs are perty up-to-date."

"We just got this house done in time," Pruiett said. "Lilly's goin' to have another baby in about a month, an' she ain't none too strong for it. You been noticin' how she looks?"

"She ain't lookin' good, by no means," Grant said. "Better be careful of her. Give her a rest on havin' them kids."

"I took her to Hot Springs, Arkansas, with me last fall, when that damned swellin' rheumatism hit me, an' just made her take a rest. But, it didn't help her like it did me. I think there's somethin' wrong that Doc Young can't locate. I'm awful worried."

Pruiett's prominence as a lawyer and citizen was evidenced by the invitation he received to make the principal address at the Old Settlers Reunion in September of 1900. The reunion, rodeo and basket lunch was the foremost function of the cattle country's social season, and was being held, that year, at Hull's Crossing, across the Washita River, west of the valley. Garvin and Grant nodded with approval when he told them that he had selected, for a subject, "The Bounty of Nature in the valley." Pruiett and Garvin had made up.

Pruiett took a stiff charge of white corn and mounted the bunting-draped platform. After a flowery introductory he got down to the 'meat of the coca-nut', as he chose to term it.

"It's climate, to begin with, is the finest in the world, equal to that of lovely Greece or that of renowned Italy. Its winters are never too cold nor its summers too hot. The fragrant balm of its atmosphere and the steady, bracing breezes that ever blow from the south and east add zest to living that can be obtained nowhere else. Truly, I would not be surprised to some day learn that Mount Olympus, the abode of the Gods, had been somewhere in those Arbuckle Mountains which skirt us to the southwest, and I am persuaded, from looking into the faces of the fair and lovely women here present, that Venus, the goddess of love and beauty, must some time in the distant past have made her home here in the classic vale of the winding Washita, and bequeathed as a heritage to her daughters that beauty of face and form—that loveliness of character—which made her the universal favorite of the gods."

Pruiett paused to sip from a glass of water on the rail of the stand. As he saw his quiet listeners look at one another, and nod their commendation, his thoughts went back to Hackett City and the hooting mob of the school room, who drove him from the platform with chalk pellets and paper wads.

"I have read of the delta of the Nile," he continued, "the fame of whose fertility has come down to us from Biblical days. I have read of the Congo, and the fertile valley of the Ganges, upon whose broad acres the teeming millions of blacks and Indians have subsisted since Buddha and Vashti lived and taught their moral precepts. I have taken the wings of the morning and crossed the undulating prairies of Kansas, Missouri and Illinois. I have viewed the rich, dark loam that borders the banks of the great Mississippi for two thousand miles. I have read and learned in song and story of the lands far away—where rivers bright wander o'er sands of gold—where rubies light up the secret caverns and where frail man has but to stretch out his hand to garner the richest bounty which nature could ever bestow. But his sunlit vale, extending from the Llano Estacado on the west and to Red River on the south, through which the Washita winds itself like a silver thread, is far and away the crown jewel of all the lands of which I have ever read, or been blessed of with vision. May we not believe that the poet had this valley in his mind's eye when he sang:

'Know ye the land of the cedar and vine
Where the flowers ere blossom, the stars ere shine.' "

He paused to survey the breathless group before him. His complete mastery, his power, made his eyes shine and his coal black hair shimmer in the afternoon sunlight. As in a trance, he gazed into the purple mist above the distant Arbuckles, and flung a sweeping gesture for an accompaniment to the handily recalled rhyme he had carried, stored in his great brain.

" 'Where the light wings of zephyrs oppressed by perfume
Was faint o'er the gardens of Gull in her bloom,
Where the citron and olive are the fairest of fruit,
And the song of the Nightingale never is mute;
Where the tints of the ocean and hues of the sky
In color, though varied, in beauty may vie.' "

This was no powder boy, with the grime of smoke and the grit of granite dust about a ragged, hungry body. This was no inmate of the correction house, marching in regulated step with the felons to their lonely cells. It was a born leader. There was no lineament to mark him as the struggling son of the ever-changing frontier, reared on the hardships and privations which inexorably attend the route of its never-settled outline.

"My friends—we have here a foundation upon which to rear a great empire; a commonwealth that will be the peer of any in our proud galaxy of states. Civilization is pressing us from all sides, and asks admittance to come in and transform these great, grass grown prairies, these rich, wooded, alluvial lands, into an agricultural paradise; to make the wild wastes bloom like the roses in the valley of Sharon. Let the question of land titles be once settled and there will be an influx of people from every point of the compass. The east and west will be brought into competition and side by side they will vie to outstrip each other in the race of material progress. The whirr and hum of industry will be heard on every side, and smiling mother earth, beneath our sunny skies and vernal showers, will pour wealth into our laps beyond the dream of avarice. This is the last great undeveloped section on our continent, and we whose lots have been cast here, in such fair lines, should feel proud, indeed, for to the generations yet unborn we will tell the thrilling story of the Old Settlers, and how they laid, deep and strong, the foundation of a mighty state."

Pruiett hammered at a local jury until it turned Frank and Mike Henderson out of the prisoner's pen, to freedom in April of 1902. He went back to Paris to defend Dave Putty.

"Old Judge Bryant was the one that admitted me on his own motion," he explained to Claude Weaver, on his return. "I went up to shake hands with him an' tell him good-bye, after the jury came in, an' he was stiff-necked as hell. 'I didn't believe that proof you put on,' he says. 'The jury believed it—they turned Dave a'loose,' I says, laughin' an' tryin' to thaw him out a little. But, he wouldn't thaw. He acted like he was sore at me 'cause I won it."

"Some of them old Federal Judges gets funny ideas," Weaver winked. "Are you lettin' Henry Furman get you in the Bud Watkins case?"

"I agreed to help him try it," Pruiett answered. "He wanted to try it up here in the valley, instead of down at Ardmore."

"You know why, don't you?" Weaver asked. "That's where they convicted him the last trial, an' they sentenced him to hang. It's a damn nasty case."

"I know all about it," Pruiett said. "I knew Wyatt Williams, the guy he killed, an' I'm entitled to say that Bud done a noble public service when he killed him. I know why Henry Furman asked me to get in the case with him, too."

"How's that?"

"Old Overton "Sobe" Love down at Marietta made him do it,"

Pruiett answered. "Sobe's the old Chickasaw envoy, an' he's Bud Watkins' granddaddy. He owns most of the land south of the Arbuckle Mountains an' north of Red River, an' he couldn't tell you within a hundred thousand of how many head of beef he's got. He helped Furman to reverse that hangin' conviction, an' he's heard about your uncle Fuller. He's hirin' him to empanel the jury this time?"

"Bud was the first duck to get a capital sentence in the Sandy Land Court," Weaver observed.

"An' he's still out runnin' around alive an' loose, but that buryin' ground at Ardmore is runnin' over with dead convicts right now," Pruiett said. "My ideas on that subject ain't all wrong. Have a little jack—get a little extra consideration. Have the bad judgment to be busted, an' you get your neck pulled in two. What the hell do I care about old Bryant's cold shoulder. Dave Putty paid me a $1,000 cash to pull his nuts out of that fire."

"Tuesday and Wednesday were consumed in the trial of the notorious Roberson murder case, and this morning the jury brought in a verdict of not guilty. W. B. "Bill" Johnson, prosecuting attorney, was assisted by Max Hill of Texas and T. M. Robnett. For the defense was Moman Pruiett. Mr. Hill opened the argument for the government. Moman Pruiett, for the defense, followed with an impassioned oration which is said by all who heard it to be Mr. Pruiett at his best. If the case lacked evidence on behalf of the defense, and it seemed that the issues were close joined, Pruiett's masterful speech tipped the beam in Roberson's favor. For forty minutes he seemed to have blended his own identity with that of his client, and certainly he could not have been moved to greater eloquence or deeper earnestness had he himself stood like Roberson in the very shadow of the gallows."

" 'Gentlemen of the jury,' said Judge Townsend, 'it is a matter of regret to me—to see this verdict. It will be utterly useless to attempt to enforce the criminal law in this country so long as murderers can be turned loose when they are without a shadow of a legal defense. You can be discharged, and I never want any of you on a jury in this court again'."

"I told 'em I'd do it," Pruiett exulted to himself. "I'll keep the thieves an' murderers in circulation, so's they can keep up their good work. Old Townsend's screamin', Bryant's squawkin'. All you got to do is put on the proof an' have a fair shake of a jury. I hope Jake Hodges gets a reprint of this story."

He shifted into the trial of the Hancock case at Ardmore. Stillwell Russell, chief counsel, came up from Dallas.

"I been hearin' things," Russell told him. "There's rumblin's of another government commission to settle with the Indians, an' statehood for the Indian an' Oklahoma Territories. I get it straight from Washington."

"What was I tellin' you on the train from Decatur, Texas?" Pruiett reminded. "Didn't I say statehood? She's comin' as sure as hell, an' there I am, got me a hell of a practice, a new house paid for; own a half a dozen bottom farms I took in for fees, an' all I got to do is let statehood skyrocket my values. I'm settin' pretty."

"I been thinkin' about gettin' out of Texas an' comin' up here—somewhere. Where's a good place?"

"The hot spot's Oklahoma City, a hundred miles north, in Oklahoma Territory," Pruiett replied. "They say she's a bitch. Liquor an' gamblin' and prostitution wide open. Killin' an' robbin' on ever' corner. She ain't twelve years old, an' spread over twict the territory of Ardmore, here. Two railroads an' goin' to get more. If I didn't have such an investment in the valley, I'd pull out an' get up there. I mean it."

"This here Ardmore looks awful good to me," Russell said.

"She may make it; but, she's stalled here for five years. With all the government business they've had, it looks like she should have grown more than she has."

"I'm thinkin' serious about leavin' Dallas," Russell said. "How are we fixed for this George Hancock case? Know any of the jury panel?"

Pruiett grinned and winked. "I ain't never seen a one of 'em before—much."

"The Hancock murder trial at Ardmore last week resulted in the acquittal of the defendant, who was represented by Moman Pruiett and Stillwell H. Russell of Dallas. Hancock was charged with killing City Marshal Chas. Liddell of Thackerville." The editor of the *Chickasaw Enterprise* was matter-of-fact about it. In its following weekly issue it said: "Moman Pruiett is stepping high these days. In addition to the glory he won in the Hancock case, Mrs. Pruiett has presented him with a son and heir. We understand the young Mr. Pruiett will be named after that brilliant lawyer, Stillwell H. Russell, of Dallas."

Pruiett was stepping high, and he had to be. The inflammation of his knees and ankles was beginning to recur, and he couldn't find time to give them the rest and mineral baths that they needed. He had a new son, Stillwell Russell Pruiett, and a sick wife, and murder on the docket. Betty was able to help fat old Mrs. Fisher with Lilly and the children and the house work, but Lilly wasn't coming out of it. Something was wrong.

He and Furman tried Bud Watkins; the jury disagreed. Pruiett traveled to the Pontotoc country, to Ada, and defended Lawrence Walker, charged with murder. "Moman Pruiett, of Pauls Valley, made a masterful defense in the Lawrence Walker murder case last week, in which the defendant was acquitted," the *Ada News* observed.

Molly and Jack Lanier were jailed by the government at Ardmore. Molly's seven year old daughter, Jack's step-child, died in fits, and a strychnine bottle was dug up near the back door of their farm home. The child's viscera was shipped by express to Dr. Ira Chase, a chemist at Fort Worth. Pruiett, counsel for Molly and Jack, caught the next train out of the valley to Texas. He was gone a week, and when he returned, he was able to confirm the general report—the bottled vitals had been lost in transit. The government was goin' to have a hell of time convictin' without 'em.

He made bond for the accused pair and accompanied them—he had brought Colonel Garvin along—to the farm, where he collected his fee. He sat carelessly in the saddle while he watched Lanier's and Garvin's riders cut two hundred head of young beef from the big herd. A south breeze rumpled the shining contour of his bulky hair.

"That's four-footed gold; solid gold on the hoof," Garvin grunted, leaning forward so that his ponderous belly rested on the saddle horn. "What you goin' to do with it?"

"Have the boys drive it up to the old Walter Bennett place, above here on Rush Creek," he answered, carelessly.

"What the hell for? You got it sold already?"

"Nope—that's my place now. I took a deed to it."

"How's that? I could've sold you better property than that."

"I didn't buy it. I took it for services."

"You mean," Garvin asked incredulously, "that Indian gave you sixteen hundred acres for gettin' him out of that cattle stealin' jam?"

"Yep."

"An' now Jack an' Molly are stockin' it for you, with two hundred head of beef—for services rendered?"

"That's right, Colonel," Pruiett laughed.

"I sure did get in the wrong business," Garvin lamented. "They

PRUIETT'S PRIVATE HOME WAS AT THE END OF PAUL AVENUE, JUST BEFORE RUSH CREEK, ON THE WESTERN SIDE OF PAULS VALLEY. SEATED CENTER ARE MOMAN PRUIETT AND HIS FIRST WIFE, LILLY, HOLDING THEIR DAUGHTER GAIL HAMILTON. PRUIETT MARRIED LILLY BELLE THRASHER IN MAY OF 1896. SHE DIED IN MAY OF 1902. COURTESY *MOMAN PRUIETT: CRIMINAL LAWYER.*

must ever' damn one be guilty, to be willin' to put up so much for legal services."

"You told me one time that all I needed to do, to make a lawyer out of myself, was to learn to fix fees, didn't you? How am I gettin' along?"

"You ain't no amateur no more," Garvin replied. "You ain't no amateur."

The South Canadian River was the boundary between legal and illegal drinking liquor. The Oklahoma Territory, on the south, was dry—at least it was dry within the intentions of the United States Government. The Box Saloon, on stilts in the sandy bed of the stream, brought the spirits as near to the sheltered Chickasaw Nation as it could. The line was the center of the usually dry sandy bed. The Box was perched in the middle of the river, barely north of the survey.

In late November of 1901 a cattle man named Rufus Choate, with a fresh roll, was there; Bert Casey, outlaw, with Jack Swofford, of the same vocation, and Joe Mobley and Tom Powell, two weak, shiftless kids, were there, also. Everybody was drunk. Powell, youngest and weakest of the Casey group, was afflicted with a ponderous pair of flat feet which flapped inward. He was so shiftless that he didn't object to being called 'Pigeon Foot'.

Choate and the roll went whooping out the door. Powell and his flapping feet skulked quietly out after him. Silence, two shots and more silence followed; when the gang from the Box got out with their lanterns, Choate was dead and his pockets were empty. Great, pigeon-toed tracks of one man led across the moist sand of the river bed toward the north bank and solid ground.

"I realize he's your brother, Nora, an' you're a nice girl. I'd like to help you, but I can't perform miracles," Pruiett was saying between coughs and squirts of tobacco juice. "I ain't feelin' good, here of late, an'..."

"You've just got to defend him, Mr. Pruiett," Nora Powell insisted. "You cleared Clarence Douglas and you cleared George Hancock. didn't you? Why...?"

"This is different, that's why," he answered. "Those were bad murder cases, but there was some foundation in 'em for buildin' a defense. Hancock killed a marshal, but we was able to prove the marshal had been pushin' him around and mistreatin' him. Douglas had that bad blood between him an' Jimmy Williams for stackin' a self-defense plea on. But here, you got robbery for a motive. That's bad. It's as bad, if not worse, as the killin'. They got them tracks in the quicksand, an' they got lots of witnesses to swear they was big and toin' in. Tom was there, he left just before Choate was shot, an' when they caught him up in the Creek Nation, he was drunk an' had a part of Choate's big roll still on him. If I could make roses bloom on a black-jack sprout, I might get him off with life, but that's the best anybody could do."

"We've always been honorable people, judge," Nora said. "I can't stand to have Tommy hung. I'll pay you $300—cash. Won't you take it?"

"Where you goin' to get that kind of money, Nora?"

"I've already got it. I've saved it from my school teachin' job. I've been savin' an' a hoardin' it for years."

"You ought to keep on savin' it, honey," Pruiett said. "Plead him guilty an' take a chance on the court givin' him leniency. He'll get life, an' that's all you can expect for him. I got to go to Paris this week. That Bud Watkins case, the one I got a hung jury in here last term, is set down there. We got a change of venue. I got to go to South McAlester an' argue my appeal in the Frank Hunt case. I got stuck there for fifteen years. Doc F. B. Tyree's killed another man an' I got to work out a defense for him, an' I got a sick wife. Ain't you goin' to let me out of tryin' Tommy?"

"You got to take the case, Mr. Pruiett," Nora cried. "You just got to. I'm goin' right from here to Mr. Garvin's about it if you turn me down."

"Give the money to the girl out there an' have her give you a receipt for it," he said, wearily. "I hate to walk into one like this; but, I'm the guy that can swallow the sour right along with the sweet. Pay your money in an' watch close to see what comes out. There won't be no refunds. I can't guarantee to win one like this."

Doc Young hailed him and stopped him on the street.

"Moman," he said, "Davenport an' I are agreed on what's the matter with Lilly, an' it's perty serious. We ain't goin' to be able to help her."

"What you mean—you can't help?" Pruiett asked, with alarm.

"Not that. Don't get excited. I mean it's goin' to take a surgeon; some one that's equipped to perform a serious operation. She's strained down there from havin' her first baby, an' she's got a little worse, gradually, ever' time. There's Doctor Bacon Sanders and Doctor Thompson at Fort Worth, they're specialists on that kind of work, an' if they was to get a'hold of her right away, they could straighten her up."

"I got to try a case down at Paris next week," Pruiett said. "Could we figure on takin' her to Fort Worth the next week after that?"

Young shook his head. "She's awful weak an' run down, an' here the last few days she's been losin' fast. Davenport an' I both say if we don't get her worked on in a day or two, it's goin' to be too late."

"Let's catch the train in the mornin', then, an' get it over with. If she's in shape, after the operation, I can leave there an' go on to Paris. If not, I can pass the case or get out of it. I'll phone down for a reservation. Bacon Sanders? Is that what you said?"

"Yeah, an' Thompson. They both ought to take part in it," Young replied.

Pruiett looked hopefully across the white bed in the half-dark room. A carved crucifix, above the head of the bed, stood out in the dim light. "What about it, Doctor?" he inquired.

"It was quite satisfactory," the doctor answered. "Quite a delicate operation, and not a moment too soon; but, we agree that it was quite satisfactory. She should recover quickly."

"Let me see you in the hall a minute, will you, Doc?" he suggested.

When they were outside the room, Pruiett got to the point.

"I got a murder case set in Paris tomorrow," he said. "If she's bad, or if I can help here, I'll wire 'em to get along without me. But, if it's all right, I could run down there for three or four days, an' then get right back..."

"If you'd pardon my being frank, Pruiett, I don't think you ought to go down..."

"Then you wasn't tellin' the truth in there?" he interrupted. "She's bad? She's..."

"She's all right, like I said she was," Doctor Thompson said. "It's you I'm talking about. You haven't had any rest or sleep for three days, two, anyway—and you've been drinking a lot. I really don't think you'd be in very good condition to try a man for his life."

"Hell." Pruiett grunted. "I'm as fresh as a wild onion sproutin' through a fresh chip. Don't bother yourself about me. When I can get good licker like they got here in Fort Worth, I don't want no sleep. Did you ever drink any of the Longhorn beer, one percent, with pepper-sauce an' alcohol in it for kick?"

Thompson laughed. "I've heard about your Chickasaw Longhorn," he said. "No—if you want to consider this strictly on Mrs. Pruietts's condition, you may as well go. She has her special nurses and the hospital will provide everything she needs. She must have complete rest; no visitors, and it would probably be best for you to go away a few days."

"Thanks, Doc," he answered. "I can make enough out of old Sobe Love on this trip to take care of most of your bill."

Pruiett's charm on the Paris juries was still working. Bud Watkins came clear, but Pruiett wasn't there to hear the verdict, or to collect the bonus he had coming from Bud's Chickasaw grandpa. His blistering final argument had been bawled with an empty, aching dread in his heart. A wire in his pocket, from Fort Worth, had said that Lilly was worse and for him to come as soon as he could. He had time before the train, so he made his speech, and co-counsel, prosecutors, jurors and spectators winced at its ragged viciousness. He didn't look back as he rushed out of the courtroom.

"What is it, Doc?" he begged in the hospital corridor. "She looks like wax, like she was dead, an' she hardly knows me. What's wrong?"

"She started hemorrhaging right after you left, Pruiett," Thompson said. "Sanders and I couldn't stop it. At first we didn't think it was serious, but she kept on, and she almost bled to death. There wasn't anything spared. Everything we had, and everything we knew, we tried; but, nothing worked. We wired you when she got..."

"She's all right now, ain't she?"

"I'm afraid not," Thompson answered, shaking his head. "I'm afraid that there's no hope. There's nothing can be done."

Stillwell Russell had abandoned Dallas and opened offices in Ardmore in 1899. After the funeral, he pronounced a eulogy over Lilly's grave in May of 1902:

"Our sister and friend whose body now rests within the open grave, will have all that is mortal of her soon mixing with the elements of the earth; the clods will soon cover her, and that which is natural of her will be hidden from sight. But to those to whom she was near and dear—her spirit will escape from its tenement of clay, and will shine as a beacon light beckoning them to follow the paths of right. The manly youth, whom she as a girl selected as her heart's mate, is still amongst you. These two came years ago as a matter of choice, and cast their lots in this beautiful valley, amongst these good people. I knew them in their earlier days, and I knew them well. They struggled hard to establish themselves in the good opinion and esteem of this people.The picture is now somewhat changed. The right hand of the husband is gone, and obligations a thousand fold are added to his already heavy responsibilities. It will be your privilege, my friends, as it is your duty, to aid and encourage him to do right. Let him know that it is your will and desire that he live in your good opinion, and, by conduct warmly manifested, make him feel that in every purpose and endeavor to do right, he will receive your hearty commendation. Let us revere the dead; let us love the living."

Russell's thoughts were winging, as he spoke from the open grave, to the events of the years before at Paris, and of what he knew, and what he had heard. It was a frail thread, that line between genius and lunacy—between good and evil. He dreaded to see what the result of this loss would be.

"I'm checkin' out for a few weeks," Pruiett, with muddy boots on a banker's table, was talking to Garvin and Grant.

"You been needin' a rest," Garvin agreed. "Where you goin'? Hot Springs?"

"I'm goin' to Washington," he replied. "I want to see Charley Culberson, an' I can get well if I can get a parole from the President for Frank Hunt. I..."

"Won't that be a hell of a rest, now?" Grant observed. "Right now, when it looks like you're blowin', you got business to take care of."

"Business in Washington is the best rest I can get," Pruiett answered with a wan smile.

"It's the kind you don't need," said Garvin. "You're drinkin' too much."

"That's what ever'body says, but I'm doin' all right. I just need to relax."

"What you doin' about the kids?" Grant asked.

"I moved Betty an' the old man into my house," he answered. "With the hired help I got an' them two, the kids'll be in good shape. I got to get away from here for awhile."

"It was too bad about Lilly," Garvin suggested, cautiously.

"She didn't hate to die, she wasn't afraid of dyin'," Pruiett said, easily. "She just enjoyed life so much. That's why it was hard to see her go. She thought I was the greatest lawyer in the world. She thought our kids were smarter, an' pertier than anybody else's, an' that that house down there was a palace. Just happy an' contented with livin'—an' she had to die." He looked casually into the distance.

"It looks like them high-priced doctors could've done something. Why did you bring her back so soon?"

"They told me, when I got back from Paris, that it was a matter of a few days, a few days at the most. I wanted to argue about it, an' to call more doctors in, but after I talked to Lilly I knew it was no use. She told me just what the doctors had said, an' they hadn't been talkin' to her about it, neither. She said she wanted to be near the babies, an' to see the green of the valley, an' hear the thrush an' the larks in the alfalfa across the creek. I could see it in her eyes; so, we fixed it up for movin' her on the train. I wanted her to have what she wanted."

"Old Stillwell Russell spoke a perty piece for her," Grant said.

"He's my friend," said Pruiett.

"What about business while you're gone?" Garvin inquired. "There's liable to be a little shootin' an cuttin', an' maybe a little cow an' horse stealin'. Shall I tell'em to hold their guts in 'til you get back, or just let'em go ahead an' puke 'em up?"

"I ain't licked by a hell of lot," Pruiett assured him. "I'll take all I can get when I get back, an' nobody'll have to hire new counsel in these cases pendin'. I ain't sure when I'll be back, but I ain't goin' to be gone long."

Ain't he the damndest feller you ever saw?" Grant mused as Pruiett swung slowly down Paul Avenue.

"He's a' outlaw at heart," Garvin answered. "He's always grindin' that axe that got chipped down in Texas. He told me after he come here that he was goin' to keep a vow he made to turn criminals a'loose on society because society wasn't fair in dealin' with people that was charged with violatin' its rules. I thought he was foolin'. I thought he wanted to work all the time 'cause he wanted the jack; but, hell's fire! He keeps pluggin' in his damn criminal cases, an' workin' all the time, when his legs swell up as big as watermelons, an' when his heart's busted like it is right now."

"He's takin' this loss of his wife perty easy, it looks like to me," Grant said.

"Pruiett's like a damn Chickasaw," Garvin replied. "They look the same all the time, when they feel good or when they back into a brandin' iron. You couldn't tell by the way he looks what he's thinkin'. I knew how close he was to that girl, an' what plans he had for his kids through her. He's makin' this little business trip to Washington to keep from goin' plumb loco. That business is part of the act."

Pruiett's Washington visit was terminated by tragedy. He had been there all summer, it was September, 1902, when he got the bad news from Betty. The baby boy named for Stillwell Russell was dead.

"I was out at Cabin John's bridge with Charley Culberson," Pruiett said, "and I heard that rumblin', ringin', noise in my ears that had bothered me off an' on since before little Hayden died. I says to Culberson, 'Charley, I got bells ringin' in my head. I had 'em a few years ago, an' right away after my baby died. They started ringin' again on me this spring, an' Lilly Belle up and died. They kind of got me bothered; I've called 'em the bells of death. Do you believe in the kind of crap?' Charley laughs in my face, an' he says, 'Son, I call'em the whiskey bucks, when my head goes to blastin' like a light house bell. That's all that's the matter with you.' So, I kind of pass it off, but my head keeps ringin'. I think when I get back to the hotel, I'll wire home, an' find out if everything's runnin' smooth, an' what do I find when I ask for my key. A telegram that my kid's dead."

"It's a coincidence, that's all," Claude Weaver assured him. They were visiting in Pruiett's valley office. "I don't believe in this mental telegram stuff."

"I feel like I can trust them bells," Pruiett answered. "The next time I get to hummin' in my head like that, I'm goin' to start lookin' an' dodgin'. Us Pruiett's is down to me an' a' orphan girl, an' we got to look out."

"You've had lots of tough luck here lately, Moman," Weaver said.

"An' I've had plenty of good, too. I learned a long time ago that the sun don't shine under the same dog's tail all the time. If you got a dollar, spend it. If you got a drink, drink it. If you don't, you'll be sorry when hard luck overtakes you, an' she's bound to catch up sooner or later."

"You're in a nice peaceable frame of mind," Weaver observed.

"Ain't I got a right to be?"

"I ain't sayin' you ain't," the agreeable Weaver acknowledged. "There's a term of court comin' up an' you got an awful batch of cases set. What you doin' with 'em?"

"I'm continuin' all I can an' tryin' all I can't," Pruiett answered. "Bill Johnson ought to do some good this session. He's holdin' Tom Powell over my head, an' I ain't got a chance to get away."

"What about them Lanier cases?"

"What about 'em?" Pruiett laughed. "Them lights an' lungs is missin', an' until they show up the government can't make a sign of a case."

"It was awful stupid of some one, sendin' them things by express, an' lettin' them get away like that."

"It was stupid lettin' 'em get away, all right."

"What do you suppose could've happened to 'em?"

"Bill Johnson says I received 'em at the other end an' destroyed 'em," Pruiett answered. "Hell, you've heard that around here."

"Yeah, I've heard it," Weaver said, "but, I ain't heard it from you."

"No, an' you ain't goin' to," he said. "I've done said all I'm goin' to say about your damn wheelbarrow."

Bail had been arranged for Tom Powell. Pruiett and Nora and Tom were having daily rehearsals in the lawyer's office.

"Good God, Nora, can you stand there an' say you love him, even if he is your brother?" Pruiett stormed, pulling his black wool. "Good God, Tommy, use your head. Can't you remember nothin'?"

Pay attention to Mr. Pruiett," Nora begged. "Why don't you listen. We're tryin' our best to help you. This case is comin' up next week, an' he wants to be sure you know what to do an' say in front of the jury."

"Well, what is it now?" Tom sulked.

"You ain't pigeon-toed," Pruiett bellowed. "That's all a mistake. When you walk, you stick your toes out at right angles like a goose full of clabber. These reports around here that you're pigeon-toed are all a mistake—see? Nora's got witnesses to prove that you was born with good feet an' that you never did walk pigeon-toed. Do you understand? I got to have somethin' to argue to this jury."

"It ain't my fault I was born with feet like that," Tom said, rolling a cigarette.

"Let 'im hang. Let me kill'm myself," Pruiett raged. "What's the use of us goin' to all this trouble for this no good lout?"

"Please, Tommy," said Nora. "Can't you understand? They got these government witnesses that testified at the preliminary, before the commissioner. They say that the tracks of the man that killed Choate were pigeon-toed. They expect to connect you up with it that way."

"My head ain't no sack," Tom answered. "I know what you're gettin' at, an' I'm doin' just what you want me to."

"There ain't a thing the matter with his feet, Nora, except they're so damn big," Pruiett insisted. "I took his shoes off an' showed you. He's just so god damn triflin', an' lazy an' sloven that he don't pick 'em up or care how they flop. He'd ought to be hung."

"Help Mr. Pruiett, Tommy," Nora placated.

"Help Pruiett, hell," Pruiett gritted. "All right, Tom, pull off them boots. Now walk over to the door. Point 'em out. Out, god damn it; out, not in. Duck walk! Point 'em out. There—that's it."

Pruiett met Johnson's brigade of witnesses man for man. For every one to swear that they knew Tom Powell, had known him for a long time, and that he was unusually and noticeably pigeon-toed, the defense produced two who testified to the contrary. They proved a good alibi for him besides, and when it came time, at the practical close of the evidence, to put the accused on the stand, the case was in good shape. Pruiett whispered a final admonition on 'turnin' those damned toes out when you show'em to the jury,' and put him on the witness stand.

Concluding a satisfactory examination of his own witness, Pruiett inquired: "Now, Tommy, certain people in this community, who don't know you very well, have intimated that you are pigeon-toed. Are you?"

"Naw sir," answered Tom.

"Have you ever walked with a pigeon-toed gait, that is, with your toes turned in, like this?" Pruiett made a gesture with his hands and fingers, laying them across the table pointing inward.

"Naw sir," Tom said.

"Tommy, I want you to take your shoes and stockings off, and walk down here to where I am." Pruiett asked the question and waited. The awkward youth twisted about in the witness chair, removing his heavy shoes and coarse socks. When Tom had completed, Pruiett put the final touch of polish to him.

"Now, son," he said. "I want you to walk down here to where I am, an' remember, walk in your most natural way. I mean, the way you walked when you took your first steps, hangin' to the hem of your mother's apron, an' as you've walked about naturally, to this good day."

The question was too strong for Tom; it had been formulated for the jury. But Tom, studying a moment, followed the directions literally. He stepped down with his big feet toed-in in a natural step, the toenails raking the ankles of the opposite foot with each languid stride. Even the resourceful Pruiett couldn't think of a quick question to ask, in an attempt to recover and cover up.

"No cross examination," was all the grinning Johnson had to say.

The jury gave Tommy life, and Nora, with tears in her eyes, thanked Pruiett for saving him from the gallows.

"That's the first case I ever lost an' was damn glad of it," Pruiett confided, patting her consolingly.

"I'm glad you lost it, too, Mr. Pruiett," she sniffled. "You were right. They should have hung him."

Bert Casey, and Joe Mobley, his youthful apprentice in the field of frontier crime, were murdering and pillaging in the ranch houses and on the roads of the Oklahoma Territory north of the river, while their friend Powell was being tried. Near the town of Anadarko, in Caddo County, they were engaged in a gun battle with Sheriff Frank Smith and Deputy George Beck, and a posse of farmers and ranchers. Both Smith and Beck were killed in the battle; and, although the tough Casey managed to escape again, young Mobley was captured. Pruiett took employment in the case, merely to flaunt the gallows. The tears of Joe's mother, rather than any considerable fee, moved him to attempt the difficult defense.

He changed the venue and tried the case at Hobart, the principal town of the Kiowa country, west of the valley. Frank Gillette of El Reno was the Federal Judge. The government was represented by Horace Speed, the United States District Attorney, an able running mate for Bill Johnson. He had an enviable string of convictions behind him. The Court, the prosecutor and the bulk of the populace, shook their heads in disgust and despair when the jury forsook their gallows, and meted out a measly five years on a manslaughter conviction for little Joe.

But Casey didn't fare so well. With Fred Hudson and Ed Lockett, apparent escapees from the Federal Jail at Guthrie, and sufficiently calloused to ride with Casey and his pal, Ed Sims, they started an expedition up the Canadian River to rob the bank at Cleo Springs in late October of 1902. Gathered around a guarded fire in a rocky canyon, and with Sims asleep on his saddle blanket, Hudson and Casey methodically cleaned and shined their six shooters. Hudson, noting that all of Casey's cartridges were laying on the blanket beside him, and that he was squinting through the cylinder of his pistol as he slowly turned it between his eye and the flickering fire, slipped several lead slugs into his own gun and let Casey have it, low. Sims, jumping up, saw what had transpired, but couldn't react fast enough to save his own life and went the same way as his leader. It developed that neither Hudson, nor Lockett, were escapees. They had been liberated by government authorities, tired of being eluded by Casey, to perform the particular job. Some one else got Hudson; but, that was the way it went. It was the story of the territory.

CHAPTER EIGHT

HOW PRUIETT SHOOTS A MAN OVER AN OVERCOAT, AND ANOTHER FOR PULLING A DRUNKEN PISTOL UPON HIM. AND, HOW HIS DESTINY, AND HIS FAULTLESS LUCK IS PROVEN, AS THE CARTRIDGE WHICH FAILED TO EXPLODE OVER HIS HEART IS READY TO GO WHEN GIVEN A SECOND AND SUBSEQUENT TEST. AND, WHEREIN HE CLEARS A CROSS-BREED WENCH WITH JURY BOX APPEAL, AND SAVES A MURDEROUS DOCTOR FROM PENALTY FOR HIS LATEST KILLING, BUT PAYS A FINE FOR ASSAULT IN HIS OWN BEHALF, AND IS CAUSED TO APPEAL AN UNSUCCESSFUL MURDER CASE TO THE UPPER COURT. AND, HOW HIS INFANT DAUGHTER ACQUIRES A NEW MOTHER, AND THE PRUIETTS AND THE GARVINS TOUR THE PACIFIC NORTHWEST, SO AS TO FORGET THE VALLEY AND GIVE IT A REST.

When the English walking coat came, he put it on and strutted before the hall-tree mirror. Betty bit her lip and patted her foot.

"Put it in the box an' ship it back," she said, threateningly.

"Ship it back, nothin'," said Pruiett. "Them big houses in Saint Looey don't make exchanges an' give money back like Thomas L. Kendall does. What's wrong with this walkin' coat? I like it?"

"You ain't wearin' it out of this house," she retorted. "Look at the yellow an' green in them plaid checks, an' them buttons is a big as saucers. You look plum ridiculous."

Pruiett grinned. "This here's the style," he said. "See that split up the back, an' how she stands open when I button her up tight."

"That waist-line is under your armpits, an' the split starts right between your shoulder blades," Betty sniffed. "A man that would wear a double breasted barber pole like that ought to be examined by a head doctor. You look like you had a bustle on."

"She cost me seventy-five bucks, an' I done paid for her at the C.O.D. window. I say I ought to wear it."

"An' I say if you ever go on the street in that outfit, I move out of the valley," Betty challenged.

"I can set that outfit off right," the Captain called from his rocker.

"Give'er to me. I need a ' overcoat anyway."

"You two are framin' me," Pruiett laughed. "That's why you wont let me wear it, Maw, you want it for your old man."

"He can get his old army bonnet out an' wear it with that coat, an' look like somethin'—a Chickasaw chief or a Mexican general; but, you ain't wearin' it. I wouldn't be surprised to see it on one of these wild Indians that wear red an' green blankets around here, or a town dandy, but not you, Mawman. You're a big lawyer now."

"Maybe if Izora Alexander was to see me in this she'd get struck," Pruiett ruminated.

"That's just the type that would go for such trash," Betty agreed. "A half-breed hussy with calf-eyes an' white teeth an' a appetite for ever' man in the valley, black, white, or red. She'd like you in it, all right."

"Then I guess I'll have to overrule you, Maw, an' wear it," he said. "I got to please my clients."

"You don't have to have truck with them kind of clients," she objected. "You got a right to defend her, she's charged with murder an' you're her lawyer. She's entitled to make a defense. But you don't want to get your taste down on the level with that kind of people, even if you do have to associate with a lot of 'em in your business. Izora's a wanton, an' everybody knows it."

"She's a fine lookin' strumpet," the Captain cackled.

"Maybe White could wear the coat," Pruiett said. "I'm joshin' with you about it, Maw, but it's a damn shame to let it go plumb to waste. It's expensive wool, an' it'll keep somebody warm when the cold weather hits."

"The Captain's got to have a' overcoat an' nobody but a man like him could get by with wearin' such a garment," Betty concluded. The argument was over. The Captain got the coat.

"Is that louse friend of White's still eatin' an' sleepin' on us?" Pruiett inquired.

"Yes, an' I don't like it," she answered. "He keeps White out all night, an' they come in drunk ever' mornin'. They pile up in his bed an' sleep 'til afternoon, an' then get up an' holler for food."

"I'll stomp his head off," Pruiett grated. "What's his name?"

"It's Charley Wiseman," Betty answered. "Let me try to straighten it out before you start anything. You lose your temper too quick. I'll see if I can't freeze him out without no trouble."

"How's Gail been doin'?" Pruiett asked. "How's her appetite?"

MOMAN PRUIETT AND A FEW OF HIS FRIENDS ENJOY ONE THE VALLEY'S BOUNTIES—SWEET, JUICY WATERMELON. SAMUEL J. GARVIN, SEATED RIGHT, STATED "HE [PRUIETT] COMES OUT EVER' SUNDAY AND WE FRY UP CHICKENS, AN' LOAF AROUND ALL DAY. HE SAYS HE LIKES TO GET MY SLANT ON THE CASES HE'S GOIN' TO TRY." SEATED LEFT TO RIGHT, PRUIETT AND GARVIN. STANDING, LEFT TO RIGHT, CLAUDE WEAVER AND RICHARD YATES. COURTESY CARL ALBERT CENTER CONGRESSIONAL ARCHIVES, UNIVERSITY OF OKLAHOMA.

"She's the liveliest kid I ever seen," the Captain said.

"She's fine; but, she's awful spoiled," Betty said. "She..."

"She needs a mother," Pruiett said. "She's goin to have all the advantages you an' I didn't get, Maw, an' she's got to have a mother for that."

"Ain't I takin' proper care to suit you?" she began.

"The best in the world," he interrupted, grabbing her and hugging her. "A kid like Gail is entitled to a mother an' a grandmother, too—not just a combination. She lost a good mother; but, I'm goin' to get her another one. I wisht you'd let me wear that English walkin' coat."

The winter term of court, and cold weather, came to the valley together early in 1903. Pruiett was immersed in two murder defenses; one for Izora Alexander, the statuesque cross-breed who had slain her black lover; and, the other for Jim Morehead, who killed the husband of the woman he was handling in a sordid rural love affair.

Morehead had become enamored by the corpulent charm of Elsie, the middle-aged wife of Frank McMeniman, who farmed in the bottoms south of town. Elsie was no bargain on the adultery board; but, Frank loved her, and he wanted to keep those paths he had trod alone those fourteen years since the marriage unsullied by the track of a libertine. He designed a premature return after an announced absence of considerable length, and upon executing it, found Jim and Elsie in the kitchen—instead of the iron bedsteaded boudoir as anticipated—and Jim, unorthodox always, had off his shirt instead of the item usually missing when disarray of raiment becomes justification for attempted homicide. As the evidence indicated, Jim and Elsie were seated opposite each other with a tub between them, paring apples and letting the shavings drop into its intervening abyss.

When Frank came in and caught them together, Jim attacked him with the apple knife. He didn't stab him with a well directed thrust, or even a pair of them. He cut him down like a wormy apple, until even the hardened officers, who came in to try to identify the bloody hulk, shuddered and backed away. Morehead had literally hacked him to pieces, while Elsie ran gibbering to the neighbors, a mile away, to tell them of what was going on at home.

It was bitterly cold, and Pruiett was pondering over the complexities presented by such a state of facts. A wood fire roared in his big office stove. The door opened and the Captain, humped up with cold, ambled in.

"Where the hell's your overcoat?" Pruiett bawled. "Ain't you got sense enough to dress yourself when you got to get out in such weather?"

"I can't find it," the old man shivered. "I looked all over the house, but it ain't there. I thought maybe I left it down here in your office the last time I was here."

"It ain't here. I ain't seen it at all," Pruiett answered. "You sure you didn't overlook it out at the house?"

"Me an' Betty looked good for it," he answered. "I like to froze myself comin' down here."

"It was awful important that you come down an' ask me how I'm gettin' along with my business, all right," Pruiett answered, with veiled sarcasm. "If it had of been ten below, you'd a had to come down an' take a look."

The Captain held his hands close to the stove and kept quiet. Pruiett went on with his reading.

"I hate to lose that fine walkin' coat," the old man finally ventured. "It was sure a han'some coat, an' it was the warmest one I ever had."

"We'll find it, or get you another one," Pruiett answered, without looking from his work. "You set down an' think, now, an' try to remember where you left it."

"I'm perty sure I left it at the house," the Captain mused.

"I'll be god damned!" Pruiett had jumped from his chair and was staring out the window. "There comes your coat now, right down Paul Avenue. There ain't but one of them coats in town, an' there she comes. Who's that a-wearin' it?"

"I cain't tell, but he's acomin' this way," the Captain answered, after he had hobbled to the big window. "Cain't you make it out?"

"Yeah, I can make it out—now," he replied. "It's that no good Charley Wiseman, an' White. I told him in a nice way to quit botherin' us, an' eatin' an' sleepin' on us out at the house all the time. Ain't Betty spoke to him, too?"

"She was tellin' him last night to stay away from White an' let us alone, an' he tells her it's none of her business. He laughs in her face."

"He does, huh?" Pruiett growled. "Well, he looks good in your coat; so, I'm goin' to lay him out in it." He pulled his pistol from the desk drawer and bolted, bare-headed, for the stairway. The Captain grinned and held his place at the window. He knew action was coming to Paul Avenue.

"What you doin' with the old man's coat on?" Pruiett demanded.

"What's it to you?" Wiseman leered. He was a hardened drifter and full of whiskey. He thought he was tough. He didn't quit leering, nor did he retreat, as Pruiett pulled out his hardware.

There were no threats or demands. Only the roar of the big pistol. Wiseman leaped so high that his head struck the corrugated metal canopy above the board sidewalk. He landed on his back, clutching his shoulder and writhing in pain.

"Good God, Pruiett, don't kill me," he screamed. Pruiett calmly fanned the hammer again. He shot him as he lay begging at his feet.

The second slug rolled Wiseman across the walk and into the muddy gutter. The walking coat was a sad sight, with bright blood and dull mud mingling in its yellow and green plaid. Pruiett cocked his gun again and as he did, Wiseman leaped up and started to run through the frozen slush of the main street—both arms dangling uselessly beside him. Pruiett's third shot broke his leg, and he lay moaning and begging for mercy.

"You can't fool with a guy like Pruiett," Doctor J. A. Young was saying, as he bound the splints about Wiseman's bloody leg. "Conventions an' rules don't make a damn to him. He ain't askin' the law, or nobody else, to help him fight his battles. All that stuff comes under the limits of his own strength, an' he takes care of things, or lets things take care of him, that a'way."

"I didn't do nothin' but borry his ol' man's coat," Wiseman whimpered.

"You done enough that he thinks you ought to be killed; so, he'll do the public service of killin' you, whether he has a penalty to pay or not. If you don't develop pneumonia or gangrene, an' happen to get well, you'd better clear out of the valley."

"As soon as I can use crutches, Doc, let me know, will you? I'll get so far from this damn town that you'll never hear of me again."

"I knew a fellow that used to be a room-clerk in a hotel in Texas, that went a long ways off an' is stayin' a long time, on account of gettin' in bad with Pruiett. Ain't nobody heard of him in years."

"Cure me up so's I can get out, an' nobody'll hear of me," Wiseman promised. "What'll they do to him for shootin' me up this way?"

"He's been charged with attemptin' to kill you," Young answered. "He's beat the same charge two or three times around here, though, already. If you want to get even with him, just lay down an' die. Then they'll have to indict him for murder, an' he might get stuck on that."

"I ain't that mad at him," Wiseman grinned. "I'd rather see him with my own eyes, aloose, than to hear about him gettin' hung, while I was in Hell."

The jury disagreed in the J. W. Morehead case in May of 1904. Izora received twelve stares of ill-concealed admiration, and a vote of acquittal, from the good men who heard the evidence in her case in November of that same year. Pruiett packed his necessaries in the old carpet bag and followed the court east to the Pontotoc Country. There were killings there, as in the valley, and Pruiett fame had traveled up and down the rivers and across the hills and gulleys. Gold Brady, a wealthy rancher, had been shotgunned to death. Lon Goff and Frank Driggers, rival cattle raisers, were being held, without bond, for Gold Brady's murder.

Ada, in the eastern edge of the Chickasaw Nation, was the principal town and the seat of government. Pruiett had a room at the Byrd Hotel, the fanciest hostelry in town.

"What you doin' down here?" he hailed across the narrow lobby. He had seen A. C. Cruce, his varying colleague and adversary, from Ardmore. "You come over for court?"

"I got a little case set that I'm tryin' to continue," Cruce explained. "You here for Lon Goff and Frank Driggers?"

"Yeah, an' I'm ready for trial," Pruiett answered. "If the government's ready, we ought to start in the mornin'. I figger on bein' in town all week."

They talked together of business and Ardmore, of Stillwell Russell, and prospects of statehood. "What's the matter with you?" Cruce demanded. Pruiett was slapping violently at his ear and neck.

"It's them god damn bells," he answered, deliberately. "My head goes to buzzin' an ringin'."

"What do you mean, them bells?" Cruce inquired.

"The bells of death," Pruiett said. "They don't fail me. They mean trouble; serious trouble. Tragedy."

"You ain't drunk, are you?" asked Cruce.

Pruiett laughed. "No, I ain't, but that's an idea. I got some licker in my suit case, an' it's most time to eat. Let's step up an' have a shot, an' then go eat supper together."

"You're talkin' sense now," Cruce agreed, as they stalked up the lobby stairway. "Say, what is it about these bells? You got my curiosity excited."

"If you don't believe in predestination, an' the supernatural transfers of thoughts an' wishes, you ain't goin' to take no stock in what I mean by it," Pruiett laughed, trying to lead him away from the subject.

"Stillwell Russell told me not long ago that you hypnotized the jury in the George Hancock case. He said you threw yourself into a trance, an' gave 'em that cold, glitterin' eye, an' that they was in your power. You ain't pleadin' guilty to bein' no hocus-pocus feller, are you?"

"People with lunky heads are just like country telephone exchanges with weak batteries," Pruiett confided, lighting the lamp in the room and pulling the blind down. "They can carry a little distance, but not very far. People with strong minds shoot out a lot of current, an' they got a faculty for pickin' current up out of the atmosphere. With a little reasoning, an' a little understanding of the circumstances you see a man in, an' you ought to know perty well what he's thinkin'."

"You mean you got one of them telegraph heads on you?"

"Don't be funny, A. C.," Pruiett insisted. "I'm serious. I hear them bells ringin' right now, while I'm tellin' you this. I ain't braggin'. I'm just tellin' you that I can understand people's thoughts up to a certain point, an' I get flashes that put me on my guard. I've learned to trust 'em."

"You said somethin' about the bells of death. What did you mean by that?"

"I feel tragedy a'comin'," he answered. "I've had three deaths on my hands in just a few years, an' ever' one was told to me before it came. I didn't understand what the message was the first time—or the second. That's why experience is such a good teacher. If you got any sense at all, you learn after you've been knocked down a few times. I heard the bells ever' time, just before the trouble came."

"That's bunk, if you'll pardon my sayin' what comes to my mind first," Cruce grinned.

Pruiett had fished his bag from under the bed and thrown it open across the quilts. The blue six-shooter nestled amongst his rumpled clothing; a bottle of whiskey lay snugly in a protected spot away from it. Pruiett handed the bottle to Cruce while he put the pistol in his hip pocket.

"What you goin' to carry iron for?" Cruce inquired.

"Just in case," Pruiett replied. "The bells maybe for me, this time. It won't hurt to carry it around for awhile."

One drink called for another, and each demanded and required a story. The two lawyers had entertained each other for an hour, when Pruiett jumped up from his seat on the bed.

"I can't keep them flashes out of my head," he muttered. "You wait here an' I'll go down an' make a 'phone call to home. I got to ask Betty if Gail's all right, an' if the rest of 'em is all right. There's somethin' wrong, or there's somethin' goin' to be wrong. I got to find out."

The assurance he received from Betty didn't relieve him. Gail was fine. Everything was quiet and satisfactory. There was no need to worry at all. Just work hard and win the case, and hurry back to them. Betty was still dreaming and praying him up the path he was climbing.

A man was pounding the clerk's desk as Pruiett passed. "I got to have a room," he demanded. "I drove in here today from Allen in my buggy, an' I'm tired. I want a room so I can go to bed."

Pruiett recognized the speaker as Doctor Waller C. Threlkeld, a casual acquaintance. "How are you, Doctor?" he said, offering his hand.

"Hello," the older man answered, uncertainly. As he shook hands he swayed, and the lids of his glassy eyes sagged. "What's your name?"

"It's Pruiett—Moman Pruiett," he said, smiling. He could see that Doctor Threlkeld was carrying a heavy load. "I was goin' to say that I had a nice room with a big bed, an' if the hotel was crowded, it'd be all right for you to use the room with me."

"You're the man that defended Sam Ashton, ain't you?" Threlkeld asked, still swaying unsteadily.

"Why, yes, I tried the Ashton case," he answered.

"Charley Dismukes was a personal friend of mine, an' that Sam was a dirty son-of-a-bitch," Threlkeld cried. "He ought to have been hung."

"I ain't discussin' my business here in the hotel lobby," Pruiett said, shortly. "I just wanted to offer you an accommodation..."

PRUIETT IN HIS PAULS VALLEY OFFICE JUST AFTER THE BEGINNING OF THE 20TH CENTURY. HIS THICK BLACK HAIR AND CIGAR BECAME HIS COURTROOM TRADEMARKS. NOTICE THE INK, TOBACCO, WHISKEY STAINED DESK TOP. ON HIS LEFT HAND IS THE FAMOUS DIAMOND RING THAT HE WORE. COURTESY HUGH AND SHANNON SMITH.

"Who the hell asked you for it?" Threlkeld demanded.

"I beg your pardon," Pruiett said, starting to walk on past him.

Threlkeld pulled a pistol from his coat pocket and pressed the muzzle of it against Pruiett's chest. Instead of an explosion, there was a metallic click, hollow and faint. Pruiett leaped behind a square column, which supported the upper floors, as Threlkeld's second effort produced better results. There was a deafening report, and a handful of splinters flew from the beam by Pruiett's head.

The battle was on. The clerk was down behind the counter, and guests huddled behind chairs and couches, or flew for the two street openings. Pruiett, sighting around the protecting column, was hitting Threlkeld every time he pulled the trigger, but the old Doctor wouldn't go down. Through the smoke of the lobby, he could be plainly seen, holding the gun in both hands and firing deliberately; with feet widespread, he trembled from head to feet each time Pruiett's lead entered his body. When his six shots were gone, he threw his weapon at the offensive post an staggered indifferently across the room and out the side door. Those who followed him, cautiously, by his bloody trail, found him halfway up the stairway leading from the street beside the hotel. He was unconscious, but alive. There were four gaping wounds in his body.

"Pruiett was sore as hell at the jury's givin' Lon Goff eight years for manslaughter, for killin' Brady." Grant was talking to Garvin. They had their customary box in the front window of Grant's bank, where they could watch life on Paul Avenue.

"The jury's got to say 'not guilty' unless they want to hear Moman belly-ache," Garvin replied. "He ain't satisfied with workin' his head off tryin' to beat the law. He wants to win 'em all. His wife dies an' his kids dies, an' he won't quit. He ain't satisfied to beat the rope; he wants 'em all to be turned out, scot free. I was surprised he went up to the Cherokee Strip to help prosecute that Riggin, in the cattle war cases."

"He done a fair job of turnin' murderers loose in that last thirty day term here. He made a plumb fool out of Bill Johnson. Hung the jury for Morehead, an' there wasn't a defense in the world to that case. There was Russell and Henry Furman, an' them high sailin' Cruce brothers, a'gettin fifty years, an' life sentences, an' hangin', an' then old bushy-headed Moman comes in an' spits all over the courtroom, bellers 'til the jury thinks the roof is comin' down, an' they say 'Not Guilty'. He's a dandy."

"When he tried that cross-breed wench that killed her sweetie at the festivule," Garvin began, "I thought..."

"Her name was Izora Alexander," Grant supplied.

"Yeah," said Garvin, "Izora. She killed that buck in one of them voodoo fits, an' there wasn't no particular reason for it, that I could see."

"What's the idea of them festivules?" Grant asked. "Somebody gets killed or hurt ever' time. The government ought to stop 'em."

"As long as I been in the Chickasaw country, they been havin' festivules," Garvin laughed. "The niggers never did hav'em an' the Indians never did hav'em. The cross breeds just cross bred'em a name, an' started havin' em regular as a good excuse for gettin' drunk. They get a barrel an' fill it full of candy an' apples—mostly candy. They get rock candy an' old-fashion stick candy an' then they melt candy in their corn licker an' they eat candy all the time they drink. When they get a certain heat, along about morning, they start to ring aroun' the candy barrel—a whoopin' an' a skippin'. I been to 'em an' seen how they go. They dance an' kick an' skid off a waist or a jacket as they go. When the inside of the shack gets to foggin' about like a boar's nest, they start droppin' out, a buck an' a wench here and a buck an' a wench there, headin' for the bushes. Izora caught her buck slippin' out with the wrong wench."

"I wasn't so surprised to see 'em turn her aloose," Grant said. "When she twisted across that courtroom goin' to the witness stand, with that calico gimp stretched around her hips, it looked like a couple of possums a'fightin' in a tow sack. When she rared back in the witness chair an' stuck them cods out, they looked like fence squash."

"I'll bet them bastards on her jury was lined up in the plum thicket behind her shanty that night, waitin' for the payoff," Garvin grinned.

"An' she didn't show up all night, an' neither did her lawyer, so I hear," said Grant. "Do you suppose he told the bitch to come to court half-naked like that? He knew it'd make them nesters set up an' get tenderhearted, don't you think?"

"He said he was a'goin' to do it; but, I thought he was jokin'. He said that was one case he had to back-pedal on, to keep the jury from acquittin' her an' convictin' Bill Johnson in the same deliberation."

"Pruiett can think of more ways of twistin' a murderer or a horse thief out of jail, an' keepin' 'em out, than a hungry freedman can of milkin' a fresh jenny," Grant grinned. "How come he tells you so much about his business?"

"He's my friend," Garvin answered. "He never crossed me but once—in that damn Sam Ashton case—an' I just couldn't stay mad at him about that. He comes out ever' Sunday and we fry up chickens, an' loaf around all day. He says he likes to get my slant on the cases he's goin' to try."

"That's his secret," said Grant. "He don't ask the other lawyers about what to do in a case. He goes to the home-folks, like you an' me, an' the boys in the barber shop. When he gets that slant on a question, he's a damn near got a jury's slant, an' he knows just what to offer in his case."

Jake Hodges had succeeded in getting John Stevenson a ten year sentence in the third trial of his case at Paris. With Gaines's ghost partially avenged, Jake withdrew, and Stillwell Russell, surviving counsel, took Pruiett into the case. Pruiett and Russell took another appeal, and following it to a hearing before the Circuit Court at New Orleans, Louisiana, obtained another reversal. Stevenson's mistake had ruined him, financially, but he wouldn't give up. He wasn't going to jail.

"A letter received here yesterday morning, June 29, 1904, from St. Luke's Hospital, St. Louis, where Mr. C. J. Grant was taken recently, states that he is not improving, and it is thought he might as well be cared for at home. Dr. Young, Moman Pruiett and Cody Witten left at once for St. Louis."

The Santa Fe rocked northward. "It's too bad about old Cal," the Doctor observed. "Maybe he ought to stay in the hospital awhile."

"I know how he feels," Pruiett responded. "Lilly Belle insisted on bein' brought back to the valley, when she knew that she had to die. I guess we'll all feel the same way."

"We could've made these arrangements for bringin' him back, without it interferin' with your trial docket," Witten suggested. "You didn't hardly have time to catch the train."

"I got time to serve my friends, an' men like Grant an' old man Garvin don't come along ever' day," he said. "When I got through with that Mobley case at Hobart, I came right home. I got off lucky to that jury up there, too."

"Joe was just as guilty as Bert Casey, an' if they ever catch him, he won't get a trial. A mob'll tear him to pieces." That was Witten's appraisal of the situation.

"I never did have the details of that murder straight, exactly," Doctor Young said.

"You remember Tom Powell, the pigeon-footed little devil I defended, an' they gave a life sentence to?" Pruiett said. "Well, Casey put him up to killin' Choate that night, an' he took part of the money Tom stole. Tom an' Joe Mobley was just kids. Casey took Joe an' drifted out into the Arapaho country, an' they got to robbin' an' mistreatin' farmers, an' burnin' down their houses an' so on. The sheriff, his name was Frank Smith, an' deputy George Beck, organized a posse an' cornered

'em in a farm house, over near Anadarko. There was a hell of a gunfight, an' Smith an' Beck was both killed. Bert Casey got away, as usual, but they caught Joe. They tried him before Judge Frank Gillette for murder."

"An' the jury gave him five years?" Young asked.

"That's all they gave him—just five," Pruiett laughed.

"How come?" Witten inquired.

"We just made a good show out of it," Pruiett answered. "I made 'em think about Joe's pore old mother instead of the dead sheriff an' his deputy. They was feelin' right sorry for Joe's Maw before we got through."

"You didn't do so good in the John Riggins case, up at Enid, did you?" Young wanted to puncture his ego.

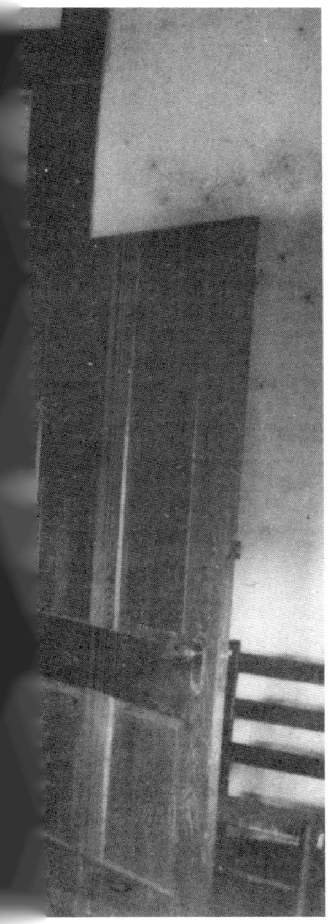

"I can't get my dander up in a prosecution," he answered. "The jury turned Riggins loose, an' I knew they was goin' to. We wasn't tryin' Riggins for murder, we was tryin' Temple Houston for bein' a good fellow, an' his daddy for being a great national figger. Old Temple is a great lawyer, all right, an' with his ability, an' havin' ever'body on the jury fixed, the blind goddess gets the prong put to her."

"On August 5, 1902, the editor of the *Daily Ardmoreite* said that that was one of the most important cases in the country; that it was a test, to determine whether the big cattle companies were goin' to be able to hold the ranges, or whether the farmers that were comin' in an' fencin' homesteads were goin' to be able to break 'em up. What about that?"

MOMAN PRUIETT CONVINCED LEDA SNIGGS TO QUIT HER JOB AS A SCHOOL TEACHER AND WORK FOR HIM IN HIS LAW OFFICE. PRUIETT NEEDED TO KNOW IF SHE HAD THE QUALITIES HE REQUIRED TO BE A MOTHER TO HIS YOUNG DAUGHTER FROM HIS FIRST MARRIAGE. HE DISCOVERED THAT SHE WAS VERY WELL EDUCATED, REFINED, AND FROM A GOOD FAMILY. PRUIETT AND SNIGGS WERE MARRIED JULY 7, 1903. COURTESY HUGH AND SHANNON SMITH.

MOMAN AND LEDA SNIGGS PRUIETT WERE MARRIED ON JULY 7, 1903 IN LEDA'S HOMETOWN OF ALVA. LEDA PROVED TO BE AN EXCELLENT MOTHER TO MOMAN'S DAUGHTER BY HIS FIRST WIFE, LILLY. PRUIETT AND LEDA'S MARRIAGE LASTED FORTY-ONE YEARS UNTIL HER DEATH IN 1944. COURTESY HUGH AND SHANNON SMITH.

GAIL HAMILTON PRUIETT, THE ONLY DAUGHTER OF MOMAN AND LILLY BELLE THRASHER PRUIETT, WAS BORN ON NOVEMBER 25, 1899 IN PAULS VALLEY AND LOST HER MOTHER IN MAY, 1902. HER FATHER MARRIED LEDA SNIGGS THE FOLLOWING YEAR. COURTESY ARCHIVES & MANUSCRIPTS DIVISION OF THE OKLAHOMA HISTORICAL SOCIETY.

LEDA SNIGGS WAS THE DAUGHTER OF AUGUST T. SNIGGS OF ALVA, OKLAHOMA TERRITORY, AND THE SISTER OF HIS JUNIOR LAW PARTNER VICTOR SNIGGS. LEDA BECAME PRUIETT'S SECOND WIFE AND MOTHER TO HIS DAUGHTER GAIL. COURTESY HUGH AND SHANNON SMITH.

"It might look that way, Doc, but I don't agree with it," Pruiett replied. "Sears was a nester all right, an' Riggins killed him because he homesteaded a hunk of his range. Temple Houston cleared him of murder, an' gave me a nice little court trimmin' along with it; but, that don't take care of the livin' an' eatin' question. The families are comin' in fast, an' they all got to have a roof over their heads an' food for their hungry kids. Them government ranges are fit for farmin', an' the majority wants to break 'em up an' let the farmers have 'em. That's what's goin' to happen, no matter how many of the farmers get shot before it's finally done."

"You ain't been at home in the valley but a few days in months," Young said. "Does your folks take care of the kid to suit you, an' keep her agoin' all right?"

"It was good while she was a baby; but, she's getting' a little older an' she's got to have a mother. I'm getting' married as soon I get back to the valley."

"Who's the lady?" Witten inquired.

"Leda Sniggs," he answered.

"She's workin' in your office, ain't she?" Young asked.

"I had her quit her teachin' job an' go to work in the office, so's I could find out whether she's got the qualities I need for Gail. She's educated an' refined, an' out of good stock. She's loyal, an' she's terribly fond of me. She understands the situation I'm in, an' about what will be required after she marries me. We got it all worked out, on a' intelligent basis, an' I know character when I see it, an' study it awhile. She's a good one."

"I hope you'll be happy," Young replied. "Say—by the way. How much did you get for defendin' Joe Mobley?"

"Not a damn cent," Pruiett grinned. "In fact, I paid the expenses of goin' up there, an' transportin' some witnesses—an' the old lady. It really cost me about $200 of my own money to try it."

The ceremony was over in early July of 1903. Leda Pruiett was in charge of the house with the curving veranda and the pecan orchard. The first frost of fall brought a creak and clatter to the side yard.

"What's that?" Leda inquired.

Pruiett looked out the window. "It's old Spencer Bias," he laughed.

"He's makin' his annual payment on my fee for defendin' Charlie."

"How's that?" she asked.

"It's his first bale of cotton," he explained. "For three or four years, now, he's been skiddin' that first bale off in my yard. He ain't the only one that does it. Old Uncle Henry Gordon delivers me a bale, an' so does Caesar Franklin. You'll know Caesar when he comes by his coonskin cap. Bill Yoder usually dumps a bale, an' old Uncle Henry always brings a sack of apples an' a sack of pecans or hickory nuts with his payment. All that stuff goes to you."

"The cotton, too?"

"I'll watch the market for you, an' when it's right, sell it," he answered. "It goes for things for the house, or for Gail. Lilly used to send to Dallas an' get things like them Dresden China pieces, on the sideboard, there, an' one year she bought that cherry secretary. You just do whatever you want to with it. It runs into perty good money."

"Why do they leave it here for you like that?"

"It's for services," he said. "I defended Yoder up in Oklahoma Territory, an' I went to Washington, D. C., to keep Spencer's boy from bein' hung. Old Caesar Franklin killed a nigger an' I defended him for murder. They didn't none of 'em have money; but, I went ahead an' defended 'em anyway. They're under eternal obligation, so they'll pay as long as they live, I guess. Ever' year they dump me one bale of cotton.

"How long do you think the jury'll be out, Moman?"

"There ain't no way of tellin'," he answered. "We must've waited two hours at the courthouse before we came to the office. They might be hung up, and the Court might keep 'em together for a couple of days."

The customary entourage had trailed him from the court. There was Claude Weaver, Doc Young and John Webb, and F. B. Tyree, the defendant. Doctor F. B. Tyree, from McGee, an inland settlement east of the valley, was the principal in the production. The jury was deliberating over what should be his punishment, if any, for killing Joe Mode, a recent citizen of McGee.

"What you think they'll do?" Webb inquired.

"You can't tell," Pruiett answered, carelessly. "A god damn jury can't be figgered. For instance..."

"What you think about it, Doc," Webb asked Tyree. "How you feel?"

Tyree looked up from the floor with an evil gleam in his weasel eye. He opened his thin lips, as if to speak, and then clamped them back together again.

"You see this cartridge?" Pruiett hastened, as if to avert an inquiry into Tyree's black frame of mind. "This here cartridge is what old Doctor Threlkeld gave me for a souvenir. When they were sure the old man wasn't goin' to die, they let me in to see him, an' he gave it to me. You see the little hole drilled in the middle of that cap? That's where the firin' pin hit'er. It damn near run through the cap, but she didn't explode, an' the muzzle of that pistol was pushed half way through my tit, right over the heart. Ever' other bullet in the cylinder was fired, five of 'em, but this first one missed."

"What was the matter with that old bastard?" Young asked.

"On a mean drunk," Pruiett said. "He bawled an' carried on like he was broken hearted, an' said he loved me like a brother. He made a statement assumin' full blame for the fracas an' said that he wisht I'd a killed him. He says, 'Son, take this here ca'tridge an' save it for a lucky piece—not for yourself, but for me. If that cap had a'popped, it would'a got you all right; but, it would a'got me too. If they hadn't hung me for murder, I'd a'committed suicide over it.' The old man was as sick on remorse as he was from loss of blood."

Claude Weaver examined the metal cylinder. "That cap had hell rapped out of her, all right," he said. "Do you suppose that it's a dud, or do you think she just didn't tickle the right spot?"

"Let's try'er out," Webb suggested. "Ever'things quiet out here in the back. Put it in the chamber an' point it out the winder. See what she does."

Pruiett unlocked his table drawer and brought out the .38-caliber pistol. Dumping the contents of the full cylinder into the palm of his hand and transferring them into his side pocket, he placed the single shell into the cylinder and slid it back into place. When he squeezed the trigger, with the barrel pointed toward the ground outside the open window, a cannon-like roar shook the interior of the room. The gun leaped upward with the recoil.

"Jesus Christ," Pruiett muttered through the blue smoke. "I knew I heard them bells a'ringin' that day."

"You must keep your pledge paid at the church," Weaver observed.

"A guy with that kind of luck can't lose," Young said, aside to Tyree, "an' here you are a'ridin' on his shirt-tail. You're as bound to come clear as a nickel is for a barlow."

"I got a belly full of you stupid bastards," Tyree cried. "Ain't you got sense enough to keep still an' let a man alone?" He looked about the room with quick jerks of his head, like a cornered animal, and then turned and ran out the door.

"That varmint ain't got no right to be out on bond," Webb said. "He's plumb wild. What's got the matter with him, do you suppose?"

"Doc's jumpy. He's been actin' queer for two or three days," Pruiett explained.

"Shootin' that gun off didn't do his nerves any good," Weaver said. "I guess I'd be jumpy too, if I had as much killin' on my conscience as Tryee's got."

"He ain't got no conscience, or nerves, neither," Pruiett laughed. "He's hot at somebody about somethin', an' I think it's me, over the way I defended him. He don't seem to think I did it right."

"He didn't seem to object to your gettin' him an acquittal two years ago, when he killed that pore kid he claimed was prowlin' his young wife's drawers," Webb said.

"He just had got his fee paid in that case when he killed Joe Mode," Pruiett said. "I think he put it off several months, just 'til he got able to afford another killin'. Old Doc is a murderin' maniac—as long as he's out, he's a menace to the peace and safety of society."

"Then he ought to be hung an' put out of the way," Weaver interrupted. "If that's..."

"This here's a democracy we're livin' in," Pruiett reminded, with mock gravity, "an' every citizen accused of a crime is entitled to a trial by jury. If the jury says you're not guilty, when you are, then you're not guilty. An' vica versa, if you're innocent, but the jury says you ain't, then you're a god damn felon. Let's make the rule work both ways, boys. Don't let's try to substitute our own little opinions for the majesty of the law."

"You better watch your client," Webb advised. "He's got a murder in him that may not wait 'til he's saved up another defense fee. He might kill his lawyer."

"He ain't so tough I can't handle him," Pruiett grinned. "I'll take my chances with him. Old Doc got in a killin' up in Missouri, around Springfield, an' things got so hot he had to leave out, real sudden an' unannounced, like. He got over to El Dorado, Arkansas, an' when that old Guy Tucker–John Parnell feud got hot, Doc couldn't hold his fidgets, so's he kills himself another man or two. The law wasn't worryin' him, in that case; it was some of the tough birds in the other camp. Doc shoved off an' settled over at McGee."

"Nice background he's got; but, I don't need his history to know he's a killer. It's wrote all over his mean, evil face," said Young. "The jury ought to convict, just on his face."

"They've convicted on a hell of a lot less, lots of times," Pruiett agreed. "The law an' the evidence can go to hell. Say, it's startin' to get dark. The sun's plumb down. What do you say we move down to William G. Kimberlin's drugstore an' see if we can't shake up a drink or two? If that jury don't report perty soon, I'm goin' home to supper."

Pruiett furnished the money; Kimberlin furnished the ingredients. The proprietor didn't try to compete with the saddlery, the Hampton House dining room and Walker's Hardware Store. His line was drugs, prescriptions and pills. Chewing and smoking tobacco constituted his only digression from type.

"Ain't you got too much distilled water for that much alky?" Webb half asked, half suggested.

"Don't try to tell Uncle Fuller how to make his licker," Pruiett grunted, shaking the quart bottle vigorously under the counter.

"I know damn well you got it too sweet," Weaver complained. "You put too much pepsin syrup in it."

Pruiett pulled the cork out and gulped from the neck of the bottle. "If it ain't as good as Manhattan Club, I'll drink it all myself," he said, passing the bottle.

"I don't care if the damn jury stays out all night," Doctor Young volunteered, as the bottle was going around the second time.

"I'm goin' home to supper when this bottle's gone," Pruiett said. "Wait a minute. There's my client comin' in. Hey, Doc. Wanta little drink?"

Tyree leaned on the front counter, staring at the men in the back. There was evil and insolence written on his furtive face. He said nothing.

"That bastard might as well be civil; I ain't goin' to charge him extra for that," Pruiett muttered. "I think I'll just call his hand. I might as well hear his yelp now as later."

Pruiett marched up to where Tyree was slouching. "What the hell's the matter with you, Doc?" he demanded. "What you so nasty about?"

"You know what's the matter," Tyree retorted, sullenly.

"Get it out of your guts," Pruiett challenged. "If you got a kick to make, let's hear it. I want to keep my records straight."

"You double-crossin' son-of-a-bitch," Tyree cried, "don't try to get wise about it, after you sold me out..."

Tyree grabbed a heavy glass bottle from the nearby case and hurled it at Pruiett's head. Pruiett ducked, and taking the quart liquor bottle, which he had been holding beneath his coat, he smote the doctor squarely between the flaming little eyes. The men, who had been standing in the rear of the store, rushed between them; but, Tyree needed little restraint. The blow had stunned him, and had opened a free-bleeding gash down his forehead.

"What's got the matter with that damn fool?" Pruiett demanded. "Ain't he got brains enough to understand that nobody besides me's crazy enough to represent him? If he was to kill me, he'd have to cut out his promiscuous murderin'."

Kimberlin was holding his needle in the flame of the gas light. He didn't want any microbes to interfere with the operation he was preparing to perform.

"What you want to jump Moman for, Doc?" the druggist asked, while he bored suture holes through the tough hide of the injured man's forehead. "Looks to me like he'd be the last one for you to fall out with."

"He made a deal with the government for me to be convicted, this time," Tyree stormed. "He never tried to get me off. He was layin' down all the time he was actin' like he was pleadin' to the jury. But, I'll get him before I swing, the dirty sell-out bastard. I'll kill him as..."

"Ain't that gratitude for you?" Pruiett demanded, as he led his crew out into the darkness of Paul Avenue. "A clean outlook like his is almost indispensable in our friendly, sociable little world."

The jury reported at ten that night; the *Pauls Valley Enterprise* made brief comment upon its findings in a current issue. "Jury in the F. B. Tyree case returned a verdict of not guilty." There was nothing said about the defendant, with his head swathed in a white bandage, rushing to thank—and apologize—to his counsel. Tyree stalked out of the courtroom with his ugly lip raised at one corner in an insolent sneer, and a defiant look of hatred in his eye.

"It ain't been six months since old Doc Tyree was acquitted over here, has it?" Sam Garvin inquired.

"I was in the courtroom when the jury came in," Doctor Young replied. "An' now he's dead—killed at Stratford by Leonard Hyden. He got tough once too often."

"That Leonard Hyden won't back up for nobody, whether they got a reputation for being a killer or not. They say old Doc was shot up somethin' turrible."

"Hyden's a client of Pruiett's," Young said. "I tried to patch Tyree up; but, it weren't any use. He was too leaky."

"I guess old Moman's got him another murder case to try," Garvin grinned.

"I'll bet he don't charge Leonard a damn cent for defendin' him in this case."

"You don't suppose...?"

"No, I don't suppose," Young supplied, "but I'll bet you a calf he clears him."

"I'll give you a calf if you need it," Garvin laughed, "but I ain't makin' no fool bets. Come over an' see me."

Pruiett obtained a change of venue for Driggers, in the Gold Brady murder case, and tried him in the valley, instead of the Pontotoc. Jim Morehead faced his second jury for the killing of Frank McMeniman. On the same docket, the clerk called the case of the *United States vs. Moman Pruiett* in October of 1904. He was charged with assaulting a citizen of the valley in an apparent attempt to take his life.

Buck Garrett of Ardmore, whose name was to become the synonym of everything that was wild and reckless and rough in Oklahoma history, was in a jam at Oklahoma City, the territorial Gomorrah to the north. Buck and his buckaroos went to town to attend the Southwestern Livestock Show and Exposition in March of 1906; Eva Ryan's place, upstairs on California Avenue, near the Santa Fe Depot, had rough visitors from the Chickasaw Nation. The windows of the street level hardware store, crowded with ploughshares and kegs of nails, winked tolerantly at the buffoonery which went on every night on its broad shoulders. Boys would just be boys.

A little difference arose in the parlor. Buck and another patron, named James Peters, started to settle. The Chickasaw marshal tried the case, and after hasty deliberation, found his adversary of contempt and assessed the maximum for punishment. Afraid of a successful appeal, he entered hasty execution—a pair of lead slugs through the bowels. Jim Peters died; Buck was held on a charge of murder.

The defendant in *U.S. vs. Pruiett* was too busy to stand trial; so, he entered a plea of guilty, to carrying a weapon, and paid a fine in November of 1904. It set an unhealthy precedent. In rapid succession, juries found Morehead and Driggers guilty of murder; but, recommended that the necks be not unjointed.

"Things are gettin' in a hell of a shape with me," Pruiett growled. "I'm gettin' stale. Two cases to take to that lousy appeals court, an' I ought to have won 'em both."

"You did win 'em," Garvin's Choctaw princess assured him. "The men can thank you for saving their lives."

Pruiett rocked in the shade and gnawed a chicken bone. "I try'em to win'em," he said. "When I get through representin' a man, I want to see him go walkin' down Paul Avenue a free man."

"He rolls an' pitches an' tosses all night while these murder cases are goin' on," Leda, Gail's new mother, said. "He makes the child so nervous she can't eat. I want him to get a room at the Hampton, or stay over with Betty an' his paw. It's terrible."

"Your damn joints'll start risin' with a little of that," Garvin predicted. "Take a little time off an' get down to Mineral Wells. Don't try to run the wagon without grease."

"I felt so bad about old Cal Grant dyin' in March of 1905 that I got behind with a case or two, an' before I knew it they had slammed hell out of me. They like to have whipped my ears off."

"Cal's counted his last stack of buggy washers," Garvin mused.

"He's somewhere where they extend the note ever' time it comes due, an' that's what'll tickle the old banker. He sure hated to go crowd a customer."

"Yep," Pruiett agreed. "Instead of collectin', he's payin; throwin' the gold out to them that needs it. No more mortgages to foreclose. The stockholders won't get to hurt him no more by tellin' him to move a farmer off."

"Sam misses him more'n anybody, even if he tries to be so hard an' indifferent," Mrs. Garvin smiled. "I see it, an' I understand it. Calvin was such a nice man."

"We all need a rest—a change," Pruiett declared. "I been handlin' murder and distress for ever'body, an' my friends an' people have been dyin' on me, 'til I'm gettin' a morbid twist to all my thinkin'."

"That ain't out of the ordinary for you," Garvin interrupted.

"There's a big fair goin' on up northwest, the Lewis and Clark Exposition, up in Portland, Oregon. I'll pay the expenses, an' the four of us, an' Gail, will take'er in. What do you think about that?"

"Would you actually take a little time off from your god damn murder cases, if the rest of us would agree to it?" Garvin asked.

"I can get away in a week," he replied. "An' we can get drunk as the train pulls out, an' we don't need to sober up 'til we get back."

"Didn't you get your snoot full up at Oklahoma City, while you was up there?" Garvin laughed. "Say, there's a bright spot for you, clearin' old Buck Garrett."

"Buck's a privileged character," Pruiett said. "He's got a technique to his killin' that makes it artistic. People don't mind gettin' killed by Buck Garrett."

"They say that there's quite a city up there," Mrs. Garvin said. "A cattle buyer that was out here said it was spreadin' out an' shootin' up. He said it was lookin' big city-like, like Dallas."

"I gave it a close inspection, for reasons," Pruiett answered. "They got five an' six story buildings up already, an' more on the way. I been thinkin' about movin' my practice up there. She's got ever' thing it takes to make a city; railroads, markets, an' rich land. The Kickapoo flats out east of the main settlement are damn near as rich as these river bottoms. They got upland, out west in what they call the Mustang section, that's damn near as rich as the bottom. You remember my speech at Hull's Crossing?"

"I'll say I do," Garvin laughed. "She sure was flowery."

"You're damn right," Pruiett said. "Remember what I said about the roses bloomin' in the Valley of Sharon, an' wealth beyond the wildest dream of avarice, ready to pour into your lap?"

"That's what you said," Garvin agreed.

"I thought about it when I got in that rush up in that town," Pruiett confided. "Maybe I had my lines crossed, an' was havin' the wrong way. After I had an eye full of the way business is rushin', an got pushed around on them nice dry brick-sidewalks, with the Indians an' niggers an' Jews an' chinks, I says to myself that maybe the valley ain't the best spot on earth. There's some awful good pickin's for a good lawyer up there."

"Do we take the vacation trip together?" Garvin interrupted, softly. "Fifty-fifty on the expenses, an' we go up the California coast seein' the scenery an' enjoyin' ourselves. It would help us all."

"Yes," Pruiett said, running greasy fingers through his glossy hair. "Let's go away for awhile an' rest, or maybe give the old valley a little rest."

CHAPTER NINE

WHEREIN PRUIETT FINDS MORE BUSINESS IN WASHINGTON, AND HOW HE TAKES THE LONG FLOUNDERING HAMILTON OKLAHOMA STATEHOOD BILL FROM ITS HOOK, THROUGH THE INDIRECT MEDIUM OF HIS CENSORED PAST, AND SEES THE PROMISE OF STATEHOOD DAWN AGAIN FOR THE DESPAIRING TERRITORIALS. AND HOW HIS VERSATILITY TAKES HIM TO A CONSTITUTIONAL CONVENTION, AND HE SEES THE SUBDIVISION OF GOVERNMENT—NAMED MOMAN IN HIS HONOR—CHANGED TO SUIT THE CAPRICE OF A POLITICAL BOSS. AND, WHEREIN, HE RE-STATES HIS VIEWS ON THE ILLS OF THE PREVAILING PENAL SYSTEM, AND ANNOUNCES HIS DISCONTENT WITH THE CONFINES OF THE VALLEY.

Early January, 1905, found Pruiett back in Washington, D.C. It was one of his few trips there which did not involve, directly or indirectly, executive clemency for a convicted criminal, or special privilege for a political ally. He was lobbying—"creating interest in and good will for"—the Hamilton Statehood Bill, which was before Congress, and as the Territorial residents complained, was staying before it too long. Stopping at the elegant Raleigh Hotel, he was making up the constant deficit in his expense account with contributions from his own purse.

An organization known as the Democratic Executive Committee of the Indian Territory had been gasping an inactive and useless existence since its sun-dried birth by mishap. Pruiett grasped it by the ears, and blowing an alcohol-laden gust of his own breath into its failing lungs, gave it a figurative boot with a substantial cash contribution and the presence of his own vigorous person. The Committee sent him as a delegate to promote action at the Capitol. George Barefoot, lawyer and land man of Chickasha, west of the valley, accompanied him as a delegate. They were supposed to "get some action." The people wanted statehood.

"I see the Oklahoma outlaw is back in town," U. S. Senator Albert Jeremiah Beveridge of Indiana observed over his evening paper.

"How's that?" his companion across the table inquired. It was U. S.

Senator Charles Allen Culberson of Texas. The senators were dining at the Willard Hotel.

"Pruiett," said Beveridge, "and he's still getting that front page. How does he keep doin' it?"

"He's just as smart as hell," Culberson smiled. "What's he doing now?"

"Beveridge began to read from the January 20, 1905 issue of the *Washington Times-Herald:* "The people of the Indian Territory are as a unit in favoring the Hamilton Statehood Bill, said Judge Moman Pruiett of Pauls Valley, who is in the city..."

"The press boys didn't call him 'judge' the first time he was here; the time he jumped on the Attorney General, and tried to whip him in his own office. So it's judge now?"

"The action of some senators on this question passes all understanding," the Senator continued reading. "Just why they will get up and talk and talk and talk for months at a time, day in and day out, about the Philippines and the Filipino, and about Panama and other foreign matters and things, when there are 700,000 patriotic American citizens in the Indian Territory, who are clamoring for admission as a state in the Union, is beyond me."

"Sounds like he's talking about me," said Culberson. "I hope the judge's in a better humor when I run into him. He's got his fire hot over something."

Beveridge kept reading. "Just what the Republicans will eventually do I cannot guess. But I am shocked and surprised that a large number of Democratic Senators, comparatively speaking, are opposing a law to admit Oklahoma and the Indian Territory into the galaxy of the states. Of course, we will not guarantee that the new state will be either Democratic or Republican, but the congressman who will let this fact stand in the way of 700,000 citizens enjoying those privileges which are theirs by divine right, is a demagogue, and nothing more."

They both laughed as Beveridge concluded. "He's got your number, as sure as hell," he agreed. "If he really knew how you and Bailey were blocking him, with your stupid plan to have two states out of the territories instead of one, so as to have four senators out of it instead of two, he'd have you impeached. But how does he get so much notice, all of a sudden?"

"Pruiett's quite a big man in the territory, now," Culberson explained. "I've watched him pretty close since, well, it's been five years that he was here in the Bias case. Five years; maybe a little more. He's had a lot of success as a criminal lawyer, and he's made a lot of money." Culberson was talking earnestly. "That's all it takes to upset an otherwise sensible young man, and turn him into politics, and that's all that's the matter with mister Pruiett. The Bias case made copy out of him; so, all he has to do is call in a reporter and go to popping off. Judge! Judge Pruiett. Jesus Christ!"

"Does he want to come to Congress, or the Senate?" Beveridge inquired.

"No," Culberson answered, "he doesn't want an office for himself; he wants it for someone else. He's smart enough to see that statehood for the territories can't be stalled much longer. He's picked himself a man to be the first governor, and he's giving him a lot of backing. Guess he's got ideas like some of your friends, and mine. Wants a few quiet contracts, and a pardon or two."

Beveridge took a quick drink. "He can make more damn noise up here than any other rube I ever saw," he said. "He's got a knack for that. He ought to get the governorship for himself. Who's the man he thinks can win?"

"Cruce," the Texas Senator said. "Lee Cruce. I got a letter from Pruiett about him not so long ago. Pruiett says he's found a natural, a regular Abraham Lincoln. You know how the boy is, gets worked up and excited in a hurry. He said Cruce was just as honest as Old Abe, and even looked like him. He's a banker—but Pruiett insists he's honest in spite of that. He's the brother to a lot of lawyer friends of Pruietts."

"He jumps on the United States Senate like he was making a speech to a cow-hand jury," Beveridge grinned.

"Who's got more right to cuss the Senate than Pruiett," Culberson demanded. "If the track's open at Havre, U. S. Senator Ollie James Murray of Kentucky has to have him go down there, an' get drunk. You and I get him drunk out at Cabin John's if we can get him there, just to hear him tell those wild stories. Remember how he could tell about 'the holler of the screech owl'? And down at Marlborough, with U. Senator John Sharp Williams of Mississippi, and the newspaperman Mark Goodwin. He told me he put old Ollie under the table by swallowing a square of butter between drinks; that the grease pad kept the fumes from coming up to his head and making him drunk. He ought to have a hell of a lot of respect for the Senate, all right."

"I'd like to see the little devil," Beveridge said. "If you run into him, and get a chance, bring him around."

Culberson had laid his napkin on the table and was standing. "Here he is now, speaking of the devil. He must have spotted us from the outside."

"Howdy, governor," Pruiett hailed. "Still careless, I notice, in who you eat with." He was shaking hands, in turn, with the Indiana senator.

"Carrying your own copy around?" Beveridge inquired, nodding toward the bundle of newspapers Pruiett was holding under his arm.

"Hell yes," he replied promptly. "They sent me up here to make some noise, and I want 'em to know they're gettin' their money's worth. I'm puttin' a big circle around the stuff I got printed today, and mailin' these copies back to the valley. Can I eat with you?"

"Pull up a chair," said Beveridge.

"Now look here," Pruiett began, as he was seated and had his elbows planted on the linen, "you two are doin' more to block statehood for us than any other two in Washington. I'm glad I found you together. It won't take me long to show you how wrong you are, and get you straightened..."

"Take yourself a drink," Beveridge invited, waving toward the bottle. Pruiett paused long enough to accept.

"You got to get right," he continued. "Republicanism ain't goin' to benefit none from this stallin'. It's goin' to be injured. Look at the national revenue goin' to waste, the difference between what these little old territorial agencies produce, and what it costs to operate 'em. Another state, greater national strength, another star in the flag. Hell! Just think about it."

"Play the Star Spangled Banner and I'll stand up for you," Beveridge agreed. "You sound like a Fourth of July speaker. Take another drink."

Pruiett complied. "An' what the hell's the matter with you, governor?" he asked, turning to Culberson. "Here I been writin' you all these letters, an' tellin' you what we want down there, an' why we want it, an' what do I get? A lot of crap that don't say yes or no; just something to put in a free-postage envelope. If you're against us, say so. I been tellin' them nesters you're the right kind of folks; that you'll get us a vote on this damn draggin' bill, and put it over for us. An' what's the fact? You're lined up with a bunch of damned Republicans; playin' right into their hands. They're against any kind of expansion unless its guaranteed blue-belly. You help 'em out by tryin' to be a hog. Two pore states, beggin' and scrapin', instead of one rich and powerful one, just for two more democrat senators. Ain't that a hell of a note?"

"What did I tell you?" Culberson winked at Beveridge as he spoke. "Didn't I say the judge would give me hell as soon as he caught me? Say, where do they get that Judge stuff? Gettin' pretty classy, aren't you? Let's all take another drink."

Culberson's pride in Pruiett, and Pruiett's love for Culberson, couldn't be concealed under sarcastic banter or affected discontent.

"It's like this, son," Culberson continued, "I been in this business a long time. You're all right, you're sharp as a tack, and I'll go to the floor with any man that says you're not, but look at it my way. Us good democrats are in a miserable minority. We got to take what the blue-bellies, as you call 'em, leave over. Northerners. Aristocrats. Federalists, like that evil lookin' one across the table. We need numbers to combat 'em, and by god, let's have more southwestern states. Let's even up..."

"If your plan's so damn practical, let's partition Texas," Pruiett interrupted. Beveridge began to laugh; Culberson squirmed. "Wouldn't take nay more than a Constitutional Amendment, maybe just a bill through Congress, and if its started, I'd bet my last dollar it'll pass. Ever' one in the country says you're too rich and powerful—just plain too big. Divide it up into six or eight, maybe ten, states, an' give each state two votes in the senate. That way you'd..."

"I got a good notion to give that to the press," Beveridge said as he laughed. "Mark me a bunch of copies and mail 'em to Texas. I think I'll introduce a bill..."

"Now, look here, boys," Culberson insisted, "that's different. Why, Texas..."

"A third of the folks in the territory is from Texas," Pruiett said, "an' you won't find a single one of 'em, Oklahoma Territory or any of the Indian Nations, that won't fight over this two state idea of yours an' Joe Bailey's. They all say you're traitors, linin' up with the blue-bellies like you have. Try to divide Texas, and look at the fight you've got. Try to divide the Oklahomas, an' you'll have just as tough a time."

"He's got you, Charley," Beveridge cut in. "Might as well shut up. Take a drink and admit you're licked in debate."

Pruiett's eyes were shining. "Take it all together," he said, "an' it's a great country. Them Washita bottoms are as rich as your Trinity River black land, or the Brazos River bottoms, either. An' the songs you sing about your Wabash River don't make it any richer, or any sweeter, Senator Beveridge, than that crooked, muddy stream through the Chickasaw Nation. Minerals, livestock, agriculture, and men. We got some real men down there. Wait 'til you see Lee Cruce, an' hear him. He's going to be the first governor, and by god..."

Culberson reached out and patted the clenched fist which was pounding the white table. "All right, son," he said, "I won't be the one to stand in your way. You can count on me. Do you hear that, Beveridge? We call this damn thing off. The Hamilton Bill goes on through."

"I hear you," laughed Beveridge. "I hate to see it go over, but I see the fix you're in. I'll call off the blue-bellies."

Pruiett swayed to his feet. His bristling black mane looked purple in the bright dining-room light. "To Oklahoma! To the State of Oklahoma," he said. "One great commonwealth, with the fairest portions of nature's vast domain intact; with the blood of the red and white, mingling in the honorable institution of marriage; with the wealthiest and healthiest race and people, of all the states of the Union." Beveridge and Culberson clinked glasses with him and drank.

"Say," Pruiett said, as he got his elbows back on the table. "I'd like for you to see Izora Alexander. Now, there's..."

Pruiett left the rest to the Texas senator and hurried back to Pauls Valley. He had the Alex Matlock and Dan Danna murder cases to try there, and word from the office had convinced him that the efforts of his associates, to acquire another continuance because of his absence in the capitol, was not going to be successful. The defendants, Alex Matlock and Dan Danna, had been arrested and charged with the murder of Robert L. Price, almost six years before. They had been tried once; but, the jury hadn't been able to agree, and every conceivable device for delay had been successfully employed since that one trial. The Federal Judge was determined to stop at least a part of the procrastination, and he expressed his determination in such terms that Pruiett received an urgent wire in Washington. He hurried home.

On February 22, 1906, the *Pauls Valley Sentinel* reported: "The well known and even noted case of the United States against Alex Matlock and Dan Danna was tried this week and resulted in an acquittal of the defendants. In 1900, Bob Price was shot down at his own house at Table Mountain, and said to have been robbed. There was nobody present but his wife, Belle Price, who has since married. The conjectures and suspicions as to who did the deed were and are various. But one thing is settled, Alex Matlock and Dan Danna were not the men, as the jury said. As a fact, on the Saturday night of the killing, they were 30 miles away, at Lexington, Oklahoma, as was proved by several witnesses. A confusing thing in the investigation was the different description of the murderers by Mrs. Price, made at different times."

Pruiett read the account with a smile. He could see and appreciate the uncultivated irony of the hack on that country paper, who was telling the populace in a nice way that the defendants were secure in their alibi because Pruiett's defense witnesses said so, and for no other reason. He smiled again at the reference to Mrs. Price's miserable attempt at identification in the second trial. He wondered if the writer of the article knew, as he did, how the lonely and destitute Mrs. Price, after the expiration of her unfortunate first mate, had married a man under undying obligation to Pruiett, and how things had brightened about their humble cabin, in the material way, by her tendency to be utterly at loss to faces, on the witness stand.

"The case had in it many peculiar circumstances. It was presented by U. S. Attorney G. W. Walker, recently appointed, in a dignified speech." Bill Johnson, the former federal attorney, who had lost out with a shift in the political lineup, had never received such a favorable notice on his vicious and venomous courtroom attacks, although his more undignified manner had obtained an occasional conviction. " and by J. E. Humphreys, First Assistant U. S. Attorney, who represented and pressed with all his zeal and ability. The defendants were represented by J. B. Thompson and Moman Pruiett. Mr. Thompson was not well. Moman Pruiett was at his best and fully grasping the situation, pressed every argument home with his fiery, rugged oratory. It was a great victory for the defense."

With the conclusion of the Matlock-Danna case, Pruiett published and circulated his "Call to Arms" letter on February 10, 1906, designed to impress the settlers at the creek forks with the political prominence of Moman Pruiett. It was a hastily-prepared composite of the Declaration of Independence, Patrick Henry's famous liberty or death speech, and his own oratorical effort at the Hull's Crossing reunion.

Pauls Valley, I.T., Feb. 10, 1906.

To A. F. Pyeatt, Chairman, 17th Recording District.

Dear Sir:

As a part of the Democratic Executive Committee of the Indian Territory, I this day mail you a copy of this letter and appeal to you and your committee. I urge you, and each of you, to bring together the members of your club, if you are already organized, and if you are not to proceed at once to effect an organization of your community, and every adjacent community where the same can be done.The time for united, aggressive action is near at hand. New and vital questions are arising every day, and no unorganized mass of men ever achieved a victory over a solid and alert foe.Within a few weeks at most the Indian Governments will be forever dissolved. The eighty thousand Indians will be added to nearly a million of other citizens, who live without representation, without a voice, not as citizens but as subjects, in the very heart of the greatest republic in the world.The dull ear of Congress has been reached, but faintly, and our remonstrances have been partly heard. Justice travels with a leaden tread but an iron heel. We are going to be emancipated and rehabilitated with the garb and rights of freeman.We believe that the hope of the territory and of this nation dwells in the name of the Democratic Party. Let party lines be drawn in every election and on every candidate from school director to president. Organize your club, communicate with me or other members of this committee, that we may enter all future contests with the discipline and strength of an organized army of American Freemen.

(Signed)

Moman Pruiett, Committeeman."

The boys on the Washita had a sublime subject for song and celebration, on that morning of the following June, when Pruiett made known the content of the wire he had just received from Senator Culberson in the National Capitol. As the *Pauls Valley Enterprise* handled it, in it extra edition, in June of 1906, the biggest type head was followed by a pertinent quotation.

"Be it enacted," so it said, "by the Senate and the House of Repre-

MOMAN PRUIETT DESIGNATED HIMSELF AS A SPECIAL DELEGATE FROM THE DEMOCRATIC EXECUTIVE COMMITTEE TO OKLAHOMA'S FIRST CONSTITUTIONAL CONVENTION. OKLAHOMA'S CREEK COUNTY MAY HAVE WELL BEEN NAMED MOMAN COUNTY IF NOT FOR POLITICAL ENEMY WILLIAM H. "ALFALFA BILL" MURRAY, WHO CHAIRED THE STATE'S CONSTITUTIONAL CONVENTION. COURTESY ARCHIVES & MANUSCRIPTS DIVISION OF THE OKLAHOMA sentatives of the United States of America in Congress assembled; that the inhabitants of that part of the area of the United States now constituting the Territory of Oklahoma and Indian Territory, as at present described, may adopt a constitution and become the State of Oklahoma, as hereinafter provided:..."

The Hamilton Statehood Bill was off the hook.

The Chickasaw Nation's proudest contributions to the Oklahoma Constitutional Convention, when it convened at Guthrie, Oklahoma Territory, on November 20, 1906, was William H. Murray. He was called 'Alfalfa William', "Bolivia Bill', "Cockle-burr Bill'. His occasional contact with the complete library which he kept 'neath the shelter of his log hovel and the frequent expostulations of what he had gleaned thereby, from the curb in front of the Indian Courthouse at Tishomingo, had earned him the additional title of "The Sage of Tishomingo." Murray was never reluctant to exercise the stentorian, fog-horn vocal equipment he had been endowed with, and it was as much his manner, as much as what he said, that appealed to the Indians and poor whites.

Pruiett and Murray were bitter enemies, with Pruiett, in his frequent moments of indiscretion, swearing to 'kill Bill Murray on sight'. Murray had referred to him as an 'ex-convict' while making a sidewalk speech from the shallow curb at Maysville, in a panic-stricken attempt to stop Pruiett's rapidly rising political popularity, which began with his issue of the 'Call to Arms' letter.

Murray's frank observation put Pruiett back to his pen, for the creation and publication of an epistle which attracted more comment than the 'Call to Arms' letter. The original was registered to Alfalfa Bill. Two hundred thousand printed facsimiles were distributed over the territories and the Indian Nations.

"Wm. H. Murray, Esq., Tishomingo," he began. "Sir: In a speech delivered by you at Maysville some time ago, you took occasion to speak of me as an ex-convict. For the purpose of this campaign, my personality, of the past or of the present, is of no interest to any one. I am not a candidate for public office. I am supporting for Governor, however, a man who is, in every respect, mentally, morally, humanely and otherwise, your superior."

"You are a candidate for the office of Governor of this State, an office which requires much honor, and which should be filled by a man whose home life and whose treatment of his family is an example to all the good people of this State. It is not to be recalled by any one who knows you that your family life is exemplary, or ever was. Although you are the father of several children, the bringing into the world of each one has brought you, coincidentally, some three hundred acres, making you today master of some seventeen hundred acres of land. (Murray had an Indian wife.) It is not to be recalled that you ever displayed any great characteristic of affection toward your family except when you could use your wife or children for political purpose, as, for instance, when you had your family photographed barefooted, for the political effect."

The theme then lapsed into a retrospect of Murray's ulterior motives in sponsoring the 'grandfather clause' in the Oklahoma Constitutional Convention, in helping a Washington firm of lawyers to bilk the Chickasaws during the operation of the Dawes Commission, and in fixing the election of the Chickasaw Governor in 1902.

"Notwithstanding you, as the first and original ballot mutilator of this section of the country, had perpetrated a crime so obnoxious," he continued in the letter, "to every one and everything decent, still you have the effrontery to charge me, because of a misfortune in my youth, with being an ex-convict. You certainly must be in a bad way for campaign material, and you must be forgetful of every sparkle of manhood that is supposed to exist, even in a man of your character, when you attempt, in your desire to attain public office, to bring misery to innocent people."

"You have lied about and vilified every man who had the temerity to disagree with you politically or otherwise. You have so taken on, politically speaking, the 'Holier than Thou' character, that at times in your madness, you have shown actual signs of incipient imbecility. With the honors that the people of this state have heretofore given you, why don't you stand up like a man and fight your battles fairly, treat all men honestly, speak of all men properly, and at least be honest with yourself?"

"I have my weaknesses. So have you—and many of them. I have erred often. I have been abused and maligned, but 'In the fell clutch of circumstance, I have not winced nor cried aloud; Under the bludgings of chance my head is bloody, but unbowed. Beyond this vale of wrath

William H. "Alfalfa Bill" Murray was one of Oklahoma's most notorious governors. Moman Pruiett and Murray were bitter enemies and on several occasions Pruiett was overheard swearing to "kill Bill Murray on sight." After Murray called Pruiett an ex-convict and moral pervert, Pruiett lashed back claiming that Murray, who was an intermarried member of the Chickasaw Nation, had children only because it would increase the number of allotments his family was entitled to. Courtesy Archives & Manuscripts Division of the Oklahoma Historical Society.

CHARLES N. HASKELL, OKLAHOMA'S FIRST GOVERNOR, WAS A RAILROAD PROMOTER AND A NEWSPAPERMAN—A MASTERFUL ORGANIZER AND WIZARD AT ANTICIPATING THE PROCESSES OF HIS OPPONENTS. WHILE THE OTHER FELLOWS WERE MAKING SPEECHES, HE WAS WORKING AND SCHEMING FOR HIS NEXT BUSINESS CONQUEST. HE ALSO WAS A POLITICAL ENEMY OF MOMAN PRUIETT. COURTESY ARCHIVES & MANUSCRIPTS DIVISION OF THE OKLAHOMA HISTORICAL SOCIETY.

and tears lies but the horror of the shade; And yet the menace of the years finds, and shall find me, unafraid'."

"I have tried to help many a man politically. I have done what I could for my friends, but I have never sought to advance their interests by bringing down upon the heads of innocent women and children the burden of brutal sorrow or by picking out one of my fellow citizens and attempting to besmirch his good name by resurrecting from the smouldering ashes of the past, what was, at the worst, a simple youth's misfortune."

"In your rush for political preferment, have you entirely forgotten your manhood? Are you to prove yourself a man utterly unworthy, utterly insensitive, without character—without one single sympathetic trait? Have you lost all decency—all pride? Is your self-respect dead? Has it died in an agony of indecision and self-reproach? Has it died, struggling in tortured resurrection—beaten to its knees—lying prone—- heedless insensible to the alarms of honor, duty and self-respect? I hate to think of a man seeking the greatest office the people of this State can give, as profligate in his brutality of speech as you are—passing from dread of defeat to anger—enduring the ceaseless need of a fair mind and clean conscience, but never to suffer even the shadow of their conduct; a man who has forgotten the words of the Master when He said, 'Let him who is without sin cast the first stone'."

"What manner of ambition is yours, with its birth not in noble things—not in things of mind—but its beginning, its origin in everything profane and debasing—founded on nothing—nurtured on nothing except your self-conceit and arrogant abuse of others? If you are an honest man, not entirely devoid of manhood in its better sense, you will not let this letter pass unnoticed. If what I have said is true, you will acquiesce by your silence. If it is not true, you will resent it in some way at the very first opportunity. In either event, your silence or your resentment will be synonymous—the last expiring hiss of a bruised and dying serpent."

Murray was elected President of the Constitutional Convention in November of 1906, which success was all that was needed to render the well salved and greased ego hard to stop. He appointed his committees with an obvious intent of insuring his nomination to the Governorship, more than for the efficient accomplishment of business, which the populace was so anxious to have done and accomplished. Word went out with the elevation that Murray should be President of the United States.

Pruiett writhed in agony and distress when he read of Murray's success at the convention, and that with the governorship in his grasp, he was talking himself for the national ticket. The law office was closed; Pruiett went to the convention. Murder trials had to wait. What he had up in the way of cash on a winner for Governor, was secondary to the utter contempt he had for Bill Murray. He went as 'a special delegate', representing the Democratic Executive Committee. He declared that the committee had authorized him to lobby at the convention, to see that the fundamental principles of the party were not disregarded in the formulation of the new constitution. As he was the committee, he went self-appointed, and as there was no provision in the enabling act for a special delegate, he was without official authority.

But Pruiett didn't need official authority. His presence, his personality and his force, was authority personified, and the vital issues of the meeting were met, fouled and delayed, as the fiery and oratorical lawyer required, or alternately demanded, that they should be. The local press noted and failed to understand his unofficial influence.

In January of 1907 the *Wilburton News* reported that "Moman Pruiett seems to be cutting quite a high dash in the convention, but as he has no connection with it whatever, it is hard to understand why this is. He was allowed to name a new county, and it is the only one that has a Republican name. He was also mixed up in a bribery charge. Isn't he the same Pruiett that used to live at Hackett City, Arkansas? Then, whence comes this high flying?"

He read the article and gnashed his teeth. It was the same Pruiett. It was the kid who had blacked the boots at Fayetteville, and who rode atop the splintery lumber of the wagon truck as he followed a struggling mother's direction that he go to Fort Smith and hear the imported Voorhees. It was the same one, but that wasn't what they were getting at. It was the trail of the serpent. He thrust out his blunt jaw and glared with venomous hate. The damned cowards would never let it die.

The delegates were permitted to select a name for a county in the

LEE CRUCE, STANDING IN THE WAGON, MAKING A POLITICAL SPEECH DURING HIS 1910 GUBERNATORIAL CAMPAIGN. MOMAN PRUIETT SERVED AS LEE CRUCE'S CAMPAIGN MANAGER IN HIS RUN FOR THE OFFICE OF GOVERNOR. LEE CRUCE SERVED AS OKLAHOMA'S SECOND STATE GOVERNOR AND SERVED FROM 1911 UNTIL 1915. A MORALIST, CRUCE'S TERM WAS CALLED A RIGHTEOUS CRUSADE. COURTESY WESTERN HISTORY COLLECTIONS, UNIVERSITY OF OKLAHOMA LIBRARIES.

new state. Pruiett had been accorded the honor, despite his rather unofficial status, because of what he had accomplished in Washington. He named it Moman County.

The man whom Pruiett feared and respected, politically, was Charles Nathaniel "Charley" Haskell. He had transferred his expansive personality and extensive financial backing from his native and over-developed Ohio Valley, to the town of Muskogee, in the Creek Nation. He was a railroad builder, and was familiarly known as 'Railroad' Haskell. While he kept the eastern speculators satisfied with his profitable promotion and development of the Frisco line, he formed and developed, for his own use and benefit, the Midland Valley Railway Company. His intellect and foresight was much like Pruiett's. He could carry two tunes at the same time.

But Pruiett liked to stand up and exercise his eloquence; to proclaim to all his natural brilliance. Haskell kept his mouth shut. While the other fellow was talking, he was working and scheming. A masterful organizer and a wizard at anticipating the processes of his opponents—and heading them off—he was always a dangerous factor in politics. Murray and Cruce divided the majority. Haskell quietly took up the balance, and gathered enough from the two deadlocked factions to have a passing majority on hand for every issue.

"Charges of graft were carried into the county boundaries committee today," stated the *Kansas City Journal* in its March 9, 1907 issue. "Moman Pruiett, a prominent member of the Democratic Executive Committee, was accused before the county committee with favoring Sapulpa for the County seat of Moman County for an alleged consideration of $1000. Pruiett heard of this and appeared before the committee. He denied the charge as absolutely false, and presented a counter charge that a prominent citizen of Bristow had offered him $5000 to use his influence to make Bristow the County seat."

That was Pruiett's kind of money, and an inconsistency begins to appear with lowly Sapulpa's successful bid for the courthouse, the square, the graft gravy, and the bums that went with it. The sponsorship of Moman County was adroitly disserved from its namesakes, as was its good name; and, by official act of the convention, the name was changed to Creek, in memory of the extra-dark aborigines who peopled the shallow soil of its hillsides.

Haskell called for a showdown, and when one called for that with Pruiett, he got it. Haskell was unquestionably stronger in the convention than President Murray, but the margin was not sufficiently wide to permit him to go about without apprehension. The calm of the Cruce group was baffling him. Pruiett acknowledged that he was for Cruce until the last, bar one contingency, and that was the probability of a Murray nomination. Then, he was for Haskell.

The railroader advanced a plan of coalition, with the Cruce group behind him for governor and the united strength of the two behind Cruce for United States Senator. Pruiett considered it and submitted it to the Cruce brothers by telegram. He would have liked to see his candidate in the senate, and he knew such a maneuver would insure the defeat of Murray. But, the Cruces couldn't be compromised; Pruiett stuck with his guns. Haskell gave him advance notice that he would be sorry. It was open warfare thence forward, and regardless of the advantage, it was the kind of fight that Pruiett most enjoyed.

The *Wichita Eagle*'s special representative was quick to perceive and relish the first of what promised to be real activity. On April 3, 1907, he reported "The manner in which the Cruce contingent of the Democratic party took 'Railroad' Haskell by the seat of the trousers and threw him out of the executive committee meeting at Tulsa, last Tuesday, is still the principal topic of discussion among politicians gathered at the hotel of this city. It develops here today that prior to the meeting at Tulsa 'Santa Fe' Thompson, of the executive committee, was rather inclined to give Haskell a chance to speak before the committee, but Moman Pruiett went to him on Tuesday last and told him emphatically that if he permitted Haskell to appear before the committee his own political head would be laid on the chopping block.The threat had the desired result, and the committee went into executive session for the express purpose of keeping Haskell out."

Current sequel installments of the story appeared rapidly according to the *Quinlan Mirror,* which reported on April 25, 1907:" 'Now just for that, Mr. Moman Pruiett, you shan't have any counties in the new state of Oklahoma named after you', is what 'Railroad' Haskell is stated to have said this morning, when he got revenge on Pruiett for the latter's work against him at the Tulsa meeting of the Democratic Committee. Moman County was changed to Creek County as a rebuke to the Pauls Valley statesman for having opposed the candidacy of 'Railroad' Haskell for Governor. Silently, but most impressively, Haskell's henchmen in the constitutional convention assented to the decree of their boss, and the change from Moman to Creek went through in easy fashion. At a meeting in Tulsa, several weeks ago, Pruiett made Haskell look like the proverbial thirty cents. and naturally, he made a solemn vow to get 'even.' The opportunity came today, and, when Pruiett wasn't looking, he got a heavy swat in an unspeakable portion of his anatomy. Reports reached here this afternoon that Pruiett is on a rampage."

Thus Pruiett saw the monument to the name he had founded and given himself, set up and tumbled down. The right to allocate the seat of government, to which reports attached a considerable cash value, went winging with it. For once, the local press took up the Pruiett cause, and the petty-fogging tactics of Haskell and his efficient majority were broadcast and censored.

The *St. Louis Globe Democrat* was matter-of-fact about it on April 18, 1907. "The convention also voted to change the name of Moman County to Creek, in honor of the Creek tribe of Indians. The county was named originally for Moman Pruiett, a democratic politician, who recently bolted Delegate Haskell, democratic floor leader, in his candidacy for governor, and this changing of names was intended as a rebuke to Pruiett."

That same day the *Muskogee Phoenix,* principal publication of Haskell's home town, was less prosaic, and editorially it berated the favorite son's tactics. "Moman County has been changed to Creek County. Moman Pruiett after whom it was first named became an active Cruce supporter, and this evidently did not suit the machine that made and named the Counties, and in order to impress on the country at large the fact that they are statesmen duly impressed with the solemnity of their duty in writing a constitution for a great state, the delegates to the convention, under the lead of the machine, takes this method of administering a personal rebuke to one having the hardihood to oppose its boss for governor."

"Henceforth it will be Creek County. Moman has been completely wiped off the map because he has been an impudent little boy." Thus another territorial organ referred to the farce.

"He didn't fall into line at the crack of the master's whip, so the master proceeded to crack his southern extremities with the aforesaid whip," according to the *Quinlan Mirror.*

All good things must have their endings editorialized the *Atoka Citizen* on March 28, 1907. "At the adjourning of the convention, Haskell and Murray shed tears, and delegates Pruiett and Henshaw had a fist fight in the Royal Hotel bar, thus furnishing the blood to complete the sentiment and spirit of the fiasco. Tears and blood! Blood and tears! O tempore! O molasses! O heck!"

Oklahoma was admitted as a State. Cruce was defeated in his race for the governorship; but, Pruiett wasn't crestfallen. Bill Murray didn't beat him; it was 'Railroad' Haskell, and he and Pruiett talked the same language. Hadn't Pruiett labored in the ditches of the railroad Haskell had promoted through Arkansas? The bonds of understanding between Pruiett and the governor were like those between Pruiett and Senator Culberson. They could sit down and talk—and reason.

"Among the democrats to call on Mr. Haskell during the evening was Moman Pruiett, of Pauls Valley, a delegate to the constitutional convention and whom Haskell's paper, The *New State Tribune,* recently characterized as 'an ex-convict and moral and mental pervert'." Pruiett had raised hell with Bill Murray for less, but Haskell had slipped into the Governor's job while no one was looking. Pardons and contracts were going to come from that source. Pruiett paid him a sociable call.

Pruiett was back in the valley with his murder business, but something was amiss. The musty mists, which arose from the Washita sloughs in the morning, to pick up the aroma of the alfalfa bloom and clover and carry it up past the house amongst the pecan trees, were not as sweet as they had been in those years before. The whistle of the quail from the field just beyond his fence annoyed him. He sat in his office alone, brooding and pondering in a morbid reverie.

"What's the matter with you, son?" Sam Garvin inquired, as he sat beside his desk and placed a manure-covered boot amongst the litter of papers across its top. "You been acting kind of peevish here lately. Ain't you well?"

"Yeah, I'm all right—just a little tired, maybe," he answered, "but I'll be all right. Got a hell of a lot of work to do."

"You've had as much ever since you come to the valley an' it ain't never made you act this way; not even when your joints swelled up. Why don't you try it over at Hot Springs, Arkansas, or down to Mineral Wells, Texas?"

"I been foolin' around too much. I'm way behind with my work. I can't be runnin' off ever' time I get a belly-ache."

"The belly-ache don't make a man look like you been lookin' here lately. You been goin' down for a year. Take my advice an' see a good doctor. Ask old Doc Young what's ailin' you."

"Colonel," Pruiett inquired, earnestly, "don't you ever get tired of this damn place? Two trains a day, bum food, mosquitoes as big as grasshoppers, and mud? Sticky mud on your feet all the time? Don't you get disgusted, and just not give a damn?"

Garvin studied. "You're gettin' too big for the valley; is that it?"

"Well, its not that—exactly," Pruiett hesitated. "Hell no, I ain't too big, but I don't seem to be doin' anything but stand still..."

"You're a liar," Garvin interrupted. "You think you've outgrown this place, an' by god, I do too. With me, it's different. When I fall out with the valley, it's gonna be because there's too many trains; too many people; not enough open acres for runnin' the cattle. You're a lawyer. I'm a stock raiser. When a country is ideal for me, it's wrong for you. The boom's over here an' we're settled down to holdin' on to what we grabbed during the free settlement period. If you don't get out, you're a damn fool."

"I don't want you to think I'm gettin' too good..."

"I won't," Garvin replied simply, "and neither will any one else with any sense. Don't apologize—just git up and git."

"I think I'd feel better if I did," Pruiett said. "I got Oklahoma City in mind. That's a hell of a town; they got some fast promoters up there. If she don't spread out—if there ain't a lot of money goin' around up there—I'm badly mistaken."

"What you goin' to do with your stuff down here, the farms and stuff, an' all the stock? Have a sale?"

"When I pull out, I pull out. I shake the dust off, and scrape the mud off, too," Pruiett said. "I'll sell as fast as I can, 'til it's all gone; that is, all but one piece. The little square lot I own out south of town, I'll keep. It'll keep bringin' me back, and prevent my stayin' long, after I come back. The memories are mostly what's makin' me want to leave here."

"How long's Lilly Belle been dead?" Garvin inquired. "Been nearly four years, ain't it?"

"Five years," Pruiett replied. "Been a lot happen to me in five years. My baby boy dead; layin' out there with his mother. Say, did you see the shaft I put up over their graves?"

"Yes, son, I saw it," Garvin said. "I thought it was kinda flashy for the valley. We ain't used to that sort of thing down here, even by the ones that can afford it."

"I paid $3,000 for it—cash," Pruiett said. "And I felt a little ashamed, for bein' so cheap. She was a wonderful woman, Colonel."

"I guess it's all right, if you can afford it. The only trouble is it makes neighbors envious; makes 'em distrust you. You ain't supposed to have all the money in the country, you know, even if you are a good lawyer."

"I got it off your friend, Matt Wolfe," Pruiett laughed. "An' you did your best to keep me from makin' it. Like I told you, I had to win that Ashton case to make a profit."

"We're talkin' serious, now, son, and let me tell you somethin'. We was both wrong in the Sam Ashton case. Fixin' juries is like burnin' your own barn; you usually don't cause nobody harm but yourself. I brought you here, an' I'm proud of the way you've developed yourself. You didn't have much chance as a kid, an' I don't blame you much for bein' kinda radical in your views. But when you leave here, don't take crooked money. Don't let the crooks capitalize on the wonderful talent you've got. Stay with Lee Cruce, and the things he stands for, like you been doin' this last year, and you'll do a heap better than you will workin' for murderers like Sam Ashton, and crooks like Matt Wolfe."

"You've been my friend, Colonel, the best one I ever had I guess, or I wouldn't tell you what I'm thinkin'," Pruiett said. His face was flushed, and there was a hard look in his eye. "The way I feel right now, I don't care whether I ever try another damned lawsuit in my life or not; but, if I stay in it, it'll be for the poor devil that the law is pushin' around. We elect a punk lawyer to a public prosecutor's job an' he thinks he's a god-damned king. He'll cut ever' corner and fudge ever' shot, just to convict. He does it to satisfy his own vanity and dangerous ambition, not to see that justice is done. An' the damned courts help 'em to do it. They drink, an' play, an' louse together. An' they send innocent men into hell on earth, just to be able to say they won their case."

In the summer of 1907, Moman Pruiett purchased this home at 900 Northwest 17th Street in Oklahoma City, just a few blocks from another home he purchased for his parents. According to Pruiett "the servant's quarters at this house were a damn sight better than the house that the entire family lived in at Rogers [Arkansas]." The family dog can be seen in front of the house. Courtesy *Moman Pruiett: Criminal Lawyer.*

"I've heard you say that before, son," the old man replied, "but you're wrong. No system is perfect, much less one that ain't been tried no longer than this one we've got; but you got to have law an' order. You got to protect your home, your property an' your kids, from murderous bastards like Sam Ashton. How'd you feel, actually, after they turned that one aloose?"

"I slept like a possum," Pruiett said, "never had no conscience whatever. How would you have felt if they'd a convicted him and sentenced him to hang?"

"Hell," said Garvin, "that man was guilty. He needed to be convicted. Ever' one knew he was guilty."

"Then what did you want to put a sinker on the jury for? If he was so damn guilty as that, an' our system's so good, was it right for you to butt in, and make sure of his hangin'?"

"No, it wasn't right," Garvin answered. "It wasn't right, but that's what I'm tellin' you. I ain't makin' no excuses. You caught me, but the reason I fixed John Webb was because I knew you was up to somethin'. I never did find out what it was."

"Well," said Pruiett, "I'll just tell you. I had Adkins fixed."

"No man on God A'mighty's earth could fix Squire Adkins," Garvin protested.

"Maybe no man could, but a god damned woman could," Pruiett chuckled. He was amused at Garvin's complete discomfort "That little widow was Sam's half-sister, an' she was workin' for me in that case."

"I couldn't compliment you on your tactics, even if I believed you," Garvin sniffed. "The old man didn't know it, even if he was fixed."

"Now you've got my point," Pruiett said, rising and walking around beside Garvin. He put his arm about him and patted his shoulder affectionately. "Juries are moved by personal feelings, likes and dislikes, little things that don't have a damn thing to do with the guilt or innocence of the one accused. The pens are full of men that were stuck because the jury didn't like the way his lawyer parted his hair, or didn't like the color of his necktie. The bastards fall out with a witness; maybe it's his religion, maybe he made eyes at his wife sometime years ago; so, to satisfy his small feelin', he uses his power; he convicts the man in the box. I take a chance on the humane side. If I can get them acquitted, society ain't hurt much, even if there is a mistake made. But, if it's on your side, and the one convicted happens to be innocent, then society couldn't straighten it up at all, not if it could mortgage eternity. Nope, Colonel, where you find Pruiett, you'll find him doin' just about what he's doin' here in the valley; bucking the system and tryin' to help the poor devil that society's pushin' around."

WHEN THE MORE DECOROUS PRACTICE REQUIRED PRUIETT TO DISCARD THE SHOE-STRING TIE FOR THE MORE ORNATE FOUR-IN-HAND, HE DID IT WITHOUT THE LOSS OF HIS INNATE EASE. COURTESY HOWARD K. BERRY PHOTO COLLECTION.

CHAPTER TEN

WHEREIN PRUIETT ABANDONS THE VALLEY AND ATTEMPTS TO ABANDON A PORTION OF HIS CRIMINAL LAW PRACTICE, BUT IS CATAPULTED BACK INTO ITS MAELSTROM BY HIS BRILLIANCE IN THE RELUCTANT DEFENSE OF A CERTAIN RUDOLPH TEGELER. AND HOW HE TIPS THE SCALES IN A DIFFICULT NON-MURDER CASE BE WELL CALCULATED PSYCHOLOGICAL MANEUVER, AND DELIVERS, ALONG WITH THE DELIVERANCE OF HIS CLIENT FROM THE CLUTCHES OF THE LAW, DISTRICT JUDGE W. N. MABEN, A FATAL BLOW TO THE GUBERNATORIAL ASPIRATIONS OF A FAVORABLY CONSIDERED LITTLE ATTORNEY GENERAL, AND, WHEREIN HE LENDS HIS EFFORTS TO A POLICEMAN, CROW, WHO IS CHARGED WITH MURDER, AND ACQUIRES HIS ACQUITTAL WITH LITTLE, IF ANY, EVIDENCE OF JUSTIFICATION, PLEADING CONFUSIONAL INSANITY.

Introducing Pruiett to speak at a Statehood banquet, Chief Justice Monroe Osborne of the Oklahoma Supreme Court observed that "the history of the Sooner State would be incomplete without the life story of Moman Pruiett." The story of his life progressed with the story of the new commonwealth, and changed with the changes which came with the dissolution of the Indian Nations and the gradual removal of the customs of the last frontier.

In a remarkably short comparative period, the rough pioneer manners had disappeared. The frontier lawyers were gone. P. Watt Hardin had been dead so long that the substance from his mouldering carcass no longer aided the unproductive soil which strove to push up a wild flower in the shade of the stone on his grave. Dan Voorhees, The Tall Sycamore of the Wabash, was but a vague, pleasant recollection. The barrister of the boots and pistols was gone. The ones of the frocktailed coats and spoon-derbies, who chewed their straight cheroots as they poignantly watched the turning century take all the color that had been theirs from them, had wheeled into the limbo of change and progress. A new type was rapidly assuming their place in the unsettled plan of sectional affairs.

The more sedate practitioner, who winced at the mention of pistol-toting S. Morton Rutherford or a reference to the peremptory justice of hanging Isaac Parker, were hurrying to their fifth and sixth story offices on the jolting and rocking trolleys. The free lands were taken up. The runs and land-lotteries were over, and their turbulent aftermaths of gunplay and bloodshed had diminished with the gradual regulation of a more pacific populace. The railroad lawyers, the corporation lawyers, were illustrating to the old school's rough and ready membership that the day of specialization was fast approaching. Instead of a perfunctory execution or two at the beginning of a boundary dispute, followed, as in the old days, by a homicide persecution, the claimants went to court in the beginning in a civil lawsuit, and two groups of lawyers, instead of one, had employment, activity—and emolument.

Pruiett, an old-timer at thirty-five, was definitely not ready for the discard. With the same effortless ease which attended his graduation from the ranks of the lawless to the roster of the Texas bar, he stepped from the shell of his old identity and assumed the most prominent place in the new order of things. As the pioneer's dugout on a windswept prairie grew into a neat and comfortable bungalow, or the commercial institution which opened tent-flaps to trade in its beginning blossomed into a towering building in a metropolitan city, Pruiett grew and developed with the growing commonwealth.

When the more decorous practice required him to discard the shoe-string tie of the cow-country court for the more ornate four-in-hand, he did it without the loss of his innate ease. When the boots had to be replaced by the more conservative buttoned shoes, and the brim of the hat had to be curtailed to conform to the more sedate headgear of the new period, he made the changes with a natural grace. When the gradual metamorphosis was complete, the result was the same. He was a masterful and commanding individual, holding, in the new system, the same superior position he had held in the old.

While his manners changed with the requirements of the customs,

Downtown Oklahoma City in the summer of 1912, Oklahoma City was known as the "Territorial Gomorrah," when Pruiett opened his law office above the Florida Bar in the 100 block of West Main Street in 1908. The Florida Bar attempted to survive the "dry" mandate as a nickelodeon theater for a while but finally settled on becoming the Olympic Theater. Later Pruiett moved his office to the Baum Building, one of Oklahoma City's most prominent addresses and among the community's first high-rise office buildings. Courtesy Western History Collections, University of Oklahoma Libraries.

and were in a sense modulated and toned down, the fierce, smoldering viciousness which had had its inception in dungeon cell suffering and physical privation and hardship could not be eradicated. The billowing black brush of hair crowning his shaggy brow was the same—flashing, bristling, forbidding. Until the fingers of the frost of years began to touch it, and streak it with fern-leaf, glaring white in contrast to its original blackness, no style, craze, custom or regulation could convert or disguise it.

Upstairs over B. H. Powell's Florida Bar, at 112 West Main Street in Oklahoma City, Pruiett, Lawyer, held forth. A block to the east, the Santa Fe, between regular runs, backed and shifted its strings of cars. A block to the north, the Choctaw, Oklahoma & Gulf Railroad pulled and backed its rumbling trains. To the south, one block, the Bucket of Blood Saloon was gasping and clotting. The new Constitution had dried the territory. String bands and piano players and dancing girls and free lunch counters couldn't be supported on the revenue brought in by soft drinks and near-beer. The Florida Bar was on the down trail, too, and shortly was converted into a movie house.

Progress, and refinement, was discernible in the Pruiett office. Brass cuspidors, girdled in the middle, with wide bottoms and mouths, had supplanted the rusty coffee cans. There was carpet on the floor and a picture, in variations of brown, on the pink calcimined wall. His old table had been replaced by an oak desk with a roll top standing back above pigeon-holes stuffed with a disarray of stained paper. There were traces of brown expectoration in the corners and along the baseboards.

"I'm tryin' to thin out my murder practice," he said. His feet, as usual, were atop his desk. "I'm gettin' to the place where I got to think of my family, an' to try to lay up more cash."

His caller was Daniel Burns Welty, one of his principal competitors for local law business. "You haven't any more chance of gettin' away from defendin' criminal cases than the wagon yard has of gettin' away from the manure pile out behind," Welty said. "You belong in a murder case."

"I been gettin' a good run of civil practice since the Constitutional Convention," Pruiett argued. "I just had to take that Jim Stevenson case. He was accused of killing Marshall R. W. Cathey. I'm attorney for the family. That was as tough a murder case as I ever got into, an' I've had some bad ones in my time."

"It was the worst one I ever heard of," Welty agreed, "an' that's why my clients insist that I take you in to help me try this one."

"Jim Stevenson was the brother of John Stevenson, my client in the valley," Pruiett explained. "Jake Hodges an' Stillwell Russell defended John for killin' a United States Marshal, an' he got a hangin' sentence. They reversed it, an' when they tried it again, they got a hung jury. When they tried it a third time an' got him ten years, why, Jake got out an' I went into it with Stillwell Russell, that's the same Stillwell Russell that's the District Judge down at Ardmore for Carter County now, an' we went down to the Circuit Court at New Orleans on an' appeal. After we reversed it again, I was gettin' ready to go to Paris, to defend old John in another trial, when he got drunk an' went trouble huntin' down on Paul Avenue, carryin' one of his big six-shooters. Old man Thomas L. Kendall, that ran the main grocery, was plumb full of John's foolishness, an' he could see John was paid for, carryin' the gun an' all. Kendall pushed his Winchester up over the cake counter an' let John have it in late December of 1908. The government didn't have no more case to prosecute."

"You must've had some hellish times down in that Indian Territory in those days," Welty agreed.

"I like to broke my back defendin' Dave Putty, to keep the government from hangin' him for killin' a Marshal, an' what was the benefit from it? In about three years from the time Dave come clear, he went to a country picnic an' tried to drink up all the licker. The Marshals was layin' for him, anyway, so the first time he gets out of line, they give him just enough trouble to get him to start out with his hog-leg. They shot him as dead as hell."

"What did Jim Stevenson want to kill a Marshal for?" Welty asked.

"Them fellers were all outlaws," Pruiett said. "On the outside, when they was sober, they was fairly peaceable; but, just giv'em a few drinks, an' their true natures began to show up. Jim hated officers 'cause of the way John was pushed around for killin' Joe Gaines. All he needed was a chance to kill Cathey, an' he took it. It just ran in his family to kill officers."

"How in Christ's name could a jury acquit him? There wasn't a man in this town that thought you could win that case."

"I talked 'em out of it—cold turkey," Pruiett said. "I liked to have killed myself doin' it. She was thin on proof, but I had some self-defense to talk on, an' I had to act out that fall that Stevenson took. I wanted to show by the line between bullet holes in the wall that Jim was flat of his back when he shot. Cathey had knocked him down—see? I crumpled up in front of that jury an' sprawled out. My god damn head hit the floor so hard I thought I had killed myself, an' I had to lay there. Ever'body thought it was part of the act, me just layin' there so still for so long, but it wasn't. I couldn't get up for awhile."

"A man that can try murder cases like you can has no right to deny people in tight places the benefit of your services," Welty said. "And, another thing, after all of 'em you've tried, and won, don't it get in your blood? Don't you crave to get into the fight?"

"I'd rather try a good murder case than play stud poker, an' that's sayin' something," Pruiett answered. "But, they burn up your energy. I can't sleep; I can't think nothin' but defense schemin' when I get in 'em. Licker takes the place of lost sleep, an' a little licker calls for more licker with me. I been makin' good money on pardons since Charley Haskell's been Governor, an' that's nice clean practice. Outside of my old clients, like the Stevensons, I been savin' myself, an' turnin' down a lot of damn murder cases."

"I'm not goin' to let you turn down this Tegeler case," Welty insisted. "These people have got money, and property. You can get a hundred an' sixty acres farm, right close in, an' you know how this town's growin'. That's a good fee."

"It's a good fee if the case ain't too tough," Pruiett agreed. "I don't want to get in one that'll make me look ridiculous."

"I'll tell you about it," Welty said, lighting a stogie. "Rudolph Tegeler was charged back in 1907. You was probably so busy with your State politics an' elections that you didn't notice it much."

"I noticed it, but I didn't take no stock," Pruiett interrupted. "The facts has slipped my mind. I must've been in Washington."

"Well," Welty continued, "he's charged with killin' James R. Meadows. We tried him to a jury an' they convicted him; gave him life. They slipped him up to Lansing, Kansas, to keep him 'til we get our pen finished, an' I start to take an appeal to the Supreme Court. The District Judge that tried the case died before the transcript was certified, an' the upper court said they couldn't affirm an incomplete record, so they ordered a new trial."

"That was almost as lucky for you as Statehood was for me in the Frank Driggers case," Pruiett laughed. "The gave Frank life in June of 1905 for killin' Gold Brady over by Ada. The old three-man Federal Appeals Court at South McAlester affirmed the conviction just about the time the State government was ready to take up the Territorial slack. Bob Williams was over there, an' I couldn't be there, so I had asked him to watch the case for me, an' if it was affirmed, to file a petition for a re-hearin'. Bob scratched the petition out in long-hand, on a rough piece of scratch paper, an' filed it right there. The Supreme Court took the business over right after that, an' Oklahoma Supreme Court Judge Jesse Dunn wrote an' opinion, allowin' me a re-hearin', an' reversin' the conviction in April of 1908. I went back to the valley to try it, an' won it. Old Frank's a'loose today."

"It won't be that easy in Tegeler's case; but, his folks swear that you can bring him out with better than a life sentence," Welty said. "I don't want you to go into it under any misapprehensions. It's tough. This fellow Meadows was an employee of the Pioneer 'Phone Company here, an' they thought a lot of him. Sam H. Harris, their chief counsel, was special prosecutor, an' he's as hard to hold down in the courtroom as Tegeler's guts. Tegeler made a confession once, you know, an' he wants to talk, all the time."

"I didn't know nothin' about it," Pruiett answered. "That may make a hell of a lot of difference. How did you get around it?"

"We didn't get around it," Welty answered. "We just kind of evaded it. We had a combination plea of harmless ignorance an' temporary insanity on the signin' of the confession. Here's the way it was. Rudolph was charged along with Lila Meadows—Jim's widow. They proved that Lila an' Rudolph had been hangin' their meat together for two or three years, and that Jim had a fat insurance policy they wanted to split, in addition to gettin' him out of their way. Meadows disappeared; Rudolph rushes up an' offers a reward for any information on his whereabouts; but, he doesn't throw the officers off the track. The telephone company tapped the wires at Lila's, and listened in on some conversations between the two of 'em to further confirm the suspicions that they already had."

"That's pretty fast work, and hard stuff to combat in court," Pruiett observed.

"Here's the real sinker," Welty went on, "there's a damned old Sioux fortuneteller out at Elk City that does business as Mother Rosa Myers.

She is a medicine-woman—see—a mind reader and future predictor? It was kind of a fad out in Lila's and Rudolph's neighborhood to write Mother Myers for information, for instance, they had an' argument as to what kind of dress Lila's mother was buried in, an' it seems like the old lady gave them the right answer when somebody wrote an' asked her. They paid a little for the information, you understand? Well, Lila and Jim were going to put the old lady in good. They wrote her a' unsigned letter, tellin' her that Jim Meadows had been murdered an' robbed by a bunch of thieves that had gone to Mexico. They sent along a little map, of a cornfield South of town, where Meadows body was supposed to be buried."

"I don't get it," Pruiett confessed.

"Nobody got it. It didn't get far enough," Welty replied. "The play was for Lila to suggest that some of the neighbors write Mother Myers an' ask her what had become of Jim Meadows. They figured the old lady would pretend to have a vision; wouldn't say anything about this unsigned letter they had sent, an' would send them to the grave. That map was what really disclosed the buried body. It might have worked, but for one thing. Rudolph wrote so bad that the Elk City looked like Okla City, an' they delivered the letter to a Mrs. Rose Meyers, right here in town. She turned it over to the police."

"It sounds plenty bad, so far," Pruiett said, "but not impossible. What's the rest of it?"

"Anybody could see the letter was in Rudolph's handwriting. They picked 'em both up an' put 'em in separate parts of the jail. Then they pulled the old squeeze play—an' it worked. When they told Rudolph that Lila had confessed, an' put all the blame on him, he confessed an' put it all on her. Rudolph signed his statement before he found out that he had been fooled. That's about all there is to it, except the family's been here a long time, an' grabbed off some choice ground. They're pretty well fixed."

"God Almighty usually looks out for a lunk-head, an' I can see that this Tegeler ain't no mental giant," Pruiett grinned. "I'm kind of itchin' to get in a good rough case. It might advertise the joint. Get me a deed to a good farm, an' leave the complete file up here at the office. I want a chance to do a little work before trial."

Sam Harris, the special prosecutor in the second Rudolph Tegeler murder trial. Harris called Pruiett the "black stud of the Washita" during the trial. Courtesy Archives & Manuscripts Division of the Oklahoma Historical Society.

The Pruiett home of the period surpassed the Rush Creek manor of the pecan grove in both external proportion and architectural elegance. Pruiett had had it built in the addition being used by the new town's elite. The house was of smooth brick, two stories and a half in height, with sharp sloping gables and carved, ornamented cornices. It stood on a corner. Methodically spaced elm and fir shrubs supplied the neat lawn with the cooler and shade, which, in the valley, the volunteer pecans had furnished.

The carriage house and quarters for the negro servants faced the East on the side street. "Them quarters was a damn sight better than the house our whole family lived in at Rogers—or Paris," Pruiett observed. There was an inviting air of subdued richness about the corner which was not exactly like Pruiett. It did not conform to his growing flair for gaudy manifestations of wealth, which he was then entitled to make.

And down the shady side street lived other migrants from the valley. A white cottage, with hedge fence, and a garden, and trees, was home for Betty and the Captain. No roomers and boarders to feed and clean up after now. Moman was paying all the bills, and they were taking it easy. Betty's dream had finally come true.

Rudolph Tegeler ran afoul the law in 1907. When he was finally discharged, a free man, in 1913, after being twice convicted and sentenced to life imprisonment at hard labor, the trail of the trial had led through the baffling maze of two trips to the Appellate Court and back, and into the blind bog of two hung juries. When the State's dogs had taken the scent, for the fourth time, and had bayed into the courtroom rafters and the box-car headlines of the southwestern press with all the yowling promise of a catch and kill, only to wind up on the blind trail of another hung jury, they despaired and gave up the chase. Pruiett's client walked out with slightly deferred, but inevitable, Pruiett justice.

A shapely shank had jury box appeal in the shaping period of the Southwest, as Pruiett well knew. Hadn't Izora Alexander proved that? Lila Meadows had been tried for murdering her husband, after Rudolph had first been convicted and railroaded, and she had been acquitted. Pruiett capitalized on her acquittal in Rudolph's second trial. His first bomb was loaded with powder scrapings from Lila's hearing.

"The defense will prove," he stated, evenly, making his opening statement to the jury, "that the State is unable to make a semblance of a case; that it is not only unable to prove that Rudolph Tegeler is guilty of the murder of James Meadows, but that it can't even prove that James Meadows is dead."

"I will prove by witnesses, who were here for the trial of the Lila Meadows case, that as the jury went out Lila said, "whether they find me innocent or find me guilty, I'll walk out of this courtroom a free woman." She knew that all she had to do was to make known the identity of a disguised man, sitting amongst the spectators in the courtroom, to insure her release. That man was James R. Meadows."

Pruiett carried the baby. Pruiett popped the blanks in the accused's pistol. Pruiett kept the jury entertained—and awake. The courtroom was packed. Spectators brought their lunches so that they wouldn't lose their places during the noon recess. It was apparent, from the moment Pruiett shook his fist in the face of the giant Sam Harris and shouted that "Tegeler is being persecuted by the soulless telephone trust, on evidence manufactured in the ambition-drunk minds of a bunch of corporation detectives', that the fight was going to be rough, and worth watching.

Sam Harris was a courtroom wildcat. "He was as mean as Bill Johnson," Pruiett said, "and twict as smart." Harris had come to Oklahoma from the 'phone company's general offices at St. Louis. He was big and burly, physically and mentally. As special prosecutor, acting at the direction of his company, he took charge of the prosecution and handled it like the murdered or missing Meadows had been his favorite brother.

Harris's capacity for invective rivaled Pruiett's. He referred to one of the defendant's female witnesses as 'a battle-axe harlot.' He called Pruiett's star witness 'a cigarette pimp.' In one of his bawling addresses to the jury, he referred to Pruiett as 'the black stud of the Washita.' The name stuck, and Pruiett was known by it thenceforward; thenceforward and long after the blackness of the mane had faded away.

"Should Meadows be found living, beyond the natural consternation which the discovery would create, a condition never before duplicated in criminal annals would come to pass," observed a reporter for *The Daily Oklahoman.* "It would establish Meadows as one of the smoothest and cleverest insurance swindlers in the country; it would disclose a nature and disposition never paralleled in that it would reveal that Meadows, becoming annoyed with his wife's immoral relations

Judge J. J. Carney, who oversaw Rudolph Tegeler's second murder trial for the killing of James Meadows. Pruiett defended Tegeler. Courtesy Archives & Manuscript Division of the Oklahoma Historical Society.

with Tegeler, had disappeared after securing a dead body and burying it as his own, in order that his unfaithful wife might collect an insurance policy of $5000.00."

"It would reveal a character not only ready to give up friends, position, wife and home, in order that his wife might admit without disturbance a paramour into affections. Not only has such a character never been heard of, but was never conceived until the versatile attorney for Tegeler became interested in the case."

The hack was not only minimizing Pruiett gall; he was letting the theme of the wild defense escape him. "Hell," Pruiett scoffed, "I'm provin' double-barreled duplicity. I don't know where Meadows got the stiff, an' I don't give a damn. He got one, an' dressed it in his own clothes, put his own shoes on it, an' buried it in the cornfield. Him an' Lila get the insurance that a'way, an' he gets to lay low an' see the guy that was poachin' on his preserves hung for killin' him."

"What about the note to Mother Myers, in Rudolph's handwriting?" a skeptic inquired. "What about that?"

"It's easy," he answered. "Old Rudolph was plain an' simple; fruit for a bunch of fast crooks like Jim Meadows an' Lila. Lila wrote the letters out, took 'em by Rudolph's an' asked him to copy 'em for her. She told him he wrote a better hand than she did, an' she wanted it to look good."

"Is he goin' to testify to that? It sounds pretty thin."

"You're damn right he is."

"What about the signed confession Sam Harris has got layin' on the table, just waitin' for Rudolph to take the stand?"

"The bulls whipped it out of him," Pruiett answered, promptly. He lets his thoughts wander, for the instant, to Jake Hodges and drear days at Paris. "Hell yes, that's what they did. They forced him to sign his name to it while they was third degreein' him. There ain't a word of truth in that statement."

Tegeler's defense produced Mike O'Brien, a self-styled private detective, who swore that he had known Meadows for years prior to his death, and that less than six months before the beginning of the second trial, he had seen him catch a fruit boat at New Orleans, Louisiana, heading for the Panama Canal Zone.

JAMES MEADOWS, WHOM RUDOLPH TEGELER WAS CONVICTED OF MURDERING. WHEN THE APPEALS COURT ORDERED A NEW TRIAL, PRUIETT SUCCESSFULLY DEFENDED TEGELER BY CHALLENGING THE PROSECUTION TO PRODUCE MEADOWS'S BODY. COURTESY ARCHIVES & MANUSCRIPT DIVISION OF THE OKLAHOMA HISTORICAL SOCIETY.

"You mean," Harris inquired, on cross-examination, "that you knew Meadows, intimately, before his disappearance?"

"I certainly did," O'Brien replied, low and out of the corner of his mouth.

"And you want to tell this Court and jury that you saw him in New Orleans, alive, as recently as six months ago?"

"That's what I said, ain't it?" O'Brien leered.

"Do you understand any of the obligations of an oath?" Harris demanded.

"I got as much honor as you have," O'Brien shot back.

Harris lashed out with his big fist, catching the unprepared witness squarely on the chin. As O'Brien slumped in his chair, Pruiett charged at Harris, and the bailiffs and other members of counsel rushed between them.

"I want to apologize to the Court for that," Harris said to the trial judge, as they helped the glaring O'Brien out of the room, "but I want to limit my expression of regrets. They don't extend to anybody connected with the defense."

"I object to his heroics before the jury," Pruiett bawled.

"I will personally offer $1,000 reward for the disclosure of the whereabouts of James Meadows, alive," Harris went on, talking to the Court.

"I object, an' move that Court declare a mistrial," Pruiett cried. "Counsel hasn't got that much money, in the first place, and his bragging before this jury is detrimental to the defendant's right to a fair trial."

Judge John J. Carney rapped in desperation. "I'll have to sustain Mr. Pruiett's contention," he said. "These matters have no proper place in this trial. Any suggestion of a repetition of mistreatment of witnesses will be censored by this Court. The jury is the one to pass on their credibility. Let's proceed."

Harris stood doggedly before the bench. "The State moves the Court to grant a continuance, in order for it to send investigators to New Orleans to obtain evidence to impeach this last witness."

"The defendant will agree that his motion be allowed," Pruiett said, jumping from his chair. There was a pause, as the Court looked at him in surprise. He went on. "Of course, the defendant will be entitled to a continuance, in order to send to New Orleans for witnesses to impeach the witnesses that the State produces to impeach our witness. Then, the State can have another continuance, to get witnesses to impeach... "

Pruiett's point was clear. "There'll be no continuances," Carney cried, slamming his desk. "Court's recessed until tomorrow morning; and, unless the State's ready to proceed with this trial, then, the Court will declare the case dismissed."

With a brown blast at a cuspidor, Pruiett turned and grinned at Harris. A fine mist sprayed the papers on the table. There was murder in Harris's face as he reached for his handkerchief, and walked away.

The advantage shifted back to Harris's side when the first rebuttal witness took the stand the following morning. It was Mrs. J. T. McGraw, Mike O'Brien's mother, who said she lived in Little Rock, Arkansas.

"Do you know the man who testified here yesterday?" Harris inquired, "and who said his name was Mike O'Brien?"

"I do," she answered.

"How long have you known him?"

"For a great number of years."

"Did you know him as Mike O'Brien, or by some other name?"

"I knew him as Milton McGraw—that is his real name."

"And what, if any, relationship is there between you and this witness?"

"I am his mother," she answered, quietly. Pruiett twisted perceptibly.

"Was your son in New Orleans some six or seven months ago?" Harris asked.

"No, he was with me, at Little Rock," she answered.

Harris was thorough in rebuttal. He put her husband, the purported father of the witness on the stand, to corroborate her. He did it, and more. He said that Milton, alias Mike, had tried to poison him in Fort Worth.

Did Pruiett care? O'Brien, or McGraw, went back to the stand. "Without wincing, Mike O'Brien sat in the witness chair in the District Courtroom Friday afternoon during the Tegeler trial and met the gaze of the man and woman who claim to be his father and mother, Mr. and Mrs. J. T. McGraw. He denies that he knows the two people who are claiming him as their wayward son, or that he tried to assassinate his father in Fort Worth, Texas, some years before, in order to get hold of a landed estate. O'Brien referred to the would-be mother as 'that old canary', and to the purported father as 'the old garbage man'."

"He offered us bribes, at first, and then threats, to keep us from exposing his false identity," the parents responded.

The black stud, Pruiett, the murder specialist, had never hoped to prove that James R. Meadows was still alive. He was artfully engaged in attracting the attention of the jurors from the magnitude of the crime committed and the magnitude of his client's guilt, and in centering it upon a less pretentious issue. He succeeded. For a full month, the mighty efforts of the able Harris were concentrated, not on proving that Rudolph Tegeler was a vicious, calculating murderer, but that a broken down old floater named O'Brien, or possibly McGraw, was a prodigious liar.

And over the vicious, pathetic, objection of Big Sam Harris, Pruiett squared off and read a telegram to the gleeful jury. "Mike O'Brien is a man whose reputation for truth and veracity cannot be assailed," he roared. He turned to leer at Harris before he finished his play to the jury. Waving the yellow slip he continued, "This telegram is from Governor J. Y. Sanders, of the State of Louisiana."

While Harris and Pruiett were sparring, reinforcements, marching on the Telephone Company's fat expense account, were coming to the front. As Mike was rubbing his bruised chin in the corridor, Claude Nowlin, lawyer assistant to Harris, and Webb Jones and O. W. Lawler, detectives, were hurrying to the depot. Their ad in the *New Orleans Picayune* newspaper brought volunteers to the grog-shop in their hotel. A fair per diem and all traveling expenses helped them to know something about the case.

"Under the direction of Sam Harris, three citizens of New Orleans were brought to Oklahoma City Sunday, and they were on the stand Monday and Tuesday. The testimony they gave, supported by public documents, some of which have not as yet been admitted in evidence, went to show that McGraw was never in the employ of the United States as Assistant Labor Inspector of the Port of New Orleans" as he had claimed. The Court, jury, spectators and reading public, had forgotten about Rudolph Tegeler. Just how big a liar was this fellow McGraw—or was the name O'Brien?

The ruinous effect of Pruiett's bombardment was showing—after five weeks—on the mountainous physique of prosecutor Harris. His massive shoulders were drooping dejectedly, and the Indian summer sweat had yellowed the white cuffs of his wilted shirt. But, there was an air of malignant, ghoulish revenge about his tired torso as he arose and began to address the Court. The State was surely ready to close.

"Your Honor," he said, painfully, "inasmuch as you permitted Governor Sander's telegram to be read to the jury, without what I would call proper identification, I feel that I am entitled to announce, in the presence of the jury, that the State rests, except for the proof of one more witness. He will be here tomorrow; it will be Governor Sanders of Louisiana, whom I have talked with on the 'phone. He will testify that the Mike O'Brien he had reference to in his telegram is a member of the railroad construction firm of O'Brien Brothers, who have been operating in Louisiana for a number of years. Governor Sanders will say that he knows absolutely nothing of the Mike O'Brien who is testifying in this case."

There was no change of expression in Pruiett. He took a fresh chew, stuffed a litter of papers into his brief case, and winked at a juror as he went by. He was unable, however, to control his feeling when the first edition of the evening paper came out.

"While making an alleged attempt to get out of the jurisdiction of the District Court Tuesday afternoon, Milton C. McGraw, alias detective Mike O'Brien, was arrested in the alley back of the County Jail. He was arrested by Deputy Sheriff Leslie Skaggs. He is being held on a warrant sworn out by Claude Nowlin, charging that he gave false testimony in the Rudolph Tegeler case."

The stud's tail flew up. He tossed off a huge drink and wheeled on his circle of loungers.

"Why the hell did he have to get caught in the alley?" he demanded, scowling viciously. "That makes it look bad for the case. That makes it look like we got an alley rat for a witness; a damned alley rat."

When the evidence was all in, the Court read his instructions of law to the jury, and there was a lull, like the quietude of sunset between the stages of a Spring storm. But with the night the wind came up again, and the lightning began to flash and roar. "At one time Thursday afternoon, Moman Pruiett's rhetorical assault upon Sam Harris was so severe that the Court was appealed to, but the speaker was so intensely in his theme that the words of Judge Carney did not reach his ears."

On its first poll, the jury was in unanimous accord. Mike O'Brien was the biggest liar in the United States of America. With the second ballot, they agreed upon the next issue; Pruiett was just as good as the press had him cracked up to be, and he had put on a whale of a performance. But, as to Rudolph? That was different. They played poker, told stories and ate meals being charged to the taxpayers who fumed in the corridors downstairs, waiting for the verdict. When they had been out three days, they announced that they were in hopeless disagreement, and a weary, frustrated trial judge was glad to discharge them and declare a mistrial. Six had wanted to turn him out, because Lila was free and she was as guilty as he. Six had wanted to hang him, because he was such a stupid, blundering dolt. The evidence relevant to the murder charge was seldom, if ever, mentioned. Whether Meadows was living or dead was never considered.

Pruiett always considered his successful defense of W. N. Maben, District Judge indicted and tried for corruption and abuse of authority, one of his most noteworthy accomplishments. The quality of a Pruiett triumph was gauged by the volume and nature of the evidence against the defendant, and by the capacity and ability of the prosecutor handling the people's case. In the W. N. "Bill" Maben case in December of 1909, Charles J. West, Oklahoma's first Attorney General, was conducting the prosecution in personum. He was a diminutive, belligerent, little lawyer who had left Georgia for the territory; he was running over with energy and political ambition. The entire county government, involved in the scandal with Maben, had turned State's evidence, and was lined up as witnesses for the prosecution. The pimps, prostitutes, gamblers and bootleggers were doing the best they could for themselves while the heat was on. They were cooperating with the majesty of the law.

The current press furnished a fairly accurate word-picture of Maben. "Judge Maben has been one of the most prominent democratic leaders in the State. He was a delegate to the National Convention at Denver and has had a great deal to do with shaping the political destiny of the State since the advent of Statehood. He was elected Judge of the District in 1907 by a large majority. He is a native of Texas and began the practice in Fort Worth several years ago."

Maben was Pruiett's friend; he was capable of doing no wrong. Like Pruiett, he was indefatigable physically, mentally and morally, and an all night session at whiskey and poker left no tell-tale mark of wear on his faultless courtroom bearing next morning. His precise manners, and dress, suggested that he wanted to acquire and keep all of the feminine good will that he could.

As practicing lawyers, they had met at the Sandy Land Court, with its transitory judge, clerk and marshal, shifted about over the Indian Territory. Pruiett, licensing murder and cattle-theft in the valley, would drift East and North to Maben's stronghold in the Seminole Nation, the town of Shawnee. Maben, an authority on relative civil rights, had occasional call to visit the valley. When they were together, there was a bottle, and a good time.

After Statehood and Maben's elevation to the bench, Pruiett had had occasion to appear before him. He was arguing a motion for a severance for one of his murder clients. They had been together nearly all night at Mabens, and Pruiett had taken a stiff stimulant before he could

CHARLES WEST, OKLAHOMA'S FIRST ATTORNEY GENERAL WAS NAMED A SPECIAL PROSECUTOR IN THE POTTAWATOMIE COUNTY CORRUPTION CASE. THE MAIN TARGET OF THE INVESTIGATION WAS DISTRICT JUDGE W. N. MABEN, WHO PRUIETT SUCCESSFULLY DEFENDED. COURTESY WESTERN HISTORY COLLECTIONS, UNIVERSITY OF OKLAHOMA LIBRARIES.

push himself out of bed that morning. He had taken several more for breakfast. He was hesitant and backward as he tried to express himself in court. Pruiett was mumbling.

"The Court can't hardly hear you, Mr. Pruiett," Maben called from the bench, cupping his ear.

"That's perfectly all right, your Honor," Pruiett assured him. "I can't hardly see you."

"You should have known that a majority like you got would start the wolves to howlin'," Pruiett said to Maben. "Ain't you learned that when you start goin' up that all the bums in the gutter go to grabbin' at your coat tails?"

"They've got me in a corner," Maben agreed. "I wasn't lookin' for such a gesture of appreciation for all the hard work I been doin' for these bastards."

"Charley West's got ever'body that was indicted to turn against you," Pruiett said. "He's got leniency to offer, an' all he wants is you. You got a political future, an' so has he. If he can ruin you, he's made."

"What we goin' to do?"

"We're goin' to raise hell, an' lots of it," Pruiett answered, vengefully. "This is Oklahoma's first dirty didy. I'll show 'em that the guy that is changin' this State's first soiled linen is doin' it for a grandstand act, an' I'll jab his nose in the mess that's in it. I coined this one on the train down, for a statement to the Press. 'Charley West is trying to cover-up his own official incompetency by smoke from the sacrificial fire he has built for his fellow officer. It is a gigantic conspiracy with two purposes, one to advance West to the governorship, and the other, to let Ben Blakeney get the revenge he wants of Maben, because Maben is an honest and impartial judge. Men of Maben's type are constantly beset by petty conspirators like West and Ben Blakeney.' How's that?"

"It sounds good, an' it sounds true," Maben replied. "There I was, partners for years with Ben Blakeney, splittin' fees with him an' workin' my head off for him, an' just because I got to be a judge, he had to get envious. I can't understand it."

"You don't need to understand but one thing, Bill. Blakeney's a good lawyer an' he's well thought of down here. With him in this prosecution, it's bad—I mean it's worse. That dirty little Charley West makes it bad."

"If I ever get out of this mess, I'll resign," Maben sighed. "It ain't worth the trouble it takes, walkin' sideways an' lookin' back all the time, to see which one of your friends is close enough to bite a hunk out of your butt. Those politics is dog eat dog, an' I don't mean like the Seminoles an' Shawnees do it. They have broiled young bitch an' fricassee of hound pup on their regular menu right out in the open."

"Charley West is runnin' his governor's race right here in this trial," Pruiett said. "He's usin' your skeleton for a ladder to climb a notch higher—he thinks. Don't lose your nerve an' start to talkin' about resignin' 'til the scrap's over. You got to stand behind me an' fight."

"You're the boss hoss," Maben grinned. "What did Sam Harris say? The black stallion?"

"The black stud horse of the Washita," Pruiett laughed. "We'll have to do some stampedin' to get over Charley West an' the organization he's got down here, but watch me trot. A good farmer's got more'n one way of gettin' to town."

Tecumseh, the council camp of the remnant of Shawnees and Pottawatomies, who survived the transfer from the East, had become the seat of government for the County named after the Pottawatomies. The whipping and shooting tree, where stern tribal justice had once been dispensed, was a great elm, shading the spotted and unkempt lawn of the Court House. Like the town, and the surrounding country side and the inhabitants, the brown-stone Court Building was somber and plain. The sleepy placidity of the place refused to be disturbed by the crowd of curious jamming the rooms and wagon yards, in town for the Maben sacrifice. Mid-May was resting season for the blanket man, and dozing and smoking, they accepted the comfort of the shade or stoically gave it up, as the marching sun dispensed it and retracted it. They ignored the bustling whites who breezed in and out with their important looking brief cases, and their more important gesticulations and loud talk.

The path ahead of Maben was rocky. "The grand jury returned indictments against W. N. Maben, Judge of the Tenth Judicial District, and Virgil R. Biggers, County Attorney of Pottawatomie County, and other county officials, charging them with misconduct in office in conspiring with others to permit unlawful sales of intoxicating liquors, gaming, and other violations of the law within their jurisdiction. They were charged with the acceptance of bribes, and in agreeing and actually taking $2500 per month, payable of the 15th of each month and beginning September 15, 1908, (ending through discovering of the situation February 15, 1909) thereby indemnifying the bootleggers, gamblers, and other criminals from prosecution from official interference."

"A Woman Started It All," the *Shawnee News* had said in May of 1909, explaining the break of the unusual case. "The information which resulted in the trial of Judge Maben on a charge of receiving money to protect bootleggers, dates from the writing of a letter by Mrs. Brown Howell, the wife of a converted jointest. Brown Howell has testified that he is one of the men who gave the $800 which Judge Maben is accused of having accepted to protect bootleggers against indictment. He was converted at the Bulgin revival, and is now a member of the Presbyterian Church. Howell had been a saloon keeper twenty-seven years; and, after his conversation, he drove to his joint and gave all his interest in the establishment to his partner. Mrs. Howell wrote a letter to the Rev. Mr. Bulgin telling of the alleged corruption in Pottawatomie County. She then put her statement into the form of an affidavit, the reading of which at the Bulgin revival brought the earthquake that is still shaking things in this county."

Pruiett and Maben sat on the bridge, watching the rats scurry down the hawsers. "They're runnin' to Charley West awful fast," Pruiett said. "Ever' one that pleads guilty an' agrees to take a suspended sentence is a witness for Charley, against you."

"There's a few that ain't gone yet," Maben said. "Biggers, the County Attorney, is still with us, an' he's the main witness."

"I'm afraid of him," Pruiett mused. "He don't look like the right kind of folks, to me. I predict that he'll take the stand against you before the State rests."

"I might as well try to trade out myself, if he does," Maben replied.

"You couldn't cop out if you was to plead guilty to murder an' agree that they hang you tomorrow," Pruiett scoffed. "Ain't I told you? This is Charley West's campaign for governor that is goin' on here, an' our great judicial system is payin' the expenses—what you ain't furnishin'. This trial is front page for the crusadin' little Attorney General. They don't want the policemen, or the commissioners, or the County Attorney. They want the District Judge that has a big political following, an' that's you. Charley's got a hand-made basket to catch your head."

"He'll catch a hell of a headache when he does," Maben grinned.

"That stuff you shook up last night like to have killed me."

The bells had told Pruiett the truth. "Virgil R. Biggers, the suspended County Attorney, and against whom an indictment is pending, will be called as one of the State's witnesses, according to a statement from the County Attorney's office, and he will likely be one of the next witnesses to be put on the stand."

"SAYS HE GOT THE BOODLE" proclaimed the *Shawnee News,* on May 15, 1909, of Biggers. "In a sensational statement made to Attorney General West today, County Attorney Virgil Biggers confessed having accepted bribes from gamblers and bootleggers of this city. He implicated District Judge W. N. Maben and County Commissioner Robert Hager. A rumor is afloat that on Monday Police Chief W. F. Sims will also turn State's evidence, and in case it proves to be true, it is thought that other prominent officers will be accused."

"What do you say now, my black stallion?" Maben laughed, shoving the paper toward Pruiett.

"I say pass me a drink," he answered. "Wasn't I right about Mister Biggers. I say Sims'll go the same route. It's all cooked up, an' Charley'll pay'em back with interest when he gets to be Governor."

"Shall we stop the show?" Maben inquired, quietly. "We can throw the towel in any time you say. There ain't no use in lettin' 'em whip our heads plumb off."

"Whip hell," Pruiett grated. "I got a hunch, an' I'm the guy that plays hunches. We're goin' to get a break in this case, an' I think the groggier we are, when it comes, the better off we'll be. Let Sims go, an' all the rest of 'em. We'll try to make the jury understand that the State's case is too perfect—too damn complete to be anything but a well laid an' developed conspiracy. Get my point?"

"I get it," Maben answered, "but I don't think much of it. We ain't got nothin' to bluff with."

"We'll just let little Charley shoot his wad," Pruiett said. "Sit tight in the buggy an' watch me egg him on. When he gets to steppin' his highest, watch old Moman. Somebody's head, besides yours, may roll into that sawdust."

The trial and progress of the case found the lawyer with the bushy black hair in a most unusual, and unnatural position. He was on the defensive, actually and figuratively. The diminutive Attorney General

BENJAMIN B. BLAKENEY, A SHAWNEE LAWYER, WAS WILLIAM N. MABEN'S LAW PARTNER UNTIL 1903. HOWEVER, WHEN THE POTTAWATOMIE COUNTY CORRUPTION SCANDAL EXPLODED IN 1909, BLAKENEY WAS MORE THAN WILLING TO SIDE WITH STATE PROSECUTORS AGAINST MABEN. COURTESY ARCHIVES, OKLAHOMA HERITAGE ASSOCIATION.

JUDGE MALCOLM E. ROSSER PRESIDED OVER THE POTTAWATOMIE COUNTY CORRUPTION TRIAL OF DISTRICT JUDGE WILLIAM N. MABEN. ROSSER WAS ONE THE MOST RESPECTED JUDGES IN THE STATE. THE SCANDAL RESULTED IN THE RESIGNATION OR REMOVAL OF OFFICE THE COUNTY COMMISSIONER, COUNTY ATTORNEY, SHERIFF, CHIEF OF POLICE, AND NUMEROUS OTHERS WHO TESTIFIED AGAINST MABEN. ALTHOUGH THE EVIDENCE AGAINST HIM WAS OVERWHELMING, MOMAN PRUIETT'S DEFENSE RESULTED IN MABEN'S ACQUITTAL. COURTESY *MEN OF AFFAIRS.*

had beat him to the punch with a scathing statement of what he expected the State's testimony to develop, and he had kept the advantage by constant barrage of leading and suggestive questions put to the already damaging witnesses, and a stream of suggestive, discourteous and insulting comment across the counsel table. He had Pruiett so punch-drunk and bewildered, apparently, during the first week of the trial, that the jury was pitying him. Hadn't the papers said something about this Pruiett—about his being smart, and hard to handle?

MAIN STREET IN DOWNTOWN SHAWNEE. SHAWNEE WAS THE COUNTY SEAT OF POTTAWATOMIE COUNTY, THE SITE OF A 1909 CORRUPTION SCANDAL INVOLVING DISTRICT JUDGE WILLIAM N. MABEN. WHEN MABEN WAS INDICTED AND TRIED FOR CORRUPTION AND ABUSE OF AUTHORITY, HE HIRED MOMAN PRUIETT AS HIS DEFENSE ATTORNEY. PRUIETT WON AN ACQUITTAL IN WHAT HE CONSIDERED ONE OF HIS GREATEST LEGAL TRIUMPHS. THE FLAMBOYANT ATTORNEY GAUGED HIS TRIUMPHS BY THE VOLUME AND NATURE OF THE EVIDENCE AGAINST THE DEFENDANT, AND BY THE CAPACITY AND ABILITY OF THE PROSECUTOR. MABEN, LIKE PRUIETT, WAS INDEFATIGABLE, PHYSICALLY, MENTALLY, AND MORALLY, AND AN ALL-NIGHT SESSION OF WHISKEY AND POKER LEFT NO TELLTALE MARK OF WEAR ON HIS FAULTLESS COURTROOM BEARING THE FOLLOWING MORNING. COURTESY WESTERN HISTORY COLLECTIONS, UNIVERSITY OF OKLAHOMA LIBRARIES.

West was an effective prosecutor. His lack of physical height—he was scarce more than five feet tall—was never noticed after his energy and activity was once set in motion. His small body was muscular and wiry; he moved about with a nervous, springy stride which made one think that he was bounding to his toes with each step in an effort to increase his deficient perpendicular measurement. His head, large and out of proportion to his body, was indicative in both size and shape of mental prowess. A slight baldness accentuated the height of his brow, while beady black eyes and a large, slightly hooked nose, gave the immediate impression of a big bird—a hawk.

The inconsistent booming voice which emanated from his broad mouth caused consternation in the first observer and listener, and invited more careful attention. It was incredible that one of such slight stature should be equipped with such a medium. The store of invective, which he had brought to the new State from his native Georgia, was both revelatory and revolutionary, even to the forked-tongued Pruiett, whose superiority in uttering vicious figures and phrases was generally recognized, and respected.

"He's just like a god damned little fightin' chicken," Maben whispered behind the back of his hand. "Watch him bounce. Watch him strut. How are we goin' to stop it?"

"He's the worst I ever saw," Pruiett answered. "That chicken's a good name for him. He's so mean that bein' tough with him won't help a bit. Let's keep on bein' real meek, an' let him go. Maybe he'll wear himself out."

But West's bouncing energy wouldn't be exhausted. He put preacher Bulgin on the stand and kept him there until he had succeeded in parading before the jury the hearsay and gossip of the revival tent. Oats Johnson and L. B. Howell, gambling joint operators, who handled whiskey, swore to having delivered various sums of money, at various times, to the defendant District Judge. They testified that he agreed to deliver them protection for the payoff. Pruiett's cross-examination failed to cross them up.

Biggers, the deposed and confessed prosecuting attorney was most liberal with the consideration he was to deliver for the immunity he had been promised. There was no doubt, at the conclusion of his testimony, that if the incrimination of Maben was a part of what he was to deliver, that the State was in his everlasting debt. Hager, the County Commissioner, corroborated Biggers; and, when he was done, a three day procession of pimps, prostitutes and petty gamblers went by, halting long enough at the witness chair to say a few words against the former judge.

"You were good," Pruiett said to Maben, during recess. "You acted so meek an' apologetic, while you were testifyin', that I like to have cried myself. I'm turnin' you over to West for cross-examination as soon as we re-convene, an' remember—our strength is in our utter weakness. Ain't the meek supposed to inherit the earth?"

"I've got a lot of respect for your judgment, Moman," Maben said. "I turned the defense over to you, an' you're the director, but I sure hate like hell to be pushed around this way."

"Let him go," Pruiett insisted. "Our day's a'comin'. He'll make ever' dirty inference that can be made, an' he'll violate ever' rule of evidence in cross-examinin' you, but I ain't goin' to object. He's done enough of that while we was tryin' to tell our side of this story. You are a lawyer, an' ought to be able to take care of yourself. Whatever you do, don't let the jury think you're mad, or that your temper's got away from you. I want your word on that."

"If you say let him rape me, I'll do it," Maben grinned, "an' I'll promise to put on the act. I just can't agree to like it, actually."

"I like it less than you," Pruiett said. "I'm lettin' him build himself up; swell up on his ego. It'll make him overbalanced, an' easier to handle when I start takin' him apart."

"He'll probably take a poke at you," Maben reminded. "You know what I mean."

Pruiett studied. He had never succeeded in flailing the serpent's trail from the sand behind him. "If he's got that little judgment, let him go," he grated. "You've stood him, an' I can too, for a little longer, anyway."

Charley West proved Pruiett's prediction. When he had concluded his vicious cross-examination he asked, with mock politeness: "Did your consciousness of guilt in this case have anything to do with your selection of a disreputable criminal lawyer, for your defense?"

Maben pondered. "No," he answered, meekly and quietly.

"It'll be two convicts instead of one, when the jury gets through with him," West hissed over his shoulder to Blakeney, as Maben stepped down. The whisper could be heard over the entire room. "Pruiett looks like he needs company."

Both sides had rested when the noon recess was taken, and the Court's instructions to the jury had been read. The courtroom had cleared, and Pruiett was sitting alone at the counsel table. Judge Malcolm E. Rosser passed on his way out of his chambers; he paused to speak to the meditating lawyer.

"Aren't you going out to eat, Moman?" he questioned. "With arguments ahead, you'll need a lot of vitality. You ought to go out."

"I haven't got any appetite," Pruiett replied. "I feel all right; but, I'm just not hungry. I think I'll rest a little during the noon hour."

"Are you too mad to eat?" Rosser inquired, bluntly. Pruiett showed his surprise; the judge had overheard the whisper.

"I never felt so much like killin' a man before in my life," he answered, truthfully. "He's gone out of his way to offer me every insult known to depraved ingenuity, an' then... "

"I heard it," the Court interrupted, "and I'm sorry. I can't subscribe to those tactics; but, I can't say anything about it in front of the jury. I advise you to keep your head."

Pruiett didn't answer, but continued to look down and scowl. The judge went on: "I want to congratulate you on your defense of Maben. You've done a good job; but, there's just too much evidence against him. Frankly, I think the jury is going to convict him. But, don't lose your own head and make matters any worse. If you try to get mean, or get even with West, when you talk to this jury, you are apt to do your client an injury."

"I've been savin' up a week, thinkin' up and savin' things to say about that little cracker son-of-a-bitch, an' you know it." Pruiett was laughing and the strain was over. "If Mrs. Rosser needs a new sifter, tell her to come by the Court House this evenin' and pick it up. I'm goin' to take Charley West's hide off right in front of that jury, an' punch it so full of holes that it won't hold sand. She'll be able to shake flour or nutmeg through it, and... " Pruiett stopped himself, for the laughing judge had already passed out of hearing through the courtroom door.

The courtroom representative of the *Shawnee News* noticed that the hide slipped. "Moman Pruiett of Oklahoma City, attorney for the defense in the Maben case, concluded the afternoon arguments with a scathing arraignment of the Attorney General and Attorney Blakeney.

He charged the former with prosecuting the case in the interest of his political ambition, and the latter with having personal animosity toward Judge Maben. Toward the end of his speech, he grew extremely vitriolic.

Pruiett's argument to the jury was sandwiched between the opening and closing arguments of the prosecution. Blakeney opened, and in an able, although unnecessarily brutal manner, interpreted every point in evidence as conclusive proof that Maben was an arch-rascal who should be given a long term in prison. He exhibited bad taste and bad judgment when he offered an insinuating reference to Pruiett and his past, and suggested a similarity in the makeup of the defendant and his counsel. His argument as a whole was an analysis of the evidence, for he was leaving, with abiding trust and confidence, the complete stultification of Maben and Pruiett to the gentleman from Georgia, the Attorney General who had the last say to the jury.

Pruiett talked for an hour before he mentioned a phase of the case other than those developed by his own client's testimony. With quiet control, he reconstructed the life story of the defendant; an humble birth with a struggle against poverty through childhood; but, gradually gaining, slowly rising, with accomplished position within his grasp, the rafters crashed around him and threatened to crush him. There was an old mother, of course. Pruiett paid a tribute to Betty as he placed roses on the altar of Maben's mother's memory. There was a faithful and steadfast wife, and innocent children. These, all of these were suffering, and why? He pondered, as if uncertain. Then, in an instant, he became transfixed, rigid, wild-eyed. He wheeled upon the complacent little attorney general and thrust a trembling finger under his nose.

"You Judas! You Brutus! You Benedict Arnold!" he roared. "You, the sum total of cowardice and treachery through the ages; why have you persecuted this innocent man? Why have you abandoned the courtesies and decencies of courtroom practice, and vomited up your putrefaction and avarice—by every cheap and despicable violation of the rules of evidence—if you don't feel that your case is inadequate to support a conviction on its merits?"

West was obviously searching for an answer as he scrambled from his chair.

"You object, do you, you cowardly little braggart?" Pruiett continued. "You cry for the protection of the Court? Why have you stood on your hind legs and objected a thousand times to what a man would introduce in his own defense into a court of justice; when he is fighting a conviction that would ruin him and rob him of his birthright?"

The rising Attorney General was being hauled back into his seat by Blakeney, who was tugging at his short coat. "Let him alone," Blakeney whispered to West. "He's only trying to get error into the record. Don't make an objection. We've already got the case won."

"How many times have you heard it, gentlemen of the jury?" Pruiett inquired, turning to them. "How many times have you heard it? 'The State of Oklahoma objects! The State of Oklahoma objects.' I'll tell you... as many times as this defendant has opened his mouth to say a word in his own defense. And West always says 'The State of Oklahoma,'—have you noticed, gentlemen? 'The State of Oklahoma objects!' His desire to impress his authority is but a manifestation of his attitude of coercion and intimidation. It is as if to say to the honest judge trying this case, 'this court will take notice that a District Judge is now on trial, and if this prosecuting power is crossed, another one, maybe you, will be next..."

West was rising again. Pruiett turned on him.

"Stand up and crow, you cowardly little capon. Flap your wings and cry for mercy. I knew you would do it; it's as old as the story of man. When the going gets rough, the weakling is the one that begins to cry. You've harassed me throughout this trial by your cowardly interruptions and side remarks. Stand up and object again; stand up and object."

West couldn't afford to take the dare and Pruiett knew it. He sank slowly, wearily, back into his chair. Pruiett went back to the jury.

"This little capon from Georgia, with his yellow comb and loud crow, is being milk fed in a private pen so he can be shown to society company. He wants to be Governor. So, the gang that thinks he can make it, goes out and hatches up their dirty conspiracies, and sets the stage for him to rush in and make a big noise. He's to capitalize on the publicity. That's the deal, and it would be all right, if it wasn't for the fact that innocent men, innocent men and their families, have to be sacrificed for the cheap show that he wants to put on."

"In his sequestered ease the little capon doesn't have to scratch. They crack his corn and warm his milk, and when the time comes for him to get out and rough it—he objects! He objects to an American citizen exercising the right that God Almighty and the Constitution of the United States guarantees to him. The great State objects. It sounds better that way, and he thinks he can intimidate the defendant, and intimidate me. He wouldn't object if Judge Maben were to sit quietly by and let him ram the roast of his crooked conspiracy down the throat of the people; let him ravage and discredit this defendant and his innocent family, for his own selfish political benefit. Stand up and object, little capon, stand up and object!"

But the little lawyer couldn't stir. Uninterrupted for the first time during the two weeks trial, Pruiett proceeded to take the few favorable circumstances of the case and set them up in such a way that they seemed to surpass, in importance, all of the injurious testimony which the State had produced. He skinned West without mercy, and punched the sifter holes in his hide with his own small bones. He pilloried Blakeney with his burning vituperation and matchless ridicule, and charged that Biggers and the pimps and prostitutes were a part of the scheme to sacrifice Maben to Charley West's political aspirations.

When Pruiett had worn himself completely out, he thanked the jury and walked out of the courtroom. He wanted them to understand that he didn't intend to make any objections to West's answer. He wasn't interested enough in what West thought of his chances to convict, to sit in the courtroom and listen.

Pruiett has struck the Attorney General's most vulnerable spot when he likened him to a Georgia capon. West was not entirely without self-consciousness where his resemblance to the fowl family was generally concerned. Somewhere, and at some time, before, some wag had drawn a similar comparison. Try as he might, the little bantam could not recall the vim he had had before Pruiett's denouncement. He floundered through his carefully prepared closing speech.

Maben had his resignation prepared. Three hours later, when the jury returned and announced that they had agreed that the defendant was guiltless of the crime charged, he shook hands with Judge Rosser and handed the document to him.

"I would thank you to submit this to the Supreme Court for me," he said simply.

Maben left town with Pruiett. While he was figuratively shaking the dust of the Pottawatomies from his boots, they were literally washing it from their dry gullets with illicit whiskey from Maben's grip. As the little train lurched and bumped along, they were talking of Charley West and the next election. Their comments were interrupted by frequent flights of laughter, laughter that was unreserved and a little vindictive. Who was going to be Governor now?

Action in the Tegeler case re-united Pruiett with his destiny. What was political preferment and fat civil-case fees, when memories of Little Rock and Rusk had to be avenged? Could he be untrue to power which had sustained him, and made him, in the valley? He thought of his vow as he journeyed back to White Bead. Sam Garvin had died in July of 1908, and Pruiett went to the burial. He abandoned affectation. He became the murder specialist. "It was along about this time that Pruiett began to get higher types of murderers for clients."

Patrolman S. G. Crow blushed as he asked for his ten day Summer vacation. "My wife's about ready to have her baby," he mumbled.

"Don't let 'em clip the end off of it, if it's a boy," the Chief roared, slapping him on the back. "He won't be a hundred per cent American that a'way. Good luck to you, son."

The baby came that night. On the next, Patrolman Crow, in plain clothes, was dragged out the back door of Nick Kaufman's southtown bootleg joint, and deposited amongst the empty tin cans and beer bottles.

"That stuff don't work with me," Nick said, dusting off his fat hands. "They don't shoot craps 'til their money's all gone, an' then pull a star an' demand it back, an' get anywhere with it. We didn't kill him, did we, boys?"

"Naw," one of them growled, "but we done a good job of markin' him up. He'll have you pinched, as soon as someone takes him to town. You know how cops are."

"I can pay a fine in the City Court better'an I can give him back all he lost," Nick grinned.

When the man with the warrant came, Nick went quietly. "These boys here, one of 'em is my brother; can they go along for makin' my bond?"

"Sure," the officer replied, "there's plenty of room in the wagon. If they don't mind ridin' in the cage, it's fine with me."

"It's fine with us," the bondsmen agreed. "She's nice an' black, like a hearse, an' them fine black horses would look good for a funeral. Well, just play like it's a ceremony, an' we're leavin' the church in the stiff-wagon. You're the head man, Nick. You get in and pick out the best seat."

It was Nick's last ride. "Brawl Ends In Killing," the morning paper announced on August 14, 1910. "T. Nick Kaufman shot by Patrolman Crow. Suspecting no violence, the customary proceedings of searching the prisoner was started. Kaufman had been brought to the window of the cage, a place about 25 by 20, cut off from the rest of the large basement room by wire netting. His two friends, Evans and Miller, with others gathered around. They were bunched up at the window, eager for news of the charges to be preferred."

"Crow walked into the room. Very deliberately, he drew his revolver and slipping near the cage window, fired. 'You dirty dog, I've got you, and I want your brother next'."

"A brother rushed to the man's side. In the blood that was streaming the floor, he knelt beside him. He felt his heart, and moaning, mumbled a prayer for life. Kaufman, with blood in mouth and nostrils, clothes soaked with blood, with ghastly, distorted face, was dead.

Crow had sent three forty-five slugs through Kaufman's midsection before the pistol could be wrested from him. Evans and Miller, innocent by-standers, had been wounded by lead that had already passed through big Nick. "After Crow was taken to the County Jail and charged with murder, he refused to talk, in accordance with the instructions of his lawyer, Moman Pruiett."

Samuel R. Cunningham was recognized as the new city's ablest medical doctor. He lived in a big house next door to Pruiett.

"I want a' expert to testify to Crow's mental condition," Pruiett said, bluntly. "I'm pleadin' insanity, an' I want a doctor to prove it."

Cunningham put his sock covered feet against the rail of his veranda. He and Pruiett were discussing the case non-professionally, at home. "I'd have to say that he had a very slight paranoia," Cunningham replied. "I understand that he had been mistreated, and that these men had inflicted a rather serious head injury when they beat him up the day before; but, that doesn't make insanity."

"I ain't got no use for that paranoia stuff, an' inferiority inhibitions an' so forth," Pruiett said. "Like I told 'em at the preliminary, Crow was sufferin' from confusional insanity. He didn't know... "

"Confusional insanity?" the doctor inquired. "I never heard of it."

"I never did either, before, but what difference does that make? There had to be a first time for some one to hear of this paranoia crap you just mentioned."

"What do you mean by 'confusional insanity'?"

"He was confused when he killed Kaufman," Pruiett answered. "He was kind of nutty, even before that gang out there whipped him. I got witnesses to prove that he'd pick up old pop bottles out at the ball park, an' pour them little drippin's from the bottle into his ear. He claimed that it was a sure cure for earache he always had."

"That sounds silly to me," Cunningham said.

"What's silly about it?" Pruiett demanded. "Here's a man that's off to start with. A sane man don't pour soda water in his ear. He goes out an' a bunch of thugs whip him 'til he comes unwell; 'til they have to take him to a hospital an' patch his head up. If he's a killer, premeditatin' a crime, is he goin' to have his victim arrested, an' hauled up before the police, so's that he can get a pot shot at him? Why, hell no, not if he's normal."

"That's what he did do, isn't it?" Cunningham asked.

"Sure, but don't miss the logic. He signed a complaint an' had Kaufman arrested, just like you, or any other citizen would have done. He was goin' to let the law take its course. When they brought Kaufman in, an' he saw him, a cog slipped somewhere. He got confused. He forgot that the law was in charge of him. He forgot ever'thing but one, an' that was that he had been injured by this fellow Kaufman. He started shootin', an' hit two innocent men while he was doin' it."

"You might be a good lawyer," Cunningham laughed, "but you'd better stick to your own field. You've no business trying to invent a new kind of psychological state. It'll make you ridiculous, this confusional insanity stuff."

"What the hell do I care if it does, so long as I win my case?" Pruiett answered. "Pourin' pop in his ear, an' bein' confused about what was goin' on, is all the defense I'm goin' to have in the Crow case."

Pruiett was ordinarily ready for trial; he trafficked in delays and continuances in only occasional cases. The Crow case came up early for hearing in January of 1911. "The case promises to be one of the hardest fought ever tried at the courthouse." Pruiett had found the right doctor and was promoting his insanity plea. "At this juncture, Attorney Pruiett read a hypothetical question embracing two typewritten pages, for the purpose of eliciting from Dr. Rily an answer to prove that Crow, after having been terribly beaten and under the influence of whiskey, was irresponsible for shooting Kaufman."

The hard fought ones were the ones that Pruiett liked better. He had the jury so well in hand that the evidence didn't make much difference. A charming, brilliant fellow like Pruiett was entitled to win his case. They couldn't turn him down. " 'Not Guilty' Is Verdict In The Crow Murder Trial. Five minutes after the foreman announced the verdict, Crow walked from the courtroom, a free man."

CHAPTER ELEVEN

How Pruiett encounters an enemy in need, and saves him, for a valuable consideration, from the penalty which is usually provided for the crime of murder. And how he displays his prowess in the scenes of his childhood, to postpone, and render more sweet and profound, his vengeance for an old, but never-to-be-forgotten injury.

"The most shocking and dastardly crime that has occurred in this section of the state in a quarter of a century took place between 3:30 and 5:30 o'clock yesterday afternoon, when Mrs. John Winkleman was brutally murdered at the family residence on Spring Street, three blocks from the public square." The shocking announcement was being made by the *Fayetteville Daily* on August 27, 1909, under the bold head, MOST SHOCKING MURDER. "The boldness and audacity of the crime stunned the citizens of Fayetteville with its fiendish enormity."

"In the old two-room house in the back of the yard, Mr. White opened the buttoned closet door and a most gruesome sight was presented." There lay the dead body of Aunt Carrie Winkleman, her clothes bespattered with her own blood and her head fearfully crushed. In searching the room this morning, a large iron bolt with a nut on the end was found wrapped in a bloody bonnet between the mattresses of the bed. This is undoubtedly the bludgeon the villains used."

"It has been understood for years that Mrs. Winkleman carried a large amount of money on her person. She lost some money once in a Nebraska bank failure, and she was afraid of banks. She had about $10,000 when she left the restaurant yesterday. Her daughter testified before the coroner's jury to this fact, and that she carried the money in a ducking wallet attached to a belt worn under her clothes."

The reward for the apprehension of Aunt Carrie's murderers, offered by the governor, the family and public-spirited private agencies, totaled $3,500. Two drifters, who had been renting a shack on the back on the Winkleman lot and who were indelibly connected with the crime, were captured. Gus Sartain, with efforts to resist extradition defeated, committed suicide by hanging himself in his Sacramento, California, jail cell.

N. H. "Red" Fox, an Oklahoma gambler, was arrested at Sulphur, Oklahoma, and brought back to Fayetteville, charged with murder.

Pruiett, the lawyer, had built a more stately mansion for his soul, or in terms more probably correct, the Moss and Mark Baum estate had built a more stately one for his murder clientele, and he was contributing by the month for the use of a portion of its elegant interior. The Baum building on the corner of Grand Avenue and Robinson Avenue was the class of Oklahoma's principal city, six stories of fluted stone blocks, with gray marble slabs about its lower extremities, and marble pillars supporting its ornamented ground floor entrance and arcade. Although the dusty atmosphere was full of talk of taller ones, and finer ones, the natives scoffed. The Baum was real big town. It couldn't be surpassed.

The floor of the fifth story offices was covered with Brussels. The surplus of fine mahogany which furnished the place spoke of extravagance—slightly vulgar extravagance—and explained, after one became familiar with the proprietor's background, how he was attempting to compensate a youth starved soul with long coveted luxuries.

What the dealers in the young city lacked he had required them to get, because a combination plan of the Washington offices of Silas Hare and J. F. McMurray were what he had in mind when he started out to furnish his new suite, and as the cost was not being considered, he got just what he wanted. Blood-colored drapes, of such voluminous folds as to almost obstruct the passage of sunlight from the outside, curved and drooped from above the tall window casements to the green carpeted floor. Strong electric lamps, close to the ceiling, reflected themselves from the shining polish of the desks, tables and chairs, and caused them to shine like a multitude of mirrors. A great iron cabinet safe, plain of exterior and as high as a man's head, and so broad that it seemed to cover the entire wall space of one end of the office, shouted out to attract the attention of the visitors, so inconsistent was it with the ornamented splendor of the other furnishings within the room.

The master was prosperous. He was as resplendent, personally, as the equipment of his office. The hair was as shimmering in the light of the lamps as the polished top of his desk, while it carried a congenital quality of luxury about it that could not be reproduced in the inanimate things—even in the superior craftsmanship of the woodwork. His features, a little less bronzed and rugged, yet more mature and handsome, retained their two salient features, the undershot jaw and the shaggy eyebrows.

His high white collar was bat-winged, as the prevailing style for men of his position and of the period dictated, while the black silk four-in-hand, tied loosely beneath his chin, was surmounted by a diamond stud as large as a sling-shot pebble from the shallows of White River. His black broadcloth coat was outlined at the lapel with black braid; his dark striped trousers were immaculately pressed, while a pair of black shoes were shined in the same efficient manner as he would have shined them himself in that distant day of his boyhood. A hand, which nervously twisted a black cigar, or passed it back and forth from a scowling mouth to the ash desecrated elegance of the table top, bore a diamond larger than the one in the scarf at his throat.

Pruiett had developed an eloquent scowl. He scowled and glared at his office girls; he practiced it in the mirror or on the neighbors kids who romped across his immaculate lawn, and on the clients who paid so dearly to see him. He could scoop the chin forward, contract the bushy brows into a single furry line, and bite the big cigar until he had a picture of brutal and abandoned ferocity. He had found that the scowl simplified the handling of business about the office—in weeding out the undesirable element which he couldn't find time to represent.

"Pruiett!" he bawled into the transmitter of the upright telephone which set on the corner of his desk. It was his own way of answering a 'phone. He didn't say 'hello' or announce the number; he merely bellowed his name. "Yes—this is Pruiett. If you got any one there that wants to talk to Pruiett, put 'em on the line. I'm waitin'."

"This is Red Fox, judge," he heard a coarse voice over the wire. "Remember me? Fox, in the Chickasaw Nation?"

"Hell yes, I remember you," Pruiett yelled. "How old would I have to get to forget about you? What do you want?"

"I'm in jail, down here at Fayetteville," Fox said. "They got me for..."

"Why certainly," Pruiett interrupted, "they got you for murder an' I know all about it. What's more, you're guilty as hell. They got you in the right place."

"Look here, judge," Fox pleaded, "I'm in a bad scrape. I got to have some help. What I called you about, I want to apologize. I want to square up that old trouble; let's forget about it, an' you represent me. I just got to get you to help."

"I ain't interested," Pruiett announced, bluntly. "I don't try cases for you, or your kind. I wouldn't help you out of hell if your back was broke. I wouldn't..."

"I got some money..."

The receiver was passing between Pruiett's ear and the 'phone hook, with a vicious gesture of disgust, as Fox said it, but Pruiett heard it. Pruiett paused to reflect. So, he had some money, did he? The old woman was supposed to carry ten or twenty thousand around in a pouch under her bustle. Maybe Red had some real money. And wasn't he the kind of rat that would make the public miserable so long as he was at large? Wouldn't society be better off if Red got his neck stretched? Wouldn't the system gloat, if it put a plug in for justice in Arkansas, the same as in Texas, the territory, or Oklahoma? Pruiett picked up his 'phone.

"Is that you, Red?" he inquired, when the connection was complete again. "This is Pruiett. Maybe I was a little hasty in the way I talked to you; sometimes I pop off a little too quick. Would you still like to talk to me?"

"You're damn right, I would," Fox answered.

"I got some other business in Fort Smith in just a few days. I got to come to Arkansas anyway. I'll just get me a ticket on up to Fayetteville, and come in an' see you. We might be able to make a deal."

Pruiett drummed his desk and smoked. He could see through the fog-like haze of the office the rough interior of the old courtroom at Pauls Valley, with a jury in the box and Jeff Aiken in the prisoner's pen. He was fighting for Jeff and the contingent fee that went with Jeff's liberty. The defendant had given him a note for seventeen hundred and fifty American dollars, payable at the Madill Bank, if and when Pruiett set him on the ground a free man. He smiled as he recalled some of the crude, but none the less effective, maneuvers he had resorted to in proving Jeff's innocence.

And, he remembered the victory. It had been sweeter then, he ruminated. Pay was better now, courts were more refined, more cultured and more discreet, although the juries were just as gullible and he cleared his clients just the same, but there was something lacking from the savor of the winning. Yes; he readily recalled the exhilaration he had experienced when Jeff and Marie, his wife, broke their own long embrace to inflict it, jointly, around his neck, while the woman kissed him and thanked him again and again.

"Jeff," he had said, "that note you made was put up at the Madill bank, by your dad. I wasn't to get any more fee if you didn't come clear; but, if you did, the note was to be paid. Is that your understandin'?"

"Yep—an' I'm glad to pay it, Mr. Pruiett. You just don't know how happy I am to pay it."

"Is it good—now?" Pruiett inquired. "Have you got the cash?"

"The bank's got it, an' they'll pay it and hold the note. Any time you want to go over there you can get your money. An' I sure am much obliged to you..."

Pruiett smiled as he remembered the payment; the banker counting out the stack of money, and pushing it over to him. But, the smile froze, and he chewed his stub cigar savagely, as he recalled the sequel; his visit to a frame shack of a drug store; his customary quest for a drink of whiskey.

The clerk had worn a striped vest. "I'm Moman Pruiett, from Pauls Valley," Pruiett told him.

"How are you today, Mr. Pruiett?" the clerk said. "Seems like I've heard tell of you before."

"I ain't no Federal," Pruiett continued.

"No, you ain't no Federal," the clerk repeated.

"An' I'm dry as a chip. I got to have a drink."

"Sorry," answered the clerk, shaking his head, "but I ain't got a bit of licker. An' I don't believe you'll find any in town."

"I want it for myself," Pruiett assured him. "I ain't got no Indians I want to feed it to. I'm dry, an' I got the money to pay for a drink, so why can't I get a drink?"

"I'd be glad to give you one, if I had it, but I just ain't," said the clerk. "I just ain't got her."

"You got a pretty good drug store here," Pruiett observed.

"She's perty good for Madill," the clerk agreed.

"An' you got some alcohol, for filling prescriptions, now, ain't you?"

"Yep. I got the alky."

"An' you got some distilled water, for mixin' up stuff to sell to the customers, ain't you?"

Yep, I got the water; got plenty of water."

"An' you got syrup of pepsin, right there on the shelf, ain't you?"

"I shore have; more than I need by a hell of a lot."

"Then let me have a little of each, an' I'll show you how to mix up the best god damned drink you ever saw," Pruiett urged.

The druggist was unimpressed. "Let me see that prescription," he said. "You know how these Feds are. They get real inconsiderate of guys sellin' alky in this Injun territory. That's all I need to see—the prescription."

Pruiett pulled a bulging wallet off his hip and selected a flapping $20 bill. The druggist's eyes glittered as he quickly inspected the contents of the purse. "There you are," Pruiett grinned. "There's the doctor's orders. Give me the stuff."

"Just step this way, back in the back," the man smiled. "I can see you're the right kind of a feller. We'll mix it up back here."

"Have one?" Pruiett inquired, as he went through the final motions of shaking the ingredients together.

"Don't care if I do," was the agreeable answer.

Sitting on a keg, Pruiett had several. The druggist did likewise. "Ever play any poker?" the druggist inquired casually.

"I play for keeps," Pruiett boasted. "I ain't been beat in a long time, an' if you got real genuine affection for your money, stay out of a game when you see me in. I wins."

"They have a game upstairs, ever' once in awhile, but I don't get in much," the confidential friend continued. "I don't savvy it so much, an' I'm just unlucky as hell. Some guys that don't play near as much as I do will win my money ever' time. The guy that relieves me, owns half the joint, is so lucky he could fall in the toilet an' come out smellin' like a tulip. But not me..."

"What time you get off?" Pruiett asked.

"I ought to be off any time, now," he said. "I got a relief man on the way. Supposed to be here at noon. Let's have another drink out of your bottle."

"You want to see a real poker player in action?"

The druggist laughed. "Maybe I could pick up a little learnin', watchin' you. What's on your mind?"

"I got plenty of time, an' plenty of money," Pruiett announced. "Maybe you'd take me by an' make me acquainted with the boys in the game. I'd like to play awhile."

"Well," mused the druggist, "I'll try it for you. I don't know whether the boys'll like it, but I'm pretty solid with 'em. Soon as my man gets here, we'll go upstairs an' see about it."

It had been Pruiett's first meeting with N. H. Fox. He grimaced at the recollection. The steps of the rickety wooden stairway up the outside of the frame building were as vivid in his retrospect as were the notches on the marble staircase there in the Baum, which he frequently traveled, when the iron-grilled car that lurched up and down the shaft in the building's entrails was out of order.

Three men were sitting beside a round table in the center of the barren room. "This is Mr. Fox—Mr. Pruiett," the drug man explained. Pruiett, flushed with the rapid drinking he had been doing, was conscious of an involuntary shiver between his shoulder blades as he shook hands with the gambler.

"What's the deal?" the druggist inquired.

"No game," Fox said. "Just waitin' for some of the boys to drop in. I'm ready any time."

"I got a little to invest with you in some stud," the man from the drugstore stated, "and Mr. Pruiett wants to make expenses on his trip over here before he starts back. Shall we start somethin'?"

"Whatever you boys say," Fox agreed.

"Let's get started," said Pruiett.

Fox took a box of heavy bone chips from a wooden cabinet on the wall. Pruiett noticed, while the door was open, that a heavy caliber pistol, with white handles, lay on the upper shelf of the cabinet. He cut himself a chew of tobacco and sat down at the table.

"I'm out'a chips again—an' out'a dough, too." The man from the drug store pushed his chair back. "Deal me out this time. I'll go downstairs and get a lamp, an' bring it up."

"Jesus Christ," Pruiett growled, "I been here all afternoon. Say, shake up another quart of the pepsin licker, will you?"

"Sure thing," he answered, "Anything else?"

"Might send up a nigger wench," Pruiett muttered. "I got to change my luck pretty soon, or go busted."

The druggist clattered down the stairway with a coarse laugh. Pruiett and Fox butted it out, head to head. By eleven, Pruiett was down his $1,800 and had six checks, for a hundred each, in the game. The dim light, and Pruiett's increasing drunkenness, made Fox both bold and careless. Pruiett saw why he was losing—and why he couldn't win.

He pushed his chair back. "I'm gettin' screwed," he said, looking Fox intently in the eye.

Fox flushed and assumed a half threatening, half defiant look. "What do you mean by that?" he growled.

"There ain't enough chips in that pot," Pruiett said.

"Oh," Fox said, with obvious relief. "Maybe I'm short; maybe you're short. Let's check it up."

Pruiett stood beside the table and pretended to count the heap in the middle. When he had a handful of the heavy chips, he drew back and hurled them with all his strength into the face of the gambler. Blinded and dazed, Fox staggered toward the wall cabinet, with blood spurting between the fingers spread over his face. Pruiett, mindful of the gun there, slipped out the door and down the old stairway.

Why not represent the red-headed outlaw? He questioned himself, interrupting his reverie. If he was in serious trouble, and had the money, what mode of revenge would be sweeter than making him pay? Would representing him in court make any difference later—if favorable opportunity presented itself—in him killing him, as he had always wanted to do? What would be nicer—a front row seat at Red Fox's hanging, or seeing him walk out a free man, to bilk, and cheat and murder some more?

Fox was in an inside cell on the second floor when the officers ushered Pruiett in to see him. The prisoner, confined and in trouble, had to grin and try to be conciliatory. The visitor was as cold and tough as his superior position entitled him to be.

"I'm glad you came, Pruiett," he said, trying to sound cheerful.

"I had some other business over here an' was comin' anyway. I only came a day or two earlier than I had planned." Pruiett had his reasons for lying.

"Sure," said Red, "but I'm glad you came. They're trying to give me a bum rap, and I need some help."

"All right," said Pruiett. "All right. Where do I come in?"

"Let's forget that other stuff, you know what I mean. Let me square myself and tell you I'm sorry. Maybe it wasn't all my fault, but I'll say it was, and say I'm sorry besides. What do you say?"

Red was straining to talk through the bars, and talking fast. His manner suggested that he considered a willingness on his own part to admit a fault and apologize, all that any one could ask for or expect.

"All right," Pruiett repeated the phrase. "Say you do. Where do I come in?"

"Go to the bat for me," Fox said. "I want you to take my case. I'll get you five hundred bucks."

Pruiett sneered. "You steal $2,000 from me, and tell ever' one on the Washita River I moved out of the valley because I was afraid you were goin' to kill me, an' you'll pay me $500?"

"But I'm broke, Pruiett," the gambler lied and begged. "I've had a lot of tough luck. I lost a lot of money..."

"The old girl had twenty or thirty thousand on her hip an' ever' one in town knows it. You got two or three good farms an' plenty of money stashed away. If you called me up here for a joke, I can't laugh. I got a cracked lip." Pruiett was gathering in the revenge like Red had scooped in the blue chips on that previous occasion well remembered by both of them.

"I didn't do this job, judge," Fox replied, with an offended look on his red countenance. "I told you this was a bum rap. They got me all wrong, an' I can prove it."

"Well, if you've got such a good defense, you can put it on by yourself," Pruiett said, as he started to back away from the bars. "You won't need me, an' I haven't got time right now for a charity job."

"How much will it take? Maybe I can get some help?" Red said.

"Five thousand, cash, an' I hope you can't make it. I don't want to take the job." Pruiett was carelessly rolling a fat cigar between his hands and watching the prisoner.

"You won't double me, will you, Pruiett?" Fox inquired, pleadingly and searchingly. "You won't hold that old grudge agin' me? I know you can get me off if you start into..."

"You come clear," said Pruiett with the finality of a judge passing judgment. "You come clear an' you don't even have to thank me; but, who puts up that five? I have it in cash before I make a move."

Fox motioned for him to come close to the iron. He whispered the name of a man to see and a message to give him, then dropped heavily to a sitting posture on the metal bunk. What a spot to be in. The way Pruiett hated him he could take his cash and give him the twist. He could lay down and let the jury braid the rope. Red turned his head slowly from side to side and rubbed the bulging swells of his muscular neck with apprehension. He was remembering the stories about old Ike Parker and Arkansas justice. What a hell of a spot to be in.

The day for the trial of the case entitled the *State of Arkansas vs N.H. alias Red Fox,* in Washington County, Arkansas, was at hand. The state was demanding its forfeit, for Red, according to the language of the indictment, "did kill and murder one Carrie Winkleman by striking, beating and wounding her, the said Carrie Winkleman on the head and body with a hard substance, a deadly weapon, the name and character of which is unknown to this Grand Jury..."

A group of men stood about the judge's bench in the courtroom. It was time for court to open. Voll and Wythe Walker, distinguished members of the Arkansas bar, had been hired as special prosecutors. Hugh Densmore, and Homer Peel, Congressmen, were there to lend the weight of their good position to the prosecution while the jury was being selected. Enoch Fagan, of the old Paris, Texas, firm of Brants and Fagan, was with them.

"Who's the man with the sinister countenance?" Wythe Walker inquired sarcastically, jerking his head in the direction of the main entrance into the room.

They all turned. "I don't know," Voll Walker drawled, toying with the sharp tip of his van dyke, "but from his general cut, I'd say he was a son-of-a-bitch that would fight on state occasions. He looks like he's got some guts."

A stylishly dressed man, with shining black hair, was looking about, inquiringly, as he stood near the door. He wore a high bat-wing collar and a black tie. Diamonds sparkled from various points on his make-up.

"That's Moman Pruiett," Fagan muttered. "He's our competitor. I heard he'd been hired in this case; but, I wasn't sure."

Pruiett was striding toward them. "Do you suppose he heard what I said?" Voll Walker whispered.

Fagan and Pruiett shook hands. "This is Pruiett, from Oklahoma

City," Fagan began, introducing him around. "He used to crowd into my little old office, down in Paris, whenever he could pick up a stray case. Maybe he'll let me use his, now that he's going so good, after I lose out, and don't have any."

"I remember you, Mr. Walker," Pruiett was saying, as he shook hands with Voll. "I used to shine your shoes, every day, on the porch of the old Van Winkle Hotel. And, I remember you, too, Mr. Densmore. I've shined your shoes many a time."

"What you doin' down here, Moman?" Fagan inquired.

"I'm hired in the Red Fox case," Pruiett answered. "What you doin' down here?"

"I'm in the Fox case, too."

"You mean, they got a special prosecutor hired?"

"They got some prosecutors hired, all right," Fagan grinned, "Voll and Wythe, but they ain't hired me. I'm donatin' my services."

"What the hell for? You ain't kin to the Winklemans, are you?" Pruiett asked.

"Nope, but I'm the prosecutin' attorney for Murray County, Oklahoma, where Red was arrested, and where he's been livin' for the past five years. I couldn't convict him of nothin' down there, but he's wore me out, tryin'. I figured I'd come over and help the boys. I know his record—and maybe I can help get him hung. That way, I won't have half so much work to do at home next year."

"What if Red comes clear?" Pruiett laughed, "you'll have a' extra load of ill will to carry. He'll really cause you some trouble."

"I ain't worry'en about that," Fagan laughed, winking broadly at the Walker brothers.

"Attorney Wythe Walker, assisting with the prosecution, made the opening statement yesterday afternoon on April 27, 1911. He said that the state would prove that Fox was in Fayetteville on Saturday, before the murder on Wednesday, and that he ate a chicken dinner at the restaurant which the murdered woman operated; that he was accompanied by Gus Sartain; that he exhibited $2000 in a roll of bills to witnesses at Sulphur, Oklahoma; that he was overheard, telling Sartain in a pool room, that 'she carries the money on her person'."

Gus Sartain was the hapless hop-head who had saved the state the trouble and expense of a trial by hanging himself in his jail cell. He evidently hadn't heard of Pruiett. And, try as he would, Pruiett couldn't keep references to Sartain's self-destruction out of the evidence in the Fox trial. One witness was informed that Sartain died in California, in the city of Sacramento. Every syllable on Sartain's consciousness of guilt was extra load for overloaded old Red Fox to carry.

Pruiett destiny—Pruiett luck—was seated on the defense side of the table. Seated in the jury box, fully qualified to serve, were two ancient reminders of the Arkansas wanderings of the Pruiett family. Pruiett felt that, when the time came, he would know how to handle them. One was F. L. Van Zant, the quick tempered Beau Brummel of his run-away experience, now concealing the stern conceit of his countenance with a network of furrows and wrinkles and a square-cut white beard. The other was old Noah Stockburger, of Winslow. Pruiett, as a lad of twelve or thirteen, had gone to the Stockburger farm for a heifer calf, bought by the itinerant butcher for sale to the railroad crews.

Van Zant was still the fashion-plate, as preened and immaculate, with his dress and his snow white hair and beard, as he was in the days of the old Van Winkle's glory. Stockburger was bald, wrinkled and debilitated; he squinted to see the witnesses and cupped his hand behind his ear in an attempt to hear the evidence; but, Pruiett knew him. Neither of the jurors had a suspicion of having seen the overbearing defense counsel before; but, the counsel had recognized them on the instant. The inexorable artist of age and decay could not paint a disguise to deceive the keen eye and the photographic memory of Pruiett.

"The examination of witness on the part of the state is being carried on by Wythe Walker, and by Attorney Prewitt [sic] for the defense. Judge Maples found it necessary to reprimand the crowd for 'laughing out loud'. It was when Attorney Prewitt asked Mr. King, who was on the stand, if he knew the present whereabouts of Mr. Isgreig, a defense witness. The witness replied that Isgreig was dead, and that he didn't know where he was."

In the face of the disheartening proof, Pruiett set out to make an alibi stand up. While the plan of operation was practically the same as in the old John Evans and Doc Richards case, the technique was immensely improved. Washita witnesses, who had not seen active service since Pruiett's lamented removal from the valley, swore that Red had been with them, miles removed from the place of the tragedy, at the time when it must have occurred. With self-defense and the un-written law eliminated, the alibi was about all that he had left to offer. It was enough to raise a fact question, something to talk to the jury about, and that was about all he wanted. He had some things to say to that jury.

Charles Hillman Brough, Arkansas's Governor from 1917 to 1921, was holding down the chair of Economics, Law and Sociology at the State University. On the day the Fox case was to go to the jury, the courtroom balcony was reserved for Brough and his law class, in order for them to hear the arguments. The Walker brothers were the big guns of the Arkansas Bar. The Voll Walker Memorial Library on the University campus is an exhibit to support his claim to fame. The Winklemans were prominent citizens. Red Fox was a no-good Oklahoma convict with an Oklahoma lawyer who didn't show the proper amount of diffidence toward the Walkers, Judge Maples or the Arkansas courts. With it well settled that censor, in the form of a death sentence for Red, was about to be made, Fayetteville, with its budding lawyers, turned out *en masse.*

Wythe Walker opened the arguments for the State. According to the *Fayetteville Daily* "with clear and sweeping words reviewed the testimony of the witnesses, analyzing the testimony and showing the strength and weakness of each. Now and then, in a burst of mighty eloquence he would tear the testimony of a witness to shreds. Then again, with sarcasm which burnt like red hot caustic, he would show the falsity of the testimony of a witness. Mr. Walker's review of the testimony was masterful and his conclusions were almost irresistible. He has been in nearly every big criminal case that has been tried in this county for the past twenty years, but he has rarely equaled, and never surpassed, his efforts in this case."

By agreement, Wythe Walker was to open, Fagan was to follow him for the state and then the defense was to have time for its plea. D. B. Horseley, the regular prosecutor, who was to begin the rebuttal speeches, was to be followed by Voll Walker. The State wanted the jury to have the strongest medicine just before it went out. Old Voll stroked his pointed mustache and shot his personality across the jury box rail. He was goin' to show old Red, and his insolent, shoe-shinin' graduate, a few tricks in Boston Mountain prosecutin'.

Enoch Fagan had his coat off in a quarter of an hour. In a half, he was lathering around the collar and at the armpits like a trotting mare in the breeches. Enoch's tough Texas manner, cradled with Colonel Jake

Hodges's, as was Pruiett's, was hardened with the callous of his Indian territory and early statehood practice. He disheveled his hair, tore off his collar, and ranted and stalked. Prejudices instead of laws; personalities instead of facts. Give the jurors a good time, and raise hell. He tried cases *a la Pruiett,* to the best of his inferior ability. He made a hell of a lot of noise.

"Gentlemen," he cried, rushing up to Pruiett and grabbing him by the arm, "I know this man better than any of you! He comes from my own state, and there, in the trial of a murder case, a bad case, where the defendant is utterly guilty, his services are indispensable."

Fagan was holding Pruiett's left hand above his head, and turning it so that the reflected brilliance of his huge diamond shone squarely in the juror's eyes.

"This man, when he leaves his State to defend a murderer, commands a fabulous fee. Look at that rock! See it sparkle? See it shine? Look at it, and tell me if you see in it any of the money that poor old Aunt Carrie saved to protect her against want in her declining days of helplessness? That's where he got it! That's it! He took the wealth to buy the diamond from the murderous paws of Red Fox, who killed and robbed Aunt Carrie. The red that shines there, with the blue, is the lifeblood of the poor old soul, trickling down from the wound which Red Fox made with his iron club."

Pruiett sat quietly, making no effort to draw his decorated digit from Fagan's unnecessarily rough grasp. He assumed an expression of tolerant lack of interest, and patiently waited for such time as the demonstrator would select for replacing his hand back in his lap.

"He commands fabulous fees," Fagan roared, "because he gets the result the murderer wants. I know him. I have seen him before a jury, and I realize his power. As I have seen it, you will feel it, and permit me to warn you against him. Don't be swayed by his matchless eloquence; do not abandon your understanding of truth, your conviction of right, for a siren song. This man, with his forensic perfection, has been trained and schooled by the great masters of the land, and he comes now on the blood money of our departed sister to gain a pardon for her murderer."

When Fagan released his hand and went into another phase of his argument, Pruiett was happy and his soul was at peace. It was not that he was glad to see Fagan let up on him, but that he had seen Fagan, by his own unsuspecting hand, open the gate of the avenue direct to Van Zant and Stockburger. While he had known how he wanted to approach them, the proper lane had not until then been opened to him.

But the hour, which was and was to become, the anathema of law and order and the men who had to try to assert it, had to come. The master of all fanatical forensics, the advocate who hypnotized his listeners, who fascinated them by his utter abandon in oratory, and who dazed them by the heights he could reach in ragged, uncouth vituperation, had to have his say.

Pruiett realized that regardless of the evidence, his client's unsavory record, known to the jury, and the brutality of the treatment meted out against a worthy citizen, made the balances sag away from him. Some one ought to be punished, and Red Fox was the only prisoner in the bull pen. He wasn't worth a damn, anyway, so let's don't let all the money the state's spent tryin' to hang him go to waste. Pruiett could usually figure pretty close to how a juror viewed a murder case.

He looked the jury in the teeth, told them that his client was guiltless, and demanded that they acquit him. Then, he proceeded to tell them why; and, when he had thoroughly disposed of the material issues, he moved into the realm of his most accomplished endeavor—the manipulation of emotion. The partisan *Fayetteville Daily* wasn't impressed, as it had been by Wythe Walker, but the speech mustn't have been so bad. "Attorney Prewitt [sic] made a strong plea for the defendant, reviewing the evidence at considerable length," was all the newspaper had to say, ten hours before the verdict.

"My friends," he said, warming up to his real task, "Counsel has presented me as a product of the far off lands of the masters, where I have been schooled in law, logic and oratory."

He paused, to press a slightly disturbed black wisp back into the bulk of his exuberant crown. He was speaking low and slow, from a confidential crouch. He was close to his dubious listeners. Gazing sadly at his diamond, he continued:

"...and the luxuries I have obtained at such a dear price, he says I have purchased with the blood of your townswoman. I see blood in it, and that white you see...," he was holding its shining brilliance in their very faces, "the white you see is sweat, sweat from my own brow as I labored an' suffered with you to lay the rails that carried the first train through this section of this state. The blood is from my own torn palms, carryin' burdens heavier than my youthful strength would permit me to carry, but toilin' on, and complainin' not."

The jury was impressed, but not understanding. There was a puzzled interest in their faces which he had purposely put there, preparatory to a climax which they would hear, feel and understand.

"I? I trained by the masters? The sum and total of my life's schooling was ten months, ten months spent in the country schools of Arkansas."

He lifted his face to the listening law class on the balcony above.

"Doctor Brough," he cried, "as a purported product of the masters, I commend you for the development of a wonderful institution. You have made this the Athens of a proud State, a State that is proud of you and your accomplishment here. I have crossed your campus, admired your fine buildin's and envied your handsome an' carefree students; but, I must confess, as a native of your state, I have never crossed the threshold of a single one of 'em, nor was I ever, in all my years, within the interior of a school of higher learnin'."

He was masterfully building to his climax. He had purposely avoided the direct gaze of Van Zant, whom he intended to make the brunt of his slow gathering attack. His attention went back to the diamond again.

"The utter privation of my boyhood is responsible for this weakness in me, this vulgarity, which I confess I am unable to control. As I washed dishes in the kitchen of the old Van Winkle Hotel for my supper, breathed the odor of the fine food as it went by me on its way to the dinin' room, an' saw the guests on the veranda in their fine clothes, an' jewelry, I promised myself that I would overcome my poverty, and that when I did, I would permit my hungry soul to partake of those things which then excited my interest an' envy."

He stole a quick glance at Van Zant. He was stroking his white beard with quick nervous jerks. He was ready for the thrust.

"And counsel, who would prostitute the truth to discredit me in my countrymen's eyes, for the sole purpose of prejudicin' an' convictin' my innocent client, will say that I lie, and that I borrow these references to the past from my fancy, for an ulterior an' unseemly purpose. I should then have corroboration for my story from one of repute; from one who can vouch for the truth an' correctness of my statements."

He strode to a position before the nervous Van Zant; he was still stroking the beard and pondering, but unable to penetrate the veil between those things the strange lawyer had suggested, and the indistinct, distant past.

"A fine gentleman strolled the veranda of the old Van Winkle," he barely whispered. "An undernourished boy with a blackin' box was slaving for nickels, sleepin' in a livery stable loft an' washin' dishes in the kitchen for his supper. The kid held the gentleman's horses for pennies and nickels, an' shined his fine boots, on the veranda, ever' day. And, one day, the careless boy let the brush slip, while he was blackin' the gentleman's shoes, an' the blackin' smeared his clean white socks. He lost his temper an' delivered a kick, an' the boy was cryin' in the cinders of the pathway..."

Van Zant saw it with the reference to the white socks. He turned helplessly from side to side in his chair, as if looking for a means of escape. He stroked the white beard frantically as he fought to restrain the tears which threatened to come. He saw the whimpering boy he had mistreated; remembered how he had bathed and aided him; saw Betty, his poorly dressed mother, coming for him and taking him home. "Can you vouch for me, Mr. Van Zant?" he whispered, "Can you do that much for me now?"

Pruiett whirled and strode to the corner occupied by the aged Stockburger. He pointed his finger at him dramatically, and cried:

"And you, Mr. Stockburger, can you vouch for me? The butcher's boy, who came that mornin' in the Spring to lead away your Mary's pet calf?"

The juror was confused. The events of that day were now as clear and complete in the Pruiett brain as they had been the day after. He had worried, childlike, about the grief of the coarse farm woman.

"You fastened my rope round her horns before you took your chain from around her neck," Pruiett reminded. "And I paid you the money my father had given me for you; the seven miserable dollars. You took it, reluctantly, like you felt that you were betrayin' a friend, sellin' your Bess to the butcher. But you were so poor then, my friend. You can understand my vulgar desire to wear this stone now, now that I can afford it, after those years of want and privation? You patted the calf, and when I started away, your wife, your Mary, called me back, and had me to lead her to the chimney corner, by the rough joint in the logs, while she gave her a farewell pinch of salt..."

A sob broke in the old man's throat as the word picture came suddenly upon his understanding. He cried convulsively.

"I can see her there now, with that salt in her poor work-worn hands, while the heifer licked it out. And she was cryin'. When I saw the tears in her eyes, runnin' down her cheek, I wondered. I was but a child. I wondered how she could be concerned over partin' with a yellow calf. And then she told me to go ahead an' her voice broke in a sob. I can understand it all now, Mr. Stockburger; we were all so very poor, an' she knew that you needed that money so desperately..."

Juror Stockburger had spread both hands across his face and was crying like a child. Fagan jumped up.

"Your honor," he said, "I must object to this line of argument. It is outside of the issues, and is too plainly..."

"You're overruled, Mr. Fagan," the Court ordered savagely. "You injected this issue in the case, and he has a right to answer. And I caution you not to interrupt counsel, or the Court, again..."

"...when I got to the road, she was still standin' there, in the same place. She hadn't moved, an' as I glanced back, I saw her take that faded old apron she was wearin' and with those red hands, wipe the tears from her eyes. She waved timidly, an' I know now that she wasn't wavin' at me..."

"I am one of you, gentlemen, an' I say counsel is tryin' to deliberately deceive you when he paints me as a mystic, a spell binder, a product of the masters..."

Voll Walker had arisen and walked to the side of Horseley, the State's attorney.

"Pruiett's got this jury and it's all over," he said. "I won't face them in a final argument. Tell the Winklemans they can keep the part of the fee that was to go to me. And tell that wild son-of-a-bitch to come by the hotel before he leaves town. I want to get down and give him the best shine he ever got in his life."

He strode to the crowded hooks along the wall, and taking down his broad brimmed hat, marched from the courtroom.

"For if it is not true, why should he have told you?" Pruiett was concluding his appeal. "His purpose is to degrade me, to the detriment of my client. Unless the prayers of a devoted an' sacrificing mother an' the unswerving application of an underprivileged boy constitutes a course under the great masters, counsel is wrong an' his declarations to you are false. By the same measure his charges against the defendant are unfounded, and crushed truth should rise to its innate glory by your righteous verdict of acquittal!"

Horseley had to close for the State. His effort was laborious and painful. He tried first to discredit, by flippant reflection, the good purposes of Pruiett. He met a solid front of hostility. He tried to argue the facts; but, he found that they had left his mind, and the bored expressions on the jurors arose to erect a barrier against their return to his distracted brain. Fine talk of classic verse and prose brought no semblance of interest to their passive faces. Walker had been right. Pruiett had taken the jury over and the case was won; the prosecutor's final floundering remarks were as good as concessions of defeat.

Crushed truth rose to mingle with the fleecy haze about the green crowned Boston Mountains. "At 3:40 o'clock Saturday afternoon, Homer Jackson swung back the doors of the Washington County Jail and N. H. alias 'Red' Fox passed out a free man for the first time in more than a year." He offered to shake hands with his lawyer, but the lawyer contemptuously ignored him.

Dr. Brough invited Pruiett to address his law class at the University. Voll Walker, with proud reference to the shoe shines he used to get, introduced him to the students. Pruiett hobbled to the front of the auditorium platform, suffering intensely from a recurrence of the inflammatory ailment of his knees and ankles. He couldn't resist the temptation to make an address to a bunch of collegians:

"Make hay while the sun shines," he said, "and be sure of one thing; your sins will always find you out."

"Young Tobe Lowry, of Hardin County, Kentucky, was indicted for the theft of a blue barrow," he told them as he concluded a short talk. "Colonel Lowry, the young thief's uncle, hired P. Watt Hardin, for whom Hardin County was named, and whose fame as a lawyer ranked with that of Vallandingham and Voorhees. Colonel Lowry was not so much concerned about the penalty his nephew might receive, upon conviction, as he was with the reflection against the name of Lowry, which would attach with a conviction."

" 'Good God, Judge,' the Colonel had cried, 'the Lowrys bear the noblest name in Kentucky. We must avoid this taint; you must lift us up out of the dust. Don't let a conviction for theft occur under the

Lowry name.' And old man Hardin had promised, with great gravity, to do his best for the family name."

"Colonel Lowry was waiting in Hardin's office to hear of the outcome of the trial. When the lawyer walked in, the old Colonel stood up, speechless in agitated anxiety. 'Young Tobe was adjudged not guilty', Hardin said, and before he could go further, Colonel Lowry interrupted him. 'Thank God,' he cried. 'Thank God. Our good name is preserved; the fair name of our family shall not be trampled in the dust'."

" 'Yes, we have been able to preserve the honor of the Lowry name,' Hardin replied, 'From external appearances the honor is preserved. But you know, and you must always know, Colonel, that every time we hear the name of Lowrys mentioned, the blue barrow will always squeal'."

While Pruiett was having his first contact with an institution of higher learning, the local police took Red Fox out of a saloon and tossed him back in the cooler. D. B. Horseley, abetted by the chagrined Enoch Fagan and the Winkleman heirs, pulled an old robbery charge on him. They charged that he "feloniously and violently, did by force and intimidation take from the person of Carrie Winkleman the sum of $10,000 in money—gold, silver and paper money, current specie of the State of Arkansas."

"Do you mean to say that you'll leave town without goin' down to see your client, Mr. Fox?" Voll Walker inquired. He and Pruiett were having a farewell drink in a saloon on the square, just before train time.

"I mean to tell you, Colonel, and others who might be concerned, that I don't go near the son-of-a-bitch," Pruiett answered, before he went into a spasm of laughter. "I sure ain't goin' down to see him."

"He's been sendin' word out ever' minute, suh, for you to hurry down there. Ain't he your client no more?"

"Maybe I defended him once; but, that don't make him my client, nor me his lawyer. I hope he stays in your jail 'til he rots."

"He's just bound to have a lot of money, somewhere," Walker observed softly. "Right now, after you've showed him what you could do, you'd be in a handsome position to fix a fee."

"There ain't enough money in the State of Arkansas to get me to set through another trial beside that red-muzzled bastard," Pruiett said, as he went into another fit of violent laughter.

"Here's to your good health, and your sense of humor," Voll said, holding up his drink. "I don't see the point, but I see that you can see it. To your good health, and your continued success."

Pruiett was convalescing at Mineral Wells, Texas, when word of Red's second trial came to him. With the same evidence, in the same courtroom, before the same judge and to a jury of the same county—but without Pruiett—Fox was convicted of the theft of Aunt Carrie's money, and sentenced to three years at the state prison in Little Rock.

The invalid lay in his wheel chair and laughed until the tears chased themselves down his face. "He's off," veranda strollers whispered in pity. "I wonder what could be so utterly humorous?" others observed. Like old Voll Walker, they knew little of Pruiett's hatred, nurtured by the years in his unyielding recollection. Red Fox at Little Rock. The dungeons were dark and damp. The foul atmosphere made your joints swell hideously, and produced an agony in them which rivaled the desolation of one's imprisoned soul. He knew Little Rock. He would never forget Little Rock.

The strollers continued to stare, and to turn aside; Pruiett forgot his pain, and rocked with the uncontrolled production of his mirth.

CHAPTER TWELVE

HOW PRUIETT IS DEPRIVED OF A FAT FEE AND TWO CLIENTS AT THE SAME TIME, BY THE INTERVENTION OF FEDERAL JUDGE LYNCH, AND HOW A GROUP OF MURDER CASES, WITH POSSIBILITIES, ARE NEVER TRIED. AND WHEREIN THE MURDERER'S FRIEND SITS AT THE WRONG SIDE OF THE COUNSEL TABLE, AND A THEATRICAL KILLER IS SENTENCED TO THE HENCEFORWARD IN CONFINEMENT FOR HIS MISDEED. AND HOW PRUIETT ATONES FOR HIS ASSISTANCE TO THE SYSTEM BY SUBVERTING IT WITH A DEAD CAT, AND THE LAW AND ORDER LEAGUE HOLD ITS COLLECTIVE NOSTRIL AS THE JURY SAYS 'NOT GUILTY'. AND HOW IT BEGINS TO APPEAR THAT GOOD MURDER CASES ARE NOT PRODUCED WITHOUT PRUIETT, AND THAT, ALTHOUGH A PRETTY MURDERESS GOES UP FOR LIFE, DESPITE HIS DEFENSIVE EFFORT, HE IS FURTHERING THE INTENT OF HIS UNHOLY PURPOSE AS THE MAJORITY OF HIS CLIENTS GO FREE.

"Take any of that money? Me? Hell no! Why, I ought to kill you." The expression of the man in rough ranch clothes showed that he was seriously considering murder as he spoke.

"Look here, Jesse West," the one he addressed answered, "I had to do it. I'm a Deputy Marshal now, and Jim Harbot shouldn't a'come around here, when he was so hot. Hell, anybody could have found out if I'd a'passed him up. That's what you call duty, Jesse. I didn't care a damn about the reward; but, I'm goin' to cut it with you; I'll give you..."

"Not none of that blood money, you don't; not a god damn cent. Jim Harbolt was my friend, an' he thought you was his friend. Maybe he did rob a few banks, an' a few trains; but, the Texas laws ought to be able to catch him. That's where he done it. Duty, hell. If you'd double-cross Jim, you'd double me, and..."

"You ain't got no call to say that to me, Jesse. We been together too long. Let's cut this reward, and get on about our business. We can't fall out over no damned road agent."

"Jesse West and A. A. "Gus" Bobbitt have fell out—they've split,"

RESIDENCE SECTION, ADA, OKLA.

MAIN STREET, ADA, OKLA.

the word was whispered along the curbs and hitching rails.

"Jesse West has gone in partners with his brother-in-law, Joe Allen, out in west Texas, at Canadian, and he's talkin' pretty dirty about Gus." The town talkers continued to dwell on the old partners' affairs. "Gus Bobbitt got to him in the ranch deal; he stole a lot and didn't pay for what he admitted he got; and what he says about Jesse and why they quit doin' business together ain't very complimentary."

Bobbitt couldn't be stopped. His brood mares brought mare colts

BROADWAY, ADA, OKLA.

DOWNTOWN ADA, OKLAHOMA, COUNTY SEAT OF PONTOTOC COUNTY, AND THE SITE OF THE LYNCHING OF JIM MILLER, B. B. BURRELL, JOE ALLEN, AND JESSE WEST IN APRIL OF 1909. THE FOUR MEN WERE TAKEN FROM JAIL BY A GROUP OF OUTRAGED CITIZENS AND HANGED AFTER BEING ACCUSED OF MURDERING A. A. "GUS" BOBBITT. COURTESY OKLAHOMA HERITAGE ASSOCIATION.

and his cows dropped heifer calves. "He's so damn lucky they drop twins, lots of time, and just as sure as he ships a trainload out, the market goes up. He must be livin' right," less fortunate stock raisers complained. Adjoining tracts were bought, or stolen, and added to his already extensive ranch. He hired all his work done and proceeded to lay back and rule the ranch-hands. As the years sped by and he lived high, his jowls began to sag and he pushed a prodigious belly about in front of him.

"Jesse West's back in town," the electric word went through the crowded stores and streets. "He's back in town, and Gus Bobbitt's in, too. There's a lot of trouble comin' up; you can watch out for a killin'."

"Who's that Jesse's got with him?" was the quiet inquiry. "That guy that looks like a Baptist preacher? Wonder where Jesse an' Joe picked up such a queer lookin' duck?"

IN EARLY 1909, JIM MILLER, JOE ALLEN, B. B. BURRELL, AND JESSE WEST WERE ARRESTED AND JAILED IN ADA FOR THE MURDER OF A. A. "GUS" BOBBITT. AWAITING TRIAL THE MEN LOUNGED IN THEIR JAIL CELLS, EATING MEALS PREPARED IN THE LOCAL HOTEL DINING HALL, AND BRAGGING THAT THEIR LAWYER, MOMAN PRUIETT, WOULD SOON BE ARRIVING TO HAVE THEM RELEASED. UNWILLING TO RISK THEIR ACQUITTAL, A MOB BROKE INTO THE JAIL, DRAGGED THE MEN TO A NEARBY LIVERY BARN, AND LYNCHED THEM IN APRIL OF 1909. HANGING, LEFT TO RIGHT, ARE MILLER, ALLEN, BURRELL, AND WEST. COURTESY ADA PUBLIC LIBRARY COLLECTION, WESTERN HISTORY COLLECTIONS, UNIVERSITY OF OKLAHOMA LIBRARIES.

"Is that a wig he's got on, or is it real hair?"

"Hell, it's real. I've seen it lots of time, down to Fort Worth. You know what it looks like? A damn possum's back, don't it?"

"That's the funniest lookin' guy I ever saw."

"That's Jim Miller."

"That's who?"

"That's Jim Miller. That's why I said to look out for a killin'."

"Jesus Christ! Is that Miller? Looks like a damn preacher like I said, doesn't he?"

"Well, Jesse West ain't runnin' with him for nothin'. He brought him in here for reasons. I'm gonna lay low, an' I'd lay low as well, if I was Gus Bobbitt."

Jim Harbolt was still behind steel in Texas. Statehood had come to the territory where he had been betrayed and captured, and where the partners West and Bobbitt had divided their lots. Talk, years of talk, that the talkers wouldn't forego, had augmented the smoldering feeling between the men, so that with the prospect of an ultimate meeting, what had began as a passive hatred was nearing the verge of an active, murderous feud.

West, in a plaid jumper, leaned against a muddy wagon wheel on the sunny side of the street. It was warm there, in out of the reach of the sharp February, 1909, gusts which made the opposite side uncomfortable. "Been seven or eight years since I seen old Pontotoc," he reflected. "These scrubby hills look pretty good, after all that flat sand out the panhandle way. Seems pretty good to get back."

Joe Allen, his tractable young brother-in-law, was beside him, as usual. "Ain't changed a bit," he chirped, "looks just the same to me as it did last time I was here."

A tall, sallow-faced man with splotched black and white hair, stood between Allen and West. He held both hands in the side pockets of a black overcoat.

"Just as many of these god damned Indians as ever, and just as lazy and dirty," West continued. "Ought to be some way the whitefolks could get rid of 'em; not have to have 'em around in the way, all the time."

"Ought to kill 'em," the man dressed in the black overcoat observed. "That's the best way. Kill 'em, ever' damn one."

West laughed. "That's all you think about, Jim, killin' somebody. But let me tell you, you don't need to waste no lead on these bastards. Just give 'em enough money to buy a little corn, an' they'll kill themselves. Likker, an' T. B. That'll get 'em all an' damn quick, too.

"It'll take too long, that way," Miller disagreed. "Christ, I get tired of seein' 'em ever' place I look. I say, line 'em up an' plug 'em."

"You give me the creeps, Jim," said West, bracing himself as if to suppress a shiver. "Think about somethin' else once in a while. Get them ideas..."

"There's Gus Bobbitt." Joe Allen interrupted them.

West set his jaw, and his eyes narrowed, as he watched the fat form of his old partner saunter out of a store across the street. "I don't know about that; maybe you got the right idea, at that," he said to Miller. "Remind me to talk to you about it... later."

Jim Miller's extensive reputation for being a professional assassin—he would kill anyone anywhere for $500—didn't seem to impress Bobbitt. He strolled up and down the opposite side of the Main Street, grinning insolently across at West and his two companions. Like kids, afraid to fight, Bobbitt spent the afternoon on the one side of the main street, West on the other, silently daring each other to stick his toe across the line. When Miller, West and Allen drifted off to a liquor joint, Bobbitt moved on down to the wagon yard.

"Jesse West's just as yellow as he always was," he told the man who was working there. "Him an' that god damned murderer he's got with him don't scare old Gus. Hitch them mules up an' get me out of here. I got a long drive out to the ranch ahead of me, an' I want to get started on it before night. An', if anyone asks you, just tell 'em the cow thieves don't scare Gus Bobbitt; not a damned bit."

When the sweating mules pulled the heavy load of cottonseed meal into the ranch yard that night and stopped with their chins over the wooden gate of their pen, no driver ambled down from the wooden seat. A ranch hand, swinging a lantern as he hopped up, recoiled from the headless hulk which sprawled back in the load of yellow feed. Bobbitt's head had been torn off by a shotgun's blast.

Jim Miller was caught in Texas, weeks later, and brought back to Ada. Jesse, with Allen trailing, kept out of sight for over a month, but the search that had been made for Jim Harbolt, those years before, was mild compared to that which was being carried on for them. West knew that he'd be implicated in the killing and that he'd have to stand trial for it, eventually, but he wanted to let the Pontotoc country cool off. He was going to surrender, but he wanted to make an arrangement or two before he did. There was a certain lawyer he wanted to have interested in his case.

"My name's Jesse West, and this here's Joe Allen; I married his sister." He was introducing himself to Pruiett. "I got an idea we're gonna need a lawyer."

"I wouldn't be surprised," Pruiett agreed, dryly, "but you ought to get a premium, instead of a rap, if you really killed Gus Bobbitt. That guy was no good."

"Did you know Bobbitt?" West took the hook and began to run with it, but quickly recovered. "I'm innocent. I didn't have nothin' to do with it an' I can prove it."

"Sure, if they'll give you a chance," Pruiett said, "but that's what you'd better make sure of. I knew Bobbitt, an' I knew his gang down there. They tried to shift a cattle stealin' job off onto Caddo Gordon, one of my nigger clients down in the valley; but, I cleared him. And, that guy Alexander, that Bobbitt hired to lie against the nigger, stole the cattle hisself, an' I proved it on him. They filed on him, then..."

"I heard somethin' about that, Pruiett, but what about us?" West was under a strain. "I got money, and I'm innocent. Will you represent me?"

"Such a hell of a question," Pruiett laughed. "From now on I'm your lawyer. An', for your first piece of information an' advice, I'm tellin' you that they've caught Jim Miller, an' got him in Ada. They're tryin' to keep it quiet; but, I had a fellow 'phone me. Will he talk?"

"Hell no," answered West.

"I don't know how they've missed you," said Pruiett, "hot as you are. But, I got to have a little time to study; to decide on what's the best thing to do. Duck in a roomin' house for tonight an' get me some word about where you are tomorrow. I'll try to see if it's safe to surrender; see if I can get a deal, a good stiff bond for immediate surrender."

West and Allen were captured as they stepped from Pruiett's office building onto the sidewalk. West didn't mind the end of the flight; but, he did object to being taken back into Bobbitt territory. "When the men were in the Oklahoma City police station here in April of 1909, they talked quite a little, and both of them said they would be killed if they were taken back to Ada, one of the officers who arrested them said. West, in particular, was sure that his trip to Ada would be his last. West told the officer the only reason he never killed Bobbitt was because he didn't get the chance. 'I would have killed him on sight,' West said. ' I didn't kill him—but that was the only reason why—I didn't get the chance'."

"These deputies say they'll take care of you, an' they're the law," Pruiett consoled him as the train was preparing to pull out. "Miller's preliminary's already set, an' I'll get an early hearin' for you. I'll be through with the case I got here in two days, an' I'll be right on down to Ada. We'll make a deal on the fee, an' leave it to me. Remember Sam Ashton?"

West smiled. "Sam had a rabbit's foot; I ain't that lucky. And them god damned friends of Gus'..."

"Sam had Pruiett," the lawyer corrected. "That's the difference. I got a formula that I know'll work in this case. All you got to do is make it worth while, like Sam's uncles did. See?"

"I see," said Jesse, "an' I got the stuff to make it damn interestin'. Just go to work, an' leave the pay to me."

Pruiett whistled gaily as he tipped the depot porter and sauntered up to the confection stand. He was catching the early morning train in late April of 1909 southeast to see West and Allen in jail at Ada. It was real business, and real money. "Got the mornin' paper, honey?" he inquired of the girl behind the counter. "Got to have somethin' to read on this rattler. Give me the *Oklahoman.*"

"I just barely can," said the girl, "they just got in. I haven't had time to look at it myself."

"I like 'em fresh," agreed Pruiett, "here's your money. Say! What the hell? Jesus Christ! Well, can you imagine that?"

The girl stared at him in frightened astonishment.

"Them's my clients," he howled, drawing back his nickel and flailing wildly at the paper. "That's where I was goin'; down to defend them guys. Look at it, will you? Hangin' there by their necks, dead as hell. The sons-of-bitches down there beat me out of a $5,000 fee."

The front page was smeared with the photo of four dead bodies, swinging by distorted necks. Pruiett recognized Jesse West's plaid cowboy shirt; he didn't need to read the accompanying story. He pulled his hat down and hurried out to the line of waiting hacks. He was going back to his office. He hadn't paid for the paper he clutched so viciously; his leather bag sat unnoticed beside the news counter in the station.

According to the story in the April 20,1909, issue of *The Daily Oklahoman:* "Four men, charged with the murder of A. A. Bobbitt, a wealthy cattle dealer of Ada, were quietly taken from the Pontotoc County jail at 2 o'clock this morning by a mob of sixty men and hanged to the cross-beams of an abandoned barn, a few feet from the jail. The mob dispersed as quietly as it was formed and the town knew nothing of the affair until the bodies were found early this morning. In the undertaking establishment of L. T. Walters lie the bodies of James Miller, B. B. Burrell, Joe Allen and Jesse West."

Pruiett was shaking his head sadly as he read the account under the photograph. Five thousand anyway; maybe he would have been able to hike it to seventy-five hundred, maybe ten thousand. Such a hell of a break. Such a case to try; to rant, and roar and raise hell in. It was gone. Why did he have to have all the hard luck?

According to the newspaper "When the mob entered the jail they encountered James McCarthey and Joe Carter, night guards, who, upon

WASHERWOMAN AGNES GILBERT SHOT AND KILLED HER ABUSIVE HUSBAND, ANDREW GILBERT, IN THE FRONT YARD OF THEIR HOME. WHEN NEIGHBORS TRIED TO CARRY HIM INSIDE AGNES ANNOUNCED "YOU AIN'T GOIN' TO TAKE HIM IN THAR AN' BLOODY UP MY CLEAN BED." WHEN MOMAN PRUIETT FIRST APPROACHED GILBERT IN HER JAIL CELL SHE REFUSED HIS HELP, BUT AFTER MUCH PERSUASION, SHE AGREED FOR HIM TO DEFEND HER. PRUIETT SO CONVINCED THAT SHE WOULD BE ACQUITTED HE PREMATURELY CELEBRATED HER RELEASE. HE WAS DUMBFOUNDED WHEN THE JURY FOUND HER GUILTY AND IMMEDIATELY FILED AN APPEAL THAT HE WON. COURTESY *MOMAN PRUIETT: CRIMINAL LAWYER.*

attempting to prepare for resistance were securely bound and left under the guard of a party of masked men. The mob then entered the sleeping apartment of Deputy Sheriffs Walter Goyne and Robert Nester, and compelled Goyne to deliver his keys to the cells. The leaders then entered the cells corridor, opened the cells in which the alleged murderers were kept and took them out without trouble save for West, who fought like a demon. He was struck over the head with a revolver and his skull fractured. The mob then repaired to an old barn forty feet from the jail, strung the men to cross-beams, and quietly dispersed."

Pruiett grinned as he reflected over the story. Old Jesse West went down battling. He was a real man; tough as buckskin, and always ready to fight. Old Jesse wasn't afraid of their ropes; he wasn't afraid to die. Pruiett knew that. He wanted to see how many of Bobbitt's gang of crooks he could mark before they got his feet swingin' off the ground like a big pendulum. Like a demon—was that what it said? Yeah! He could see him crumple—not all at once—but slow, and defiant, when they broke his head with the gun barrel. Pruiett could have experienced genuine sympathy for his friend of the new and short friendship, if it wasn't for his recollection of the lost fee.

"The crime for which these men were lynched was the murder of A. A. Bobbitt, a very prominent cattleman and former Deputy U.S. Marshal. Suspicion pointed to Miller, and after considerable search he was located near Fort Worth. The others were arrested at different places, West and Allen being the last captured, at Oklahoma City."

" The prominence of the parties in the case gives it additional interest. Miller was under indictment for murder committed in Johnston County, and it is talked freely on the streets that he is suspected of numerous other killings. West and Allen, who were brothers-in-law and lived at Canadian, Texas, were well-to-do stockmen. While living in Seminole Nation, a very bitter feeling arose between them and Bobbitt. Burrell lived at Fort Worth, but formerly lived in the Indian Territory, holding at one time a position of cashier of a bank at Duncan."

Pruiett leaned up toward the hack driver. "That's what old dog Tray gets for runnin' with the sheep-stealin' pack," he hollered. "Buck-shot in his butt. That Burrell kid didn't have no connection with the killin' at all, no more than you did."

"Don't know nothin' about it," the driver replied. "Keeps me busy tendin' my own business. Wouldn't hurt other people to do the same."

Pruiett leaned back. "The dumb son-of-a-bitch. Wonder how much interest I ought to have in it; how much I ought to lose, before I'd be entitled to just mention it?"

Editorially, the local press approved the mob's conduct and took it's customary poke at Pruiett. The satisfaction of getting to hear society's organ howl was all he got out of his experience with the case. "As a sequel to a violent assassination that occurred in Ada, in February, last, four men suspected of the crime were lynched. Lynchings are to be deplored; but, Oklahoma juries are permitting too many murderers to escape the penalty of their crime."

" 'She killed me,' he gasped, as he propped himself on his hands and looked into the indistinct blur of curious faces around him. 'I guess I shouldn't have come back here'," reported *The Daily Oklahoman* on February 24, 1910.

Andrew Gilbert was like the farmer boy grazing the mule. When he got tired of holding the rope he tied it to his leg and laid down for a nap. He realized and admitted, as soon as the mule became frightened and started to run away, that he had made a most grievous mistake.

His good wife, Agnes, who was rapidly becoming a widow, was standing quietly beside and over him, a defiant expression on her hard Irish countenance. Wispy smoke was still trickling from the nozzle of the bull-dog revolver she held in her dangling right hand, and was drifting into invisibility with the steam which rose from the wash tub sitting across two chairs, on the porch nearby. The hand holding the pistol was big and red. Splotches of wet on the front of her course apron suggested that her activities in dispatching a lead slug through her prone mate were but briefly removed from her labors over the tub and washboard.

There was enough drama in the situation to arouse the literary in the news hound on the police run. "The man fell backward and after a few convulsive movements all was over. A large crowd had collected in the yard, attracted by the sound of the shooting and the sight of the speeding police buggy, and pressed morbidly forward to watch the death throes of the dying man."

Selecting an arm and a foot apiece, a quartet of the kindly kibitzers lifted the inert remains and started toward the house. Agnes vaulted the steps ahead of them. With her arms folded across her extensive chest and with the pistol still uncomfortably prominent, she placed her ragged figure across the opening into the kitchen.

" 'You better lay it on the porch,' she said coolly. 'He'll be all right. You ain't goin' to take him in thar, and bloody up my nice clean bed'." When they locked her up, and later when they filed the murder charge against her, she was as unperturbed as she had been there on the back porch. Her's was a sodden soul made listless by long suffering and utter lack of hope. If she saw light in the fruit of her desperation, delivery from the discouraging repetition of seeing Gilbert stagger in at night, stuporous from drink, it did not reflect from her tired eyes. If there was remorse with the realization of his death, a stolid and unquavering chin concealed it.

Pruiett claimed that he offered his services to the washerwoman without figuring on a fee, and that the development of a choice piece of cash after the conclusion of the case was but the inevitable reward which follows the righteous. The agile tongue was thrust into a grinning cheek as he said it. A whispered contrary contention established that he knew the money was there, and would be forthcoming, all of the time.

"Agnes," he said, squinting through the bars at her, "This is Mr. Pruiett. Moman Pruiett. I want to talk to you."

"I don't want to talk to you," answered Agnes. "I didn't send for you; so, don't bother me. I ain't got no use for lawyers."

"You just think you ain't," Pruiett corrected her. "I been at it quite awhile, and I can't remember ever seein' anyone who could use a lawyer to a better advantage than you could, right now. You've got a pretty rough road to travel."

"Not so rough that I can't stand it, an' it's my own business," said Agnes. "An' it won't be no rougher than it has been behind me, an' I stood that for a long time. I'm guilty. I ain't got no excuses, an' I ain't got no money. I guess you won't bother me anymore, now."

A soft laugh came in between the rusty bars. "Who said anything about money?" he said. "I'm not lookin' for money. I've got enough to get by on for awhile; an', I've got enough business to keep me busy. I came down to try to help you."

"Then I'll say I'm much obliged to you, Mr. Pruiett, but I don't need none of your help. I know what I want to do, an' it ain't fightin' the case. I want you to let me alone."

There was a minute or two of silence. "I got a little girl out home; just twelve years old, same age as your kid. She reads the papers, and she saw that little girl of yours with her picture in it. She's made me explain all about the trouble to her."

There was no reply from the interior of the cell in the brief pause which followed. Pruiett continued. "She made me promise I'd come to see you, an' offer to help you, before I left home yesterday mornin'. When I got home last night, an' told her I hadn't done anything about it, why, it hurt her—an' that hurt me. It was that young lady that decided you needed a lawyer."

He paused again, and listened, but he heard nothing. "She's got some dolls an' things together, an' we're takin' 'em by to her in the mornin'—out at your sisters. It was her idea, understand, not mine. I believe..." he almost whispered, "that I couldn't hardly stand to have them take me away from that kid of mine. These blood-thirsty prosecutors around here'll cause you plenty of trouble, even if you fight. But, if you just lay down, they'll give you more than you'll be able to stand. Ten or fifteen years ain't so bad, unless it drags you away from someone that means a lot to you, an' then its worse than life. Say—would you mind if me an' my kid picked that girl of yours up tomorrow evenin', and took her out to my house for supper?"

The jailer had to call time on the Pruiett-Gilbert visit that night. Their plans for her defense, started there through the cell bars, promised to last until morning, unless interrupted.

An organization known as "The Law and Order League" had sprung into being and was flourishing in the Southwest. Its object was to procure a more adequate and proportionate punishment for crime than the regular system was meting out during the period. The liberation of the fiendish Red Fox, the apologetic clean slate given Judge Maben, Jim Stevenson's acquittal, the day before the lynchings in Ada, and in short, Pruiett's depredations in gutting the pens and letting the gallows go hungry, was the stimulus for it's inception and rapid growth.

"There is always two sides to every story" proclaimed the *Garvin*

County Herald on April 23, 1909, "and God forbid that we should cry aloud for vengeance or demand an eye for an eye, a tooth for a tooth, but if the courts of Oklahoma declare every man innocent who shoots down another then indeed anarchy will reign. No one blames a man for using every effort in his power to be freed, for life and liberty is sweet, but the law abiding people deplore the fact that, seemingly, it is impossible to convict a man in Oklahoma of homicide, that is, a man who can employ astute lawyers or bring influence to bear on the courts."

While the editorial writer didn't utter the name, the subject was understood, for Pruiett had just cleared Stevenson for killing Cathey, the City Marshal of Pauls Valley, and the populous, as well as the press, was screaming. Pruiett read it and grinned as he thought of Rusk and Little Rock. He was making money so fast that he couldn't deposit it in the bank; he didn't want them to know how fast he was taking it in. He stowed sheaves of bills and sacks of coin, the origin of which was oftentimes subject to censor, in the massive iron safe in the corner of his office.

The dream, that had been his solace in the hours of darkest despair, had come true; and, the anti-social vow, that he had uttered as he was being dragged away to his prolonged discontentment, he had kept. He ground his teeth and rumpled his raven hair with a trembling hand, as he told himself and the horde of hangers-on, who trailed him about, that it was only the beginning; that his best was yet to come.

The poet, Eugene Ware's, better known as Ironquill, 'Washerwoman' was the nucleus for a pre-meditated tear jerker which Pruiett delivered, intended for the deliverance of red-handed Agnes. The defense of the case had exerted an uncanny influence over him, and his conduct through its trial had been unusually brilliant. A banker jury sat in the box. He knew that the propaganda of the Law and Order League, with its constant editorial fortification, would find fertile beds for sprouting and growing in their complacent bellies. Pruiett had realized it and tried to avoid it by a heated attack against the entire panel, charging that the individual members were prejudiced by the placards, posters and editorials which the semi-secret organization had succeeded in circulating.

Unsuccessful in his attempt to disqualify the panel, he took up the challenge. By his own main strength, and exposure of the stupidity of the prosecution, he would make the League, itself, turn one of his clients loose.

Pruiett wouldn't let them forget that his connection with the case was based on nothing save his client's utter friendlessness and innocence. As in "The Washerwoman's Song" by Ware:

Just a trifle lonesome she,
Just as poor as poor could be;
But her spirits always rose,
Like the bubbles in the clothes,
For the woman has a friend
Who will help her to the end.

The personality was being turned on. Standing close to the front row of jurors, so that they could feel the charm exuding from his well groomed frame, he was engaged in deliberately shoveling spades-full of maudlin sentiment into the eyes of their sound judgment.

I have seen her rub and scrub,
On the washboard in the tub,
While the baby, sopped in suds,
Rolled and tumbled in the duds,
Or was paddling in the pools,
With old scissors, stuck in spools.

He was bringing back the aching damp of Ozark poverty; Betty, stooped and sweating as she labored for the cursing laborers from tie-cutting camps or the fills of the frontier railroad. The methodical rise and fall of the washboard stroke was in his dogged gestures; anguish of mind, agony of body, suffering of despair, came up with his voice and hung like limp, wet garments about him there in the crowd, even after he had ceased to speak and stood gazing appealingly into the floor or ceiling of the courtroom.

Human hopes and human creeds
Have their roots in human needs,
And I should not wish to strip
From that washerwoman's lip

Any song that she can sing,
Any hope that songs can bring,
For the woman has a friend,
Who will keep her to the end.

The old Pruiett vanity, after it had recovered from the shock which Agnes's conviction gave it, had to call on a friend to keep her from an unanticipated, and rather ignominious end. The jury found her guilty of manslaughter and gave her four years. With the verdict coming in late at night, he had sent an office associate to receive it, while he stayed with the celebration he had prematurely opened in a downtown hotel room. He was so sure of another acquittal that he had partially completed the speech of congratulation on himself. When the phone message apprised him of the unexpected outcome, he swayed unsteadily, and glass in hand, extemporaneously supplied a brief conclusion.

"The sons-of-bitches cried to easy," he said as he swayed. "When you get a bunch of smooth bellies that sweat easy from the eyes, watch out. A cryin' jury will go out and pray for you, and cry like old women while they vote to send your soul to hell. I don't never want another cryin' jury."

Washita farm land on the washerwoman's bond kept her out of jail until the appeal, which reversed the conviction and gave her another trial, was complete. Everyone but Pruiett considered the outcome a victory; that four years for such cold blooded murder was a triumph and that he was taking an unnecessary risk with the old woman's welfare by exposing her again to a trial that carried a possibility of death, or life imprisonment, with a murder conviction. Pruiett scoffed.

As the appeals court stated, "It is true that appellant is only a poor washerwoman and is without friends, without influence and without money, and is dependent upon the charity of her attorney for her defense; but she is a human being, and her rights are as sacred in the eyes of the law as though she was the wealthiest and the most influential society favorite in Oklahoma. It is the duty of this court to see that the poor and friendless are fully protected in the enjoyment of the rights given them by law."

Thus the Criminal Court of Appeals echoed Pruiett's repeated assertion that 'the woman has a friend, who will keep her to the end.' The next jury to hear Agnes' story had dry eyes and horny hands instead of dripping orbs and agate hearts; and, as they opened the figurative gates of prison to the washerwoman, they commended her for her steady hand and clear aim. Pruiett took half the night to deliver the congratulatory speech he had prepared to deliver on himself the year and a half before.

Another month rolled by. Rough old Agnes was sitting in Pruiett's office, as conspicuously out of place there as the fashionable lawyer would have been in her steamy kitchen. He was talking on the telephone, and employing his most professional dignity.

"Smith," he was saying. "Mrs. Gilbert is in my office, and she has a paper with her, a paper she says she found in with some of her husband's old clothes. It looks like a life insurance policy for $2,500, and so far as I can tell, it was in force two years ago when Gilbert was—er—a—when he died. Would you check up on it, and . ."

"Check up on it hell," Smith replied. "We did that a long time ago. I've been wonderin' how long you'd wait after gettin' her off, to spring that policy on us. I've got a letter back from the home office about it, already."

Pruiett abandoned his affectation.

"Well, what do they say about it," he snapped. "The premiums are all paid and you'll pay on the damn policy or..."

"The company says pay it," Smith laughed. "If you've got the policy there I'll bring the check over. We've got it made out to you and Mrs. Gilbert, jointly. Just a lonesome washerwoman. Just as poor as poor could be—hello—hello? Hell! He hung up on me."

The history of the Miller murder cases, tried in the fall of 1911 in Temple Houston's old bailiwick at Woodward, Oklahoma, present an example of the versatility of the lawyer Pruiett. Acting as a special prosecutor in one, he obtained a conviction and sentence of life imprisonment. As attorney for the defendant in the other, where the appearance of guilt was so great that he 'had to gouge himself in the rump with a peggin' awl', as he himself termed it, before he could get started, he gained the complete acquittal of his client.

Woodward was a plains relay for the endless train shipments of cattle out of west Texas into Dodge City and on to Kansas City. The

Alphonso Jackson "Al" Jennings, one of the Old West's most famous outlaws and lawyers; however, according to Moman Pruiett "Al wasn't no gunfighter. He wasn't no lawyer and, so far as that goes, he wasn't no outlaw. He was just a little petty larceny fellow that was willin' to take a plea in a felony case, and do a stretch in the federal penitentiary just to acquire a bad man's reputation . . . Al tendered his career as a horse thief and train robber as his chief asset of citizenship." Courtesy Archives & Manuscripts Division of the Oklahoma Historical Society.

Raven's, as Sam Houston was known, son selected it as a locale for testing his own deflected genius, because it resembled most the limitless ruggedness of his native Texas. The verdant sod of the buffalo grass had not been violated by the implements which were to pulverize its surface and make it sport for the eddying gusts, and were to ultimately make it a barren, dust-blown waste. It was a cattle kingdom in its own right, and the grass pastures, which stretched away between and beyond the purple mesas where the headwaters of the North Canadian arose, and on to the sandy stretches of the Cimarron's wide bed, were spotted with great herds of market beef.

Statehood and prohibition had removed the back panel of Woodward's color when its double row of Main Street saloons and sporting houses had been closed; but, even after the end of the first decade of the century, there was a suggestion of the untamed west in the jingling recklessness of the bronzed men who rode clatteringly down the brick pavement on horseback, and left their mounts at the livery barns while they rode away on the cabooses of the cattle trains.

The Indian fights, the overland cattle drives, the building of the Orient and the Santa Fe, were typical reminiscences in gatherings during court sessions; but, the topic which surpassed them all in the fancy of the old timers—was Temple Houston. The memory of the brilliant son of Texas' liberator, who came to Woodward to avoid the confining influence of his sire's greatness in Texas, was fast in the hearts of Woodward.

He was dead, died on August 15, 1905, and buried in the hard packed earth of the town's Elmwood Cemetery, in Woodward County; but, the echoing eloquence of his 'plea for the prostitute', drifted back like a reverent musical accompaniment as his admirers retold their stories of his many courtroom achievements.

And, as they told the whole story, the muffled roar of his big pistols, blazing death in feud and folly, reverberated like distant thunder along the horizon of the plain. He was reproduced in their provincial phraseology. The collar of his buckskin coat was foul from the grease of his long black hair, which he saturated and twisted into tight black rolls, Mexican fashion. He stalked into a Main Sreet saloon to settle a difference with the Jennings Brothers. Ed Jennings was dead, and Frank Jennings, his brother, lay under the same gambling table critically wounded, as Houston holstered a smoking pistol and strolled out into the evening atmosphere. And on the street the children gathered about his

TEMPLE HOUSTON, STANDING THIRD FROM THE LEFT, WITH HIS HAND ON HIS CHIN, IN FRONT OF THE MCFADDEN SALOON AT TALOGA, OKLAHOMA TERRITORY. THE GENTLEMAN WITH HIS HAND IN HIS POCKET IS W. H. MCFADDEN. THE MAN WEARING THE DERBY IS WINDIELF MCFADDEN. MOMAN PRUIETT AND TEMPLE HOUSTON CLASHED IN A MURDER CASE THAT TOOK PLACE IN 1902 AT ENID, OKLAHOMA TERRITORY. DURING THE TRIAL, PRUIETT DESCRIBED HOUSTON AS A LAWYER "WHO WORE BUCKSKINS AND TWISTED HIS HAIR UP LIKE A MULTITUDE OF RAT'S TAILS" AND WAS WARNED BY THE JUDGE THAT WHEN THE TRIAL WAS OVER TO LEAVE TOWN BEFORE HOUSTON KILLED HIM. THE TWO MEN MET THE EVENING AFTER THE TRIAL AND SHARED DRINKS TOGETHER. THE NEXT DAY PRUIETT RETURNED TO PAULS VALLEY AND HOUSTON HAD HIS HAIR CUT. COURTESY WESTERN HISTORY COLLECTIONS, UNIVERSITY OF OKLAHOMA LIBRARIES.

Anheuser
Busch
LAGER B

THE FIRST GARFIELD COUNTY JAIL AT ENID. LOU STEPHENSON IS STANDING IN THE DOOR, WITH A BALL AND CHAIN AROUND HIS ANKLE. THE TWO OTHER PRISONERS, STANDING ON THE LEFT, ARE CHAINED TOGETHER AT THE WRISTS. THE SECOND MAN FROM THE RIGHT IS JOHN RILEY. TEMPLE HOUSTON, ANOTHER FLAMBOYANT PIONEER ATTORNEY, LOCATED HIS PRACTICE IN WOODWARD AND DREW MANY CLIENTS FROM THE COUNTY JAIL IN ENID. ONE OF HIS MOST SUCCESSFUL CASES IN ENID WAS THE DEFENSE OF JOHN RIGGINS ON A CHARGE OF MURDER. HELPING WITH THE PROSECUTION IN THE CASE WAS MOMAN PRUIETT. COURTESY WESTERN HISTORY COLLECTIONS, UNIVERSITY OF OKLAHOMA LIBRARIES.

boots to play, and to taunt and tease him about his peculiar hairdress. He laughed, and joked, and played with them.

Al Jennings, a brother of Frank and Ed, was a mediocre prairie lawyer. He claimed that he turned outlaw and train robber because a jury refused to convict the killer of his brother, when he was tried for the murder. Speculation on what would occur if and when Temple Houston and Al Jennings came face to face was rife, more abundant than the gossip over the Jesse West-Gus Bobbitt relations; but, Al saw to it that a true solution was never available.

"Al wasn't no gun-fighter. He wasn't no lawyer; and, so far as that goes, he wasn't no outlaw. He was just a little petty larceny fellow that was willin' to take a plea in a felony case, and do a stretch in the Federal penitentiary, just to acquire a bad man's reputation." That was Pruiett's private opinion. He went on record, in his defense of Senator Thomas P. Gore, to charge that Jennings "tendered his career as a horse thief and train-robber as his chief asset for citizenship." Pruiett even refused to take employment in a good murder case, at Guthrie, because his mis-guided prospective client wanted him to go in as co-counsel with Al Jennings.

Pruiett was more than casually familiar with the legend of the Al Jennings-Temple Houston feud when he went to Woodward to try the Miller cases. His own relationship to the panhandle's pride was in the feud fringe, or had been until the time of Houston's death six years before. It had been so since a night in October, 1902, when the two had met in the bar-room of the old Frantz Hotel at Enid, the principal town of the Cherokee Strip country.

Pruiett had traveled the long trail from the valley to the plains at the insistence of Bill Whittinghill, an Enid attorney and his friend, who was trying to prosecute cases for the government in the Northern Territorial District. Houston was getting away with murder in the Cherokee

Strip like Pruiett had been on the Washita, and his reputation for being good, and effective, was extending from the south of Kansas across No Mans Land and into the stretches of west Texas. Pruiett had hoped that the long haired Texan would move south into the territory and cross swords with him on his home, or at least a neutral battle-ground; but, Houston was too wary for that. Against his better judgment, Pruiett gave in to Whittinghill and agreed to help him prosecute John Riggins, charged with the murder of Harry F. Sears. The Sears family had put up an attractive cash inducement, however, before his great friendship for Bill overpowered him and the cattle-war case, as it was called, was getting a lot of territorial publicity.

The October 2nd issue of the *Enid Events,* 1902, chronicled an account of a Pruiett defeat. "Mr. Pruiett made the closing argument in the Riggins case. His remarks were characterized by a fiery zeal for justice and law and order. He made a remarkably analytical argument and wove a web of circumstantial deductions from the evidence which was conclusive and convincing. His 'fiery zeal' caused him to tread on the blunt toe of the figurative Houston boot. He told the jury that 'the defendant's lawyer, who wore buckskins and twisted his hair up like a multitude of rat's tails, had but one virtue and claim to fame, and that was the undying reputation of an illustrious father'. He shook his fist under Houston's nose, and cried, 'Spawn of the tee-pee!' "

Pruiett contended that Houston's attitude of utter contempt for him throughout the trial of the case had provoked the accusation, one which he well knew would arouse the unconventional Texan. Garfield County Judge James K. Beauchamp made a noble gesture. He warned Pruiett to stay off the streets and to get out of town as soon as he could, lest Houston kill him; then, under the guise of court business, took Houston by the arm and insisted that he leave the court building with him.

Pruiett pondered his problem in his hotel room. He didn't want to stay, and he hated to leave. The kind of trouble that appeared to be hovering in the offing wasn't new to him. Outraged ego and offended conceit had been the spark for the violent physical encounters he had been associated with since early childhood. A paddy, who backed off the fill just because his adversary was approaching with a pick and a wild look, wasn't worth keeping. He was yellow. The cowhand, who ignored a threat or backed up at a dare, soon had to ride on to another settlement. The better element of the community shunned a coward.

Tossing his old carpet bag to the bed, he unbuckled it and took out the blue-steel pistol. Pushing the front end of it down into the waistband of his trousers, he sauntered downstairs for a drink.

Pruiett looked over his bottle and glass and into the back mirror of the bar, and saw Temple Houston, with three or four companions, when they came in. They ordered, laughed and talked in a little group at the opposite end of the bar. Pruiett knew that Houston was conscious of his presence; had seen him there as he entered the room and walked up to the rail. He watched them, by looking into the mirror, and saw that Houston, with a glass in his hand, was edging down the polished counter toward him.

"The young gentleman from the Chickasaw country is a pretty talker," Houston said sarcastically, holding his glass awkwardly in front of him, as if in readiness to toss it into his listeners face. "He makes a very pretty speech."

Having no answer to make, Pruiett remained silent. He stood looking unwaveringly into Houston's deep eyes.

"But the jury was not misled by it," Houston continued. "I guess you have heard that Riggins is at liberty? That he was found not guilty?"

"I hadn't heard of it, until now," Pruiett replied, using the same terse tones as did Houston, and never letting his stare waver from its level path into Houston's eyes. "I hadn't heard of it; but, if that's the jury's verdict, I must necessarily concur in it. The jury is always right."

Houston continued to hold his glass and to stare. "Would the young gentleman from the Chickasaw country condescend to drink with the son of the immortal emancipator of Texas—the one who wears his hair on his coat collar, like a multitude of rat's tails?" Houston was menacingly sarcastic.

"The young gentleman from the Chickasaw country confines his professional feelings to the courtroom," Pruiett replied. "He tries to give satisfaction to those who trust him enough to employ him. When he has done that, he is able to look any man in the face, even his adversary, without an apology. He would be glad to drink with Temple Houston, an able lawyer."

Houston weighed the remarks briefly, and gave a quick nod of approval. "He is indeed a pretty speaker," he murmured. He raised his glass and the drinks were tossed off. Each nodding, they moved away from each other; neither changed the focus of the intense eye-to-eye gaze. Pruiett moved toward the exit; Houston back toward his companions. Each appeared to be uncertain, and cautious and apprehensive, as to what kind of a move to expect from the other.

Pruiett left Enid on the midnight train. Houston dropped into a barber shop on the square, next morning, and left his greasy curls. During the balance of his stormy career, he wore his hair close-cropped, in cowboy fashion.

Pruiett's successful defense of Jim Stevenson, and Judge Maben, and Agnes Gilbert, had broken the morale of his chief heckler, the Law and Order League. The League, persuaded that it couldn't beat him, decided to enlist him, and through the agency of $3,000 in cash, engaged him to go to Woodward to act as a special prosecutor.

N. L. Miller, the accused, had purportedly slain a Mabel Oakes, long the object of his illicit affection. Always theatrical, Miller had committed his crime on the stage of the 'Opera House,' an unused theatre in the town of Alva, and had set the props so that a suicidal end might be deduced. The scene was so crudely laid that it failed to fool anyone but the prosecuting authorities who were politically allied with the prominent Miller, and who wanted to be deceived.

The dead girl's relatives, the populous, and the League, cried for a trial; but, Miller leered and grinned, and the County Attorney stalled. When Pruiett moved in, the gang around the courthouse, although they agreed he couldn't compare with Temple Houston, did acknowledge that a lawsuit was going to be tried.

Miller was a strange quantity in himself. He was a typical western villain, with the handle-bar mustaches curling back around large white teeth. He had been educated in medicine; but, for unknown reasons, had not practiced the profession. He was a studious, scholarly sort of man, well past middle age, who was prominent in the local church, apparently devoted to his plump wife and interested in the welfare of two handsome, nearly grown daughters. He had shifted with the territorial land lotteries and contests as a trader and speculator, and settled, shortly after the last opening, at Alva. In 1911, when the trouble came, he was the Justice of the Peace, with his office in the upstairs front of the two story building which was principally occupied by the 'Opera House.'

"Mabel Oakes was an innocent country girl who left the farm and entered Miller's office as a stenographer; during the time she was in Miller's employ, she was seduced by him. During this time, Miller and his wife were separated and he had promised Miss Oakes that he would get a divorce from his wife and marry her." So did *Renfrew's Record,* the Woods County paper, view the appalling situation on September 15, 1911. Miller's villainy was summed up by the ladies of the Missionary Society in a whispered and simple, yet eloquent charge of shame. "He keeps a couch in his office, the wretch," they horrifiedly whispered.

Mabel had not been the first to suffer wrong at the hands of the 52-year-old Romeo, although she was the first to lose her life. He was an addict to booze and his own ego. The periodical separations from his wife and family usually lasted during the period of an affair with a new stenographer, who either saw things his way or looked elsewhere for a place of employment. He kept his liquor, which was alternately bootleg, or the confiscated evidence of his own constable, secreted in various out-of-the-way places about the old theatre building. When an affair was getting cold and the whiskey bucks were overtaking him, he would repent and go home for forgiveness. His was the life of the typical upland libertine.

Both sides claimed that they were unable to receive a fair trial at Alva; so, by agreement, the venue was shifted to Woodward, the adjoining county seat on the west.

"The theory of the State is that Miller wished to put Miss Oakes out of the way as she was about to become a mother, and that he wanted the recent reconciliation with his wife to continue. Miller had approached Dr. Saffold, at that time owner of the Alva Hospital, and tried to persuade him to perform a criminal operation on the girl, which the doctor positively refused to do; that failing in this he informed the doctor that if he had the necessary instruments he could perform the operation himself." *Renfrew's Record* was reproducing a part of the opening statement of Sandor J. Vigg, the son of a Swede farmer, who had worked his way through the law school and had been appointed Prosecuting Attorney when Claude McCrory had resigned. McCrory quit rather than prosecute Miller, when public sentiment had arisen to such a peak that he had to do one or the other.

Miller had had a medical education. "If he had the equipment," as

Doctor Saffold quoted him, "he could do the job himself." He had acquired the instrument, a physicians speculum, through a mail order supply house in Chicago, Illinois; but, it had been discreetly ordered, and received, by McCrory, who was then County Attorney. Pruiett could prove that the order had been filled and shipped, through the testimony of the employees of the supply firm; but, he couldn't prove that Miller ever received it, unless Miller took the stand and gave Pruiett a chance to cross-examine him. The State could prove by McCrory, were he available, how Miller had had him order the appliance, and how he had given it to him on it's reception; but, McCrory had quit when it appeared the case was actually coming to trial, and the Law and Order League was depleting it's stable treasury in a wild but futile effort to run him down.

"Dr. Bilby described the condition of the body and stated the girl would have become a mother in a few months if she had lived. He believed that the girl died from strangulation at the hands of another person, by means of her scarf which was wrapped tightly around her neck. The indications were that it was a case of murder, and not suicide." *Renfrew's Record* was speaking again—this time commenting on the evidence. "Dr. Edwin DeBarr, of the State University at Norman, testified that he had held the chair of chemistry there for 19 years, that he had received the stomach of Mabel Oakes from Dr. Bilby, by express, and that he had analyzed it and it's contents. He stated that he found strychnine and morphine there, but not enough to cause death."

The Black Stud was as fully cognizant of the prosecution's one vulnerable spot, as he was aware of the potentialities of the rest of his case. The fact that the girl was dead, or that Miller had discovered the dead body, was no circumstances indicating guilt. Miller and the deceased, as occupants of the rented front portion of the theatre building, were logically the ones who might have access to it; and, if the girl had wished to kill herself, her morbidity could not have invited her to a more appropriate spot than the musty shadows behind the rotting drop. The defense was not going to deny that the girl was about to reproduce, nor was it going to admit that the defendant was the one responsible for her condition. That was part of what had to be proved.

The case hinged on the speculum. If Miller had sent for it, and if he got it, then the chain of circumstance was complete. The patient had refused to submit to the operation; so, he had given her a drug in a drink of whiskey. Then, he had guided her, sans the customary white gown and wheeled cot, down the decaying staircase and through the cob-web matted passageways to the improvised surgery table backstage. When he had removed a part of her clothing and had proceeded so that his purpose became apparent in her drug befogged brain, she had rebelled, and Doctor Miller, instead of administrating a little more anesthetic, tightened the struts of the Alpine scarf she was wearing about her neck, until her remonstrances ceased. Then a conclusion of the operation had become unnecessary.

The men associated with the prosecution, who scoffed at Pruiett when he said that Miller would never take the stand unless McCrory was produced to establish that the surgical instrument, which he ordered from Chicago, was for the defendant, looked a trifle less skeptical when the trial judge refused to permit testimony on the speculum "unless counsel would assure him that it would be connected, by competent evidence" to the accused. The League's runners and detectives hadn't located the hiding ex-County Attorney, and hope of finding him had been practically abandoned.

Thus, the State's case was clearly incomplete. The defense had devoted its time to discrediting the dead girl and proving that any number of men about town might have been responsible for her unfortunate condition. The almost savage Pruiett could feel the reasonable doubt which existed, and which would probably continue to exist, until he could demonstrate that the accused was the one who had first wronged her. When the production was down to routine testimony in support of Miller's general good reputation, he despaired. He knew that the accused was going to claim his Constitutional privilege. He wasn't going to testify.

Pruiett tousled his bushy hair as he meditated. Then, with apparent languor, he arose and walked into the corridor, crowded with curious people craning to see the activity through the open door. After he had been out but a moment, he bolted back through the crowd and up to the counsel table.

"Vigg," he said in a hoarse whisper, "Vigg! They've got McCrory. They just brought him in—the Sheriff—and they took him into your office. Go out an' talk to him; I'll watch this record. Have him ready for our first rebuttal witness."

Pruiett was lying but Vigg didn't know it. He hurried out of the courtroom. Neither did the defendant nor his attorneys know he was lying, and they had heard every word of the excited communication.

When Pruiett declined to cross-examine the witness, the defense held a brief, whispered conference, and then—Miller, with his black mustaches drooping dejectedly, marched wearily to the stand. He had been well coached for the emergency—the appearance of McCrory—but his dread of Pruiett and the ordeal he was approaching was evident in his every movement and expression.

Miller's hope was to beat the prosecution to the punch. What he knew they would prove by McCrory, now that he was there, he would admit himself. He had to acknowledge that he ordered the speculum in McCrory's name and that, when it came, he was the one who got it. He positively had to deny that he used it, or intended to use it, on dead Mabel. But any route he took, away from that denial, led him into a field beset with danger. Miller was no fool; he realized the precariousness of his position.

"And, when this speculum came, which you admit you ordered, you attempted an illegal operation on this poor dead girl, didn't you?" The ever accusing, trembling finger was in his face as Pruiett roared at him in cross-examination.

"I did not," he replied with spirit. Miller's wife sat in the courtroom between their two pretty daughters. Pruiett glanced in their direction as he formulated his next question.

"Did you order it for use on your wife?" he inquired.

"No," he answered. "I didn't intend for her to use it."

Pruiett glanced at the innocent looking girls. He saw his opportunity to further discredit the defendant and at the same time impress the jury with a benevolent gesture on his own part. He took a significant last look at the daughters.

"I won't proceed further in that direction, Mr. Miller. You may stand down."

With one well calculated sentence, he had made a beast of Miller and a martyr of himself.

"The State rests." Pruiett made that brief announcement when the trial court invited its rebuttal at the close of Miller's testimony. Then, he turned to the defense side of the table and laughed audibly. They understood, without going out to look, that McCrory was not there—had not been there. They knew that they had not only been tricked, but that there position in the case had been speedily reversed. The *Oklahoma News* at Oklahoma City on September 12, 1911, in a brief bulletin, concluded the story. "The jury in the N. L. Miller murder case returned a verdict of guilty and fixed the penalty at life imprisonment, after having been out one hour and fifteen minutes."

Pruiett was occupying a room with Dr. Edwin DeBarr, head of the chemistry department of the state university. He had helped to establish that Mabel Oakes had been drugged before she was killed.

"When can we get a train out of here?" Pruiett asked, as he stirred a drink on the dresser.

"I don't know," answered DeBarr, "but it doesn't make much difference to me. I don't get away for a few days; I'm a witness in another murder case. It's a woman, this time, and her name's Miller, too, Maggie Miller."

"The Miller's up in this country must be a tough outfit," Pruiett observed. "But I'm not in any hurry, an' I've got plenty of liquor. I think I'll wait and see what the jury does to this Justice of the Peace we just tried. What they got the Miller woman for?"

"You ought to watch that liquor, Moman," DeBarr advised. "It's habit forming, and it's tissue destroying. At the rate you go, and after that speech you just made to the jury, your system shouldn't have any stimulants at all. That stuff will get hold on you before you know it."

Pruiett laughed. "It can have all the hold on me it wants," he said. "That's what I take it to do. It gives me lots of good ideas. I don't just take 'em after; I take 'em before an' after. When I get so I can see the jurors' faces, real clear, I know it's time to ask for a recess, so as to get a drink, or to quit. Forget about me; what about this old Miller girl?"

"Her name's Maggie Miller. She's charged with giving a kid a batch of strychnine. They sent the stomach down to me for an analysis; so, I've got to be a witness."

"Did you find anything in the stomach?"

"I found enough poison in that kid's belly to kill ever' body in Woodward. Old Dr. J. M. Workman, who lives here in town, is goin' to testify that they soaked up three dozen towels, with froth, before the kid died. He had an awful dose."

"Who's kid was it?" Pruiett inquired. "What was her idea? What was her motive?"

"It was her husband's kid, Roy Gordon Miller; she was the kid's step-mother. It was one of those family fights where the ex-wife and the next wife had trouble ever' time the old man visited with his kid. There's plenty of motive, and it's a cold-blooded one, too."

"Being a step-mother is enough to get her convicted," Pruiett said. "There's a lot of prejudice against step-mothers anywhere you go. Who's defendin' her?"

"I don't know, whether she's got a lawyer or not," answered DeBarr. "I believe that Vigg said she couldn't get anyone to defend her. There's a lot of feeling up here in the case."

"Anybody prosecutin' besides Vigg?" Pruiett asked.

"No, not in this case," DeBarr laughed as he answered. "He won't need any help in this one. It's just a case of whether they'll let her off with life, because she's a woman, or whether they'll make the court appoint a lawyer to defend, and then send her to the chair. Between Workman and I, that woman is already convicted."

"Roy Miller died August 5," Oklahoma City's *Daily Oklahoman* explained in a special article on the case on September 12, 1911, "and, acting on advice of his mother, Ellen Miller, the divorced wife of the father of the boy, an examination of the viscera was made by the State Chemist, Dr. DeBarr, and a State Bacteriologist, Ellison. It was claimed that Maggie Miller broke up the home of Miller and his first wife in Chandler five or six years ago. Miller afterward divorced Ellen Miller and married Maggie Miller.The theory of the state is that Maggie Miller poisoned the boy in order to remove the last tie between her husband and his divorced wife."

Pruiett received his next intelligence on the strychnine murderess, the 'tiger lady' as *Renfrew's Record* had tagged her, while getting a cold water shave in Bill Miller's two chair barbershop. Pruiett had once thrived on worse shaves than the Miller parlor dispensed; but, the recent lush years had softened him. When the barber dashed un-cut Bay Rum on his smarting countenance, he squirmed and cursed, and observed that the barber "ought to be down in jail with the tiger bitch that killed her kid." A pained expression, with an uncomfortable silence, told him that he had said the wrong thing.

"I guess I talk too much, old man," he said. "I'm sorry."

"That's my wife," said Bill, frankly and quietly, "and it was my kid, too."

"I'm really sorry," Pruiett repeated. "I had no business sayin' such a thing. Just tryin' to be funny, I guess. I hope..."

"It's all right," said Bill, but there was pain in his voice. "It's not the first time I've had to take it."

Pruiett was embarrassed by the effect of his own inconsiderate slip. At loss for anything to say, he paid for his service and went out. But, he was back in the shop the next day, where he waited about until dark, and closing time. Then, he and Miller took a walk together, talking in low, confidential tones. When Pruiett got back to the hotel that night, he had agreed to defend Maggie Miller, without compensation. It was his way of straightening himself up with Bill.

Pruiett was puzzled. He had agreed to defend Maggie; but, he couldn't think of a defense. At that stage of his career, agreeing to defend a person charged with murder was synonymous to agreeing that he would gain an acquittal. The dead boy had been but eleven years old. Self-defense or the unwritten law wouldn't work. He couldn't set up an alibi, because dutiful Maggie had stood by and passed up fresh towels to the country doctor who was absturging the frothy secretion from the convulsed countenance of the child. The boy had been robust and healthy the one day; beset with frothing fits the next. His step-mother had given him the last breakfast he had eaten, and had been alone in the house with him until the doctor was called at mid-morning. DeBarr said. DeBarr said too much. It was no assistance to him, in his quandary for an intelligent explanation, what DeBarr said.

Trusting that it would come to him, as it always had, he browsed through his Edgar Allan Poe and communed with his liquor. Half full, and half dreaming, he climbed up into the twisted steel high chair with foot rests, which Bill Miller's porter used as a stanchion for his shoe shine customers, and gazed through the back window into the warm brightness of the autumn afternoon, casually observing a vista of rusting cans, sun dried weeds and paper scraps and refuse dumped from the street. Of a sudden he arose, and walking out the back door strolled slowly to the back of the lot to a clump of weeds and brush, and then back to his elevated seat.

"What you doin', Mr. Pruiett?" A negro boy was trying not to be too curious.

"I'm thinkin'," Pruiett snapped.

"I know you is now," the boy grinned. "But I mean, what you get down out of my stand for, an' run out into them weeds behind the shop, an' fool around out there for so long?"

"I didn't wade through your old tin cans an' filth for nothin'," Pruiett growled. "Hand me that empty shoe box off of the shelf back there, an' give me that piece of string," he commanded, next, pointing toward a tangled mass of twine lying with dead hair in the corner. "Hand it up here."

The boy obeyed.

Miller, the proprietor, was half asleep in his own barber chair. There were no customers in the place; only Miller, the negro and Pruiett.

Pruiett stuck his finger through one end of the shoe box, so that a little round hold perforated the section of heavy paper; then, he tied one end of the cord to the box, by looping it through the hole he had made. Straightening the string out, he tossed the box to the floor, where it landed on its flat bottom. As he reeled the twine in, hand over hand, the box slid slowly toward him across the floor.

"Which one of you killed that cat?" He said it so quickly that the barber and the negro started, as if they were being accused. They looked at each other, inquiringly.

"What cat?" Miller finally answered, almost inaudibly.

"That one out behind," Pruiett snapped. "The bones and skin's out there where all the flies are. Been there a couple months; it's almost gone. Who killed it?"

"Oh!" said Miller. "That old dead one. Nobody. It just died."

Pruiett scowled at him balefully.

"I said who killed it? Killed it? Can't you understand. Which one of you killed that damned cat?"

"Well, I did, I guess," Miller replied weakly, trying to look wise but betraying his utter lack of understanding.

"Hell yes, you did," said Pruiett viciously. "He was havin' fits around here an' you killed him. Now, that was in the hot weather, about the first of August."

"Yes sir, that's just when it was." Miller was still in the dark, but the open mouthed negro nodded his head violently in positive agreement.

"The kid was playin' with the cat. Say; the boy played around the shop here a little, didn't he?" Pruiett appeared to be cross-examining himself.

“Sure,” said the barber, truthfully, “he was just visitin’ us up here, and he didn’t stay up at the house much. He played down here around the shop almost all the time.”

“All right,” said Pruiett. “All right. The kid was playin’ with the cat...” He had climbed down from the shine stand and was arranging his shoe box and string behind him. “He would put the cat in the box; that was his wagon, see? An’ he’d pull him across the floor, like this...” Pruiett took a number of short, side-wise steps across the linoleum floor, dragging the little box as he went. “An’ when he moved the box a little, that cat would jump out. Wouldn’t he, boy?”

He had turned on the wondering African, who nodded with violent assent. “He cert’nly did, Mr. Pruiett,” he said, “that’s just what he done.”

“And so, the boy grabbed the cat and stuffed him back in the box a few times, and then, the cat bit him. Not a bad bite; not enough to worry you. Just enough to make it bleed a little. In the next day or two, the damn cat began to have fits around here, an’ you had to kill it. The next day or two after that the boy died. He had hydrophobia, see, from the cat bite, and that’s all there is to it.”

Pruiett was standing in the middle of the barbershop floor with his arms outstretched in a magnificent gesture, as though he had just concluded an appeal to a jury. Miller and the negro shoe-shine boy were looking from him to each other in wonderment.

“That’s right,” they agreed. “It sure is right.”

The theory of Maggie Miller’s defense was typically Pruiett; it was an idea conceived and delivered with brief, intense labor, like the babies of the Chickasaw squaws on the Washita, they dropped when they were ready; under a bush or behind a corn shock. It was flawless. Inadequate, of course, at birth, it was the perfect nucleus for the master to shape and mold into that which would serve his exacting requirements best.

“Did you tell me Maggie called Doc Workman when Roy got sick?” He was addressing Miller.

Miller nodded.

“I’ll see you in the mornin’,” Pruiett said. “Get me some witnesses. See how many of the boys around here remember the cat, an’ about the shoe box. An’ put that box up where it won’t get lost. I’ve got to go see a doctor.” With that and a knowing wink, he was gone.

Pruiett might have saved his introduction of himself to Doctor Workman.

"We all know you up here now, Mr. Pruiett," the doctor said. "And we are all grateful to you. Your service in that Miller trial was needed, and appreciated."

"Thanks," Pruiett answered, a little dryly. "I'm staying over next week, tryin' the other Miller case. I'm appearin' in her defense."

"I'm sorry to hear that; sorry and disappointed," Workman replied. "And I'm sure there are many others here who will feel the same as I about it. I know about that case myself, and..."

Pruiett interrupted him. "Don't make a lot of talk before you know what you're talkin' about." He had no restraint to employ in this visit. "I'm interviewin' you professionally. I know you're a witness in this case; you know now that I'm the lawyer for the defense. I don't want to hear any of your pet theories. Let's talk facts."

"I'll tell you what I know of the case," Workman said, coldly, "but I don't think it will help you, in your position."

"Doctor," Pruiett said, looking at him keenly, "haven't you reported to Dr. DeBarr that, when you first got to the Miller boy, he was beginnin' to slobber, an' that you gave him two bella donna tablets from your kit, to dry the saliva up?"

"Why, yes, I have," Workman replied. "That's just what I did. I gave him one tablet when I got there, and another in about an hour, when..."

"You didn't get the desired, usual, results from them, did you, Doctor?"

The doctor shook his head.

"No," he answered. "The boy grew steadily—even rapidly worse. The froth came so fast that we used up all the towels and cloths in Miller's house. I carried the boy to my office; but, he got worse. Do you know, Mr. Pruiett, we saturated three dozen fresh towels, thirty-six of them, with froth from that childs lips before he died. He had terrible convulsions. He had a monstrous dose of strychnine."

"I know he did, doctor, an' you gave it to him," Pruiett charged. "That wasn't bella donna you took from your kit—it was strychnine! You gave the boy the strychnine tablets, and you're the one who killed him! You've killed one person by your stupid blunderin', and now you're tryin' to kill another." Pruiett's voice had risen with the gravity of his subject, and he was shaking the finger accusingly at the doctor.

Workman was pale and trembling. His agitation was being produced by anger, not by fear.

"If that is going to be your attitude, Mr. Pruiett," he cried, "I don't care to discuss this case with you any further. I will have to ask you to leave my office."

"Sure. You'll ask me, but I won't go," stormed Pruiett. "I've been hired to defend this woman, an' my position as her lawyer requires that I develop all the facts. I'd hate to ruin you, but I'm goin' to do it. This is a case of one man's reputation against an innocent woman's life, and by God, the woman ain't goin' to die. I'm in a position to prove that that kid was bitten by a rabid cat, two days before he got sick, an' that all you did was to put him out of his misery with an overdose of poison. They found strychnine in his belly, alright. Hell yes, they did, after you got through blunderin' around with him. But, did you test him for rabies? Did you do anything besides cut out his mid-section and ship to DeBarr? Hell no! You were too anxious to cover up your own stupidity."

"I tell you, it won't work," Workman insisted. "You can't bluff me! Get out of here!"

"Can't bluff you, huh?" The lawyer was menacing, "I'm wirin' Carter and Hollingsworth at Wichita, Kansas, to be here Monday at my expense. I'll let some good doctors testify to what that much bella donna would've done to a kid. It would'a dried him up so that he couldn't have spit for a month. They'll get to answer some questions on the symptoms of hydrophobia, an' when they do, an' when Maggie Miller comes clear, you can look out for an indictment, Doctor Workman, for the murder of little Roy Miller!"

"What is it—what about this cat?" The doctor had become interested. "That's the first I ever heard about that. Is there anything to it?"

"Anything to it?" Pruiett was scornful. "Bill Miller says he tried to tell you, but that you wouldn't listen to him."

"No," Workman said, weakly. "I don't know anything about it. I didn't want to talk to him after I learned he was staying with that woman, and she—after his own little boy was..."

"That's just it," Pruiett cut in. "You won't listen to but one side of an issue. That's what's wrong with our system. If you get in jail, you're guilty until you prove yourself innocent, instead of the way the boys put it that wrote up the Constitution. I venture..."

"What was he going to tell me about the cat?" Workman persisted.

"Well," said Pruiett patronizingly, taking an easy chair, "well, the kid had a shoe box, with a string in it, an' the cat hung around the barber shop. He took..." Pruiett was concluding the narration an hour later, "... an' Miller's still got the box, an' all the boys around the shop remember how the cat had those fits just before the kid took sick. Now, doctor, on that hypothesis and based on your experience with this particular case, what, in your own opinion, caused this boys death?"

Doctor Workman mopped his forehead and looked much further away than his pale eye would carry out through the little window. He wasn't seeing the future alone; he was only considering it, as he looked into the past. All he had worked and striven for, his hopes, for himself and others, was about to end in shame and disgrace.

"Hydrophobia," he whispered, "he died from hydrophobia, a cat bite. And I was about to do that woman a terrible injustice. That's what makes it so bad. A terrible injustice."

"What about DeBarr," Pruiett pressed on. "He's goin' to swear that he found poison in the stomach. What are we goin' to do with him?"

The doctor shook his head, still gazing limply out the window. Pruiett had his answer ready for him.

"These chemists can make mistakes, can't they? Are their tests infallible? Everybody makes mistakes. DeBarr just gave that stomach the wrong test, and he's mistaken in his conclusion. That's the way it looks to me."

"Yes, that's it," Workman agreed. "I gave the boy bella donna, and he had a cat bite. DeBarr is wrong about it. I'll testify that it's possible, that it's easy, for chemical tests to go wrong."

"We'll need help; lots of it," Pruiett said. "Get out in the sagebrush in the mornin' and round up the country doctors. I want at least ten to testify, an' be sure you know how they'll answer my hypothetical question on the sick cat before you bring them in. They'll be helpin' you, more than they will Maggie Miller."

Pruiett won his case. As the staff man for *The Daily Oklahoman* saw it; "The defense alleged that the boy died of hydrophobia and experts testified in support of both theories. Several physicians testified that all the symptoms shown by the boy previous to his death denoted that he was suffering from hydrophobia. It was shown that he was seen playing with a sick kitten a few days before his death and that the kitten afterward died in convulsions."

The Law and Order League rued the ill day it hired Pruiett to go to Woodward. Their cheers turned to jeers as they followed the progress of Maggie's trial, and to groans as they read its final chapter.

"After deliberating from 10:30 Saturday morning to 4 o'clock in the afternoon, the jury in the case of Maggie Miller, charged with the poisoning of her step-son, Roy Miller, brought in a verdict of not guilty. " At the end of the long column, rehashing the weeks events at the trial, it was casually stated that "Moman Pruiett of Oklahoma City was counsel for the defense."

Pruiett traveled three thousand miles to try his tricks on a Pacific Coast jury in the celebrated Frank H. Carr-Atkinson murder case at Montesano, Washington in June of 1913. His client was acquitted. He had experienced a gnawing curiosity to try the sector since his trip there in '05 when he and Colonel Garvin had visited the Lewis and Clark Exposition at Portland. After he had cleared the wealthy stockman, the matter of the attorney's fee was considered. Pruiett told him that he wouldn't charge a fee; he would just charge mileage. They agreed that a dollar a mile would be both fair and adequate. After the railroad receipts had been figured, Carr gave Pruiett his check for $2,950. He got as far as Denver with it, where he threw a party at the Albany Hotel and let his guests carry off what was left as prizes of the poker game.

He got back to Oklahoma in time to stump the state for Lee Cruce, who was out again for governor. When Cruce won, Pruiett assorted $17,000 worth of canceled checks, representing sums he had spent since the Constitutional Convention, in the furtherance of Cruce and his campaign for governor. In Pruiett's book, it was about time for dividends to begin; in Cruce's, it was time to start being careful. The cautious governor, not unappreciative, was so sensitive and so spotlessly scrupulous that he was afraid to give Pruiett a decision in a perfectly square deal. He thought that he would be charged with bias, with trying to pay a political debt; so, he leaned backward. Where Pruiett had realized a fortune from his services in procuring pardons while "Railroad" Haskell, his arch enemy, was in office, the boys learned that hiring Pruiett, while Cruce was in the saddle, was all right if you wanted to be turned down. Cruce gave Pruiett one pardon, and it was handed to the applicant lawyer three weeks after his convict had died in the McAlester prison hospital.

"When the persons who caused the death of Thomas J. Gentry on the night of Saturday, January 6, 1912, mixed egg-nog and prepared food in the kitchen of the Gentry home before the killing took place, did they leave any prints on the utensils they used?" That pertinent question was being propounded by the current press. "Has evidence which might have been valuable in identifying the person or persons who murdered Thomas J. Gentry been destroyed?"

It was a conundrum. Pruiett had been employed to defend the sad eyed, handsome widow, Alverta Gentry, almost before Tom's body had been carried out of the house. There was respectable authority to support the insinuation of interested parties, which suggested that if Pruiett was in the case, and some fast work hadn't been done in covering up evidence, that it wasn't like Moman Pruiett.

Alverta Gentry was one of the few Pruiett clients who had to pay for her infraction of the legal precepts. No person or thing could minimize or justify the one night's depravity which she inadvertently admitted and then tried to deny. The jury, which convicted and sentenced her to life imprisonment, signed the verdict with the stink of what Pruiett called 'the most brutal crime I was ever connected with' rising and reeking in its nostrils.

The twenty-five year old defendant, with a good home, a good husband and a five year old son, started an affair with a grocery delivery-boy six years her junior according to the *Oklahoma News* on January 9, 1912. "The witness said he knew J. K. Mackey by sight as the man who frequently stopped for a period of a year at the Gentry home. He said that Mackey's wagon stopped so often at the home that his family remarked about it. He said that Mackey would stay for long periods at the house, and that one time, when he timed him, he stayed for an hour and a half."

Maurice Weightman was the nineteen year old brother of the accused. She referred to him, after their arrest, as 'my baby brother'. "Mackey's account of the killing, as detailed by Chief of Police Tilghman to the corner's jury, was as follows; ' Mackey claimed that he met Mrs. Gentry in front of a pool hall and walked with her to the post office. There they were joined by Weightman, and the three went to Gentry's home together. Mackey claimed that on the way out they drew straws, Weightman securing the short one, which decided that he should be the one to kill Gentry'."

The three jolly conspirators had a number of drinks before the man of the house came in, whether the detectives on the case could find finger prints or not. "One witness said he saw two empty whiskey bottles in the kitchen of the Gentry home, a pitcher partly filled with egg nog, and several stained glasses." When Gentry came in, and sat down in his easy chair before the fire, one of them stepped through the kitchen door and sent a pistol bullet into the back of his head. "The bullet entered Gentry's head at a point below and to the left of the crown, and came out between the nostrils, splitting the septum. It pierced a large artery of the brain, and death was instantaneous."

What shocked the conscience of the gory murder fans—even offended Pruiett's ideas on homicide etiquette—was the conduct of the three after the crime had been committed. They caught a street car and rode to a downtown rooming house, the Oke Hotel, where they took adjoining rooms, and the newly made widow went to bed with her grocery carrying paramour. There was a sweet serenity of conscience with the realization that at long last the embrace was not adulterous.

The little brother took another drink and went tranquilly to rest in the next room. As their confessions disclosed, as the *Daily Oklahoman*'s reproduced the story, and the corroboration of it by witnesses: "Mrs. E. R. Ferris—was called. She produced the register of the hotel, on which appeared the names of 'J. K. Mackey and wife,' followed by that of 'Harry Ratcliffe.' Mrs. Ferris stated that Mackey and Mrs. Gentry came to her hotel about 2 o'clock Sunday morning, and asked for a room. She assigned them to room number two and they retired." Harry Ratliffe was identified as Morris Weightman.

Mrs. Gentry affected some genuine horror and surprise when she walked in at mid-morning on Sunday, while her neighbors were starting to Sunday School, and found Tom sitting so still in his chair with that nasty looking brown stuff running out of a hole in his head. She ran screaming into the yard, and the crowd gathered. When they began to put that ever embarrassing interrogatory to her, 'where did you stay last night?' She got panicky. It had never occurred to her, or to the kids she had liquored up the night before, that that would make any difference. She stammered and blushed like a school girl, and they told the truth. By noon, J. K. and Maurice were in the bull pen. When they told Alverta, in her cell atop the city jail, that the boys had talked, all they had to do was get another tub. What they had omitted in the somber details, she supplied.

And then came Pruiett. According to the *Oklahoma News* on January 11, 1912 "Moman Pruiett maintains that third degree methods were resorted to in securing the confessions. 'Those confessions will not stand up before any court of law because they were obtained by such methods,' he said." The Press gave the Gentry case a lot of space; it excited a lot of local interest. "County Attorney Sam Hooker received a letter Thursday night ostensibly signed by twenty over-zealous individuals, who gave fictitious names, threatening to hang Mrs. Gentry, and her two confederates charged with the murder of Thomas J. Gentry, if the widow is permitted to attend the funeral."

The dead man had been long on fraternity, and it was a day when fraternal vows carried weight. "The Gentry funeral will be held Saturday midnight, at the Masonic temple, and further services at the First Christian Church Sunday afternoon. The temple services will be under the auspices of the consistory, and those Sunday afternoon, of the Blue Lodge." When Alverta read the notices in the evening paper, she decided to go. They wouldn't let Pruiett make her bond; so, he requested, then demanded, that they guard her with a couple of deputies and take her to the burial services. The lodge said they didn't want her there, and the members were all old enough to vote. The prosecuting attorney refused to permit her to go, and the District Judge backed him up.

Pruiett was mad; and, when he was mad, he swore. That is, he swore more, and louder, when he was mad than he did when he was in a good humor. Swearing promoted ideas, and a protracted delivery of profanity, and a couple of drinks of whiskey put his anger-swollen head to working. He grabbed the two-paragraph instrument, which he had just dictated, as it came out of his stenographer's machine. It was a power-of-attorney, where Alverta Gentry, as the widow and surviving next of kin, delegated all authority for the making of funeral arrangements and burial of her deceased husband, to Pruiett.

At 10 o'clock Saturday night Marshall and Harper's Funeral Parlor, on Broadway, was ablaze with light and alive with lodgemen. They had their long robes, ostrich hats and nickel-plated swords. The procession was about to begin to the temple, where a final tribute was to be paid to Brother Gentry. And then, things not on the program began to happen. A rickety wagon, with a thin, whinnying nag, blowing clouds of steam out into the freezing January night, pulled-up and stopped in the drive in front of the mortuary. A man with a black hat and overcoat jumped down from the seat beside the negro driver. It was Pruiett.

"I don't like the way you've handled this business," Pruiett said, handing the undertaker a sheaf of currency, "and neither does Mrs. Gentry. You're fired. You've got your money for embalmin' an' the casket, an' all you've done so far. I'm takin' this with me." He motioned for the negro driver to help him lift the casket.

"You can't do this, Pruiett," Marshall said. "The notices are out on this funeral, and the lodge is..."

"The hell I can't," Pruiett replied. "I've paid you off, and you're fired. You've got my authority from the widow right in your hand. This State makes it an offense to detain a dead body and you know it; but, if you don't recall right off, ask the judge, he'll tell you."

Pruiett flipped a finger toward a gowned lodge member, standing with the scowling group which surrounded him. It was the District Judge who had refused his client permission to attend the funeral that same forenoon.

When the casket was carried out, Pruiett had hold of one of the handles. He waived from the drivers seat at the swearing lodge members, all dressed up but with no one to bury, shivering on the illuminated porch. Pruiett announced that the funeral was postponed indefinitely, 'pending the arrival of relatives.' When the high ups of the order had apologized to him, and the consent was given for his murderous client and her guards to attend the ceremony, he turned the body back to them.

They convicted Alverta and gave her life in March of 1912. Her lawyer told her, as they put her on the train for the State's prison, that so long as his friend Cruce was governor, she couldn't hope to get a pardon or parole. He hated to lose a case; to see a client being sent up. He cheered himself by saying that it might have been worse, that she should have had the chair. He always said, 'it was the worst damned case I ever fooled with.' Alverta served less than three months. She developed stomach trouble, and Pruiett got her a parole in November of 1912.

He defended Maurice Weightman, 'the baby brother.' Profiting by his experiences in the sister's case, he ranted until he obtained a change of venue. The case was sent to El Reno, a neighboring county seat town to be tried in late June of 1912. Too much publicity, and too many unsavory expressions in editorial comment had biased the populous, so he charged. His client was unable to obtain a fair and impartial trial. He was probably right; surely more successful. According to the *Norman Transcript* "It is considered that Moman Pruiett secured quite a victory in the defense of Maurice Weightman, on trial at El Reno last week, for the murder of Thos. Gentry, when the jury brought in a verdict of first degree manslaughter, and gave Weightman a sentence of only five years. It was believed that he would be convicted of a much graver crime, and given a much heavier sentence." There was considerable comment on the grocery boy. "The attorney for the defense was vicious in his denunciation of Jesse Mackey, who had turned state's evidence against Mrs. Gentry and Weightman, and everybody seems to admit that the denunciations were thoroughly deserved. 'Unclean,' was the local cry against Mackey when he appeared as a witness. He was just as guilty as Mrs. Gentry or Weightman. He now goes free by reason of turning informer."

With the litigation closed, Mackey moved West. He took a job as ranch hand in New Mexico; but, he didn't hold it long. He was found by a gate in the field. He was dead; shot to death. A slight investigation was made into the circumstances, but no one came forward to claim credit or commendation for the deed. The Gentry case was finally and completely concluded.

Pruiett was borrowing energy from the neck of a bottle and keeping up the pace. A Turkish bath and a rough barber, preceded and followed by a stiff charge of liquor would sustain him, after a nights drinking, gambling and carousing, in the trial of the most exacting case. It was the Texas at Fort Worth or the Baltimore at Kansas City. There was business at St. Louis, or Chicago, and regularly to Washington. He had so many criminal cases on his docket that he knew he couldn't try them all, so he philosophically determined that he would try as many as he could, and when he could, 'and dissipate a little' in between.

In August of 1909 "Jim Bothwell and Edward Mitchell, charged with holding up a gambling joint operated by Lon Ammerman and

Frank Buxton, were acquitted this afternoon. Moman Pruiett of Oklahoma City represented them." The *Sapulpa Light,* principal publication for Creek County, born Moman County, chronicled the usual arrival, fan-fare and departure of Pruiett.

The *Dallas News,* in mid-August of 1910, saw enough of interest in a business call, in contrast to his numerous pleasure visits, to comment upon it. "Frank Holloway, known to many as Robert Hunley, charged with being implicated in several bank blowing exploits in Texas, was released on bond by Judge Simmons of Fort Worth last Saturday. Holloway protests his innocence of all the charges preferred against him and asserts that he can prove an alibi. His picture is in the possession of the local secret service department, and he is known as a dangerous man. He has spent $25,000 defending himself against the Texas charges, he says. Moman Pruiett of Oklahoma City is his attorney."

That was the kind of money that Pruiett liked to find on clients. And, as to the alibi? He would be better than a green hand at making one stick. Were Doc Richards and John Evans at-large as the result of anything else? Could Red Fox be dealing from the bottom of the deck in the Wichita Mountain gambling joints if Pruiett didn't know how to make an alibi stand up? Holloway, or Hunley, or whatever his real name might have been, was in good hands, even if he did growl, as he walked from the old Tarrant County, Texas, Courthouse that 'he thought his lawyer might come to court for him once without smelling like a damned mash barrel.' Pruiett laughed him into a side street saloon and handicapped him the morning start; then, he put him under a back room table, drink for drink. The *News* had said that 'he was known as a dangerous man.'

"Moman Pruiett, the renowned criminal lawyer, had been secured by Allison Ooley, the Deputy Sheriff who is charged with the murder of 'Bronc' Heath, for his attorney. Ooley's release was obtained Wednesday by Pruiett through a habeas corpus proceedings. The release was made on a $5000 bond, which was given by local citizens." *The Courier,* in the county originally named for Pruiett, was printing what was to be the foreword to another acquittal story for Pruiett and his clients.

Katherine Snodgrass killed husband Frank in their Harvey Street residence in Oklahoma City in January of 1910, and Pruiett got her off with the payment of $17.50 court costs. The house went to Pruiett, along with an assignment of a fair bank account; but, she was free, and rid of Frank besides. She acknowledged that it was a bargain.

CHAPTER THIRTEEN

WHEREIN PRUIETT LOSES A HARD FOUGHT CONTEST BEFORE THE CANADIAN KING'S BENCH, AND SEES HIS ACCUSED MURDERESS EXTRADITED TO THE UNITED STATES FOR TRIAL. AND HOW HE COUPLES VIRTUE AND VICE TOGETHER TO RAISE FUNDS IN OLD SEATTLE, AND TREATS THE PACIFIC SLOPE PRESS TO A LIBERAL PORTION OF HIS PRE-TRIAL PROPAGANDA BEFORE HE ASTOUNDS THE WESTERN CITIZENRY, AND HIS FRIEND THE GOVERNOR, BY WRINGING A VERDICT OF ACQUITTAL, FOR HIS CLIENT, FROM A HOSTILE JURY.

It was June again, and there in the vale of the Swinomish, as on the Washita River, the air was full of its dank sweetness. Pruiett was in Seattle, Washington. The business was murder; the respite, for the instant, was poker. June, with its bracing night application from the Pacific and Puget Sound, bore no comfort to Pruiett. The lights in the bar room of the old Seattle Hotel were bright, and the man with the coal-black hair roached over his ears was puffing and chewing a long cigar at the main table in the adjoining gambling room. A huge diamond glittered in the square black knot at his high-collared throat, while a gaudier one shone from the knuckle of his immobile left hand.

A long-necked quart bottle at his right, with a single glass beside it, was taking his attention away from the game before him. The last portion of its content went out of sight with the last of the chips that had stood before him. He stood disconsolately, and placing a large black hat carelessly atop the bulging contour of hair, he adjusted the tie and stone as he walked toward the bar.

"One more glass of whiskey," he said evenly. "One more and I'll go on up to bed."

"Yes, sir, Mr. Pruiett," the bar-keep replied briskly. "The same kind?"

"Yes, the same kind," Pruiett growled.

The boy put the bottle on the polished bar, feigning interest. "Was your luck bad tonight, Mr. Pruiett?" he inquired.

"I lost a $1,000," Pruiett said, "an' I never won a pot."

"Yes," he agreed, "Your luck must be down a little."

"Either that, or your game's awful god-damned crooked," Pruiett observed.

The bar-keep appeared not to hear. The speaker tossed a coin down on the bar and strolled out.

Pruiett's picture, with a full account of the nature of his business in Seattle, had been in both the *Star* and the *Intelligencer* earlier that day. He was acknowledged about the hotel, by guest and employee alike, as a visiting celebrity. Nodding to the girl at the telegraph desk, he sent a telegram to his office associates at Oklahoma City, advising that he was out of funds, and requesting that $500 be sent immediately. He had already ascertained that the Hotel wouldn't like to accommodate him for that amount on a check, even with the big send-off in the press, unless he had a substantial endorser.

His reply was waiting at nine the next morning when he stepped briskly into the lobby from the elevator. It was a frank, even vulgar refusal. Concluding, the missive read, "and why not come home by way of Cape Horn?" Pruiett was evidently off his course, as it was now easy for him to go, and he grinned, biting the end off a cigar. He envisioned the black frame of mind his less imaginative but more profoundly practical associates must have been in on receiving his night message. Instead of going to breakfast, he stepped over the negro, on hands and knees scrubbing the marble step into the bar, and ordered Green River whiskey.

Pruiett was traveling with a client, a middle-aged woman and her fifteen-year-old son, and his lack of cash was embarrassing. His associates at home had turned down his plea for aid. His wife knew how much money he had received with his last wire from home, and how recently he had received it. The bills were running up at the hotel.

It was luck, in place of resourcefulness, that came to aid him first. A lobby bell-hop was paging him. He hurried to the phone booth.

"Pruiett?" He heard a male voice over the wire. "Pruiett? Is this Moman Pruiett of Oklahoma City?"

"Yes, this is Pruiett," he replied readily. "Who is this?"

"Doctor Carter Helm Jones," the voice supplied, "of the First Baptist Church in Seattle."

There was genuine cordiality in Pruiett's tone as he told the caller he was glad to hear his voice. The Doctor Jones, or Reverend Jones, was a Baptist minister, and had before his assignment to the West Coast, been the pastor of Pruiett's church at home. He was a man of position and prominence in Seattle, and that was what the Oklahoma lawyer needed more than anything else at the particular time.

"We saw your picture in the paper last evening," the preacher was saying. "Mrs. Jones wanted me to call you; but, I knew you would be tired, so I waited 'til this morning. How are you, and how is Mrs. Pruiett?"

"I'm a little tired," Pruiett confesses. "I had a bad evening; however, my health is good. Mrs. Pruiett is not with me."

"Can you come out to dinner? Mrs. Jones is anxious to see you, and she insists that you come."

"No," Pruiett replied, "My train leaves at 1 o'clock and I have a number of things to take care of before. And, by the way, I'm a little embarrassed, out of funds, and was just preparing to wire the bank at home for an order. I was just wondering..."

"Not at all, Pruiett, not at all," came the prompt and welcome interruption. "My bank is right across from your hotel. If you can't come out here, we'll come down there to see you."

Pruiett and the Reverend Jones met in the hotel lobby a few minutes later. Mrs. Jones was with him. Pruiett wrote a check for $500, the preacher endorsed it, and the three of them walked to the hotel desk to present it for cash. The clerk came back with an apologetic expression.

"I'm so sorry," he said. "So very sorry. We don't have enough cash to handle it this morning. If you'll bring it back a little later..."

Doctor Jones interrupted. "It's the bank right across the street, where I do business," he said, pointing through the plate window. "We can walk over there and cash it."

The obliging clerk had a suggestion to make. "I can call over and identify Mr. Pruiett, and tell them he is coming over with it. I'll save you a trip."

Pruiett agreed. The three chatted a little longer before the minister and his wife departed.

"The Seattle Bank across the street is where I do most of my business," Dr. Jones advised as he departed, "but, if anything goes wrong, you can go to the City National Bank a block up. Our church has a big deposit there, and I know they will be glad to handle it for you."

Complimenting himself on his unfailing good luck, Pruiett hurried to the closest bank. The officer he had been referred to greeted him considerately; but, he remained in the back office so long that the waiting applicant's suspicions arose. When he did appear, he wore the same kind of an apologetic look as Pruiett had seen on the face of the hotel clerk.

"I'm very sorry, Mr. Pruiett," he said, "but this kind of an item is very unsatisfactory to our officers. The exchange fee is very slight, and while we know of you, and acknowledge the sufficiency of the endorsement, there is always an element of difficulty connected. We would just rather not handle your paper."

Pruiett gave him the poker face as he thanked him and turned away. Knowledge of another bank where he could take his righteously endorsed check was not enough to keep him from being apprehensive when he reflected over his actual plight, and what he would have to do if this plan didn't work.

The vice-president of the other bank took time for conference and consideration after the check was presented to him; but, his decision was the same. As he stroked his white vandyke, or patted his slick and utterly bald head, he gave Pruiett to understand that, while he hated to do it, he was required to turn down the endorsement of Reverend Carter Helm Jones. Pruiett went back to the bar at the Seattle Hotel for a glass of Green River. He was trying to elect between sending a wire to the wife, or one to his banker. Under the circumstances, having to approach either for cash was the same as an admission of extravagance, and what went with it, on the road.

But, he retained his Pruiett luck. They were paging him again, and as he began to realize that it was his own name that was drifting in between the velvet portieres, he was not so quick to respond as he had been to the last exploratory bellow. He sipped his drink and mused. It would not be Doctor Jones. He wouldn't be calling back so soon, and so near to train time. He didn't know any one else in Seattle, unless—. Yes, that was it. The banker had reconsidered; probably had decided that he couldn't face his preacher and admit that he had rejected his friend's check. Surely, that was it. He was going to get the money; be spared that embarrassing appeal to home for relief. He left the bar and hurried from the bar room.

"Pruiett!" He hurled his most business-like bellow into the tilted transmitter. "Pruiett."

"Hello, Moman," a soft sweet voice cooed in his ear. "Is that you Moman, dear?"

"Who the hell is this?" he cried. He was surprised and disappointed. "This is Pruiett."

"I saw your picture in the paper, and I was scared to death you would get out of town before I got to see you," the sweet voice continued, sweeter than ever. "How are you, dear?"

"I'm all right," he managed to answer, "but who is this?"

The caller was playful.

"Don't you know?" she blandly catechized. "You're not at all as flattering as you used to be. How is R. J.? Is he still trying to get hold of all the money in Oklahoma?"

That was a cue, and Pruiett almost caught it; but, his troubles were resting so heavily that it got away from him. He had to ask her again who she was.

"This is Josephine," she said. "I've married again, since you got my divorce for me; so, you wouldn't know my last name. Josephine Hall? Remember?"

Pruiett remembered, with a flood of recollections.

"How are you, Moman dear?" she inquired again.

"Well, I'll tell you," he said. "I'm not so good. I'm a long ways from home and I'm flat broke. I was just ready to wire home for cash and I hate like hell to do it; but, I can't get a soul out here to cash my check."

The frank confession and its dolorous tone brought a peal of merry laughter.

"Bless your heart," she laughed. "Bless your heart. Come on out here and I'll cash your check. I've just got to see you before you go. I'm dying for some one who can answer some questions about some of my old friends. Come on out here."

"Out where?" Pruiett questioned bluntly. "Where are you?"

She was still laughing merrily as she answered him. "My place is 2912 Pine," she said, "put it down so you won't forget it. 2912 Pine, and hurry on, dear. And bring the check."

Pruiett was taking stock as he went through the wide door of the Hotel toward a line of waiting taxicabs. He had less than $2.

"How much to 2912 Pine?" he inquired of the first driver.

"A buck," was the prompt response.

"Let's go," said Pruiett, stepping through the low door into the uncovered, hard seated driver's compartment.

"You'll find it a lot better in the back," the driver volunteered. "These cobblestones is kind of rough, and that seat ain't none too soft."

"Let's go," said Pruiett again, impatiently. "I want to ride up here with you."

As soon as they were off, Pruiett turned to the driver. He lost no time in getting to the point.

"What kind of a place is 2912 Pine, where we're going?"

"It's the fanciest whore-house in Seattle," was the prompt, proud response.

"Well, hurry it up," said Pruiett. "What are we waiting for?"

The place on Pine set far back from the curb and sidewalk. It was of brownstone, a two-tone creation in light and dark brown, with curving glass in the bay windows behind the colonnaded porch, and shining green and blue prisms in the diamond-shaped openings above and between them.

Pruiett marched to the carved door and pulled the old fashioned door bell. A yellow wench with pierced ears and straight, oily hair admitted him. The nap of the Brussels carpet covering the floor of the mirrored hallway tickled his ankles, and as he tried to view the magnificence of the tapestry on the walls between the mirrors, and the leafwork of the elegantly plated chandeliers, he had to shake off a pack of dogs that leaped up about him. There were little ones, with bald bodies tied in bright ribbons; great flat-footed ones that wore steel spiked collars, and dogs of all other colors and sizes ranging in between. The grinning wench helped him to push them down as she guided him into a high ceilinged sitting room, elegantly fitted, and slid the tall panels together behind him.

"Miss Josephine will be down in just a minute," she said. "She told me you was comin', an' to make you comfo'table."

"All right," he said, "I need a drink. Can you get me a drink?"

She departed with her grin but without an answer. He had scarcely time to look around at a part of the elegance of the old place when she returned with a pail of ice, with two bottles of champagne, and glasses. Then Josephine came in.

"Moman, dear! I'm so glad to see you," she said, as the twist of her rapid approach across the soft floor caused the feather-trimmed hem of her long skirt to wave and billow. "So glad to see you, again."

He gave her the kind of embrace which the approach suggested, or required. Turning her loose and holding her back for a second look, he could note that the seven years elapsing since he had seen her last had been more than gentle, regardless of what he had just heard and understood about the nature of her business.

"It's been a long time since I saw you, Josie," he said. "But, you're as young and charmin' as ever. I've often wondered what had become of you."

"Don't lie," she smilingly rebuked. "You were as cross as you used to be, when I called you. I really believe it made you mad."

"I'm so damned worried, I can't think," he explained. "What I was tellin' you, about the expenses, is the truth. I lost my roll in a game at the hotel last night, and it's goin' to be embarrassin' as hell if I can't cash a check. I'm worried about it."

Josephine, fondling a bubbling glass, had twisted into the far corner of the silken seat. She was beautiful, with flashing eyes, teeth and diamonds. Her bare arms were plump and white. Her busts and hips were over, but not disproportionately, developed.

"Whatever became of Joe?" Pruiett inquired.

"I don't know," she said. "I heard he went to California. I guess he's still the proud, struggling baggage clerk."

"How did you happen to marry such a bird?"

"I was stuck on him, an' I thought he was smarter than he turned out to be. I didn't think he was so damn straight."

They laughed together. "Did he ever know who promoted the divorce?" Pruiett asked.

"He knew you were my lawyer, if that's what you mean. He knew that, and cussed you for it."

"That ain't what I mean. I said, who promoted it? I'm talking about R. J., the money-bag."

"I don't know whether he did or not?" she answered. "But, I don't think so. He didn't seem to pay any attention, much, after the divorce."

"When you took up so quick with R. J., afterward, I thought he might have got suspicious. A lot of people know that R. J. paid me a good fee for representin' you."

"If Joe knew it, or suspected it, he never let on. He never tried to cause us any trouble," she said.

"How about R. J.?" Pruiett persisted. "Did he know what the deal was between us? Did he know we was splittin' his dough, an'..." She cast her glance toward the bubbling glass, while a perceptible flush mounted her fair forehead. Their hands met across the cushions in an affectionate clasp.

"How you talk," she smiled.

Pruiett looked at his watch and started. "I meet my people at the station in an hour, an' I've got to get my things out of the hotel. What about this check?"

"How much is it, dear?" she asked.

"Five hundred," he answered. "I'm stoppin' at Denver to take depositions in this case, an' I've got a lot of expenses. I need all of that, an' maybe more."

"Well, all right, you can get it," she said soothingly. "I don't have it here this morning, but it's in the bank. I'll put my name on it and you can stop by on your way to the station. No, I'll have my boy drive you there, and then take you to the hotel."

Pruiett handed her the check, dubiously.

She took a gold pen from the tall mahogany secretary. "Now," she said. "You take this to the City National Bank and present it to Mr. Barbour, and tell him I sent you. You'll get the money."

"Is Barbour a bald-headed fellow with a vandyke?" Pruiett inquired.

Josephine smiled and nodded as she answered. "Yes, that's Mr. Barbour. He'll take care of you."

"No, he won't, either," Pruiett disagreed. "He's the one who just turned me down. Can't you let me take it to some other place...?"

Josephine picked up a small 'phone and called a number from memory.

"Mr. Barbour?" she said, when she had had a response. "Mr. Barbour, this is Josephine. I have a friend, a very dear friend, from out of town, who wishes to cash a large check, and I've endorsed it for him. I'd like for him to have the money, immediately. Do you understand? Thank you, Mr. Barbour—thank you, dear."

"I don't like that guy," Pruiett insisted, as she was holding him and helping him toward a big car waiting in the shaded drive. "An' I hate like hell to see him again; but, I've got to have that jack..."

The contents of the champagne bottle were dancing and sparkling in his dark eyes as he reclined in the car seat and mused over the strange, unorthodox happenings. It seemed that there was always an answer, an aid, in his every dilemma; and there was usually a lovely female connected with it. He could recall similar situations, such as.... His thoughts were interrupted by the uniformed negro who had already opened the car's door in front of the bank.

Barbour was no happier to meet him again, under the circumstances, than he was to meet Barbour. They smiled and bowed while the banker took the check. He returned almost immediately with the money.

"You forgot to deduct the exchange fee," Pruiett reminded him, very politely.

"No," said Barbour, even more politely. "The charge is slight and we are remitting it. We are glad to accommodate you, Mr. Pruiett."

"But, I don't like for you to do that," Pruiett insisted. "This is business, and I'd like for it to be handled that way."

Barbour was beaming with indulgence. He was stroking his white stub of a beard and smirking. "We have our own way of handling things out here in Seattle," he beamed. "It may seem a little different, or odd, to a stranger, but it's our own way. We like it, doing it different. Our ways are big. It's the influence of the Rockies, and the Pacific, you know?"

Pruiett shook his head as he started to leave. "You will pardon the observation," he drawled, "but I've noticed that you do handle things differently here to any other place where I've been, an' I've been to quite a few places. It's the first god damned town I ever saw where a man with money in the bank had to have his check endorsed by the pastor of its biggest church and the madam of its most flourishing whore-house, before he could get it cashed."

"The common law ain't nothin' but common sense," Pruiett maintained. "A successful lawyer's no freak. He's just a level-headed guy with brains enough in his head to reason things out."

Pruiett was a profound and practical thinker. He was loud and boisterous, and his sensationalism oftentimes attracted attention away from his learning, and understanding, but it was always present to aid him.

"Come right in, judge," Pruiett exclaimed, rising with unusual deference and shaking hands. His caller was an associate justice on the Oklahoma Criminal Court of Appeals.

"I'm here on serious business, Moman," the judge said, abruptly. "I want to hire you in a white slave case."

"You mean...?"

"No, it's not me," the judge smiled. "I'm not old enough to be gettin' my tail in that kind of a crack. It's my father-in-law, the wife's old man."

"Has he been indicted?" Pruiett inquired.

"No, but he's in for it. There's a Federal Grand Jury in session an' a subpoena out for the gal. I don't see any way of blockin' it, at all, once they get her story in the grand jury room."

"Give me the dope," Pruiett invited, holding a box of cigars toward the judge.

"The old man owns a lot of land down around Cero Gordo, Arkansas," the judge began. "He's got some poor-folks for tenants, farmin' it on shares, an' they got a buxom daughter. She's a good lookin' bitch about seventeen or eighteen. He took'er up to Kansas City an' bought a bunch of fancy clothes an' stuff, an'..."

"An' when she got home, the folks wanted to know who the Santa Claus was? Wasn't that it?" Pruiett inquired.

"That's right," the judge said. "An'..."

"An' then they wanted Santa Claus to come again, or they'd have to protect Sal's virtue with a criminal prosecution?"

"There ain't no use of me tellin' you, when you're able to tell me," the judge laughed. "You must be readin' my mind."

"They're all alike," Pruiett said. "The difference between rape an' mutual lust is in the check book. I'll bet I can settle with the outraged parents for less than the old man can defend for in K. C."

"We're willing to pay off," the judge answered. "Can you handle if for us?"

"I'm on my way to Cero Gordo right now," Pruiett said. "When I wire, shoot me the money orders. Maybe that little girl'll have to answer to that subpoena the Federal Grand Jury's tryin' to serve on her; but, if I get down there in time, I don't think she'll have much to tell 'em."

Pruiett sauntered into the chambers of United States District Judge Orba S. Van Valkenberg at Kansas City. The insolent grin of perfect confidence was spread across his handsome face.

"The clerk over at the Baltimore Hotel said you called a' hour ago," he smiled. "Sorry to keep a Federal Court waitin', but I was tied up in the barbershop an'..."

"The Grand Jury's the one being detained," Van Valkenberg said, sternly. "Mr. Frank Wilson, Assistant United States District Atorney, "has asked me to commit this child for contempt, and it appears that you are the one that is really in contempt of court—and the Grand Jury. She says she refuses to answer, on your counsel!"

Pruiett looked at the frightened Arkansas girl and gave her a reassuring smile. "Our Constitution provides," Pruiett said, speaking to the judge as if he were a law student, "that one does not have to incriminate or degrade one's self. I advised the child of that much."

"The District Attorney, and this Court, has guaranteed full immunity to the witness." Van Valkenberg gritted. "Did you tell her that when she had her immunity, that she had to testify, or be subject to punishment for contempt."

"I did, your honor," Pruiett answered. "If this court could grant her full immunity, my client would not hesitate to answer; but, until that is done, she shall refuse to testify."

"Young lady," the judge said. "This court assures you, again, here in the presence of your attorney, that you need have no fear of criminal prosecution, from anything which you disclose in your testimony. Now, go back to the jury room and answer the questions the District Attorney asks you."

The girl looked at Pruiett. Pruiett shook his head and smiled.

"That isn't full immunity," he said. "That isn't even half-assurance that she won't be prosecuted. She will continue to refuse to answer any questions that you put to her in this investigation."

Van Valkenberg turned purple and red. "You are in contempt yourself, Mr. Pruiett," he choked. "Why shouldn't you be punished for deliberately opposing this Court?"

"But I'm not your honor," Pruiett assured him. "When my client has all immunity which she is entitled to as a citizen, then I'll tell her to answer."

"What's your point?" the prosecuting attorney demanded.

"You are tryin' to make a white slave case on this child's testimony,"

Pruiett replied. "You can guarantee her immunity from criminal prosecution, and liability, but can you immunize her from the badge of disgrace she'll carry to her grave if she gives you the information you want?" Pruiett struck a heroic attitude in the middle of the office floor. "You pin the scarlet letter of shame upon her young breast, an' send her out into the world degraded by her own admission, and you have no semblance of power to guard or protect her. You can refrain from prosecution, but how many wagging tongues can you stop? How many heartaches can you abate? How many dragging strides, as she walks the street peddling the lack of virtue which you exposed to public knowledge, can you retrace?"

"You have your law to enforce, but she has her reputation as a chaste woman to protect. Unless you can enforce your writ without transgressing her holiest right, then you must retire and let your statute suffer. You are powerless to deliver the immunity which you must guarantee before you can compel her to answer. She will not utter the words which drop the cloak of virtue from about her shoulders, and you may send the child to the dungeon, and her oft-erring counsel along with her, if the laws of the land are so unjust as to require the one or the other."

The Court drummed on his desk. "What about that?" he inquired of the District Attorney.

"I haven't had the question raised before," Wilson answered, frankly. "It doesn't appeal to me, however, as being sound logic, or law. I..."

"It appeals to me," the Court said. "Have you any authority for your position, Mr. Pruiett?"

"The authority of common sense," Pruiett answered. "I haven't read any cases on it, but the law's just. If you want to give me a little time in the library, I'll see about it."

"We'll continue this matter until after lunch," Van Valkenberg said. "I'd like to have some cases on that question."

Women's virtue was safe in the robed embrace of justice. Pruiett found his cases, although he went back to the court's of old England. The girl didn't have to talk and the government couldn't make out a case without her. The Washita stallion had dropped another stumbling block in the pathway of law enforcement.

To win a concession of concurrent life sentences for his client from Judge George W. Clark, Pruiett quoted Langdon Smith's poem "When You Were A Tadpole And I a Fig." When asked what the difference between two life sentences that would run concurrently or consecutively, Pruiett remarked that "I had to win at least one round of this case, an' they'd beat me at ever' turn up to that one." Archives & Manuscripts Division of the Oklahoma Historical Society.

Persistence had its reasonable limits in Pruiett practice. When a jury convicted W. T. Maness of murder for the death of Cecil Jones, and fixed his punishment at life imprisonment, Pruiett, his lawyer, knew that the time for resistance was past. The State had another charge of the same character, for Maness had murdered two Jones and Sherman Morton before his blazing pistol had ceased to fire. Pruiett announced, when formal sentence on the first conviction had been made, that his client would plead guilty to the content of the second charge in late 1926.

'Very well," Judge George W. Clark observed. "It will be the judgment and sentence of the court that you be sentenced to life imprisonment on the second charge."

"Might I inquire," Pruiett asked, rising carelessly, "whether those sentences are to run concurrently, or consecutively?"

There was a titter from the gallery. "Are you trying to make fun of this court, Mr. Pruiett," Judge Clark demanded, belligerently.

"Not at all, your honor," Pruiett answered. "This is a matter of the utmost gravity, both to me and my client. I insist that the record show whether the sentences in the two cases run concurrently or consecutively."

Clark pondered. He didn't want to be ridiculed, and he didn't want to commit judicial error. Pruiett's manner of complete sincerity confused him.

"What difference could it make?" he demanded. "This man's been sentenced to life imprisonment. He hasn't got but one life, so any sentence rendered after that is actually surplusage. I sentenced him to life just to be consistent with the sentence in the case where a jury convicted him. What's the difference?"

"I recall the sweet words of the poet, Langdon Smith, in 'When You Were A Tadpole And I A Fig', " Pruiett said, advancing into the opening before the bench:

"God wrought our souls from the Tremedoc beds
and furnished them wings to fly;
He has sown our spawn in the world's dim dawn,
and I know that it shall die.

Though cities have sprung above the graves,
where the crooked-bone men made war,

And the ox-wain creaks o'er the buried caves,
where the mummied mammoth are.

Our lives are old and our loves are old,
and death shall come again,
Should it come today, what man may say,
We shall not live again?"

His tones were like the whispers of time. His gestures, and expressions, gave him the air of utmost sincerity.

"I believe in the Christian religion," Pruiett said, devoutly, "but my client believes in the reincarnation of the soul. He believes that after this mis-spent life, he'll come back to earth again, in some other form or in some other body. He doesn't want another lifetime of imprisonment hanging over him."

Clark scratched his head. There was something to that argument. Pruiett wasn't poking fund at the court. He was too devout, and too serious for that.

"Let the record show that the sentences are to run concurrently," he said, as he folded his papers and moved down from the bench.

"That may not be much consolation to you; but, it is to me," Pruiett said to Maness. "I had to win at least one round of this case, an' they'd beat me at ever' turn up to that one. If you come back as a bird-dog or a jackass, you can look the cops in the eye without a flicker. When you serve that one life sentence, you are even up with the majesty of the law."

Governor Lee Cruce was distressed. His Chickasaw Nation colleague, his former campaign manager and financial backer, had invaded the Dominion of Canada and was creating such a disturbance with the King's Bench that international complications were threatened. It was Pruiett, resisting the efforts of the State of Oklahoma to extradite Lorena Mathews, a buxom widow wanted for the murder of her wealthy, ranch-owning husband. The legislature was in session and the sensitive ear of the chief executive could hear the whispers of political opposition: "He's overlooking Pruiett's outrageous conduct because Pruiett backed him in his campaign." Cruce demanded that the legislative

WS. DENVER, COLORADO, THURSDAY, DE

Negro Trails Woman 4,000 Miles

Held as Slayer of Her Husband

PRINCIPALS in the chase and capture of Mrs. Laurena Matthews, who is being taken to Oklahoma to stand trial for the murder of her husband four years ago. Above: Mrs. Lurancy Harris, the Canadian police officer, who has Mrs. Matthews in charge. Below: Mrs. Matthews.

Black Gets Revenge After Four Years Dogging Footsteps of White Employer.

LAURENA MATHEWS, SHOWN HERE, AND HER HIRED HAND, A BLACK MAN, BRUTALLY KILLED HER HUSBAND AND THEN CARRIED ON A VERY OPEN AND PUBLIC AFFAIR IN PAYNE COUNTY. THE ROMANCE WAS ON THE ROCKS IN LESS THAN A YEAR AND MATHEWS FLED TO CANADA WHERE SHE WAS CAPTURED. THE WOMAN IN THE FUR HAT IS CANADIAN POLICEWOMAN LURANCY HARRIS WHO ACCOMPANIED MRS. MATHEWS WHEN SHE WAS RETURNED TO OKLAHOMA FOR TRIAL. COURTESY *MOMAN PRUIETT: CRIMINAL LAWYER.*

body appropriate $5,000 to pay the expense of concluding the proceedings, and insuring the return of the accused woman.

The act and its performance was a trifle hard on Pruiett, who, until that time, was having the fun of his life with the white-wigged Canadian justices. He had made four trips to Edmonton, in Alberta province, in one year, and had each time successfully resisted the efforts of the United States authorities to move the woman across the line. They had arrested her again, in Vancouver, British Columbia, in June of 1913 according to the Seattle *Post-Intelligencer* and had been holding her there, when the Governor gave the push that was to cause her to be extradited.

Back in Oklahoma, Pruiett badgered the courts until they set her bond; but, they set it so high that they thought she wouldn't be able to make it. Pruiett scheduled a portion of his own unencumbered real estate on the $25,000 bond to make it without assistance. Then, he took her on a trip back through the Canadian Northwest, developing evidence by deposition which he intended to use in the actual trial of her case.

When Lawrence Mathews had been put away, he was considered to have been the victim of a perfectly legitimate mishap. "On the night of December 5, 1908, between eight and nine o'clock, Mrs. Mathews went to a neighbor and told him the mules were kicking Lawrence to death in the barn. The neighbor then went back with her and assisted in carrying the body from the barn to the house." It was the *Advance-Democrat* of Stillwater, Payne County, on January 16, 1913, recounting and recollecting, as best it could, the strange circumstances around Lawrence Mathews' death.

According to the account, "the ranch owned by Mathews at the time of his death lies principally in the Stillwater bottom and is one of the finest in Payne County. His family consisted of himself and his wife, and a boy and a girl about eight and ten years, respectively." He had actually owned, along with a great variety of livestock, a span of young mules that were unusually mean and vicious, what Mathews called 'fighters'. The accused woman's version was that on the night of the tragedy the young mules started to fight, causing such a commotion in the barn that Mathews went out to try to stop them. When he was found, there were mule-shoe prints on his face and cranium, and the cause of his death was perfunctorily attributed to the rough treatment, which it appeared, the mules had given him.

Jim Chapman was a common laborer employed on the Mathews ranch. He was a stalwart specimen of physical development, with skin as black as anthracite and with muscle as solid. Chapman was to later tell an amazing story of a love affair between himself and the middle-aged farm mother which culminated in a plot, and its execution, with the murder of Mathews. The negro said that he choked the man as he sat in a chair, while his wife beat him in the head with an iron poker. Then, they carried the fresh corpse to the mule's stalls and flung it at the animal's heels, so that the hoof tracks, apparent with his removal, became evident.

It was almost a year after Mathews' burial that the first rumble came. Mrs. Mathews and her negro hired-man had become careless with their relations, in fact, were flaunting them in the community's collective faces. A move was started to take the children away from her—'to remove them from the injurious effect of such lascivious conduct ' "Mrs. Mathews and Chapman had unbridled all caution and were constantly together, at her home or at Chapman's house, or at work on her farm. She was seen to take refreshments to him in the field where he was at work, and while Chapman's wife was in Texas, she was at Chapman's place almost every night and would leave somewhere from ten to two o'clock in the morning. They were seen to take their fishing rods and go fishing together—Mrs. Mathews went with him to Perry—she went with him to negro picnics—she had him constantly with her at her table, and with her family, when he was at work for her. They had been seen together on the creeks west of Stillwater, and were seen to enter a stairway, in Stillwater, which led to some upstairs room which were, at the time, vacant.They were seen walking through Donart's field one morning with their arms around each other." The little *Advance-Democrat* either knew what it was talking about, or had a wholesome contempt for libel suits. It was going pretty strong on Mrs. Mathews.

Acting under the authority of the State Juvenile Law, a neighbor filed a formal complaint against her. "The trial of Mrs. Mathews to take her children away from her lasted twenty-one days.The feeling on both sides was bitter—the colored population armed itself. The jury rendered a verdict taking the children away from Mrs. Mathews. On the evening that Judge Burns came up from Cushing to pass on her motion for a new trial, Chapman and Mrs. Mathews went to the home of a negro tenant of hers and wanted to stay overnight together. The public had not lost interest in the case and the negro would not allow them to stay, but they were furnished some bed quilts and they went into the cotton patch, where they spent the night together. Within a few days, Chapman left and went to Canada—finally landing at Edmonton. Mrs. Mathews also left and went to Canada."

The black and white romance was on the rocks in less than a year. When Mrs. Mathews tried to shake the negro, he wouldn't shake. The liberties which he insisted on taking about the Clover Bar Ranch, a wheat farm which she had bought and had been operating with his help, were beginning to embarrass her. "He became such a nuisance to her that she complained to Police Chief Lancey. When spoken to by the chief, the negro stated that he had murdered Mathews, and implicated Mrs. Mathews. His statements were very contradictory when he was placed under a grueling examination by the police, who soon abandoned the case. They did not place any credence in his remarks. Then, Chapman went to the mounted police, who arrested him and the woman also on his statement. "

On May 17, 1913, the *Edmonton Daily Capital* had had that much, and more to say. This organ contended that Mrs. Mathews was being persecuted by the negro and the officers who persisted in extraditing her. In a later edition it stated: "The life that Mrs. Mathews led while she was in Edmonton and Calgary and the fact that she had the intimate friendship and good-will of a large circle of eminently respectable and well-to-do people of both cities, should absolutely prove the falseness of the scurrilous attack made on her character by a confessed murderer, who says she conducted a house of ill-repute in this city."

Chapman waived extradition, came home and started doing twenty-five years which they gave him on a guilty plea. A public-spirited lawyer named James L. Springer started a campaign, from Chapman's cell in the State Penitentiary, which was to result in the recovery of the suspected woman, whom they had tried so hard, and for so long, to grab. In an open letter, published over his own signature, Springer told of the progress of his maneuvers.

Stillwater Advance-Democrat: "A committee of five citizens called on Governor Cruce and the Attorney General for the purpose of interesting them in appointing me special consul for the prosecution of this case and making a trip to Canada to bring about the extradition of Mrs. Mathews. They both promised to aid in every way they could; and, on October 3, 1912, Cruce appointed Springer to represent the State of Oklahoma in extradition proceedings. I immediately took the matter up with the State Department at Washington, D. C., and had the Governor of Oklahoma to request the arrest of Mrs. Mathews in Canada. She was arrested on the 16th day of October at Vancouver, B. C., Canada."

And so they took her back to Oklahoma. The *Denver Daily News* on October 12, 1912, carried her picture, being guarded by a Canadian Policewoman, who wore a fur hat. The Canadian good will had extended south from Puget Sound, for the *News'* attitude was decidedly sympathetic. "Trailed by a negro, who twice baffled in efforts to cause her indictment by an Oklahoma Grand Jury, shadowed her for more than four years and finally brought about her arrest through the Canadian Mounted Police, Mrs. Laurena Mathews, 37, is being taken back to Stillwater to stand trial for the murder of her husband, a crime alleged to have been committed December 8, 1908. In the custody of Mrs. Lurancy Harris, the first woman police constable of Canada, and James Springer of Stillwater, Mrs. Mathews arrived in Denver yesterday and was confined for several hours in the quarters of the police matron at the city jail."

Jim Springer lamented the laxity of the American procedure which, in his estimation, was less disciplinary than that of the Dominion. "As soon as Mrs. Mathews had been committed for extradition, she was sent to the penitentiary at New Westminster and put in what they call the death chamber. No one was allowed to see her, not even her counsel, without an order from the King's Bench, and the order would state who it was to see her and just the number of minutes she might talk to any one. When she was brought here, it had been arranged that she might be kept guarded in one of the best hotels in the city, and allowed the privilege of receiving whoever wanted to see her. In fact, she kept open house" Pruiett had made the advance arrangements. He considered those little expressions of thoughtfulness a part of the requirements of his employment. He always tried to keep his clients in a peaceful and serene state of mind.

And Pruiett couldn't understand why Springer was so impatient to have the case tried. As he looked at it, Mathews had been dead for five years already, and another year or two, to prepare for the trial, shouldn't make much difference. Every conceivable subterfuge was indulged for delay, and the black stud could do an unsurpassed job of conceiving when dilatory tactics in a criminal prosecution were ordered. As a final gesture, he took his client and made another tour of the Northwest, taking statements and depositions of witnesses to be used, one way or another, in the eventual trial.

Back in Edmonton, Pruiett took a final verbal poke at the prosecution. According to the *Edmonton Daily Capital* on May 19, 1913, "That Mrs. Mathews has been practically ruined financially through the heavy expenditures necessary in her defense of the charge of murdering her husband leveled at her by James Chapman, a negro farmer, who is now serving a 25 year sentence in the McAlester, Oklahoma penitentiary on the strength of his own confession of the crime, is the statement made to the *Capital* by Moman Pruiett, Oklahoma City, Mrs. Mathews' attorney."

They were lionized at every stop on the way back. At Seattle, press photographers met them at the station and gave them the front page for any kind of statement they wanted to make. Mrs. Mathews and the boy furnished a picture in a pose of devoted tenderness, but Pruiett did the talking. The *Seattle Star* on June 9, 1913, was more than kind.

"Mrs. Lorena Mathews is a guest at the Seattle Hotel. She is the central figure in the sensational Lawrence Mathews murder case which has been before the courts of Oklahoma and Canada for the past number of years. Accompanied by her son James, a boy 16, and her attorney, Moman Pruiett, of Oklahoma City, Mrs. Mathews is on her way from Vancouver, B. C. to stand trial. A dishwasher in a restaurant, an old man named Baker, complained to the Juvenile Court that Mrs. Mathews was not a fit mother for her children.The prejudice, often ordered Jim to hitch up and take her to town on shopping and business errands.The negro followed her to Canada. You perhaps do not know the nature of the southern negro farmhand. His name had been coupled with that of a white woman, and he was mighty proud."

The Seattle *Post-Intelligencer* concluded a similar story with a flattering recollection of the attorney in the affair. "Pruiett, the attorney in the case, is known in the Northwest. Two years ago he came to Montaseno for the defense of the Carr-Atkinson murder case, in which case Carr was cleared. Mrs. Mathews is said to be still wealthy, although a large part of the fortune left by her husband has been spent in the courts of Oklahoma and Canada."

When they laid over in Denver, the accused woman had a suite at the Albany Hotel, instead of an iron bunk in the woman's ward at the municipal prison, as she had had on her latest visit. The *Denver Daily News* on June 13, 1913, remembered her. It was still friendly, and solicitous. "Mrs. Mathews has spent the bulk of the fortune left to her and her two children, James, 16, and Fanny, 18, in defending herself of the charge. The only part of the vast sum left the family is a few thousand dollars which he bequeathed to the son. With Mrs. Mathews were her son James, and Moman Pruiett, an Oklahoma City Attorney. Following her release on bond, Pruiett accompanied her to Canada to get certain documentary evidence, which, the defense hopes, will offset the evidence given by Chapman."

When Pruiett had baited the exponents of justice and order to the point where they were near madness, and had aroused them to such a pitch that they were editorializing him and his client, he knew that he had gone far enough. It was as far as he cared, and had planned to go, at any rate. According to the *Stillwater Advance-Democrat* on June 12, 1913. " It was great disappointment to those interested in the prosecution of the case to see Mrs. Mathews admitted to bail. In England, 80 percent of the murderers are hanged, while in the United States, 80 percent of the murderers are acquitted. It is because the efforts of those who undertake to prosecute crime in this country are hampered by the courts in allowing bail; then, continuing the case from time to time, and efforts of attorneys through newspapers to throw sympathy and a feeling of persecution about the defendants."

Pruiett attached a copy of that editorial to a motion for a change of venue, and got what he asked for. the cause was sent to Guthrie, first capital of Oklahoma, in Logan County. Once off of Springer's dunghill, Pruiett was ready for battle. The trial, which opened on September 2, 1913, continued over two weeks. According to the *Stillwater Daily Press,* on June 4, 1913, nearly two hundred witnesses testified in the case and the defense had fourteen depositions from Canada, where it was claimed the accused and the negro went after the death of Mathews."

Jim Chapman was brought from the penitentiary to testify for the prosecution. He was a willing witness. "That man died with my hand over his mouth and my fingers on his neck, and he knew me, too." Thus the current stories carried it. " 'Mrs. Mathews,' he said, 'is one of the pleasantest women I ever knew, and I believe she is the smartest woman in this courtroom; but she is the deceiven'st woman I ever saw, too', 'But from your story,' suggested counsel, 'you indicated that she was the principal in the murder, and that she persuaded you to help.' 'Well,' said Chapman, 'I wouldn't say that. She persuaded me into it. We arranged the details right by the corner of the courthouse, the day before the murder. I got the stuff for her and she was going to do the job; but she wanted me around. After she hit him with the poker and he didn't die, she came out and called me in, and that man died with my hands over his mouth and my fingers on his throat.' "

The defense had had that kind of testimony to combat all the way through. Pruiett was disconsolate when the jury went out, and fearful of conviction. When they had been out two days, he began to feel better, although he was drinking heavily to sustain his ceaseless corridor pacing. He envisioned a deadlocked jury and relished the visitation. He could give a lot of newspaper interviews, and create a great deal of feeling in the public in the time which would elapse before another trial could be had. He remembered the damaging testimony and consoled himself with the thought held in readiness, for use in every case. You can't win 'em all; a hung jury is better than a conviction.

And then, trouble marched into the courthouse. Lee Cruce, Governor of the State which had absorbed the Indian Nations, hadn't gone to the field house to see the game. The contest had been over for over two days, the umpires just hadn't posted their decision, when the Governor arrived. The Guthrie Free Fair was in full country swing and the red and white yokels alike showing their yams and pop corn and trying to outwit the pitch man who manipulated walnut husks over inoffensive green peas. The Governor was down to give that part of the citizenry, which was still grieving over the loss of Guthrie's status as the capitol, a word of encouragement, and to make a little political swamproot for himself by delivering a speech from the rail of the race track. A. H.

"Harry" Huston, District Judge, who had heard the Mathews case, was to introduce him and the Governor's party had merely driven by to pick up the court.

Cruce pretended that he didn't see Pruiett pacing in front of the courtroom, as he ducked into the door of the judge's chambers. Pruiett walked into the bailiff's vestibule, outside the chambers, and dropped into one of the numerous empty chairs. No one else was in the room. With his eyes on the print of a country paper, but with his ears, and attention, focused upon the wide cracks around the door into Huston's office, he emulated interest in the smeared print. Cruce had already injured his case; so, he was instantly suspicious of him when he saw him about the court.

"This is awful," he heard Cruce's voice after the trial judge had given him a profane explanation of the status of the case. "It's simply awful. That woman's guilty and ever'one knows it. She should have been convicted long before this. It's awful."

"I can't help it," Huston answered, weakly. "I'm worn out, tryin' to hold that fellow Pruiett down. I've tried cases with him in 'em for fifteen years, way back in the territory courts at Ardmore an' the valley, but he gets worse instead of better. I stopped court and called him in here, an' told him I was goin' to lock him up if he didn't stay within the bounds of reason in cross-examinin' witnesses, but it didn't do any good. I jumped him for the same thing before the jury, an' he made a record of me that'll reverse the case as sure as hell if she's convicted, an' he takes an appeal. I don't know what to do."

"This case has been spread all over the country," Cruce growled. "It's news even in Canada, and we're being criticized for spendin' so much money on it. A lot of 'em up there think that we're wrong, and that she's innocent. A hung jury, where a quick conviction should be had, is goin' to make a joke out of this State, and this Court, and," Cruce added, "the Governor, too."

Pruiett heard Huston speak to his bailiff. "Go up and get Bob Hancock, the jury foreman, an' bring him here. Bring him in here; this office."

There was a short pause, with complete silence.

"Mr. Hancock, meet Governor Cruce; Governor, Bob Hancock, the foreman of the jury."

There was an exchange of greetings before Pruiett heard Huston continue. "Are you any nearer an agreement?" he asked.

"No, sir," came the reply. "There ain't been a vote change all day. We're hopelessly hung."

There was a weariness in the answer to give Pruiett hope. He wanted them to hang if they couldn't acquit; he didn't want any outside influence, even a Governor's , to interfere with that order of results. But the Governor was going to have his say.

"Surely twelve sensible men can agree on as clear-cut a case as this one," he said. "These trials cost money; the State has spent a great amount on this one. Petty impressions should be set aside and the public good considered.

Pruiett gnashed his teeth as he fixed his stare into the little paper.

"The Governor is right," Huston put in. "A verdict ought'a be reached in this case. We can't afford to try it again, or let the public know it has to be tried again. Can't you do anything to help things along?"

Hancock's answer was not immediately forthcoming.

"Well," he said slowly, "I might, but it is goin' to be hard. We might possibly agree,—but,—I—, but—- ."

The Governor interrupted his stammering.

"This case should not result in a disagreement. It should not be tried again. You intelligent men should agree, even if it is hard, as I have said..."

The judge interrupted him.

"Bob," he said, " I am goin' to rely on you to line those men up. Bring us in a verdict—it can be done. Go back up there an' tell 'em the Governor is waitin' so I can go to the fair grounds to introduce him, and that I'd like for him to be present in the courtroom when they return a righteous verdict in this case. I want you to put an end to this quibblin'."

When Pruiett took his ear from the keyhole he was purple with old fashioned Washita anger. While the judge, or the Governor, had said nothing as to how they wanted the case decided, he knew that his client was having an instruction put in against him. The commendatory slap which he heard Huston bounce off Bob Hancock's back was as much as to say 'Bob, old boy, the Governor wants this bitch stuck. Let's you and I and the boys give him what he wants."

When the jury filed into the box, rundown and bleary, Cruce and

Huston were beaming. Pruiett looked like a prairie tornado just ready to swoop to earth for a havoc-wreaking instant. When that foreman announced that she was guilty, he was goin' to hear a denunciation such as no courtroom ever before had been privileged to hear. A certain judge and a certain Governor were to be included. Pruiett was ready to scream.

The clerk read the verdict. "We find her not guilty." Huston looked like he had opened the election reports and found that his constituency had forgotten to remember that he was running for re-election. Cruce looked equally surprised; but, there was a tinge of sheepishness about his expression. He realized how his attempt to influence a conviction had resulted in an acquittal, which otherwise would not have occurred.

The Daily Oklahoman carried the official report on the outcome on September 21, 1913. "The jury in the case of Mrs. Mathews, charged with helping James Chapman, a negro farmhand, murder her husband, Lawrence Mathews, on their farm near Stillwater brought in a verdict at 4 o'clock Saturday afternoon acquitting her of the charge. The case was brought to Guthrie from Payne County."

There was nothing in print about the star chamber session where the jury foreman, the trial judge and the Governor discussed procedure without reckoning in the precepts of justice and civil liberties. No word was written on old Bob Hancock, who gave up his abiding opinion on the guilt of the accused in order that a verdict could be brought in while the Governor was there to see it. The chronicle could have truthfully said: "The foreman and one other were for conviction, and would have so remained until the others had joined them, or they were excused from deliberations on the case. They gave up their position so that the State could be spared the expense of another trial."

CHAPTER FOURTEEN

WHEREIN THE VENERABLE BADGER GAME IS TURNED INTO BLIND MAN'S BLUFF, AND PRUIETT HASTENS TO THE AID OF A SIGHTLESS UNITED STATES SENATOR. AND HOW OFFICIAL WASHINGTON, D. C., IS STARTLED BY AN EXPOSE' OF A BACKSTREET CHAPTER IN ITS OWN STORY, AS BIG-TIME POLITICIANS AND LOBBYISTS, REVENGE BENT, CRY FOR THE COMPLETE DISCREDIT OF A BROTHER. AND HOW THE HUSH-MONEY AND BRIBERY MARKET HITS THE SKIDS, THE PETTICOATS OF THE LITTLE WOMAN IN THE CASE SHOW SOILED THROUGH THEIR STARCH AND LACE, AND THE EDITORIAL COMMENT OF THE NATIONAL PRESS ECHOES THE EXPRESSION OF THE PRESIDENT OF THE UNITED STATES—PRAISE FOR COUNSEL FOR THE DEFENSE.

The *Kansas City Star*'s western correspondent had acquired a buzz from his evening's gin-swilling which the night man on the desk had been unable to identify, classify or diagnose. When the rewrite men had turned down his wired copy, it was sent on up to the make-up department, with a shrug. If the big bosses raised hell, he'd let'em in on where it came from. That, he was certain, would be an adequate explanation for anything,—anything, that ever happened. It appeared on February 10, 1914.

" The lawyer for the defense," so his story went, "removed a large part of his clothing and piled it up before the jury. This was regarded as a shrewd legal move and probably had immense weight in deciding the case, as the other lawyer, in addressing the jury had removed only his collar and tie. The lawyer for the accused, having torn his coat into shreds and trampled on it, hurled his vest and suspenders to the floor and proceeded to a calm and dispassionate review of the law and the evidence. His learning and eloquence moved the audience to the wildest demonstrations; and, when he clinched his argument with the statement that he had formerly blacked shoes in the streets of Fort Smith, a member of the jury requested a few moments delay while he stepped out of the box and choked the plaintiff. The lawyer with the fewest clothes on them announced his readiness to engage in personal combat

Mrs. Minnie Bond and her husband. Minnie accused Oklahoma's United States Senator Thomas P. Gore of attempted rape, and when prosecutors in the District of Columbia refused to file criminal charges against Gore she sued the senator in a civil case asking $50,000 in damages. Courtesy Howard K. Berry, Sr.

with any lawyer or witness on the other side, with or without shirts or collars. Courteously handing the measurements for his coffin to the judge, the attorney calmly awaited a taker for his challenge. Flinging his impeding cuffs from his wrists, he mussed his hair up in the wildest disorder and advanced on the jury in a crouching attitude, uttering shrill cries. Reaching the jury box, he walked around the rail on his hands amid thunders of applause, cracked his heels together in the air; and, after landing by a spectacular handspring in the middle of the counsel table, announced his purpose and ability to carry his home county by six thousand in the fall election."

The amateurish satire of the bored reporter had caught Pruiett's portrait, his mannerisms and characteristics, like a master. The line on the Fort Smith boot black—although unnecessary—was a dead giveaway, for Pruiett had the exclusive rights reserved on the use of that phrase. He was back before the national eye, engaged in one of the strangest cases ever to attract the attention of the gullible, sensation loving public.

The Bond-Gore case, being tried in Oklahoma, was the unorthodox consequence of a fast first-round of the ancient indoor exercise known as the 'badger game.' The playground had been Washington, crowded with the curious throng which attended the Wilson inauguration in March, 1913, and stayed over to gawk and play, and look for jobs. The participants were; for a fall guy, United States Senator Thomas Pryor Gore of Oklahoma; for the closest peepers, two big time political organizations, one disgruntled over patronage, and the other over government business resisted by the Senator on the floor of the Senate.

Tom Gore was blind. His marble-white optics had received no sensation of light since he had been an eleven-year-old child, and in 1913 he was forty-two years old. The strength of his lost sense had fortified some of those which he retained, as is not unusual, and although sightless, he was gifted with a ponderous mind and a matchless oral eloquence. His opposition in debate was not invited on the floor of the Senate, not even by the most able and keen eyed, of the nation's statesmen.

And while his sightless orbs, aided by the mind of genius, could gaze beyond the grooved walls of the halls of state and see the rocks and shoals of the political sea, he had his little faults, his mundane weaknesses, and as in the universal flesh, they played him false. While he saw not the beauty and symmetry of the female form, his mind's eye had a constant picture, and with his gold-headed cane pecking a laborious way down the marble halls, he would edge toward the titter of maidenly laughter and the rustle of silken petticoats, even when affairs of government should have been foremost in his mind, and restraining him.

According to the *Kansas City Times* on February 18, 1914, "The courthouse shook with the stamping of hundreds of feet upon the floor today when Moman Pruiett, attorney for Senator Gore, in his speech to the jury exclaimed; 'You, Senator Gore, are on trial here today because on the floor of Congress you stood between the helpless Indians of this State and the thieves and crooks who wanted to rob them'"

Pruiett was talking about J. F. "Frank" McMurray, of the Washington law firm of Mansfield, McMurray and Cornish, which organization had collected a single $750,000 fee for services in National Indian litigation. McMurray was a Texas product who had stopped long enough in the Indian Territory and the new State, as the latter was absorbing the former, to be able to identify himself as a citizen of both. Since he had gotten in the big money, he confined his trips out of Washington, D. C., to New York City and adjacent points East; but, he managed to keep his stick in with the delegations from the West. He was in on the ground with everyone but Gore, who didn't like him to start with, but who literally cut him to pieces on the Senate's floor when the details of the $750,000 attorneys fee, filched out of the Indian's buck-skin pouch, were made public, and plans of another, and larger one, were advanced.

On February 19, 1914, The *New York World* had quoted from a speech made by Senator Ashurst of Arizona, debating on the Tariff Bill, to give a thumb-nail sketch of this J. F. McMurray. He was described by the western Senator as "'the smoothest lobbyist I ever met. McMurray could carry a bundle of eels upstairs and never drop a one."

Continuing with the sketch, the *World* had observed: "McMurray is a member of the law firm of Mansfield, McMurray and Cornish, which collected a fee of $750,000 for ridding the tribal roles of the Choctaw and Chickasaw Indians of the names of 3,600 interlopers who sought a share in rich farming, mineral and timber lands. In 1897, McMurray moved into the Indian Territory. The Dawes Commission was breaking up the rich tribal estates of the Five Nations. The government concluded the Atoka agreement with the Chickasaws and Choctaws a year later, undertaking to sell off their lands before 1907. Mansfield, McMurray and Cornish became the counsel for the Indians at an annual retainer of $10,000. There were some 4,000 persons on the rolls who, in the view of the redskins, were not entitled to share in the pro rata distribution of the proceeds of the sales of the lands. McMurray's firm undertook, for a consideration, to purge the rolls. The agreement was that, as every person put off the rolls meant $4,500.00 to the firm's clients, 9 per cent of the value of the lands thus added to the Indian's treasury should be paid to the lawyers. McMurray went to Congress and procured the creation by Congress of the Citizenship Court; and, before this tribunal, his firm drove out 3,600 persons from their Indian citizenship, adding to the value of the Indian owned lands."

As Pruiett said, with reference to the deal, "McMurray wasn't satisfied with makin' a fair fee ($750,000), he had to be a hog. He wanted to get rich, an' that's what he and the Senator fell out about."

"McMurray and Senator Gore came to a clinch when Gore opposed a bill approving Indian land contracts, under which McMurray's firm was to collect $3,500,000 fee." That was to be in coin of the United States Government, and not Indian wampum—$3,500,000. " Senator Gore, on June 24, 1910, arose to a question of privilege and told the Senate he had been offered a bribe of $25,000 to withdraw his opposition to the proposed legislation. The persons named by Senator Gore were exonerated by the Senate, but the McMurray laws were defeated."

There was that angle, and still another, to the attempted badger swindle. President Woodrow Wilson had to have a cabinet, and the West had long contended that it should have recognition, and representation, on that select board. Colonel Robert A. Rogers, a prominent businessman and attorney in Oklahoma City, who had left the South for the East when he was being educated, and who had sought the boundless traces of the Indian country when he had fulfilled the purpose of his quest, had all the qualifications for that office. At least, he acknowledged that he had them. He had the family background. He had land; money and lots of it, and he had been a graduating classmate of Woodrow Wilson, when that prominent chinned student had marched with the others at Princeton commencement exercises.

It was real Alma Mater stuff, and Rogers knew that with a senatorial recommendation he would go over. Oklahoma's United States Senator

Robert L. Owens, had already gone on record for him. If Gore would go, the far west would have a cabinet post, a Secretaryship of the Interior it was being sought.

Pruiett contended from the first that Rogers was the creator and principal backer of the plot to destroy the blind Senator. Rogers was no novice in playing badger; he had had a lot of experience and Pruiett knew it. The Colonel's experience had seen him in the place of the victim; instead of that of the victimized; but, Pruiett surmised that a greater impression and knowledge of the intricacies had been gained from the position he had occupied, than from any other position or contact he might have had with the old shake-down. Rogers had been successfully hooked for a large sum of money, and he would have lost more had it not been for the maneuvers of an apt attorney who stalled in court until he could compromise the compromising little widow who was after him. Coincidentally, Rogers' attorney in that case had been named Moman Pruiett.

The trial of the Colonel's case had been well under way on December 20, 1911, which was about two years ahead of Senator Gore's difficulty, and was drawing its share of headline and bold type in the *Oklahoma News* on December 10, 1911, published and circulated in Oklahoma City.

"Sensation was added to sensation in the case of Catherine Rogers against Robert A. Rogers, called for trial before Judge Oldfield in the Superior Court Tuesday. Catherine Rogers is suing for $100,000 alimony, and for $10,000 additional to pay for the education of her nine year old child, who she claims is the son of Robert A. Rogers. No case has been tried in the Southwest which caused wider interest than the suit of the woman who calls herself Catherine Rogers, against Robert A. Rogers, a corporation lawyer of Oklahoma City, who is widely known in nearly all of the southern states.When asked whether any marriage ceremony had ever been performed between them, Mrs. Rogers said, 'One time he asked me to go down on the beach at Galveston with him. One other woman went along. When we got down there, he made me hold up my hand and swear to forsake all others and live with him. He told me if I ever broke that promise, I'd never see my mother in heaven'. Rogers was a classmate of Woodrow Wilson, and is the president of the Woodrow Wilson Democratic Club of Oklahoma."

Colonel Rogers maintained a mighty lobby in the city of the Potomac. He had the kind of money that it took to hire fast fixers, even after he had settled with Catherine, and he had them working. When they had failed, and they knew that they had failed, they took advantage of being already organized, and set out to scuttle the blind Senator's prairie schooner. Gore hadn't been able to see Rogers, either literally or figuratively, and the Colonel, and the crowd that saw good jobs winging with his future to receive the appointment, knew that their loss was directly attributable to him. They moved over to the Ebbets House, mixed a few with Frank McMurray, and talked the situation over.

But the bait? What about the bait? Who ever heard of a badger sequence, even one with a blind villain, and with prominent politicians for heroes to appear in the nick of time, without a fair damsel to be rescued? With facial and physical pulchritude abundant in Washington, the producers of the drama picked a dumpy little matron of near middle age, whose sorrel hair and rats spiraled above her head like a bee hive, and who squinted at the world through a pair of thick lensed, Prince-nez glasses. Setting the stage for a blind one, who was ultra-imbued with his own amorous inclinations to start with, must have been an exacting task for the revenge seeking job-seekers, who had the free advice and direction of such high priced producers as Mansfield, McMurray and Cornish.

Her name was Minnie. Minnie Bond was born Minnie Ballinger; and she had a husband. By strange coincidence her man had failed to catch any of the pie that the Gore wagon had been delivering, and there they were, a thousand miles away from home, broke, and with no jobs. Jim Jacobs, and Kirby Fitzpatrick, and Thaddeus E. Robertson, from their adjoining rooms in the Winston Hotel, had watched the coveted pastry with dripping lip, and looked apprehensibly, as if in fear of cannibalism from their lank consorts, when the loaded cart had passed on and out of sight in the distance.

They were an able crew. Jacobs was an accomplished lobbyist. "He had been there [Washington] a long time, and seemed to know the ins and outs; seemed to know where to hang his hat."

Fitzpatrick, until late enjoying plenty in the government land service, was a Tennessee adventurer who had seen the world, and had most recently soldiered in the Philippines. As he stoutly advised the Attorney General of the United States, after the Bond-Gore incident had begun to smell, "I am no vagabond; my people have not been strangers to the halls of Congress, nor laggards on the battlefield of the Republic; I followed the flag ten thousand miles from home and offered my life on the alter of my country's honor. I am a graduate of two universities and the governor of my state does not blush to call me friend."

Robertson, the fourth of the principal participants, was the youngest, and the most gifted. At 27 he was playing for big stakes and with the big boys. His stature, smaller than average, was surmounted by a large, swarthy-skinned head. He had a black, beady eye, and a quick answer. When Pruiett asked him what he was doing in Washington, he instantly replied, "I went there to see the inauguration, for one reason, and then I thought Bob Rogers would be appointed Secretary of the Interior, and I wanted to be in on the ground if he was."

"This is a plot to destroy me." Thus the sightless Senator labeled the lawsuit from the witness stand as reported in the *Kansas City Post* on February 16, 1914. But, if he was going down, he wasn't going alone; he was dragging under, in his fierce and frantic clutch, all of the conspirators connected with it. When Gore had bowed his neck and refused to reconsider on the patronage proposition, Minnie Bond and the trio of eye-ball witnesses gave the story to the press. When Gore countered with charges of blackmail and attempted extortion, the conspirators had to make good, or suffer the consequences. They went to the District Attorney for the District of Columbia and gave information, and asked that the Senator from Oklahoma be arraigned on a charge of attempted rape. Their statements, as given to the officers of the district, and as they later developed in court, were as disconcerting to the political idealist, or moral idealist, as they were refreshing to the scandalmongers and sensation-seeking courthouse loungers.

The District Attorney refused to file charges. The Senate declined to act, although each individual member was invited, in well-couched terms, to make an official inquisition in the matter. They gave their blind colleague a vote of confidence. Washington's lawyers wouldn't touch the civil angle of the case, although the Bond-McMurray-Rogers combine shopped the district. Back in Oklahoma, and just before election time, the Senator on a visit to his constituency, received the greetings, which apprised that he had been sued by Minnie in the Oklahoma County District Court for damages, $50,000 worth of them, for assault, and for defamation of character. The trial, and it's evidence developing ramifications, produced not only a sordid revelation of the official Washington manners and mannerisms, but revealed a back-street section of the lives of both the principals, which had theretofore been studiously and successfully concealed.

But, back to Washington, or rather to the events of Washington as they developed in the testimony of lobbyist Jacobs, on the witness stand. Jim, responding nicely to the careful handling of Minnie's lawyer, was beginning to tell how the trouble all began.

"On the 24th day of March, 1913, in the afternoon, I will get you to state if you had a conversation with Mrs. Minnie E. Bond?" The question was propounded by Mr. Ross N. Lillard of Minnie's counsel.

"I did," Jim replied truthfully.

"About what time was it, if you remember?" was the next question.

Jim had a good memory.

"My recollection is that it was between five and six o'clock," he promptly answered.

"What was that conversation, Mr. Jacobs?"

"I met Mrs. Bond in the little aisle that you come in, it would not be called a lobby, I don't think, about four feet wide, on the first floor of the hotel, right where you start to walk up to the elevator, and she made a remark to me that she had an engagement with Senator Gore, and that she didn't know where she was going to talk to him. Well, I could understand why without her telling me; she went on to say, you see that both the men and ladies' parlors are congested with people, stopping there, a lot of tourists stopping there, and very much congested at that time. I says, 'Mrs. Bond, take him to your room.' She says, 'Oh no, I would not do that—I would not go to a private room anywhere with him.' I says, 'Why?' She says, 'you don't know Senator Gore.' I says, 'I will go along with you if there is nothing private you want to discuss.' She says, 'I would like to have you to go, but I don't want to take you up to my room. I have unpacked everything to repack and it is not in proper shape for you to go in,' and she says, 'I am expecting him most any time.' I says, 'take my key and go to my room.' She says, 'will you go up with us?' I says, 'No, I will either go up with you or come in afterwards and hang around and make it a point to be in if I don't go with you,'—so, I leave her the key and walked out on the streets."

Jacob testified that he 'just hung around the front of the hotel, talking with Bill Tilghman until he saw the Senator come along'. As he stated it:"about that time I saw the Senator and his brother-in-law, the one the government has employed to lead him around, coming across the campus toward the hotel." The Winston Hotel was near First Street and Pennsylvania Avenue, across from the park of the Washington Botanical Gardens. When counsel asked Jacobs what he did then, he replied:

"Well, Fitzpatrick was going by and I caught up with him and caught him by the arm and says, 'Fitz, lets go up to your room.' He says, 'all right.' I took him by the arm and walked part of the way towards the hotel from the corner of First and Pennsylvania Avenue, and held on to his arm, I think, until we got to the little alley—my recollection is—and, when we got to that, I turned his arm loose and I says, 'Fitz, there is a matter I am going to watch.' I passed right on through and went on upstairs."

The lawyer didn't like for him to stop there.

"What did you and Fitz do then?" he inquired, as if he didn't know what the answer was going to be.

"I went on ahead, and I met Thaddeus E. Robertson on the way. I says, 'Rob, lets go to your room. He went on ahead of me, unlocked the door, throwed it open, and he and I walked in."

Fitzpatrick and Robertson shared the room next to Jacobs; the one he had loaned Mrs. Bond for her interview with the Senator, and there was a door connecting the two rooms. The conference had already started when Jacobs and Robertson stealthily entered the latter's room.

Mrs. Bond, testifying by deposition, had explained her business in the National Capitol—how and where she had first contacted the blind Senator—and how they had reached Jacob's room after making the general appointment to meet at the hotel. Mr. Lillard, was examining her.

"I will get you to state when was the first time you saw Senator Gore in Washington," he asked her.

"I visited him in his office, in the Senate Annex," Mrs. Bond replied.

"And on what date, if you remember?"

"I don't remember the date, sometime between the 4th and 24th?"

"For what purpose did you visit Senator Gore at his office?"

"To discuss Mr. Bond's appointment with him."

Lillard was being ponderous and methodical, as if he was much in the dark about the affair. The ground was being carefully covered.

"Did you discuss that appointment with Senator Gore at that time?" he inquired.

"I did," she answered.

"I will get you to state who, if anybody, was in his private office, at the time you had this first interview with him?"

"There was nobody in his private office," responded Mrs. Bond with a significant, suggestive, toss of her head.

"Please state, Mrs. Bond, what occurred upon your entering Senator Gore's private office, and during this interview which you had with the Senator?"

Mrs. Bond shifted about in her chair before answering. Her preparation was a suggestion of a spicy disclosure.

"On entering his office, Senator Gore shook hands with me. I sat at the corner of his desk in a chair, and while we were discussing Mr. Bond's appointment, Senator Gore first reached over and took hold of one of my hands. I moved back a little bit, and then he put his hand on one of my knees. I shoved it off gently with my fingers, and moved back farther."

"What else occurred there?" Lillard took advantage of a slight hesitation to put another question.

"Senator Gore said he didn't have time to see Mr. Bond's references, although I urged him to see them. I was in there a few minutes when he reached down and took hold of my foot, and after he had held my hand and foot, I decided it was time for me to go. I got up and said I didn't want to monopolize his time, and tried to get away without appearing to observe anything. When he went to shake hands to say good-bye, he pulled me up to him. He said he didn't see how he could place Mr. Bond in that particular position, but that he would be very glad to have me call on him socially."

She was interrupted with another question.

"When did you see Senator Gore after that, or when did you have another conversation with him, either in person or over the 'phone?"

The witness studied for an instant.

"Well," she finally said, "I remember I called him over the 'phone to make an appointment with reference to the matter we had been discussing. He suggested that it was a matter he didn't care to discuss over the telephone. I said I expected to go away at a certain time, and asked him if he would come by the hotel."

"Did he invite you to his office?"

"Yes, he invited me to his office."

"Now, Mrs. Bond," Lillard persisted, "on the 24th day of March, I will get you to state if you had a telephone conversation with Senator Gore?"

"I did," she replied.

"What did he say in that conversation?"

"He asked me to come up, and I said I couldn't—I was busy; he said he thought he would be able to come down."

"Did you talk to him over the 'phone any more?"

"Yes, I talked with him at another time."

"What did you say in that conversation, and about what time was it?"

"I judge about three or four o'clock. I am not positive about the time. He said he had some people in his office he thought he would soon be able to get rid of, and that he would come to the hotel; he would call me before he did come."

Mrs. Bond continued to explain how her packing, and the return of her laundry, had caused her own room to be in temporary disarray, and how she aired her dilemma in the presence of compassionate old Jim Jacobs, on the mezzanine. She told of how Jim had given her his key, along with curtailed rights and privileges to use his room.

"Immediately afterward," she said, "And while I was downstairs, I just walked over to one side, and somebody remarked, 'there's Senator Gore,' or 'here is Senator Gore,' some such remark as that."

"What did you do then?" catechized the ever curious Lillard.

"Senator Gore came on inside," she answered, "I walked up to him and shook hands with him. He turned around, excused himself from his attendant, and walked with me to the elevator."

"Where did you go to?"

"When we got upstairs, I told Senator Gore that we would go to that room, the parlors were all crowded. He said he had noticed the confusion. When we got upstairs, we went down the corridor and into this room."

And so the little blind fly felt his way into the mesh of the spiders' adjoining webs. His silk hat and gold-headed cane were placed upon the pillows at the head of the bed while he adjusted the lapels of his long, black, Prince Albert coat. The crease in his afternoon trousers were as true and immaculate as the black and grey stripes themselves, and there was an expression of benign patience on his childlike face as he turned his head from side to side, to better hear to the swish of the petticoats as his little hostess bustled about the room. The shades were down, the lights were on, and a dresser had been pulled in front of the connecting door—to provide peeping space for the conspirators—as if they needed camouflage or cover to conceal them from their victim. Gore couldn't have seen them if they had lounged in the easy chairs under the reading lamps.

Jim Jacobs's version of the episode established that no lights were turned on in the Robertson-Fitzpatrick room when he and Robertson stealthily entered it. He said that Robertson asked him who it was in his room.

"I says," Jacobs testified, "It is Senator Gore and Mrs. Bond. I says 'I am going to watch them.' About that time, Fitz came in and I proceeded to ease the door open. The door is connecting door, this Robertson and Fitzpatrick room, and the dresser sat in my room in front of this door. They used to go back and forth to use my bath-room; and, sometimes, we would leave the dresser moved enough for them to pass. I eased the door open a little tiny crack and proceeded to look in there. When I got the door eased open, Robertson was leaning against me looking in and I looked around and there was Fitz, looking in through a crack. You see, the glass in that mirror hung on one of those apparatuses, a little hole, or groove, and all we could see of it we could see through this hole, for the dresser was three and a half or four feet high."

The blind Senator and bespectacled Minnie talked about the things that senators and female applicants for jobs usually talk about in sequestered hotel rooms. "Mrs. Bond was sitting on the foot of the bed and Senator Gore was sitting in a rocking chair. I noticed that he seemed to want to catch hold of her—he asked her some questions about her weight and looks. There was a scuffle and she sat back down on the bed. Senator Gore attempted to pull Mrs. Bond down on his knees, and she shoved herself loose from him, or rather shoved up and he pulled up with her, and in a very short while they were both over on the bed. He had his hand on Mrs. Bond's face, his left arm—he took his right hand and placed her left here under his hand, no, under this right knee, and then crawled astride her; he then attempted to pull her skirts up and succeeded in getting them up about her knees." Such was a portion of Robertson's sworn version of the incident.

Jim Jacobs's account of the Senator's approach was slightly different in substance but essentially the same in conclusion. "Well, they talked along awhile there, he first tried to kiss her hand; but, she pulled it away and told him he must not do that. Then, he caught hold of her arm and she would push it off and asked him to behave himself. He would say something back, I could hear his voice but could not distinguish what he would say. I think he finally put his hand up on her face—or up towards this way—and when he did that, and when she raised her back on the bed and she was not entirely laying on the bed, she caught hold of the foot of the bed with one of her hands. When she reached over she just was close enough to catch the foot of the bed and she made a remark, immediately when he got her down, that if he didn't let her up she would call the police. He jumped up and begged her pardon."

The ever helpful and oft-interrupting Lillard didn't recognize Jacobs's pause as a proper place to stop. He prompted him with another question.

"What did he do after jumping up?"

"Well," he said, "he sat back down in his chair, and Mrs. Bond sat up a little more towards the head of the bed and then she began to reprimand him, said he ought to be ashamed of himself, and that she was not the kind of a woman he might think she was. Of course, he replied back all the time but I did not understand anything he said. Then, they went on talking again, about her uncle, friendship between them and so on, and they finally got this straightened up, this little episode, and commenced to talk about the position again. They talked on awhile about that and he made some kind of advance, I could not see on account of the dresser; my judgment from the demonstration that he made was that he commenced to catch hold of her feet. She said, 'behave yourself, I want you to stop that.' He put his hand on her arm and put his other hand over her mouth and shoved her back on the bed and got right up over her. Fitz took hold of my arm and says, 'boys, he's going to rape her in spite of hell'."

The coy plaintiff had her own recollection of the events of which she made complaint.

"What did he say; did he or not ask you as to your looks, and as to whether or not you were good looking?" her counsel asked.

"He did," she answered tersely.

"After asking you that—and after your reply to him—what did he do; did he or not reach up to your face?"

"Yes, he reached up to my face."

"For what purpose?"

"I don't know what his purpose was, he didn't tell me. I importuned him to keep his place, and he begged my pardon."

"What further conversation did he have with you as to the position in Washington?" That was the next question.

"He told me that, if I were a little widow, he would be able to take care of me in Washington." She said it with an emphasis intended to imply that such a declaration was not fully warranted by senatorial privilege.

"At that time had his actions become more marked?"

"They had."

"What did he do then?"

Mrs. Bond summed the situation up in her next answer.

"He caught hold of me and tried to push me on the bed," she said. "I told him I would call the police and that he would have a brass button to take away as a souvenir, if he didn't desist. He grabbed hold of me, shoved me down on the bed with his hand over my mouth, and piled down on top of me."

"What occurred then," her counsel inquired, breathlessly.

"Mr. Robertson burst into the room. I held my clothes down with one hand and pushed him off with the other. When his hand slipped off my face, so I could, I gave a smothered scream. Then, Mr. Robertson burst into the room.

So there was the dignity and the culture of the Senate. With Prince Albert coat askew and afternoon trousers at half mast, he sat on the wrinkled counterpane and gazed bewilderedly about, as if trying to penetrate, with his gaze, the blackness which encompassed him. Thwarted in his original design and unquestionably understanding, by that time, that he was being victimized, he retained his polished manner of complete nonchalance. "He jumped up and asked who it was, and," Robertson was saying, " 'Robertson from Oklahoma City.' 'How do you do, old man, how do you do,' the Senator replied. 'I am glad to see you. So very glad to see you'."

When Minnie's attorney asked Jim Jacobs a rather delicate question, Jim proved his lobbyist's tact by the way he answered it.

"Mr. Jacobs," he inquired, "can you state what condition Senator Gore's apparel was in at that time?"

"Well," said Jim, "the part of the flesh that was visible wouldn't look very well in print."

In response to the same question, Robertson said that 'the front of his trousers were open, or rather, unbuttoned. They were not open.' After Robertson had hurried to the rescue, knocking down the dresser which sat in front of the door, for the realistic effect it would give the charge, Minnie began to scream and blubber. The Senator tried to get her to state, before Robertson, and Fitz and Jim Jacobs, who had followed Robertson into the room, 'that everything was all right and that he had been a perfect gentleman.' This Minnie declined to do. Robertson hustled Gore out while Minnie went into the bathroom, and it was while he and the blind man were waiting for the elevator, that Robertson claimed he noticed the condition of the striped trousers, and it was there that the Senator straightened the situation up. "We were waiting for the elevator to come down and he asked me if his clothing was not all right, and I pulled his coat back to see. I noticed that his trousers were unbuttoned, and I told him so."

The storm of notoriety which started immediately after the incident and continued, for over a year, contained the various conflicting contentions of the various parties. The Minnie Bond backers, and there was plenty of them, contended that Gore sent a representative to the Winston the next day, and 'asked her what she wanted, saying that she could get any job the senator could give, if she'd keep her mouth shut.' Fitzpatrick and Jacobs always maintained that they were offered lucrative positions in the government if they would respect the senator's wishes for a complete silence in the matter. Gore and his backers claimed that the exposure never would have been made if certain demands for patronage had been met by him.

In cross-examining Mrs. Bond, Pruiett asked; "I will ask you if you didn't have a conversation with Mr. Linebaugh, the next day, after you claimed Senator Gore assaulted you, where you said that you had some strings on Senator Gore, and that if he didn't lay down, and if he didn't come through and help you out, that you were going to pull them on him."

The more generally accepted, and more plausible, version of that angle of the case, was that the participants, who might have some interest in getting a political job from the senator, had no voice in the direction of the production after they played their parts. Minnie's husband met Colonel Rogers, the man who could thank Gore for the loss of a cabinet position, in Memphis, and the two of them rode the train together to the National Capitol. There was a midnight conference in the Jim Jacobs room at the Winston, where Fitz and Robertson, Rogers and Bond were present, and the names of Frank McMurray and Jake Hamon, the millionaire Republican politician from Ardmore, were mentioned. Rogers left the next afternoon for New York and Robertson followed him. These two met at the Martinique Hotel there, then journeyed back to Baltimore, where they met Jacobs and Fitzpatrick. The large amount of cash which Rogers gave Jacobs for distribution amongst the group was called a loan by Jacobs, a payoff, by Pruiett. Minnie Bond and her husband went to the District Attorney's office and demanded that Gore be prosecuted. The press ate it up.

The *Kansas City Journal* for February 7, 1914, reporting the trial progress, made reference to the conditions as they existed at the time of the expose. "The Senator denied that he had ever attempted to settle with Jacobs or the others for a cash consideration, or that he was asked by Senator Kern to appear before the Committee of Privileges and Elections of the United States Senate and explain his conduct." In the same article, the *Journal* stated that "Questions asked Senator Gore as to whether he was not guilty of accepting bribes for his vote on various occasions as a member of the counsel of Oklahoma Territorial Legislature were admitted to the record by Judge Clark just before the conclusion of Gore's testimony this afternoon. A deposition alleging improper conduct of the Senator toward a blind girl, said to have been his sweetheart years ago, also was read into the record. A number of questions read into the record related to other alleged episodes of the Senator with women in Oklahoma, Washington, D. C., and in Indiana."

While the charges and counter charges flew, the Gore forces gained steadily. On April 17, 1913, the polished Kirby Fitzpatrick addressed a letter to the Attorney General of the United States, giving mimeographed copies to the all-too-glad-to-publish-it press. "Re. Bond-Gore charges—Sir: The press reports that Sen. Gore has been made the victim of a conspiracy to blackmail, basing their conclusions on findings of District Attorney Wilson of your department. It is not my purpose to volunteer any opinion as to the guilt or innocence of the Senator, but I respectfully suggest that you examine a transcript of the evidence taken by the District Attorney, from which you will be forced to the conclusion that a felony has been committed by the Senator, the witnesses, or the District Attorney, in which case I feel that, even though you do not cause the guilty to be brought to justice, you will surely see the innocent freed from the imputation of dishonor and crime."

"When it was whispered in Washington that the witnesses in the case would be arrested, I, together with Mr. Robertson, went to the office of the District Attorney and challenged an indictment, which challenge was later laid before the District Attorney by letter, a copy of which was served on yourself and each U. S. Senator; and as I am informed you stated that this challenge, if not accepted, would free Mr. Robertson and myself from any criticism, and yet we are left exposed to the libelous attack of every editorial peon in Oklahoma, with no recourse except to the maudlin process of a libel suit. "

"I, in my interview with the District Attorney, drew the conclusion from his admissions that it is no offense in the District of Columbia for a Senator, in the very shadow of the Capitol, to attempt to commit rape on the wife of a constituent who was seeking patronage, so long as the charge of force was not clearly proven, and this, not-with-standing a confession and an attempt to bribe witnesses, which was in evidence. If this being true and the Department of Justice being unable to defend, we should at least hoist to the dome of the capitol flag of the white slave traffic as a warning to those who are not strong enough to defend their own."

"When I return to my home state, I find myself branded as a blackmailer through the action of a District Attorney, from whose attitude it is reasonable to infer that he is willing to stand like a guardian eunuch at the portals of a senatorial harem so long as his patron does not leave his finger marks on the throats of his victims. Respectfully submitted, Kirby Fitzpatrick."

And young Mr. Robertson was no neophyte in guiding the scurrilous pen. He petitioned each member of the United States Senate a letter, asking them to hold an official investigation on the conduct of their blind colleague. With these letters, he enclosed carbon copies of two missives, one which United States Senator Charles S. Thomas of Colorado had written him, and the other, the reply which he had made to that communication. Senator Thomas had been given particular advice to the incident, in that he was the chairman of the Committee on Womans Suffrage.

In his letter to each of the members of the Senate, Robertson said: "Sir: As there seems to be some misunderstanding as to the position occupied by myself in the Bond-Gore matter, I beg your indulgence in the reading of the two enclosed letters, the letter I received from Senator Thomas in answer to my former communication, and my letter to him in reply. I want it distinctly understood that I do welcome an investigation of this matter and think that it is the duty of the United States Senate to investigate the charges growing out of this affair. Certainly the people have a right to know the real facts concerning this salacious episode in which one of your honorable body is inseparably connected. I am, with great respect, Yours very truly—T. E. Robertson."

Senator Thomas, on franked stationary, showing that he was Chairman of the United States Senate Committee on Woman's Suffrage, and under date of April 15, 1913, had addressed T. E. Robertson, Esquire, Oklahoma City, as follows: "Sir: Your letter of the 9th inst. with enclosure received. The action of the District Attorney in Washington to which your letter refers was in my judgment perfectly proper. I regret, however, that he did not follow it up by the institution of criminal proceedings against those connected with the effort to compromise the standing of Senator Gore, in whom I have entire confidence and whose statement concerning the matter was long ago accepted by myself without hesitation. Yours truly, Chas. S. Thomas."

Robertson's reply to this terse attempt on Senator Thomas's part to put him in his place did not indicate that he was abashed. On April 21, 1913, he sent the Senator from the Rocky Mountain sector a truly enlightening epistle.

"Sir," he said, Your letter of April 15, received. I wish to commend you for your loyalty to Senator Gore, a loyalty which causes you to go on record in his behalf favoring and admitting as perfectly proper the action of the District Attorney in Washington who failed to thoroughly investigate a charge of attempted rape alleged to have been committed by a United States Senator within the very shadow of the Senate Chamber, and this notwithstanding the fact that it is the sworn duty of the District Attorney to thoroughly investigate all charges of crime and diligently prosecute all criminals."

"In my letter to you and of which you acknowledge receipt, I asked for a thorough investigation of the affair and offered you personally my assistance in any way to a full, fair and impartial investigation. I, again, request such an investigation and renew my offer of assistance. I assert with perfect confidence and I think my actions will bear me out, that I have done all in my power to bring about such an investigation, and while I agree with you that there is cause for 'regret' that the District Attorney in acting 'perfectly proper' did not do his duty; yet, I do not want to create the impression that I believe in the sincerity of your 'regret,' for I do not."

"You are possessed of a great power and influence as a member of the United States Senate; that a word from you would bring about the institution of criminal proceedings against all those connected with this affair will not be questioned, and that you could at least bring about a senatorial investigation cannot be doubted. Surely, a request upon your part for an investigation would be welcomed by every member of the Senate, not excepting Senator Gore, who is laboring under this great suspicion. If you are sincere in your desire to see the truth prevail and the guilty brought to a deserving punishment, and certainly you do stand for that, then ask for a Senatorial Investigation. By this means, you can obtain your desire and place yourself where you will cease to have cause for regret."

"Certainly you can have no objection to an investigation by the Senate as you have entire confidence in Senator Gore. You, no doubt, would gladly embrace the opportunity to sit as a juror in this case and render a verdict expressing your 'entire confidence' in Senator Gore, basing it upon his statement concerning the matter which you have long ago accepted without hesitation as being the truth. A request upon your part for an investigation will show the sincerity of your 'regret' and a failure upon your part to make such request will, in my opinion, show that your 'regret' is a mere banter of words, exposing the vain and vaporing imaginings of a mind whose judgment has become abhorrently subservient to the sinister demands of bias and prejudice."

"If purity and morals cannot be maintained by those occupying high positions of honor and trust; if virtue of our womanhood cannot be protected from the lecherous assaults made by men whose daily sustenance is taken from the public till, then I say, take down from the dome of the Capitol the likeness of the Goddess of Freedom, and place in her stead a statue of the diseased form of a hag from hell; tear down the red, white and blue, emblematic as it is of liberty, and hoist in its place the blood-stained banner of carnal triumph; let chaos be king, and let the American people view with awe the wreck of their glorious republic, the result of the joint efforts of failure to enforce the law and the pollution of public office by men whose estimate of morality proves insufficient, even when judged by the standards of Nero."

"In order that there will be no misunderstanding concerning the position taken by me in this matter, I have mailed a copy of your letter and this reply to the Attorney General, and to each of the other Senators. Yours very truly, T. E. Robertson."

The Senator from Colorado should have encountered no ambiguity in the terms employed by the young Oklahoman, although subsequent developments did not disclose his attitude toward the expression. If he had an answer for it, or if he made answer, the content of it was never given over to the public, which was being kept currently informed by the *National Press.*

Robertson's letter to the District Attorney was explanatory of many angles of the issue, and served to illustrate the feeling which existed between the parties involved in the controversy.

"Sir:" he said, "In-as-much-as there was no record made of the conversation between yourself, Mr. Givens, Mr. Fitzpatrick and myself this morning [April 5, 1913] I deem it most advisable to present my views to you in writing and to that end I register you this letter, which sets forth fully the view I took of the charges and counter-charges growing out of the Mrs. Minnie E. Bond-Senator T. P. Gore controversy."

"Your statement to the paper that there was no justification for further investigation of this matter confirms fully your statement to Mr. Fitzpatrick and myself, and in my opinion it creates the impression as suggested to you by me, that there is no truth in the testimony given by myself and Mr. Fitzpatrick. This is the question I want to discuss in this letter."

"As stated to you in my conversation, one of two things is absolutely certain, either Senator Gore is guilty of the crime of which he is charged, or else a conspiracy was framed to blackmail him. It is also equally as certain that a crime of some kind has been committed, or, if Senator Gore is guilty that crime should be investigated, and if he is innocent of the charge then the crime of blackmail on the part of the witnesses who testified against him should be investigated, with the end in view of exonerating Senator Gore completely."

"It is a matter of record in your office, testified to as I understand it, by Mrs. Bond and Mr. Jacobs, that Senator Gore had Dr. J. H. Earp of Oklahoma come to him at his [Gore's] special instance and request, to ascertain what could be done to shut this matter up. Dr. Earp did not come to me in person on the matter, but I understood that he advised three or four other people that Senator Gore had confessed this entire matter to him. The names of the parties I will be glad to furnish if you desire them."

"With these facts in mind, I am constrained to the belief that a fair and impartial investigation should be had and that the imputation of blackmail upon myself should either be proved, or else I should be entirely exonerated on any blame. Surely you, yourself, and Senator Gore will agree to this. If he had been blackmailed, he would certainly want, as a matter of justice, his blackmailers punished, and you as prosecuting attorney in whose jurisdiction this crime has been committed, would certainly use every means at your command to give the blackmailers sue and speedy punishment."

"While I appreciate your frankness in telling me and Mr. Fitzpatrick that the prosecution against Sen. Gore would be dropped and considered no further by you, yet I feel that the stand you have taken imputes to me the crime of conspiring to blackmail Senator Gore. This should, in justice to me, be fully and completely investigated, and it is found that I am not guilty, then I should be exonerated. I therefor respectfully, but earnestly, urge that you make a thorough investigation of this matter. Respectfully, T. E. Robertson."

Senator Gore was in the corner. He had to fight. His first six year term in the Senate, which had begun with statehood for Oklahoma in '07, was nearing its end, and he was more than reluctant to give up the advantages which Washington offered, amorous and otherwise, over the accommodations of his native Texas and Indian Territory. When the Bond story broke, he had but one choice of program to adopt. He had to whip it so decisively that it could be used as campaign capital in his coming fight to be re-elected, or he had to sit by and watch it as it overwhelmed and defeated him.

He employed Pruiett, paying him $5,000, when the retinue of talent already volunteered would gain his equivalent to an acquittal, along with relief from paying the $50,000 Minnie prayed for, if legal ingenuity and skill could accomplish it. there was Charles B. Stuart, a lawyer who had moved to the new state from Gainesville, Texas, when his law partner, Joseph Weldon Bailey, was elected to Congress and moved off and left him. A. C. Cruce, Pruiett's old alternating ally and adversary was on the list, as was W. I. "Bill" Gilbert, who in later years acquired prominence as the leading legal light of the Pacific Coast, and who, in his suite in Los Angeles, California, advised the movie stars as to their rights and obligations, contractual, marital and otherwise. In a hotel room conference, the lawyers agreed that Gore should know how, and by whom, he wanted his defense handled. The sightless Senator pecked the floor a few times with his fancy cane before he answered.

"The rest of you boys get the law ready, and take care of the detail. I want Moman to cross-examine their witnesses, and I want him to take charge of getting our evidence together. And, another thing, I hired him to give this case to the jury."

Pruiett started after Minnie Bond in full cry. The plaintiff had had an unfortunate prior marriage or two, and a child born that didn't survive. A country town burial, with forced economy apparent in the utility of a shoe-box for a casket—and with the services of the embalmer and preacher dispensed with—gave him license to charge that she had murdered her progeny. On January 22, 1914, he took the sworn depositions of witness at Caddo, a hamlet in the old Choctaw bogs in the southeastern part of the new state, to expose a few of Minnie's apparent many indiscretions. His detectives had learned that she had lived in that community as the wife of Dr. Farrar, a dentist.

His first witness was 55 year old P. L. Rogers, who testified in a deposition taken on January 22, 1914.

"Do you know whether or not Minnie Ballinger was a married woman when you knew her?" he asked.

"No, she wasn't married," the witness replied.

"Do you know whether or not she married in Caddo?"

"Yes, she married here in Caddo."

"Do you know who she married?"

"A man by the name of Dr. Farrar."

"Do you know about the time she married Dr. Farrar?"

"I don't know the exact time, but it must have been along in the fall of 1903."

Pruiett had a purpose in developing that particular kind of testimony, as it appeared from the witnesses answers a little later on.

"Do you remember the circumstances of the birth of a child after the marriage you have spoken of?" he inquired.

"Yes sir," came the prompt answer.

"Do you know how long it was after the marriage that this child was born?"

"Not exactly, but it was a short time."

"Fix the time with reference to months, as best you can."

"As well as I remember," the witnessed answered, "it was in February the child was born; it seems to me they hadn't been married but six weeks or two months. I don't think they had been married but a short time."

"Do you know where they were living when this child was born? I mean the house?"

"It was on this street and on the north side, this is Buffalo street. It was the third house from the old ice house."

"Did you see that child?" Pruiett pursued.

"Yes sir," the witness answered.

"State where, and under what circumstances you saw the child you speak about?"

"This man Slaton was plowing in the garden back of the house where they lived, breaking the garden for Spring, and plowed the child up." The old man showed that he attached considerable importance to the incident he was narrating, and a like amount to himself as the narrator. Pruiett was glad to give him the opportunity to strut in the light of his own self-importance. He stayed on the same subject.

"Describe the appearance of the child with reference to probable age, weight and sex," he commanded.

"It looked like a well developed child." came the reply. "Its finger nails were full grown, and it had hair on its head. I believe it was a male child, and it looked to me like it ought to weight between six and eight pounds. I didn't think it could have been buried but a short while, it had a dark place around its neck and one little spot in the stomach darker than any other about it."

"From your examination of the external appearances of the child, what conclusions, if any, did you arrive at as to the manner and cause of the child's death?" Pruiett was cold and deliberate as he asked the question. The witness was just as cold in making response.

"It was my opinion that the child had been killed, and there were a lot of rumors around town, to the same effect, at the time."

"I will ask you to state if you knew Minnie Ballinger's reputation, at the time she was married to Dr. Farrar, and just prior thereto, as to being a virtuous woman?"

"Well," the witness replied, "she would make dates with Dr. Farrar and meet him in a thicket. Her reputation was bad."

When Rogers, and Slaton, who followed him to the stand had concluded their testimony, Minnie Bond's reputation was as rough, and seamed with furrows, as had been the back lot where Slaton's one mule plow had disturbed the buried remains of the infant in the shoe box. He proved that she had been indiscreet, actually promiscuous with all the big boys of the town, and that she and the dentist slipped away and out of the county to avoid prosecution for the murder of the new born baby.

Then he disclosed that Dr. Farrar had not been free to wed; so, shortly before the arrival of the baby, because of the existence of an undissolved prior marriage which he had contracted in Georgia. To make things perfectly regular, and to satisfy the luckless Minnie's father, the dentist had procured a divorce from his first wife, and then gone through with the second ceremony with Minnie. Pruiett had the records where they were married twice, and then that Minnie divorced him before the ink on the second certificate had scarcely more than dried.

The interests behind the plaintiff weren't idly absorbing all the punches that Pruiett was throwing them. The Senator hadn't been much more discreet in his youth than he had been after his elevation to the Senate, and a blind man with a natural abundance of enemies, political and otherwise, who would march into a strange hotel room without the report of a trustworthy lookout, and conduct himself as it appeared had the Senator, must have had an uneasy conscience when he knew that men like Robertson, Jacobs and Kirby Fitzpatrick, backed by money-bags like Jake Hamon, Bob Rogers and Frank McMurray, were scouring his old haunts in search of skeletons for shaking in his public face.

They produced mild-mannered, soft-voiced Myrtle Holder, who gave a deposition at Chico, Texas, on January 26 and 27, 1914. Myrtle saw the world and its wonders through the tips of her fingers, as did Senator Gore. She gave lessons on stringed musical instruments to provide funds for the education of her nearly grown child. Myrtle Holder didn't have, and never had had, a husband. She claimed that the blind statesman from Oklahoma was her child's father, and had so insisted through the years, long before he had gained political advancement and preferment.

Theirs had been a romance which began in the soft balm of gulf nights at old Galveston, Texas, where Myrtle was teaching music. Gore, with a brother-in-law who was taking lessons, would call and idle while the two of them would play on their guitars together. She later moved to Corsicana, Texas, and she and Gore, both blind, renewed their associations there. Her testimony with reference to this association was being taken by the attorneys for Minnie Bond in the parlor of the old Brown Hotel at Chico, Texas.

"I will ask you if you ever gave birth to a child, along about the year 1896 or 1897?" Mr. Lillard asked, after he had elicited general information establishing that she had known the Senator for a long time.

Pruiett interrupted with an objection.

"Objected to as incompetent, irrelevant and immaterial, and for the further reason that the question, or its answer, is not germane to any issue in this case and is only propounded at the suggestion of a lot of politicians who are seeking to give publicity to this testimony in order to injure United States Senator T. P. Gore, of Oklahoma; and for the further reason that the lawyer who propounded it knows as a lawyer that it is incompetent, irrelevant and immaterial, and can only be used for the purpose of a bunch of political vandals in the State of Oklahoma who are seeking to destroy Senator Gore politically."

"I move that the speech be expunged," Lillard laughed.

"You are going to get a lot more speeches in this record," Pruiett promised, vengefully.

When the witness answered the question in the affirmative, her counsel asked her for the name of the father of her child.

"T. P. Gore," she answered, simply.

"Were you ever married to T. P. Gore," he asked her.

"No sir."

The witness hesitated for an instant, and when no one prompted her with a question, she continued, slowly and methodically.

"I was engaged to the man and I loved him, I believe, as well as a child, for I was at that time a child, in mind and heart, as well as a child could have loved anyone, but I did not submit to him of my own free will."

"I will get you to relate how you came to submit to him, if you did submit to him, and how it came about the first time." Her counsel was on the job again.

"There was no resistance that I could possibly make that would have availed anything," she answered dramatically, "he overpowered me and I could do nothing."

They were leading her smoothly along toward the climax of the build-up.

"In what way did he overpower you?" she was asked.

"Well," she said, "I could not scream; he placed his hands over my mouth and overpowered me in strength."

When she began to talk about the hand over the mouth, Pruiett recognized the Minnie Bond touch. When he had first taken her on cross-examination, he thundered:

"Now, when did you first tell anyone that Senator Gore placed his hand over your mouth?"

Then in rapid succession he asked her;

"When did you first meet Mrs. Bond? When did you first hear that Senator Gore placed his hand over Mrs. Bond's mouth? Who told you, her husband?"

The blind woman who plunked the banjos in the moonlight didn't appreciate Pruiett's boisterousness, and didn't try to conceal the fact from him.

"Unless I am treated with absolute respect, I refuse to go one bit further," she firmly and rebelliously said.

"I suppose you are posted not to got further," Pruiett answered, dryly. "So just so you won't be embarrassed by my tone, I will say that I am talking to you in my natural tone, as I talk to all people. I hope you will understand that my tone is not for the purpose of embarrassing you, but simply to try to elicit the truth. With that understanding, I will start in now again."

The assurance which Myrtle gained, if any, from his patronizing confidence must have been short lived, but she forgot to invoke her reticence with his violation of the bargain he had made.

"How did Mrs. Bond put it, when she told you about her experience with the Senator?"

"She just told me the facts of the case," Myrtle said, "that he had placed his hand over her mouth to keep her from screaming and that she struck him, now wait a minute, anyway, that she fought to be released and that he broke her glasses, and I think that is all she said; I mean in regard to that particular phase of it."

"You told her that you had been a pure girl before he had violated you, didn't you?" Pruiett was leading her, and with a purpose.

"I certainly did," was the spirited answer she gave.

"Did she tell you that she had been a pure woman—that she had always been a pure woman?"

"Why, I don't think there was any need for her to tell me that; but, I thought she was."

"Miss Myrtle," he bellowed at her, leveling his finger in apparent ignorance of her inability to see it. "Did she tell you anything about being fired out of a hotel in Little Rock, with her corset and little panties on, and nothing else on her body?"

"No," came a weak, shocked answer, "She said nothing to me about anything like that."

"Did she tell you anything about how she made $130.00 by being intimate with men over at the old confederate reunion at Little Rock?"

"No!"

"She didn't tell you anything about having intercourse with a fellow named Rogers, did she?"

"No."

"Did she tell you anything about living in a whore house at Fort Worth, Texas? Did she?"

"No."

"So she didn't tell you that? Well, did she tell you that she had given birth to a child three months after she was married, and that she buried it in the garden, and that a nigger plowed it up?"

"No."

"She didn't tell you anything about a Mrs. Sean begging her not to murder the baby, did she?"

"No."

Pruiett produced the records of cases number 5132 and 5133 of Navarro County, entitled *State of Texas vs T. P. Gore,* and had the witness agree that they had been filed, one for seduction and the other for procuring an abortion, on the witnesses testimony before a grand jury. Then she admitted that the cases had been disposed of on directed verdicts in favor of Gore, with the agreement by herself and the prosecuting attorney that there was not sufficient evidence available to convict. The latter charge, which made reference to the abortion, they could not hope to substantiate. It had been nothing more than an attempt, and an unsuccessful one, for by her own declaration the child had been born, and was still living.

And poor unfortunate Myrtle was living at the time with an oft-divorced and married Mrs. Paul Hemphill, the record of whose matrimonial and divorcement score lay in Pruiett's fat brief case. The Gore intelligence service had long arms. Pruiett referred to her as Mrs. Paul Norwood Noble Jones Hemphill, and when he had exhausted his invective in discussing Mrs. Bond, and in making insinuations against the character of the blind witness, he turned on Mrs. Hemphill.

"Anticipating that Mrs. Hemphill will be a witness and testify in this cause, the defendant wishes to ask these questions for the purpose, first of showing and general reputation and character of Mrs. Hemphill, and second, for the purpose of showing the character and kind of people this witness has associated with and lived with, for a number of years, to-wit; that Mrs. Hemphill's reputation in the community in the various places where she has lived, is for murdering a husband and poisoning people, and we expect to show the records where Mrs. Hemphill's husband filed suit for divorce, alleging that she was a—that she had attempted to poison him, and threatened to murder him."

During another phase of the long cross-examination, he went into the financial backing of the plaintiff's case.

"Do you know that Mr. Bond is a poor man, and working on a salary?" he inquired.

"Why, he told me he was a poor man," she agreed.

"Did he tell you who was paying the expenses of this case?"

Myrtle knit the brows that shaded her sightless orbs. "I think not; if he did, I do not remember," she replied.

"Did he tell you there was plenty of money behind this prosecution? Tell you anything about Mr. McMurray backing him in this fight, or Jake Hamon?" Pruiett inquired.

"If he did, I did not understand them," the witness said. "But, he did name some names—he read me a letter or two—some names something like that."

"Something like McMurray? Was the name Rogers?"

"I could not tell you the names, I do not remember."

"Well, what was the purpose of the letter; why did he read it to you?" Pruiett was persistent.

"Why, I think it was from a friend of his, telling him that with clean hands and true hearts they wanted nothing but the truth, or something to that effect; in a way, it was sympathizing with him; I don't remember anything else of the letter."

"How much did the letter say was enclosed," he shot at her.

"I don't know," the witness answered wearily.

"You don't know his object in showing you the letter?"

"Why, I suppose it was to show me how the good men really felt. I did not think of it in any other way; just to show how good men felt."

"Good men," he roared, "how do you know whether they were good men or not?"

"Well," she stammered, "I guess from the way the letter read they must have been; no one with clean hands and clean hearts could have been otherwise."

"You don't know whether it was from the thieves who had been robbing the Indians for years or not, do you?" That was his final shot in her darkness.

And so the immaculate, clean-cut issues were tried. The Senator was a political and moral despoiler who violated the chastity of a blind girl, and who sold his vote in the senate to whoever would offer him the most for it. Minnie Bond was an infanticidal prostitute who parceled out her virtue, for a consideration, to the besotted delegates of a traveling man's convention. The Department of Justice and the Senate of the United States was bought by the influence of one of its sponsors and members; the million dollar graft lobbys and disgruntled seekers of cabinet positions were persecuting an innocent, honest official, after they had conspired against him. With that calibre of subject matter, and with Pruiett in the driver's seat, charged by Minnie's organization with bribing and intimidating witnesses, and fabricating perjured evidence, it was little wonder that the Oklahoma Capitol, where the case was being tried, was attracting the attention of the national paper-watching public.

" 'I knew they had framed up on me. I told Dr. J. H. Earp when he called at my office on the day following the occurrence that I would see them in hell before I would make terms with them. I did not tell Earp to hush Mrs. Bond and get her out of Washington. At no time, neither in my office nor in the Winston Hotel, did I ever offer Mrs. Bond any improprieties or take advantage of her'. So declared Senator T. P. Gore in testimony in his own behalf today in the $50,000 damage suit against him by Mrs. Minnie E. Bond."

The St. Louis *Globe-Democrat* on February 17, 1914 had opened its daily two-column front in that manner. "Speaking in a loud, clear voice, Senator Gore denied every essential part of the testimony of Mrs. Bond, Dr. Earp and the other members of the alleged conspiracy against him."

"The feature of today's events, other than the testimony of Senator Gore, was the appearance on the stand of Al Jennings, ex-outlaw and present candidate for Governor on the Democratic ticket, as a witness for Mrs. Bond. Jennings contradicted the testimony of Mitch Bonner, Oklahoma City banker, and said that in Jacobs's conversation with Bonner, Jacobs did not say he would 'call off' the Gore charges for $25,000."

The St. Louis paper told the senator's side of the story as he told it himself. "I talked with her only a few minutes. I told her I would have to go. I rose to start and extended my hand, and when she took hold of it she kind of seemed to go down on the bed. I said 'What does this mean?' She gave me some kind of an answer which I didn't understand and then I heard someone come in who said it was T. E. Robertson of Oklahoma City. We exchanged salutations. Mrs. Bond began to make an outcry and carry on, and Robertson told her to 'stop that squalling.' He and she passed some remarks and she went into the bathroom. I told Robertson to get my hat. He did so and then I told him that I wanted to talk to Mrs. Bond. I said to her 'Mrs. Bond, what have you got to say about this? I must explain here that my relations in the past with Mr. Robertson had been unpleasant. She said 'I don't want Bond to know you have been in my room.' I put the same question to Robertson and he said he had nothing to say. Neither made any suggestion of any impropriety. My intention was to summon the hotel keeper if there had been any such suggestion."

The *Kansas City Star* on February 19, 1914, likened it, editorially, to the New York scandal involving Funk and Sulzer. "The Gore case, like the case of Funk and Sulzer, has exposed once more the methods used by unscrupulous politicians to discredit men who are in their way. Sulzer they punished, not for his misdeeds, but for his refusal to obey the mandates of the boss and turn over the State of New York to politicians to plunder."

The Associated Press to the *Post Dispatch* at St. Louis on February 18, 1914, was able to glean a little of homely interest from the smelly bulk of the subject being considered. "On her arrival in the courtroom today, Mrs. Gore brought with her hundreds of messages addressed to Senator Gore, from friends over the country and constituents, in Oklahoma, expressing their sympathy in 'his persecution' and their belief in his vindication by the jury."

Moman Pruiett's argument to the jury, at the conclusion of the evidence and the reading of the law by the court was typically his own. The satiristic scribe had said that he "tousled his hair and walked the jury-box rail on his hands." The national press, commenting in a more serious vein, gave it so much favorable notice that the author was swamped with calls, telegrams and letters, asking for reproductions of the speech. The none too modest Pruiett had it transcribed by the official reporter, and bound into an engraved booklet, with a bushy haired portrait of his own for a frontispiece. He spent $2,000 on the speech before the wave of orders subsided; that sum did not include the $500 he paid for postage in sending it out.

The *Kansas City Star* editorialized on February 18, 1914: "Such a speech as that arouses the sympathy of even those who see the ridiculous character of the procedure. What he said is so essentially sound, the object of his strange eloquence is so fundamentally righteous that all his 'crouching like a tiger,' all his dramatics of removing his collar and tie, all his evident genius for going to the heart of an issue and ap-

OKLAHOMA FARMER

Volume 24 | March 15, 1914 | Number 6

The Verdict

WE, the jury empaneled in the case entitled Minnie E. Bond vs. Thomas Pryor Gore, find that the evidence is insufficient upon which to predicate a suit, and that said evidence wholly exonerates the defendant, Thomas Pryor Gore.

Senator Thomas P. Gore Is Vindicated

His Statement

THE verdict confirms my faith that truth will triumph. It confirms my doctrine that a public servant should perform his public duty without calculating upon the consequences, either personal or political.

FAILING TO publicly dishonor United States Senator Gore, his political blackmailers are said to have ruined him financially, and the club they used with which to sandbag him was a court of justice. The plot of these political shysters to disgrace Oklahoma's blind senator shows how easy it is to use our courts for criminal purposes, or by means of them to perpetuate an injustice. In this case the court actually was made a party to the plot to ruin the blind senator, for the conspirators used all the court's legal machinery to carry out their vengeance. Senator Gore stood between these political grafters and their plans to loot and plunder the Indians. He declined to make the appointments they wished made. It costs a public man a small fortune to defend his honor in a court of justice and takes a poor man's all, and it was here that the court of justice became a party to the crime in the Gore case. This perversion of courts might be prevented and the cause of justice be advanced by having a public examiner, or his assistant appear in every court and cause. Let this man take the place of the prosecuting attorney, whose very title implies injustice, and make it his duty to clear the innocent as well as convict the guilty. Justice, absolute justice, so far as that is in the power of man, should be the aim and purpose of his work, not a deliberate effort to send as many men as possible to the penitentiary, whether guilty or not. A public examiner would make justice a less expensive luxury.

UNITED STATES SENATOR THOMAS P. GORE. ALTHOUGH BLIND, GORE WAS ACCUSED OF ATTEMPTED RAPE BY MRS. MINNIE BOND AFTER THE TWO MET IN A WASHINGTON, D. C., HOTEL ROOM. GORE CLAIMED THAT THE CHARGE WAS AN ATTEMPT TO DESTROY HIM AND HIRED MOMAN PRUIETT AS HIS DEFENSE ATTORNEY. PRUIETT SUCCESSFULLY CLEARED GORE OF BOND'S ALLEGATIONS. COURTESY CARL ALBERT CENTER CONGRESSIONAL ARCHIVES, UNIVERSITY OF OKLAHOMA.

pealing to the hearts of jurymen and onlookers seems to fit in well with the achievement of justice, if not with its administration."

And another, the *Daily Globe* of Joplin, Missouri, said: "Probably the man who has profited most from the Gore case is the man who cared least about profiting. Moman Pruiett, one of the Senator's attorneys, won a lasting place in the hearts of every Gore sympathizer throughout the country by his burning castigation of the men behind the plaintiff. There is no gentility to Pruiett's eloquence. Even his sarcasm is blunt and ragged; it has no razor edge. He simply strips a proposition naked and redresses it with homely, striking word pictures, or peppers it with trip-hammer blows of wilting invective. Naturally, he is deeply loved, desperately hated, and profoundly respected. And above all else, he is immensely interesting."

A quart of good whiskey had put Pruiett on the point he had been working up to for months. He kicked restraint under the counsel table and jumped upon 'the hell-inspired conspiracy' as he called it, and the conspirators.

"First comes Jacobs," he roared, "the arch-conspirator who, with criminal ingenuity, created within his own perverted mind and debased soul the sickening details of this horrible crime. Jacobs, according to the testimony, was an eye-witness to the result of his own hellish scheme. He addressed a long written document to the Senator confessing his guilt and gloating over the fact that he had been successful in persuading others to take part in his high carnival of perfidy. With the sneaking malignity of the hyena, he has pressed the wolf dogs of persecution on and on, until today there is presented to the world the sad and sorrowful spectacle of a blind man, high in the councils of the government, who has hitherto led a life of honor, forced to meet the unmerited indignity of a political persecution. This man Jacobs, the ring-leader of a criminal gang, the brains of all that's dirty, low and debased—this monument to depravity whom they were afraid to put on the stand. He held off, so he could turn states evidence when these conspirators are arrested and prosecuted for this crime. Jacobs and McMurray are wily old coyotes, too cunning to be witnesses in the case; they planned it all, then coward like, they shrink in the shadowy background, and dare not come out to testify."

The underlying logic of his theme was eve apparent in his violent vituperation.

"Now remember, that Jacobs was the man that wanted Robert A.

Rogers appointed as Secretary of the Interior, and Senator Gore refused to endorse Rogers. And remember further, that McMurray is the great Indian grafter whose numerous attempts to rob the defenseless Indians of this State have been successfully defeated by Senator Gore. Bear those facts in mind and you will catch the full force of Jacobs's remarks, and arrive at a complete understanding of this diabolical scheme."

One of the plaintiff's attorneys, E. J. Giddings, was an oratorical sort of person with considerable of a start toward a political career. He had stated, during the progress of the trial, that his own political future was involved along with his, and his client's, good faith in the prosecution of the case. Pruiett went into that.

"My friend Giddings said that he would stake his political future upon the conduct he has displayed in this trial," he cried. "Let me say to you, gentlemen, that Giddings is playing for small stakes. He need not worry about his political future: he hasn't any. If he is not already politically damned, he will be at the end of the trial of this case."

"Now, let us divide our time with the great soldier in the case," he cried. "Let us pay our respects to that distinguished military genius. But, let us recall, and let us not forget, he is also a disappointed office seeker. He followed the flag, did he? Let me tell you, gentlemen, he would follow the bedraggled petticoats of a degraded harlot ten thousand miles where he would follow the flag of his country one. This brave soldier, who stood there in the darkened room in a Washington Hotel, and peeped through a crack at a blind man who had been lured into a lighted room by a woman, is a brave soldier indeed, spying upon a blind enemy!"

One by one, he took them up and took them apart. Robertson. Bond, the pale, sickly imitation of a husband, as he called him; Minnie Bond, her character and her motives. One of counsel had challenged the defendant to 'say that Al Jennings lied.' Al, although his book 'Beating Back' was a current best seller, and he was running for Governor of Oklahoma on a reform platform, still carried a bad man reputation, and a great portion of the populous tried to let him alone. Pruiett interpreted the challenge as the threat of a pistol ball in the back.

Ready for his inevitable dramatic climax, he struck a heroic pose before the jury.

"And now, my friends," he cried, "here's where I get killed. Call the bailiff to measure me for my coffin, and have the sexton dig my grave. This bad man Jennings, this outlaw who is making political capital of his every criminal act, who tenders his career as a horse-thief and train-robber as his chief asset for citizenship, has threatened to kill any man who dares to call him a liar. I call him a liar. I call him a perjurer. I say he is unworthy of the respect of any honest man. I say all this, and what is more, I say that Al Jennings is afraid to even so much as crook his little finger at me!"

With a borrowed bar from Burns and a whispered reference to Milton's sonnet on his blindness, he was through. "Let me ask you after all is said, to consider this case in the light of the facts, and by a righteous verdict, to give back to the world, unsullied by the assaults of foul conspiracy, the name of Blind Tom Gore." The itinerant butcher's boy had been making another speech, and the entire nation had been listening.

The *Baltimore Sun* was prompt with its commendatory editorial on February 20, 1914. "We congratulate Senator Gore on the verdict which has so emphatically given the lie to the trumped-up charges against him. He performed a fine public service in refusing to make terms with the blackmailers, and fighting them in the open."

That same day the *Washington Post* said: "All men in public life will feel reassured by the outcome of the sensational trial in Oklahoma, in which Senator Thomas P. Gore was the defendant. He was promptly exonerated." The *Philadelphia Press* also noted the outcome in that day's issue. "It looked like an attempt at blackmail from the beginning, and the contradicted testimony of the plaintiff and her witnesses did not remove that impression before the defense had said a word. Senator Gore bore himself with great dignity and good sense through his unpleasant ordeal."

In a letter bearing date of March 4, 1914, addressed "My dear Pruiett," the blind Senator had a word of gratitude to offer. "It would be gratifying for you to know how many congratulations I have received and am still receiving from every quarter of the country and from every class of people, from the lowliest working woman to the President of the Republic. The President was especially enthusiastic in his congratulations, as was Colonel [William Jennings] Bryan and other members of the Cabinet. I am under deep and enduring obligations to you for your splendid faith and efficient service. Let me hear from you from time to time, and keep me advised as to the course of events. These people will of course exhaust every recourse in an effort to trump up some other cause of embarrassment, but all the world has now foreclosed the matter in our favor. Truly yours, T. P. Gore."

Gore went back to the Senate. Standing before the roster of that great body, he opposed the war policy of the President; he told his colleagues of what his sightless eyes could see across that horizon which blocked their view, but they abandoned him in an unpopular minority, to be defeated in the primaries of 1921. When his stand was justified by the development of historical events, he went back, and served another, his third term, as a member of the Senate. When he stepped down the second, and last time, he uttered an open letter to his constituency, which conveyed, more than anything else available on the life of the blind statesman, the quality which bound Pruiett, as a lawyer and a certain type of idealist, to him. "At midnight, January 2nd, [1937] the curtain comes down forever on my political career. The people of Oklahoma have been generous to me, and I am grateful to them."

"As you know, I was defeated for the Senate in 1920 on account of my attitude toward the war. I had promised the mothers of Oklahoma that I would never vote to ship their sons across the sea to die in the bloody shambles of Europe. I kept my word, although it lost me my seat in the Senate. Some may doubt my wisdom, but they can hardly doubt my sincerity. When I left the Senate in 1921, I was confident that I would one day return. In 1930, my dream came true; but, I now indulge no such dream as to the future. No one knows better than I do that politically my day is done; the people giveth and the people taketh away."

"I repeat in parting that I love Oklahoma; I love every blade of her grass, I love every grain of her sands. I am proud of her past and I am confident of her future. I honor the Oklahoma Pioneer as I honor the American Pioneer. Their example is our riches heritage. The virtues that made us great in the past can keep us great in the future. We must march, and not merely mark time. We must indeed solve new problems, must meet new conditions with new measures, but they should be met with the same resolute and courageous spirit as of old. Anyhow, let us bet on America to win. Unless we quail we cannot fail. Whether I fought a good fight or not, I have kept the faith. Good-bye and goodluck."

CHAPTER FIFTEEN

WHEREIN PRUIETT ADDS JUSTIFICATION FOR PATRICIDE TO HIS LIST OF ACCOMPLISHMENTS, AS HE GOES IN STYLE TO THE OLD KIOWA-COMANCHE-APACHE COUNTRY, AND TRIES A CASE WHICH OFFERS BUT LITTLE OF EARLY PROMISE OF SUCCESS. AND HOW HIS CLIENT, AS USUAL, IS SAVED BY AN ABSOLUTE ALIBI, AND THE STATE'S STAR WITNESS CHARGES THE CIRCUMSTANCE TO A VISITATION OF THE SUPERNATURAL. AND WHERE THE OUTRAGED CITIZENRY OF THE LOCALITY ATTEMPT TO REVERSE THE USUAL ORDER OF THINGS BY LYNCHING THE ACCUSED AFTER THE TRIAL OF HIS CASE, INSTEAD OF BEFORE, AND INCLUDE IN THEIR PLANS AN ATTACK UPON THE LAWYER, WHO HAD CAUSED THE LIBERATION OF THE ACCUSED.

"L'affaire Hopkins," was one for the Pruiett legend. Its locale was Lawton, in the Kiowa-Comanche-Apache country. The settlement had literally come into municipal existence through the spinning of the wheel of chance. Nestling amongst the rough slopes of the Wichita Mountains, so close that the shadow of each passing cloud, trailing its path across Mount Scott could be seen from the green courthouse square, the town was a mixture of the sturdy whites, who had settled to a substantial, but not too opulent existence, and the long-haired Comanches, who had given up their fight to retain control of the rocky upland.

By 1901, the land runs had become impractical. There were so many claimants for the limited Indian land remaining, that a race would have precipitated a war—not a riot. "Eighty-three thousand families were registered at Fort Reno for 13,000 homesites,"reported the *Daily Ardmoreite* on July 19, 1901. The government took advantage of the sporting inclinations of the pioneers; they gave them numbers and rolled the wheel. The land-lottery gave homes to a few; disappointments to the multitude. Lawton was a hard city and had produced some hardy citizens. Tom Gore had gone to the Senate from Lawton.

George Hopkins was tried in the brick courthouse there for the murder of his own father, and he was acquitted. The Sheriff, who had previously been beset with the problem of guarding George, to prevent his escape, had to guard him after his acquittal, to keep a mob from lynching him. Pruiett, the mouthpiece who had promoted the outrage, was spirited away with the defendant and out of town, an equal object of the mob's wrath. It was fitting that such an episode should occur in a chance-begotten city.

Old A. T. Hopkins, of fairly pure strain Scotch, had cracked the rocks of the rough hillsides, hoarded the trickling rains in the many gullies of his farm, and made money. His one extravagance had manifested itself in a love for horses, and with typical Scotch ingenuity he had commercialized it. He owned a string of the finest race horses in the Southwest; and, in addition to the revenue he received from sale, trade and breeding, he entered them in race events over the county. His combined business and hobby was housed under the corrugated iron roof of the section's most complete and prosperous livery barn.

The roughest boulder on the hillside of Hopkins' thrifty existence had been an unsatisfactory family. Mary and George, his daughter and son, had been left motherless in early childhood by the death of his wife. They had passed through an adolescence of varying neglect and over-indulgence. No one could satisfactorily explain the passionate hatred which the girl developed for her father. George, the older of the two unusual offsprings concealed an utter disregard for the 'old man' with an affected attitude of concern and consideration. This enabled him to avoid the restraints of the father's penuriousness, and to obtain funds at the same time, for the promotion of certain innate vices which ran the gamut of drink, females and gambling. Naturally, his pursuit of these devices required that he spend more than he had, or could get. He was alternately broke, flush, or in trouble for petty confidence ventures and larcenies.

Mary had scarcely passed her majority before she married a young lawyer. She abandoned the sire she so cordially hated to the crudities of his humble tastes. George moved around. When confronted with an ordinary dilemma, he would take a job and do a little work. If it was an emergency, such as the brig in the offing, he would petition the pater and invariably receive the discounted face of his request—for which he had made allowance—and the admonitory word of advice which would accompany it. Nothing pleased the old man more, as his years grew, than to have George go to the race-meets; to ride the caboose to New Orleans or Chicago, or to Hot Springs, where the Hopkins' ponies were running.

On the morning of November 9, 1915, the German advance on Paris during World War I and the likelihood of President Wilson issuing a proclamation throwing the United States into the holocaust had to give way, in its front page prominence, to an item of local interest which superseded it. According to the *Lawton News* A. T. Hopkins had been found dead, murdered, just inside the door of his livery barn. A blood spattered axe on the ground beside the body, and the dents, notches and grooves in the cranium of the corpse suggested to the ordinarily deductive mind that the twain had met in violent contact.

Son George was away, training a trio of colts that were to perform in some specially matched races at the Fair Grounds in Oklahoma City. Tom Coley, a negro who had worked for the Hopkins Barn at Lawton, and who had left his job there for unknown, at least uncertain-reasons, was working at the sheds with George and the horses.

When word of the tragedy was out, George rushed home. In rage and grief, he made the funeral arrangements, and worked in the wide search being organized for the slayer. When the final ceremony was over, George, with Walter C. Stevens, the old man's lawyer in Lawton, went to the office of the livery barn to check the status of affairs and business. A will in a strongbox, inside the iron safe, provided that a dollar should go to daughter Mary and that the residue should go 'to my beloved and dutiful son, George.'

Solution to the murder mystery came to town with Tom Coley, who showed up with a bankroll. He flourished it as he bought a new green suit for $30, confidentially telling the clerks that from then on he was on velvet, because Dolly V belonged to him, and would thenceforward be doing her running for him. Dolly V was the fastest and highest priced filly in the Hopkins barn. With nothing to lose, the baffled police picked him up and put him away for questioning, with a bunch of vags, in the Hopkins case.

John Froneberger was just a yokel yegg-catcher; a plateau patrolman. He was equipped, however, with all of the predominant attributes of a metropolitan sleuth. He was tough lawman!

"What did you kill old man Hopkins for?" he bawled at Tom Coley.

"I don't know nothin' about it, Mr. Froneberger," Tom answered.

Froneberger knocked him out of his straight-back chair with an open handed slap across the ear, then resumed his methodical, big-footed pacing of the floor.

"What did you kill old man Hopkins for?" he howled again.

"I didn't do it, Mr. " Tom couldn't complete his denial. Froneberger had hit him across the opposite ear, sending him whirling into the opposite wall of the room.

The methodical floor pressing was resumed; and, each time the prisoner was passed, he dodged and covered. Pausing before the swollen face, Froneberger placed his hands on his hips and glared balefully, as if waiting for the proper time to put the question.

"What did you... "

"Mr. George put me up to it," Tom interrupted him. "He paid me money, an' showed me how he wanted it done. He's the one that got me into this."

"Who do you mean, nigger?" inquired Froneberger suspiciously, "Who do you mean, Mr. George?"

"Mr. George Hopkins," chattered the negro. "He's the one what done it. He give me the race mare an' $100. He give me the axe an' brought me down here, too. It's a fact, Mr. Froneberger, Mr. George made me do it."

Froneberger stared incredulously. Nigger-whipping was but routine, and he had been about ready to let Tom go. He couldn't believe what he was hearing. "Then you was the one what did it?" he asked, doubtfully. "You killed the old man with the axe, and took his pocket-book?"

"Yes, suh, I sure did, Mr. Froneberger, but I give the pocket-book to Mr. George. He was waitin' in the car, he was, an' we drove right on out of town. Mr. George he's the one what thought this up; he's the one what made me do it."

Froneberger suspected that Coley was lying about George and his participation in the crime. His deductive mind could already glean a motive sufficient to involve the confessing negro.

"You used to work for old man Hopkins," he recited, "an' the old man fired you. Didn't he?" Froneberger drew back his big hand as if to swing again.

"No, suh!" answered Tom. "I didn't neither get fired; I quit. I quits 'cause I don't want to stay down here in Lawton no longer."

"You and the old man fell out over somethin'," Froneberger insisted. "Come clean now, that's why you killed him. You had it in for him, 'cause he fired you."

"No, suh," Tom repeated. "It was like this. Mary, she wouldn't stay down here at Lawton 'cause Mr. George wasn't here, an' I wouldn't stay here 'cause Mary wasn't here. I could of had the job as long as I wanted it; but, I wanted to stay up there with Mr. George and Mary."

Mary was Tom Coley's wife. She was an ebony animal with limbs as trim as the stable thoroughbreds, but with negroid features as dull and ugly as a zombi. She worshiped the dissolute George Hopkins with dumb devotion, and Tom, her husband through assumption and convenience, though that his fealty to the house of Hopkins required that he share her with George.

"Look here, nigger," Froneberger menaced. "Don't get clear off, now. Are you tellin' me that George Hopkins has been layin' up with that wench of yours?"

"Yes, suh," said Tom. "Mr. George an' Mary an' me, we been good friends for a long time. Before we left here, Mr. George, he came to our place to drink home-brew, an' lots of times he stays all night. Him an' Mary was awful good friends."

"Good friends, huh?" asked Froneberger. "How good a friend was he of yours? Who did he sleep with?"

"He sleeps with Mary," Tom answered promptly, "but, it's all right with me. I had Mary all the time Mr. George wasn't there. Me an' Mr. George was awful good friends."

Froneberger was obviously puzzled. "Yeah," he said. "You must've been. But, by God, you'd better not be lyin' to me about this. You know you're goin' to be checked on it, don't you?"

"Yes, suh!" said Tom. "Check me all you please. Ask the colored folks in the city, as lived in the same house with us, an' the white folks what lived next door. They'll tell you all about it."

"Tell me about what?" asked Froneberger. "You mean that George and Mary and you layed up together the same way up there?"

"Well, you see, this is what happened," the negro said. "Mr. Hopkins sends me an' Mr. George up to the Fair Grounds with the horses; an', we takes Mary along, like we usually do. Then, Mr. Hopkins tells Mr. George to keep the horses in the Fair barns 'til some man gets his horses down from Chicago, an' they's goin' to run some races, horse for horse, you see? Mr. Hopkins told me to come back here an' go to work; but, when I got ready to leave, why, Mary says she was stayin' with Mr.

George. I just decides I'd rather stay with them than have the job, so I didn't come back."

As the negro's weird story unfolded, and as the testimony taken at the trial of the case confirmed him, George Hopkins lived with the negroes in open disregard of convention. He slept in their various beds or on their floors and pallets, as conditions required. He ate the meals which black Mary prepared, from the oil-cloth covered table in her kitchen. Changing conditions, it developed, were governed by the excesses of the African guests of the evening and night before and by how many of the guests were unable—or indisposed—when time came to depart, and had laid down and gone to sleep where it was most convenient.

"He sure did, Mr. Froneberger," said Coley. "He took Mary right down to the grocery on the corner, an' told the man to sell her anything' she wanted, an' just put it on his bill."

"What about this killin'?" asked the officer. "How did you happen to decide on it? Did Mary have anything to do with it?"

"No," said Tom. "Mary thinks we better not do it. Mr. George, he said the old man was too tight with his money. He said it was all comin' to him anyhow, an' Mr. Hopkins, he done live too long and got too old. He said he'd help me, an' nobody'd ever think about me doin' it. He tol' me he'd pay me $100 an' give me my pick of any horse in the barn. He said somethin' else, too. He says if I don't help him I get an axe in my own head."

"How long did you plan it?" asked Froneberger.

" 'Bout a week," answered Tom. "We had to wait 'til Mr. George could borry a car from a friend of his'n. He gets us some corn, an' this car, it was a Hudson tourin' car, an' we left the city about dark. We got some eats about midnight an' drink a lot of whiskey. Mr. George, he done all of the drivin'. We come down through the old reservation an' the fort, an' we got in Lawton about four in the mornin'."

"Who got the axe for you, Tom?" Froneberger asked. His manner indicated that he was beginning to believe the negro. "Where did that new axe come from?"

"Mr. George bought it in the city," Tom said. "He got it an' had it aroun' the house the day before we left. He threw it in the back seat when we was leavin', an' he says 'Tom, this is what you make yourself a rich man with. You can fix Mary up an' show her off to your cheap nigger friends'."

"Mr. George tol' me what I was to do on the way down. I worked in the barn for a long time, an' I knowed when Mr. Hopkins opens up. I'm to wait by the post in front 'til Mr. Hopkins swung the big gate an' got inside; then, I was to go right in behind him. An' that's just what I done, Mr. Froneberger. It was awful. I knows I killed him the first lick, but I kep' right on, jus' like Mr. George tol' me. He wanted me to be sure. I hacked him about ten times, I guess."

"What did you do then, Tom?" whispered the officer.

"Well," pondered Tom, "he was layin' on his face an' all I have to do is to take the pocket-book outa his hip pocket. Mr. George tol' me to be sure an' get the pocket-book, 'cause that'd make folks think it was just a plain robber. An' I done just ever'thin' that Mr. George tol' me to."

"Where was George Hopkins when you were doin' this job, Tom?" asked Froneberger. "Did he come up there, or drive up, to get you when you were through?"

"No, suh," answered Tom. "He waited for me in the auto. We was parked by a string of box-cars 'bout a block and a half from the barn. He was right there where he was when I left, when I gets back."

"What did he say when you got back?" inquired Froneberger.

"He asks me if I did a good job, an' says, 'Where's that pocket-book?' He says 'git in here an' let's get the hell out. Mary'll be worried 'bout us if we don't get back to town'."

Judge Walter C. Stevens had scarcely filed the Hopkins Will for probate when he had a call from the police. George Hopkins was under arrest, being charged with murder. The police had a complete confession from Tom Coley, and part of the cash that George had paid him for the part he had played in moving him up in the livery stable business. Stevens, after a brief conference with his client, left the jail with a hopeless look. He started a long-distance contact for Pruiett as soon as he returned to his office.

George Hopkins, typical of the petty criminal apprehended in an attempt to cover too much territory, tried to talk, to explain, his way out of his difficulty. He made and signed a detailed statement wherein he attempted to show that Tom Coley had lied in every particular, and that the funds in Coley's possession had been actually stolen from him.

"Hell, no," he told Froneberger, "I never had nothin' to do with his wench. I never liked to have them niggers around me. Tom stole that money from me, and cooked up this story to try to keep me from prosecutin' him."

"Where were you when you found out your Dad had been killed?" inquired Froneberger.

"I was out at the Fair barn, workin'," answered George.

"Where were you the night before?"

"Let's see," mused George, seriously. "I was home all night. I was in my room, up in the city."

"And where did you say that was, George?" asked Froneberger.

"It was at the Allen Rooms," said George. "At Fatty Allen's Hotel on California Street in Oklahoma City. That's where I stayed while I was in the city this last trip."

"Now look here, George," said Froneberger, "we got it pretty straight that you were stayin' with the niggers down on Noble Street. Tom Coley says so, and we got some witnesses names; some white folks. You'd better tell the truth about this, because I've got to check up on you."

"A god damned nigger never did tell the truth, John, an' you know it. You don't need to check me; but, it's O. K. if you want to. But you ought to take my word in place of that nigger. He never told the truth, an' he never will."

George believed that his story would stand to discredit the negro, without verification, for his alibi was being manufactured as he went along. He could expect no support from any of the pre-arrangements which the casually smart criminal would have provided for himself. The utter falsity of his statement, once checked and established, tended to indicate an utter consciousness of guilt, and to entangle him more hopelessly in the circumstances.

Tom Coley had entered his own guilty plea and accepted a sentence of life imprisonment when, those four days later, Pruiett dazzled the square and courthouse with his presence. He was using an automobile, a long one, with his initials on the back door and a combination chauffeur, valet and body guard to drive.

W. F. "Dutch" Webber, as the Pruiett associates heard the driver addressed, was as proficient at ferreting out mechanical defects in the gradually developing Cadillacs as he was at locating home brew joints or corn likker 'leggers. His face was prompt admission of the privys of that then select trade; his manner contained that assurance of safety the operators required before they condescended to deliver the poison and slop which their fly-infested closets and basements produced. He had done a stretch on McNeil's Island for transporting a hot car to the Pacific, and another at Jefferson City for a St. Louis kick-in. His capacity for keeping quiet endeared him to his employer, who liked to do the talking and to see his prolix orders followed exactly as he gave them.

For an overnight stay out of town, Pruiett would take a week's change of wardrobe. With the rear seat piled high with leather luggage, he would get in front beside the dead-faced Dutch, and regale himself with accounts of Pruiett in Washington, Pruiett in the backwoods, or Pruiett in a big case somewhere else.

There was no touch of gray in the black mane as he removed a soft felt hat and laid it on a dusty stand. He patted his moist brow gently with a silk handkerchief. It was exceedingly dry and warm in the day time, although near winter, and the walk up the one flight to the second floor of the jail, and lack of ventilation in the small room where he was about to interview George Hopkins, caused the beads of moisture to dot the scant forehead visible between the dark of bushy black brows and the black hair that dropped down before it began to roach back atop the head and about the ears.

Pruiett was past forty, but no sign of sparseness had appeared in the raven brush. It was more luxurious and abundant than it had been back on White River, when he had first become conscious of its comparative excellence, and began to groom it. It shone with an oily splendor which the constant care and studious grooming of his prosperity permitted. He was tailored and attired to match the perfection of his natural ornament, in the neatest and finest raiment, and in the exactly correct style, of the period.

George Hopkins sat in a straight-back chair with both hands obscuring his face. He was weeping like a child. Pruiett eyed him with mild concern, unable to conceal all of the surprise and contempt he had for such a reception. The officer shook the prisoner roughly, and with a half-apology to the waiting lawyer, said that he would be waiting outside when the conference was over.

"Oh, God! Mr. Pruiett," the miserable George bawled. "Can you save me from the chair? Can you save me? Can you save me?"

"Is that all you want?" Pruiett inquired, contemptuously.

"God, yes," Hopkins cried. "Just don't let 'em give me the chair. Judge Stevens said he couldn't save me, but that you might do it. Can you save me?"

Pruiett's answer was indirect, going into the more material realm of what George had, and what he would be willing to put up. After a short conference, he stepped to the door of the small, hot chamber. With a word to the waiting guard, he hurried down the steps, and was soon talking to Steven's office on the 'phone.

"Send your girl down here with a bunch of blank deeds and bills of sale," he said. "I'm about to take this case off your hands, an' I need some blank forms. Send a bunch of 'em, and be sure you give me a girl that's a notary."

When Pruiett walked into Stevens's upstairs office latter that afternoon, he carried title to every foot of ground and every item of personal property that Hopkins, senior, had owned when he died. Stevens, the family lawyer, had had a startling report from the girl who spent the afternoon at the jail with George and the criminal lawyer. He intended to make an objection; but, he was uncertain as to how to begin with it. Pruiett saved him the trouble.

"Well, I took the case," Pruiett said, carelessly. "It's a hell of a thin one, an' I've got a lot of things I'd rather do than try one like this; but, we made a deal that's satisfactory."

"What did you take?" inquired Stevens.

"I took it all." The tone of the reply showed provocation, for he knew the girl had had time to detail the events of the afternoon.

"You mean you took it all? All that property?" Stevens's tone and expression showed disapprobation.

"Hell, yes," said Pruiett. "Ever' damn bit. An' it'll be worth it before I get through."

"Look here, now, Mr. Pruiett," said Stevens, with patronizing formality. "I represent the boy, and I have his interests to look after, even in his contract with you. I called you, you know, and I can't permit him to be fleeced in such a manner. That property will bring $40,000 at a quick sale, and you know it. I won't permit you to impose on his desperate state of mind, this way."

Pruiett stared at him in amazement.

"I'll be damned," he said. "You call me and beg me to come down here and take this mess off your hands...You didn't say you were going to fix my fee, or guarantee I'd get one, even. I..."

"But you're taking all he's got—everything," Stevens interrupted. "You're leaving him penniless."

"What good will he get out of it if he burns?" Pruiett asked quickly.

"Well, he... "

"What right has he got to it? How did he get it?" The questions, with the second interrupting a stammering answer to the first, left Stevens speechless. Pruiett continued.

"If you mean to uphold this bird who killed his daddy; think he's got a right to keep any of this stuff, an' can be conscientious in it, you'll be able to represent him yourself. In that case, you don't need me, an' you an' George can keep the farms an' the plugs. But, if I stay, the stuff stays with me. What do you think about that?"

He tossed the bundle of legal conveyances he had taken to the desk in front of Stevens in a gesture to emphasize his attitude of complete independence. Stevens pushed them back and shook his head. He knew that, if he ran Pruiett out of the case after George had hired him, and something happened, he would be in a position as inextricable as was George himself. Pruiett was starting out in the case with his customary advantage.

Froneberger was detailed to check the purported Hopkins alibi. Arriving in Oklahoma City, he gained the assigned assistance of John Hubatka, a plainclothes expert of the Oklahoma City Police Department and later Chief of Police for Oklahoma City. They found the substance of the alibi false before they had fairly begun their investigation. Then, they began to collect verification, which was plentiful, of the Tom Coley story as it pertained to conditions at and around the Coley house while the details of the plot to kill were being hatched.

The proprietor of the Allen Rooms was a portly person of two hundred and fifty pounds, whose short stature in connection with such prodigious weight made him a natural recipient for the nickname of

'Fatty'. Fatty Allen kept a nine-stool 'grease joint' on the ground floor with furnished rooms on the upper level. He had a tall, gaunt wife. They relieved each other at letting out the upstairs accommodations and serving up the unsavory food which an occasional customer called for across the counter.

"We're officers," said Froneberger crisply, showing a rusty badge stuck to the shoulder strap of his loose vest.

"Yes, sir," answered Fatty. Fatty had the same affected respect for authority that a petty thief had for a police uniform.

"Do you know George Hopkins?" inquired Froneberger.

"Hell yes," answered Fatty.

"Seen him around lately?" was the next question.

"Hell no," answered Fatty.

"How long's it been since you seen him?" asked Froneberger, casually.

"Been a hell of a time," said Fatty.

"Did he ever stay in your hotel here?" Allen was asked.

"Sure, a lot of times, but not lately," Fatty insisted.

"You keep any record here of roomers, and when they come in and go out?"

"I sure do," Fatty said, giving Hubatka the benefit of a big wink, "the law says I keep a register, an' I do just like the law says."

"We're checking up a little," explained the officer, "and we want to know if George was here in October. Where's your register book for October?"

"It's upstairs," said Fatty. "I'll just go up and get it for you. Just wait right here a minute."

"We'll go along with you, Mr. Allen," interrupted Hubatka. "We'll look at it upstairs."

A black bound ledger was laying on a home-made shelf, built desk-fashion along the wall at the head of the stairway. Hubatka and Froneberger reached it ahead of the proprietor, and studied it for several minutes before turning to him with more questions.

I see George was here October 14th," said Froneberger. "I thought you said he hadn't been here for a hell of a time?"

"That's a hell of a time in my book," grinned Fatty. "He ain't been here for over a month. You asked me was he in here lately."

Froneberger handed Allen the book. "Was George Hopkins in this joint on the night of November 8th? Just last week?"

Allen studied the register, turning the pages slowly. "Nope," he answered, "he was with me just one night, an' that was last month, in October. It was October the 14th, just like it shows up in the book."

"Is that Hopkin's signature?" asked Hubatka.

"Yep," answered Allen. "I seen him sign it. I know his writin' anyway, but I seen him sign that. I know it's his."

"Do you let people stay here without signin' up?" asked Hubatka. "Could Hopkins have stayed here without registerin'?"

"Hell, no, Mr. Hubatka. You know I wouldn't do that," wheedled Allen. "Anytime these guys stay in the Allen Rooms, they put their John Henry right in that little book. I don't get myself in no trouble with the city laws."

"Do you remember about this George Hopkins," persisted Froneberger, "do you remember when he was here, and how many nights he stayed, regardless of what the book shows?"

"Hell yes," said Fatty. "He was here one night, just after the fair closed and business fell off. I remember it was just after the fair an' he was tellin' about his horses. I know damn well that it was close to fair time, an' just one night was all he was here."

"Hopkins says he was here ever' night for three weeks, an' that he was here on November 8th, the day his old man was murdered down at Lawton. What do you say about that?" Froneberger was watching Allen narrowly as he talked.

"I say it's a damn lie," Fatty answered, without hesitation. "I ain't seen him for a month, an' he ain't been in my rooms here but about twice in the last year. He's just a god damn liar if he says different."

"You won't alibi for these crooks, will you, Mr. Allen?" suggested Hubatka. "They don't use you that way, do they?"

"Hell, no," Fatty beamed, swelling with the compliment. "This is a respectable place, an' the crooks don't use Fatty's hotel for no alibi."

"Then I guess we'll have to make a witness out of you; you and your little black book," said Froneberger. "That is, if we have to try George. With the case we'll make, he'll prob'bly try to cop out, even if he has to take a chance on the chair. We got a signed confession by his buddy, an' this blows his alibi all to hell. Can you keep good care of this book, or shall we take it?"

"I'll take care of it, an' damn good care, too. I'll get me a new book an' put this one up in the trunk. When ya need it, just call on old Fatty. He'll be ready to tell 'em what's what."

It was March of 1916, the twentieth day of Oklahoma's windy spring month, when the George Hopkins trial was begun. The old man's unfilial daughter, who had shown nothing but animosity for him during his years of living, was unable to condone brother George's alleged liberty in murdering him, especially when she learned that the entire, and rather bulky estate, went to George alone. She saw that her lawyer husband, James A. "Jim" Diffendaffer, offered his service to Comanche County Attorney T. B. Orr as a special prosecutor. Calculating the customary outcome of a case defended by Pruiett, and in an attempt to avoid it, she arranged for the assistance of A. C. Cruce, Pruiett's old friend from the valley, who had marched to prominence and success in his own line, along with Pruiett. He was the brother of Governor Lee Cruce, who had tried to stop a Pruiett landslide in the Lorena Mathews case.

Pruiett admired and respected this particular member of his opposition—even feared him—so far as his technique and courtroom ability was concerned. But, he would give him no quarter, no matter how badly he needed it. Pruiett's objective in the trial of a lawsuit was victory, victory complete and at any price. He liked to win and he hated to lose. Those were his personal feelings in relation to the outcome of a case, but above all else, he hated to see the system triumph over his efforts to subvert it. His fierce fight for a client's liberty of life was a re-enaction of his struggling exit from the old Texas courtroom, when and where, as a boy, he had been dragged away to the miseries of a prison cell. His defense of a dangerous case was a figurative writhing, kicking and screaming, with claw and nail flailing in a fierce effort to find a vulnerable spot on his adversary.

According to the *Lawton News* of March 23, 1916, "Witness after witness was introduced by the State in the trial of George Hopkins, Wednesday, in an effort to tighten the cordon of evidence around the defendant, attorneys for the defendant contesting stubbornly every inch of the ground covered." Thus the *Lawton News* viewed events. "Cross-examination of the witness in chief, Tom Coley, failed to materially weaken the force of the negro's testimony. With a memory almost uncanny for an uneducated man, Coley repeated again and again on cross-examination, and almost word for word, his previous statements."

Pruiett's apparently casual defense of Hopkins was actually long cal-

CONSTRUCTED IN 1902, THE COMANCHE COUNTY COURTHOUSE IN LAWTON WAS THE SITE OF MOMAN PRUIETT'S SUCCESSFUL DEFENSE OF GEORGE HOPKINS FOR THE AX-MURDER OF HIS FATHER. COURTESY OKLAHOMA HERITAGE ASSOCIATION.

culated and carefully timed. It was pitched first on the proposition of discrediting Coley, impeaching the more or less immaterial portions of his confession and accusation, and then proving the defendant a positive alibi. There was Hopkins' signed statement to be reckoned with, the one the State had taken before counsel had been employed. He had to keep his witness stand version fairly consistent with that, unless he intended to further discredit his client.

"I'll prove," said Pruiett, making his opening statement to the jury, "that Tom Coley is a motivated liar, and that his effort to incriminate my client is based on fear and spite. I'll prove that George Hopkins never was in the Coley house on Noble Street, like Tom says he was, while the plot to kill Hopkins was being hatched. My evidence will show that during the three weeks preceding the murder, George Hopkins spent his days at the Fair Grounds race barn, and his evenings and nights at Fatty Allen's rooming house down on California Street."

"By proving the one, I'll automatically prove the other. If Hopkins was staying at Allens, then Tom Coley's a liar when he says he was laying up with him and his friends on Noble Street." He gave the prosecution a half-defiant, half-contemptuous look as he said it. Cruce, who had just completed a narrative of what the State would conclusively prove, had said that he would offer the testimony of Allen, himself, to show not only that Hopkins was not there before and on the night of the murder, but that he had deliberately, and with guilty design, lied when he told the investigating officers that he had been there.

Tom Coley was the State's star; but, Fatty Allen was given a disguised supporting role.

"You say your name is Allen, and that you operate a rooming house in Oklahoma City?" County Attorney Orr inquired.

"Yes sir," said Fatty.

"Mr. Allen," said Orr. "Directing your attention to the month of October, last year, were you then engaged in the same business?"

"Yes sir," repeated Fatty.

"Do you know George Hopkins, the defendant in this case?"

"I certainly do," said Fatty.

"How many times did the defendant stay in your rooms, if he did during the month of October, 1915?" inquired Orr.

"He was there one night, an' that's all."

"Do you remember the night he was there?"

"I remember 'cause it was just after the Fair shut down. That's how I remembered so well. It was the night of October 14th that he was there." Fatty was bolstering himself a little as he went along.

"Was Hopkins there on the night of the 15th, or the 16th, or the 17th, or any other night later that month?"

"No, sir, he wasn't. He certainly was not."

"Was George Hopkins there in your hotel during the early part of November, say during the first week of November?"

"Nope," answered Fatty. "He was there on October 14th and that's all. He hasn't been in that hotel a minute since then."

"Was George Hopkins in your hotel of the night of November 7th, or the early morning of November 8th, 1915? Was he there then?"

"He certainly was not." Fatty was emphatic.

Orr lifted a rough package from the counsel table. It was the register for the Allen Hotel, preserved by Fatty in a thick wrapper of newspaper. It was exactly as it had been when Fatty had put it in storage, that night after the Froneberger-Hubatka visit. Orr handed the bundle to the court reporter and had it marked as an exhibit. Then he handed it to the witness.

"Mr. Allen," he continued, very formally. "Do you keep a register, or guest entry book, in your hotel?"

"I sure do," answered Allen. "It's a city ordinance that says I got to. I mean, it says, anybody what operates a roomin' house or hotel has got to keep a register. That's so the police, maybe, can check up on who's been stayin' there, an' whether they really have or not." He grinned knowingly at Pruiett and his client as he completed his explanation.

"This package," said Orr, "has been marked as a State's exhibit. I will ask you to examine it, and then tell the court and jury whether or not you recognize it, or know what it is."

"Sure I do," the witness answered. "I know what it is. I brought it down with me from the city, like the subpoena I got told me to. Do you want me to say what it is?"

"No, not just now," answered the prosecutor. And turning aside to the Court, he said, "We will reserve the offer of this item at this time. This is merely for preliminary identification. We may offer it later."

When Pruiett took Fatty Allen for cross-examination, the Hopkins cause emitted a dire prognostication of the impossible; of Moman Pruiett losing a major case. Self-professed courtroom authorities observed that the defendant's chief counsel had tried to take in a little too much territory in his statement of what he intended to prove, and that his inability to make good on it was 'goin' to do a sight of harm'. The khaki clad youths from the Fort Sill Post, who crowded about the jammed entrance-ways, ribaldly remarked that the difference which the outcome made was slight; that you might as well have that portion of the anatomy singed off at home, as shot off at Metz or Verdun. While others had varying comment to offer, at least varying in form, it was not diverse in substance. The prevailing opinion was that George Hopkins was a goner.

"Mr. Allen," Pruiett inquired, respectfully, "did you state on direct examination that the ordinances required you to keep a daily register of all the guests of your rooms?"

Pruiett had had ample time to complete his regular analysis of the witness. He knew that he was a man of slight culture and of course taste and habit, who was enjoying the prominence which he believed was his by reason of his being a material witness in the trial of the case. His corpulence was attended by the usual physical distresses accompanying such a physical condition, high and rapidly fluctuating blood pressure, shortness of breath, and a pronounced tendency to perspire. Spring had come early to the Wichitas, and in the early afternoon sunshine, with the crowd and the confinement of the old courthouse, Fatty was sweating copiously. Pruiett asked him a number of questions that were easy to answer. His purpose was to lead his ego out and exercise it. He might be out of condition by the time the hard pull began.

"I sure did," responded Allen, without apparent cranial exertion.

"Then why didn't you keep one?" There was a suggestion of an attempt to trap the witness, both in the suddenness of the query and a slight increase in the volume of his tone.

"I did, ever' day," said Fatty, looking about with a smirk, as if to placate the jurors, and assure them that he was master of the situation.

Pruiett assumed an air of slight chagrin, and hesitated, as if in a quandary.

"Then why didn't you bring it down here with you?" Pruiett finally came back.

"I did," Fatty cried, triumphantly. He was taking the bait like gullion. Cruce shifted uneasily in his seat. No one could make him believe that Pruiett didn't fully understand what was wrapped and tied in that newspaper package on the counsel table, even though Allen was gloating over the surprise and shock he was going to inflict if the stupid lawyer kept going in the same direction. Cruce began to feel that something was wrong. Pruiett feigned amazement.

"You did? You have the register, here? Well, where is it?"

"Right behind you, on the table." Fatty unfolded a pair of ponderous hands which he had kept folded across his bulging expanse of belly, and pointed a pudgy finger, with childlike glee, at the roughly bound package. It was some dumb lawyer that couldn't have guessed that he had just identified the book.

"Is this it? Is this the register book?" Pruiett inquired doubtfully.

"Yes sir, it sure is," replied Mr. Allen.

"How did it get down here?" Pruiett was examining the package, and questioning, as an idle curiosity.

"I brung it. I brung it down myself. That's what I just got through tellin' Mr. Orr."

"Well, what is it doing in this shape? You can't register guests with your book baled up like this?"

Allen grinned indulgently, as if he was going to let Pruiett in on a big secret.

"Well," he said, "when Mr. Hubatka and the other gentleman came down and looked at it, and saw Hopkins' name wasn't in it, like he said it was, they said I was liable to have to be a witness, an' I said, 'will I have to have the book?' and they says 'yes,' so just to be sure, I gets me a new book, an' I tied the old one up, an' I locked it in my trunk. When the time comes for me to go to court, I gets the book out an' carries it along. I just want to be sure all the time that nobody fools with my register, you see?"

"If that's the case," said Pruiett, "this register ought to be just exactly the same now as it was the night Mr. Hubatka an' Mr. Froneberger called on you, to check up on Mr. Hopkins' story?"

"Just exactly," said Fatty. "Nobody has it but me, and nobody fools with it."

"When you checked it up, and showed it to Mr. Hubatka and Mr. Froneberger, didn't you see Hopkins' name there for the night of November 7th, and for three weeks before, every night?" Pruiett was still being casual.

"I certainly didn't," said Fatty.

"Do you say now that your book doesn't show Hopkins was there, or do you want to change your testimony, an' say it does?"

Allen was so astonished by the audacity of the suggestion that he didn't answer immediately.

"No I don't Mister," he said finally. "Allen don't change his story, now, or no other time."

Pruiett began to pace the floor in deep reflection. His right hand ran repeatedly, nervously, through his thick hair, and made it stand out further about the square contour of his well shaped head. Finally, as if in desperation, he took the register and handed it to the witness.

"Mr. Allen," he said slowly, "will you untie this bundle so I may see what it is?"

"Do it yourself," said Allen shortly. "You look able-bodied to me."

Pruiett looked appealingly to the trial judge. He wanted Allen to feel that he was hurt, in addition to being completely at his mercy.

"You will accommodate counsel," advised the Court. "Please do as counsel requests."

The witness produced a pocket knife. Slashing savagely at the heavy cords, and pawing the triple thickness of newsprint aside, Allen proudly produced the black ledger which he had previously used as a rooming house register. He handed it to Pruiett. Pruiett handed it right back to him.

"Is this the register you say you used at your hotel?" Observers, less involved with their own importance than was the witness, could have seen that Pruiett's demeanor had changed. The Pruiett scowl was stamped on a contracted brow and undershot jaw. The shaggy ends of his heavy hair seemed to snap and crackle like the sharp crisp words that flew from his throat.

"It ain't nothin else," replied Fatty flippantly.

"Turn to your sheet for October 14, the one day you say the defendant was there, and show me where he registered." The change in Pruiett's tone caused Allen to look up, but not to comprehend.

"Do it yourself, you... "

There was no appeal to the Court this time. "Do as I tell you," Pruiett cried, standing close and holding a taut finger in the witness's fat face. "Do as I tell you. Turn to your entry for October 14th, and show me where Hopkins registered on the night you say he was there."

Fatty glanced up and about; toward the jury, toward the Court, toward Cruce at the counsel table, as if to see if something had occurred to upset his advantage, while he had received no notice of it, himself. Their somber faces seemed to bring him back to reality. He grinned weakly, mopped his brow, and opened the book.

"There it is," he said, when he had turned a number of pages. "Right there it is; George Hopkins, on the night of October 14th."

"Now turn to the fifteenth, the next day, and tell me if Hopkins' name is on that page." It was no request; it was a command.

"It ain't here, no more," said Allen, without attempting to obey. "It ain't here. I showed it... "

"Do as you're told," Pruiett roared at him. "Do as I tell you. Look and see if Hopkins' name is in there on the next page, for the fifteenth."

Fatty acquiesced. Turning the page gayly, he glanced at Froneberger, sitting behind County Attorney Orr at the counsel table, and winked. Then he let his gaze wander idly over the lined page of the register. Pruiett was standing belligerently before him, his arms folded across his chest and a malignant black scowl on his countenance.

The witness gazed at the book for a full minute. Then he looked up slowly toward the State's counsel and the officers, grinned weakly, and jerked his head back for a quick second look at the book. Inserting a fat finger between his wet neck and his utterly wilted tight collar, he pulled lustily, in an eloquent gesture of stifling discomfort. He looked up at Pruiett, but found no understanding in the beetle-browed scowl which met his gaze. The silence of the courtroom was complete. Allen looked at the Judge, who was squinting quizzically at him by that time.

"Judge, there's spooks in this god damn case!" he said.

Pruiett wouldn't let random dumb wit detract from his climax. "Mr. Witness," he roared, "Will you answer my question? Does the name of this defendant appear in your register for the date of October Fifteenth."

Fatty couldn't hear him. He was looking toward the only compassionate expression in the courtroom, that of the Court, and clutching frantically at the wet collar which threatened to shut off his air.

"There's spooks in this god damn case, I tell you, Judge, spooks. I never saw such a god damn thing in my whole life..."

"I will remind you that you are in court, Mr. Allen, and that your alley language will not be tolerated." Such was the compassion of the Court. "You will answer counsel's question, in seemly language, or I shall be required to penalize you for contempt."

"Answer my question, Mr. Allen," Pruiett shouted as he shook the saber-like finger in his face. "Does..."

"Yes," the witness interrupted the question which he had heard before, with a quick, weak, affirmative "Yes."

"What about the next day, the sixteenth, do you see his name there?"

"There's spooks, Judge, I know there is. Spooks is in... "

"Read him the question, Mr. Reporter," Pruiett interrupted.

"Yes," was Fatty's same weak reply.

"Now, Mr. Witness," Pruiett continued, without looking toward the amazed Cruce and his colleagues, "I want to direct your attention to this entry for the fourteenth of October. Is that George Hopkins' signature? I mean by that, did you see him sign it, himself?"

"Yes sir."

"Does the name George Hopkins, you see written on the next page, appear to be written in the same hand?"

"It appears to be wrote by spooks," was Allen's dogged answer.

"Let's not be ridiculous, Mr. Witness," Pruiett cautioned him, as he would have reprimanded a child. "Does it appear to be the same hand?"

"Yes it does," said Allen frankly, "but... "

"I know, spooks," Pruiett interrupted him as he waved him carelessly aside. He introduced the register into the trial record. In the defendant's undeniable scroll, the register was stamped for every day of the controverted period, including the day and night of the murder.

The attempt of the prosecution to recover was necessarily ludicrous. The register had been in the trunk in Fatty's attic; the defendant had been shivering through the gusty winter in the upstairs cell of the county jail. Fatty had severed the strand which bound the original wrapper about the volume, and then Allen swore on his redirect examination that the names, save one, had not been between the pages on that November eve when he tucked the precious book in and patted it goodnight. Detective Hubatka, whom Fatty was so anxious to please, swore vehemently that he had examined the pages of the book, and that the pages had not had so much as a suggestion of a Hopkins signature. Froneberger chimed in with his denial of the existence of the registration; but, it was all meat for Pruiett.

Suave and smiling, ultra-polite, he would require their recognition of the likeness between the first name, admitted to be the defendant's and the others following. He called their attention to the varying positions of the entries on the pages, the color of the ink and its resemblance in shade to the established genuine. He tested their knowledge of the defendant's winter-long jail wait. Then, he would casually inquire: "Do you believe in spooks?"

On March 26, 1916, the *Lawton News* reported "The Hopkins case was closed by the arguments to the jury of two of Oklahoma's greatest lawyers, Moman Pruiett for the defense, and A. C. Cruce, for the state. Mr. Pruiett is recognized, and so characterized by Mr. Cruce, as one of the greatest criminal lawyers in the country, while, on the other hand, Mr. Pruiett, in his address told the jury that he feared A. C. Cruce, his wonderful analytical mind and his power over a jury. Both gentlemen were but stating facts that are well known to the public. The Hopkins case is the 188th murder case in which Moman Pruiett has participated while A. C. Cruce was for years a prosecutor for the government, and has a reputation more than state wide."

The *News* was being prosaic and conservative, but just as well, for it would have been impossible to catch, in a word picture, an adequate reproduction of Pruiett in action. His timing was so superb, as he produced his thought and gesture, that he presented the intended drama of the moment in an exaggerated proportion, and what the one lacked, if it happened to be lacking, the other supplied. His every movement and expression was a continuing climax.

"Mr. Pruiett reviewed the testimony of practically every witness who had been placed on the stand, forcibly bringing to the front the substance of the witnesses for the defense and reducing to a minimum the substance of the state's testimony as he so capably knows how to do. He attacked the state's witnesses in roughshod language, and enlarged upon what he called villainous conspiracy on the part of the state and the detectives employed by it to destroy a man for the greed of gold."

"County Attorney T. B. Orr and Officer Froneberger of the City Police force came in for a bitter arraignment at the hands of Mr. Pruiett. He grew eloquent as he referred to the love of George Hopkins for his father, and said that the state had not produced one scintilla of evidence to corroborate the testimony of Tom Coley with the main facts of the crime as required by law."

Cruce, with all the admiration he had for his more daring and gifted adversary, detested defeat. He could see it settling its dark cloud about his shoulders, but he went down fighting.

"For almost two hours, Mr. Cruce argued to the jury, confining much of his attention to the defendant, for whom he said, he was surprised the attorneys had not contended insanity. With biting sarcasm he held before the jury a picture of the defendant as he strove to secure evidence which would smirch the character of his own sister, all for money. He said there were attorneys in the case whom two years ago would not have presented such a case as this one, not even for the $25,000 for which he was striving, and said that he believed that not only nations, but individuals were going mad."

The current press had carried the edifying intelligence of "the peaceful Meuse running red with the blood of the Germans and

French." If his reference to cases and attorneys included Pruiett, he was overlooking Red Fox and Rudolph Tegeler, and twenty-five grand was small change compared to what he had already taken from George Hopkins.

The jury took the case at 10:30 on Saturday night. Pruiett slept soundly and got up early, to drive with Dutch through the budding vistas of Medicine Park and the contrasting martial bustle of Fort Sill. The post was teaming with the crop that was soon to sail for France. When he drove by his hotel at two in the afternoon, he was told that he had been called from the courthouse, that the jury was ready to report. The word had circulated rapidly in the small town, and the curious were gathering, hurrying in across the shaded square from every direction.

The *Lawton News* proclaimed on March 28, 1916, the jurors returned a verdict of "Not Guilty." The court excused them briskly, and Hopkins, who had been brought from the jail by the Sheriff, pumped their hands with maudlin gratitude as they marched out. The trial judge congratulated Pruiett, avoided Hopkins and took his leave. The liberated defendant, his lawyer, and the Sheriff were left alone. Pruiett and Hopkins were talking about leaving town, when a granite stone crashed through the window. Pruiett stood motionless; the Sheriff hurried toward the break to peer out.

"You're in for trouble," he announced, as he came back. "It's a big crowd, a mob, out in front. They ganged a time or two before, when Hopkins was first arrested, but we were able to scatter 'em out. They're pretty sore."

Pruiett strode to the window. Another rock crashed through. As he peered cautiously over the sill, he saw that a large crowd had gathered and was milling about beneath the trees below. He had some knowledge of mob conduct, and he realized that he stood in the same light, with them, as did the hapless Hopkins. He knew that if they went outside, or if the mob came in, he and his client would be roughly treated, beaten and stomped, or worse. He shuddered as he ruminated. If they had a rope, and they got started.... He was thinking of old Jesse West.

"I'll have to lock you up 'til we can clear this up," the Sheriff said. "I can't take any chances on your gettin' hurt. We'd better get downstairs an'..."

Pruiett interrupted him. He was familiar with the courthouse and jail arrangement, the jail occupying a two-story brick wing on the west side of the building, making the general plan of the entire edifice irregular. The jail wing extended almost to the street on the west side of the square.

"Dutch'll see that crowd an' he'll know what to do," he said. "He'll drive to the only exit that's near the street, an' we can make it to the car."

They had been moving down the unlighted stairway all the time he was speaking. When they reached the main floor level, where they could see the light that streaked in from three outside entrances of the building, they saw that the leaders of the muttering crowd were pushing through the east and north doors. The three men slid quickly through the adjacent opening into the jail wing. The barred gate, first, and then the pine door, slammed shut behind them.

Through the dirt stained and bar shaded windows of the Sheriff's office, Pruiett could see that the south lawn, too, was cluttered with a milling, pushing throng of the excited farm and townspeople. He likewise noted, with an appreciative and understanding eye, that his car was moving slowly along the curb in the shaded street west of the square, toward the point, where in his mind's eye, the reliable Dutch knew he would need it.

"Sheriff," he said, "if we can just get out of town, you won't have any trouble. They may wreck your building, or some one may get hurt, if we stay here an' you have to protect us. If we can get out a window, or anyway, out this west side, my car's out there, and...."

"The coal hole for the heatin' plant is right up against that street," the Sheriff replied. "We can go to the basement, an' boost you out that way. If your car is there you can make it easy, an' there's no one on that side, yet."

Dutch had cased the job well. When the Sheriff boosted the elegantly attired Pruiett, a little soot stained and mad, but otherwise his resourceful self, through the scuttle, the driver assisted him directly into the back seat of his own limousine. When Hopkins had followed him, and the door and scuttle were closed, Dutch drove quietly past the mob and away.

"Shall I drive by the hotel, Mr. Pruiett?" he inquired. "We have your bags there, and."

"Hell no," said Pruiett, savagely. "We might be killed tryin' to get 'em. Let's get out of this god damned place as quick as we can, an' stay away, as far as I'm concerned. They sure give you a hell of reception when their own jury finds out they've had the wrong man in jail all winter. That's the way with our courts; they've raped justice and persecuted the innocent so long that the people have got used to it an' like it. Yes, by God, they demand that some one be convicted in ever' case. It's a great system, I'll say."

A Bohemian woman in a side road shack was getting rich peddling home brew to the boys in training at the post. They gulped her slop and joked about the champagne they would soon be having in Paris. She was hostess to Hopkins and his cynical lawyer that night; the drinks were on Pruiett, for Hopkins was unqualifiedly broke.

Hopkins was happy. He had heard the hum of the dynamos and felt the first shock of the heavy death current. Breathing free air again was an experience he had not permitted himself to dream of during those endless nights of his pre-trial confinement.

Cruce and Diffendaffer, and County Attorney Orr, were pondering the events in the County Attorney's office. Ideas and theories were being advanced in an attempt to explain one problem, the reason for Hopkins' acquittal. That was, how did Hopkins' registration get in Fatty Allen's book?

"Allen may have been right," Diffendaffer said, sarcastically. "It might have been spooks."

"I see it all, now," Cruce said. "We left that book layin' around here, and Pruiett slipped it into that big black briefcase he had, and when the court let them use his office for a private session, they just had Hopkins sign it up. You know, he had Hopkins in there for a time or two, with the deputy guardin' at the door. That's how he did it."

"It's simple," said Diffendaffer. "They untied all that cord, unwrapped all that paper, made nineteen entries at the same time, wrapped it up again and brought it back and put it on the table, and none of us ever noticed it."

"They never were in there more than ten minutes at a time," Orr insisted, "and they couldn't have untied that much string in that time, alone. Besides, they would have changed the appearance of that wrapping so that Allen could have noticed it. I know, and I'll swear, that the book, wrapped, was on that table all the time they were in their private conferences. I saw it, and by God, I had it with me in my own hands, all the rest of the time."

"Yeah," said Diffendaffer, turning the pages of the offending register slowly. "And what about this ink. It's not fresh, an' it's not all the same. Not by the same pen, either. Maybe they slipped a little age to the ink, and to the paper, while they had it in the chambers."

"Well, you can say what you want to, but that briefcase of Pruiett's was too big; he got it for this particular purpose. I know he's had the book in it, and they just slipped it over on us, right before our eyes." Cruce was persistent, but the manner and tone of his delivery showed that he had not even convinced himself.

Pruiett maintained that Hopkins was innocent, and that the signatures in the register were genuine, both as to the signer and the dates of the entries. But rumor, as it will, continued to circulate; and, when Mrs. Allen was confronted with evidence of the inevitability of the struggle, and was attempting to straighten up a corner or two of her rather neglected house, she called Fatty to her bedside. As she told him her truth of the George Hopkins case, he choked and reddened, and emitted the smelly perspiration like he had those years before, when Pruiett had blasted him on the witness stand.

"You mean," he gasped, "that you stole that book out of my trunk and let some lawyer have it, and then slipped it back?"

The sick woman nodded weakly.

"Good God," cried Fatty. "That's how it happened. But how in the name of God did you think of it? Whatever made you do it?"

"That was the winter we was havin' so much trouble, Fatty," she said, "an' I went to see a lawyer one day about it. When I told him who I was, an' who you was, he told me not to get no divorce from you. I was awful glad he did, for I was just mad at you and didn't mean what I was sayin'. He said he knew somethin' about this Hopkins case, an' that he could sure use that register book you had hid down here somewhere. He told me he'd give me $200 just to look at it for a few days, an' that I could slip it back without you knowin' it, and no one would ever know the difference."

"Was his name Pruiett? Was that the lawyer you talked to?" The unpleasant memories caused Fatty to bark at his sinking mate.

"No," she whispered, shaking her head, "that wasn't it. I've tried to think of it lots of times, but I just can't remember it. It wasn't Pruiett, but it was somebody that knew about George Hopkins' trouble."

"That got me in a hell of a jam," whispered Fatty, trying to conceal, in a gesture of respect for her critical condition, the anger which enveloped him. "Why didn't you say somethin' about it, sooner? Why did you want to let 'em get away with such a hell of a stunt? You could'a squawked when it came out, an' blowed the whole thing."

"It wasn't that, Fatty," she whispered. "I wasn't tryin' to help 'em, an' I wasn't tryin' to do you dirt. When he gave it back he says, 'Here it is, just like you give it to me, we ain't even opened it up. We decided we didn't want to mess around with the state's evidence,' an' when I looked at it I could tell it never had been untied or touched. He give me $25 more when he brought it back, that I wasn't expectin' to get, an' so I just swiped your keys again an' slipped it back in your trunk. When I found out what they had did, I was too scared to say anything. I thought the laws would grab me up for it, an' I knowed what you would do to me. I was just too scared, Fatty, that's all."

The old man who carried the keys at the Comanche County Jail had his own chapter to write in the story of rumor. For more than two weeks, he said, after Mr. Pruiett came into the case, a young man who's name he couldn't remember, but who said that he was one of Hopkins' lawyers, would come to the jail to visit him, each time with an unusually large and bulky briefcase. And, the visits were at most inopportune hours; early in the morning when the inmates were scouring the concrete floor of the cell-block with the big hose, or late at night, when the prisoners were supposed to be asleep. And strangely, too, after a few weeks of calling, and strange, prolonged whisperings through the bars, the young man quit, and came not back to see his client.

The account of a certain commercial photographer, as an illustration of one of the unusual experiences of his calling, dovetailed with various chapters in the rumor story. "A fellow brought an old package, just a plain one wrapped in newspaper and tied with old string. He had $20 worth of pictures made of the darn thing; front, side, bottom and top. He even had enlargements made, and waited around there two or three hours 'til I got through, just watchin' that old bundle."

And years later, George Hopkins let corn liquor loosen his tongue to such an extent that some of the loose ends of drifting gossip and speculation were connected together.

"That damn book had its picture took before it was unwrapped. There was some pretty smart guys lookin' out for old George, that's why there wasn't no slips. They knew just how to tie it up, with the big pictures they had, so that it would be just exactly so, an' not make nobody suspicious."

"An' I had one hell of a time gettin' my name in the damn thing. They had to bring it in that old jail a hell of a lot of times, before I could ever sign it up without no one catchin' on. That was a job of writin' that had to be done just exactly right. What I mean, the i's had to be dotted and the t's and to be crossed."

Pruiett proceeded on his complacent way. He had won another impossible victory, and had made enough out of it to supply more of the things which had been denied him in his unpleasant youth. With half closed eyes, he viewed the scene in the light of retribution. The thieves and murderers shall be liberated, turned back into their midst, he had vowed, and a little of the outside cheer had filtered through his cell bars with the thought, and had sustained him. He saw the line marching by in lockstep, hands on shoulders and eyes dressed upon him in his comfortable reverie. There was old John Evans, and Doll Wilson; Sam Ashton and Red Fox. Agnes Gilbert, Maggie Miller and Lorena Mathews sauntered by. When shivering, whimpering George Hopkins fell into line and step and looked toward him, smiling his appreciation, Pruiett smiled in return. You can get a guilty one acquitted, by God, just the same as you can convict an innocent one.

CHAPTER SIXTEEN

WHEREIN, UNDER THE HEAD OF MISCELLANEOUS MURDERS, PRUIETT DEFENDS A PROFESSOR WHO KILLED HIS PUPIL; A WOMAN WHO KILLED HER BROTHER; TWO WOMEN WHO KILLED THEIR HUSBANDS; A STOREKEEPER WHO SLEW AN INOFFENSIVE PATRON; AN AGED MAN WHO KILLED HIS AGED BROTHER; AND A RICH MAN WHO KILLED A HARPY, AS PROSTITUTES COMMONLY WERE CALLED; AND HOW ALL OF THE GUILTY ARE ACQUITTED; BUT, THE AGED MAN, WHO WAS INNOCENT, IS CONVICTED. AND HOW HE VOWS THAT HIS CLIENT WILL NEVER GO TO PRISON, AND AFTER AN APPEAL TURNS UNSUCCESSFUL, THE OLD MAN MAKES GOOD FOR HIM BY COMMITTING SUICIDE. HOW DISGRUNTLED SURVIVORS OF A MURDER VICTIM ASSASSINATE A MISSISSIPPI LAWYER, AFTER PRUIETT HAS MANEUVERED HIM OUT OF CONFINEMENT, AND OUT OF THE SHADOW OF THE ELECTRIC CHAIR.

Professor Corley P. McDarment was a disciplinarian of the old school. 'Spare the rod and spoil the child' had always been his slogan. When he drew a class of high school boys, larger than he is in stature and handier than he with what it took to flourish the birch, he called upon his native Kentucky resourcefulness to help coin an appropriate amendment to his guiding precept. He ordered three of his rebellious pupils to a room in the school basement, and, after following them there and bolting the door, produced a rod and began to apply it to them. The rod was of .38-calibre, and would shoot six times in rapid succession. One dead and one seriously wounded was the score when the janitor broke down the door and disarmed him.

Pruiett was reading a week's accumulation of mail and soiling the polished brass of his own office cuspidors. His secretary slipped though the door and stood nervously before his desk. The black stud was not an easy task-master.

"What you want?" he growled, without looking up.

"There's a man waiting to see you," she said. "He said... "

DENVER, COLO., MONDAY, ...

Pretty Widow on Trial for Murder Of Husband, Victim of Conspiracy

Mrs. Laura M. Reuter.

Reuter Home, Where Charles J. Reuter Was Slain.

Mrs. Laura Reuter Faces Charge in Oklahoma City Court.

Sweetheart Hires Thug to Kill Man Who Stood in His Way.

Charles J. Reuter and Their Children, Marcella and Johnny R...

CHARLIE REUTER, IN THE CENTER; LAURA REUTER, ON THE LEFT; THEIR CHILDREN ON THE RIGHT; AND THEIR HOUSE IN THE BACKGROUND. LAURA AND HER BOYFRIEND WERE ACCUSED OF MURDERING HER HUSBAND. PRUIETT SUCCESSFULLY DEFENDED LAURA, WHO SPENT A TOTAL OF 48 HOURS IN JAIL AFTER THE KILLING. COURTESY *MOMAN PRUIETT: CRIMINAL LAWYER.*

"I told you I didn't want to see any one," he snapped. "I got to get right on out of town. Let one of the boys take care of him."

"He won't see any of them," she replied. "He's been in several times in the last few days, and he says it's most urgent. He said it was a big murder case."

"Send him in," Pruiett said, "but understand... I won't be in town the balance of this week, an' I don't want to see any one else."

"My name's Wright, Mr. Pruiett," the well-dressed man began. "I'm authorized to say that I represent the Teachers Association..."

"The school teachers?" Pruiett interrupted.

"Yes, the school teachers," the man smiled. "I know you're busy, so I'll be brief. One of our members is in jail, up in eastern Oklahoma, on a murder charge. We want to employ you to defend him."

"How bad do you want to employ me?" Pruiett asked. With murder waiting to be heard on a dozen dockets, he couldn't afford to be tactful.

"We'll pay $1,000," Wright said.

"I wouldn't touch it for two," Pruiett snarled. "Why, hell's fire... You're talkin' about McDarment, ain't you?"

"That's the case," came the answer.

"The daddy of the boy he killed is a lawyer, an' one of my friends. His uncle is the District Judge in that County, an' he'll probably try the case. I couldn't afford to get into it at all."

"It's a very unwholesome situation, for McDarment," Wright agreed. "That's the reason why our committee selected you. We figured that position and influence didn't make any difference to you."

"I'm awful busy," Pruiett argued, but Wright's smart flattery had not missed its mark."They'd have the court an' jury both against you with that set-up. I don't want to get mixed up in it."

"I'll guarantee the payment of a $3,000," Wright suggested. "I don't want to haggle."

"Will you put that in writin'?" Pruiett demanded.

"I'll be glad to," Wright replied.

"How long will it take you to pay off?"

"I'll agree to pay in full in one week."

Pruiett pushed the buzzer beneath the desk ledge. "Call Tulsa an' get the County Attorney; tell him I'm sick—I've had a stroke, or a fit, or somethin'," he said to the girls, "an' get that case over there passed." Then, he turned to Wright. "Say, where are they holdin' McDarment?"

"At Muskogee," Wright smiled.

"See when's the first train to Muskogee, an' get me a ticket on it," he continued. "An' remember, I don't want to see anybody before I leave."

"Do you want me to outline the facts of this case for you?" Wright inquired.

"No," Pruiett answered, shortly. "I'll outline 'em for you. It was self-defense. He shot to save... No, that won't work. Say, what the hell are you goin' to say for a professor that shoots hell out of the kids in his class. That's pretty stern teachin', ain't it?"

"I'll tell you," Wright began, "The... "

"Did McDarment have a kid sister? We'll use the unwritten law." Pruiett gnawed the end from a big cigar and was spewing the dry fragments over his vest. "What about that kind of a deal?"

"I'll tell you, if you'll hold on a minute," Wright said. "This McDarment is a small man; he doesn't weigh more than a hundred and thirty-five or forty. This happened in the high school up at Wagoner, up north of Muskogee, an' the boys involved were bigger than the teacher. Edgar Watts, the dead boy, weighed twenty pounds more than McDarment. Clay Moss, the one that got his eye shot out, weighed more than Watts. There was another one, named Dick Jones, and he was a big-armed bully, too. They... "

"I may be able to make the self-defense stick," Pruiett interrupted. He was so nervous that he couldn't be still. "These boys were bullyin' some of the little children, an' McDarment was tryin' to protect..."

"If you please, Mr. Pruiett," Wright persisted. "Let me give you the bare outlines; then you can add all the theory you wish. We'll pay you to add enough to keep McDarment from going to the chair. These over-grown yokels bragged that they wouldn't be bossed by a teacher that wasn't as big as they were. They barked like dogs and howled like cats, so that he couldn't hold classes. He was dodging beans and paper wads all the time, and they had a game that was called 'high and low', where one would get on his hands and knees behind the professor, and another would push him backward, over him. They told him when he got tired of it he could quit his job and leave town; that it'd be all right with them any time."

"That's bein' pretty hard on the professor," Pruiett agreed. "We used to rough 'em up a bit down in Arkansas, but we never had the guts to get that rebellious. Did McDarment just get tired of it an' take his little pistol to school with him?"

"We don't know about that," Wright answered. "It seems like McDarment and these three boys were alone in a chemistry room they had in the basement of the school. We have two members who tried to teach in this school, who were driven out by these same boys, and they have reported the situation to us. We're sure McDarment was justified in taking the course he did, whatever it was. He's in jail; and, so far, none of us have had a chance to talk to him."

"Tell your membership that Pruiett don't give a damn about District Judges an' State politics. All he's interested in is justice." He arose and held out his hand, the signal that the conference had been concluded. "Tell 'em McDarment's as good as acquitted, an' not to let the fee matter drag along. Let's clear that thing up an' get it out of the way."

"Have you signed up a nice little statement for the County Attorney?" Pruiett was squinting between steel bars as he asked the question.

"No," McDarment answered. "I've had plenty of chances, but I told 'em I didn't care to make a statement until I had consulted my attorney."

"All school teachers ain't damn fools," Pruiett grunted. "Our Constitution says a man don't have to incriminate himself, but prosecutin' attorneys don't know nothin' about that. They usually take a signed statement, an' then add a little about 'this here can be used against me as evidence if the prosecution finds anything in it of value'. You know?"

"I know," McDarment agreed, listlessly.

"I like to have the cooperation of my clients," Pruiett said. "It helps to beat hell. Are you willin' to help me win this case?"

"Perfectly," McDarment answered.

"All right. Now, who owned that pistol?"

"I did."

"Now look here," Pruiett objected. "I thought we was goin' to cooperate. It would be a hell of a lot better if one of the boys had brought that gun to school that day."

"I can't help it," McDarment replied. "It was mine and every one around here knows it. We can't get anywhere going that way."

"You're right, if that's the case," Pruiett agreed. "What was you doin' in that basement room with the three boys?"

"I sent 'em out of a classroom upstairs; told 'em to go down there, and then I followed them. That's... "

"Just a minute, now," Pruiett interrupted again. "That don't sound so good. We've got to be careful... "

"I don't care how it sounds," McDarment cried, hysterically. "I had a belly full of those god damn apes so I just slipped the pistol in my pocket after breakfast, and carried it to school with me. They were drivin' me out of my job, an' I had a wife an' baby to feed. I had to fight, and those boys were all bigger than I... "

"You ain't feelin' well today," Pruiett said, stopping him. "There's no use of us discussin' it here. We'll wait 'til they have the preliminary next week, an' just fish out the facts they got against you. We're not puttin' you on the stand, see? Then... " Pruiett peered intently into the dim light of the cell. "Say, what's that stain on your sleeve? That one just above the elbow?"

"What does it look like?" McDarment countered.

"It looks like a burn, a scorched place, to me," Pruiett replied.

"Yeah, that's what it is," the professor said. "The wife scorched it with the iron, when she was ironin' it. She had to do all that kind of work for us."

"Did you have your coat on when this trouble came off up there?" Pruiett inquired. Before McDarment could reply, he reconstructed the question. "You didn't have your coat on, did you?"

"No," said McDarment, "I didn't have my coat on."

"Wait just a minute," Pruiett said.

The Pruiett defense delivering head was at work. Stepping down the corridor, he called to the jailor and an assistant. He asked them to come down to the door of McDarment's cell. When they were there, he asked the professor to stick his right arm through the bars.

"Take this pen and put your initial on the sleeve of that shirt, up there near the shoulder," he said, handing his fountain pen to the jailor. "That's all right, let it smear; just make 'em big enough so's they won't all run together. That's it. Fine." He approved the way the bewildered officer made his mark, and then handed the pen to the other one, who was waiting.

"Now, you, please sir," he continued. "Down here below, on the cuff. Put your initials. That's it. That's fine."

Holding McDarment's arm out in the light, as he placed his pen in his pocket, he pointed to the scorched place at the elbow.

"You see that yellow burn? That scorched place right there?" he said to the officers. "That's what I want you to witness and remember. I've had you put your marks on the sleeve, so you'll know the shirt if you ever see it again. Now, Mr. McDarment, take it off so I can stuff it in this 'folio of mine. I'll see that you get another one right away."

That had been the substance of Pruiett's first interview with his client. The burned shirt had suggested something, possibly a remote likelihood of utility in the future; so, he preserved it. If a place was made for it, and it fit, it would be heard from later. If not... The most dutiful housewife scorches a garment occasionally. No harm was done.

"Professor C. P. McDarment, instructor of Wagoner High School, was late yesterday afternoon, after preliminary hearing before Justice R. E. Doggett, held for the District Court on the charge of murdering Edgar Watts, an 18 year old student. Two men and two boyhood companions of young Watts [told their stories] of what transpired behind the locked door of the High School laboratory at high noon on February 10, [1916], and when they had finished the tragedy remained as much a mystery as ever." So did an early account of the case appear in the *Muskogee Daily Phoenix* on March 1, 1916. "McDarment himself did not take the stand [at the preliminary hearing]. Neatly attired, he sat beside his attorneys throughout the day, seldom even so much as suggesting a question to be asked. Moman Pruiett, chief of his counsel, at several times thrilled the courtroom with dramatic declarations which gave intimations of what the young teacher's defense might be."

"We got to be awful careful," Pruiett whispered behind his hand to McDarment. "That's Thomas H. Owen, the Muskogee City Attorney and the special prosecutor in this case and former member of the Criminal Court of Appeals. He's in charge of the prosecution, an' the guy with the big ears is Fred Branson, the prosecuting attorney. They're both as smart as hell, an' good prosecutors."

"What's the matter with the public prosecutor they had up here?" McDarment whispered. "Isn't he supposed to have charge of these kinds of cases?"

"Special prosecutors," Pruiett answered. "The interested parties are entitled to hire 'em if they want 'em, to back the State's attorney up. They didn't need to hire 'em in this case. The Wattses are so prominent up here they got a lot of volunteers."

"I think you can handle the situation," McDarment encouraged.

"I'll show 'em some tricks," Pruiett boasted, swelling with the compliment. "Somethin' they can't pick up on an appeals bench. Who's that kid they're bringin' in for a witness?"

"That's Clay Moss," McDarment said. "He's gettin' out of the hospital early."

"He sure as hell is," Pruiett agreed. "He must be perty tough. Is he hurt as bad as that big bandage on his head would make you think?"

"He lost his eye," McDarment whispered. "I'm glad it wasn't worse."

Moss gave a damaging account, damaging for McDarment, of what had transpired in the high school basement room. The State had the professor charged with deliberate, premeditated murder, and Moss had received an injury at his hands. He made a willing witness in support of the theory the State had to prove if it was going to win its suit against the spare-built little school teacher.

" 'Where were you the night before the tragedy?' Pruiett demanded of Moss on cross-examination. 'At the basketball game,' the witness answered. 'Did you see McDarment there?' 'Yes, sir.' 'Did you have a conversation with him that night?' 'All he said was that he wanted me to take charge of the game and to referee. Then he gave me his whistle.' The witness mumbled his last sentence. Pruiett shot out of his chair. 'His pistol?' he cried. 'His whistle,' the witness corrected. 'I didn't know he had a pistol'."

When Pruiett resumed the seat 'he had shot out of', as the correspondent for the *Muskogee Phoenix* had observed, the panorama of the McDarment defense was finally clear before him. The imperfect diction of the witness in answering, or his own inability to understand, had opened the door of credible explanation to him. He saw the dead cat. He heard the flap of the wings of his attending spooks. He conferred with McDarment, in whispers, before he resumed his cross-examination of Moss.

"You did referee the basketball game that night, didn't you?" he demanded.

"Yes I did... "

"And, isn't it a fact that Professor McDarment, or some other member of the faculty, usually acts as the official at the school games?"

"Yes...but..."

"You took the whistle out of McDarment's pocket?"

"He told me to. He said for me to get it out of his coat, hangin' on a post, an'..."

"McDarment was supposed to referee this particular game? He went there to act as referee, didn't he?"

"Yes, but... "

"And you and your friends Watts and Jones pushed the professor backwards a time or two, an' told him if he didn't set up in the stands with the girls, where he belonged, that you were going to whip his ass, right there before the basketball crowd, didn't you?"

"No," Moss shouted. "Nothing of the sort. I... we... "

"That'll be all," Pruiett drawled, waving the witness aside. He arose to address the Court. "I'd like to have this matter continued over until tomorrow, for further cross-examination of State's witness and possibly for some evidence for the defendant."

"We object," Tom Owen cried. "We want to close our case now. After this hearing is over, we are willing that he have fifteen weeks to manufacture his defense."

"I never have been handed such a beautiful bouquet of courtesy in all my life," Pruiett said sweetly, making Owen a profound bow, "as from my distinguished friend, the judge of the Criminal Court of Appeals."

"The request for a continuance will be denied," the Court barked.

"Thank you, your honor," Pruiett said, bowing again and smiling.

"I'm givin' you back nine of them fifteen weeks you offered me," Pruiett grinned at Owen and the prosecution as he swaggered into the District Court courtroom before trial. "I'm announcin' ready."

Owen and Branson, with others interested in the prosecution, pretended not to hear him. Pruiett looked closer to see that none of the family of the deceased were within hearing; he was always compassionate and considerate of those who survived his client's misdeeds.

"I see you're runnin' for the Supreme Court," he continued, talking directly to Owen. "I'm glad to see it, an' I'm for you, a hundred percent. Who shall I make my check to? I'm sendin' a little contribution to your campaign."

"Thanks," said Owen, indifferently. "Just send it to the office, if you're really going to the bother."

"I sure as hell am," Pruiett grinned. "I think we ought to have more public-spirited lawyers that're willin' to sacrifice the gain of private practice for the good of the people."

"Thanks," Owen repeated.

"I hope you win," Pruiett went on. "I hope you get a better chance of winnin' that judge's race than you got o' winnin' this case. You boys are off... " Owen got up and walked away.

"I got his fire hot already," he beamed to McDarment. "Did you get that stuff I sent you to study?"

"I got it." McDarment answered.

"Have you got it straight? Want to ask any questions?"

"I understand it, I believe."

"I intend to reserve my openin' statement until the State has finished its case," he whispered. "We're goin' to coast on the cross-examination, just cut 'em a time or two, to let the jury know we ain't pleadin' guilty. We'll blast 'em when we put you an' our other witnesses on the stand."

"I'm sure your plan is a good one," McDarment agreed.

"When I start to make the openin' statement, act like you're too tired an' indifferent to listen, but have your ear over ever' thing I say. I'm goin' over that statement I sent up to your cell, an' I don't want you to fall down. Follow it, close, in the statement."

When the State had concluded its case, it had been established by Jones and Moss, who survived the basement fracas, that McDarment was the heartless aggressor. He had ordered the three boys from class, had directed them to go to the room in the basement, and after following them there, had bolted the door before he made known the purpose of his private interview. Then, he had drawn the pistol, and began to shoot.

Pruiett began his narrative of what the defense evidence would show. He was the embodiment of defiance, and assurance. His newly tailored suit, a trifle ash-cluttered, hung easily about his rugged frame. His black mop of hair was in faultless array, and shone brilliantly in the dim light of the courtroom. There was a trace of brown tobacco stain about the corners of his mouth, but he was close-shaven and freshly manicured. His voice was deep and booming. His gestures, his smiles of assurance and his grimaces of pathos, were always in harmony with the tempo of his restless footwork, as he moved up and down in front of his listeners. The eyes of the jurors followed him. They reflected his moods and feelings as he expressed them.

"Gentlemen," he said, "you understand, from my cross-examination of State's witnesses that our defense is based generally upon the doctrine of self-defense. Our proof, which will follow this statement, will show that Edgar Watts was killed accidentally, in a struggle over a gun which might have caused the death of McDarment, or to the other boys, as well as it did of Watts. These boys had driven two teachers out of school, out of town, by their rough tactics, and they were enraged because McDarment had defied them and refused to give up his job."

"Professor McDarment didn't carry that gun to the basement room," he said, with tones and gestures which caressed his listeners' ears. "Our proof will show that—beyond all reasonable doubt." He made an oratorical play on the 'reasonable doubt,' and glanced slyly at Tom Owen as he let it roll out. Owen knew he was going to hear a lot about 'reasonable doubt' before the trial was over, and he frowned.

"McDarment sent the boys out of the classroom so that he might have a talk with them in the privacy of the basement laboratory; to reason with them and to try to make peace with them. He wanted to try once more to show them that they were being unreasonable, and were wrong. He wasn't carrying a pistol. He had no design to commit an assault of any kind on the boys."

"The pistol was going to be the subject of the interview in the basement. The pistol was missing. There's going to be no contention that the gun used in this unfortunate affair was not the property of the defendant. He admits it. He will continue to admit it; but, he didn't carry it to the basement on this fatal morning, and it was not in his hand when the tragic shots were fired." There was soul-stirring pathos in Pruiett's deep voice as he moved artfully toward his climax.

"The professor had taken that pistol to the basketball game on the night before, to use it as a timing gun. In other words, when the half period was reached, and when the game was over, he would discharge the gun. The whistle was for stopping plays when the ball was out of bounds, and when fouls had been committed. I'm not familiar with the game, but it has been explained to me in that way. This pistol was in his coat pocket, just before the game started, hanging by the basketball court. The whistle was attached to a string, or little strap, and the professor carried it about his wrist or in his hand."

"The trouble came up about who was going to referee, and as it is partially in evidence, the Moss boy won the argument. He says that McDarment asked him to referee, and told him to get the whistle from the side pocket of his coat which was hanging there. That is not true, as our proof will show. Watts, Jones and Moss called McDarment aside, and told him that he was going to sit up with the girls, where he belonged, while Moss refereed the game. They told him that they were going to whip him, before the crowd that was coming in to see the game, if he went out on the court to referee. One of the boys grabbed the whistle and twisted it from McDarment's wrist. In confusion and embarrassment, and in an effort to avoid an embarrassing scene, McDarment withdrew, and permitted Moss to act as referee. He didn't think about the gun until he was on his way home, after the game, and it was then that he missed it."

"He didn't know whether it had been stolen, or whether he had lost it from his pocket. He intended to inquire about it, at school the next morning, merely to ask the students if they had found or heard of a gun being found about the school; but, when he got there, a girl student told him that she had seen Watts stick his hand into his coat pocket there at the basketball game, and take something out of it. Was it unreasonable for him to deduce that the incident explained the whereabouts of his missing time gun?"

"Yes. McDarment sent the boys to the basement. Does that show premeditation of murder, sending three big boys, when he knew that one of them might be armed, down to a secluded room in the basement? Or you may think to ask me: 'Why did he send them out, and follow them away, as he did?' Our proof will show, gentlemen, that his acts were motivated by concern and kindliness for the boys. He will tell you that he didn't want to accuse them, publicly, of having robbed him; of having picked his pocket. He was going to ask them, privately, to return his property. Then, he was going to demand its return, and then, if they refused, he was going to file a complaint against them, charging that they had stolen his pistol, and seek to recover it in a legal and proper manner."

"The boys went downstairs first. McDarment followed them. They were in the room first. McDarment will tell you that as he stepped into the dim light of that room, the Moss boy moved in behind him, and slamming the door shut, bolted it. Before the professor had time to ask about the pistol, Edgar Watts pulled it out and pointed it at him, held it right against his belly, and called him a bunch of vile names. He called him names that reflected upon the character of his mother and questioned the good purposes of his father, and told him that he had hung around their town too long. 'We don't like you and we've told you so,' they said to him, 'and we've told you to get out. Now we're goin' to beat the hell out of you, and you'll have to hire somebody to carry you out'."

"Watts held the gun on him while Moss aimed a blow at his head. The Professor ducked and grappled with Watts, grabbing at the hand holding the pistol. As they struggled, the gun went off, it was right between them. The first shot didn't hit any one. That's the one that lodged in the window frame near the ceiling. The next one grazed Moss's face; he had jumped into the fight, and he hollered, but kept right on swinging and slugging. It went off again, and the bullet went through Moss's eye; he fell unconscious, but Watts and the professor went on fighting, struggling over the pistol. There was another report, and the bullet went squarely though the boy's face. He fell to the floor—dead. McDarment stooped over, picked up the gun which had fallen from Watts's grasp, and the janitor pushed the barred door in. The gun which wounded Clay Moss, and which killed Edgar Watts, was in Edgar's own hands all the time, during all the times that it was being discharged."

"We will offer for your consideration the testimony of the girl who saw the boys taking something from McDarment's pockets at the basketball game, the one who reported what she had seen to the teacher the following morning. We will have the testimony of firearms experts, who have made examinations of the shirt McDarment was wearing on the morning of this unfortunate occurrence. They will say that the shirt was scorched about the elbow of the right sleeve, and that with their microscopic examination they found tiny granules of burned gun-powder. That scorched place on Professor McDarment's arm was a powder burn, and if he had held the gun in his right hand, deliberately firing it into the bodies of his victims, as these victims have testified, it would have been impossible for the sleeve of his shirt to be scorched and burned by the blast."

Tom Owen mopped a fine film of perspiration from his forehead as Pruiett concluded his outline. Owen was a good lawyer; he knew a good defense when he saw one. The prophecy of acquittal was written across the dingy walls of the old courtroom, and the prosecution didn't need a prophet to interpret the message for them. The pilfering of the inoffensive whistle, suggested by the resemblance in the pronunciation of whistle and pistol, made a perfect base for the construction of a homespun Pruiett defense. Owen saw why he was going to be beaten, at the same time the inevitable became apparent. He gnashed his teeth. Fred Branson cursed under his breath. The black stud leered and swaggered.

Defense witnesses swore that Moss had slipped something from the professor's pocket. Moss said it was a whistle. The professor said he discovered that his signal pistol was missing after he left the ball game. What was the Court going to say about reasonable doubt, when he instructed the jury? If there's a reasonable doubt in your minds at the conclusion of all the evidence, you must resolve in favor of whom? The defendant? The accused? Why certainly! Why hell, yes! This here's the United States of America. This ain't revolutionary Russia. Will Pruiett think of that for his argument? Just you let Pruiett alone, and watch an' listen. You'll have some fun when he goes to burnin' the State in this case.

The old jailor and his assistant came, under compulsion, to identify the scorched shirt which McDarment had yielded into Pruiett's briefcase. The County Attorney'll get us fired for this, but there's our initials on that shirt, an' that wild-eyed devil defendin' McDarment will hang a perjury rap on us if we try to back up on him. That's the shirt we signed, all right. Signin' a shirt! Who'd a thought of such a thing, except that gimlet-eyed Pruiett? That's the stain all right, right there by the elbow. It was there the day Pruiett came to the jail, an' it was the same shirt that the professor had on when he was brought into jail. Let 'em fire us. It's a hell of a lot better to be out of a job than to try to hedge with a wild man shakin' his fist under your nose, there in a crowded courtroom. We're tellin' the truth about that shirt.

And Pruiett was right about the ballistic experts. They came, and they testified.

"Do you mean to tell this Court and jury," Tom Owen screamed, "that a flaming pistol would make a different appearing scorch on a piece of fabric than a hot iron would?"

"No sir, I don't," the expert replied.

"Then why are you so positive that his burned shirt shows powder burns, instead of some other kind of burns?"

"Because I made microscopic tests of this fabric, and I find particles of burned gun-powder in it, burned right into the scorched fabric."

Owen produced his big handkerchief and began his deliberate, desperate, face moping. "Could you take a piece of fabric that had been scorched in ordinary use, say as in being ironed, or coming too close to a hot stove, and after it had been discolored, fire a revolver in such proximity to it that particles of powder might become imbedded in the scorched surface of the fabric?" Owen was no fool.

The witness pondered. "Well, yes," he answered. "I believe that it would be possible to imbed the powder in the fabric, with such a process."

Owen glared triumphantly with the admission, and stalked toward his chair. Pruiett gave him an insolent smile and wink. Was he going to let a jury convict a man on such an unreasonable hypothesis? Let him argue that the powder was a Pruiett trick. What was reasonable doubt in that old Constitution for, if they could get by with that kind of stuff? Did the boy filch a pistol or a whistle? If he had stolen the pistol, would he admit it, in the face of the proportions of the tragic result which followed? Was a jury going to convict, when they couldn't ever decide, with definite certainty, what that kid had found in the professor's pocket? Pruiett was serene. He had acquired, in his rounds, something of a knowledge of homely human nature.

When the forensic fireworks, which came after the evidence, were over the jury went out—and came back. According to the *Muskogee Phoenix* on June 18, 1916, Pruiett's client was not guilty. McDarment pumped each juror's hand in gratification; Pruiett complimented each of them for a smart verdict. Tom Owen and Fred Branson made strange muttering sounds under their breath as they tried to console the weeping, half-hysterical, parents of the dead Watts boy.

"Have you had any experience in shooting a gun?" A polite young clerk in a small town hardware store was leaning across the counter and asking the question of a plump, middle-aged woman. She wore a black dress and a black hat.

"No sir," she answered, "but… "

"Then I would suggest that you get a shotgun," he said. "A mad dog, any kind of dog, would be very hard to hit, and this small gun wouldn't be very satisfactory."

"I think I'll learn to use it all right," the customer answered. "Do bullets go with it, or do you have to buy them extra?"

"The cartridges will be extra," the man corrected.

"How many do you want, a box?"

"Just enough to fill it up," the lady in mourning replied.

When the clerk had loaded the gun, a short barreled revolver, and cautiously complied with her request for information as to how to shoot it, she paid and walked out. Fifteen minutes later, the crowd of farmers, who packed the town's principal store for the Saturday afternoon shopping, was in a panic. A woman, holding a pistol in both hands, was pumping it empty and into the body of a man who tried to stagger away from her.

The killer was Callie Pence, the recently widowed survivor of Sid Pence, a farmer of the community. The victim, begging from the floor of the store was her own brother, Lee Sharp. Sharp was under indictment by the District Court of McClain County for killing Callie's husband in an argument which arose over the occupancy of a farm which Pence owned, but which Sharp farmed for him, on half-shares. He was out of jail on bond. Before all the 'bullets' acquired in the neighboring hardware store were exhausted, Sharp was fatally wounded, and two scurrying female bystanders had been less seriously injured.

Pruiett took the case and a deed to the Pence property. Temporary insanity was the plea, and even the staunchest Pruiett supporter expressed a doubt as to whether or not he could explain around the cool premeditation which the hardware clerk's testimony was going to supply. It appeared that Widow Pence had fairly well decided to kill her brother, before she began to put the decision into successful execution.

Callie's case came up for trial in District Court at Norman, County Seat of Cleveland County. She was out on an ample Pruiett property bond. A conference, pre-trial, was being held in local counsel's office near the old courthouse.

"That hardware clerk is listed as a State's witness, an' he's goin' to testify about that mad-dog business," Pruiett said. "I ain't sure whether I like it or not."

"I can deny I said it, if you want me to," Callie agreed.

"What other reason you goin' to advance for buyin' a six-shooter?" Pruiett asked.

"Whatever you say," Callie answered.

"I got a hell of a headache today," Pruiett said, pressing his temples between his finger tips. "My head's bustin'. I can't hardly think."

Callie waited. She didn't need to inquire about his health. She was a woman of experience, and Pruiett's slightly sour breath and shaking hands were explanatory of a prodigious hang-over.

"We won't bother to change it," he said, finally. "You said a mad dog, so we'll stay with it. I hate to have my witnesses change their testimony, anyway. If my head wasn't hurtin' so bad, we might cook up somethin' better; but, if we go at it right, it's goin' to be hard to beat."

Callie sat patiently. Pruiett arose, and pressing his temples again, began to pace the floor.

"You had a dog out at the place that was actin' mad, an' you wanted to kill him. You came to town on Saturday afternoon, an' bought you a little gun for shootin' that dog, an' you put it in your pocket-book. You was over there at Rucker's store, doin' some marketin', an' in walks Lee Sharp. You didn't know he was in town, an' you wasn't entertainin' no ideas of givin' him any lead treatment. You got that?"

Callie nodded. She had it.

"When you saw Lee Sharp in that aisle, the lights went out. I mean they went plumb out, an' ever'thing got black before your eyes. You didn't do nothin', an' you didn't say nothin'. It was plumb blank. Then somebody turned them lights back on for you, an' there you was; standin' there with your teeth in your face an' a wild look in your eye. There was that damn smokin' pistol in your limp hand; there was the apple baskets turned over and the cracker barrel spilled all over the place, an' old Lee layin' there in a pool of nasty lookin' red stuff, but you didn't know nothin' about it. You follow me?"

"I'm right behind you," Callie chirped, cheerfully.

"Somebody screams over behind the cheese counter an' you see a bloody woman layin' over there, kickin'. 'You killed him,' she hollers, 'an' you shot me.' 'Who—me?' says you. 'What's goin' on around here? What's happened?' You don't know a damn thing about what's happened around there at all. See?"

"I'm temporarily insane, am I?" Callie inquired.

"Exactly," Pruiett thundered. His headache was gone. He was acting out each movement there on the rough pine floor. "You say, 'I didn't mean to kill him—if I did.' Get it? 'If I did,' ever'time. You got to act like you're still confused, that you can't realize, even now, that you shot your own brother. Then, you tell the Alabama story, an' how much you loved old Sid. I'll make 'em hang their eye balls in their vest pockets when I go to tellin' 'em the truth about how that ingrate brother took your soulmate away from you. I'll... "

"No just law would condemn me for what I did; put me in jail an' try to send me to the penitentiary, or the electric chair," Callie interrupted. "It's like you say, an' I think you're perfectly right. If they'd do that to me, I'm justified in doin' anything I can to defeat them."

The other side of the Pence case contained high-gravity pathos. It was murder, all right, if designed killing constituted murder; but, there was a lifetime of justification for it. Pruiett was back before a jury, according to the *Norman Transcript,* in December of 1921.

"Callie and Sid grew old together," he whispered, leaning close to see if tears had started down the weather-beaten cheeks of his farmer jury's faces. "She was fourteen; he eighteen, when they married. Penniless kids on poor old Alabama farms, and in love." He paused to push a loose wisp of hair back into its black bulk, and to let his message sift down. The head would catch it, but the heart had to have it before it took effect. "Babies wouldn't come to them; they wanted them but they wouldn't come; so, they directed the love that they would have had for their children back into each other. They lived alone, and worked hard, and loved one another. They had no one, nothing else to love."

He was building slowly—carefully. "They moved out to this territory; and elbow to elbow, they toiled and saved. We know, you and I, of the hardships they endured. We were here with them, struggling as Callie and Sid were struggling, for the things that would make life in our declining years a bit softer—a bit sweeter. They relied on the comfort that the one would be to the other, in the eventide of life, as they struggled and saved and loved."

"Old Sid's hands were rough and work-worn. His face was wrinkled and seamed with the wear of age, and weather, and hard labor—but,

Callie loved him. He wore patches on his old overalls so that she might have a new churn, or a new gingham apron." Pruiett paused. They were coming, now. Number three in the back row was brushing them away with the back of his hand and trying to look unconcerned; he was feigning interest out the window. An old one in the front row, with gray hair, was indifferent about it. He let them drop off the end of his nose.

"And they sent back to Alabama for Lee. Callie was kind-hearted, she cherished the recollections she had of childhood frolics on the old pine-studded Alabama hillsides. Lee wasn't gettin' along so well, and they had an adjoining farm they would let him have, and let him work it. Sid agreed, just because he thought it would make Callie happy; so, they sent him money, and had him come on out to Oklahoma. Lee was Callie's brother, but let me tell you, my friends, that there's one thing stronger than the tie of family blood, and that's the bond of love that a man has for a woman, or a woman has for a man, that's been molded in the pit of joint-suffering and baked in the oven of self-sacrifice."

"Selfish, little-minded Lee Sharp killed Callie's life-mate over a line dispute between the farms, an' the Pences owned both of them. He just took his shotgun an' shot Sid to pieces. The law stepped in, and was going to prosecute Lee for it, I am sure, and I am sure that my client had no intention of interfering. By the force of her dull mechanical will she went on the train with the body; she carried Sid back to his Alabama hills, and saw him unloaded and dropped into the sandy ground. Did she come back here for vengeance, as the State contends? Did she come back here to slaughter and kill? It was her home here, the one she and Sid had suffered and bled for, and she had no other. She was an' old woman—and she was alone. Her dreams of what was to come, the comfort that was to be hers, had been shattered."

He spread his hands in an appealing gesture. "She had been awakened from her dream, but she moved about as if she were still asleep. Every ripple of the wind-blown grain field, the field that she and Sid had sown, was like a ponderous blow upon her heart. The sight of the trees he had planted, the fences he had built, were torture for Callie. She had to work to forget, or go mad, so she tried to run the farm. She didn't know Lee was in town. She had no desire to see him, or to harm him. She was going about the hard business of running her farms, and had been required to buy the pistol, when Lee Sharp had to march back into her tortured mind. The sight of him tore apart her last line of understanding. The last fragment of reason and control snapped—and she couldn't remember. She couldn't remember."

The jury disagreed according to the *Norman Transcript.* A hung jury was half a victory, Pruiett always said, and it was an indicator. When he had hung a jury, he had enough of the State's case in his mind to strengthen his next attack upon it; and, he could make up for some of the flaws that had appeared in his defense. When he had produced the drama the second time in 1923, the jury accepted it at par. Callie bought the gun to kill a mad dog. The jury said that she was not guilty of murder, as charged.

Pruiett liked to play with that dangerous property called 'temporary insanity.' He invoked it in the defense of cases where other, and more feasible defenses, were available. On one occasion, when the wisdom of his program was being questioned by co-counsel, he made his typically frank outburst.

"Hell's fire! I've got to have somethin' besides self-defense. I'm developin' rheumatism in my right shoulder from grabbin' at my hip pocket an' arguin' the old gun pullin' act."

He undertook the defense of Sam St. Mary. According to the *Oklahoma City Times* on February, 15 1917: "As the result of a misunderstanding regarding the use of a telephone in the Gray-Graham Tailoring Company's store in the Skirvin Hotel Building, W. F. Henry, baggage driver, is dead, and Sam St. Mary, manager of the store, is in the county jail charged with murder. The shooting occurred shortly before noon today. Spectators saw Henry run from the tailoring shop and turn the corner into the alley which flanks the Rock Island depot. As the fleeing man turned the corner, St. Mary is reported to have dashed from his shop with a .38 calibre revolver, and fired three shots which took effect at the base of Henry's spine."

Charles Baxter "Charley" Selby was the County Attorney and headed the prosecution. "I'll let Sam plead guilty an' recommend a life sentence for him if you'll save the State the expense of a trial," he said.

"An' relieve it of the chance of gettin' beat?" Pruiett inquired.

"There's not a chance of his gettin' away," Selby scoffed. "There was the noon-day crowd on the street, an' a big gang on the station platform waitin' for a train to come in, an' they all saw Sam shoot him in the back. I got fifty eye-witnesses in this case."

"I wonder what that crowd on the depot platform thought, when they saw that scared baggage man a flaggin' down the bricks, an' old Sam burnin' his coat-tails with pistol bullets?" Pruiett laughed heartily.

"I don't know what they thought, but I do know what a jury's goin' to think. They'll give Sam the chair as sure as hell."

"I can't agree with you," Pruiett smiled.

"You'd better take this life sentence I'm offerin' you," Selby said, "before I change my mind. I can't leave a proposition like that open after I get the subpoenas out for my witnesses."

"Old Sam said he didn't want to go to the pen," Pruiett said. "He ain't extra smart, but he's got that much sense. He gave me specific instructions to clear him."

"You ain't got a chance," Selby answered.

"I ain't got a chance," Pruiett repeated, "but we ain't pleadin' guilty, not even to a simple assault, if you wanted to reduce it to that. Me an' Sam'll be ready for trial when they call his case."

"SAM ST. MARY FOUND NOT GUILTY," the *Oklahoma City Times* reported on June 6, 1917. How in the hell could a jury acquit a man under those circumstances? Shoot a man in the back, at high noon, before an army of witnesses, an' he's not guilty of murder? What's this guy Pruiett got? Can't the State get a conviction against him a'tall? The masses were grumbling. Charley Selby was tearing his hair.

A week of rough and tumble Pruiett trial had left Charley distracted, but still confident of victory. Insanity wasn't going to work in this case; Pruiett was wasting a lot of his gas. When the verdict came in, and Pruiett was starting his grin across the table, Selby rushed out of the courtroom. Before Pruiett and his client could get out of the courthouse, the Sheriff had served another warrant on Sam, and was leading him off to the iron cells.

"I never heard of such a thing," Pruiett gasped. "How they goin' to keep holdin' this man after the jury's acquitted him?"

Selby smiled, weakly. "I went before County Judge an' signed a' insanity complaint against him in probate court," he answered. "You proved he was insane; brought the doctors an' others here to swear to it, 'til you convinced the jury, an' me, too. I'm askin' the County Judge to send him to the Hospital for the violent insane, for the rest of his no-good life."

"I'll be god damned," Pruiett managed to say. "I never saw such a poor loser. You ain't no sport at all."

"Not if lettin' that murderous son-of-a-bitch run loose is a requisite for sportsmanship," Selby agreed. "Bein' a public officer don't keep me from complainin' against nutty folks, an' ain't you just proved he was nutty? I guess bein' his lawyer won't save you from testifyin' in the sanity hearing."

"If I ain't mistaken," Pruiett said, "a guy that's accused of bein' insane is entitled to a trial by jury, the same as when he's accused of anything else. Ain't that what the Constitution says?"

"Maybe it does," Selby laughed, "but you can't blow hot an' cold at the same time. The judge, or the jury, is goin' to hear the same evidence that this one heard that found him not guilty, by reason of being insane. They can't find both ways."

Within a three week period, Pruiett twice produced his jury-thunder; each time for Sam St. Mary. In the first case, where Sam was charged with murder, Pruiett screamed that he couldn't form the criminal intent necessary to make murder, because he was insane. In the second, where he was charged with being insane, he maintained that he was mentally quite sound. The doctors, who had testified for him in the first hearing, were necessarily against him in the second. Testimony from the record in the first case was read into the record of the second. The verdict, finding him not guilty because he was insane, was introduced in evidence, and exhibited to the jury hearing the sanity complaint.

"This is a farce," Pruiett roared, while the brass chandeliers in the room vibrated with the echo. "This is a fair example of a petty-fogging attempt of a poor loser to misuse public office, and public funds, to satisfy a personal desire for revenge. Charley Selby's a poor loser, and he wants to get even. I took him to a good trimmin' in a murder case less than a month ago, an' he wasn't big enough to swallow it. He got it lodged in his craw; let the cockle-burr hang under his tail; so, he thinks he'll spend a little more of you tax-payers money in parading his incompetence—tryin' to get even with me an' Sam."

It was plain language, but it was Pruiett speaking. He didn't indulge in ambiguities. He had bilked the State, and he might as well proclaim it. Wasn't he admitting it when he said he had trimmed him? He had gotten something he wasn't entitled to; but, he could afford to acknowledge it because the law wouldn't allow a man to be twice placed in jeopardy. The murder case was a closed episode.

According to the *Oklahoma City Times* on July 7, 1917, the jury found Sam not guilty on the insanity charge. They found that he was sane; and, they liberated him. Society ground its gold-filled molars and Selby started using the side streets and alleys. He was afraid that some one would make an insanity kick against him and have him picked up. He wasn't certain in his own mind, as to whether he could beat it or not. Pruiett brushed a curving section of the black plume back over his ears as he toyed with a tall drink. There was a sparkle in his black eye and the trace of a half-smile about the corners of his big mouth. Was he thinking of the double fee the State had helped him earn by repeating its effort to take Sam St. Mary out of circulation? Or, was he glancing into the dim chambers of years gone by, when the serpent's trail was visible on the western sands, and a theatrical threat of retribution was being uttered by a penniless, friendless boy?

Lee Bird was old enough to be held accountable for his own acts, however indiscreet, so the county officers drew murder charges up against him, and filed them. He was 62 years old when he shot his 57 year old brother to death. When running workmen from the industrial houses along the Missouri, Kansas, and Texas Railroad tracks had arrived at the place where a number of rapid pistol shots had been heard, they found sour-faced old Lee with a pistol, and with blood running from a gaping wound on his left hand. Anderson Bird, his brother and partner, was lying dead on the rough floor. An unsatisfactory warehouse partnership had just been dissolved.

The outcome of the Bird case was a stimulus for Pruiett's already cynical attitude toward the court and jury system. The old man was not entitled to be convicted. He had been attacked by a morbid and disgruntled brother, armed with an axe, and the shots which he had fired to stop him had begun only after he had suffered a vicious wound from the flailing weapon. Pruiett, in Bird's defense, presented the facts just as they were, witness for witness and circumstance for circumstance. The jury found him guilty of manslaughter, one of the minor offenses embraced in the charge, and sentenced him to four years in the penitentiary.

If Bird's counsel had slumbered or coasted as he negligently relied upon the prevalence of justice to protect his client at the trial, he made up for it as he presented his motion for a new trial, after the old man had been convicted. When he had concluded a lengthy and laborious tirade, which included a denunciation of the good faith of the individual jurors and the fairness of the trial court in instructing the jury as to the law, he arose to his toes and shook a menacing fist in the face of the trial judge.

"An' I give you my word of honor as a lawyer and a gentleman, that old Lee Bird will never serve one second of this infamous sentence. The Court may as well set it aside right now, and give him a new trial, for the dark walls of prison will never surround this suffering old man."

The court understood Pruiett's meaning. He was saying that he would keep the defendant out on bond until he had completed an appeal, that he would reverse the conviction on appeal, and that he would obtain his acquittal in another trial. He was skeptical and unimpressed, however, and the motion was denied.

The Criminal Court of Appeals, passing on the Bird appeal almost a year later, affirmed the conviction on December 13, 1922. Pruiett had had the news long enough to take the bottle from the desk and have the battleship jaw out-thrust. It galled him to lose any kind of a case; but, in this one, with his courtroom threat and promise fresh enough to be revived with the publication of the outcome of the appeal, he was doubly annoyed. He didn't leave his office until after dark; and, although he had imbibed freely during the afternoon, he could still see, by the light of the corner street lamp, that considerable notice was being given to the Bird decision. He had bought a late edition of the paper.

Pruiett was pondering and scowling over the outcome of the case and its relation to his violent prediction, and trying to figure some technical way to continue the fight until he could make his word good, as he stepped into the living room of his home.

"The coroner just called, Moman," his wife said, without the preliminary of a greeting. "Lee Bird's dead." According to the *Oklahoma News* on December 14, 1922, "he shot himself in the chest with a rifle, and the coroner said it was despondency over his conviction that caused

Mrs. Lottie Baker, (above) shot and killed her husband, Lusco W. Baker, (below) at 7 p. m., Sunday, March 16, while church bells were ringing for evening worship.

One shot was fired, and the man fell dead at the alley entrance on N. Harvey-st., between Main and Grand-av.

Brandishing her pistol, Mrs. Baker is alleged [illegible] Agnes Smith, the girl with Baker, to go to the police station where the gun was surrendered and the story told.

LOTTIE BAKER KILLED HER HUSBAND, LUSCO, AS HE WALKED AWAY FROM HER WITH ANOTHER WOMAN. PRUIETT THREW THE UNWRITTEN LAW IN REVERSE, AND SCREAMED SCRIPTURES LIKE A HOLINESS PREACHER. "IF AMERICAN MANHOOD WON'T RESPECT AND PROTECT ITS WOMANHOOD, THEN I SAY, LET THEM TAKE UP ARMS AND PROTECT THEMSELVES," PRUIETT SHOUTED TO THE JURY. WHILE THE JURY WAS DELIBERATING BAKER'S FATE, THE OKLAHOMA COUNTY PROSECUTOR STATED TO THE PRESS THAT "IF I EVER SHOT SOMEONE IN THE BACK, DELIBERATELY AND COLD-BLOODEDLY, THE FIRST PERSON I'D RUN TO SEE WOULD BE MOMAN PRUIETT." COURTESY *MOMAN PRUIETT: CRIMINAL LAWYER.*

him to do it. He had a copy of the paper with the story of it by his bed, when they found him. The poor old man won't have to serve the sentence, after all, will he?"

"That fellow Guy MacKenzie was the sorriest little piker I ever saw, or ever heard of," Pruiett observed, as he spat and spewed. "If he'd a-been on the veldt in the days of Kimberly, he'd a got him a job on a little sand dredge, an' scraped the surface for day wages, rather than take a chance of diggin' for a fortune in the diamond cuts."

The boys who had dropped in to hear some Pruiett lore, from the stud himself, listened in quiet anticipation.

"There he was, a well-driller by trade, an' the big oil strikes around Tulsa had crude runnin' over the derrick tops an' floodin' the country, but old Guy just set still. William G. "Bill" Skelly, an' Frank Phillips, an' Tom Slick borrowed a little money an' put a few extra lengths of stem on their drills, and made billions of dollars. Guy goes right on drillin' water wells for a $150 a month, an' keepin' his friends' wives company when they was out of town or away from home."

"He got life for that killin', didn't he?" one of the fans inquired.

"Yeah," Pruiett answered, "an' the guy that defended him did a good job. I wasn't sure 'til it was over that they wasn't goin' to fry him. I couldn't get into the case on account of the one I got to try next week; but, I was watchin' it awful close. That was a' awful murder."

"Did you know old Charley Reuter, the one that got it?" someone asked.

"He was a personal friend of mine," Pruiett said. "He was a lawyer over there at Tulsa, an' a perty good one. He'd a' been a rich man if that baggage hadn't a' messed him up. He was a member of the School Board, an' he'd organized his own oil company. They say that he had some good holdin's, but he was too swanky to drink city water. He made his big mistake when he started to have that well drilled in his back yard. I ain't never seen a well-digger you could trust."

"What's the real facts about it, Moman? Give us the dope."

"It's just exactly like it came out in the paper while they was tryin' MacKenzie," Pruiett answered. "Reuter had a wife that was gettin' middle-aged; but, she had them perpetual youth ideas in her head. They had two kids, eight an' ten years old, an' old Charley didn't want any more, so he quit work. Laura, that's the old lady, had saved her figger an' didn't want to be a sedate little housewife. She wanted to play; so, when old Charley'd come home an' read his paper, an' go off to bed by hisself, she opens up for the well-digger. Guy wasn't no piker when it came to housewives. He'd spud into the preacher's bedroom if he got a half a chance."

"Laura always had a sign so Guy could tell whether Charley was at home or not." Explained the *Tulsa World,* on September 27, 1913. "When the shade in a back window upstairs at Reuter's house was down, it meant that Charley was at home; and, when it was up, it meant that he was away an' the coast was clear."

"Charley found out about it, an' started to kill 'em both. He got to thinkin' about the kids, an' he was really that kind of a father, an' he decides to just keep his mouth shut an' get along the best he can. They lived in a great big house out on Cheyenne Avenue in Tulsa, an'

Charley moved all his things into a single room up near the kids' room an' stays away from Laura altogether. They lived there like that for over a year before Charley got his head shot off. It was right in that room that Joe Baker shot him. Laura let Joe in the basement window, an' as soon as he'd killed Charley, she jumped out on the roof by her window an' went to yellin' an' screamin'. They wanted to make it look like robbery, an' Joe grabbed all of Charley's diamonds. That was to be part of the pay, what he got off of Charley an' out of his room, except he had to split the diamonds with Laura."

"Where did the hitch come in?" one of his listeners inquired.

"The hitch was in it all the time. Ever'body knew Laura was mamma for Guy MacKenzie. They just rounded up Guy an' his gang an' started puttin' the pressure to 'em, 'til one squawked. They had a mixed-breed name Grover Bellew, he even had some Mexican in him, besides Greek, an' Choctaw an' freedman. He puked up a tubful, an' the show was over. Guy an' Joe Baker are down at that state prison in McAlester doin' life, an' Laura's out on bond. That's one case that's got me worried."

"What's your defense?"

"We just don't know nothin' about it. Guy ain't squealed, nor neither has Joe Baker. It's just Bellew an' some unfavorable circumstances about the house that's against us. I got the venue changed away from Tulsa, too much prejudice there after trying MacKenzie an' Baker; so, we're tryin' it up at Bartlesville. It'll be bad enough up there."

"DETECTIVES FOIL PLOT OF HIRED GUNMEN TO ASSASSINATE BELLEW," proclaimed the *Tulsa World* on September 27, 1913, in glaring red column heads. Acting on an underworld tip which advised that the half-breed wouldn't live to repeat the testimony he had given in the MacKenzie-Baker trial at Tulsa, but that Mrs. Reuter's defense plotted to have him killed, a group of special officers out of Tulsa County made an investigation. "Detectives Ed Egan and Charles McCloud, representing the prosecuting attorney's office of Tulsa County, searched the city [Bartlesville] for desperate characters. They found the quartet of gunmen ['Blacky' Anderson, 'Kid Glove' Charley, 'Arizona' Harry, and Tom Jones] in consultation in the back room of a cheap rooming house. When confronted by the detectives, the men denied that they were here to kill Bellew; but, they agreed to leave town if spared arrest."

Pruiett may have considered a plan to suppress the Bellew testimony; but, it was acknowledged to be most unfavorable where his client's interests were concerned.

" 'A few weeks before [the murder]', said Bellew, 'Guy [MacKenzie] mentioned to me about getting Joe Baker to murder Charlie Reuter. I told him I didn't think Joe would do it, but he said that Joe was hard up and he could get him to do it by showing him that he would have the protection of Mrs. Reuter. That evening, Guy told me that Joe Baker was going to do the killing for $200 and whatever he found on Charlie. He said Joe had been over to the Reuter home that afternoon, so Mrs. Reuter could show him the house. On Saturday morning, just before the killing, I saw Joe Baker and Joe said he had been shown through the Reuter home from basement to the top bedrooms by Mrs. Reuter. He said he was going to do the killing that night. He was to get $200 and what money he found on Reuter, and Mrs. Reuter was to get back the diamonds that he took from Reuter. Guy said that Mrs. Reuter was to give an altogether different description of the man than Joe was. She was to say that he was a big man. [Joe was a small man]. He said Mrs. Reuter was to place the key on the outside of her bedroom door, go to bed, keep quiet and then, after the shots had been fired, to scream. Guy said that Mrs. Reuter had said she would furnish plenty of money to hire competent counsel to defend him if he got arrested'."

" 'Guy said that after he got Reuter out of the way, he didn't know whether he would marry Mrs. Reuter or not. He said her little boy looked so much like Charlie that when it grew up he would have trouble with it. He said that Mrs. Reuter was to stake him in business after the murder, and he was going to take me to Mexico and start a horse ranch. Then Guy told me what I was to do. I was to wait in the auto for Joe, drive him north of town about a mile, where he was to burn the clothes he had on and to change into the ones I had in the automobile. Then we were to go back to town and I was to ditch Joe and then go on to MacKenzie's myself and go to bed. Guy was to be in Skiatook that night, so he could prove an alibi'."

" 'The night of the murder we drove around town a while. Joe and I went by the Reuter home and saw a light burning and Joe seemed a bit uneasy. We went back to MacKenzie's and got a suit case Joe had brought up from his room, which contained some old clothes. He put on a pair of overalls, an overcoat, a mask, cloth gloves and some old shoes.It was about 1 o'clock Sunday morning then. Just as I left in the car, Joe says to me, 'if you cold turkey me and I ever see you again, you're a dead one'."

" 'I went over to the orchard and pretty soon I heard a whistle and there was Joe all out of breath. He had the money and diamonds in a handkerchief. I asked him how Mrs. Reuter acted and he said she did fine. She was screaming with all her might when he left there. We decided to go a different route than the one agreed on; so, we went to the Pease ranch. We went up a canyon and burned all the clothes Joe had on and the mask. He put on his other clothes then. Joe then told me he had done his job. He said he went into the home through the basement [window], locked Mrs. Reuter's door on the outside and then poked his gun in Charlie's ribs and woke him up and told him to give him his money. Charlie handed him the money and then the diamonds, one at a time'."

" 'Joe then told him to turn around. Then, he shot him in the back of the head. He shot the second time, but the bullet went wild. The third time he shot him in the head as Reuter was lying on the floor. Then, he left the house [and ran to meet me at the orchard]'."

Glenn Condon, in a special to the *Tulsa World,* summed up motive and execution in a crisp paragraph. "Guy MacKenzie wanted Reuter killed so that he could satisfy his passionate love for Laura Reuter; she was no unwilling participant in the purpose. It was she who set the stage and turned down the lights for the midnight tragedy which cast an air of mystery about the home on Cheyenne Avenue."

The widow, who had cast herself into mourning, made good on her promise to 'furnish plenty of protection and stand behind' her fellow conspirators. After MacKenzie and Baker had been convicted and had been moved to the State Prison at McAlester, she disguised herself and slipped in on visitor's day, to talk to them, and to pat Guy's hand through the bars. "Pat Oates, deputy warden of the Oklahoma State Penitentiary testified this afternoon that Mrs. Reuter visited Guy MacKenzie and Joe Baker in the penitentiary two months ago. She represented herself to be a Miss Gordon, a famed detective in the employ of Moman Pruiett."

Pruiett assured the jury that Laura was completely innocent, in spite of a 'few circumstances that might look a little funny'. Things looked too funny. The jury found her guilty, and she drew next to the maximum, the henceforward in confinement, at the State Penitentiary. But, it was only the beginning for Pruiett. He filed his motion for a new trial, and Judge R. H. Hudson, who had tried the case, was so confused by the time the black charger had bellowed at him for two hours, and threatened with flailing fists in his face, that he didn't know whether Laura had received a fair trial or not. Laura's counsel, in no uncertain terms, charged that justice had aborted.

Resolving the doubt in the accused's favor, as old Thomas Jefferson had suggested that it be done in his document on the fundamentals of liberty and justice, the trial court set the conviction aside and assigned the case for trial again. The citizenry of the South and West, and especially that of the oil metropolis of the Arkansas's brink, pulled frantic hairs. Pruiett slipped across the State line to the resort where the springs were hot and the female guests from the East, strolling the hotel veranda, were similarly inclined. He had to have a little rest before the next murder trial.

Laura stood trial again, in January and February 1914, but the details of a long story can be dispensed with and a much shorter treatment of the subject substituted. She was acquitted and restored to actual liberty. Her confinement, aside from the year's figurative restraint while under bond, had amounted to a total of 48 hours in jail, in Tulsa County.

Lottie Baker shot Lusco, her husband, on a downtown street in Oklahoma City. He died before he could be conveyed to a hospital. D. V. Monroe shot Marguerite Ellis in a sporting house where Marguerite was eking out what is reputedly a tough livelihood by merchandising her charm and virtue. Her death ultimately resulted from the wound. Both were charged with murder, both were tried in the District Court of Oklahoma County, both were represented by Moman Pruiett, and both were acquitted and restored to liberty by the juries which heard the cases. Lottie was a penniless waitress; Monroe was a wealthy business man and broomcorn planter.

Monroe, although he knew it not, was helping to pay Lottie Baker's fee when he gave Pruiett $7,500. But, he was not getting full credit for it, for when Lottie's case was going to the jury Pruiett told them, in his pathetic, self-sacrificing manner, that he was serving her out of the kindness of his heart, that he was receiving no compensation for his services.

Pruiett reached a new high for acrimony in his argument in Lottie Baker's case. He coined invectives which shocked the members of his own whiskey-consuming entourage. "He's unfit to preside while a female canine whelps her pups," he roared, speaking of the Justice of the Peace, who presided at Lottie's preliminary hearing, and then came as a State's witness in the District Court trial, to impeach her.

"She had a perfect right to kill him," he howled, referring to dead Lusco. "If American manhood won't respect and protect its womanhood, then I say, let them take up arms and protect themselves. If any man had treated my daughter as Lusco did Lottie, I'd have taken my pistol..." He crouched, with his right index finger trembling taut in front of him, like a pistol barrel. He was re-enacting the Charley Wiseman incident, or the Doctor Threlkeld shooting. "I'd have taken my pistol and I'd have shot him through the heart, and as he fell to the earth I would have placed my ear over his bloody bosom, and listened with relish and satisfaction while I heard his soul yelpin' its way into hell!" When he concluded, he was on his hands and knees before the jury, with his head cocked sidewise like a listening pup. He was holding his ear over an imaginary bloody bosom.

According to the *Oklahoma News,* on January 13, 1915, "A throbbing human drama was enacted late Tuesday afternoon in a room at 700 East Fifth Street. Marguerite Ellis, 22, girl of the underworld, paralyzed from the waist down and given four years, at most, to live, was a white thing, hardly distinguishable from the snowy linen of the bed. She faced D. V. Monroe wealthy merchant of Lindsay, who is under a charge of assault with intent to kill. Since the night of Dec. 28, [1914] when Monroe shot Marguerite Ellis in a resort at 9½ West California Ave., the two had not met. The meeting was the result of the Justice Court's desire to get the girl's story of the shooting, on which, more than anything else, Monroe's fate hinges."

"On the table near the girl's bed was a small leather-bound Bible. Near it was half an orange. Above her head was a picture of Cupid, armed with his bow and arrows. Other pictures were on the wall. Attorney Moman Pruiett, head counsel for the defense, and reputed to be a bulldog when a point was to be gained, asked his questions of the girl as gently as if he were her nurse."

"That girl's goin' to die," Pruiett said, as he and his client left the room.

"What'll happen then?" Monroe asked.

"You get plumb relieved of this assault an' intent charge you got against you," he answered, sarcastically, "an' you get a nice little murder charge against you instead. That's all that'll happen."

"I'm countin' on you to protect my interests in this," Monroe said.

"I've already told you we ought to pay off in the damage suit the girl's filed against you. She's got a perfect cause of action against you. You shot her, an' she's hopelessly and totally disabled as the result of it. A settlement before she dies will help to make dyin' a little easier for her, an' it'll make defendin' you for murder a sight easier."

"It's a shake-down," Monroe growled. "She's sued me for $10,000, an' look at all the expenses I been to in this thing already."

"The fiddler always charges extra when he sees a' old bastard like you tryin' to hop with the young folks," Pruiett said dryly. "If you get out of it with payin' all you got, but don't have to go to the pen, you can count yourself lucky."

"What makes you so sure I'm goin' to face a murder charge? How do you know she won't live a long time, or get well?"

"I been talkin' to her doctor," Pruiett answered. "That bullet hit half of her spinal cord. She's paralyzed from the waist down, now, but there's a gradual sloughin' of the balance of the cord, an' she won't live thirty days. They thought at first it might be a matter of years, but not now. She's a goner."

"What can we settle with her for, in the damage case?"

"I know her lawyer awful well, old E. J. Giddings. I've tried lots of lawsuits with him. I think I can get a release, for fifty cents on the dollar."

"That's too much," Monroe grumbled.

"Would you trade places with her for $5,000?" Pruiett inquired.

"No," Monroe answered. "I ain't no whore... "

"You just think you ain't," Pruiett snapped. "What was you doin' in the whore-house, then?"

"I ain't payin' you all this money to be insulted," Monroe sulked. "If you don't... "

"I'll get out an' let you get some one else to represent you if you want me to," Pruiett answered. "You're the head man, but if you was able to handle all the things that are goin' to come up in this case, or able to tell your lawyer how to handle 'em, you'd be a damn fool to pay out money for a lawyer's service. Either give me some authority to do what I think ought to be done, or fire me an' let me get out of the case."

Monroe studied. "I couldn't have anybody representin' me in this kind of a mess but you," he said. "Go ahead an' settle with her; get the best deal you can for me, an' I'll back you up in it. I'm sure you know best what ought to be done."

Pruiett stood beside the stricken harpy's bedside again. "I ain't got no business bein' here," he said, abruptly. "I told the landlady that it might look bad for Mr. Monroe, me comin' here to talk to you, without your lawyer here, or any of the prosecutin' attorney's men."

"She told me," the girl said, "but I wanted to talk to you, an' I told her to go back an' tell you to come."

"What do you want?" he asked.

"Just to thank you, first," she said. "Mr. Giddings told me that you made Monroe settle with me for the injuries. The money I got is goin' to make me comfortable, an' help me to do some things I wanted to do, before I go."

"Don't bother about that," he answered. "You don't need to thank me. Monroe's got plenty of money."

"I want to see my mother before I die," Marguerite said.

"That's natural," Pruiett said, shortly. His eye was perfectly dry. "Where is she?"

"She lives in Indiana, at Gary," the girl whispered. "She's poor; lives up there with my step-father. I'd like to go back."

"What's holdin' you?" he asked. "I got the money for you. Why don't you go ahead?"

The girl smiled. She had lived the hard way; she was worldly wise, like Pruiett. "You ain't so tough," she smiled up at him. "You don't scare me with that loud mouth and wild eye. You're my friend. I trust you."

"What you got in your mind for me to do?" he demanded.

"I want you to go with me—to take me," she said. "I was in Mercy Hospital at Chicago, when I was a kid. I have dreams of goin' there;

that maybe they might be able to save me; but, if they can't, I'll be close to home. I've got the money, but I ain't got the strength. If I had someone like you, to cheer me an' bully me, an' give me courage, then I'd be able to stand the trip. That's the main reason why I sent for you."

"That wouldn't be right, child," he said. She looked like a child, pale with pain, and with fear of the ordeal approaching. The hard lines of life were gone from her face. In their place was the soft gleam of death. "I couldn't do that. I'm against you in all these things. I've got to try to justify what Monroe's done to you. He's paid me. We'd both be criticized for it; they'd say that you was sellin' out on the State, an' that I was influencin' you to keep you from makin' a statement against my client."

"I don't care what they say," she sighed. "I don't have a friend in the world... "

"You got your own lawyers," he argued.

"They haven't done anything for me. I wouldn't have had any help at all, if it hadn't a' been for you. You're the only one that's had a kind thought for me."

"I'm busy," he argued. "I got cases set for trial all over this country. I couldnt get away from business."

"I'm just askin' you to do me this favor, this last one," she whispered. "I'd forgive Mr. Monroe if you did. I really don't have to go, I guess, but... "

Pruiett went with the dying girl. He held her hand on the Pullmans to Chicago, and he stood by her bedside while the heads of the Mercy Hospital made their deliberate examination of her. He wiped the tears that trickled down her made-up cheek when they told her that she couldn't be saved; that she must die. In the cheaply furnished room at Gary, which was her mother's home, he was holding her hand when she died according to the *Daily Oklahoman* on March 26, 1915.

Monroe had to stand trial for murder in June of 1915. Pruiett put his painful recollection of Marguerite's trust and devotion behind him as he plunged into the difficult defense. He could go soft, and let a distressed dame lead him out on a mercy errand if he wanted to; but, when it came to murder, the State was always wrong. Pruiett's clients were never guilty.

The sordid details of the shooting, and the events which preceded them, were preserved in a statement which Marguerite Ellis signed at the hospital, shortly after she was admitted there. "I am conscious and aware of impending death as I make this true statement," the paper began.

"It's incompetent. It's heresay," Pruiett shouted. "Even if she was makin' a death-bed statement, which she wasn't, she was mistaken. She wasn't dyin'; she lived almost two months after she signed this outrage that the County Attorney cooked up for her. It's not a death-bed declaration."

The bloody document was read to the jury. "That girl didn't have any idea of what was in that paper when she signed it," Pruiett whispered to Monroe. "They talk about me doctorin' evidence in murder cases, but if I ever pull a trick as raw as this one, I hope lightnin' strikes me dead. I'll fudge a little for mercy, but these bastards that're supposed to be public officers are tryin' to fudge you into the electric chair."

They fought it out before twelve men, elated with each sordid scrap which fell from the swinging scale in the hand of the blind goddess. That phony statement made it bad, but there's lots of ways of gettin' around incriminatin' evidence when you're tryin' your case to a jury.

"Mister Monroe was met at the depot by runners from Gracie Goode's hell-house," he told the jurors, commenting on the evidence after the Court's instructions had been read. "Gracie Goode kept a few handsome girls like Marguerite Ellis—I held her hand as she died, an' she was as fair as a Grecian slave, God bless her soul—an' she kept a lot of illicit liquor. This evidence shows that through the wiles of this beautiful girl, Monroe was persuaded to get drunk. When they thought he was drunk enough to be rolled—for them to get his pocket book and all his money—Gracie came into the room, helped Marguerite with that little job, an' was sneakin' out the door with it, when Monroe caught onto what was goin' on. He grabbed his pistol an' called for Gracie to halt. She kept runnin', an' he aimed at her legs to stop her, an' fired. Marguerite screamed and stumbled into the line of fire, so that she received the bullet in her back which killed her."

He paused and scratched his head in honest contemplation of the situation. "The Court, in his instructions, told you what murder was. This is not murder. This is an accident, a wholly avoidable accident, which, except for the related circumstances which cause clean minds to become prejudiced, would never be considered with the crime of murder. If he'd a hit Gracie, as he intended to hit her, it might have been murder. But, he was stuck on Marguerite, in his drunken state he held her in the tenderest esteem, and he would never have harmed her. So, he had no intent, no premeditation, which the Court tells you was necessary before the crime of murder can be complete."

"Can you agree, beyond all reasonable doubt... ?" He launched into his highly developed analysis of reasonable doubt. He lashed them with his logic. He captivated them with his eloquence, his gestures, and his pathos. Monroe was acquitted according to *The Daily Oklahoman* of June 25, 1915. He went home sadder, wiser, and poorer by $25,000.

The victory celebration was in full swing. The drinks were on the black stud, and he was having plenty of drinks himself.

"Now that it's all over," one of the boys suggested, "tell us why the hell Monroe wanted to kill a little doll like Marguerite. I've heard all kind of theories, but none of 'em, not even the one you argued to the jury, sounds right to me. What did he want to do it for?"

"You'll laugh your head off," Pruiett grinned. "Old Monroe was worn out. He'd had his day, an' it was gone; but, he tried to hang on. Well, he got full of corn an' decided he was a buckeroo again, so he went down to Gracie's to celebrate. His mind an' his pocketbook made a contract with Marguerite, but his old wore out body couldn't deliver on it. He couldn't get his rhubarb up—see? It made him so mad, realizin' the uselessness of his old hide, an' with perty little Marguerite a'layin' there, that he just pulled out his gun an' shot her."

A lusty whoop went up around the table.

"A few of his kind would make hustlin' a god damn precarious occupation, now, wouldn't it?" Pruiett inquired, innocently.

The defense of Lottie Baker in March and June of 1919 had a catchy twist to it. Pruiett threw the unwritten law into reverse, and using it as a background for a thin plea of self-defense, screamed Scriptures like a traveling Holiness preacher, and won his case. Lottie was a hard-working hasher. Lusco, the deceased, was a shiftless pimp, who offered to sell magazines for a blind. Agnes Smith, a police court prostitute, who carried the alias of Dirty Breeches, held down the pivot position in the triangle. Lottie killed her husband, Lusco, because she caught him with Agnes. Agnes was the principal witness for the State.

She was on the stand, and Pruiett was cross-examining.

"You say your name is Agnes Smith?" he inquired.

"Yes, sir," Agnes answered, meekly. She knew what was coming.

"You are generally known, about the police station, and on California Street, as Dirty Breeches, ain't you?"

"We object," the prosecuting attorney howled.

"What's the purpose of that line of examination?" the Court demanded.

"It would go to her credibility as a witness," Pruiett said.

"Overruled," said the Court. "Go ahead an' answer."

"They call me that, but I don't like it," Agnes retorted, "an' it ain't so."

"All right. You say it ain't so," Pruiett repeated, agreeably, as he turned to note the good-humored grins on the juror's faces. "Now, you admit that you were in Lottie's room with Lusco on the day of this fatal occurrence, don't you?"

"Just like I said," Agnes answered. "I went up there to sign a contract to sell magazines for Lusco. We was there just a few minutes, an' we left to go up town an' have a notary stamp it."

"You mean you was there just a few minutes, an' Lottie came in—unexpectedly, an' you had to leave?"

"We was leavin' anyway," Agnes said. "Lusco took his magazines an' we started up town."

"Lottie asked him to stay there with her, didn't she?"

"She told him to, but he said he had to get his work done. He went out anyway."

"You went with him?"

"Yes, I went with him."

"An' Lottie followed you, didn't she?"

"Yes, she tagged right along behind us, cussin' me an' Lusco, an' threatenin' to kill us both. All I was tryin' to do was to get away from her."

"You've been layin' up with Lusco for a long time, haven't you?"

"I have not," Agnes answered, with feeling.

"You knew Lusco was a knife man, didn't you?"

"I knew he carried a knife, but I didn't know he was a knife man."

"Didn't you know he cut a playmate to death, when he was kid, up at Paris, Illinois?"

"We object," the County Attorney cried, bouncing out of his chair.

"Sustained," droned the Court.

"I'll make my proof on it," Pruiett promised. "Did you know he cut a policeman to ribbons with a knife, up at Terre Haute, Indiana?"

"We object," the prosecution howled again.

"Sustained," said the Court.

"I know what I'm doin'," Pruiett said, serenely. "Did you know that he was tried an' convicted of rape up at Terre Haute?"

"You'll have to offer that proof in the proper manner, if you've got it, Mr. Pruiett," the Court interrupted, ahead of another objection.

"All right, your honor," Pruiett grinned. "I just thought one time was as good as another for that kind of information. Now look here, Dirty—I mean, Agnes. When you got up there about a block from the police station, Lusco turned on Lottie an' told her to go back, didn't he?"

"Maybe he did," Agnes agreed, "he'd been tellin' her to go back ever since we left the roomin' house."

"An' he started to pull out this long bladed knife he always carried, didn't he?"

"He certainly did not," Agnes answered, indignantly. "Lottie had been still for a minute, an' I thought maybe she had decided to let us alone. Then I happened to glance back an' I saw her up close behind Lusco, with the pistol out. She shot him right in the back of the head, an' he didn't know she was near to him."

"How many prostitution charges against you have the police promised to dismiss for tellin' such a story?" Pruiett snapped.

"Not any of 'em," Agnes came right back.

"Then they have got a few over you, haven't they?" Pruiett grinned.

"Not very many," Dirty Breeches sulked.

The State offered the blood-spattered magazines, cheap pulps, which Lusco had been carrying when Lottie assassinated him. *Household Magazine,* with a red hen and a bunch of yellow chicks on its front cover, was amongst the lot. Pruiett picked it up and studied it.

"Was this magazine in the bunch?" he demanded of Agnes.

"It was," she answered.

"It's a' old hen, lookin' after her brood, her little family, isn't it?"

"That's what it looks like to me," Agnes agreed.

"Lottie was just tryin' to protect her husband from you, wasn't she? Tryin' to get him away from you?"

"We object," the prosecutor cried.

"I'll withdraw the question," Pruiett said. "That's all of this witness."

Pruiett produced an elaborate free defense for Lottie. He brought the testimony of Oklahoma City Police Captain Van Cleave, and Matron Catherine O'Donnel, to establish that departed Lusco had an unsavory reputation at Terre Haute. It still stunk, on warm nights, up the brick alleys of the old town. He proved that he'd raped a girl and been convicted for it, that he'd carved an Indiana policeman to shreds, and had killed a childhood playmate with a knife. Was Lottie entitled to carry a gun, to protect her life, when she had business with Lusco?

"Lusco got just what was comin' to him," Pruiett screamed at his jury. "He was a knife man. He dug his own grave with his own knife."

"There was poor, long-sufferin' Lottie, trying to hold her meager happiness, trying to keep her little home together," he whispered. He grabbed the *Household* Magazine and shook it, hen and chicks and all, in the jury's face. "O Jerusalem, Jerusalem, which killest the prophets and stoneth them that are sent unto thee;" he cried, plucking a passage from St. Luke from his unyielding memory, "How often would I have gathered thy children together, as a hen doth gather her brood under her wings, and ye would not!"

He paused to mop his perspiring forehead. "And ye would not. And ye would not," he ruminated. " 'Go away, Dirty Breeches, and let my husband alone,' Lottie begged, but she would not. She would not. 'Come home, with me Lusco! Abandon this whore and come back home with me!' But he would not. He would not. 'I'll take you back, Lusco, rotten and debased as you are, for you're all I've got an' you're mine; I'll gather you under my wing like a hen doth gather her brood and I'll work and slave for you',—but ye would not; ye would not."

He wheeled on Agnes, who was sitting with the spectators in the crowded courtroom. "The harlot looked from the casement of her window and discerned the weary youth, and she sought him; come, come to me, my bed is perfumed with aloes." He shook his fist at Dirty Breeches. "And the weary youth went straight like an ox to the slaughter."

Pruiett's argument for Lottie Baker's acquittal lasted three hours and a half. Lottie was paying him nothing; so, he received no more for his effort than he would have received for a five minute observation, except the victory. If an innocent man could be convicted, a guilty woman could be acquitted. The system should be upset and the thieves and murderers should be circulated back into society. He had to make the jury forget that Lusco had stopped that bullet with the back of his head. He had to lead their minds away from Lottie's undeniable guilt.

When the jury returned, he heaved a tired, satisfied sigh. They agreed that Lottie was free of guilt according to *The Daily Oklahoman* on June 15, 1919.

"TO MY CLIENTS: This is to notify you that while I am burdened with the charge of murder against me and while this charge is of deep concern to me and my loved ones, yet I feel that the interests of my clients should be safeguarded and every legal right should be exhausted in their defense. I have employed Mr. Moman Pruiett, who will act in conjunction with my partner, Mr. Geo. F. Short, in looking after their interests. This employment pertains to all criminal cases in which I have been employed, and I assure that your interests will be protected. (Adv.) J.M.LEGGETT." Thus read the notice that appeared in Idabel's *Democrat-Record,* on July 15, 1915.

The *Democrat-Record* for Idabel, a town in the timbered Kiamichi Mountain section of Oklahoma—on the line the Frisco had cut and trestled from Rogers to Paris—was carrying a classified preamble to a Pruiett prowl on jury justice. "One of the most horrible tragedies that has occurred in Idabel since it was made an incorporated town, occurred here Saturday evening about 7:30 o'clock, when James M. Leggett, an attorney, shot Hiram C. Strawn to death in the office of Esq. D. B. Price, in the second story of the DeBerry Building. Just seventy-one days before the killing, Virgil Strawn, a brother, was shot from ambush and killed in the northeastern part of the county, and A. W. Lail was charged with the murder. Leggett was the leading counsel for Lail, and had succeeded in getting him released on bail."

Leggett, a Mississippian, had picked the booming Kiamichi lumber district for developing his legal talent, and he had been more than casually successful. Cash circulated freely through the hills. The big companies were shaving whole mountainsides at a swoop, and the old Frisco couldn't get enough cars to keep even with orders for hauling ties and lumber out of the camps. The accused lawyer had plenty of money, and a sensational state of facts involved in his case. Pruiett was interested.

"Can't it wait a day or two?" Pruiett demanded into the transmitter. He was at the Baltimore Hotel in Kansas City, talking over long-distance to George F. Short, Attorney General of Oklahoma from 1922 until 1926. "This's the Fourth of July. We came up here where we could relax an' dissipate a little. You can..."

"I can't either," Short interrupted. "Jim's in a hell of a fix. It ain't like he was just charged with plain murder. It's not like a plain feud. This is a faction fight, an' Jim's killed one of the majority leaders. The Sheriff's guardin' him out at his house at night, an' keepin' him in the jail in the day time. He's goin' to be lynched if we don't make bond and get him out of the county."

"How do I get down there from here," Pruiett inquired.

"Take the Southern Railroad to Ashdowne, Arkansas," Short advised. "I'll have a' automobile meet you an' drive you up here. Get yourself in shape for some work, 'cause there's sure a plenty of it waitin' for you."

Pruiett called the depot before he rejoined the party. "I ain't even got time to get a shave," he complained, as he slammed his dirty shirts, and a pair of large bottles, into his bag, "an' I need a Turkish bath. I wish to god the damn killers'd recognize a National Holiday, like the rest of us, an' lay off. I'm gettin' tired of murder all the time."

According to the *Democrat Record* "Strawn, who is said to have been unarmed, was shot to death with a number of eye witnesses to prove who did the killing. When Leggett went into the building he went back into the office of the justice, where he saw Hiram Strawn sitting in a window, and with some remarks began shooting. The first shots struck Strawn in the arm, and he attempted to get away from Leggett, who was still shooting, and got across the hall, when Leggett, who had followed him to the door, fired the last shot, the bullet striking Strawn in the back."

Bill Maben followed Pruiett down from Kansas City. He and Short, and Maben, were contemplating the case as they bumped over the hill roads toward Idabel.

"I can't see much to hang self-defense on," Pruiett observed.

"Has Jim got a sister?" Maben grinned, winking at Short.

"Jim's got more than his own defense to worry him," Short said. "He's got a lot of law business pending around these parts, and he's not so sure that I can handle it just exactly to suit his clients. He want's to know, first thing, if you'll stay down here an' help me to straighten up his clients' affairs for them?"

"I can't do that," Pruiett objected. "I got so much stuff in my own office that I went stale; I just had to walk off an' leave it. I got to get through here an' hurry home."

"You know how you're able to do that, an' get away with it?" Short countered. "You've got a reputation that's so well known that ever'body knows you got business conflicts all over the country. Counsel an' courts both know it; so, they don't raise hell when you ask for a continuance like they do in other cases. It wouldn't take more than a month, an' we could hustle Jim's case for trial in that time, an' wash the whole business up."

"I can't afford to," Pruiett answered.

"We don't want you to do it as a favor. We're cuttin' fees in all the cases you handle, an' payin' you for defendin' Jim. You can make a years pay out of it." Short was painfully persistent.

"Let's get us a campin' outfit an' open up headquarters on one of these foamy creeks," Maben suggested. "We'd be right close to town, an' it ought to be cool in these pine hills. We could fish, an' drink moonshine... "

"Have you got that writ ready to file, like I told you?" Pruiett asked.

"She's all ready to go," Short answered.

"Bill's got a good idea, finally," Pruiett said. "We'll open up defense headquarters up on Mountain Fork River, an' you can take care of the office stuff in town, an' handle the detail for us. I was around these parts when I was just a kid, an' I think I'd enjoy a little rest on the creekbanks."

"I got a good camp man that I'll send out to manage camp for you," Short agreed. "His name is Goggle-eye Smith."

"That's a good name," Pruiett said. "Does he know where the stills are?"

"He knows where his own is, an' its big enough to take care of your demands. Ain't that enough?"

"That's plenty," Maben sighed from the back seat.

"That District Court ain't goin' to allow bond in this case," Pruiett grinned from his seat on a log. His gaze wandered to a point above the tent top. "Who done that?" he demanded.

"I did," Maben grinned, as he calculated the subject of Pruiett interruption inquiry. "Me an' Goggle-eye did it. It looks real professional, don't it?"

"It looks like hell," Pruiett differed. Nailed across the stalk of a big pine was a yellow plank, bearing the inscription 'Moman Pruiett, Lawyer'. "It looks like the valley," he said. "Where'd you get the lamp-black?"

"It's burnt cork," Maben said. "Me an' Goggle-eye thought you'd like it."

"I'd like it if I could make a little headway with this Leggett case," Pruiett muttered. "That E. G. Nelson, the McCurtain County Attorney, is the meanest guy I ever saw. An' them lawyers from Arkansas, Steel an' J. S. Lake, that're helpin' him, are real grudge fighters. This makes three writs, an' the Court denies bond ever' time."

"George Short told you it was a faction fight, an' that Strawn was a big shot in the majority," Maben said. "What you think you'll do?"

"I want Jim to get sick," Pruiett said. "If it looks like confinement is goin' to wreck his health, the Criminal Court of Appeal will make 'em give bond. I don't think they'd turn me down in the State Court if I could make a good showin'. I'll see that the fancy food Jim's folks're carryin' to him in the jail is flavored with gun-powder. That old black-smoke powder out of a shotgun shell'll make him sick as hell, if I can make him eat it."

"He'll eat worse than that if you tell him to," Maben said. "He'd eat... "

"He may have to before he gets bond," Pruiett interrupted, anticipating the conclusion of the comparison. "Let him puke up about four meals straight an' the County doctor'll have to agree there's somethin' wrong with him. I'll spring a writ an' put the jailor on the stand. That ought to work."

According to the *Democrat-Record* of September 9, 1915, Leggett was released from jail after 33 days of imprisonment because of illness on $15,000 bond.

When Leggett's bond was approved and he was released, Pruiett was still dreaming on Mountain Fork River. He was unwilling to break camp for home and old business. "I got things in good shape at the office," he said. "Ever'things bein' passed until I get my rest over an' my health back. Let's get it circulated around that Leggett ought to be tried right now instead of at the regular fall term of court. The natives would pick it up an' think it was their own idea before night. They'd get a special judge appointed down here, which would beat the regular one, an' we could try the case an' have it over with. We could get ready right here in camp."

"Suits me," Leggett said.

"You're the doctor," Maben agreed.

"I'll go to town in the morning, then, an' send a telegram to the office, sayin' that if they don't set a special docket down here in a day or two, that I'll be in. I'll say that I hope to hell they don't, 'cause a delay of the case would help Leggett. That damn operator is kin to the prosecution, an' he's been givin' 'em copies of ever' wire I've sent since I've been here. They'll pick it up an' have a docket with a special judge workin' in three days."

"This looks more like a hardware store than it does like a courtroom," Pruiett whispered to his client in September of 1915 as the trial started. "There ain't a son-of-a-bitch here that ain't carryin' a gun."

"I know it," Leggett replied. "Harrison Branch, Strawn's brother-in-law, is carryin' a forty-five, an' he's said if the jury don't give me the chair he's goin' to drill me, right here in the courtroom."

"That guy next to him is workin' for me," Pruiett assured him. "If he pulls a gun, it'll be knocked down. But, these prosecutin' attorneys are armed. I ain't never seen nothin' like this, not even in the Sandy Land Court."

"Nelson's carryin' his gun in a shoulder holster," Leggett observed. "That's why he keeps his coat buttoned up in this hot weather."

"An' look at old G. M. Barrett, the prosecuting attorney for McCurtain County, up there makin' the State's opening statement. Smotherin' to death, an keepin' his coat buttoned up clear to his chin. He's got one slung in his arm-pit." Pruiett was pondering as he talked.

"This imported judge don't know about the feud down here," Leggett said. "You think we ought to get a recess, an' tell him these lawyers are armed? I'd like to have a little protection, or the right to carry a gun myself."

"We'd have to amend the Constitution to get you the right to carry a pistol while you was bein' tried for murder," Pruiett grinned. "I got a' idea. I'll get 'em unarmed or get us both killed, an' ruin their damn case at the same time. Wait 'til I make my statement."

When Barrett had concluded, Pruiett began to address the jury. He was making a narrative outline of what the defense proof was going to show. He was immaculate of manner and appearance. He smiled, and he nodded and he bowed, as he interrupted himself and paused before the Court's bench.

"It's extremely warm in the courtroom, this morning," he observed, "and this promises to be a long trial. I wonder if your honor would grant me permission to remove my coat, and proceed in my shirt-sleeves?"

"We have no formal rules here, Mr. Pruiett," the Court said. "You may remove your coat if you care to." Pruiett slid out of his coat and draped it over the back of a chair.

"You other gentlemen may do the same, if you wish," the Court continued. "We might as well be comfortable—all of us. I think I'll take mine off."

Pruiett watched the prosecutors quizzically as the Court stood up and peeled off his coat. They shifted uncomfortably, but made no move to unbutton their coats.

"You can see, gentlemen of the jury," Pruiett continued, in a barely audible hiss, "that I am unarmed. With the might of right behind me, I'll deliver my innocent client from the shadow of guilt, unless I am struck down by a bullet in my back. That's the only way the State will stop me in this case. If the County Attorney, and his special assistant, were to remove their coats, they would display the arms which they deem essential to their program of intimidation and oppression. They may shoot me down, but... "

"Here, here," the Court interrupted. "What kind of an opening statement is this? We're not up to arguments, and I won't stand to hear such charges being made against the State... "

"I demand that Nelson and Barrett be searched by the bailiff," Pruiett roared. Nelson grabbed a bundle of papers from the table and hurried toward the door into the Court Clerk's office. Barrett was close behind him.

A juror in the front row of the box leaped up. "I saw Nelson's gun under his coat, your honor," he cried. "I know about this feud and I've tried hard to keep out of it. If they are goin' to carry it into the courtroom, I'd like to be excused from service in the case. I got a family to support."

"An' so have I," cried another, rising. "They both had guns on. I seen 'em."

"We'll take a recess," the Court ruled. "All the attorneys in this case come into my chambers. I want to talk to you."

"The shows over," Pruiett whispered to Leggett. "That jury's on our side now, an' I'll see that they don't get away. I don't give a god damn what they prove. That jury is goin' to turn you loose."

Leggett was acquitted reported the *Democrat-Record* on October 7, 1915.

How, and why, will continue to be one of the mysteries of the system. When the evidence was all in, including the portion establishing that Strawn was shot in the back, a long-haired fashion plate with a demoniacal glare in his eyes and whiskey odors on his breath, began to parade before the enraptured jury. He defied God Almighty to strike him with lightning if his client wasn't innocent. He challenged the prosecuting attorneys to shoot him in the back if they wanted to keep Leggett from being acquitted. Pruiett, Maben and Leggett slipped out of town before Branch and his surprised associates had time to pull their pistols. Leggett was a free man.

Pruiett and Leggett met six months later. They were on depot platform at Nashville, Tennessee, in April of 1916.

"Where you headed, now?" Leggett grinned.

"I got to go to Lafayette, Tennessee," Pruiett answered. "I got to meet a kid named Jess Knight down there. He's charged with murder back home, an' I'm to bring him in an' surrender him."

"That sounds like a good deal," Leggett agreed. "Goin' to make a lot of money out of him?"

"Naw," Pruiett said, dubiously. "His dad, David H. Knight, is a Baptist preacher, an' I want to do somethin' for the church. They got his brother, John Knight, in the can now, they're both charged in the same killin', an' the old preacher got me to agree to represent 'em. I ain't sure I'll be able to get expenses back. Where the hell you been, an' where you goin'?"

"I've been on slow starvation down home, down at Hattiesburg, Mississippi" Leggett said. "There ain't a livin' for a lawyer down in that country. I'm goin' back to the Kiamich, where there's some dough, an' some fun."

"You ain't goin' to Idabel, are you?" Pruiett inquired.

"I sure as hell am," Leggett grinned.

"You won't last no time. Why, hell's fire, that Harrison Branch is a killer, an' he never will get over wantin' to kill you. You're crazy."

Leggett continued to smile. "It's been six months," he said. "They've all forgot about the trial by this time. I want to get back down in them lumber hills an' make some money. I'm flat."

"You'll be a hell of a lot flatter if you go back in that country," Pruiett said, with finality. "I ain't your lawyer any more, but take my advice an' stay away from there. It ain't healthy."

"Much obliged," Leggett answered, "but, I never was much of a hand to be a' scared. I can take care of myself."

"So long," Pruiett said, extending his hand gravely, for a farewell handshake. "Don't be hollerin' back across the river, an' tellin' me I didn't warn you. When you feel that hot lead a'cuttin' through your guts, just think of old Moman an' what he told you. So long, son."

Pruiett read about it in the paper when he got back to Oklahoma. "I knew it," he said, folding the paper and tossing it aside. "They shot him down on Main Street," according to the *Democrat-Record* of April 20, 1916, before he had time to get his trunk out of the baggage office. Poor old Jim. I heard them bells ringin' in my ears ever since I saw him at Nashville."

CHAPTER SEVENTEEN

WHEREIN THE BLACK STUD CROSSES THE ARIZONA DESERT TO TRY A TRAINROBBER WITH THEATRICAL INCLINATIONS, AND HOW THE BELLS IN HIS EARS CAUSE HIM TO LOSE HIS CASE, BUT SAVE HIS NECK, AND THE NECKS OF HIS DEFENSE ASSOCIATES, FROM THE BLADE OF A FEDERAL COURT INDICTMENT. AND HOW HE DEFENDS HIS OFFICE ASSOCIATE ON A MURDER CHARGE, AND GAINS HIS ACQUITTAL, WHILE THE COUNTRY WAITS TO SEE IF THE ACCUSED IS TO BE SPARED FOR ITS SELECTIVE DRAFT. AND, WHEREIN, BETTY AND THE CAPTAIN MAKE QUIET WITHDRAWAL FROM THE SCENE, AND PRUIETT, WITH MURDER AND DRAFT EVASION BUSINESS ON THE DOCKET, PLEADS GUILTY TO A FEDERAL COUNT OF PURLOINING AN EXTRA DRINK FROM THE FORBIDDEN WELL. AND HOW THE GOVERNOR OF HIS STATE IS MOLESTED BY A DRUNKEN DEPUTY, AND A PRUIETT CLIENT PROMPTLY RELIEVES THE SITUATION BY MURDERING THE OFFENDING OFFICER ON THE SPOT. AND, WHEREUPON, THE OBLIGING PRUIETT DEFENDS AGAIN, AND ACQUITS AGAIN, AND ADDS THE NAME OF AN ILLUSTRIOUS OUTLAW TO THE ALREADY LONG AND DISTINGUISHED LIST OF HIS CLIENTELE.

"The Golden State train robbery case, for which Joe Davis and Jeff Spurlock are being tried in the Federal Court, probably will go to the jury this afternoon, since United States Attorney Flynn had practically closed his address for the government before adjournment at noon. Judge Sawtelle's instructions will follow. Attorney Moman Pruiett, of Oklahoma, sustained his reputation as an eloquent and able advocate in closing for the defense. He explained that the defense had introduced no evidence because they believed that the government had shown nothing against Davis and Spurlock except a mass of suspicion, which he believed unworthy of refutation. He then proceeded to argue that there was no direct testimony to connect the defendants with participation in the holdup, except that of Berthoff, the confessed bandit, and Hynes, the hobo soldier, and that they were unworthy of credence." It was the *Tucson Citizen*, on February 27, 1917, giving its current impressions of events developing at the Federal Court Building at Tucson, Arizona.

The Golden State Limited, crack Pacific Coast unit of the Chicago, Rock Island, and Pacific Railroad lines, had been stopped and looted in the fringe of the southern Arizona desert, near Apache, Arizona, in a throwback to the theatrical stage coach and train holdups of a quarter century before. The apprehension of part of the cash on one of the bandits, and a confession by him, had resulted in the arrest of Joe Davis and Jeff Spurlock. Davis called for Pruiett, who was the saltiest thing in the West, including Earl Rogers and the waning reputation he enjoyed with his local Los Angeles clientele. Spurlock had employed Charles Owen of El Paso, Texas. Owen was a mouthpiece of no mean ability, whose time was occupied, principally, in representing a certain non-resident named Francisco "Pancho" Villa. Villa was encountering numerous legal complications in his operations on the upper side of the Rio Grande.

"I was late gettin' away," Pruiett said as he slid his suit case under the bed. "I just got checked in. Here... One of you can sit on the bed."

"We were gettin' worried about you," Jim Davis said. He was the father of Joe Davis, whose trial was set. "We got a lot of work to do, an' just a couple of days to get it done. What was the matter?"

"My maw's sick," Pruiett answered briefly. "She's dyin'. I started once to wire you I wasn't comin'; but, I decided I might just as well. I figured she'd insist on my comin' if she was in any kind of shape. She always insisted I take care of lawsuits ahead of ever'thing else."

"No hope for her at all?" Owen inquired, sympathetically.

Pruiett shook his head. "Betty—I call her by her first name most of the time, like the old man—was just about the best half of me. I can look back over my whole life an' the only bright spots in it are the ones where she was givin' me a wrinkled hand an' helpin' me over rough places. She told me one time... "

"What did she say?" Davis inquired, as he trailed off.

"It don't make no difference, now," Pruiett answered. "I ain't the one to bother others with my own private troubles. Let's get down to business. Is there any chance of gettin' severances, an' tryin' these cases one at a time?"

"Not a chance in the world," Owen replied, "And... "

"What's the chance of a continuance?"

"Not any better."

"We don't want no continuance," Davis cut in. "We got a bunch of witnesses here, an' it costs a lot of money. They're high-priced witnesses, an' we want to put'em on an' get it... "

"Shut up," Pruiett hissed, in a whisper. "I've had this room reserved ahead of time on a telegram. It may be tapped."

He turned up the mattress and examined the bed springs. He looked behind the pictures on the wall and in the drawers of the writing desk.

"Check that bathroom, an' be sure you do it good," he whispered to Owen, while he turned from the light-fixtures to the corners of the run on the floor. "Don't overlook nothin'. They got a bug in here."

"What the hell you so suspicious about?" Owen demanded. "You an' me aren't charged with anything. You think they'd put a dictograph on us?"

"There ain't nothin' the government won't do to win this case," Pruiett declared. "I had a tip from a con that was on the train. He said that this town was as hot as that gold out of the Golden State's express car that they ain't found yet. He was a guy I can rely on."

"Everything looks all right to me," Davis, senior, said from under the bed.

"I can't find a thing; but, I can feel it, plain as hell," Pruiett grated. "Now, listen. Let's put this gabbin' off 'til tomorrow mornin', an' we'll meet in the cafe for breakfast. I'm all run down an' I got to get some sleep. We can... "

"We ain't got much time to... " Davis started to make an objection.

"We got plenty of time, 'til we locate that bug or get a place to talk where we won't be talkin' into some dick's ear," Pruiett rejoined. "An' do a little thinkin' about my suggestion that we continue this case, will you?"

"I been up a' hour," Pruiett announced, as Owen and Davis came up to his table in the restaurant.

"You smell like it," Davis answered. "I didn't think the saloons opened up that early."

"I didn't think you ever thought," Pruiett snapped. "Joe inherited all the brain you got, an' he's eatin' his breakfast out of a tin tray up in the federal jail."

"That stuff won't get us anywhere," Owen observed, stuffing his napkin into his vest. "Let's talk some sense. What're we goin' to announce when the government calls these cases?"

"Not ready, an' have a motion an' a bunch of affidavits for a continuance ready," Pruiett answered.

"I'll be damned if we do," Davis cut in. "I got a perfect alibi right here in town, an' its cost a'plenty. We're goin' to trial."

"I learned enough, while you was stuffin' your shirt-tail in this mornin', to satisfy me that we ain't got no chance tryin' to make a defense play work," Pruiett said. "That boy on the train said this place was as hot as hell, an' he was just touchin' it. The guy that fixed my drink this mornin' ain't no regular bartender. He's a federal agent in there with his ear drooped over the counter, to pick up all the information he can. There was a punk at one of the front tables actin' drunk—but he wasn't. He's there to listen, an' he goes back to the can ever' few minutes to make a bunch of notes. Ever' joint's goin' to be the same way, an' ever stranger in town is bein' watched and shadowed. My friend said there was four hundred dicks in here—Feds, express company and insurance company detectives—to try to find where the rest of that loot is, an' to send ever'body connected with the defense to a Federal penitentiary."

"I don't believe it," Davis said.

"You won't believe nothin' I tell you, but Joe wouldn't believe anything anybody told him, either," Pruiett retorted. "That's the trouble with the whole bunch of you. Why, I saw a bunch of Mexicans goin' down the street—part of this celebration that's goin on. What'd you call it?"

"Fiesta de los Vaqueros," Owen supplied.

"Yeah, the fiesta," Pruiett continued, "an' they was pullin' them red an' green shawls up around their little tight seats an' lookin' back like they was expectin' a knife in their back. Ever'body's scared; ever'body's suspicious. I can feel the tension in the atmosphere; the bells are ringin' in my head, an' I know it ain't no time to go to trial."

"We'll either try it with you or without you," Davis snapped.

"Can you do anything with him?" Pruiett inquired of Owen.

"I couldn't if I wanted to," Owen answered.

"You mean you want to go to trial in this mess?"

"Might as well, an' get it over with."

"It's two against one," Pruiett announced. "I'm willin' to announce

ORBAN CHESTER PATTERSON, MOMAN PRUIETT'S JUNIOR LAW PARTNER AND BROTHER-IN-LAW, KILLED PURCELL BANKER SAMUEL "SAM" WILLIAMS ON A CROWDED OKLAHOMA CITY STREET. WHEN ASKED FROM HIS JAIL CELL HOW HE WAS FEELING HE REPLIED "DID YOU EVER PICK COTTON AN' DRAG A HEAVY SACK 'TIL YOU THOUGHT YOUR NECK WAS GOIN' TO BREAK, AN' KEEP WATCHIN' THE SUN AND HOPIN' IT WOULD GO DOWN, SO YOU COULD QUIT AND GET THAT AWFUL LOAD OFF YOUR BACK? AND THEN, THE SUN GOT CLEAR OUT OF SIGHT, AND IT BEGAN TO GET DARK REAL SLOW LIKE AND YOU COULD SEE THE OLD MAN AND THE WAGON AT THE END OF THE ROW AN' YOU TOOK THAT STRAP FROM ACROSS YOUR SHOULDER AND AROUND YOUR NECK, AND YOU STOOD UP STRAIGHT AN' TOOK A DEEP BREATH. DID YOU EVER DO THAT? WELL THAT'S HOW I'M FEELIN'. I'M FEELIN' AWFUL DAMN GOOD." PRUIETT WON A NOT GUILTY VERDICT FOR PATTERSON. COURTESY HOWARD K. BERRY PHOTO COLLECTION ready, an' let the boys get a good long stretch, if you two insist, but I'll be damned if I'll let the two of you insist me into goin' along with 'em. That phony alibi is out. We'll let the boys tell the stories they told in the beginnin', follow the statements they gave the government, an' stand on it. We ain't offerin' no corroboration."

"Oh, yes, we are," Davis said, looking toward Owen for support.

"Davis," Pruiett said patronizingly, "anyone listenin', an' I ain't so sure that they ain't, would think I had hired you to give me advice, instead of vica versa. Now get this... It's my final expression in this case. I won't offer a word of that stuff that's been cooked up, an' I'll bet you $500 that any one that does is goin' to the Federal penitentiary, right from the courtroom or the witness stand. I can see it, an' I can smell it, an' I can hear the bells ringin' in my ears. There's the damnedest system coverin' the preparation of this trial that was ever got together. My room's wired, whether I can find the bug or not. Yours is too, both of you, an' all your witnesses have been makin' up a volume of information for the prosecution durin' these last two or three days, but they don't know it. We'll try it straight, on what we got, or old Moman don't even go to the courthouse."

"Quittin', are you?" Davis sneered.

"You're damned right I am," Pruiett snapped.

"I guess we can get along without him, can't we judge?" Davis inquired of Owen.

"I won't stay in the cases without Pruiett; he's been the head man all the way through," Owen said. "If he withdraws, I'm makin' application to the Court to get out myself."

Pruiett picked up the check. "I'm walkin' around on the street for a few minutes, an' then I'm goin' to my room," he said. "Let me know before time to get ready for the noon train, what you want to do about it."

Davis and Spurlock were convicted, according to the February 25, 1917, issue of the *Daily Oklahoman,* and given 15 years apiece. As Pruiett was hurrying out of the building towards his train, he was stopped by Flynn, the District Attorney in charge of the prosecution.

"Pruiett," Flynn said, as he extended his hand, "I've heard a lot about you, and I've wondered about you a lot since I found that you were going to be active in the trial of these cases. I've enjoyed meeting you and trying the case with you."

"Thanks," Pruiett said, dryly. To himself he said: "What you heard wouldn't be to my credit; but, I don't give a damn."

"The government was prepared to resist a studied attempt to acquit these men," Flynn said, as if his dictograph was hooked to Pruiett's head, and he was hearing him think. "We had authentic information showing that a perjured conspiracy was being considered. And, we have information that you are the one who prevented it and kept the defense on a clean, and safe, plane. I want to commend you, and thank you."

Pruiett watched him closely. He didn't know whether Flynn was sincere, or sarcastic.

"Davis's people ought to thank you, too, and a few others—some lawyers," Flynn went on, significantly. "If that thing had gone on, if they hadn't listened to you, there would have been twenty-five indictments out in connection with it by this time. We would have played their perjury back to them on phonograph records, and... "

"Thanks for the information, old man," Pruiett interrupted, as he grabbed his hand and gave it another hurried shake. "I've got to go. Got to make a train. Stay on the level, is my motto... Always stay on the level. I'm glad to have met you, Flynn, and glad to have had this little chat."

Betty was dead when he got back. Her obituary appeared in the March 25, 1917, issue of *The Daily Oklahoman.* He took her to the valley, to the plot beneath the marble shaft he had raised over the grave of Lilly Belle and Stillwell Russell Pruiett, and as he heard the last rites being said over her casket, he supported the stooped, trembling husk of the old Captain. The lingering look which the Captain gave the spot as they guided him away was as much as an assurance to the fresh remains that it would not be long until he was back with her.

Fourteen months later, when the May zephyrs were whipping the blooming branches of the redbuds along the Washita, the Captain returned, and he was lowered to the place which had long been waiting for him. He died in Oklahoma City, and his obituary appeared in *The Daily Oklahoman* on May 27, 1918.

Pruiett was 45. The gusts which disarranged his bared black plumage as he stood there beside his father's grave, were unable to expose a single fading strand. His stance was straight and square, and his emotion, as always, was concealed by the straight line of his set lips and the advanced, defiant jaw. He stole a glance about while the benediction was being read. There was Colonel Garvin's Choctaw widow, hiding her grief with typical aborigine stoicism. Her presence made him conscious of the absence of old Colonel Sam, and Grant, the banker. And there was Jeff Aiken, and Cal Stewart with all the lineaments of old men, looking on with expressions of dutiful sadness. He had saved them both from the gallows; and, could it be, was it possible that the coarse-dressed slattern, worn and shapeless, was the lithe cross-breed who had once so appealed to his fancy? A look of added sadness crept across his countenance. The years had been unkind to his—to Izora. It was his client, Izora Alexander.

Grief had to be combined with business on the docket. Congressional ratification of President Wilson's war proclamation on April 6, 1917, made the United States an ally of the European majority. The machinery of the selective draft revolved about the drive of one Hugh S. Johnson, an Oklahoman, and an intimate friend of Pruiett's; a country-school classmate of Pruiett's wife. It was whispered that Pruiett could get things done in Washington. He never made an appearance before the exemption board; but, the majority of the applicants who contributed to the expense of his constant travel between Oklahoma and the national capitol received favorable consideration on their applications for exemption. He had taken a lesson from the wily Jim Jacobs, and learned where to hang his hat.

While Pruiett had been traveling in the Pacific northwest in 1906, and making his plans for scraping the valley mud from his boots, a valley jury had convicted Dr. Price Patterson of manslaughter for killing Dr. G. W. Harrod at Maysville, and had sentenced him to confinement in the penitentiary for ten years. The doctor had stalled the conviction through a four year appeal, and upon an unsuccessful conclusion, had managed to get a parole from the Governor.

His boy, Orban Chester Patterson, finished law college and Pruiett found a place for him in his office because he was raised on the Washita.

"I'd like to see you make yourself into a lawyer," Pruiett said. "Get them valley feudin' ideas out of your head an' work hard. I'll help you get started."

"I'll try to make myself handy," Patterson replied.

"Things has been layin' quiet down at Maysville," Pruiett said.

"How long's it been since the old man killed Doc Harrod?"

"It's been almost ten years."

"Maybe it's over, but them valley feuds don't usually die so quick; they raise somethin' besides good cotton an' broom corn up them Washita flats, an' that's tough hombres. It ain't but a jump from Maysville over to Lindsay."

"That's right," Patterson agreed.

"Ever hear of my client Monroe from up that way?" Pruiett grinned.

"I'll say I have," Patterson answered.

"They called him the chippey's nemesis around here," Pruiett laughed. "But, no jokin', I figured, from the day your daddy shot old Doc Harrod in two with that shotgun, that there'd be a string of killin's follow it. That's the way things usually went down in the valley."

Patterson smoked in silence. He was a tall youth who looked dreamily away when office clerks and loungers poked fun at his old fashioned habit of wearing a pistol. His height, in excess of six feet, was accentuated by the high heels of his footwear. He had the tops cut from the box-towed and high-heeled ranch boots, and had them fixed with tongues and eyes and laces so that they could be tied above his ankles like shoes. The exceeding roundness of the outline of his small head was not interrupted by the sparse, fine hair which he brushed so close to it. His eye was like Pruiett's; black, and straight and cold. His sallow complexion harmonized with the inevitable cigarette which he nervously fingered or sucked, and while he seldom spoke, when he did it was a queer finality which discouraged disagreement.

"Old Bill Murray made a' awful dirty speech about me over at Maysville," Pruiett ruminated, re-lighting his frayed cigar. "Your paw heard it, an' told me about it, an' durin' the conversation I asked him if he wasn't scared of old Harrod's kinfolks, or friends, down there."

"The old man ain't scared of nothin'," Patterson said without hesitation. He was not boasting.

The buzzer in the office began to rattle. Pruiett grabbed up the telephone. "Pruiett," he bawled into the transmitter. "Pat? Yeah, he's in here. Sure. Here, son, it's for you."

Patterson put the receiver to his ear and answered the call, softly. "Is that so?" he inquired. "How long ago? Well, I guess I'd better come down. Yes... I'll see you before long."

Pruiett, with his feet in the window ledge, blew smoke rings and looked inquiringly up at Patterson as he took his coat from the back of his chair and started to put it on.

"Got to go?" he inquired.

"Yeah," Patterson answered, evenly. "Wade Williams shot the old man up. He's dead" according to the *Pauls Valley Democrat* on November 2, 1916.

"The hell," Pruiett cried, jumping to his feet. "When? How did you find out?"

"That was Sis called," Patterson replied. "She just told me. It just now happened, down home."

"Are you goin' down there—now?" Pruiett asked, watching him intently. There was an unnatural air of unconcernment about the young man.

"Sure, I'm going down there," Patterson replied. "I'm going down there—now."

Pruiett took his arm and turned him around, so that the two pairs of beady black eyes crossed their beams within a short, blunt radius.

"I'm a lot older than you are, son, an' I've seen a hell of a lot of this stuff. I've been close to it all my life an' I know what I'm talkin' about. Don't do it. Don't do what you are thinkin' about doin'. Take my advise and let the law take care of it, an' don't make matters any worse by another killin'."

Patterson made no change of face. "You want me to let him get away with it?" His eyes were unwavering. "You think I should do nothin' about it?"

"That's what I said," Pruiett snapped. "I'm givin' you some good advice. Don't do any killin'."

"Mr. Pruiett," said Patterson, with mock formality, "I understand you was from Kentucky. That don't sound like Kentucky counsel you're givin' me."

"I'm you're friend, son, and I'm talkin' to you like I would to my own boy. Let the law handle this case. Keep your hands out of it."

"All right, Mr. Pruiett," he said. Patterson had looked him searchingly in the face before he replied. He prefaced his dry answer with a wan smile. "I'll take your advice. I'll follow it... at least for awhile."

When word came to the office that Wade Williams and been acquitted at his trial for killing the doctor in January of 1917, the young lawyer sat quietly by the window, smoking his cigarettes and looking away, not even glancing up when Pruiett stopped by to reiterate his word of warning and advice. No visible change in his demeanor appeared, when, two months later, his sister, Vernon "Verna" Patterson, was found dead in the old Terminal Hotel at Oklahoma City. A dose of self-administered poison had produced her death. The two sealed notes which she had written and left on a dresser in the room were pocketed by Patterson; any questions regarding their contents were met with a patient shake of his head.

"I'd like to see you forget that hog leg, some mornin', leave it at home on your baby grand," Pruiett joked with Patterson. "It's liable to go off an' hurt somebody."

"Maybe," Patterson answered, without looking up from his desk.

"Let's get these blood and thunder ideas out of our heads," Pruiett persisted.

"I don't want to be disrespectful, Mr. Pruiett," Patterson said, rising, "but I'll have to ask you to let me handle things that don't pertain to office business in my own way."

"I been burned up with hate all my life," Pruiett confessed, "an' I think I'd a'been better off if I'd a' taken a few people into my confidence. I'm your friend. If you got to nurse these grudges, let me help you. Tell me about 'em."

"I'm not much of a hand to talk," Patterson said, "but you can't see your people killed off like I've seen mine, and expect a pistol bullet in your own back, an' not burn inside over it. I can't work, for thinkin' about it."

"Has the Williamses jumped the old grudge up this late, you suppose?"

"Hell, yes," Patterson said. "They been hatchin' it since they was sure the old man was goin' to stay out on his parole. Wade stood across the street from the bank an' watched Dad come out, an' then shot him down like a dog. An' it's the old man Williams that's responsible. He's been trainin' these boys, Wade and Alonzo, ever' since Harrod was killed, to do these jobs they been doin'."

"They didn't have nothin' to do with Verna's case, did they?"

"You're damned right, they did," Patterson answered, bitterly.

"What was the truth about that?" Pruiett demanded. "What was the matter, that she killed herself like she did?"

"That's something I can't discuss, not even with you," Patterson answered. "Don't ask me."

"So that's it," Pruiett mused, scratching his chin. "The old man wasn't in on that, though."

"He's the devil's granddaddy," Patterson gritted. "He fixed up the parties an' furnished the liquor, an' got the young people together. An' he was... "

Pruiett waited. Patterson didn't want to disclose any more.

"That old man's run crooked cattle deals up an' down the South Canadian River for twenty-five years," Pruiett said. "He was with old Mat Wolf in a lot of 'em, an' that Williams bank at Purcell never did get the reputation of bein' the farmers' friend."

"He ain't done no killin', himself, but he's engineered a dozen of 'em, just like he did the old man's," Patterson said. "When you want to stop the wolf pack, why, head off the leader. Ain't that right?"

"Get them ideas out of your head," Pruiett said, slapping him on the back. "By the way, when I used to make Purcell, the old banker was carryin' a little pearl handled thirty-two in his side pocket, all the time. Come in an' see me any time you get stuck on any of these cases."

"Sam L. Williams, banker and ranch owner of Purcell, Oklahoma, was shot and almost instantly killed by O. C. Patterson, an Oklahoma City attorney, at 10:45 this morning" according to the *Oklahoma City Times* on September 28, 1917,

The afternoon *Times* was advising the populace of the western city, still stunned by the nation's entrance into the War and the first drawing of the selective draft, of what had occurred on the crowded downtown intersection. "The tragedy took place on North Robinson Avenue, near the intersection of Main Street. Patterson shot Williams when the two met at a point twenty feet north of the Main Street line.The shooting is said to be the result of a feud of long standing between the Williams and Patterson families."

"Wade Williams, son of Sam L. Williams, killed Patterson's father, Dr. Price Patterson, at Maysville last October. This killing is also reported to have resulted from alleged relationships of Williams, and his son, with one of Patterson's sisters. When tried, Wade Williams was acquitted by the jury."

"Miss Verna Patterson, a sister of Patterson, is said to have committed suicide at a hotel here several months ago. After shooting the contents of his pistol into Williams, Patterson stood beside the body and lighted a cigarette. Patterson will plead self-defense, according to Moman Pruiett, Patterson's law partner. Pruiett has been engaged to defend Patterson."

In subsequent reports on the case, it appeared that "When asked in regard to a letter one of his sisters is said to have received from Sam Williams some time ago, Patterson said the matter would all be threshed out at the trial." As one account stated, "Justice of the Peace A. T. Early, who performed the inquest on the body of Verna Patterson, who committed suicide at the Terminal Hotel last March, declared that the girl had tried several times to call a man named Williams over the telephone before she committed suicide." And in another "A letter addressed to Wade Williams, which was found by her (Verna's) side when her body was discovered was turned over to young Patterson, and is still in his possession, according to Moman Pruiett, Patterson's attorney."

Skeptics termed the letter talk 'Pruiett convenience'. It had an aroma of a dead cat and scorched shirt sleeve. But, the defense counsel had entered the case on the ground floor and he knew how he wanted to try it. He had leaned from his upstairs office window, after hearing the shots, in time to see Williams roll into the street. He surveyed the crowd which pushed around the gory scene meticulously, for the faces of friends who would bear reliable witness. The panorama of the trial-defense was in his mind when he started to the jail to see Patterson.

"Well, son, how you feelin'?" Pruiett greeted through the bars.

Patterson looked dreamily through the tobacco smoke of his cell. "Did you ever pick cotton, Mr. Pruiett, an' drag a heavy sack 'til you thought your neck was goin' to break, an' keep watchin' the sun and hopin' it would go down, so you could quit and get that awful load off your back?"

"Hell, yes," Pruiett laughed, "I've picked lots of cotton. Why, I've..."

"And then," Patterson interrupted, "the sun got clear out of sight, and it began to get dark—real slow like—and you could see the old man and the wagon at the end of the row, hitchin' up to go home. An' then you got to the end of the row, an' you took that strap from across your shoulder and around your neck, and you stood up straight, an' took a deep, free breath. Did you ever do that?"

"Hell, yes," Pruiett repeated. "Lots of times, why... "

"Well, you asked me," Patterson replied. "That's how I'm feelin'. I'm feelin' awful god-damned good."

The foundation for Patterson's self-defense plea had been set when the coroner produced a small automatic pistol from the dead banker's pocket. The defendant's own testimony, well corroborated, would justify the first shot. What bothered Pruiett was a satisfactory explanation for emptying the smoking cylinder into the writhing body while it was prostrate on the concrete. He anticipated that the abundant proof on the phase of the case, which the prosecution meant to stress, would cause trouble after the trial judge had instructed on how far a person, once attacked, could reasonably go in repulsing the attacker and defending himself.

Colonel Jake Hodges had observed that self-defense was best; that the unwritten law was often adequate and effective, and that temporary insanity was better than a plea of guilty. The Pruiett corollary, formulated in a dark cell at Rusk and developed in the cow country courts while apprehensively looking about so as to be able to dodge a pistol ball headed for his back, had tended to combine all of them.

Patterson wasn't guilty because the old man, shifting his cane from his good hand so as to clamp it under his paralyzed arm, had meant to pull the little gun and inflict severe bodily harm, possibly death, upon him. He had wronged his sister, had broken her heart and caused her to take her own life, and that was of itself an act a true southwestern gentleman could not honorably overlook. The combination of the overt agencies produced by the dead man, the murder of Dr. Patterson, the wrong to his sister, fear for his own safety, mortal fear, dread and hate, all aroused with the single view of Williams, had caused a breakdown of his reason and intellect. He temporarily lost control, and in the blackness he continued, as witnesses glibly established, to snap the pistol in the direction of the dead man long after the last cartridge had exploded.

Pruiett scornfully ignored a valuable talking point in the Patterson trial. The accused was big, young, single and able-bodied. "Tell them the country needs men, he's already been drawn in the draft, to send him to the front. He'll probably be executed in France; make the Huns waste some powder and lead on him." Those were some of the many suggestions which Pruiett received as he was preparing to go to the jury with his final appeal.

"I don't beg 'em for a damned thing," he growled. "I may decide to go to Washington and see if I can't get this boy off with the exemption board, after I pull him out of this scrape. He told me he didn't have much preference between the hot seat and a batch of shrapnel, an' that he'd already done the world a greater service in killin' the head-dog of the Williams kennel than he would have if he'd captured the Kaiser. He's got some good stuff in him, it appears to me."

The years since Rusk and Little Rock had proven Pruiett's evil theory. John Evans and Doc Richards stood at the head of his proof column beckoning to the host that floundered in a mire of blood. What did it take to fool a jury? Credible Proof! What did it take to captivate a jury? Theatricals! The spectacular! What did it take to overpower a jury? The psychological thrust at the psychological moment! Where would Maggie Miller have been if he hadn't produced the credible proof? Would Clarence Douglas have walked out into free air if the jury hadn't been startled into belief, with his twin knife trick? Didn't pulling his coat off at the right time ruin the carefully prepared murder case the State had built up against Jim Leggett?

Pruiett played a jury like the piper played his piccolo. The astonishing recollection, his amazing ability to act and imitate, the power which permitted him to pull appropriate poetry out of his head, to remember testimony, word for word and never to forget a face, had stored up a profound panorama of murder-trial experience behind him. By inclination and instinct, and knowledge based upon a process of elimination, he knew what to offer to this jury, and what to offer to that one. Pruiett genius had reached its zenith. He knew how to stage the perfect murder trial.

Patterson's trial held from February 18 through March 3, 1918 was simply a more highly developed reproduction of a hundred others which had preceded it. It was Pruiett, jerking his laughs, tears and jeers as he willed them. He toyed with the State's attorneys and encouraged them, until he was ready to shatter them with his favorite blow; the unearthly eloquence of his final speech to the jury. The local reporters used old copies of the paper for notes; they changed the old names and dates, and left the Pruiett in. One composed a page of doggerel, as he casually watched the State's witnesses march up to the sacrificial stand for Pruiett cross-examination. A reporters poem about a stray dog befriended in the courtroom by Moman Pruiett as reported in the *Oklahoma News* on February 21, 1918.

The courtroom was crowded and quietness reigned
As lawyers from witnesses, slowly obtained
The tale of how Patterson, armed with a gun,
Discharged all its bullets, which struck, to a one -
How Williams wheeled back, how he fell, how he died,
While Patterson calmly stood off to the side.

The scene in the court as the story they sought,
Displayed little love, and of happiness naught.
The sorrowful women, the stolid-faced men,
Presented a scene for the pessimist's pen.
The talking continued, the wrangling kept up,
When through the small gateway there toddled a pup;
A pup! Yes, we mean it—a wee little hound
That clumsily tumbled and sniffled around.

A spectator grinned and a baby cried Goo!
His Honor looked solemn—what else could he do?
The hearing went on, and the lawyers all pored
O'er the books on the table—the dog was ignored,
'Til wandering around, he pulled up at the feet
Of Pruiett—Yes, Moman—the lawyer complete.

The latter leaned across his chair,
And stroked the puppy's shaggy hair.
The doggy knew he'd found a friend,
His tail vibrated to the end.
He stood upon his hindmost paws,
And smiled between his doggish jaws,
While Moman Pruiett, lawyer, sat
And gave the pup a kindly pat.

Have you wondered at the power which this Pruiett does command,
When he takes a case to try before the Court?
Have you wondered why he's able, when he takes it in his hand,
To deliver it across in finest sort?

Now perhaps here is a reason—it's the fiber of the MAN,
Who tho leader of a case of much import,
Found the time to stroke a doggie for a little moment's span,
As the creature wandered friendless through the court!

Patterson came clear in early March of 1918. "We the jury drawn, empanelled and sworn in the above entitled cause do upon our oaths find Orban C. Patterson 'Not Guilty'. (Signed) M. R. Thornton, Foreman." And charity abroad was not spite at home in Pruiett's book. Instead of rendering the Pattersons a fee bill, he took his client, and Bill Maben, who had been grinning gleefully from a front seat in the courtroom when the verdict was read, to the Baltimore at Kansas City. Pruiett paid all the bills. Papers from various parts of the country, publicizing the Patterson trial and its outcome, were strewn about the elegant suite Pruiett was furnishing.

"Who's this guy Clarence Darrow they talk about up Chicago way?" Patterson mumbled, as he admired a picture of himself in the *Star.* He squinted at its magnified proportions through the bottom of his nearly-empty highball glass. "Is he supposed to know somethin' about tryin' lawsuits?"

Maben stunned the house girl nearest him with a merry slap on the back. "He's just pretty good," he guffawed. "I always say, give me the Washita Stud."

Pruiett, standing before a mantle mirror, was brushing his hair. The relaxed lines of his face showed that he was not out of accord with the opinion of his companions.

"Now that we think of it, Harry K. Thaw overlooked a bet when he failed to engage the services of Moman Pruiett" according to the *Tulsa World.* Pruiett was reading from a recent publication, for the further enlightenment of his admirers.

When the well went dry, the black stud had his collar off, and his mane in the trough. At midnight of that memorable night in 1919 when the Volstead Act became effective, John Barleycorn became officially dead, and Pruiett was in attendance on the sad funeral service being held in the barroom of the Hotel Worth at Fort Worth. Bill Maben was with him, and when sad-eyed but resolute employees had backed them out and locked the door, they hurried to the Rock Island depot to catch the train for Oklahoma. Sixteen handsome quarts, eight of them apiece, nestled in the two heavy leather suitcases which the two men carried. They were taking favors of that long to be remembered farewell party home with them.

Waurika, a lazy settlement in the old Comanche reservation country, was a water-stop for all trains on that line. In early April of 1919, when Pruiett's train pulled in, a squad of Federal Internal Revenue officers boarded it and began a systematic process of thumping baggage. The bags which responded with bottle-toned chimes were opened; and, if spirits were then visible, the owner was invited to step forward. Fifteen luckless cheaters stood on the brick platform of the station and watched their transportation depart without them, before they began the weary march to the local jail. Pruiett and Maben were members of the fuming, swearing group.

It was almost 4 o'clock in the morning when Chamberlayne Jones, District Judge, was called out of bed to answer a long distance 'phone call. His sleep fuddled brain was scarcely capable of assimilating the jargon which entered at the ear.

"Moman Pruiett and William N. Maben, residents an' citizens of the State of Oklahoma, allege that they are bein' illegally restrained of their liberty by the Sheriff of Jefferson County, an'... "

"What the hell is this?" exploded the angry and confused judge.

"This is an oral writ of habeas corpus," Pruiett answered. "We can do it as well this . . "

"Who is this? Who's talking?" shouted the judge.

"This is Moman Pruiett," Pruiett shouted back. "Me and Bill Maben are in the Sheriff's office at Waurika, an' they're gettin' ready to lock us up on a hold charge for the Federals. We had some liquor in our grips on the Fort Worth train. I'm givin' you this writ and we want bond."

Pruiett paused, listening. "Say," he said, aside to Maben, "that damn judge is either chokin', or laughin', at me. Do you suppose... ?"

"Let me have the Sheriff on the wire," the judge said.

"A writ of habeas corpus has just been submitted to me," he said to the Sheriff, "which you may consider as signed, directing you to produce the bodies of the two prisoners, immediately. If you want to save yourself a long drive, turn them loose on their own recognizance, and on my recommendation, until 2 o'clock tomorrow afternoon."

When the liquor cases were called for trial at the next sessions of the Federal Court, the customary Pruiett sensation developed, but not in the customary manner or in the way the curious followers of the event had expected. Instead of a passionate plea in his own behalf, or the production of a maze of technical legal points, Pruiett stood up and entered a plea of guilty. He claimed ownership of the entire whiskey stock, and the grinning Maben, giving away his actual guilt, was discharged without censor or cost. Pruiett accepted a stiff fine and distasteful rebuke from the bench with a look of assumed repentance, but with his raven black mop still shining like the defiant black flag.

Charles B. Stuart was attending court. He was one of the men who had helped defend Gore; he was a former law partner of Joe Bailey in Texas, and was respected in the Southwest as a man of character, and a lawyer of great ability. He met Pruiett in the corridor of the court building as the culprit was coming out. The two attorneys shook hands.

"That was noble of you, Pruiett," Stuart said. "The good that will come from helping Maben will more than make up for the injury you may suffer. I admire your courage."

"Thank you, judge," Pruiett replied. He had a respect that was akin to awe for the ponderous-minded Stuart.

"I've watched you and the cases you've tried with a lot of interest," Stuart continued. "I never tried a murder case by myself in my life; it's out of my line, but I've been before plenty of juries. The way you handle a jury and win your cases is most remarkable. I still hear people talking about your argument in the Gore case."

"I guess I have been fortunate, is all, judge," Pruiett answered, with a modesty not entirely characteristic of him.

"No," Stuart disagreed, "there's something that helps you along, that holds you up, and you must know what it is. If you wouldn't mind, I'd like to have you tell me what it is that you attribute your success to in the trial of jury cases?"

Pruiett studied, then smiled. "It may sound a little strange to you, right here, judge, but I believe in givin' a fair answer to a fair question. I never enter a courtroom to try a case without offerin' up a prayer; not a prayer to win the case, understand, but a prayer to let me try it right, so that my client will have the best chance of gettin' what he needed when he showed confidence in me by hirin' me."

Stuart was nodding slowly as he passed on. There was neither surprise, disbelief nor scorn in his expression as he went into the courtroom.

Oklahoma Governor Robert L. Williams stood with his hands above his head while a man with a whiskey breath went through his pockets.

"Some day somebody is going to kill you," he grated at the searcher, "and if they're convicted for it, I'll give 'em an unconditional pardon, regardless of what the sentence is."

The Governor, accompanied by a County Commissioner or two, was traveling by automobile from Medicine Park near Lawton to Oklahoma City. Grover Fulkerson, deputy sheriff, had stationed himself at the south end of the toll-bridge over the South Canadian and was engaged in searching every car and every person slowing down for the gates. Fulkerson liked his own liquor but he didn't like for any one else to like theirs.

The fuming Governor was scarcely out of sight down the highway when dim lights through the dust announced the arrival of another toll, and another shake down.

"Get out," Fulkerson said. He jerked back his jacket, exhibiting his badge, as he gave the insolent command.

"What for?" came a prompt, courteous response from the interior of the car. It was a small truck, and the driver, a mild appearing, medium sized man, was curious.

"None of your god damned lip," informed Fulkerson. "Get out an' be quick. I'm the law, and I'm knowin' what you got in this truck."

The driver felt a gun muzzle in his ribs as he quietly alighted.

"Put 'em up, and keep 'em up there," Fulkerson was making a methodical search with his big left as he held the gun against the suspect.

The victim seemed mildly interested, slightly amused, as he watched the procedure.

"What you haulin' in this outfit?"

"Peaches," was the short, laconic reply.

Fulkerson picked his lantern up from the ground and swung it in the direction of the truck bed. It was piled to the top of the sideboards with peaches.

"What you runnin' anyway?" Fulkerson persisted, with a disagreeable inference in his tone. "What you got under that stuff?"

"Peaches," replied the unperturbed trucker.

"So you got some more peaches, have you?" The deputy sneered. "All right, Mister wise guy, I'll see if you have. Just start unloadin' right here on the ground. I think I'll take a look at them bottom peaches."

"Have a heart, Mister, for Christ's sake," begged the driver. "I'm tired out. I can't load and unload that stuff here just to satisfy your curiosity. It'll take half the night. Can't you... "

Fulkerson waved his big pistol menacingly. "I said unload," he commanded. "Get busy and get that stuff all out of there. I want to look it over."

"You haven't got no right to do me this way," the driver retorted. "You ain't got a search warrant, an' I... "

"Do you do as I say, or do you resist an officer?" Fulkerson roared. "This is your last chance, do you or not?"

"I guess I do as you say," replied the driver with resignation. "I got a scoop in the seat. Can I get it out to unload with?"

"Get it and get busy." Fulkerson fairly gritted the command between his teeth.

The driver, without a change of expression, stepped to the door of the cab and leaned inside. He had the same indulgent, laconic look as he wheeled around, with a long forty-five in his hand, and began to shoot. Four holes popped through Fulkerson's spleen and bowels. He was the same as dead when he finished sagging into the dusty roadway according to the *Norman Transcript* on August 24-28, 1917.

The peach man kicked the lantern into the ditch alongside the truck and gave the crank a methodical twist. He made one stop, where he removed fifty gallons of corn whiskey from beneath his cargo of peaches, before he drove into Norman and surrendered. He told them what he had done, and told them exactly why.

"I know that's what you said," Pruiett argued, "but is it your real name. John Jay sounds like a name that's lost part of itself somewhere."

"That's all the name I've got, or ever had," the mild voiced prisoner answered, through the bars. "It's not as well known as Pruiett, but I've not had the chance to establish it, yet. Give me a little more time."

"You sound like a man that's had a little education," Pruiett hazarded.

"I've been to school a time or two," Jay smiled.

"You think you're goin' to set this prairie afire with your brilliance, you say?" Pruiett asked.

"I'll make you a good client," Jay answered. "You treat me right, an' I'll see you collect a lot of fees."

"What business you goin' to be in, if I might inquire," Pruiett demanded.

"Whiskey," Jay said.

"What about this little murder charge hangin' over you, for killin' a Deputy Sheriff? Are you goin' to let that interfere with your plans?"

"That's what I've hired you to straighten up," Jay grinned. "Of course, these big fees I pay you in the future are contingent on my beatin' the electric chair for cop killin'."

"You got a good healthy slant on life," Pruiett laughed. "I'll give you a little extra effort. Leave ever'thing to old Moman, an' the verdict'll be not guilty. If you follow the directions on the bottle, I'll make a little bet with you on how long the jury's out. Take it easy, now."

Pruiett and Jay against the field wasn't a bad venture. Fulkerson couldn't say anything; so, Jay could present his self-defense story as he liked it best. The load of peaches he had had when he surrendered at the side of the Sheriff's office had been inoffensive enough in its appearance, and when they had found the dead deputy, the gun was lying beside him exactly as Jay had told them it would be. The unsavory odor of Fulkerson's overbearing disposition was constantly wafted from the defense side of the table to the nostrils of the jurors, and never a whiff of it strengthened their stomach to convict. The defense was in good shape when Pruiett started to pump his final blast, his hypnotism act, full in the jury's face.

Governor William's ultimatum to Fulkerson had been transmitted to Pruiett, not by the Governor—by one of the County Commissioners. Pruiett wouldn't rely on the security suggested in its content any more than would the accused; but, he saw a chance to use it to an advantage. Governor Williams was the same Bob Williams, who, as a territorial lawyer had scribbled a long hand petition for rehearing in the Frank Driggers case, at Pruiett's request, and filed it for him.

Pruiett addressing the jury, had thrown the State's attorneys off guard by a lull in his wild forensics. He became confidential.

"The Governor of this State promised a pardon to any one who would kill that coward and relieve the highways of the disgrace of his conduct. You should show your respect for his judgment by acquitting Jay, and relieving Governor Williams of the trouble."

"What's that?" cried Thomas Cheatwood, the Cleveland County Attorney. "I didn't get that. What did you say?"

Pruiett smiled indulgently as he turned toward him.

"I said," he roared, "that the Governor of this State promised a pardon to any one who would kill Fulkerson and get him off... "

"I object," cried the prosecutor, "it's incompetent, and prejudicial, and... Why, your honor, it's monstrous! He charges the Governor with being an accomplice; with abetting this murder. I move that the jury be admonished not to consider it, and that counsel be censored for such conduct."

"Your remarks are wholly unwarranted, and improper, Mr. Pruiett," the frowning Court told him. "It is indeed a serious charge you make against our Governor. I think... "

"I know what I'm talkin' about, your honor," Pruiett replied. "But, if you say... "

"I do say it," the Court interrupted. "Keep within the record; the evidence. The jury will not consider any of the remarks just made by counsel. Proceed."

But the mere admonition couldn't remove the advice from the minds of the jurors. If reasonable doubt hadn't been in their minds before, it was then, and it was bound to remain there. A verdict of 'Not Guilty' was returned, and Jay walked out of the courtroom with his counsel, a free man.

CHAPTER EIGHTEEN

WHEREIN THE STUD BREAKS FROM A GALLOP TO A TROT, AS HE DECLINES TO GO TO THE DEFENSE OF THE HANDSOME WOMAN WHO KILLED HIS FRIEND, THE REPUBLICAN NATIONAL COMMITTEEMAN. AND HOW A PISTOL BALL FINDS A VITAL SPOT IN THE BODY OF A BOOTLEGGING NEGRO CLIENT, AND PRUIETT, THE DEAN OF THE FELON EMANCIPATORS, MAKES HIS OWN BOND UNDER A TECHNICAL CHARGE OF MURDER. AND HOW HE COMES CLEAR IN THE COURT, BUT CONTINUES CLOUDY IN HIS OWN MIND AND HEART, AND HE SUFFERS DEFEAT IN HIS DEFENSE OF THE WORST MURDER CASE IN THE ANNALS OF ROCKY MOUNTAIN CRIMINAL HISTORY. AND HOW HE GAINS THE ACQUITTAL OF THE COY LITTLE WIDOW OF A WEALTHY GAMBLER, WHO WAS CHARGED WITH MAKING HERSELF A WIDOW, AND COINS, IN THE TRIAL, INVECTIVE AND ABUSE MORE SCURRILOUS THAN ANY HE HAD ORIGINATED THERETOFORE IN HIS VIOLENT CAREER.

Pruiett's deliverance of Sam St. Mary and Orban Patterson were classic. Nothing could have been added to perfect their records and further their desired results. No word or move was omitted which might have detracted from the theme of the defense. From the time the first jurors were called to the box to the time the verdicts were read, the scowling, black haired lawyer dominated the scene. Suave and sarcastic, or explosive and belligerent, each syllable, sentence and gesture was timed and produced to fit into the picture he had learned to create—the perfect murder trial. Ten days of his enchanting excellence and the juries, the mere men who came to try the ones accused but who only watched, and marveled, at the technique of their counsel, were under his spell.

Pruiett, as he was in those cases, would have saved Nicola Sacco and Barttolomeo Vanzetti, two political radicals executed in Massachusetts on August 23, 1927, from the New England hot seat. He would have produced some justification, some circumstance of mitigation, for William Edward Hickman's bestial Pacific Coast conduct; he would have robbed the maw of San Quentin's hungry gallows of its insignificant morsel. Leopold and Loeb, with cringing pleas of guilty, resting secure on the practical decision of a judicial mind, were not tried a la Pruiett. Was their crime less justifiable than Maggie Miller's? Was the probability of their technical guilt less certain than that of Red Fox, or George Hopkins? The black stud would have mixed them up a batch of temporary insanity in the Sam St. Mary manner, and with a jury, a group of human beings with souls, and feelings and emotions, he would have commenced the dangerous game of lives and liberties. His game was winner take all.

The towering pine exposes more of vulnerable surface to the elements than the scrub. When it has reached its full growth and height, the weight of its own structure causes it to sag and split, and with each opening a vulnerable spot is made for the entrance of a parasitic body. Decadence proceeds from excellence more inexorably than it does mediocrity. The symphony is complete and a master is acclaimed. The campaign of application, and concentration, and sacrifice, and self-denial, is over. Real genius does not stumble over his objective; he has fought for it and pursued it, and he holds it for at least a precious instant with full and complete recognition when at last it is his. With the joy of success comes the correlative pain of practical understanding. There is but one pinnacle. The classic cannot be improved.

In the defense of Joseph H. Goldstein, charged with a violation of the Mann Act, transporting a female, with immoral intent, across a State boundary in the U. S. District Court for the Western District of Oklahoma, the accused had experienced apprehension over the way his case was being handled. He was a wealthy merchant, unable to see his mischievousness, indiscretion at best, in the criminal light turned upon it by the District Attorney. The girl had been young and inviting. He had spent his money for clothes and food for her, and that, in the old Jew's opinion, was justification for using her how, and where, he was able. But could his high-priced counsel, with such an alcoholic breath, and the trace of a glass film over his black eyes, present the case so that the jury could see it his way, and understand? Pruiett stood unsteadily, adjusting the knot of his silk necktie. His argument was in his eyes, not in his voice box.

"An old man, an old fool," he mused dreamily in his smoothest tone, "but still human."

He resumed his seat at the counsel table. Nine soft words, from the throat and mouth capable of producing a thunderous volume. Spectators wondered. Goldstein glared. There was mayhem in his face, and it remained there, until he was startled into realization with a deliverance. The speech, in a single sentence, had moved him out of the shadow of Leavenworth's grim walls.

And there were other appearances of decadence, if temporary lapses from complete abandoned ferocity could be called decadence, in the demeanor of bloody murder's best friend. Jake L. Hamon, millionaire oil man, Republican National Committeeman from Oklahoma, and an intimate of the President of the country, was shot to death in his hotel room by a concubine, Clara Smith, whom he took on tour and passed off as a member of his family. The defense was offered to Pruiett. What could have been sweeter in the decade or two before? A beautiful client. A shy, softly sweet, witness. Cash! Stacks of cash, and national eye-catching notoriety. Pruiett, in his prime, had used a pretense to gain employment in a lowly washerwoman's case, just for the opportunity to fight and win. How he would have relished, in that day, the offer Clara Smith extended for services in the case where she was charged with killing wealthy Jake.

Pruiett turned her down according to the *Dallas News* on December 29, 1920. "Assailing Clara Smith as a modern vampire, Moman Pruiett, noted criminal lawyer, today set at rest rumors that he might aid the alleged slayer's defense when he sent a telegram to Mrs. Jake L. Hamon, as follows: 'I think it an outrage that no voice has been raised in behalf of the dead. I know more about this unfortunate tragedy and what led up to it than any man living, and I cannot long remain silent when this modern vampire is preparing for the movies and seeking a one-fourth interest in Jake's estate'." It was strange talk for the man who had dedicated his life to empty prison cells and rotting gallows ropes.

Jake Hamon had been one of the black stud's closest friends. Pruiett made a convert of him in his defense of Tom Gore, where Hamon was discovering the efficiency of the political outlet for surplus cash. Hamon was putting up a lot of the money that the Bond-McMurray-Fitzpatrick combine was spending to discredit blind Tom. When it was over and there was no question about who had won, Hamon went directly to Pruiett.

"We made our mistake in not havin' you on our side," he said after he had complimented Pruiett on his victory.

Pruiett didn't answer.

"I'd like to feel that I could call you when I need a lawyer in this part of the country," Hamon said. "I can let you make some, an' I'll feel a lot safer with you lookin' after me and my business."

"You can call me," Pruiett replied with slight cordiality. "I'm in the business."

Their next meeting had been in a room in the Kingkade Hotel at Oklahoma City. "They've had me before the Grand Jury all day," Hamon opened the subject with little preliminary. "I think I'm goin' to be indicted."

"What do you want done?" Pruiett asked. "What d'you think I can do?"

"I think you can block it," Hamon replied coolly. "I'm new in this politics business, and I like it, for a plaything. I don't want to be indicted."

"I never saw any one who did," Pruiett laughed.

Hamon opened one of the top drawers of the dresser in the room. "Well, I don't want to be indicted," he repeated. He was tossing little oblong packages from the drawer to the corded counterpane. "Here's somethin' for you to work on."

Hamon laid out $25,000 in $100's, five bundles of them, with fifty crisp notes to the bundle.

"Yes," Pruiett grinned, "I see you don't want to be indicted."

An indictment had been returned against Hamon when the two had their next conference, in a room in the same hotel. It was Pruiett's turn to toss out the green packages. Hamon thumbed them glumly as they landed on the bed beside him, taking a quick, professional inventory.

"You brought it all back," he said when he had concluded his count. "Didn't you do anything to block this business?"

"I sure as hell did, plenty, but it couldn't be stopped," Pruiett replied. "I may get yanked up myself for what I've done. An outfit like that would indict Jesus Christ on hearsay. I just couldn't stop it."

"How much did you spend?" the astute Jake inquired, watching close for the expression that would come with the answer.

"Three thousand, an' I had a hell of a time doin' that. I couldn't find anybody with his hand out."

"Well," Hamon persisted, "you didn't hold out anything for legal services. Don't you value your services at anything?"

"Not when I don't produce," Pruiett responded. "I'm always willin' to let my clients put the fee up in the bank, or give me a note payable when they get their results." His mind was in the valley, plugging for a win-or-you-don't-collect fee in the Sam Ashton case. "When I lose, I don't care about the pay."

Hamon handed him two of the packages. It was $10,000. Pruiett was about to make an objection to taking it when he was interrupted by a knock on the door.

"Come in," Jake called. A beautiful young girl walked in.

"Mr. Pruiett, meet my niece," Hamon said, very softly.

"Really?" the worldly Pruiett drawled. His remark was dripping with skepticism. "I'm delighted."

"Clara Hamon," Hamon continued.

Pruiett made another bow, more formal and sincere than the first. His apologetic manner was a confession of the doubt he had had of actual relationship.

The girl was twenty-three or twenty-four years old; radiant, stalwart, voluptuous. The V at her throat was a trifle low and the hem of her skirt a trifle high, Pruiett thought, for a young woman to wear for a call on her middle-aged uncle. Pale, tan freckles across the bridge of her nose and high on the smooth cheeks detracted nothing from her natural charm. They added a natural accompaniment to the picture of health which her superbly developed figure suggested. Her reddish brown hair was loose and wavy. The white toothed smile which she bestowed so opulently upon Uncle Jake seemed slightly out of proportion to the esteem, or restraint, usually accompanying meetings between those so closely related.

"I'll fix us a drink," Jake said, as he tugged with the top of ginger ale bottle.

"Your niece is a han'some girl," Pruiett observed, eyeing her frankly as she crossed her legs and reclined in a big chair.

"Ain't she," Jake beamed. Clara took a package of cigarettes from her hand bag.

"How many drinks you fixin'?" Pruiett demanded.

"One apiece," Jake laughed. "You ain't so old fashioned you won't let the little girl take one, are you?"

"Not me," Pruiett grinned, trying to conceal some of the surprise he felt at Jake's attitude. What the hell kind of a fellow was he—with his kin-folks?

"This is keen," Clara cooed, sipping the cold highball and blowing a blast of white smoke through her delicate nostrils.

"It's a good drink," Pruiett agreed.

"Jake knows how to fix 'em better'n anybody," Clara declared, as she got up and walked toward the men on the bed. She rested her weight upon Hamon's thick knee, and carelessly let the hand holding the cigarette steal across his shoulder and behind is fat neck.

"I got to be goin'," Pruiett announced, after he had bolted his drink. "I got an appointment I got to keep. I'll mail you a receipt for the money, an' I'll call you sometime."

Bill Maben dropped in from Tulsa. Pruiett was out of the city.

"What the hell does he mean poppin' off about Clara Smith?" he inquired. "Why don't he grab off that case an' go to town?"

"He's been actin' queer about a lot of things, here lately," Patterson answered. Pat's mind was clinging to business since he had dispatched the leader of the Williams wolf pack, and Pruiett had cleared up the likelihood of his having a penalty to pay for it.

"I thought maybe he had a' offer from the Hamon estate," Maben said. "They'll be hirin' a special prosecutor or two in it, won't they?"

"They offered it to Pruiett, but he turned it down," Pat answered. "What they offered him was equal to the runs of a Healdton gusher, an' you know what he says? He says 'Hell no. I see old Jake across the river, an' he's shakin' his head an' tellin' me not to touch it.' Can you believe it?"

"He's been leery of them prosecution cases ever since he tried Pete Thompson in Hughes County," Maben mused. "He poured it on old Cecil Mingle, charged with killing a woman, an' they gave him life after his trial in July and August of 1909. Then, he sent that amateur Romeo that was a Justice of the Peace up state in for a life sentence, an' he didn't seem to mind that. But, when that jury gave Peter "Pete" Thompson a death sentence in November of 1909, Pruiett looked sicker'n Pete. He ain't no prosecutor."

"Hell, no, he ain't," Patterson agreed. "He got so burnt up prosecutin' Pete that he forgot how strong he was goin'. He lost twenty pounds worryin' about the State burnin' a man on his help, an' then he finally went to the Governor an' got him to commute the sentence to life."

"Just the same, I don't understand him landin' on Clara Smith, an' then turnin' down a whale of a fee from the Hamons. He could grab the gravy an' pull short on the punches, couldn't he?"

"He could," Pat agreed, "but he wouldn't. There's somethin' about the damn case I don't understand. Some of the boys from down Ardmore way was up to see him, an' they had a hell of a session. I think maybe the stud was afraid to cut any cake. He thought he might choke on it."

"I'd believe he had a heavy conscience before I'd believe anybody bluffed him out of a part," Maben scoffed. "You know how him an' Jake was... an' Clara, too, for that matter. The three of 'em was stayin' in the same suite at the Raleigh Hotel at Washington, D. C., an' they went to New York an' California together two or three times. I heard Pruiett say that old Jake was the best hand to hustle a bootlegger in a strange town he ever saw."

"An' I've heard him tell how Clara used to pull their shoes off an' spread the foot blanket over 'em, after he an' Jake had passed out," Patterson recollected. "He made two or three settlements between Jake an' Clara after they started gettin' tired of their arrangement, an'... "

It takes a woman to make a final settlement," Maben laughed. "Give one of 'em a .38 an' a close shot an' she'll draw up a' agreement that'll hold."

"Pruiett's strong for his friends, like he is poison for his enemies," Patterson reminded. "He was tryin' a case one time an' I was helpin' him empanel the jury. I came in a little late an' saw a guy in the box that was no good, an' I felt like I ought to tell Pruiett about it. 'That guy in the third seat in the back row's a dirty son-of-a-bitch', I whispers in his ear. 'I know he is', Pruiett comes back, 'but he's MY son-of-a-bitch. I'm goin' to keep him.' That's the way he is."

"Maybe he thinks too much of Jake, that's why he's blastin' Clara, but it don't sound right. Well... he's got plenty of murder cases waitin'. Maybe he ought to keep out of at least one around here."

James C. "Ropey" O'Brien of Chicago, a special prosecutor, who was trying to hang as many murderers on the Great Lakes as Pruiett had managed to liberate in the South and the Southwest, took the Hamon hook. When he stepped onto the stations platform at Ardmore, a tall man with a big hat and a double hip-bulge sauntered out to meet him. It was Buck Garrett, Carter County Sheriff, and the pride of the cattle land grown rich with oil drenched pastures; the same Garrett whom Pruiett had liberated those fifteen years before, after his indiscreet gun-play in the sporting house over the hardware store. Buck was chewing, and whittling, and looking carelessly about as he approached lawyer O'Brien.

"You Mr. O'Brien?" he inquired casually.

"Why yes, I'm O'Brien," the lawyer replied, with surprise.

"Are you the lawyer from Chicago, that's going to work in the Smith case?" The lank Sheriff chipped splinters from a wooden block in his hand with a narrow, long bladed knife.

"Yes, sir, I am," O'Brien responded. "Did you have a message for me?"

"Why, yes, I did," Garrett drawled. Looking him intently in the eye, he let the block drop and clatter to the bricks of the platform, while his left hand extended to grasp the lawyer's flowery necktie. With a firm grip on it, he lashed out with the knife hand, severing the tie just below the knot at his throat.

"I'm tellin' you that you ain't wanted here, and that it ain't healthy for you to stay. That's about all I got to say."

No imported talent was chargeable with the loss of the Clara Smith case. The mild efforts of the local prosecutors were ineffective. She was restored to liberty after her trial in March of 1921.

The leg of lamb rose up and smote the butcher with a shiny cleaver. The pony stood on its hind legs in the center of the ring, puffing a cigar and popping a long whip while a male biped on his all-fours, with big-tent mustaches and patent-leather boots, galloped 'round the ring and jumped clumsily through the big hoop. Everything was in reverse. The war and the armistice, prohibition and bathtub-gin, had upset the universe. Moman Pruiett, the dean of the felon emancipators, was led into court behind counsel, held on a technical charge of murder.

Pruiett had been licensing murder for almost a quarter of a century. His business confined him to contacts with murder. His reputation limited his conversations to murder. It was as natural for a casual acquaintance, as for an old friend, when meeting him on the train or on the street, to talk of that which they presumed would be of the most interest to him—murder. He lived, ate and slept murder. He knew the signs and sequels of murder like the old settlers on the Washita knew nature's signs of the seasons.

When Cal Stewart slew Ben, his brother, in August of 1906 after Pruiett had obtained a joint acquittal for both of them for murdering old Doctor F. A. Graham at Enville, Pruiett nodded understandingly. He knew that he would have to defend one of them for the murder of the other, and that in all probability Cal would beat Ben to the punch. He defended Cal, and he came clear. When news came that Charlie Liddell had shot George Hancock to death, from a second story perch above the Main street of Marietta, Pruiett showed no surprise or concern. Liddell was the son of the Marshal who had been slain by Hancock on the Thackerville depot platform in 1901. Pruiett knew when he cleared Hancock in January of 1902, that when the Liddell kids grew big enough, one of them would avenge the Marshal's death.

Continuously under the influence of liquor, heavy doses of it, Pruiett developed a homicidal mania. Its first manifestation was in a reunion with the old blue steel revolver which he had carried so constantly during the territorial days, the same as he had used to stop celebrating Dr. Threlkeld in the crowded old hotel lobby at Ada. The bells were ringing in his ears again.

Joe Patterson, a burly negro ex-convict, was stopped in his unsavory prime by Pruiett lead. The soft-nosed slug smashing against his leather-tough chest and rough ribs, flattened and spread as big around as a silver dollar before it exploded his heart. Writhing, kicking and cursing, the dying outlaw crawled and flopped from the kitchen of his bootlegging joint to its front porch, where, in final resignation, he rolled down the steps and sprawled motionless in death according to *The Daily Oklahoman* on October 10, 1921.

Joe ran a spot in 'nigger town', the East side colored settlement along the Rock Island Railroad tracks in Oklahoma City. Cold home brew was thirty-five cents, three bottles for a dollar. Corn liquor that would strip the enamel from the molars as it rushed by, was a dollar a pint. A wench to shimmy and kick, or go to bed, could be provided on short notice. If a storage squab-chicken was seduced from the back porch icebox and fired up in the quick grease, it was two dollars more.

And, like all guys in luck, Joe didn't know when he was well off. He had to do a little hi-jacking, and buy and sell hot diamonds, in between times and on the side. His fondness for carrying a pistol caused his downfall.

Pruiett and pistol-toting Orban Patterson packed their artillery into Joe's, shortly after supper time on Sunday night. Patterson was still watching from his eye-corners for Wade and Alonzo Williams. Rush McGaffey, a negro protege of Pruiett's, who drove his car, oiled his pistol cylinder, emptied the old bottles out of his office waste basket and operated a Kelly pool game and policy racket in a Pruiett owned building, was along. The negro Patterson, who was a client of Orban Patterson's, Pruiett's junior partner, didn't like Rush McGaffey—neither did white Patterson.

Joe decorated the worn oil-cloth of the kitchen table with four sweating bottles before he sat down in the one vacant chair remaining. Pruiett, expensively tailored, and with his black mop competing with his finger and tie diamonds for shine and splendor, showed the strain of a bad drunk. Small pockets, which had formed under his dark eyes, twitched spasmodically. There was a noticeable gap between the slightly dirty edge of his white collar, and his neck.

"Git me another bottle of beer, Joe," Pruiett commanded in an unpleasant tone.

"Let Rush get it, he ain't too damn good," interrupted Orban Patterson.

Joe sat and looked defiantly for an instant; he uttered a slight sniff of contempt as he arose to obey. There was insolence in the way he slammed the fresh bottle down on the table before the lawyer after he brought it. Rush McGaffey squirmed uneasily.

"I guess I'd better go on home, Mr. Pruiett," Rush said. "It ain't very far an' I'll just walk."

"Hell no," said Pruiett. "You're drivin' my car, an' stayin' with me. When I go you go, and not before."

There was a difficult silence which lasted for several minutes. "Joe," Pruiett said, deliberately, as he eyed him through optics that were almost closed, "I've worked out all I owe you for drinks. You don't get any more free service; I don't get any more free drinks."

"That's good for me," Joe answered. "What suits you suits me. I guess there's plenty of lawyers, just like there's plenty of bootleggers." He grinned understandingly at Pat, sitting sour-faced and silent beside Pruiett.

"Pat don't represent you, not if he stays in my office, if that's what you mean," Pruiett corrected him. "I told you about those diamonds, and I meant what I said. You went right ahead an' fenced 'em, an' by god..."

Joe shot a quick look at Rush McGaffey. "God-damn you, Rush, did you... ?"

"I ain't said nothin', Joe, not a word," Rush said, half-rising. "Mr. Pruiett's been fussin' all evenin', and sayin' I was in on it too, but I ain't, an' I ain't told him nothin'."

"Hell, yes, he did, the black rat," Pat interrupted. "He's the one that squealed, an' it ain't the first time he's done it. He's a regular snitch."

Joe's massive lip curled with contempt. "You always was a damned rat," he growled at McGaffey, "an' I ought to kill you. By god..."

"Git me another bottle of beer, Joe," Pruiett interrupted. His voice was hard.

Joe Patterson glared at McGaffey for a full instant before he gave a sign of hearing Pruiett's command. He looked defiantly at Pruiett, again, as he arose. The evil look which was apparent on his face as he headed for the back-porch cooler was suspiciously absent, and supplanted by a fictitious grin, when he returned.

"No use to git mad at me, Mr. Pruiett," he said. "Ol' Joe is goin' to listen to his lawyer. He ain't got the best one in the country for nothin'. Ol' Joe ain't that dumb."

Pruiett nodded and studied the rising foam on the slightly wild brew. He might be drunk, and he might suffer from chronic ego, but he wasn't goin' to be fooled by a murderous nigger. He could hear the bells ringin', and they told him to watch out for evil action.

Black Joe changed the subject; switched to a tale of World War ribaldry. McGaffey, frightened and uneasy, forced a smile, then an African guffaw, at the smutty climax.

"Git me another bottle of beer, Joe." The insolent content of Pruiett's command had graduated with the slight lapse of time and the considerable quantity of brew he had consumed. Joe appeared not to notice it. He promptly slammed a wet, foaming bottle on the slick table before him.

Joe Patterson didn't resume his seat. Instead he stood beside it, on one foot, with the other foot planted squarely in the seat of the chair. "What kind of a gun's that you're carryin' tonight, Rush?" he asked. "Is it the same one as you always had?"

The stupid Rush laid his hand on the butt, which protruded from the waist band of his trousers. He was going to lay the weapon out on the table. "Yeah," he said, as he touched it. "It's... "

Orban Patterson's hand crept toward his belt. Etiquette and style was temporarily requiring that he eliminate the hip-bulge. He was wearing his pistol in the waist-band.

"Rush," Pruiett barked, "don't do it! Don't move that gun. They're gonna kill you."

McGaffey turned a pale brown. His hand froze on the bone handle.

"Put it on the table, you son-of-a-bitch," Joe Patterson said, with a menacing movement toward his side. "Put it on the table. You reached for it, an' you don't get no drop on me. Lay it out here."

McGaffey was as white as Pruiett or Pat. Unable to move a muscle, he could only look appealingly at Pruiett by rolling his big eyes.

"Don't move, Rush," Pruiett said. "If you start to move that gun, they'll shoot you. That's all they want you to do. Don't move."

"It's a show-down," Joe Patterson gritted. "An' I don't take no chances. Do you bring it out, or do I let you have it now?"

Joe was standing directly across the table from Pruiett. His gun was on his right hip, which was slightly distorted by the position of his right foot, resting, as it was, on the seat of the chair. He didn't suspect that Pruiett was armed; that he had a pistol in the band of his trousers, the same as McGaffey.

Joe started to drag his foot across the rough bottom of the kitchen chair. He was going to drop it to the floor and draw at the same time. The dive was as tense and still as if death was present, instead of only approaching.

"Don't move, Rush," Pruiett whispered. "They'll kill you, sure."

As the foot went down, Pruiett leaped up. His gun, and that of Joe Patterson, looked each other squarely in the eye for a recognizing instant, and but one, spoke. It was Pruiett's. The force of the big slug knocked the heavy negro almost out the kitchen door. Mortally wounded, bleeding terribly, he crawled back past the transfixed trio in the room, through the house and out the front door, whimpering and mumbling like an ailing pup.

The unexpected turn of events stunned Pat. He was standing pale and rigid, watching the wounded negro, when Pruiett's attention was attracted by a movement at his side. Pruiett cocked his big pistol again.

"Don't shoot, Rush," he cried. "Don't you kill Mr. Patterson. If you do, I'll blow your head off."

Patterson looked around into the menacing muzzle of McGaffey's gun, trained full on his head. Pruiett was at the negro's side, holding a cocked pistol in both hands, within a foot of McGaffey's head.

"I'll kill you as sure as hell if you shoot," Pruiett repeated. "Put it down; take it off Mr. Patterson. You're as dead as hell if you don't."

McGaffey seemed to reflect for an instant, not looking toward the man who was threatening his life so soon after saving it; he was sighting all the time down the groove of his pistol barrel. In the tense atmosphere, he seemed to casually seek the preponderance. He wanted to kill Patterson. Was it worth what it would cost if Pruiett meant what he said? Rush dropped the gun to the table-top. Patterson slumped into a seat.

"You better go on home, Rush, or somewhere out of here," Pruiett said. "Me and Pat'll take care of things. Maybe you better call me at the office in about a' hour. I've got to call the cops, an' I may need you for a witness."

"PRUIETT HELD ON CHARGE OF KILLING NEGRO," proclaimed *The Daily Oklahoman* on October 10, 1921.

It was 34 point type in the Oklahoma's headlines, announcing another sensational move on the part of the irrepressible Pruiett. "Joe W. Patterson, Negro," said the story which followed, "was killed Sunday night at 9 o'clock in a shooting affray at his home, 615 East First street, in which Moman Pruiett, Orban Patterson and Rush McGaffey are alleged to have been participants."

"According to W. P. Lindsay, under-sheriff, Pruiett called the County Jail immediately after the shooting and announced that he had 'shot a man', and was ready to give up. When they arrived, they found Patterson dead near the front steps. Pruiett, in a statement to Carl Glitsch, Chief of Police, said at the jail that he had shot Patterson in self-defense, following a disagreement between Orban Patterson and Rush McGaffey, in which Joe Patterson is alleged to have interfered."

The old boy had been shy of temporary insanity since the prosecution had tried to send St. Mary to a psychopathic cell. He wouldn't want to plead insanity for himself, anyway. Being an old southern gentleman, the unwritten law wasn't going to be invoked over the killing of a black man. The simple elimination narrowed it to self-defense. There was no other plea available, but wasn't it a good one, served the Pruiett style?

According to the *Oklahoma News* on October 10, 1921, "Information gained by County officials, that a plot was nipped in the bud when Attorney Moman Pruiett whirled and killed 'Negro Joe' Patterson at his home Sunday, kept charges from being filed Monday against the attorney, it was declared'."

"The mystery of the shooting rests solely in the hands of Rush McGaffey, negro bootlegger and gambling king, who operates a pool hall in a building owned by Pruiett and Orban Patterson, who are law partners. Bertillion Expert Lee Mullenix rushed to the place from the police station, and declared Monday that 'all parties had been drinking heavily' .. "

"Both Attorney Patterson and Moman Pruiett were released on personal checks of $1,500 each as bond pending investigation by the County Attorney. 'Negro Joe' Patterson was a notorious character, and was considered a 'bad actor.' Together with Rush McGaffey, the control of the gambling and bootlegging element among the negroes fell to the pair."

Was Pruiett goin' to be prosecuted? Why, Hell no! Men with money an' power, an' political pull, don't have to answer to the law just for killin' a damn nigger... That ain't the point. We don't want to see him prosecuted so as to get him stuck. We want 'em to file on him 'an try him, so he'll have to make a wild, rabble-rousin' speech to a jury, in his own defense. What a speech that'd be. The Washita's pride, the old black stud himself, up before a jury with his own butt in the balances. Can't you hear it? How he was half-starved all through his childhood, and how he blacked them boots at Fort Smith? How his poor old mother worked an' slaved so as to make him a lawyer, an' now a bunch of jealous competitors jumps on him an' tries to railroad him out of practice? That's what we want to hear.

You don't want much. Why, Hell! You've had more of that now than one generation's entitled to, ain't you? Wasn't the Tom Gore speech enough to satisfy you? One like that, an' the Orban Patterson trial, ought to be enough to satisfy anybody. Hell, yes, he'd make 'em cry. They'd sweat blood right out of their eyeballs when he got to tellin' 'em how he'd struggled. An' there'd be some cussin' along with it. Skunks? Vultures? Pigs? That's mild language to what he'd give 'em if he got to bellerin' for his own neck. But forget it. There ain't no chance, 'cause Pruiett's too strong to have to worry about more than a little old preliminary hearin'.

"Moman Pruiett was justified in killing Joe Patterson, alleged negro bootlegger and gambler, Sunday night." In instructing the jury Justice of the Peace, A. W. McWilliams, "said that he believed that it was their duty to exonerate Pruiett. He had a verdict prepared to be signed."

"The said jurors," read the entry on the magistrate's docket, "upon their oaths do say that the said Joe Patterson came to his death by gun shot wounds, said gun in the hands of one Moman Pruiett, and that said Moman Pruiett was justified in said act, and was acting wholly in self-defense. (Signed) R. Weesner, Foreman."

It was a hum-drum existence. Annabelle Edwards was insisting that at least a fraction of his time be devoted to the preparation of her case, coming on for trial in a fortnight. The Hill murder case, set for trial at Brighton, Colorado, was set, and in no uncertain terms had the Court and the prosecution told him that his application for a continuance would be denied. Napoleon Buffalohead, Osage Indian at Newkirk, who had paid him $4,500 to defend him in a murder case, after being charged with beating and stomping his eight month pregnant wife to death in March of 1920 couldn't understand why his counsel had to kill a nigger on the night before his case was to be tried, in October of 1921 nor why he didn't come on up, and help his office assistants, after the coroner's jury had promptly absolved him of blame. Buffalohead eventually was found guilty of manslaughter and was required to pay a $1,000 fine.

But there were reasons. "Pruiett In New Gun Affray," advised the *Oklahoma News* on October 12, 1921. "Attorney Moman Pruett [sic] late Tuesday faced a tragic situation for the second time this week when Attorney Sam Clement drew a gun and threatened his life at the Kingkade Hotel. Pruiett sprang toward Clement, grasped the revolver by the hammer and wrested it away. Pruiett's finger was cut when he disarmed Clement. J. W. Burns, senior member of Clement's firm, declared that no enmity had existed between Clement and Pruiett.

Clement is Burn's son-in-law. 'Whiskey was the cause of the affair, an I hope to God that Forrest Hughes [Oklahoma County Prosecuting Attorney] stops these affairs as he announced he will do,' Burns declared emphatically." A man just had to do something to break the awful monotony.

"The 10-year-old girl found murdered by drowning" near Eno, Adams County, Colorado, "late Saturday, was Helen Maxine Short, daughter of Mrs. Thelma Hill, this city. This is the bare statement of last night's latest developments in probably the most brutal murder case Adams County police annals show. Evidence found by Sheriff E. A. Gormley and Coroner E. J. Jones of Adams County, weights tied to the child's neck by wires, the clutching position of her hands, the marks made by the wires on her throat, showed, the authorities believe, that the little girl was thrown into the water alive and left to die," said the *Rocky Mountain News* of Denver on July 25, 1921.

"Circumstantial evidence and information given by Mrs. Hill here started a search for William Riley Hill, her second husband, who, she said, is a half-breed Indian, as the alleged slayer of the child."

William Riley was the son of old John T. Hill of the valley; his mother had been a Chickasaw squaw. They were Pruiett's friends and clients of a more wholesome era, who held land on the Washita, and raised cattle to augment their already substantial wealth. Pruiett was employed.

In a deed filed on August 12, 1921: "KNOW ALL MEN BY THESE PRESENTS: That I, William Riley Hill, son of John T. Hill, deceased, of Paul Valley, Garvin County, Oklahoma, do hereby grant, bargain, sell and convey unto Moman Pruiett of Oklahoma City, Oklahoma, all of the following described real estate situated in Garvin County, Oklahoma, to-wit:

"Approximately four hundred and fifty (450) acres of land situated from two and one-half to three and one-quarter miles East and South of Pauls Valley;"

"Approximately nineteen hundred (1900) acres of land situated about eight miles East of Pauls Valley; all of the above land being situated in Garvin County, State of Oklahoma, and being included in the Estate of John T. Hill, deceased, of Pauls Valley, Oklahoma, described as follows:."

Pruiett took deed to a neat fortune, for the defense of a case he knew he couldn't win. He smiled while he was preparing the conveyance, as he thought of old Sam Garvin. Them bastards at the convention had wanted to change the name of Garvin County, that he'd fought so hard to get named for his friend, just to take another poke at him. The Colonel had sure been good to him.

The utterly original explanation reported in the *Brighton Blade* of Adams County on October 25, 1921, offered by Hill didn't help Pruiett as he strove to make out a credible defense for him. "Hill still maintains that he gave the little girl to a foreigner near Derby, who promised to take her back to Denver in his automobile. He admitted that the child was with him in the vicinity the day before the murder is supposed to have occurred." Pruiett had never liked to see a witness change his testimony; tell your story and stick to it, regardless of how improbable it may seem, had been his advise to clients. Callie Pence profited by his program. He built his defense around Hill's hastily concocted statement, given to the police immediately after his arrest.

The flattering notices given him by the mountain press failed to rouse or elate him. "Pruiett gained prominence when he defended Senator Gore of Oklahoma in the sensational damage case brought against him a few years ago," said the *Denver Post* on October 21, 1921. Hill's "leading counsel is Moman Pruiett of Oklahoma City, a criminal lawyer of wide reputation in Oklahoma and Texas," said the *Brighton Blade.* "Mr. Pruiett has been the chief counsel for the defense in two hundred and sixty-nine murder cases." He was weary, and tired, and bored. He didn't get the old thrill from setting the drinks up for the press boys, and watching their eyes shine as he told them his stock murder trial stories. It was a drink, and another, and another. And he'd rather have a continuance than have the case go to trial. Maybe he'd feel better, more like trying it next term. He was beginning to suggest a delay in every case being called to trial.

But, the account of the conclusion of the trial, printed in Denver's *Rocky Mountain News* on October 30,1921, disclosed that there was the customary rally just before the whistle blew. "The Oklahoma Lawyer was perspiring profusely, and stopped long enough to remove his collar.The attorney then delved into the testimony, dissecting it and assembling it to his client's credit."

" 'I am appealing to you men,' he said, whirling again to the jury. 'I am appealing to you not to be swayed to a rabid sentiment built upon a false fabric.' Then turning and shaking his finger at Sheriff Gormley, he cried at the top of his voice, 'Gormley, you sleuth hound, with your ambition for re-election, why didn't you bring the station agent of Barr into the courtroom? This defendant asserts he talked with him. Why didn't you bring the agent in to testify?' Then whirling again to the jury, 'Gormley thinks he has a cinch on this case,' he said, 'but gentlemen, I've known dead things to crawl. There is nothing to fear but maudlin, damnable sentiment that ought to be in purgatory rather than in a court of justice'."

But the Colorado jurors wouldn't be whiled away from a true verdict in such an obvious case. They found Hill guilty of murder and sentenced him to life imprisonment in the penitentiary. When Pruiett entered the District Courtroom at Oklahoma City two days after the verdict, ready to try the Annabelle Edwards case, every one was congratulating him.

"That was a good job, Moman," the lawyers and courthouse employees observed. "It was a great victory. We knew that was all you expected to do; save him from hanging. It was a terrible case."

"Sure," Pruiett agreed aloud. "It was a'awful tough one." Aside to Pat, and beneath his heavily alcoholized breath, he muttered, "Don't you suppose them bastards know I got the book throwed at me? Don't they know they haven't got capital punishment in the State of Colorado?

Annabelle Edwards paid Pruiett $10,000 in cash for his services. She was charged and tried for the murder of W. L. "Billy" Edwards, her gambler husband, in March of 1921 yet she never knew from day to day and until the verdict was finally read, whether she would have a lawyer in court for her or not. Pruiett wasn't carrying whiskey; whiskey was carrying him. He tossed his mane and shook his fist at it, and defied it to restrain him or slow him down. The comely, Annabelle, in rage and disgust, charged him with stupid conceit, but her psychological analysis was not as true as her aim with a .38, poor dead husband Billy. Her counsel merely despaired because her case was so routine. There were no new fields for him to invade.

But Annabelle Edwards didn't take her erring counsel without notice. His shortcomings were being aired as conspicuously as were his triumphs. Southwestern papers had broadcast his censure by a Federal

Judge when he came to court weaving drunk. The anecdote of his unique display of complete independence and indifference, when criticized by an offended wife, were as well known as his movements in the latest murder case.

Mrs. Pruiett stood before the secretary's desk in his outer office. "I've been looking for Moman for three days, and expecting him to call me, but I haven't heard a word," she said. "I'm sure, from your tone, that you could give me better information about him, than you have."

"No m'am," the girl answered in confusion. "Well, yes m'am. He's in there; in his own office."

"When did he come in?"

"He hasn't been out," the girl said. "I know I told you on the 'phone that he wasn't here; but, I had instructions... "

"I understand," Mrs. Pruiett interrupted, jerking at the brass knob. "It's locked. How can I get in?"

"It's bolted from the inside."

"I'll get him out," the irate wife stormed, as she kicked and pounded on the panel. "But I don't hear a sound. Are you sure he's in there?"

"I don't believe he's been out for three days," the frightened girl answered. "He took a' awful lot of whiskey and soda water in, an' gave me definite instructions not to disturb him, an' tell any one who called that he was out. The door's been locked ever since, unless he comes out at night, an' I don't think he does."

"Call the police station and have them send some men up here, immediately," Mrs. Pruiett directed, still pounding on the door. "We've got to get in there. He may be dead."

"No m'am, he ain't dead," the girl replied. "I hear him all the time. Part of time he's talkin' loud—making speeches—an' part of the time he's laughin', loud and kind of scary like. I heard him just a little before you came up."

"Break that door down," Mrs. Pruiett ordered, when the police had arrived. "I'll be responsible for the order. Go ahead and force it." The officers began to lunge against the heavy door.

The room was filled with a smell of tobacco and human waste. The big windows were fastened down, although it was mid-summer, and the heat, with the odor, was sickening. Fine furniture was littered with empty bottles, broken glass, cigar butts and expectoration stains. The picture of complete ruin was surmounted by the figure of the Washita stud, reclining on his shoulder blades in the depths of his desk chair, grinning stupidly up at his callers.

Pruiett was dirty. What had once been a white shirt and tie was a spotted, streaked pair of raiments, yellowed with sweat and browned with filth. The long tail of the shirt hung outside his belt, about a sagging browned seat and the unbuttoned front of a pair of linen trousers, so wrinkled, stained and dirty as to positively contravert the true suggestion that they, too, were once white. One foot was bare; a soiled shoe and sock lay amongst the empty bottles on the desk. The other shoe was on the wrong foot, and its innate whiteness was imperceptible beneath a coat of tobacco juice and waste. Unsteady jerks of his head, as he looked about and tried to smile, caused matted locks of long black hair to fall across his eyes and forehead, and about a face obscured with a coarse growth of black beard.

"Bless your heart, Leda," he mumbled, "I'm glad to see you. Jus' awful glad to see you. Take a seat."

The long suffering wife glared balefully at him. She surveyed the ruin of the room with methodical glances, to return each time to the most desolate and wretched item of the interior—that of her husband.

"You beast," she cried. "You utter animal! You are the dirtiest, lowest thing I ever saw!"

"Bless your heart," he repeated. "Bless your heart. You're all excited. Fix yourself a drink, an' fix me one, too. Fix old Mome a drink."

Mrs. Pruiett patted her foot and glared in gathering fury. "Dirty! Filthy! Foul!" she cried. "I've never seen such dirt in all my life. My husband—as dirty as a hog. You're a degenerate. No human could sink lower, and get dirtier and nastier than you are this minute."

"You think not?" he answered, as he opened his eyes to inquiring slits, and grinned again. "Let old Mome show you you're wrong again."

He leaned awkwardly forward and lifted a heavy glass inkstand from the table top. Holding it tremblingly above his head, he gradually tilted it, so that its contents spilled on his scalp, and ran down to mingle with the dirt which already tried to conceal his identity. When the black fluid had covered his face, neck and shoulders, and was spreading in a huge blot downward toward his waist, he shuffled to his feet.

"Now you're right," he mumbled, disconsolately. "I'm the dirtiest son-of-a-bitch on god a'mighty's earth; the very dirtiest. Will you take me home, honey?"

The black charger bustled into the office of Edward Dewes Oldfield, District Judge of the 13th Judicial District. His pocket was bulging with an assortment of legal papers.

"Got your writ all ready?" the Judge inquired, smiling.

"Ain't interested in no writ, yet," Pruiett grinned.

"Annabelle ain't goin' to wait in jail, now. Don't tell me that."

"Not unless I lose my taw," Pruiett returned. "We got somethin' more important than tryin' to bust the State's investigation hold while they wait on Billy to die. We're suin' him for a divorce and asking for a restainin' order against his relatives from seizing his property, an' I got orders here for tyin' up a couple bank accounts, an' a safety deposit box."

"That's kind of rough, ain't it?" Oldfield inquired. "Shoot a man up an' put him in the hospital, an' then file a lawsuit against him? She just wanted to be sure she'd have him where she could get service on him, is that it?"

Pruiett grinned again. "This is the first shootin' case I ever got into where I started out with a divorce petition instead of a writ of habeas corpus," he admitted. "But, this is an unusual case from a lot of angles. She alleges in her petition that this jack is community property, that they got it together since they was married, an' that Billy's folks are liable to grab it out of the bank, an' beat her out of it. We want some restrainin' orders, to keep ever'body away from that stuff 'til we can get a hearin'."

"You ain't tryin' to restrain a little security for a' attorney's fee, are you Moman?" Oldfield inquired, as he attached his signature to the orders.

"It's goin' to be high, if Billy dies, an' I'll bet you two to one he ain't alive tomorrow night," Pruiett said. "If I'm right about that, you'll see me in here with the writ. We'll have to persuade the County Attorney to agree to bond, or make him do it in court."

Billy Edwards writhed and twisted under a retraining sheet, according to the *Oklahoma City Times* on March 30, 1921, while the Deputy Sheriff served the summons in the divorce case on him. He was dead by nightfall, and Pruiett filed his writ to compel Annabelle's release on bond. The bond was steep, but he made it, and preparation for trial was commenced.

"More shooting took place at 910 1/2 North Dewey Ave., Billy Edwards' apartment, Tuesday night. Following a report of shots heard

Whatcom County Library System
02/09/15 11:48AM
FERNDALE LIBRARY
360-305-3600
www.wcls.org

LIST OF ITEMS OUT

LL - HE MADE IT SAFE TO MURDER
3202001489106 Due: 03/02/15

Your current account balance is: $ 0.00

Whatcom County Library System
02/09/15 11:48AM
FERNDALE LIBRARY
360-305-3600
www.wcls.org

LIST OF ITEMS OUT

L - HE MADE IT SAFE TO MURDER
3202001489106 Due: 03/02/15

Your current account balance is: $ 0.00

there, Police rushed to the place and found Moman Pruiett, attorney, and Mrs. Edwards. Pruiett said some one was eavesdropping at the apartment and that the shots were fired by Mrs. Edwards' guard. No arrests were made. Pruiett said he did not fire the shots," the newspaper reported.

"What's the trouble?" a plain-clothes officer demanded, as he came to the top of the stairway.

"Nothin' a'tall, chief, nothin' a'tall," Pruiett assured him. "Mrs. Edwards and I came out here to pick up some private papers of hers, an' to reconstruct the tragedy for her defense, an' some one tried to sneak up on us. Dutch was waitin' in the car, an' he tried to stop 'em. When they ran, he took a couple of shots in the air, just to scare 'em."

"Where's Dutch now?" asked the officer.

"I sent him away," Pruiett answered. "I don't like that kind of stuff. I told him to go away an' let us alone."

"What's the matter with Mrs. Edwards," he asked, next.

"She's under a strain; you know how it is, an' I guess the shootin' upset her more," Pruiett said. He was steadying the girl with a tight grip, while she trembled and shook with sobs.

"I'm leavin' it with you," the policeman said, after a deliberate study. "Let's have things quiet around here from now on. The neighbors are raisin' hell about this place all the time."

"Okay, Chief," Pruiett agreed. "I won't bust a cap if they mob me."

"I'm glad he didn't look inside, an' see all the bullet holes we got in here," Pruiett said, as he pushed Annabelle into the apartment and locked the door. "What the hell's the matter with you?"

"I wanta die," Annabelle sobbed. "Give me that gun back, an' let me alone for a minute, an' I'll see that I do."

"Brace up," Pruiett soothed, producing his bottle. "I'll fix you a drink an'... "

"You an' your bottle," Annabelle shrieked. "That's what's the matter with me. You've got to defend me for murder, an' you do nothin' but drink whiskey. You can't help me when you're dog drunk."

"I ain't drunk, honey," Pruiett answered. "Was that what made you grab that pistol out of my pocket an' try to kill yourself? Just because I had both hands occupied tryin' to uncork a bottle?"

Annabelle sank to the bed, crying hysterically. I'll get the chair; I know I will," she bawled. "I paid you a fortune to defend me, an' I get a dopey drunk. Oh, God! Let me have that gun so I can end this misery."

"Now look here, Annabelle, honey," Pruiett answered, in a professional manner. "We got to be reasonable. What did I wrestle you all over this place for, with that god damn gun a poppin' in my ear, if I wasn't goin' to give you a good defense. When I saw you puttin' it up to your head, I knew damn well if I let you go I wouldn't have any work to do for that big fee you paid me. Why, hell, I'm paid in advance. It'd be the easiest way for me; just let you blow your head off an' have no defense to make a'tall."

"You'll send me to the chair," she groaned. "You just mark my word, I'll be convicted. I know I will."

"You won't be if you'll give me half a chance to try you," Pruiett answered. "This is the kind of a case I like the best. If Billy hadn't a left you so much dough, I'd a defended you free, or paid you to let me get in the case. I'm goin' to make monkeys out of the State's attorneys, an' you'll have a barrel of fun watchin' it, before you come clear. You know it?"

He took a big handkerchief and wiped her tear-smeared rouge. She smiled and sniffled. Pruiett had a way with his clients.

James Brooks Ayers Robertson, who managed to last his four-year term without being impeached, was Governor. John "Jack" Calloway Walton, his successor who didn't fare so well with the Senate, sitting as a Court of Impeachment, was the Mayor of Oklahoma City. Pruiett didn't like them or agree with them politically, and as the Edwards case contained a rich graft and corruption element, he decided to unload it on them.

"The defense will prove," Pruiett said in his opening statement, "that the dead Billy Edwards paid the Governor $5,000 for a pardon for George Parrish, who was his first lieutenant in the vice and liquor business, and who is the State's principal witness in this case; that Jack Walton's police force winked at open violations of law as Billy and his gang of gamblers and bootleggers paid tribute to him."

According to the *Oklahoma News* of November 18, 1921: "Pruiett, following his attack on Robertson, Walton and a number of gamblers and bootleggers, all of whom he asserted were in conspiracy against the woman on trial, declared he not only feared for her life, but for his own as well. 'They may get me, some dark night,' he said in a broken voice, 'but if they do, I hope that some other will take up the torch and carry on the fight'.' I'm only 49 years old,' he added, 'but I'll be ready to go. I've already lived a hundred and forty-nine years."

"A brawl and near-fight between Defense Atty. Moman Pruiett and George Parrish, erstwhile gambler, was the entertainment presented to hundreds of murder fans at the re-opening of the Annabelle Edwards trial Monday" according to the *Oklahoma News* on November 14. "Parrish accused Pruiett of frequenting city gambling halls; Pruiett denounced the witness as a liar, and both men were out of their seats. Judge E. D. Oldfield quelled the disorder before either had a chance to follow up the hot words."

"George Parrish was put on as the first prosecution witness. The brawl with Pruiett came near the end of his testimony. 'Didn't you operate gambling houses with this unfortunate man, Edwards?' Pruiett demanded. 'No,' Parrish retorted. 'I was at some places where gambling was going on, just like I've seen you at such places'. ' That's a lie,' Pruiett shouted, banging the table at his side. ' I haven't played cards for 16 years' 'You wouldn't call me that outside this courtroom,' Parrish answered, as Oldfield rapped for order and other attorneys moved in to quiet them. Pruiett was determined to fire a parting shot. 'Mr. Parrish,' he inquired, suavely, 'Isn't it a fact that you regularly, and recently, purchased eight and ten 100 pound sacks of sugar?' Parrish turned even redder than before. 'What about that grocery store at 23rd Street and Robinson?' the attorney demanded. 'I bought five sacks there,' the witness admitted. 'But I bought them for a friend'."

Those were the days of home brew and sugar whiskey. Mash-fed hogs brought good prices on the market; there was a ready sale for the liquor. Pruiett drank it in case of emergency, when he couldn't get the high-priced stuff which he usually imported from Kansas City. He preferred to play poker in the Baltimore Hotel there, or in Washington, but he didn't confine his talents exclusively to the big time. He knew, and so did the listeners in the courtroom, that his heated denial of George Parrish's observation was nothing more than part of the proper production of Annabelle's defense.

Behind the back of the straw man of graft and corruption, which he had set up to beguile the gullible jurors away from the real issue, he had his inevitable little plea of self-defense.

"He came upstairs and said, 'You god-damn bitch, get your clothes on and get out of this house'," Mrs. Edwards said in telling of the shooting. "He walked to the dresser and opened the drawers. I walked over to him. He snatched a diamond lavaliere from around my neck and struck me. My hand hit the side of the table. I had been sick and wasn't well enough to fuss or fight. I backed away. My hand touched a gun lying on the table. He made a movement like he was reaching for his gun. He was left-handed and he always wore his gun on the right side under his vest—" At this point she choked and sat silent for a moment. " 'Well, what did you do?' asked her attorney. 'I fired,' was the answer. 'When I picked up the gun, I didn't know whether it was loaded or how many shells were in it. I intended to scare him, but he kept coming. I knew by the look on his face that he would kill me. I shot to protect my life. I fired twice; his gun fell to the floor'."

That was all there was to the Annabelle Edwards case, except Moman Pruiett, counsel for the defense and the forensic fireworks which went with him. He managed to drag the trial of the case out over fifteen full days. He took five hours to sum it up in final argument to the jury. Even the trial judge was looking sheepish and apologetic when Pruiett had concluded his denunciation of the enforcement officers and State prosecutors who had been so ignoble as to try to perform their sworn duty. A holy light, like the nimbus over a madonna, glowed about the head of the little chippy in the prisoner's dock.

Pruiett warmed up by telling the jury that the Governor of their State was "as crooked as a pan full of hog guts."

"God deliver me from coming in contact with the shadow of this Governor us yellow dog democrats are so proud of," he bawled. "I wouldn't trust Jack Walton or the Governor, handcuffed, to carry their own grips to the depot."

And poor old George Parrish, the State's star witness, had hesitated before attending the trial, apprehensive of being picked up on an old criminal complaint. The prosecuting attorneys had written him, and in diplomatic terms, given him to understand that bygones could be bygones, even with the majesty of the law, and especially when Pruiett was hot on their heels. Pruiett's extensive underworld intelligence service had brought news of the deal back to him, and he had exposed it in the trial of the cause.

Having paid his respects to the Governor, and the Mayor, he turned to the prosecuting attorney's office. Jerking his coat off and slamming it into an empty chair, he dashed a splash of perspiration from his face and wheeled upon the hapless prosecutors with the same movement.

"There never was a more dirty or contemptible deal made, with a perjuring skunk, than your letter indicates you made with this dirty pig," he roared. "Give ME the authority of County Attorney, and give me this Edwards case, and I'LL put more crooked thieves and officers in the penitentiary than there are this side of hell."

The able E. J. Giddings, his adversary in a hundred bad cases, who had fought valiantly to discredit blind Senator Gore seven years before, was special prosecutor. He had been hired by dead Billy's parents to insure the conviction of the woman who had killed their son. Giddings was desperate. By preference, he had enjoined the whispering school that said, 'Pruiett is slippin; he's drinking himself to death.' He felt and hoped, may have even believed, that at last his opportunity for victory, and revenge, had arrived. He had made a vigorous, and effective argument to the jury, but not one that Pruiett couldn't answer in his own inimitable manner.

"That is the gentleman, Annabelle, honey," Pruiett soothed, as he pointed the trembling finger at Giddings, "who called you a harlot and a prostitute, without one scintilla of testimony to support it. The dirty, damnable scoundrel who brands a woman as a harlot is unworthy of the consideration of any jury, especially when he does it without one scintilla of evidence to justify it. When any lawyer says that a woman laid flat on her back, in the absence of proof, in old Kentucky—that lawyer is either mentally deranged or he is as mean and dirty as hell. Where is there testimony in this case that this poor little soul has ever laid flat on her back?"

Pruiett stood defiantly beside his pitiable client, caressing her shoulder tenderly. He glared at the jury, then in the direction of Giddings, and then back at the jury.

"He talks to you of the North," he continued. "I care not from what clime you come. I care not if you live upon an island in the sea; I care not if you be a Yankee, with a blue stripe around your belly six inches wide; I care not whether you hail from Georgia," which he pronounced it Jaw-Jaw, "or old Alabamy, or whether you are from the State that produces the blue granite, as cold and relentless as it looks. You're a man if you're a man, whether you came from Wharton County, Kentucky, or not, and in the breast of every real man there is a resentment against murderous and slanderous assaults against the defenseless, and a natural inclination to come to the defense of a helpless, ninety-five pound woman."

"You talk to me about the Fatherhood of God and the Brotherhood of Man, and how it is abroad in this land. You talk to me about peace on the earth, and good will toward men. But let me ask you, where can that peace ever exist when men like Giddings can take the floor to stultify pure American Womanhood, and pardons are bartered and sold by our public officials of $5,000 per each?"

The sweat which sifted through his pores and saturated every garment over his body gave off a pungent, alcoholic odor. His eyes were fixed and glassy, and with every wild vehement gesture the billowing black mass of hair atop his head rocked and rolled. His eloquence was fierce—painful. No one, not even the presiding court, dared to interrupt him. Every eye in the room was trained upon him, and not even as much as a labored breath could be heard during his dramatic pauses. And, as if his scurrility was not strong enough, he half apologized to the tense jurors for the mildness of his language.

"I wish I could coin a word to describe that man Parrish," he cried. "Do you know, I studied all night? I told my wife, 'for God's sake, honey, give me something; get the dictionary, so we can find some word to describe him'. 'Well,' she said, 'you once said "A Lizzard of Lies," what does that mean?' I says 'that don't describe him at all'."

"He said 'I am a farmer—I have got 20 acres of land; I get $90.00 a month from the Government. No wonder you lie, God bless your heart. There wasn't any use for him to try do it—but listen, the dirty liar, he wouldn't weaken. The dirty skunk—but skunk isn't a good name for George. Did you ever go to the mouth of a sewer, with fecal matter? Well, it is one of those live things, that is what George Parrish is."

"Your Honor, I have heard that on the equity side of the docket, before they can get anything from you or the rest of the judiciary, that they must come in with clean hands, but it looks like, in these piping times of bootlegging and gambling, that in the PROSECUTION, you can come in with just any old kind of hands."

"Look at Parrish. 'What did you feed those hogs out there—Sugar?' and he says, 'No, sir, I buy dairy milk.' What did you carry that sugar out there for—those hogs?' I asked him, and he says, 'I didn't carry any sugar out to those hogs.' 'What are you doing buying 10 sacks of sugar a week out there on North Robinson Street?' and he says, 'Judge, do I have to answer it? I bought that for a friend'."

When he was ready to conclude, he stood quietly in eloquent stillness, close to the front row of jurors, near to the center of the box. In a mild tone, without gesture, he started to speak again.

"In God's name, I beg you; I beg you in the name of Him who came to save, in the name of Him who met the woman at the well, be just. If the spirit of Christ and the goodness of the hand of God can penetrate this jury box, we can have no fear. Let the Godly spirit combat and destroy the wickedness, and the evil in this case—Annabelle, God bless your little heart, you need have no fear."

The conclusion of the trial was orthodox, according to the *Oklahoma City Times,* of November 19, 1921. It was chronicled for posterity by a representative of the fourth estate, who witnessed it with his eyeballs.

" 'Gentlemen,' inquired the Court, 'have you reached a verdict?' 'We have, your Honor,' replied the foreman. 'Hand it up please, Mr. Foreman,' said the Judge. There was a stir, then an intense hush. 'We find the defendant, Annabelle Edwards, not guilty,' read the judge. 'Gentlemen, is this your verdict?' 'It is,' came the unanimous statement from the jurors. Annabelle Edwards smiled a little smile of relief—and then fainted. Her grip relaxed on the bouquet that she was holding and the flowers fell to the floor. 'Three cheers for Moman!' shouted some spectator near the doorway. The bailiff thundered for order. 'Who was that man that got noisy?' growled the judge—but the man had left hurriedly."

CHAPTER NINETEEN

WHEREIN PRUIETT PROFICIENCY IN MATTERS CIVIL IS DEMONSTRATED, AND ACCOUNT IS GIVEN OF HIS CONDUCT IN THE TRIAL WHERE THE SAD EYES OF LINCOLN SAVE A MURDEROUS VAGRANT FROM THE PENALTY USUALLY IMPOSED FOR TAKING HUMAN LIFE. AND HOW THE ONUS OF HIS OWN INTEMPERANCE, AND RECOLLECTION OF THE ILL-CONSIDERED ACTION, WHICH COST THE LIFE OF A FELLOW MAN, PRESSES UPON HIM, AND HE FINDS LESS OF ENJOYMENT IN CHEATING THE GALLOWS AND PRISON PENS. AND HOW HE JUSTIFIES THE ACTIVITY OF A MILLIONAIRE OIL MAN WHO SLEW A NATIONALLY PROMINENT ARMY AVIATOR, AND PREVENTS A STAIN FROM ATTACHING ITSELF TO THE NAME OF THE ACCUSED'S WIFE, ACQUIRING A VERDICT OF EXONERATION FOR HIM. AND HOW THE DEATH SENTENCE IS PASSED AT LAST—NOT UPON A PRUIETT CLIENT—BUT UPON THE WASHITA STALLION HIMSELF, AND HE PUTS HIS HOUSE IN ORDER BEFORE GOING TO OLD HAVANA, CUBA, TO SIT BY THE BAY AND WATCH THE SUN GO DOWN.

When Uncle Joe Adams died on the fender of a Santa Fe Railroad locomotive, according to the *Oklahoma City Pointer* on September 22, 1907. After a very commonplace crossing collision, Aunt Nancy Adams would hear of having no one but Moman Pruiett for 'suin' the company'.

"It's out of my line," Pruiett told her. "I'm a—"

"I know you're a criminal lawyer," Aunt Nancy supplied. "That's what some of my neighbors said, an' that you couldn't try this kind of a case, but I know better. You have to try it to a jury, don't you?"

"Yeah, it's a jury case," Pruiett agreed. "But . . . "

"Uncle Joe wouldn't a' had anybody but you for a lawsuit," Nancy maintained. "You got to take this case an' try it for me. The company's goin' to pay me plenty."

"Look, Auntie," Pruiett argued, "there's plenty of ambulance chasers that knows how to win a railroad-crossin' case with their head in a bucket. They try 'em all the time, just like you see me tryin' murder cases all the time. It ain't that I don't want the business; I just don't want you to take a chance by havin' a lawyer tryin' your case that don't know his stuff. Get the idea?"

"What's the difference?" Nancy demanded. "A lawsuit's a lawsuit, ain't it?"

"This case of yours has got a lot of involved negligence law mixed up in it," Pruiett argued. "Just because Uncle Joe is dead don't mean that you get to recover. You got to prove that the company was guilty of negligence, an' that Uncle Joe didn't contribute to his own death. I'd have to look up a lot of law before I'd be wise on that."

"Uncle Joe said you was the smartest lawyer in the country," Nancy answered. "You've got the case. I'm leavin' it to you to get me my money."

Pruiett prepared for trial at Eva Rush's roadhouse in the Mulligan Garden District, west of Oklahoma City. He could have what he wanted there, when he wanted it. He could orate, and strut and preen with his book, paper, and bottle, in front of full length mirrors that went to make up the walls of the elaborate assignation house. An office assistant gave him a short memorandum of a brief and two books on negligence law, the night before the trial of the case. He announced ready when the cause was called the next morning.

Uncle Joe's survivors and their floundering counsel made enough of a case for the trial court to let the issue go to the jury. Pruiett, under the impression that the customs of civil procedure limited him in the lengths he could go in arguing the facts, made a quiet and conservative, although analytical and effective, speech. He wanted, in a way, to show that he could restrain himself in court and be as much a gentleman in the trial of a case, as the corporation's counsel opposing him. The Santa Fe's staff had quietly enjoyed the discomfiture which Pruiett exhibited in the trial. He was obviously not familiar with the civil procedure. They had the bad taste and judgment to drop a word about it at the close of their argument.

"Pruiett is a little off his course in this case," the defense attorney told the jury. "He doesn't know just what to do with himself. He doesn't recognize the elements of negligence, and what it takes to make liability in this kind of an action. If it was a MURDER trial, he'd know what to do, but here the poor old boy has just stumbled around, and made a miserable failure of making a case. He ought to stick to murder. Yes, sir! Old Moman just doesn't fit in where there's anything involved besides a brutal, bloody, sensational murder."

The last word went to the plaintiff. When the defense had concluded its arguments, Pruiett still had time for a short reply. He came out crouching, with mane bristling and eyes snapping. Dignity and decorum were forgotten.

"Murder?" he bellowed. "Did I hear some one say somethin' about murder? Murder? MURDER? MURDER?" Each inquiry was made with increased volume, until he had reached a rafter-shaking roar.

"Good God Almighty," he screamed. "What is this if it ain't murder? What in the name of God is murder? Why The books have always told me that murder was the takin' of human life without the authority or justification of the law. Old Uncle Joe's dead, ain't he? He was killed, wasn't he? They took his life, I guess, if they killed him. Does the law say you can slip up on people at death-trap crossin's and crush their bones, and tear their flesh apart, just because you've got millions of dollars—because you're a big corporation—an' stole a lot of land from the government along with your millions from the pee-pul? MURDER? Does the law tell them to ring their bells and blow their whistle, so to give poor folks like old Uncle Joe a little warnin' at the crossin's, as they tear through the country, after more money, an' after more gold?"

"An' he says I do all right in a murder case," he reflected. "Well, let me tell you, that this is the damnedest, meanest, most cold-blooded case of murder I ever got mixed up in my life, an' as a murder specialist, I feel perfectly at home here tryin' it."

The jury charged the railroad for $17,000 for his speech. Pruiett reflected at Eva's as they read him the verdict over the 'phone. "Maybe I been wastin' my time," he mused. "Maybe I been tryin' the wrong kind of murder cases."

"Moman Pruiett, Attorney, sprung a sensation today in the Haines murder trial following the convening of court after the noon-day recess, when he dramatically admitted that his client, A. H. Haines, charged with the murder of Claude O'Conner at Garber on the night of January 5, last, was guilty," reported the *Enid Daily Eagle* on March 8, 1921.

That was news. The fire hydrant had dribbled on the dog. It was the first Pruiett client in twenty-five years who wasn't outraged in his complete innocence.

" 'Give your good Sheriff the credit and the honor for arresting the man who did the shooting,' Pruiett said. 'As for the deceased, O'Conner, I have nothing to say in censure of him, but may God have mercy on his soul.' "

The listening, and doubtlessly surprised, jury was beginning to see more—and further. Pruiett's client was guilty, but with reservations. The deceased had done something, his conduct had been so objectionable, and base, that big-hearted Pruiett was concerned about his chances in the hereafter. An experienced observer would have sensed in an instant that it was the Pruiett prelude to a ripping old "unwritten law" of defense.

"O'Conner proclaimed his plan of leaving for California and wrote a note to Lucy Haines, this defendant's wife, asking her to go with him. She wrote him a note in reply, asking him not to bother her. When Haines learned of the note, he asked his wife why she had deemed it necessary to reply in writing."

Pruiett was warming up to his task with relish. Haines was surely entitled to be just a little suspicious of such conduct. He didn't get a very satisfactory reply. "He then followed O'Conner to the pool hall, and there he asked O'Conner to show the note his wife wrote him; and, either he or O'Conner proposed that they go out of the back door and after they reached the outside, Haines asked again to see the note his wife had written, and when O'Conner said, 'All right, I'll give it to you, and I'll give you something else, too,' and with this O'Conner moved as to strike Haines, when Haines fired the shot that killed O'Conner."

The case was being tried at Enid, the old Cherokee Strip post which had developed into a handsome prairie town with tree-lined avenues leading away from a well planned public square. It seemed to Pruiett to be the constant host to Temple Houston's ghost. He remembered the town by the Houston episode, and it was with displeasure, for he had suffered two decisive and unwarranted courtroom defeats there at the Texas master's hand.

The Haines-O'Conner killing had occurred at Garber, a mushroom camp in the Garber-Covington petroleum production area, where millions were spouting for the settlers who had participated in the last of the great free land rushes. The defendant was a pimp who had brought himself from the poor, piney districts of West Virginia. Lucy, whom he claimed was his wife, may have been; she was unquestionably his stock in trade. Pruiett didn't care. Some one had paid him a fee, and the way he would make it look, their family life and relations were spotlessly clean. He meant to turn brother Haines back on society.

He was struggling against the handicap of a prolonged hangover that had taken a morbid twist. His liquor had begun to make him periodically despondent. A shake of the head, a cold bath and a quick drink didn't do the trick like it had in the days gone by. Unwelcome thoughts would cling closer than the army of moochers and panhandlers who banged him on the back and bragged on him as a preliminary to a two-bit to a ten dollar touch. The shaft in the valley and the memories entombed around it drifted in with his morning headache, and by evening, with work, and scheming and maneuvering to keep his many interests straight and in good order, he would be staggering under an onus of sorrowful recollections which grew heavier with each succeeding drink.

The Court recessed late in the evening in the Haines case and, after the evidence was in, written instruction of the law had been read to the jury, and final arguments had been continued until the following morning. Pruiett forced himself into court for opening next morning, sick, mournful and dejectedly drunk.

Murder had become a drab subject. He had an unusually unwholesome client, and a case which offered his imagination little in the way of inspiration or stimulation. He tried his old flights into oratory, and the scriptures, and rhyming verse, but they fell from his lips listlessly and lacking in appeal or responsiveness. His ever-ready abuse of the prosecutors and the officers in the case failed to flow out when he sought to turn that current loose. His tongue was thick and sour; his head was beating and thumping.

While he knew not what the dubious onlookers were thinking, or whispering, about him, he had the more unpleasant presence of a self-accusing conscience. Was this the breakdown that Giddings and the pack he had harassed for two decades, were predicting? Was he finally through? Could it be that the whispered end, which he had held in such complete contempt, would visit itself upon him in one foul and fatal swoop?

In a later day account of it, Pruiett made explanation of his plight. "I was just ran plumb down; I was clear out of soap. I couldn't think of any old speeches, or anything else. I got scared, and I wanted to turn and run from the courtroom."

The fading interior of the old courtroom was of average country-courthouse simplicity. The dung-brown walls were two-tone, light dung above a dust catching molding rail half way down the wall and dark dung from the rail down to the floor. The judge's rostrum, straight, unornamented and ugly, relieved a little of the monotony of design at the south end of the room. Directly above the bench, and balancing precariously upon the molding rail, was a warped and faded chromo in harmonizing browns, as dour, and drab and dingy as the balance of the interior of the room. It was a whiskered portrait of Abraham Lincoln.

"When I saw the Lincoln picture, I remembered I was in a belt of Republicans; that it was a Republican Congressional District, an' that they gave the Democrats hell around there all the time," he said, describing the motives which directed his strange conduct at the conclusion of the case.

Jurors were dozing or gazing out the window. The accused was shifting uneasily in his chair. Such lame forensics were not what he had bargained for when he paid his money for representation, or what he had expected from the highly touted Pruiett. The March gale, rattling a loose splinter in the window frame so that it sounded like a neighbor's boy practicing on his cornet in the distance, was attracting more attention than the purportedly eloquent lawyer. "These Republican bastards can stand a lot of Abe Lincoln," Pruiett resolved to himself.

"Look, men!" he struck a heroic pose in the center of the floor as he startled them back to attention with a stentorian shout. "The sad eyes of Lincoln!" he roared."The sad eyes of Lincoln are upon us. The spirit of Lincoln is hovering about us today!" He held his left hand outstretched, with fingers spread wide, like a master muting the bass section, while he led their attention with an eloquent pointing finger to the melody—the faded chromo perched on the wall. "Look! Behold! The sad eyes of Lincoln!"

The men in the box were startled. Their quick, scared glances furnished the poor old picture, the remains of what had been an insurance company's calendar, with an atmosphere of the artistic, and of reality. Garfield County Judge James E. Cullison, sitting beneath the likeness, and immediately in front of it, had to turn and twist, dangerously, in his high-backed swivel chair to look, like every one else in the crowded room, at what was causing Pruiett so much evident concern. As the judge craned and twisted, and the drapes of obesity which fell from his ample jowls, partly obscuring the collar of his shirt, were drawn tight and tense, his sinus ailment attacked him, and a series of prodigious tears began to course down his fat face. "That damn jury thought he was touched; that his memory of Old Abe was breakin' his heart," Pruiett said. "They thought he was weepin' for me and my client."

Pruiett, with his clenched right fist held high above his head, began to advance upon the jury, holding them with the strange fanatical glare which seemed to create an ominous spell over those whom it encompassed. He began to recite the lines he had stored in his memory almost ten years before when he had read them in a little Kansas paper while he waited for a shave in a Topeka barber shop. They were from *The Sad Eyes of Lincoln* by Walt Mason.

"Sad eyes that were patient and tender, sad eyes that were steadfast and true, and warm with the unchanging splendor of courage no ills could subdue."

He interrupted his recitation with an extemporaneous insertion. "The spirit of him with the great heart and the sad expression, who so loved the liberty of a million slaves that he sacrificed his own life, is present now with you. I can feel his presence like the warmth of the sun, the soothing caress of a Spring breeze. What would he do, my friends, if he was in your place today?"

It was indeed a ponderous problem, what Lincoln would have done with the West Virginia pimp's murder case. When Pruiett described the magnitude of the responsibility in such terms, the upland farmers began to look at the case in a different light. What the hell would Lincoln have done?

"Eyes hard with the dread of the 'morrow, and woe for the day that was gone, the sleepless companions of sorrow, the watchers that witnessed the dawn."

"Those sad eyes will be watching for you and your return with a just verdict, like they were for the presence, the symbol of liberty on Sumter's rampart," he shouted. "The sad eyes stand guardian here today over the rights of this American citizen who had the courage to stand against the assaults of a defiler of his home, an assailer of his person, and fight for those rights which Lincoln promised, and guaranteed to the true American citizen. What would Lincoln have done? You do that which he would have done, by your verdict."

The Republican brothers found their departed leader's mind in a typically opulent state that afternoon. They declined to convict Haines of the crime charged, and looked cautiously up at the faded chromo, as if for approbation, as the Court read the verdict. Pruiett, chuckling as he gathered up his papers, nodded cordially, in gratitude, toward the likeness of the emancipator, and stalked out of the courtroom.

He struggled on, manfully shouldering the heavy burden of work, worry, and... liquor. The city of Tulsa, reflected its refinery fires in the turgid Arkansas River, as men took wealth from beneath its sandy banks and put it back into towering buildings on the hill above its sweep. Its citizenry emulated Pruiett and his own homicidal conduct on an enlarged scale. The race riots, which raged there from May 31 to June 3 of 1921, took a heavy toll of life, especially from black bodies, and consumed a proportionate toll in property destruction. When the National Guard had restored a semblance of order, the civil authorities began their customary inquiry for fixing responsibility.

Will Robinson, an educated negro man, was indicted for riot in the District Court of Tulsa County on the theory that he was the principal instigator of the mass destruction. While he was accused of but one specific killing, by inference, he would be tried at once for a hundred or more of them. An organization of negroes, designing to serve their race generally, and Will Robinson particularly, raised a fund for the employment of counsel. They met to decide to whom the employment, and the fee, should be offered. A great fundamental principal was involved. If Robinson was cleared, the blame against their race would be materially lessened; the pressure of prejudice would be relieved. Correspondingly, if he was convicted, condemnation against the race would be more definitely fixed. Serious complications might develop. Their man must be represented by the most able, by the one most likely to secure an acquittal.

Lawyer Pruiett of Oklahoma City was able, but he had killed a member of their race in a beer-joint shooting. Perhaps the negro had been wrong; maybe Pruiett had been right, as the white man's jury had decided, but still, Mr. Pruiett didn't have any right to be over there. The negro had been shot down in his own home, and the Constitution said that color and previous condition of servitude didn't make any difference where a man's rights were concerned, especially around his house, what the white folks called his domicile.

And Lawyer Pruiett was being mentioned in the papers in a way to make them believe he wasn't taking care of his business. He was goin'

JEAN P. DAY, A PROMINENT OKLAHOMA CITY ATTORNEY, SHOT AND KILLED COLONEL PAUL BECK, COMMANDING OFFICER OF FT. SILL ARMY BASE, IN DAY'S HOME AT 411 NORTHWEST 19TH IN OKLAHOMA CITY. DAY WAS SUCCESSFULLY DEFENDED BY MOMAN PRUIETT IN THE SPRING OF 1922. COURTESY *THE DAILY OKLAHOMAN.*

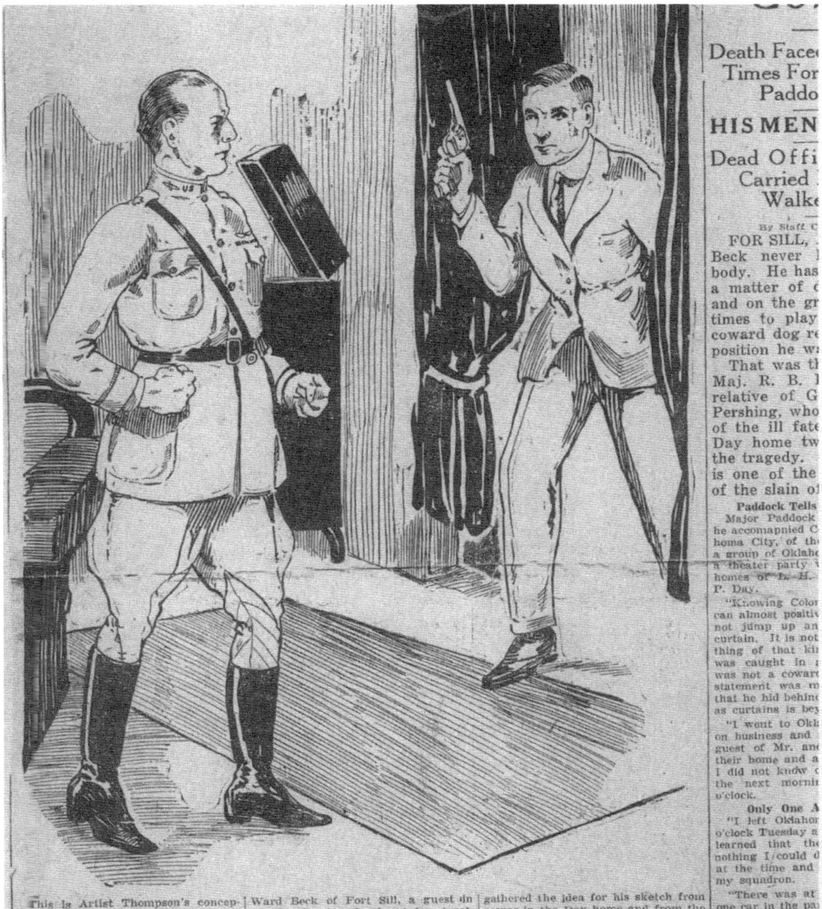

PRUIETT ARGUED THAT JEAN DAY WAS JUSTIFIED IN KILLING COLONEL PAUL WARD BECK UNDER OKLAHOMA'S "UNWRITTEN LAW." WALTER HARRISON, LONG-TIME EDITOR OF *THE DAILY OKLAHOMAN,* REFERRED TO THE SHOOTING INCIDENT AS 'THE SHOOTING OF THE DECADE' IN OKLAHOMA. SKETCH COURTESY *THE DAILY OKLAHOMAN.*

out too often, and drinkin' too much. What about that? Even if we are black, even if we are plain niggers, we got to have a man we can rely on. We got to have a man that can bring Will Robinson out clean. They've got good lawyers in Kansas City, an' Chicago. There's thousands of us, and we've all chipped in a little, so we've got plenty of money. That's no item to worry us. Who shall we get to defend Will?

Record for record, accomplishment for accomplishment, the sick fading Pruiett stood out in bold relief. He got the offer and he took the job. In one brilliant plea before the District Court at a hearing on Robinson's petition for a writ of habeas corpus, he showed that he knew his law like he knew his human nature in the jury box. With empassioned brilliance, he interrupted his intemperance long enough to decisively defeat the prosecutors, and walked from the courtroom with a black man, free, where before he had been held without bond on the most difficult and dangerous of criminal accusations.

"The charges of grand larceny, which were preferred against G. L. Roberts and W. I. Ritchey, of Fredonia, alleged bank robbers, were dismissed this morning by County Attorney Arch F. Williams." So said the El Dorado, Kansas, *Times* on May 22, 1922. "Immediately after the dismissal of the charges here, Roberts and Ritchey, and their attorney Moman Pruiett of Oklahoma City, Oklahoma, went to Eureka, where preliminary hearings are being held this afternoon for Roberts and Ritchey on charges of robbing the Piedmont State Bank last Winter. The defendants have been on bond of $15,000 each since their arraignments at Eureka several weeks ago."

"The visit of Mr. Pruiett to El Dorado recalls that he recently was employed for the 268th time, in his career as a criminal attorney, to defend a man under a shadow cast by a deadly shot he fired. This time the defendant is Jean P. Day, wealthy lawyer, politician and oil man, who killed Lieutenant Colonel Paul Ward Beck on April 4, 1922, when he surprised Beck attempting to attack his wife."

"Pruiett, with his flowing shock of hair that gave him the nickname of 'the black maned maverick of the Washita' has fought opposite prosecutors in practically every County in Oklahoma, and has defended slayers as far West as Aberdeen, Washington. His is the frontier type, grown up with the West, and though Oklahoma population has changed greatly in 30 years, Pruiett has never lost the keen perception and knowledge of people in every community that makes him clever at jury-picking and shrewd at presenting testimony."

"His western character also makes him as fast with a gun as any man he has ever defended. It was last year that Pruiett and his partner, Orban Patterson, ran afoul two negroes in a house on the south side of Oklahoma City. Though the negroes are reported to have got to their guns, Pruiett killed one of them and took a shot or two at the other, who fled."

His reputation trailed him wherever he went. Up to the time he killed Joe Patterson, he gloried in it. Afterward, he tried to slip in and out of strange places, and to avoid contacts with the Press. God, wasn't he glad that old Doc Threlkeld hadn't died that time he shot him. Wasn't it good to know that old Charley Wiseman was finally able to get up and around, after that time he shot him through the leg? This thing of havin' killed a man, even a Negro, was something to make you uneasy when you're alone, and it was something he'd rather the public would forget. If they would, and wouldn't be forever writing it up, usually wrong, in their papers, maybe he could forget it himself.

Cal Stewart had never told him that it was hard to sleep at night, or to get that awful look of a dead man's face out of your mind, and he'd killed his own brother. His partner, Patterson, said it felt like takin' a heavy load off your shoulders, the time he talked to him in jail after killin' old man Williams. He wondered. Maybe if he quit carryin' that damned pistol around he could get to feeling better, and lose that draggy feelin', the feeling of hopelessness that made him dread to go into court to try his cases. Maybe if he left the pistol at home, they'd quit writin' about him shootin' somebody every time they mentioned his name in the papers.

Murderers. Bank robbers. Dope smugglers. What was it old Walter Ferguson the editor and publisher of Alva's *Cherokee Advocate,* had said about him in his column years ago? The chicken thieves and petty criminals were turned away from his door? That he specialized in murder and defended only the big horse thieves? Maybe Ferguson was right. He said that he was the toughest hombre in the toughest Indian town in the territory. That was right, then. He'd been tough; he didn't give a damn about anybody, or anything, then; but, he felt kind of weak and squeamish inside nowadays. He'd lost somethin'; he'd lost part of his old don't-give-a-damn-what-they-say-attitude. He wished that he hadn't a'killed that nigger.

He should take a rest. He ought to see a doctor, and if the doctor said go away and rest up, he should do it. Every one had some suggestion to make; they all agreed that he looked bad; that he didn't act like the old Pruiett. Maybe he ought to cut out part of the whiskey. Hell no! That was what was holdin' him up. If he cut out any of that, he'd flop, and look at all the murder cases pending. Look at the fees he'd miss. He would cut down on the work though. Just the choice cases nowadays. The ones with the heavy dough in 'em, a bank loot, or a rich murderer, or something like that. Not so much to do, and a little more time for rest. But the rest let him think; it made him think, an' he couldn't stand some of the things that made him think of them. So, the liquor bottle came out, and the cycle began all over again. Where was he goin'? Where was he goin' to get off? What the hell was goin' to happen to him?

The little old Kansas sheet that had to garble up the shooting story told about Jean P. Day, as 'the last case for him to take employment in'. While Pruiett didn't know it at the time, it was his last murder case, the last one for him to participate in, for a long time.

On April 7, 1922, the *Oklahoma City Times* reported that on Tuesday morning, April 4, "the entire State was shocked by the news of a tragedy that involved two of the most prominent citizens within the confines of the State." Forrest L. Hughes, County Attorney for Oklahoma County, was having a formal statement published in the local press.

"The deceased, Paul Ward Beck, was one of the most prominent aviation officers in America. The man who fired the fatal shot was not only one of the ablest lawyers in the State but one of its most highly respected citizens. Since this tragedy occurred, I have been quoted in a number of papers as saying things I little dreamed of. Owing to this fact, I now take the opportunity of making my first official statement relative to this fatal tragedy."

"I am frank to admit that I have always had the highest regard for Judge Day, both as a citizen and as a lawyer. However, immediately following his statement to me, he requested me to forget that friendship and not hesitate to file a murder charge against him if I thought it my duty to do so. His attorney later reiterated this request and statement." Pruiett was Day's counsel.

The case made national news. "Jean P. Day, former State Supreme Court Justice, President of the Foursome Producing and Refining Company and Vice-President of the Continental Asphalt and Petroleum Company, is being held at his home, 411 West Nineteenth Street, in the custody of a Deputy Sheriff, following the shooting to death of Lt.. Col. Paul W. Beck, commandant of Post Field, Fort Sill, at 3 o'-clock Tuesday morning. Lieutenant Colonel Beck was one of the first four army aviators in the United States. Day returned home and found his wife struggling in the arms of the Army Officer, according to a statement authorized by Judge Day, made by a friend of the family." So said the *Washington Post* on April 9, "On the witness stand, Day and his wife told, with emotion, of the slaying of Lt.. Col. Beck. In a broken voice, but with a gleam of determination in his eye, Day said he killed the army aviator accidentally when he sought to drive Beck from his home, after finding him attempting to attack Mrs. Day."

" 'I saw Colonel Beck holding Mrs. Day on the divan,' said Day. 'She was fighting him. He had his right arm around her. His other hand was about her knee'."

The unusual events had followed a late party in the Day home, where a group of the oil elite were amusing themselves on apricot cordial—'non-intoxicating.' "Judge Day denied a statement of W. R. Withington, evidence man, that empty bottles and a glass found on the mantle in the room after the bridge party had contained intoxicants.' The bottles had contained nothing stronger than non-intoxicating apricot cordial,' he said. 'Beck was sober at the time of his alleged attempt on Mrs. Day,' the judge declared, denying emphatically there had been any drinking."

"Moman Pruiett, defense counsel, gave forth a statement Wednesday. He said it was he who advised the Days to make a sworn statement of the tragedy wherein Day invoked the 'code of Oklahoma,' that a man's home is inviolate, and shot Beck when he alleged Beck had attempted Mrs. Day's honor. 'I wanted to save them the humiliation of appearing before the coroner's jury and satisfying morbid curiosity,' Pruiett said in the statement."

Mrs. Day's theatrical account of the affair made good copy in the April 8, 1922, issue of the *Oklahoma City Times.*"Mrs. Jean P. Day, Washington and Oklahoma City society woman, half-hysterical and distracted, Tuesday night told at her home what she remembered of the tragedy early Tuesday morning. Mr. Day had gone to take the other guests home. I sat on the couch, Colonel Beck facing me from a chair. Suddenly, he sprang from his seat and came to my side. 'I must tell you,' he said... ! Then he poured out an impassioned plea that I submit to him. He grasped me, clutching me to him. I screamed aloud for him to release me. He did not heed. Instead, he held me closer, crying out that he would have me. I fought with all my strength, but he was too powerful for me. The events which followed are but a blank. I was still struggling, his arms about me, his face pressed to mine, when I saw the form of my husband before me. I ceased to struggle then, and only then, for I knew I was safe. I knew no more until I saw Beck's body there dead at my feet."

The way it looked from out West, and the way the *Los Angeles Examiner* put it on April 9, " 'I did not see the shot fired. I did not hear the report,' Mrs. Day testified. 'I looked down and saw his lips move,' she continued, 'I lifted his head, then I put his head back down and the blood surged out. Then my hands were covered with blood.' "

" 'When he was struggling with you and he asked you to come to his room, you didn't think he was trying to do anything wrong then?' asked County Attorney Hughes, explaining that he wanted to bring out the intent in Beck's mind.' 'I didn't think; I didn't know,' Mrs. Day replied. 'What would you think?' "

Pruiett conducted his prominent client's defense in his customary high-handed manner. The army board had its findings to make, and Pruiett insisted on goin' before them with Judge Day. They had their own way of doing things, what they called the Rules of the Military Court, and Pruiett had what he had long shouted was the 'Constitutional Right of an American Citizen.'

"The morning session was consumed in the examination of Judge Day. The new angle of the case that was developed, it was said, was the introduction of several letters by Moman Pruiett, Day's attorney, concerning the alleged relations of Beck with women at other posts where he had been stationed. This came as a surprise to the army men, it was said, who expected the defense only to answer questions put them."

The findings of the military board, conducted under Major Thomas George Lanphier, were slightly ambiguous as reported by the *Oklahoma City Times* on April 10, "the board does not believe the version of the Days as to the conduct of Lieutenant Colonel Beck on the fatal morning was true. However, it does not believe the testimony introduced at the inquest would justify filing a charge of murder against Jean P. Day."

Lieutenant Paul Ward Beck, Jr., son of the slain officer, viewed the conduct of the military court disconsolately, and with disapprobation. " 'My father was always an honorable man, an officer and a gentleman, and I still believe he remained so to the last,' young Beck said. Coupled with the son's statement came the intimation that a searching investigation will be instituted by the War Department, to clear up certain confused details in connection with the death of the officer."

For a swan song, according to the April 9 issue of *The Daily Oklahoman,* Pruiett gained a figurative double-acquittal at the trial of one case. Said Judge Day: "The jury did exactly what they ought, and it is absolutely a just verdict." Said Mrs. Day: "I feel grateful over the verdict. It is an honest one, and the only thing the jurors could have done. The evidence has thoroughly vindicated me, and left my name stainless."

The stoop and forward pitch of Pruiett's posture, first noticeable as he ambled in to testify at his own murder preliminary, didn't disappear when the coroner's jury decided, and said, that they wouldn't bind him over for a trial in the District Court. Whiskey would run down the arched gullet, but it wouldn't remove the hump from his back or the weariness from his manner. Pruiett slowed down, perceptibly, almost overnight.

In less than two weeks after the final hearing in the Jean P. Day case, Pruiett went to a new doctor. It was not for a recurrence of the dungeon stiffness; his knees and ankles had ceased their painful assaults upon his motion almost ten years before. His years between forty and fifty had been, fortunately, the most vigorous and healthful of his life. But, his throat had developed a great huskiness, a great pain, and the once stentorian roar, responding with his impulse, was modulated overnight to a raspy whisper. Passing food from his mouth to the stomach was torture. Letting liquor in was almost as painful, but once down, it tended to relieve the agony in the throat. He had to stand that.

"Doc," he said, "I got a lot of confidence in you. When a fellow can't believe a lot of specialists, he goes to his friends, the ones he knows he can trust. I want you to check me over, an' give me a fair verdict."

"All right, Moman, I'll decide your case," the smiling doctor replied. "I don't need a lot of evidence to convince me, either, that you're drinking too much. Cut it out and you'll be well in no time."

Pruiett was talking to Dr. Oscar M. Marchman, in his office in Dallas. Marchman, member of the Southwest Clinic of Dallas, staff doctor at the Baylor Baptist Hospital, was an established throat specialist in the Southwest. Pruiett smiled back at the doctor, but shook his head.

"It's not as simple as that, Doc," he replied. "I'll agree that your recommended course of treatment is good, but your diagnosis is incomplete. I'm sick as hell. They say I'm goin' to die."

Marchman laughed again. "You're too tough to think about it," he said. "You've got the bucks. Let me put you to bed and clean you out. Give me a week, 'til I can get the water I run through you to come out pure, and I'll have you ready to go back to work."

"I got a hole in the roof of my mouth, Doc," Pruiett complained, with a trace of a quiver in his voice. "It's as big around as a nickel an' it keeps gettin' bigger. It's plugged up with wet cotton right now, or I couldn't even talk. I'm in a hell of a shape."

The doctor's face and manner changed. He became grave. "I'm sorry, Moman," he said. "I didn't understand. Let me see now, how long has it been bothering you?"

"Six weeks, maybe a little longer," Pruiett replied. "It's been givin' me hell. I can't work. I can't sleep, an' I can't get enough whiskey in me to kill the pain that goes with it. I drink two quarts ever' day."

"I'm sorry," Marchman repeated. "What do the doctors at home say about it? What do they think?"

"Cancer," said Pruiett laconically. "But I don't believe a god damned word of it. There never was a cancer in my family, and it ain't the right place for cancer to break out. I know damn well it ain't no cancer."

"It sounds more like syphilis," Marchman said, frankly. "Any of that in your background?"

"Hell, no," Pruiett replied, just as frank. "But I wish there was. Anythin's better than a god damn cancer. I... "

"Well," Marchman mused, "you've been notoriously indiscreet. Maybe you've contracted it for the Pruiett line. There has to be a starting point for every new case, you know."

"Why hell, yes," Pruiett agreed. "But I'm regular. I ain't entitled to have no venereal diseases breakin' out in my mouth. What the hell do you think I am?"

Marchman had to laugh again. "I'll dress you in and run you through the clinic. You ought to stay three or four days. A certain laboratory test I know of will tell me right off what's the matter with you."

"If it's a Wasserman test you're talkin' about," Pruiett said, "They ain't worth a damn. I've had nine of 'em in the last four weeks an' ever damned one comes back negative. That's why they say it's cancer, but I know damned well it ain't."

Marchman's amazement was obvious. "Nine tests, and all negative? All by the same technician, or at different places?"

"Three doctors; three tests apiece," Pruiett answered. "Ever' god damned one negative."

"It's no use then, running you through," Marchman said, shaking his head. "What could I do?"

"You could tell me what's the matter with me," Pruiett said. "The Wasserman says I ain't got syphilis, an' I say I ain't got cancer. It ain't what I ain't got, it's what I have got, that I want to know. That's what I want you to tell me."

The Dallas doctor was more puzzled at the close of the three day clinical examination than he had been after he had taken Pruiett's profane history of the case. Two Wasserman tests showed negative. There was no disease in the blood. Every other clinical sign pointed to syphilis. Diagnosis by elimination, supported by some clinical evidence, suggested cancer, but Marchman, like Pruiett, didn't think it was cancer.

"In your own language, Moman, that Wasserman's a damn liar," Marchman said, earnestly. "That's not cancer. It's the logical place for syphilis to break through, where you've strained your throat, hollering your head off, and scorched it raw so often with strong whiskey. Disregard the laboratory, and take a regular course of treatment for your blood. I'll graft the palate back in, when you begin to respond, and make you well again. I'll make you so well you can go back to screaming at juries again. If I do, you pay the regular fee. If I don't, you don't pay me a cent."

"That's the way I handle cases," Pruiett said. "Win'em or you don't collect. I believe you, Doc, but I'm just not satisfied. I think I'll shop around a little more, and see if maybe some one else can't figure this out."

Baltimore, Maryland, was the next stop. Pruiett was dressed in at Johns Hopkins Hospital, to endure the trial of a thirty day clinic. The black mane, that had showed its first tinge of gray as he limped up the stone steps to Marchman's office at Dallas, had turned iron gray. His stoop was decided; his step halt. He carried the little paunch, which he had permitted to develop under the inside angle of his stoop like a pregnant squaw, and the black eye, once so sparkling and sharp, was no brighter, or smarter, than that of an old Indian woman in a family way. He would have been meat in the revengeful hands of the old prosecuting clique in the Southwest, who had so long predicted that Pruiett was through. He was so completely out that he didn't think in terms of murder trials and criminal defenses. It was two quarts a day.

"Give me something, anything, to relieve this god damn pain."

"Judge," the diagnostician at Johns Hopkins was saying, "Your frank question requires a frank answer. The infection in your mouth is malignant. It's cancer. If you take care of yourself, cut down a little on this liquor, you may last a year. But at best, it's just a year; you can't live any longer than that."

"Then why the hell cut out the liquor?" Pruiett asked, dropping his bare legs over the side of the high bed and unhitching the neck strings of a hospital jacket. "Tell 'em to bring my clothes in. If a man's only goin' to last a year an' he's got to be in such pain as this, what difference is a little liquor goin' to make?"

The doctor's answer was an unconcerned shrug as he turned to walk away. Bellevue Hospital at New York City concurred with Johns Hopkins. Marchman, with his condemnation of the Wasserman, was in a weak minority.

"We can keep you, and treat you, Mr. Pruiett, and take your money," the staff-man at Bellevue told him, "but we can't do any more than your wife could do for you at home. That's cancer. You can't impeach the Wasserman like you can a poor witness; you simply don't have syphilis. At the rate it's going, it will kill you within a year, and as we feel we should do in these kinds of cases, we're warning you so that you can put your things in order."

"Will this pain get worse?" Pruiett inquired.

"I'm sorry, but it will, much worse," the doctor said. "But, wherever you are, you can get prescriptions, of course. And I would suggest that you cut down on... "

"Oh, I know," Pruiett interrupted. "Too much liquor. What's so bad about that? Ain't it better than the needle? I can get it from bootleggers, I don't need to get a prescription, an' it don't cost so much. Why not drink plenty of booze, as long as I got to die in a year anyway?"

"It was merely a suggestion, Mr. Pruiett," the doctor answered. "I can understand how you feel. But the whiskey upsets the system so; and burns you up. You'll get about the same relief from pain, but it'll shorten your time, and that's short enough all ready."

"As long as it's that short, it don't make any difference," Pruiett growled. "I'm not criticizin' you, son, for the suggestion. If I got to die, it's all right. Two or three lifetimes wouldn't help me a hell of a lot now, for I've been ever'where an' seen ever'thing all ready. I may get on junk, an' I may quit the whiskey, but if I do it won't be because I think it'll make my life any longer. I don't care about that. It's this god damn pain all the time that I don't like. It's so useless, like killin' a man by inches when you can do it all at once by shootin' him."

"I only wish we could do more than give you temporary relief," the doctor said. "But, at the same time, think what a blessing the diseased have received since morphine and . ."

"Yeah," Pruiett interrupted. "I got off the train at Memphis, one time, and rode to Fort Smith with John Jay, in his automobile. Know John? He knows more about junk than you doctors, and makes a hell of a lot more money out of it. You wouldn't think so, the way you charge up here, but it's a fact. I defended John one time for murder. He'd made himself a millionaire on the stuff, but he don't use it himself. I think sometimes its all right, buying it and shootin' it, and then sometimes I think John's all wrong, lettin' 'em have it, don't make a damn why they want it. But, by God, I never was so scared, an' I never was so uneasy, as I was that trip. John told me about half-way out that his suitcase was full of dope. Had a hell of a lot of it; an', when we got in to Fort Smith, I couldn't stand it any longer. I ducked him. I caught the train there and let John take it on in by himself."

"Did he make it?" The doctor was both courteous and curious.

"Those birds never make it," Pruiett snapped. "He got in with his load, an' sold it and made a hell of a lot, but he's finally got to settle. He's a fugitive, accused of violating the Harrison Narcotic Act, and he'll go to Leavenworth as sure as hell, for the government'll catch him sooner or later. He's got a million salted, but it ain't worth it, not for one week in such a god damn place. I know, for... " He almost uttered the phrase which he permitted no other man to suggest or insinuate. "I've represented lots of criminals, and seen what goes on in these places," he concluded.

Pruiett returned to the West after leaving $15,000 on the Atlantic seaboard. He received nothing for it but definite information that he had a cancer in his mouth and that he would be dead within a single year. The black flag was down. A halting step and a weary stoop and supplanted the belligerent strut which had been so characteristic of him in his prime. One landmark, the grizzled and outthrust jaw, remained unchanged. The power was gone, but the spirit was intact. One look at Pruiett's countenance and one knew that his attitude was unchanged. "I ain't got no cancer. They're either wrong about it, or they're a bunch of damned liars."

Thomas H. Owen, who had survived the Pruiett assault in the McDarment case, had become Justice of the Oklahoma Supreme Court. Pruiett made him trustee of his property and accounts, with his wife and daughter as beneficiaries, and taking out $25,000 in cash for himself, moved on to Havana. He was thinking, although rebelliously, about the Bellevue doctors reference to the prescription. At the same time he was thinking about old John Jay, languishing somewhere in hiding, and what he had learned from John while he had been his lawyer and closest confidante. Pruiett knew where and how the dope came into the country from southern Europe. He knew that the West Indian Islands, with Havana and Nassau in the Bahamas as import centers, relayed the stuff into the Florida Keys, and that from there the runners moved it northward.

"That's where you find more junkies to the square mile than any other place in the country," Jay had told him. "The wise ones get tired of moochin' and hustlin' for enough to get a shot, and then landin' in somebody's stinkin' jail to do without. They got to the Keys, where it's plentiful, an' cheap, an' where they can dream on the sand in the sunshine. There's more junkies in Nassau than any other place ten times its size in the world."

In the mid-1920s, Moman and Leda Pruiett decided to move to Biscayne Bay, Florida. There was a land boom in the area and Pruiett was game for a new and easier environment. Courtesy Hugh and Shannon Smith.

MOMAN AND LEDA PRUIETT'S BISCAYNE BAY HOME AT 59TH STREET AND BAY SHORE. PRUIETT REFERRED TO THE HOME AS HIS "VILLER" AND, MUCH TO THE DISMAY OF HIS WIFE, TOSSED CIGAR BUTTS AND SPAT TOBACCO JUICE INTO ITS RIPPLING FOUNTAINS. COURTESY HOWARD K. BERRY PHOTO COLLECTION.

Pruiett put the bulk of his cash in a Dallas bank. He consumed his two quarts en route, but ran the average to two and a half after he got to Cuba. He inspected Nassau and the ragged addicts who slouched in the shade of the dirty shacks on narrow streets, or slept in dirty heaps of rags along the water front. He thought of the miserable watery-eyed addicts he had heard whine at him through the iron bars as he interviewed clients in jail corridors. He remembered their furtive, shifting movements as they jerked and scratched, and flaunted the miserable poverty which they endured for the sustenance of their terrible habit. All hell could turn its misery loose upon him; slow fire and the medieval wheel might sear and grind him, but it would be easier than going on the junk. He decided that there was one easy death he would pass up.

Palm tree shadows across sun swept boulevards and lattice stripes of swinging doors across saloon entrances endeared Havana to the failing lawyer. He had a year, possibly a little more, possibly a little less, to live. He had to suffer every waking minute of the residue, and as the high priced specialists had frankly told him, the pain he now had would gradually increase, until the time came, when final relief was near, he would have to have prescriptions, take the needle, to lift him over it. But, the needle was out. He had set the square jaw and eliminated the needle. They could start with the roof of his mouth and tear him apart an inch at a time, but he wouldn't die a damned, sniveling dope head. Hell no, he wouldn't. That was out.

He decided to drift off on liquor, like he had so often when harassed and troubled with the strain of hard cases. Just drink so much of it that the galling pain of every swallow would seem distant and far away, like a bad dream. So much that the constant drip from his nostrils with the increased loss of function of the nasal and sinus ducts, wouldn't humiliate and distress him. There was the Cuban rum, hotter at first and more searing, harder to get past the spreading sore at the head of his throat when he first sat up in bed in the morning, but which threw fresh power into his organs and the sections of his system they supplied, so that he was able to be up, and to dress and get out into the sunshine. Rum, with a punch like old territorial day longhorn, would help him up and then hold him up. Rum, it would be, in mild weathered Havana, to comfort him as he slipped from the existence through which he has recklessly passed.

Pruiett had plenty of money. There were no worries, or regrets about his family, except those of natural compunction at leaving them. His fatalistic attitude toward life was real, not an assumed one that would crumble with his own exposure to the reality of death, and leave him cringing in abandoned loneliness. Where he had started with nothing, he left a trust that he would amply provide for his wife and child. He would deny them the right to make the sacrifice he knew they longed to make, that of being with him and comforting him as the spectre of death stalked slowly, but relentlessly in for him.

It was selfishness, in a sense, for he knew that they would be no comfort to him, only stimuli for the lapses into morbidity which he could tolerate only in his solitude. What they would suffer in knowing that he was suffering, and dying, out of their arms, or the correlative satisfaction their service to him, would give them, he refused to seriously consider. He made definite arrangements to stay, so long as the thread of life would permit, in old Havana, where whiskey, and rum, was plentiful.

The stamping black stud became a stumbling, spavined old nag. His custom-tailored clothes hung on his humped-over frame in smelly, disheveled array. He didn't bother to shave; he oftentimes neglected to wash his face. Dragging along under the partial shelter of the corrugated metal or canvas canopies above the walk, he made no effort to avoid the sifting tropical rains of the afternoon. He drifted from joint to joint. He watched with dull eyes the varying movements of the interiors, or nodded as he slept in straight chairs along the wall. His thick hair had become shaggy; it has lost its striking eye appeal. It was gray; a dirty shade of white. No longer did it reflect the beams of light, like crows feathers, as it had in the days when he fought for the acquittance of Senator Gore, or tried the perfect murder case for the benefit of murderous Sam St. Mary. It was the picture of an old man, waiting—waiting for the benevolent angel to come and relieve him of his misery and distress, and to release him from himself.

CHAPTER TWENTY

Wherein Pruiett returns from the dead, and with the aid of the miracle of modern medicine, stumbles through the dim halls of half-life into vigorous health again. And how the Invisible Empire takes a new lease on life with him, and together, they unseat a Governor who had not previously enjoyed favor in Pruiett fancy. And how he trades diamonds, and felon's gold, for a villa on Florida's Biscayne Bay's blue water, and fills his sack, prior to departure for the South, with what he considers the last of western tribute.

"You get a splendid view of the bay here, and it's delightfully cool all the time," the young man with the white Panama hat was saying. "That's the Nunnelly property there, and the Candler estate over here. And you see the big place across the point there, with the pink tinge to it? On the island? That's... ," he stepped closer, lowering his voice into a confidential undertone. "That place is sold, but the buyer insists that his name be kept secret. But, just between us, it's Mr. Capone, of Chicago. Al Capone. It's one of the finest properties on the bay."

"I don't think me and that son-of-a-bitch would make very good neighbors, but I don't know," the elder man replied. "How much do you say you have to have for this dump?"

A pained expression passed across the young salesman's face. "Twenty-five thousand dollars, and it's our best bargain. These values are increasing, and these adjoining properties are being constantly improved. Mr. Capone is spending... "

"Who gives a damn about Capone?" the prospect interrupted. "Will you take some good diamonds in on the deal?"

The salesman started. The closer scrutiny he gave the man he was trying to sell, after such an inquiry, disclosed a medium sized man a little past fifty, with broad square shoulders and dark, sun-tanned face and neck. His jaw was square and hard. A wide, thin-lipped mouth, drawn wider as it encompassed a huge cigar and rolled it in its extreme corner, suggested an unsympathetic, probably cruel nature. Shaggy black brows shaded dark eyes, almost black, which were deep set and inscrutable. The broad brimmed Panama, setting carelessly aslant on his large head, failed to conceal all of a billowing mass of iron gray hair which bulged from beneath it and fell shaggily about his ears and the back of his high collar. As he gazed into the cool breeze, out into Biscayne's blue, his eyes shone with the light of youth, and the extreme vigor in the expression caused the younger man to look again at the long gray locks, as if in contemplation, and suspicion, of a disguise. The reference to diamonds startled him.

"Well, we might consider diamonds on the deal," he said cautiously, "but, you know . ."

"They're clean. Nothin' hot about 'em," the older man interrupted, correctly reading his thoughts. "I got $15,000 worth of 'em."

"We can talk about it with the manager," the salesman said. "What did you say your name was, please, sir?"

"The gray haired man darted him a look of contempt. "It ain't Capone, and it ain't Jesse James, either," he growled. "It's Pruiett. Moman Pruiett, an' I'm from Oklahoma."

"Oh, yes, Mr. Pruiett. I read about you in the paper, last week. I didn't understand it when we met at the office. You are an attorney, I believe the article said."

"Hell, no," Pruiett said. "I ain't no attorney. I'm a lawyer—just a plain one-gallus lawyer. An' this place ain't what I wanted, but I'm gettin' tired of lookin', so I'll take it. Get your manager and come by the Ta-Miami. I got my diamonds in the hotel safe. If they'll take the rocks at a fair price, I'll buy your little viller."

The Miami, Florida, *News* was publishing glad tidings on August 15, 1923. "An important addition to legal circles in Miami shortly will be the location of Pruiett and Patterson, of Oklahoma City, who have been engaged in practice there for 26 years and have been interested in some of the most important criminal trials ever held in the Southwest. Moman Pruiett, head of the firm, and Orban C. Patterson, one of his associates, are at the Ta-Miami hotel, where they have spent the last week arranging for office space in a downtown building and looking for desirable residences for their personal use."

"Mr. Pruiett handles murder cases, principally, but his firm does a general legal business. He represented Jean P. Day, ex-member of the Supreme Court of Oklahoma, who killed Col. Paul Ward Beck. When United States Senator Thomas P. Gore was sued for damages by Minnie E. Bond, Mr. Pruiett was chief counsel for the Senator. He also defended Clarence P. Douglas, former Editor of the Muskogee (Okla.) Phoenix, when Douglas was placed on trial charged with the murder of James Williams, Editor of the Ardmore (Okla.) Chronicle.

Discussing Florida, Mr. Pruiett said: 'Florida is the only State left unscratched. It is the only section for youth and talent to meet its reward; it is almost what the Indian Territory was thirty-five years ago. There is no question about the wonderful future of this city and State, and no question but that the government will recognize its claims to become an important sea port with ample ship channels. As to climate, I have not suffered from heat since coming here, although the temperature reached 107 in Oklahoma City recently."

The old Pruiett capacity for making the headlines was unimpaired. Two days later the *News,* on August 17, bowed to him again. "Thursday afternoon proved to be a gala occasion at the range of the Miami-Hialeah Gun Club at Hialeah, where distinguished visitors were amongst those present. Outside of the club's own George D. Williams, back in Miami from a northern trip for a few days, interest centered particularly in Moman Pruiett and Orban C. Patterson of Oklahoma City, who have come to Miami to make their home. Mr. Pruiett is probably one of the most famous criminal lawyers in America, specializing in murder cases, and who has handled some of the country's most sensational ones. Interest of club members centered in the two visitors as the result of rumor preceding them to the range, to the effect that gentlemen from Oklahoma never ventured forth without high-top boots, a sombrero and a pair of 45's strapped to their belt." Black Joe Patterson's fresh ghost, or old banker Williams' more mature one, may have had something to do with starting the rumor. "It turned out, however, that neither Mr. Pruiett nor Mr. Patterson sported any of the three articles mentioned, but did know how to shoot, and tallied a good score of clays with deft handling of the guns."

Pruiett was back in the murder business. From the rut in the Havana slums, he had risen in a single year to overcome disease and regain his place at the top of his profession, as if his absence and degradation had been but a holiday out of the office. His conduct in his recovery, as always, had been fantastic, and unorthodox, and unexplainable.

Routine delays and charges in the exchange, drawing on his deposit in the Dallas bank, had chafed his already irritable nature. With the specific intent of withdrawing his money, placing it in his pocket and carrying it to Cuba with him, where he could reach it and spend it as he chose, he took the boat for the mainland and the trains for Dallas. The fates who had permitted him to survive as a premature infant, who had deposited such a prodigious brain in his skull and such matchless courage in his belly, who winked at his adolescent folly and turned the key in the dungeon locks to restore him to his liberty, who fouled the cap on murderous old Doctor Threlkeld's cartridge and who furnished him with an inspiration of deliverance in every emergency, were still attending him. Staggering out of an Akard Street dive, he ran directly into his friend and medical aid, Doctor Marchman.

"My God, Moman," the doctor cried. "What in God's name has happened to you?"

Pruiett had swallowed the cotton plug with his recent drink. The opening between his mouth and the nasal chambers was unobstructed, so that he could not talk, he could only whisper.

"It's that god damn cancer," he whispered, leaning drunkenly on the doctor. "I been to Baltimore, an' New York, too. I told you I was a sick man, an' they backed me up in it. I'm gonna die...," he glanced around as if to see if any one was watching, or listening. "The fact is, Doc, I'm done dead. This ain't old Mome you're talkin' to, now."

Marchman's eyes were swimming in tears. Pruiett swayed before him on the sidewalk.

"Where's your wife, Moman? Where's your family? What are they thinking about, letting you get yourself in this condition?"

"They ain't with me anymore," Pruiett mumbled. "I'm dead, an' I'm buried down in Cuba. I'm a rummy, Doc, but by god, I'd rather be a' old rummy than a god damn dope head. What do you say, Doc?"

"How long have you been in Dallas?" the doctor asked.

"Two-three days. Just came up to get my money out of your god damn bank. Seems like they don't want old Mome to write checks on his own money, by god. I got plenty of money... " He thrust his hand into his trousers pocket, as if to produce a roll in substantiation of what he had said.

"Don't do that, Moman," Marchman restrained him be a gentle pressure on the arm. "Let's get in a cab, and go out to the clinic. I want to talk to you."

"Nope," said Pruiett. "I got to buy me some new clothes, an' get outa here. I don't like it. I'm goin' back where they let a man do as he god damn pleases, an' where he can get all the rum he can pay for. I'm a god damn rummy, Doc." He put his arm around the doctor again, confidentially. "It's a damn good place down there, Doc, an' I like it. It's a god damn good place... to die."

Marchman contemplated the sick man hopelessly. He was a drunken husk, and mentally, morally and physically sick. "You owe me the courtesy of one more visit, Moman," he insisted. "We may never meet each other again, and we've been good friends. We have been friends, haven't we?" Marchman knew how to wheedle a drunk.

"You're god damn right, Doc, we been friends... but, a man ain't got no right to his friends when he gets a cancer in his face," Pruiett argued. "He ain't got no right to his wife, or his kids, or nobody else. He's just got a right to a lot of pain, that's what, an' a lot of lonesomeness. But by god, Doc, I ain't on no needle; I ain't no junker, an' I want you to remember that."

His tired whisper was trailing. A cab swerved to the curb in answer to the doctor's wave.

"Go out with me for just a short visit, Moman," he urged. "We can talk, and maybe I can help you." When Pruiett continued to hold back, he leaned close to his ear. "I've got some good stuff out there; it's prescription, not bootleg. I can fix some hot toddies while we talk." The sick man's resistance faded.

Marchman put Pruiett to bed. Two days later he was able to carry on an intelligent conversation with him.

"I quit fightin'," he said. "I know I'm dyin', but I still don't believe it's cancer. It's something just as bad, maybe worse, so it doesn't make much difference. An' don't feel bad about the way you found me, Doctor. I'm not down an' out. I've got plenty of funds. Rum an' whiskey kill the pain, and it doesn't matter how you look when you're full of that stuff. I'll be all right 'til it's over."

"But Moman," Marchman said, "There's no sense in quitting. It's not like you. I told you before you went East that I thought you had an infected blood stream, regardless of what the Wasserman showed. I told you I'd give you the treatments to correct it, and if I was wrong, there would be no charge. I'll make you a better offer than that. I'll let you die here in Baylor, free, provided you let me treat you my own way, as long as you last. If you get well on me, there's no charge. If you die, well... you say you're dead already. You can't lose, either way."

"That's damn nice of you, Doc," Pruiett answered wanly, "but I don't see any use. Seven or eight months, and I'm a dead duck, here, or Havana, or somewhere else. I don't want to burden my friends, or my family... "

"Moman, you've given up before the verdict's read," said Marchman. "Did you ever try a tough case, a real tough one; one so tough that you thought you were going to lose it; so, while the jury was out, you slipped up to the trial judge and offered to plead guilty? Offered to plead guilty and throw your client on the mercy of the Court, just because you thought there was a probability of gettin' stuck? Did you ever do that?"

"Hell, no, I never, and you know it, Doc. Pruiett lost a few cases, but he never lost a client. An' he never lost his nerve, either. Check me up on that."

Marchman had made his point. "That's what you've done to yourself, Moman," he whispered. "You never weakened on the other fellow, but you did on yourself. You quit fighting before the verdict was in."

The sick man's eyes shone. "By god, Doc," he said, "I see what you mean. I believe you're right. I'm not so old yet; I'm 52. I'm not wore out, am I, Doc?"

"No, you're not, Moman, you've got a lot of murder cases left in you yet, unless I'm mistaken. What do you say about letting me experiment on you?"

"What are the requirements? What are the rules?"

"Complete obedience to my directions, is the first one. Complete rest, that means, stay in the hospital, in bed, is the next one. Make up your mind that I'm going to cure you, that you're going to get well, and... No liquor! Absolutely no liquor!"

"You won't make me suffer too much, will you, Doctor? You won't drag it out too far, will you? Promise me that when you know you can't make it, you'll tell me, so I can make my own plans from there on." Pruiett was pleading and directing at the same time.

"That's a bargain," Marchman answered.

"And listen, Doc," Pruiett charged. "I don't want no god damn morphine. I made up my mind I won't be no hophead. Do you understand?"

"I understand," said Marchman.

Pruiett kept the faith with his doctor. Marchman's treatment restored him to health, and after a delicate operation, grafting the palate and roof back into his mouth and throat, his vigorous roar began to echo across Baylor's wide halls.

There were but a few words, and a few tears, as Pruiett and Marchman clasped hands in the hospital lobby on July 14, 1923. Pruiett was being discharged. He was well; cured. On the 17th, three days later, the United Press was broadcasting Pruiett news from its *Fort Worth Star Telegram.* "Moman Pruiett, noted criminal lawyer of Oklahoma City, pleaded not guilty here today when arraigned on a charge of possessing one quart of red whiskey. Pruiett was released on $500 bond after his hearing before United States Commissioner Parker. Pruiett was arrested last night in his automobile while in company with several nurses from Baylor Baptist Sanitarium of Dallas, where he had been a patient. Police allege the whiskey was found in Pruiett's car."

While Pruiett had been alternately engaged in trying to die and trying to get well, John Calloway Walton, more familiarly known as 'Jack,' had been engaged in getting himself elected Governor of the black stud's native Oklahoma. He was the same Walton, who, as Mayor of Oklahoma City, 'couldn't be trusted, handcuffed, to carry his own suitcase to the depot.' He took the gubernatorial reins from the hands of J.B.A. Robertson, whom, Pruiett so bluntly averred, 'was as crooked as a pan full of hog guts.'

And while Pruiett was away, strange events, in addition to the Reverend Edward Hall and one of his parishoners Mrs. Eleanor Mills trial farce in New Brunswick, and James A. Stillman's paternity squabble, at Carmel, New York, in which he accused his wife of having an affair with their Canadian guide, were occurring. Something stronger than West Indian Rum had been shot into the long dormant organs and glands of the Knights of the Invisible Empire of the Ku Klux Klan. The hillsides and creek banks from Penobscot to Bakersfield were flickering in the light of a multitude of fiery crosses; the cotton sheet market was enjoying a decided upturn as white-hooded regalias waved themselves back into flower.

And not all being published about the rejuvenated order was to its credit. According to Albert de Silver work, *The Nation,* "the klan springs from the memory of post-Civil War lawlessness, when the Negro was disfranchised by terror. It proclaims its purpose to maintain white supremacy and to protect womanhood, the two customary cloaks for lynching. Its leader asserts its purpose to protect the security of the people 'in the absence or inadequacy of the forces of law and order.' Its membership form discloses an unmistakable anti-Jewish and anti-Catholic bias. Over the whole has been thrown an amazing haze of mumbo-jumbo, with its Imperial Wizards, its King Kleagles, its Grand Dragons, Ghouls, Goblins, and Cyclopses, its fiery crosses and the rest. It was inevitable that all this should have attracted those most easily stirred to mob action and should have led to repeated outbreaks."

Laurence Greene's expose of the Klan, "Things That Go Bump In The Night," published in the *New York World,* gave it a million members—paying five million dollars for hooded night shirts. Five dollars per suit, f.o.b. the Klan-owned manufacturing company. Its realms and domains, extending their influences into every State in the union, had contaminated fair Oklahoma, and was alarmingly 'threatening white supremacy and the purity of womanhood,' or at least so Governor Walton averred. Although conditions were not so bad as in Texas, where the *Galveston Daily News* reported on July 19, 1921, that "a young white woman was seized on a hotel porch by masked men wearing white uniforms, taken several miles into the country, undressed, tarred and feathered and returned to town,'" nor in Birmingham, Alabama, where, according to Charles P. Sweeney, "a Klansman killed a Catholic Priest in cold blood on his own doorstep, and was acquitted at the trial amidst the plaudits of the mob," they were serious enough to cause the new Governor to look around and about for counsel on the extent of his authority with martial law behind him if the hooded props for law enforcement began to interfere with things, the way he thought they should be managed.

A half-page display ad in *The Daily Oklahoman* on October 4, 1922, announced that "The Ku Klux Klan will hold a great Open Air Initiation at the Fair Grounds, Wednesday, October 4 [1922] at 8 P.M." On the following day and in the news side appeared, "With fiery crosses outlined against the sky and white robes appearing ghostly in the darkness, the Invisible Knights of the Ku Klux Klan gave Oklahoma City a glimpse of its strength and the nature of its rites at a public ceremonial at the fair grounds. A crowd estimated between 20,000 and 25,000 watched the initiation of 400 candidates into the mysteries of the order."

Florida, like Texas, Alabama, Oklahoma and every other unit in the union, was suffering from Klanitis, and as the press put it, "Just before election day 500 members of the Ku Klux Klan marched in costume through the streets of Jacksonville, Fla., following the fiery cross, 'supposedly'," according to the *New York Times,* " 'as a warning to Negroes to attempt no lawlessness at the polls on Tuesday.' It is of record that few colored people voted in Jacksonville on Tuesday. 'White Supremacy' was maintained."

N. C. JEWETT, GRAND DRAGON OF THE OKLAHOMA KU KLUX KLAN, WHOM PRUIETT SUCCESSFULLY DEFENDED IN MARCH OF 1922 IN A WHIPPING CASE. COURTESY *THE DAILY OKLAHOMAN.*

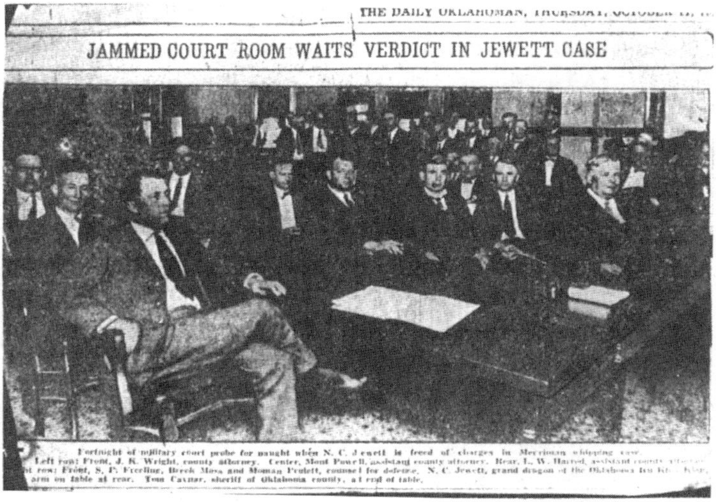

THE COURTROOM WAS PACKED DURING THE ENTIRE TRIAL OF N. C. JEWETT, GRAND DRAGON OF THE OKLAHOMA KU KLUX KLAN WHO WAS ACCUSED OF WHIPPING E. R. MERRIMAN. PRUIETT, AS COUNSEL FOR THE DEFENSE, HAD AN ALIBI FOR EVERYONE AND JEWETT WAS FREED. SEATED AROUND TABLE, LEFT TO RIGHT: L. W. HARROD, ASSISTANT COUNTY ATTORNEY; MONT POWELL, ASSISTANT COUNTY ATTORNEY; J. K. WRIGHT, COUNTY ATTORNEY; TOM CAVNAR, OKLAHOMA COUNTY SHERIFF; JEWETT, WITH ARM ON TABLE; PRUIETT; BRECK MOSS, DEFENSE COUNSEL; AND S. P. FREELING, DEFENSE COUNSEL. *COURTESY MOMAN PRUIETT: CRIMINAL LAWYER.*

While Governor Walton's courage was commendable, his judgment was unquestionably subject to criticism. The brand which he picked up and attempted to brandish was hot clear down to the handle. The wily klansmen had him on the ropes and out before the first bell rang, but the fight, while it lasted, was one to excite the interest and admiration of a true fight fan—even of Florida bound Lawyer Pruiett. Pruiett, after his recovery, proved, as a witness before the Senate Impeachment Court, that he had been right again when he so frankly appraised Walton's virtue while arguing for 'poor little Annabelle Edwards' freedom.'

Retiring Governor Robertson had left no Ku Klux good will in the gubernatorial mansion for pro-papal Walton to utilize. As the annals of his waning months in power disclose, according to the September 12,

1922, issue of the *Oklahoma News,* "Governor J. B. A. Robertson testified before the State Supreme Court Tuesday that he would have been mobbed by the Klan in Okmulgee had not National Guard officers accompanied him when he was there, seeking to testify before the grand jury which indicted him on a charge of accepting a bribe to permit the continued operation of the Guaranty State Bank, after it had become insolvent."

In addition to inheriting Robertson's Klan fight, the conduct of neighboring Governor Henry Justin Allen, in Kansas, abetted Walton in his injudicious warfare against the hooded order, and his plunge into political self-destruction. "The Kansas battle against the Ku Klux Klan, started by Governor Henry J. Allen, drew George C. McCarron of Oklahoma City, head of the K. K. K. activities in Oklahoma, Kansas, Missouri, and Nebraska, into its center Tuesday," reported the *Oklahoma News,* on October 31, 1922. "While Governor Allen, keeping up his campaign since last Saturday against the Klan was making a statement against the 'Invisible Empire,' McCarron from the Kansas City office of the Klan was answering Allen and indicating more strength than is generally known for the K. K. K. in Kansas."

HOODED KLANSMEN OPENLY DEFYING GOVERNOR JACK WALTON'S ANTI-MASK ORDER. PRUIETT WAS MADE AN HONORARY MEMBER OF THE KLAN AFTER HIS SUCCESSFUL DEFENSE OF N. C. JEWETT, A POSITION HE USED TO WIN FREEDOM FOR SEVERAL CLIENTS WHEN HE APPEALED TO KLANSMEN ON THE JURY TO VOTE NOT GUILTY. COURTESY WESTERN HISTORY COLLECTIONS, UNIVERSITY OF OKLAHOMA LIBRARIES.

Divisional director McCarron, making answer to the sunflower state's governor's threat to drive the Klan out of Kansas, and in no ambiguous terms, said that "it will be about as hard as driving out the Knights of Columbus."

While Pruiett was so studiously engaged in skidding gutterward that he failed to observe it, the fight waxed warmer. Beneficiaries of Walton's executive clemency, and there was a host of them, were being flogged, along with other miscreants, by bands of prowlers dressed as goblins. By the time Pruiett had righted himself, had been discharged from the hospital and concluded the social obligations he had made with members of the hospital staff while confined, Walton had half emptied the State penal institutions, had the State under martial law, and was directing his adolescent guards as they patrolled the corridors of the Capitol to prevent an impeachment session of the State Legislature from convening. Machine guns protruded from windows abutting the courthouse and City Hall in Oklahoma City. When Jack Walton said that Civil authority had ended, and that his martial edicts should stand in lieu thereof, he meant just exactly that.

The *Oklahoma News,* of October 8, 1923, spared enough of the front page, being pressed as they were by news of Walton's impeachment and juicy revelations of his remarkable official conduct during the brief time since his inauguration, to announce the Pruiett departure. "Oklahoma and the Southwest will lose its best-known criminal lawyer within a few months. Moman Pruiett, known in many states for his ability to bring tears of sympathy for unfortunate persons charged with murder, will leave the first of the year for Miami, Florida, where he plans to practice law. For the past year, Pruiett has been missing from courtrooms, due to a prolonged illness. Murder cases were postponed from last Winter's court term because he could not appear for the defense. About two weeks ago, Pruiett resumed active practice, and in that time he has tried five murder cases. He is now representing W. A. Joslyn, on trial for the murder of Anna Stewart, in District Judge T. G. Chamber's court. Born on a river boat in the broad Ohio, Pruiett has often remarked that he was a native of no State. As for law colleges, he says that they are mighty nice, but not necessary. For years he has specialized in murder cases, and his record for acquittals is not approached, perhaps, by any other lawyer in the United States."

If the writer of the article knew what Pruiett had had in place of law college, and why he thought it was not an absolute necessity, they tactfully kept it to themselves. References to Little Rock, and Rusk, were taboo. They were still his fightin' words.

Joslyn came close to disaster, according to the August, 22, 1922, issue of the *Oklahoma News.* He was a hardened old abortionist who had been caught red-handed with a client's pants down, so to literally speak. Current accounts stated that his victim, dying in agony, signed her name to a prepared accusation by guiding a pencil held in her teeth. Pruiett was a palsied wreck in the Havana side streets when Joslyn had committed his crime and had his preliminary arraignment. He was selling out, leaving Oklahoma for good, when Joslyn engaged him to go right into the trial of the case. Any style or plan of defense, other than Pruiett's, would have been unsuccessful, and Joslyn knew better than any one how narrowly he missed having them. His efforts procured a prompt acquittal, the hard way, tried to a jury of twelve fathers and husbands in the District Court of Oklahoma County.

On October 11, 1923, *The Daily Oklahoman* reported that "N. C. Jewett, grand dragon of the Oklahoma Klan, and L. L. Rhode and C. Whitlock of El Reno, were cleared of charges in connection with the whipping of E. R. Merriman March 7, 1922."

The actual substance of that news item had contained the punch which knocked-out a hard hitting Governor, out for the count, and out of a job so select that only forty-eight of them were available in the entire nation. The military court, directed by the State's executive as commander-in-chief of the National Guard, had fostered the procedure which resulted in the 'riot and insurrection' charges being filed against three men. A conviction of those charged would amount to some justification for the martial law, and the high-handed invasions of civil liberties which Governor Walton claimed were required to suppress the Klan and its depredations. An acquittal was to be a reliable indicator to the contrary, a civil rebuke to Walton's martial regulation of the populace.

"Sensational charges of 'darkroom,' third degree methods, used by Walton henchmen to obtain confessions tensed the large audience to absolute quiet in the final moments of the trial," said the papers.

The charges and counter charges flew. Walton's military court had contended that a band of hooded klansmen went into Merriman's Carbarn cafe on the night of March 7th, held a gun on the operator while he was being handcuffed, and then drove him to a secluded place in the country where they administered an old fashioned mule whipping. "E. R. Merriman, Charles Wallace, cook in the Cafe and Gus Marlatt, employee of the Oklahoma Railway company, testified on the stand that Whitlock and Rhode were the ones who held the gun on Merriman." A rather disreputable Mr. A. A. Maupin completed the evidence against the rioters by swearing that Mr. Jewett, the Klan's head man, took him into his confidence 'in the klan's office in the Liberty National Bank Building and told him of leading the whipping party on March 7."

Pruiett, as counsel for the defense, had an alibi for every one. The hand and mind that had delivered George Hopkins from the very jaws of retribution wouldn't be confounded with so simple a situation. "Jewett, and Cliff Saffell, his assistant secretary, said that the offices had been moved from the Liberty National to 139½ West Third Street, before March 1st, 1922."

"Rhode and Whitlock proved that they were in El Reno on the evening of March 7, 1922, by several witnesses. Chief among these were R. D. Thompkins, secretary of the Knights of Pythias Lodge, which had held a meeting that night, attended by Rhode, and A. J. Kivette, mayor of El Reno, who declared that Whitlock, a special policeman, had been at the police station at the time Merriman was taken out and flogged."

"While Maupin was on the stand, he was made a target for scathing questions by Pruiett. 'Do you use dope?' Maupin was asked.

'No,' he replied.

'I notice you scratching your ear and face all the time. Isn't it true that you took some dope before coming up here to testify?'

'I'll scratch my face, or any other part of my body I damn please,' came the hot retort."

It was a boner for Pruiett—he was familiar enough with addict characteristics, as he had recently picked them up around Havana and Nassau to recognize them, but he had forgotten that addict wit, at peak, was sharp. He backed away from that line of examination.

"The courtroom was packed during the entire trial and toward the last spectators crowded close to hear every word of evidence. Not even an indistinct murmur was heard when Whitlock told his story of how he had been arrested without a warrant, brought under armed guards to Governor Walton's residence, and then placed in a dark room at the

[Huckins] hotel, where he was asked to tell his story and go free, by an alleged friend and member of the klan."

Late in the afternoon on the day of the acquittal of the alleged insurrectionists, Pruiett answered the 'phone at his hotel. An old friend and acquaintance was calling.

"It's a little party for you, tonight," he was told. "All in your honor; call it a farewell party, if you got to have a name for it. We'll have a car pick you up in front at ten o'clock."

Pruiett got into the rear seat of a large touring car beside a prominent local business man. Two others, well known to Pruiett, were riding in the front seat. The car headed westerly from the downtown sector.

"Where's Charley?" Pruiett inquired, making reference to the man who called to invite him out.

"He couldn't come, but he's out there. He'll be there when we get there."

"Where's the blow-out goin' to be?" Pruiett asked.

"Well," came the hesitant answer from the man beside him, "that's kind of a secret. You see, this is kind of a surprise party, and we can't tell you. But we'll be there soon. It's not far out."

The car was passing through a residential section. All the occupants had relaxed into handy corners, and were saying nothing. The man in the back seat interrupted the silence.

"You see," he began, "this is kind of a surprise. We got to surprise you, not let you know where you are, see? Before we get too close, we're supposed to blind-fold you." He produced a black cloth from the corner of the seat behind him. "We better put it on; we're getting pretty close to there."

Pruiett laughed. "It's all right with me, boys, if it's a party, but remember, I'm leery of this mystic hocus-pocus stuff. I'm not used to it. You'll have to go easy, and not scare me too much."

After being led through a door, a series of halls and up a short flight of steps, Pruiett was ushered into a room. He knew by its heavy silence that it contained a multitude of people. Without a word, the guides, who had held each arm, released him, and he felt the bandage, which had been tied about his eyes, being jerked away. There was no perceptible difference. He was in complete darkness, as impenetrable as had been the blackness of the blindfold.

He waited, standing motionless. The he saw a light flicker opposite him in a large room, which wavered and grew. He saw that it was a match, first scratched, then applied to a taper. As others were lighted around the room their wavering beams began to reflect upon white bulks in the background, rounded trunks with pointed hoods above them. Some had crimson crosses and insignias across the white fronts while others were of plain white. He was amongst the Knights of the Invisible Empire and at what appeared to be a solemn and secret ceremonial. He stood and grinned, unable to identify any of them for a more appropriate or direct greeting.

"Mr. Pruiett." A voice well known to him came from the depths of an ornate nightgown. It was that of his client of the day; Jewett, the Grand Dragon. "We are indeed honored by your attendance."

Pruiett's reply was a profound bow, made more profound by mockery.

"Our principles require that we recognize and acknowledge signal service," the spokesman for the group continued. "We have asked you to come here, for one purpose, to thank you, and to attempt to show our genuine gratitude to you."

"It is my honor, gentlemen," Pruiett replied, with another, and more profound bow.

"We have abrogated every rule and regulation of our order, in bringing you here in this way and in this manner. May I say that you are the first non-member, not a subject of discipline, of course, to attend an executive session of this group." When he referred to discipline, there was a titter from the ranks. "We hope to impose upon your generosity once more today, by asking that you lend your efforts to us in correcting the breach of our regulations, which we have made in admitting you here tonight."

"I am at your service, gentlemen," said Pruiett, a trifle mystified. "I hope your requirements are not so difficult that I cannot comply with them."

The leader of the hooded band continued. "This group lives and breathes for the public good. The maintenance of law and order, the protection of the underprivileged, is what we strive to preserve. Membership is open to Americans, of good character, who are sympathetic with the high ideals which our cause fosters. We do no solicit membership. Membership is awarded to deserving applicants after their qualifications are investigated, and determined."

The leader paused, as if trying to catch the line of a committed speech which had temporarily eluded him. Not understanding, Pruiett remained silent.

"We are your friends. We have watched your fight for health with interest, and had sympathy for you in your absence and distress. When you returned, we watched for your application for membership in our order, with hope. We read of your decision to move to Florida with regret."

"By official action, I am prepared to offer to you an unsolicited membership in the Ku Klux Klan. We know you have the qualifications for membership. Your acceptance of it will correct all irregularities with reference to your attendance here tonight. You will serve us and make us happy by being a brother!"

Pruiett walked up to the speaker with hand outstretched. "ALL'S WELL ON THE POTOMAC." Jewett cried.

"All's well on the Potomac," Pruiett echoed.

There were two hundred solemn handshakes executed with solemn gravity, before the new member could work his way through the then de-hooded throng to the tables where the liquor, legislated against by the law they swore they would fight and die for, was being served from fruit jars.

Pruiett was making hay while the ground was in shape. He wanted more than car fare to Florida. He wanted to have his sack full, for he knew something about that tropical rainy season. It took more for that than it did for an ordinary rainy day. The South Atlantic boom looked good, but he didn't know whether he would find such lush pickings there, or anywhere else, as there were in his old haunts after a year's absence. He even made a contract to procure a pardon for Xenophon Jones, a long-term murderer, when he knew he had to work through his arch enemy, Jack Walton. Jack was then flailing and floundering before his senatorial accusers. The case was infested with money, and for that stuff, in sufficient amounts, Pruiett was prepared to put his pride behind him, and apologize to Jack. Maybe he could be trusted to carry his luggage as far as the depot, even with the handcuffs left off.

Xenophon, whose mention always brought forth a scandalized whisper—that he was half white and that his father was a wealthy member of the Oklahoma Supreme Court, was actually supposed to be half Negro and half Creek Indian. Rumor and pedigree were of little assistance when appearance was considered. He looked like a full-blood nigger. The makers of the Creek tribal rolls didn't try to minutely determine the ratio of black to red when they were being made up. Xenophon's allotment was belching oil over its own, and adjoining, scrub timber acres, and his bank balance was prodigious. But there he was in McAlester pining away for little luxuries which he could afford, but which the inconsiderate warden refused to let him have. "Hell, who wouldn't want out, under those circumstances?" Pruiett observed, while the facts of the case were being submitted to him.

According to the *Oklahoma News* on March 22, 1923, "Jones was sentenced to 25 years imprisonment when a jury found him guilty of shooting and killing Guy F. McIntyre, a white man, in 1917." Pruiett would have been glad to have acquitted him, win-or-you-don't-pay style, for half of the fee the lawyers collected who bungled the case, and let old-fashioned justice prevail. "After the shooting, he was placed under a $75,000 bond for appearance at preliminary hearing. He appealed from the District Court verdict, and was placed under $10,000 appeal bond, which he forfeited, and went to Tia Juana, Mexico. The wealthy negro has had one of the most colorful careers in Oklahoma criminal annals. Many attempts have been made to secure his freedom, and reports were that as much as $100,000 had been offered for a pardon."

The Pruiett contract was contingent on his procuring 'Zen' a pardon, not on the prisoner being restored to liberty. The details of how a duly executed pardon was presented to the warden, and to every other State official who might be connected with the State Penitentiary, only to be turned down, were aired before the committee investigating impeachment charges against Governor Walton.

"Testimony of Martha Jones, wealthy mother of the negro slayer, before the House Committee, was revealed. The negro woman told of a contract she entered into, about October 20, with Moman Pruiett, Oklahoma City attorney. By it, she testified, she was to pay $10,000 in cash, to be deposited in a bank, and was to turn over 120 acres of land in Tulsa County," with potential oil production, valued at $25,000, reported the *Oklahoma City Times* on November 26, 1923.

Speaking editorially the following day, the *Times* asked: "Does any one think Xenophon Jones would have been pardoned if he had not had much money at his command? There is no apparent reason for clemency in his case. His brutal crime deserves punishment. But there was a fortune behind him equal to paying $25,000 for 'Counsel'. That much has been revealed by the investigation, and that the pardon was issued. It happened to be one of the pardons that came too late, and Xenophon still is in prison—which is exactly where he belongs."

So there, Mr. Xenophon! With a handsomely embossed certificate in your lawyer's pocket and with your coffers considerably depleted, you are still behind those nasty old prison bars. Acting Governor Martin Edwin Trapp, standing at attention before the Ku Klux review, tells the warden that his name must be on the paper now, because Mr. Walton has been suspended from office by the act of his once loyal and cheering senate. If the impeachment court acquits, the pardon will be worth par value. If they convict? The pressure will be too strong, I fear. We'd better keep you where you are, Mr. Xenophon, right where you are, for just a little longer.

The uproar succeeded in involving Mr. Pruiett officially. He was called as a witness to testify before the State Senate, sitting as a Court of Impeachment for it suspended Governor. Wesley E. Disney, young Tulsa County Attorney and member of the lower house who served as the state questioner during Governor Walton's impeachment, was hard and fast on his way to Congress, prosecuting the hapless executive. He conducted the examination of Pruiett. *The Daily Oklahoman* of November 26, 1923, reported Pruiett's testimony."

" 'Xenophon Jones is your client in the matter of a pardon?' Mr. Disney inquired.

'Yes, sir,' said Pruiett.

'You visited McAlester [home of the State Penitentiary] at the call of Martha Jones?'

'Twice.'

'A week or two ago?'

'Well, once at her call, and once at my calling her.'

'The first time you went there, Mr. Patterson didn't go did he?'

'No.'

'Who went with you?'

'I went by myself. Now, I will explain that to you. I had an appointment with the Hayes boys, who I defended there for murder, and I went to the jail, saw the Hayes boys, and after goin' to the jail, I went to the penitentiary.'

'You talked with Martha Jones and Xenophon Jones there at McAlester?'

'Yes, sir.'

'Relative to representing him in a pardon matter?'

'Yes, sir.'

'As I understand it, you didn't definitely fix the matter of the fee that day?'

'We did not. It was agreed on, the matter of the fee.'

'To refresh your recollection, didn't you meet Martha at the station.'

'Yes, sir.'

'Now, who was the man who had the pardon—whom you told her had the pardon there in their grip, or portfolio?'

'I didn't tell her that. I had it right here where I have it now.' [Indicating coat pocket.]

'That was a week or two before the fee was definitely arranged for?'

'Yes, we had agreed on it that day. If you gentlemen will allow me, I will just tell it in my own way.'

'Yes, just tell it in your own way.'

'I want a sweeping investigation, so far as I am concerned about it, because I have lived here a long time, and they haven't caught me touching the hem of a jury's garment, or with the shadow of the subornation of perjury, and I am going to leave.' [His 'viller' was beckoning.] 'Now Martha Jones was over here, I don't remember the exact date, and while here some nigger woman by the name of Jennie, an old nigger that I defended for murder, and two or three of them came up to the office, and said that Martha, the mother of Xenophon Jones, was here, and she wanted a pardon. And they told me about Xenophon Jones. I had read that in the press, of course, with all the great publicity given it. In fact, I had read about it during Robertson's administration, and read of it, about Garrett carrying him over there when you gentlemen investigated it. At that time, though, I told this bank, or these people who came to me, I would be glad to help him if I could, but my attitude with the administration was such that I didn't think I could help them, but I named some gentlemen I thought might help them, and among the parties I named was Orban Patterson.' [Patterson was Pruiett's law partner.] 'I thought that I knew Jack Walton's chief virtue and his greatest fault, and I knew the connection with Patterson and Walton, and I told these parties that Walton could get the pardon.'

'You mean that Patterson could get the pardon.'

'Patterson could get the pardon. I don't know whether it was the day before or two days before, I told Patterson that he had better get that pardon if he expected to make any money out of it; if he expected to get the fee. I cautioned him in every way I could to be very conservative about his remarks; that the investigation was on and I didn't want to see him have any shadow cast on him in any way about the transaction. I told him there would be great publicity through the press. I think it was on the day that the Governor was suspended, I'm not sure now whether it was the evening before, that I told Mr. Patterson if he expected to get it he had better get it. On the day the Governor was suspended, sometime that evening, I don't remember the—sometime around five-thirty or six o'clock. Whatever the time may have been, at one-forty, before he was suspended I saw the pardon, and I only know then by hearsay as to when he got it.'

'Where did you see it, Mr. Pruiett?'

'I saw it in Mr. Patterson's office.'

'You didn't know who delivered it to him of your own personal knowledge?'

'No, I don't. I would be glad to tell you anything in the world, I know about it.'

'Do you know anything on earth that [Charles H.] Ruth' [a suspended State Supreme Court Commissioner] 'had to do with it? The question of the validity of the pardon is not before us, you understand?'

'Yes, I know what I heard. I don't mind telling you. When these niggers came to me, some nigger by the name of Jennie, I don't know—I can't call her name now—but Jennie somebody—there was three of them, telling me that Martha was here, you understand. They told me that Ruth said he had it in his pocket, and that he could deliver it. Well, I told them if that was true, if Ruth or any one else had the pardon in his pocket, that the culprit had the right to that pardon; they didn't have the right to peddle it around over the country, for the purpose of commercialism, or otherwise. That is what I told those negroes.'

'To refresh your recollection, wasn't it an Indian woman by the name of Jennie Fields, instead of a negro? Jennie Fields, George Fields' wife?'

'Yes. Well, I had forgotten, because when I came back here from the hospital; I just finished trying eight murder cases, and I have been awful tired; these things just come to me; in fact, I knew Patterson and Walton were good friends, and I thought if he could make the fee by getting it, why, let him get it. That is my attitude in the matter, exactly.'

'Do you know anything further, by hearsay, about Ruth's connection with it?'

'I think that Martha Jones, when she came over here, went to Judge Thomas H. Owen' [The same Tom Owen who had tried to prevent Pruiett's delivery of Corley McDarment, and who was supposed to be, at the time, trustee for dead Pruiett's property and estate.] 'I think she talked to him, in other words, sought his advice about it, because when these parties—the reason I have an independent recollection of this matter is, when these negroes, or Indian women or whoever it was, came to me and talked to me about the matter, I wanted to find out, if I could, the financial ability of Xenophon Jones and his mother, and I told Mr. Patterson that I would go and try to find out. I went to Judge Owen. I asked him about the financial condition. He said he had attended to the business of Martha Jones, for, oh, I think something like twenty-four or twenty-five years. He told me of the condition of Xenophon Jones—of an allotment he had. He said the value of it was very much exaggerated. It was located somewhere in Tulsa County. It was after that that Martha Jones called me and at her bidding I went to McAlester. Now, in that conversation there in the jail with Martha Jones and Xenophon Jones, I got this information. The poor old negro woman, she looked at me and she said, 'now, Judge, of course I know you have been working on this case, but how many of you gentlemen got the pardon?' Well, it was such a scream of humor that I couldn't help but laugh. I said, 'Martha, I don't know how many gentlemen have got the pardon, but I know I have been working in harmony, as you know I have, trying to get it.' She said, 'Is there more than one out?' I said, 'I don't know; I am not so sure; but I think there is more than one out.' Well, it struck me so forcibly that before leaving the penitentiary—there was a mail fellow there, who handles the mails, and I happen to know him. He said, 'Moman, I saw you talking to Xenophon Jones and his mother.' I said, 'Yes.' He said, 'Well, I understand you have a pardon for them.' I said, 'Yes, I have got it here in my pocket.' He said, 'How many is out?' I said, 'I don't know.' He said, 'Is this one from Trapp, or who?' I said, 'Well, it don't make any difference, I have got the pardon.' He said, 'Well, I understand there is another one out.' I am giving you gentlemen all the information I have.'

'Did you ever talk to Ruth about it?'

'No, I don't talk to him; I don't deal with men of his ilk. You can put that in the record. My attitude is this way—they came to me and I know that Orban Patterson had went around here and worked his head off. He and I married sisters and I was fixing to leave here; I just thought I would help him out if he could get the fee—I would put him onto it. So that is the history of it. I would be glad to come back in the morning and give you further information, as long as you will learn of it this afternoon. I would like to do it. It is no secret; it will be made public, because people who are connected with this pardon must give their testimony here or affidavits before the Secretary of State. I have nothing in the world to conceal. At the time of my first conversation with Martha Jones and Xenophon Jones, the first conversation in the penitentiary, I stated to Martha and Xenophon that I had the pardon and it mattered not whether they kept their contract with me or not, that he was entitled to the pardon, and it was to be delivered to Judge Thomas H. Owen, whether they kept the contract with me or not'."

The most amazing part of the Pruiett testimony, its background and its effect, was the sincerity of it. Pruiett's peculiar viewpoint was properly reflected in his disclosures. He saw no evil in his own purveying of pardons. The Governor was the one who was guilty of the wrong. He saw nothing objectionable in taking money from Martha Jones and Xenophon. They were niggers, in the first place, and they had too much money, in the second. Patterson's fee was half his, they were partners, but his own open enmity for Walton justified his denial of having any direct connection with the case. Pruiett was jealously proud of what he considered a spotless character and reputation; he considered the testimony which he gave before the Senate as nothing but support for them.

CHAPTER TWENTY-ONE

WHEREIN THE REJUVENATED PRUIETT ENTERS UPON THE FLORIDA BOARDS, AND LIVES UP TO FLASHY PRESS NOTICES BY CLEARING A CATHOLIC WITH A KLUCKER JURY, NOTWITHSTANDING THE VICTIM HAD BEEN A KLUCKER, AND HAD BEEN RUTHLESSLY DISPATCHED BEFORE WITNESSES ON THE STOOP OF THE MIAMI POST OFFICE. AND HOW HE DEMONSTRATES HIS POINT, AFTER CHARGING THAT DARROW HAD MISTRIED LEOPOLD AND LOEB, BY PLEADING SELF-DEFENSE FOR A HI-JACKER WITH A RECORD, WHO SHOT A UNIFORMED POLICEMAN FROM HIS MOTORCYCLE ON A DOWNTOWN THOROUGHFARE, AND SUCCESSFULLY DEFIES A JURY OF TWELVE MEN TO ELECTROCUTE HIM. AND, WHEREIN, HIS TECHNIQUE IS LABELED 'HOKUM', AND FLORIDA IS ADVISED TO AUCTION ITS ELECTRIC CHAIR PENDING HIS CONTINUED STAY ON THE PENINSULA.

When handsome Hattie Freckleton shot her husband to death on a crowded street in the Miami, Florida, business district, she was merely impelled by those ordinary passions of hate, viciousness and self-pity which invariably concur to produce such extraneous conduct. But she was rendering the lawyer Pruiett an inestimable service. She was setting the stage for his comeback; was giving him his chance to perform in the light of the flashy notices lavished by the Florida press since his permanent location in Miami.

The Pruietts were at home in the 'viller' at 59th Street and the Bay Shore. The fountains, three of them, gurgled on the front lawn, in the sun room and on the patio. Pruiett tossed cigar butts and spat his brown expectoration into their rippling basins with impunity. Pruiett and Patterson, attorneys, had offices in the Calumet Building. "Were they fixed up? Why, I paid $3,000 for the rugs we had in the place; $3,000 for the stuff we wiped our feet on," Pruiett boasted.

Legend had labeled him the black stud of the Washita, or the black-maned maverick, as he ploughed through a quarter century of murder. He was on the ascent of his second Matterhorn. He had risen and fallen. The heights which he had attained were the loftiest; the depths to which he had dropped had been like the ocean's floor, where the excrement of the whales reposed. His accomplishments and his degredations were illustrative of his nature. They contained the utmost of the good and noble; an equal content of honor and evil was there. Only such a nature, in such a physical structure as the indomitable Pruiett possessed, could have survived the rigors of exertion of body and mind, and the excesses in dissipation to which they had been subjected. It was for such a man to rise again, to scale the second, always the more difficult and forbidding, pinnacle; it was for him to write the second masterpiece; to compose the second symphony.

Slightly bent and slightly gray, he jerked about with youthful vigor. The bustle of the extravagantly promoted land boom, with its hustlers and suckers, inflated values and deflated characters, reminded him of the old valley on Saturday afternoon, when the ranchers and Indians were packed so tightly on the muddy main street that buckboard wheels interlocked, and drunken cursing vibrated like thunder, warning of a storm, before the bullets began to fly. The sandy stretches of the wastes along the coast looked all the world like the dry, sandy bed of the South Canadian River during the long summer drouths. Green citrus groves, with tangled tropical foliage along the ditches and bordering the fences, were like his Washita River, in full green to match the dark vistas of alfalfa fields, ready for their first spring cutting along its muddy banks.

He had the same desire, the inspiration and fight, which had propelled him to Washington for Charley Bias. The courage and ingenuity which the liberation of Sam Ashton and Doc Tyree had required, was hot within him. It was the old Pruiett. He was ready, and aching, for a fight.

The Freckletons, Hattie and Joseph, lived in Miami's fashionable Coconut Grove section. Joseph was an artist, designer and decorator who had moved south from New Jersey when the Florida boom and the building of the big places along the bay offered a tremendous field for his kind of service. He was a Protestant. Hattie was a Roman Catholic. Special dispensation had been made by her church before the marriage. Their existence, agreeable or otherwise, was little noticed in the booming peninsula, until Hattie put the ball through his skull which left a mural, in some unidentified capitalist's palace, unfinished. Then, the entire populous seemed to know all about them, and just how they had gotten along together in their bungalow by the bay.

Ku Klux Klan popularity was at its height. The order's impressive victory over Governor Jack Walton, marked by his impeachment and complete condemnation, had quieted executive opposition in other parts of the country. The Kansas governor's fight had been placidly postponed. Candidates for office, the nation over, adopted new campaign plans and procedure. What they would normally have invested in advertising, they put up in an attempt to purchase Klan endorsement, which was the equivalent to election.

Conscientious members would limp across town for a package of cigarettes or a box of cough drops, to buy them from a brother in the lodge, when a Jew or a Catholic was running a drug store next door to them. And, outside of its closest calculations, the Klan was stimulating the negro population. The blacks were foraging no more after night. They stayed at home and went to bed early, and layed up with their own wives as an incident to the necessity. Black babies were being born with greater frequency.

The Miami Klan had lost one of its most active members with the demise of Brother Freckleton. He had kept Hattie's Catholic past completely quiet, and starting with the early rejuvenation of the order, he had worked himself up, for personal and business reasons, to an enviable kleagleship. When news of Hattie's religious affiliation came out, following the killing, there was an executive session of the white robed fraternity. With solemn deliberation, the case was tried and the ballot taken. Hattie Freckleton was condemned to die, by the Klan, in the State's electric chair. The old Goblins and Kleagles were pretty crafty.

Pruiett's honorary klan card reposed in his bulky bill fold. He had not elected to establish his membership or affiliate himself with the Florida organization.

"We ought to join up with these Kluckers," Patterson said to him, in their office. "You got your card, and you can get me in. We won't get any business around here unless we do."

"I'm beginnin' to feel the same way about it," Pruiett said. "They're worse here than they were at home, and if you don't think that's bad, write your old pal Jack Walton a letter," he chuckled.

"Well, make a move; we can do a lot better if we start gettin' some of the klan business," Patterson said. "We got to make some money."

"Did you ever stop to think," Pruiett inquired casually, "that every damned lawyer in Miami, except a few Jews, is a member of this klan. They stick together, all right, but when one of those guys gets a little law business, he's goin' to take it to the lawyer member he knows the best; that he's known the longest. We've just got to wait, an' get acquainted. It'll take a big case to put us over."

"We won't get started any younger," Patterson replied. "I say, join up and find out who the big boys are. Get acquainted as members, not outsiders."

"Use your head a little," insisted Pruiett. "Non-membership is goin' to get business, too. While we're decidin' on just what's best, we may get some good business, that a klan member couldn't take, or get. Did that ever occur to you?"

"Freckleton was shot to death near the Real Estate Building on First street, near North East First Avenue," said the *Miami Tribune* on October 13, 1924. "Immediately following the shooting, the wife was arrested by police and later released to county authorities." When Pruiett saw her, on the same date, she was in the old jail behind the Dade County courthouse.

"Do you belong to this Klan, Mr. Pruiett?" That was the first question she asked him.

Pruiett evaded her. "I've only been here six months," he said. "I don't even know who the klan is."

"I'm a Catholic, Mr. Pruiett, and my husband was a member of the klan. He was a powerful member, too. The Sheriff, the Judges, the Court employees, they all belong to the klan." She was talking fast; half hysterically. "They'll have a klan jury too, Mr. Pruiett, and I won't get a fair trial. Oh God, what can I do?"

"You can trust me, for one thing," Pruiett told her promptly. "I don't belong to the klan, this klan down here," he corrected himself, "but, if I did, I've still got my oath to uphold the Constitution of the United States. I'm under obligation to no one in Florida, nor any lodge or fraternal order. I'm a free lance lawyer."

"Will you swear it? Will you swear to me that no matter what else you belong to, that you have no connection with this gang, this klan that Freckleton belonged to?"

"On my honor as a lawyer and a gentleman," Pruiett glibly swore. He wanted her case badly. He could see his picture on the front pages of the *Miami News* and the *Miami Herald* on December 11, 1924, as he looked through the bars into Hattie's tear-stained visage.

Pruiett got the case. In brief, simple terms, his client had killed her husband by shooting him through the head with a thirty-two pistol and bullet. All he had to do, besides avoid the difficulty which she, a Catholic, might expect from a klan jury, if the jury was a klan jury, was to prove that technically, such killing did not amount to murder.

"At the beginning of the afternoon session, Attorney Moman Pruiett, who is acting as counsel for Mrs. Freckleton, stated the case as it would be offered by the defense. He told the jury that it would be the contention of counsel to show that Mrs. Freckleton is 32, that Mr. Freckleton was 40; that they had been married about five years at the time of the homicide and were happy until after the time Mrs. Freckleton made a trip to the North for an operation; that following her return trouble existed between them; that he mistreated her; that she was allowed to come to Miami only a few times during the four years they lived at Coconut Grove; that she received a blow at his hands from which she has suffered continually since, that he filed divorce proceedings against her and that the matter was adjusted, and they became reconciled.

Following this reconciliation, they became estranged and he again started to sue for a divorce. She was attempting to effect another reconciliation just before the killing, but he cursed her and finally offered to strike her, causing her to fire the shot, in self-defense, which ended his life. 'We expect to show that she was distracted—an abnormal woman,' Mr. Pruiett concluded. 'And if we show you these facts, and I have tried not to exaggerate them, we confidently expect you men of the jury to acquit this defendant'."

Pruiett was making that opening outline to a jury composed principally of members of the klan. He had engaged local counsel, not a klucker, who knew, by reputation and street corner talk, about who was who in the klan. All his associates, and his client, had presumed that he was getting such information so that he could challenge klan members as they attempted to qualify. Instead, he challenged the non-members, and accepted those whom his client, and co-counsel, said were klansmen.

"My God, Mr. Pruiett," Hattie whispered frantically, "we've got ten klan members in the box; what in the world are you doing?"

"From now on," Pruiett answered, "I'm waivin' my peremptory challenges. I got you a damn good jury. No more challenges."

"But, the klan, they've sworn to avenge Joe," she rasped. "You've got to get 'em off; do something, not let 'em murder me."

"I'll try your case for you, Mrs. Freckleton," Pruiett told her. "That's what you hired me for. Now, please, don't bother me. We'll have our final conference on your testimony just before the State finishes its case."

The accused leaned back in her chair with a fixed, frenzied stare in her eyes. She was convinced that the counsel, to whom she had deeded her bungalow and given an assignment of poor Joseph's life insurance policies, was in with the all-powerful klan. She could see the double cross, instead of the fiery cross, sending her to death in the wired seat.

Pruiett seemed oblivious of her hostility; of her lack of faith in him. He cross-examined the State's witnesses with old time Territorial ferocity. He stalked and strutted and ranted, building his defense foundation, step by step, and using for it the same stones the State had produced for building a death dungeon for unhappy Hattie.

The State, with numerous incriminating offerings, proved by its Officer Scarborough that following the shooting he rushed to the body and demanded to know who had committed the act. He said that Mrs. Freckleton stepped forward, and said; "Oh, I did it. He's my husband." According to the *Miami Tribune* on October 13, 1924. The State contended that her declaration was with perfect candor, as if the marital ties entitled her to take such liberties as she had just taken with her spouse's skull. And it is probable that Hattie meant it just as it sounded.

Pruiett saved the best until the last. All of his evidence was in before he put Hattie on the witness stand. Her attitude had noticeably brightened since a long conference in the consultation room of the jail, at mid-trial, but she was still nervous and ill at ease. Pruiett began to question her, casually.

"Are you a native of the South, Mrs. Freckleton?" he inquired.

"Oh, no," she assured him, "I was born in the North; up in Jersey."

"And your husband, Mr. Freckleton, he was born there too, I presume?"

"Oh, no, Mr. Pruiett," she said. "He wasn't born in this country; he was born in Sicily, you know."

"What?" demanded Pruiett, affecting such surprise that he flounced from the reclining position in his chair. "What did you say, Mrs. Freckleton?"

"I said that Mr. Freckleton was born in Sicily," she repeated. "He came to this country when he was a young man."

"Well," Pruiett seemed to muse, "he was naturalized, I suppose. He was an American citizen?" He had the corner of his eye on the alien-hating klan majority in the jury box.

"No, he was not, Mr. Pruiett. I talked to him about it lots of times. I begged him to take out his naturalization papers, but he wouldn't do it. I just couldn't persuade him to take them out." The coy witness daubed a perfectly dry eye with her handkerchief.

"Yes," Pruiett said, breathlessly, as if to say—'keep it up, for Christ's sake don't stop now.'

"He refused," she continued. "He said that if they got his name on the books, he'd have to do military service, and..."

"We object," howled J. H. Swink, the prosecuting attorney. "It's immaterial."

"Sustained," droned the Court.

"Was your husband a veteran of the late war, Mrs. Freckleton?" he asked.

"We object," howled Swink again. "It's.... "

"Sustained," said the Court.

Hatties pathetic look was equivalent to a negative reply. It carried even more weight with the jury, and the jury was beginning to take interest in what the defendant was offering.

Then, Pruiett and Hattie got down to business. Freckleton was a sadistic beast in a ceiling decorator's smock. He beat her and he kicked her and he cuffed her. He denied her enough clothes to wear or enough food to eat. Her evening caress was rewarded with a fist in the face. Her prostrate supplications for consideration, and affection, were met with brutal kicks. He whipped her when she laughed and he whipped her when she cried, but his uncontrollable frenzy, with bestial attacks, came when she objected to his sending his money away when she needed it so badly for groceries and a few clothes.

"Is that so," Pruiett asked innocently. "What did he do with his money? Who did he send it to?"

"I never was able to find out who it was, for sure," she whined. "It was a foreign name; he sent it back to Sicily."

"Did he have people in Sicily?"

"I don't know, Mr. Pruiett. He had no relatives in this country at all; it may have been that he had folks in Sicily; but, I think it was a business associate, a painter. As fast as he received pay on a contract, he took just enough to keep us, that is himself, for he had no regard for me, and the balance he sent to Sicily."

"Didn't you ever receive letters from the old country?"

"He did; not I," she corrected. "He did, quite often."

"And who were they from?"

"I don't know, Mr. Pruiett; he destroyed them. He burned them just as soon as he opened them and read them."

A shapely shank and a coy manner were Hattie's natural attributes. The Sicily story and all the rest was Pruiett's creation. If an innocent person could be convicted, a guilty one could be acquitted, and no rule, law or prohibition, could stop him if his client would give him a semblance of cooperation. Hattie Freckleton worked with him like a true disciple of the doctrine.

It was privation—and Sicily. It was cruelty—and Sicily. It was want—and Sicily. Americanism in the jury box was being invited again, as when it was inducted into the robed order, "to approach the portal of our beneficent domain and join in the sacred duty of protecting womanhood, to maintain forever white supremacy in all things, to bless mankind and to keep eternally ablaze the sacred fire of a fervent devotion to a pure Americanism." Americanism and Sicily? Americanism, with beating a hungry wife, preliminary to sending hoarded American wealth to a bunch of damned lower Italians? What the hell is Americanism? Hattie was seeing and understanding Pruiett's motive in keeping the klansmen, her avowed persecutors, on the panel.

Florida saw its first fanatical forensics in the courtroom, when Pruiett argued the Freckleton cause to the jury. "Mr. Pruiett," stated the *Miami News* on December 14, 1924, "who came to Miami recently from Oklahoma, where he was attorney in a large number of important murder cases, held the rapt attention of a courtroom which was, this time, crowded to its capacity. The defendant sat motionless, almost as pale and immovable as a marble statue, while her counsel paced back and forth, hurling his bursts of oratory at the jury, or extending hands pleadingly—only to turn a moment later and shake his fists at the State's attorney."

"Mr. State's Attorney," he roared, "I throw the challenge back to you. Try her as if she were a man. Forget she is a woman. Suppose a man were on trial and had been repeatedly beaten, choked, abused, threatened, and assaulted. Would you not say that he would be justified in protecting his own life? Talk of compromise if you please, Mr. Swink. Spread before the jury's eyes the smooth vista of a prison sentence. Never! In this case it must be either the extreme penalty, or an acquittal. There can be no middle ground."

"My friends, since in the beginning of time, when the gray of creation's dawn began to drive back the flood of darkness, the true male of the specie has endeavored to love and protect womanhood, not oppress, mistreat and degrade it. The real issue in this case," he cried, "is American manhood in the jury box, protecting American womanhood from the depredations of an alien beast! There is to be no compromise. If Mrs. Freckleton is a human tigress, she is guilty and she must pay the penalty. If she is not, she is innocent and you must find her not guilty by your verdict."

"Give her liberty or give her death," he challenged according to the December 13, 1924 issue of the *Miami Herald.*

"They say that she lived in Coconut Grove? Nay! She lived in Lonesome valley, between the mountains of dread and hate. They tell you she lived on Douglas road, but she lived on the road of fear. All she had for companions were cats and dogs, and lonesome pines. This man was a brute, and when I say 'brute' I will assume the full responsibility for the use of the word."

When he had screamed of chivalry, the sanctity of the home and the purity of good woman's breasts, of blind wifely devotion and compelling mother love, and everything else that could possibly tend to excite patriotic feeling in a male structure, he mopped the perspiration away with a huge silk handkerchief and made as if to sit down. Then, with an afterthought, he rushed to the rail in front of the first row of jurors.

"When our American mothers tuck our American children in their little beds tonight, let them be able to kiss the little frowns of care from their innocent faces, and assure them, and the Maker she looks to above for guidance and counsel, that 'All's well on the Potomac!' " He gave the rail a resounding slap, as if punctuating his sentence with an exclamation point. Then, he stalked defiantly to his seat.

"Mrs. Hattie Freckleton was acquitted yesterday of a charge of first degree murder for the slaying of her husband, Joseph Freckleton, on N. E. First Street near the Real Estate Building, on September 29, 1924. The jury in Judge H. F. Atkinson's Circuit Court, which was given the case at 2 o'clock, returned its verdict of not guilty at 5:10 o'clock. Following her acquittal, Mrs. Freckleton was released from the County Jail, where she had been since the time of the shooting, and was taken to the home of Attorney Moman Pruiett, on the bay shore at Fifty-ninth street, where she will remain for some time to rest."

Pruiett, with Charley Ketcham, past Grand Master of the Masonic Lodge, who had driven from Key West to hear him try his case, went to the Ta-Miami Hotel for dinner. After dining, they lounged in the lobby, smoking Cuban cigars.

"Judge Pruiett?" A uniformed hotel employee had approached him.

"Yes," he said.

"A gentleman says he's holding a 'phone call for you in the game room. Shall I tell him you'll take it there?"

"Yes, I'll take it. Show me how to go," Pruiett replied.

The boy lead him through the back lobby to a stag room used for cards, the current craze called for hearts, but poker and rummy equipment was available. The boy stopped at the doorway. As Pruiett walked in, the door was closed behind him.

"Hello, judge." A grinning man dressed in a light tan suit offered his hand. It was the foreman of the jury that had acquitted Hattie. Pruiett looked about as he accepted the shake. He thought he saw the entire jury present, although there were actually only ten of them—the ten that he knew were klansmen. Possibly as many as a dozen other men were in the small room.

A portly man with gray hair, almost as thick as Pruiett's took charge of the meeting. "Grab him, boys," he directed.

Two or three of them, closest to him, attached themselves with restrained grips, to each of his arms. "Shake him down, now, an' see if you can find it. See if he's got it on him," the leader directed.

A man stepped forward to begin a methodical search. When it had proceeded as far as the left hip, to a bulging billfold, the search ended. The searcher held up the klan identification card triumphantly. "I told you the bastard was a klucker," he cried.

"Why didn't you identify yourself a long time ago?" the leader demanded.

"I wanted to establish myself," Pruiett laughed. "I wanted you to learn somethin' about me before I pulled the card on you."

The jury foreman stepped up. "Was Joe Freckleton really born in Sicily?" he demanded.

"Hattie said he was," Pruiett laughed. His merriment was a shaking roar before he concluded. "Hattie swore it; you heard her."

"Boys," the chief said. "You've been hooked. You've been double crossed. He talked you out of doin' what you started out to do, and made you think you were doin' your duty. It's a hell of a note."

"It's treason, that's what it is," said another. "A member, defendin' a Catholic bitch who killed a brother member, to a klan jury, and gettin' her off. Oh, god!"

"What's to be done with him?" asked the leader. "Do we revoke the card and give him the strap, or act on his application for transfer of membership?"

"Who said he applied for transfer?" chimed a voice.

"I did," said the leader. "When he said 'All's Well on the Potomac' before that jury, he was puttin' in his bid. If he wasn't, he's in a hell of a bad fix now."

"I'm ready to join up, or get the boot, either," Pruiett grinned. "It's the Constitution of the United States first with old Moman, and fraternal affiliations next. If that suits you, I'd like to come in."

"Was Joe Freckleton really born in Sicily?" insisted one of the members of the jury.

"You heard what I said about it," evaded Pruiett.

They voted him in. "It reminds me," Pruiett began, as they handed him his third drink, "of the old Sam Ashton case. Now, that was a case where I had a tough jury, and a hell of a bad client. We started out... " He told them about Pruiett here and there—in murder cases. When subsequent inquiry established that Joseph Freckleton had been born in Davenport, Iowa, and had some respectable relatives living in the North, they declined to vote as was suggested, on removal, and klan discipline, for Pruiett.

The assistant warden at the state prison in Railford brushed out the death cell and ordered an overhauling for the electric chair. The signs from down Miami way were as conclusive of death business coming, as the palm-tree stalks, snapped half-way up, were of the recent visit of a gulf storm. Company was surely on its way.

The extreme quiet around Toledo, Ohio, had driven young Walter

Valiton out. From petty to great thievery, he went with little more than a parental rebuke. Drifting across and below the Ohio River, he swiped himself an automobile, at Somerset, Kentucky, but received only a suspended sentence and a mild rebuke from a kind-hearted judge reported the *Miami News* on May 18, 1925. With the Kentucky experience for guidance, he went back to Toledo and pulled the same kind of a job. He received the same kind of lenient treatment after being apprehended.

With this experience in his mind, his appreciation for the court's good will and leniency in his heart, and a stolen automobile in his hands, Valiton sought the more agreeable clime of Biscayne's sunny bay. Napoleonically, he went post-horse, or post-auto, taking fresh mounts as whim and convenience permitted, at intervals along the route. Car owners and insurance companies were distracted by the time he reached Daytona, where he stole his last, a box-backed Essex, to carry him into Miami. There he began to put into effect his plans for bigger and better crime in Florida.

"The little bastard was tougher than a boot," opined Pruiett, who was to become his mouthpiece. Building into the weak and already criminally inclined crackers of the poor piney land, Valiton got himself a pal and a few girls. From an abandoned shack in a palmetto swamp, surrounded by enough substantial earth to support thick pine woods, he began his program of hi-jacking, pilfering and burglarizing. John Naugle, a misguided kid who had run away from a poor home in Jacksonville, Florida, received a first lieutenant's commission from the Toledo outlaw.

The warehouse of the Eli McDonald Furniture Company suffered an unusual violation. Enough furniture to furnish a small house, in selected items, was stolen with the currency and checks from the office safe. The leaky floors of the shack in the swamp, thereafterward, were covered with oriental rugs, and handsomely carved mahogany pieces rested awkwardly in its well-ventilated corners. Citizens were histed; safes were blown; property was stolen. Valiton and Naugle, in silk shirts and bell-bottomed trousers, smoked imported Cuban cheroots and drank expensive Jamaica liquor.

The carbide light of Police Sergeant Laurie Wever's motorcycle reflected from the rear of a slow moving sedan with an Ohio license. It was 2 o'clock in the morning, and police business was bad. The chief had been raisin' hell about the wave of burglaries and hi-jackin's that had the county half-terrified, and the strong language of a recent departmental bulletin on the subject was running through his mind. Here's a good one to investigate, Wever decided.

"Pull over there, you; pull over and stop." Wever had ridden to a position beside the driver. When the car stopped, two stylishly dressed boys stepped out. "What's the trouble?" the one who had been driving inquired.

The street light from the corner—by the Savoy Hotel—gave Wever a good view of them, but he augmented the illumination with the beam of his flashlight. "Kind of late for joy riding, ain't it?" he asked. "What you doin' out this time of the morning?"

The driver flashed him a personality smile. "We took our girls home, and then had a flat tire," he said. "It took quite a while to fix it, so we're late. We're just on our way home."

Wever's light continued to play on them. "You didn't get your hands very dirty, changin' that tire, or your clothes, either. How about that?"

"Oh, we washed up at the filling station—washed our hands up," the spokesman said glibly, with just a little more smile. "I'm pretty good at changin' 'em anyway."

The patrolman wasn't satisfied. "Mind if I look in your car?" he inquired, watching them closely in the light.

"Help yourself. Drive it around the block, if you want," chirped the flip speaker.

The little light arched its white ray into the back seat of the sedan. Wever switched it around, pulled the rear cushion out onto the floor with one hand and studied the display within the beam for several minutes.

"What you use these kind of tools for?" he asked.

"Tires," said one of the boys.

"First time I ever saw any tire irons that shape, or size," the policeman replied. "And, what's the use of so many? Have a lot of flats, do you?"

His hand was on the butt of the service revolver which hung on his Sam Brown belt as he walked back to where the boys were standing. "Do you always carry so much soap, an' perfume, an' cigarettes, when you're going home from seein' some dames?" he asked.

The boys didn't answer. "Got guns?" asked Wever. There was still no reply. "Hold your hands up a little, while I look around." Wever walked behind them, his hand still on the handle of his own revolver, and began a methodical search by running his hand down the exterior of their light clothing. After he had inspected the front seat and compartment of the car, by illuminating it with his little light, he turned to the boys, still standing under the street light.

"Get in, an' drive down to the station," he directed. "You look hot to me, an' I'm goin' to have you checked up. I'll follow on this motor, an' remember; no monkey business. You turn right two blocks down for the station."

Two blocks down the Essex failed to turn. With a slight increase of speed, it continued straight ahead. Wever pulled up on the driver's side. "What the hell's the matter with you," he bawled. "I told you to turn right back there... "

The driver, with one hand on the wheel, was holding a blue thirty-eight in his lap, with the other. He had slipped it from under the seat cushion, where Wever's flashlight had failed to penetrate, as he had driven from the scene of the policeman's search. Laying it professionally on the crooked elbow of his driving arm, he pointed it square at the motorcycle rider's chest, and began to fire.

" 'I was shot by a highwayman," Wever managed to gasp to fellow officers before he died,' reported the *Miami News* on May 18, 1925. Three days later a posse, composed of officers and incensed citizens stormed the shack in the swamp, which was in truth, a little fortress. They met no resistance from the two occupants. Valiton adopted the alias of William Fox, and credited Columbus, instead of Toledo, with his origin. He modestly confessed to having killed Wever, giving the Deputies, who took an occasional random swing at him, or jabbed him with the point of a pocket knife, all of the intimate details.

According to the April 2, 1925, issue of the *Miami News,* "When Valiton was brought to the jail, he was spattered with blood, his lips and face were bruised and he appeared badly battered up. 'I took Valiton' said the warden, 'placed him in a padded cell and told the officers that I would kill anybody who started anything'."

"While a constantly growing crowd milled around the courtyard and County Jail yesterday morning," observed the *Miami Herald* on

April 2, "eager to secure a glimpse of Fox and Naugle, the prisoners were spirited away before their eyes by Deputy Sheriffs posing as garbage collectors.' 'Make way for this truck there, men,' called the driver of one of Dade County's big trucks, used in road-repairing. 'Move that automobile out there.' The crowd paid little attention to the truck or the attendants who brought forth from the jail the large garbage cans with lids clamped down. The men were deputies from Sheriff Henry R. Chase's staff. Inside one garbage can huddled Fox, confessed slayer of sergeant Laurie Wever. Inside the other crouched Naugle, Fox's accomplice."

" 'The prisoners were removed from the County Jail at 9:30 this morning,' the sheriffs office notified the steadily increasing crowd at 3 o'clock in the afternoon. 'Whether they went by water, automobile or rail, we are not at liberty to state.' The Sheriff decided that under all the circumstances, it was best to remove them from Miami. They will likely be kept at the place to which they have been removed until their case is called to trial."

Startling revelations tumbled over each other as they began to come out in the case of the *State of Florida vs Walter P. Valiton, alias William Fox, and John Naugle.* "Money came easy for Fox and Naugle, and it went just as easily as it came, according to their admissions to the police. Cards, liquor, women and the races claimed their money, which they obtained through the strong arm method."

"Eleven hundred dollars, taken by Fox and Naugle from the safe in the office of the Eli McDonald Furniture Company, was squandered on the races, pool games and other forms of betting, and two hundred dollars taken from the safe of Ye Wayside Inn, obtained by them when they tied up the night watchman, went the same way. They confessed yesterday that they had in their automobile loot from a drug store which they had just robbed when overtaken by Sergeant Wever. Fox declared he did not want to be taken to jail, and shot in a frenzy of fear. He said that he had been drinking," claimed the *Miami Herald* on March 10, 1925.

The automobile—abandoned in the swamp—was the beginning of a well marked trail to the hideout. The clumps of palmetto along the way, and the thick, adhesive morass, yielded up separate articles of loot, then the suitcases used for carrying it. Word of suspicious acting occupants in the abandoned hut, and carefully spliced descriptions of the occupants, harmonized with the indications made by the flight and the trail of loot. "At exactly 2:10 o'clock yesterday morning, 14 policemen in charge of Chief H. Leslie Quigg and detective Forrest E. Nelson set out from the police station in three automobiles. All were heavily armed. The party continued as far as Fulford, then turned West on the trail leading to the shack housing the two slayers, then parked their automobiles."

"Six of the men, revolvers in hand and ready for instant action, crept up the trail about a quarter of a mile and surrounded the house. In the meantime, the remainder of the party, on signal, approached the house. Without lights of any kind, Chief Quigg drove his automobile through the underbrush to the front of the shack, then flashed the headlights and spotlight directly on the house. At the same moment, Detective L. H. Haddock, with William Beechey and Detective Pearce immediately behind him, threw his full weight on the door, which soon gave way. Four men dashed into the room, revolvers and flashlights in hand."

"The two men were asleep in the front of the house, Fox on the west side of the room and Naugle on the east side. While the three companions of Beechey covered the two men with their guns, Beechey jumped on Naugle and handcuffed him as he said: 'Did you kill Wever?' Naugle, somewhat dazed and nervous, replied, 'No, I didn't, but he did,' pointing to Fox'."

"A careful examination of the house revealed a large box of dynamite caps and several boxes of electric fuses. Throughout the house was a complete network of wires, which terminated at a point near the dynamite box. Over each door two wires terminated, and it is believed that they could be so arranged that if the door was opened, the dynamite would be ignited by a spark from several dry batteries. The circuit was disconnected when the men were in the house, and in their absence the men would close the circuit, leaving a death trap for intruders."

"Two truck loads of stolen property were hauled away from the small shack, including articles of every description. A large quantity of perfume, soap and other articles sold in drug stores was found. A complete set of yeggs [burglary] tools, including a ratchet drill, hack saws, copper headed sledge hammer and a large collection of keys was found in a box in the back room of the house. Acids used extensively by yeggs on safes and as a neutralizer for nitro-glycerine composed part of the kit. Dispatches yesterday from Columbus, Ohio, stated that police in that city have no Bertillon [a method of identification used prior to fingerprints], record of Fox," reported the *Miami Herald* on March 19, 1925.

Miami turned out en masse for popular officer Wever's funeral. His bullet scarred motorcycle was draped with black and mounted on a truck, and paraded about the city behind the hearse carrying his body. A quick trial and a speedy execution for his assassins, was the oft' expressed hope and opinion. The klan, in executive session, considered a private everglade hanging for them; they reflected on the rather irregular liberation of Hattie Freckleton, who had slain one of the brothers. Wever had been a member. But, the electric chair at Railford needed a workout, and Pruiett was a member, now. There would be no slip this time, so just let the law take its course. No official action was taken.

Valiton's mother and father, on their arrival from Toledo, hired Pruiett to defend their precocious killer. The kluckers winked and grinned when the gray-haired mouthpiece, who had tricked them once, told them in tones that could be heard in Key West, 'the Constitution of the United States comes ahead of any oath I took to any god damned secret society, and by god, I'm goin' to the front for that kid.' Let him go, as far as he wanted. Valiton would fry as sure as the tides would be in in the evening.

It was a tough case, but not Pruiett's first one. Loeb and Leopold were becoming familiar with the regulations at the Illinois State Prison in Joliet, after their uneventful trial. It's outcome had been easily predictable. A news hack, half inquiring and half suggesting, approached Pruiett.

"Are you going to follow Clarence Darrow's plan of defense in this case, Mr. Pruiett—as he defended Leopold and Loeb?" he asked.

"Hell no," said Pruiett briefly. "There will be no Clarence Darrow stuff in this case. And you can make the most of that statement. These defendants will go to trial on the real issues," he told the *Miami News* on March 28, 1925.

He had been fighting the system too long to lay down and beg it for mercy now. He'd plead him not guilty, and chance the chair trying to clear him. Anyone could plead guilty and cop life.

On the trial date, he filed a volume of pleadings. There was a twenty page motion for a change of venue, with attached copies of every article, editorial and illustration the Miami papers and magazines had carried on the crime, the capture, and the Wever funeral. He complained of the threatened mob violence which required the removal of the prisoners from Miami. He filed a fifty page motion for a continuance of the trial, and a volume of accusations against the regularity of the jury panel, which he charged, 'was drawn by the Ku Klux Klan with the purpose and intent of convicting, and electrocuting my client.'

"Its treason," whispered the scandalized klansmen again.

"Attorney Pruiett, in his demand for a change of venue," reported the *Miami News* on March 30, 1925, "stressed the fact that public sentiment had been so aroused by the press and by wealthy relatives of Sergeant Wever that the Sheriff was forced to spirit Valiton out of the jail to the north to prevent possible violence, immediately following their arrest'. The public has been given only one side of this story,' cried Pruiett, trembling as if shaken by violent emotion. 'Walter Valiton is not guilty of the crime charged; he has been forced to confess to this deed by being brutally beaten by Deputy Sheriffs, and threatened with even more serious harm. The public does not understand; it has been given an untrue version of the story'."

"Pruiett pointed out that the young men were strangers in a strange city; that at the time of their arrest they neither had money nor opportunity to hire lawyers to advise them, and that after a third degree their only course could have been to confess to anything—to prevent mistreatment. 'Why,' he exclaimed, 'many attorneys, who were asked to defend these young men, pleaded other business. On the other hand, many of the most prominent attorneys volunteered to prosecute them. And more than $2,000 had been raised to assist their prosecution.'"

But Dade County didn't want to lose the right to burn the jellybean killer, and it didn't want to lose the Pruiett production of the defense. They knew it would be futile, but if the Hattie Freckleton forensics were any criterion, they knew it would be good.

Florida Governor John Martin "PLEDGES TROOPS TO GUARD MIAMI SLAYERS," proclaimed the headline.The type of the bulletin covered the upper half of the front page. "National guardsmen will be called out in Miami to preserve order in event of a mob outbreak against Walter Valiton and John Naugle, confessed slayers of Sergt. J. L. Wever, Gov. John Martin notified Moman Pruiett, attorney for the pair, by telegraph Monday night. Shortly before noon, Pruiett wired the Governor, who is at Tallahassee, that in case a change of venue to another county is granted, he feared the two confessed slayers would be in danger of violence at the hands of a mob, presumably infuriated because of the removal of the pair to the courts of another county, and asked that proper precautions for their safety be made. Shortly afterward, Judge H. F. Atkinson refused the defense plea for a change of venue, and ordered that the trial resume Thursday in the Dade County court. Apparently still concerned over the safety of the two youths, who are being held in the County Jail, Pruiett did not revoke his plea for State protection for the prisoners. About 9 p. m., the answer of the Governor to the attorney's plea came by telegraph. The telegram said; 'Advise Sheriff take every precaution, keep down mob violence. If necessary, will call out militia. (Signed) John W. Martin, Governor of Florida'."

"Pruiett wired the Governor," advised the *Miami Herald* on March 30. "During the argument for a change of venue in the beginning of the trial yesterday of Walter Valiton, Attorney Pruiett, for the defense, without consultation, so far as he has been ascertained, with any constitutional official of the county, sent the following telegram to Governor Martin: 'My firm defending Walter Valiton, charged with murder of Sergeant Wever. Motion pending for change of venue. Believe same will be granted. In that event, I fear mob violence. Will you communicate with officers here and take such steps as may be necessary? (Signed) PRUIETT'."

During the Washita charger's brief term as a citizen of Florida, he had already placed himself in a position where he could take liberties with the Governor, and identify himself by merely signing 'Pruiett' to the communication. His dinner with the Governor, at the Flamingo Hotel in Miami Beach, had been but a resumption of a friendship which had begun in Washington. "Where I can do anything for you, Moman," the Governor had said as he left Miami, "don't hesitate to call on me." Pruiett had suggested that he put Florida's principal city under martial law, with but slight hesitation. "And, if he thought it was necessary, or that I needed it, he sure as hell would have called them soldiers out," Pruiett laughed, reviewing the incident after conclusion of trial.

"At no time, during the days hearing," continued the *Herald,* "was there any indication that aid might be needed in the preservation of order. It was obvious, of course, that should any disturbance occur, now or at any future time, the Sheriff would not hesitate to ask for help from the Governor. IT IS UNUSUAL FOR AN ATTORNEY TO MAKE SUCH A

MOVE. The telegram sent by Pruiett was dispatched at an hour when absolute quiet prevailed."

If boom-bounding Miami and vicinity wasn't going to approve of the unusual, it was going to have to rid itself of the irrepressible Pruiett. The right way, or the orthodox, was the one way he wouldn't go if he could avoid it. No one was concerned with the commonplace. He had long since learned that what roused the slumbering populace, and made them act the way he wanted, and needed, them to act, was the unusual, the unexpected and sensational. The front page ad, which his two dollar telegram acquired, would have cost an orange grove development company, or a yacht sales agency, $50,000. And maybe it would put the prosecutors on their toes. He wanted some competition in the trial of this little old case.

Pruiett was putting on proof in support of his motion for a change of venue, according to the *Miami News* of April 2, 1925. "John Talbot, deputy sheriff, the last witness to testify on the change of venue petition in the Valiton trial, climaxed the morning session when he declared that Moman Pruiett, principal attorney for Valiton, was the only man he had heard utter a threat against the prisoner. Talbot emphasized that the threat was uttered before Pruiett was retained as counsel by Valiton's parents. Pruiett himself arose and placed in the record the phraseology of the threat originally spoken near the kitchen of the County Jail while Valiton and John Naugle were at Jacksonville for safety.' If they bring those men back to Miami, old Moman, for one, will be athirstin' for their blood,' Pruiett said were his words."

Talbot had steadfastly denied that he had heard any threats made against Valiton. Pruiett persisted, trying to break him down. "The incident sent the spectators, judges, attorneys and court attaches into gales of laughter, punctuated by a spatter of applause. Even young Valiton, shadowed by the law, smiled, as did his parents, through their astonishment. Only the taciturn, poker-faced Talbot, and Pruiett himself, refrained from displaying any mirth. The defense lawyer unsuspectingly pulled the forensic trigger that fired Talbot's surprise shot. 'Did you ever hear any man utter threats of violence against the life of the prisoner?' 'Yes,' Talbot replied dryly.' Tell the Court and jury about it,' urged the lawyer.' It was you, Mr. Pruiett,' continued Talbot. 'You were the one man I heard speak words of violence against the life of the prisoner'."

"For one moment Pruiett was dumbfounded by the sudden turn. Then he sprang to his feet to make the best of it. 'Then you did hear a citizen of Dade County,' he thundered at the witness, 'in the act of threatening violence upon the defendant'."

His motion for a change of venue was denied, but his appeal for a reasonable continuance—in order to prepare for trial—was granted. On the last day of the proverbially ill-fated month of March, the Christians filed into the arena to view the gory drama. "Harlan Miller, *Miami Daily* news staff writer, is reporting the Valiton-Naugle trial for the *Miami News.* Mr. Miller covered the Loeb-Leopold murder trial in Chicago. He has written the story from the packed courtroom in the Dade County courthouse." So spake the *Daily* editorially on March 31, 1925.

"Lack of Jurymen May Delay Trial of Murder Pair," announced the *Miami Tribune* on April 1. "All Jurors Challenged," reported the *Herald.* "Lawyer Defending Valiton Declares Whole Panel Illegal." The news items, written under the foregoing column heads, tended to demonstrate that correspondent Harlan Miller knew whereof he spoke when he observed that 'Pruiett had begun to swing the shield of a complex defense, without an apparent loophole,' between his client and the Railford electric chair.

"Pruiett announced to the court his challenge of the entire list of veniremen summoned, and moved that the indictment against the defendants be quashed. In his motion to quash the attorney said: 'Dade County had a population in January, 1925, as shown by the last census, of 85,000. Under the laws of the State of Florida, the board of county commissioners is required to provide a list of not less than 2,500 to 3,500 persons to serve as jurors. We allege and maintain that the board of county commissioners has failed to comply with this provision of the law by its failure to provide such a list of qualified jurors, and the panel therefor provided is illegal. This entire panel of 750 jurors, instead of the 2,500 required under the law, is disqualified," reported the *Miami Herald* on March 31.

Perhaps the point was a trifle technical for a self-educated territorial lawyer to raise. The Court overruled him. But it didn't discourage the movant, or endear the trial judge to him. Thenceforward, the Court came in for his share of the arraignment, which Pruiett usually reserved for the prosecuting force and the arresting officers the reporter for the *Kansas City Times* wrote:

"Your Honor," said Pruiett, "since reports and modern law are not sufficient to convince you, let me read this section from Blackstone, the father of the Common Law and undoubtedly an authority. He supports my contention precisely."

"You may as well sit down, Mr. Pruiett; I have decided the point against you," replied the Court. "You need not cite more cases. I have overruled your motion and do not care to read the section."

"I know you have, Your Honor; I know you have," sarcastically said the lawyer. "I know it, but I just wanted to show the Court what a fool Blackstone was."

"Yesterday, the third day since the Court called Walter C. Valiton to the bar for trial, was occupied entirely with the selection of the jury and the questions and arguments of attorneys," stated the *Miami Herald* on May 14, 1925.

"Very few of the men examined said they had formed no opinion as to the guilt or innocence of the accused, and of those who said they had formed such opinions, several declared their opinions were of such a nature that they could not render a fair and impartial verdict according to the evidence. Some said their opinions were so strongly formed that it would require convincing evidence to overcome them."

"Scruples against the death penalty caused many jurors to be excused by the court. When questioned by the State's attorneys, E. C. Miller, a resident of Dade County during the past 30 years, admitted he had formed and expressed an opinion, but said this opinion could be swayed by evidence favorable to the accused. Questioned by Pruiett, he said he would go into the jury box with his opinion fixed, and that convincing evidence would be required to change that opinion."

"In reply to questioning by Judge J. A. Rose, Miller said his opinion was not so strongly fixed as to prevent his rendering a fair and impartial verdict exclusively on the evidence he heard from the witness chair. Miller admitted expressing his opinion on one occasion."

"Pruiett objected to Miller's acceptance, but the Court overruled his objection. The jury was sent out of the courtroom and arguments of counsel began. Pruiett objected to the Court questioning the jurors."

"This Court must be extremely careful," Pruiett cried, shaking his finger in the Judge's face, as if he was cross-examining an alley witness. If this Court is going to lean at all, he should lean toward the defendant. The Constitution says a man is presumed to be innocent, until proven guilty, and our appellate courts have construed that to mean that a reasonable doubt must be decided in favor of the accused."

The prosecutors blanched. The great crowd in the room was hushed. It was worse than treason; it was contempt. The little murderer's counsel had the same as accused the trial Judge of leaning, of being biased and partisan. He was going too strong; he wouldn't get by with this.

"Do you realize what you imply, Mr. Pruiett?" the Judge demanded, sternly.

"I am as conscious of every syllable of my remarks, as I am of the terrible responsibility which rests upon my shoulders," Pruiett roared at him, never retreating a step. "I'm defending the life of an American citizen and I want every word I am saying to go into the record of this case. No man will ever say that Moman Pruiett was derelict in his oath to our Constitution, or his duty to his client."

"Watch your language," barked the Court.

"The record will watch my language," howled Pruiett. "And let me say, that this Court has no right to interfere, and question jurors, as it did this man Miller." The prosecutors gasped again. "The State is well and ably represented here by its attorneys, and they are questioning these veniremen properly. You are the Judge. When you go to examining jurors, you are having an influence over them, and depriving this defendant of his right to a fair trial. A juror's first impulse is to say 'yes' to a question asked by a judge." The exasperated Court had to recognize the logic of his argument and the correctness of his position. Miller was excused.

"After exhausting a panel of 250 talesmen from the box and a special venire of 70 others, a jury was at last selected and the State began the presentation of its case," said the *Miami News* on May 14, 1925. Keep the line open to Railford. Don't let the dynamos get cold.

"Nostrils acquiver and lips tightened with mature fear of a whipping, 18-year-old Walter Valiton, the stigma of neurosis shadowed on each feature of his face, watched his lawyer attempt to swing the shield of a complex defense between him and the death penalty, as his trial opened," wrote Harlan Miller in the *Miami News* on April 26, 1925. " 'There will be no Clarence Darrow stuff,' Moman Pruiett, the prisoner's attorney had said, and Monday morning he laid a foundation for a defense that left not a loophole unguarded."

So much for Harlan Miller's comparative impression on Pruiett's technical efficiency. Speaking more intimately, and personally, he said: "Pruiett is of the type so tremendously effective with a jury. Juries, as a rule, are filled with men who prefer their dramatics mellow; and Pruiett gives them what they want. He paces back and forth, whispers and roars at them alternately in intimate nearness. Very nearly he caresses them with persuasive phrases and gestures, and pours pathos on their susceptibilities. He is master of the histrionics of the homicide trial; deft is his appeal to home and fireside, to patriotism and community pride. Watching him face twelve of his peers, one sees him, in the mind's eye, addressing a Fourth of July crowd, or memorializing the soldier dead on Decoration Day."

Pruiett philosophy had long held that a guy who would steal, or murder, would squeal. He was all set for the leniency-dispensing prosecution to prime an accomplice against him, to turn State's evidence, as the stock phrase put it.

"Stunning news that Naugle had turned State's evidence went through the packed courtroom as deputies brought him into the room at 12:05 P. M., and it flashed through the courthouse and out on the streets, bringing crowds which could not jam their way into the already filled courtroom. As Naugle went on the stand, he threw one long look toward Valiton, a look which caused one spectator to murmur, 'He seems to say "I'm sorry, but I've got to do it".' Valiton exhibited signs of nervousness as his erstwhile companion walked into the courtroom; and, as Naugle sat down in the witness chair, Valiton's hands were shaking and his hair, usually polished closed to his head, was rumpled from his fingers which had been pushed through it," reported the *Miami News* of May 18, 1925.

It took Pruiett to plead self-defense for a hi-jacker who had admitted shooting a uniformed policeman off his motorcycle. " 'Yes, I shot him,' he told the jury in the Circuit Court, where he is being tried for murder in the first degree. 'I shot him because I believed he was going to shoot me. He threw his light into my face and into John's, and then he went from the left side of the automobile to the right side and examined it. He looked under the seat and saw the tool box and asked what it was. I told him we had been changing a tire'."

" 'Drive on down to the police station,' he said. He never told us he was a policeman, or said who he was. He never said we were accused of any crime, or told us what he wanted. He just said 'drive to the station.' He was standing on the right side of the automobile when I started up the motor. Then he said; 'pull up to that curb or I will kill both of you.' He reached into his right hip pocket and pulled out a gun. I thought he was going to shoot. I did not mean to kill him, but just wanted to scare him, because I thought he was going to kill me'," according to the *Miami News* of May 18.

The crackers whispered in the courtroom and on the streets. "Where does that Oklahoma lawyer think he's goin' with that kind of stuff. It's sickenin'. He's frying the kid as sure as hell; such a defense is ridiculous." But, Pruiett wasn't lost; he just didn't have anything better to offer. The flimsiness of the story was indicative of the load he was going to carry when he went to the jury for the last time. Anything was better than a guilty plea, for with that, the Court would discharge the jury and direct the application of the current himself. He just wanted an issue, something to keep away from a directed verdict, and self-defense was all he could think of.

But was he giving up? Valiton was trying to keep away from an unsavory record; he lied about his previous convictions. But Swink and Fred W. Pine had the goods on him, official records of his car thefts and suspended sentences, and the squawk of another old buddy.

"Did you plead guilty to stealing an automobile an Federal Court at Toledo, Ohio, on July 1, 1924?" Prosecutor Pine inquire politely.

"No," Valiton answered shortly.

"Did you plead guilty in Federal Court, to stealing an automobile at Somerset, Kentucky, on April 19, 1924?"

"No," Valiton insisted. "I have never been arrested on any charge whatever."

"Then Moman Pruiett, chief of defense lawyers, jumped to his feet with a motion to strike from the record, the testimony given Friday by Police Chief Quigg, in which the chief recounted a statement made to him by Sergt. Laurie L. Wever, for whose slaying Valiton is being tried. Chief Quigg had said that as Wever lay dying in the hospital the wounded man told him: 'I was shot by a highwayman.' Pruiett now contended that the State had no right to introduce this testimony, as Sergeant Wever did not know whether or not his assailants were highwaymen. Then Fred Pine prepared for his smashing thrust at the very heart of the defendant's plea that Valiton was not a highwayman, had never been arrested, and is now on trial for the only offense of his life."

The first thrust was the witness's own criminal record. The second was the testimony of young Cleo Butler, Valiton's cousin 'who testified that he came to Miami from Toledo with Valiton, and stayed here one month.' " What was Valiton's occupation? The defense objected. Then Butler answered. 'His occupation was... stealing'."

Pruiett's efforts to shake him, on cross-examination were unsuccessful. 'He had no occupation except as a thief,' Butler insisted.

'Did you help him?' Pruiett asked.

'Yes, I did on two occasions,' Butler answered.

'Then, you are a thief yourself?' Pruiett surmised.

'No,' the witness replied, 'I am not a thief'."

He was entitled to his opinion, and he was going to stick to it.

And Pruiett's professed fidelity to the Constitution, superior to that he had for any fraternal oath—had to come out.

"Parker Henderson was the third witness called by the State in its rebuttal testimony. He testified that he was driving north on N. W. Second Ave., on the night when Wever was shot. He said he saw a large crowd in front of the Savoy Hotel and stopped there. He saw Wever, and added that he saw the policeman's pistol and holster, with the pistol in the holster."

"This testimony was brought out by the State, it is believed, in answer to Valiton's assertion that he saw Wever draw his pistol, and fired in self-defense. The fact the pistol was in the holster after the wounded sergeant fell to the ground is considered by the State as proof that he had not drawn it before Valiton fired."

"Then Pruiett started cross-examining. 'Did you belong to the same secret society as Wever?'

'I am not sure,' Henderson replied.

'Don't you know for a fact that you do belong to the same society?' Pruiett insisted.

'I refuse to answer,' said Henderson.

'You must answer,' Judge Rose interposed.

'I do not belong to the society,' he said.

'Don't you remember,' asked Pruiett, 'that you and I and Wever were present at the lodge rooms together on one occasion?'

'No, I was not there,' repeated Henderson. As Henderson left the stand, he threw a dirty glance at Pruiett, which was seen by almost every person in the courtroom. There was some laughter, and applause. Judge Rose cautioned the spectators to keep silent."

Pruiett swung the heavy load across his back and started up the hill. He looked the hostile jury in the face and without a blush declared that the State had failed to make out a case of murder; that his client was guiltless, and that they ought to turn him loose. "Arraigning the attorneys for John Naugle as subjects for a whipping boss, and State's Attorney Swink and Assistant State's Attorney Pine as crying for blood, not justice, Moman Pruiett closed the argument for the defense with one of the most bitter, personal attacks made in the history of Dade County courts."

The staid southerners would have to insulate with asbestos if the pride of the Chickasaw Nation was to continue to try cases in their midst. "I took the hide off them prosecutors, like I did Charley West in Bill Maben's case," Pruiett chuckled. "They thought they were ready for what was comin', but they weren't. They thought they would send that boy to the electric chair, but I knew damned well they wouldn't. I wanted to persuade a couple of 'em to turn him loose, so the stickers would get scared and come across with a compromise. And another thing, I wanted to show Harlan Miller that Clarence Darrow didn't try Leopold and Loeb right. Hell, what's the bar comin' to, when it pleads a fellow guilty, and then crawls and begs for leniency?"

"Is there no God In Florida?" he screamed at them. "Is there no Christ in Miami? Are the monsters of hell really lurking in the everglades, ready to crawl out and breath fire from their nostrils on your dance of death, while you gloat over this friendless boy's death agonies, like a swarm of cannibals?" the *Miami News* reported on May 17, 1925.

He revived his old Jeptha story from Chapter 11 of the Book of Judges in the Bible for them. They could acquit Valiton and send him home to mama and papa, if they had the guts and stamina of a biblical

MOMAN PRUIETT AT THE HEIGHT OF HIS LEGAL CAREER IN 1929. ALTHOUGH HE HAD LOST MANY OF HIS INVESTMENTS IN THE FLORIDA HURRICANE OF 1926, PRUIETT WAS STILL A FORMIDABLE LEGAL OPPONENT OF PROSECUTORS. COURTESY *THE DAILY OKLAHOMAN.*

bastard. The way the Valiton case was put up to them, they were bastards if they did and bastards if they didn't.

"The money changers need to be chased from the Temple," he added, then turned on State's Attorney Swink, and Assistant State's attorney Pine with the challenge that they had made electrocution and vengeance a personal matter, going back to the old Mosaic law of 'an eye for an eye, a tooth for a tooth.' Since that law was written, I have heard of a New Testament, and of a Christ who was crucified on the cross."

He paused, deliberately taking the cue for his next thrust from his own reference to the Scriptures. "On the cross?... On the cross?... On the cross!" He had graduated from a gaunt whisper to a buxom roar. "Your actions in deciding this case will be guided by the sign of the cross. Perhaps you can, perhaps you may, weigh the issues of human flesh and blood, of a human being's soul, in the shadow of the cross—the FIERY CROSS. But by the memory of my mother's prayers, offered up for the guidance of my feeble childhood steps, I'll cling to the Cross of Calvary, where Jesus died for weak, misguided mankind" quoted the *Miami News* of May 17.

He was so utterly sincere and devout, or so utterly vicious and abandoned, that he never failed to startle his listeners. Before the jury took up the issue of the case they tried to decode Pruiett. "What the hell kind of a man is he? One that can make me feel this way—I've never felt like gettin' religion before—must have somethin' on the ball. How can he be so good, an' so tough at the same time? Can a body that can generate such viciousness have any good, at all, in it, or is that Bible stuff all a part of his act?" Each deliberation over Pruiett was an advantage for Valiton. The old partridge was crippling down the hedge row, leading the hunter away from the nest.

" 'Is Walter C. Valiton in the Courtroom?' " asked Judge Rose.

'He is, your honor,' answered Bailiff Garnett.

'Let him stand up,' said the judge. To Valiton he said: 'You, Walter C. Valiton, have been found guilty of murder in the first degree, and the jury has recommended you to the mercy of the Court. Have you anything to say why the sentence of the law should not be imposed upon you?'

'I am sorry all this happened,' said Valiton. 'I know I am not a murderer in my heart.'

'You have had a fair trial by an impartial jury,' Judge Rose continued. 'You were protected by the Court in your legal rights. Your counsel was zealous in his defense of your rights. Their verdict was fully warranted by the evidence in the case. The evidence, in the opinion of the Court, showed a cruel and unprovoked murder of an officer in the discharge of his duty. Under the law, whoever is convicted of a capital offense and recommended to the mercy of the Court by a majority of the jury in their verdict, shall be sentenced to imprisonment for life'."

" 'It is therefore considered, and it is the judgment of the Court that you, Walter C. Valiton, be imprisoned by confinement in the State Penitentiary for the remainder of your natural life.' Valiton did not quail as he heard the sentence pronounced."

Miami Life of May 23, 1925, made the last official lament. In its current editorial it arraigned Pruiett, and the brothers in the lodge who were so derelict in their instructed duty. "What the jury gave Valiton is, as a matter of precedence and fact, a sentence of eight or ten years, and we venture the prediction right now that Valiton will never serve longer. Just the same as there are otherwise sane jurymen who will allow a wildly gesticulating criminal lawyer to pervert their judgment with hokum, there are mildly imbecilic men and women who conceive it their highest duty, the moment anyone is imprisoned for murder, to start pleading with the Governor and pardoning board for his release."

"Hokum—and we say this with all due respect for the Court and the lawyers, for no one knows it better than they—saved Valiton from the chair. And Hokum will free him in a few years. *Miami Life* is going to petition Governor Martin to sell the electric chair that was recently installed. Junk it, blow it up—do anything to get rid of it. Erase the law authorizing capital punishment. After the Valiton trial, we are convinced that we have no use for either."

CHAPTER TWENTY-TWO

How Pruiett obtains the acquittal of a man charged with slaying his sweetheart while she is confined in jail, and how the experience crystallizes his previously entertained ideas on abandoning the Gay Coast. And, wherein, he expresses his disapprobation with the locality, and predicts its destruction, almost on the eve of the blast which blew a land boom away and materially reduced the status of the precocious peninsula. And how gentle nature takes a hand to obtain the result for which enforcement bodies and public prosecutors had long striven for, and the Stallion makes a humble and unostentatious exit.

The reflecting lights of the Flamingo Hotel's thousand windows were multiplied into millions as calm Biscayne Bay's mild ripples sparkled them across the bay. The Pruietts were watching in quiet darkness as they sat on the veranda of their shore home.

"It won't work, Leda," Pruiett said. "It ain't meant to be, so it won't be. This place won't last."

"It's heavenly," she murmured. "What I have dreamed of, and prayed for. There's no place on earth like it. No.... "

"No, and it won't be here long, either, by god," he interrupted. "There never was so much wickedness, and so much evil, got together on god's earth before... an' I don't suppose you dreamed and prayed for any of that."

"Moman," she said softly, ignoring the harshness of his tone, "what's come over you? What's happened to turn you against Florida—against Miami? The way business has been and the way things have gone, I was sure you were contented here."

"Why, hell yes, I'm satisfied, but that ain't it," he persisted, "a coral reef ain't strong enough to make a foundation for such a structure of sin and degradation. There ain't no sound basis for this place. We've got a fortune involved here—I know its small compared to what the others around here have got—but we can't afford to stand a loss like they can."

He waved generally toward the Candler, and Capone, and Nunnally estates.

His wife laughed. "That's funny, from you, Moman. You sound like an evangelist. Leave off the courtroom act for me; let me understand you. What's bothering you?"

Pruiett chewed his unlighted cigar savagely before making answer. "I want to sell out and get out of this damn place. I want to go back West—to Oklahoma—somewhere."

"Not for anything in the world," she replied. "This is the first place where we've found peace, and contentment. No references to your misfortune; no slurs at me in connection with it. No cold; no dreariness. It's the first place where I've had happiness, and I won't give it away; at least without a reason. Do you see hell fire and brimstone descending on the palm groves?" She was trying to cheer him.

"Do you remember the trip we made to the Lewis and Clark Fair, up in Oregon state? The one we made with old Sam Garvin and Mrs. Garvin right after we was married? That was twenty years ago; can you remember it?" He asked the question softly, musingly.

"Why, yes," she replied. "I'll never forget... "

"An' remember the week in San Francisco, when we took all the excursions, and went to all the old joints and dives?"

"Yes, I remember," she said.

"An' we went to China Town, an' Barbary Coast, an' old man and old lady Garvin was so shocked by what we saw, an' the whiskey I drank?"

"Yes, Moman, I remember all about San Francisco."

"Well," he said, raising his voice, "can't you remember what I said, when we were on the train comin' home, about San Francisco?"

There was a moment of silence. "No," she finally answered, "not particularly. What do you mean?"

"Hell," he said, with provocation. "I told you, right before the Garvins, that that damned place was too wicked. I said it's like Sodom and Gomorrah; God Almighty won't let it stand. He'll wipe it off the earth, right level with the ground. Wasn't that what I said, and wasn't it about six months later that I carried the paper in to you, and showed you the pictures of what God done to it? Everything that wasn't shook down was goin' up in smoke. Didn't I tell you that very thing?"

"Yes, dear, you did," she replied slowly, "but that was nature; that was the law of nature. What the people of San Francisco were doing had nothing to do with that earthquake, and the fire."

"Why, hell no, and neither did the people of Sodom have anything to do with what happened to them, and their damn town. But she was leveled off, shook apart and burned up."

"You were guessing; anyone might have said the same thing. And you were drinking, too. You were more surprised than anyone else, that your prediction came true. If you had believed in it yourself, the realization of your power, your gift, would have driven you crazy."

"Just a minute, honey," he interrupted. "I didn't guess at it, and I didn't know it. I felt it, like the god damned bells I hear ringin' in my ears. I felt old Doc Threlkeld tryin' to kill me, an hour before he pulled the pistol. I felt the destruction of that wicked city, an' I feel the destruction of this one. She just can't last."

"Will it be an earthquake," she inquired, with mock interest. "Will the Lord shake the walls of Miami apart, and burn the ruins 'til they slide back into the swamps. What does my soothsayer see?"

He chewed his cigar silently, as if intending to ignore the sarcastic question. "Typhoon," he said, laconically. "A god damn gulf twister, an' she'll blow the whole damned works away."

Mrs. Pruiett laughed. "Right away?" she inquired. "Will I have time to pack my bags, and run for it."

He ignored her levity again. "Maybe this season; maybe next; maybe next after that. I don't know, but they've been gathering in the Caribbean for centuries and centuries, and comin' this way ever' once in a while. An' when they come, they'll put the ground where the water belongs, an' blow the water up where the ground used to be. They can't fix the foliage up after one of 'em, they have to grow a new crop, palm trees and all. It's just a matter of time 'til another one comes by."

"Oh, we've had storms since we've been here, but nothing like that; nothing to do great damage," she rejoined. "I... "

"I'm talkin' about a hurricane, not a tropical shower; a wind that'll blow a wall of water a mile high across this peninsula, an' carry a mahogany saw-log across from Cuba and blow it into the side of that Flamingo Hotel, and knock the hell clear out of it. One that'll strip the tillable top off this ground, an' leave twisted pine stalks on white sand dunes. That's what I mean; where the one's that live to tell about it will be damned few, an' damned lucky, an' where there won't be a house or buildin' standin' like in San Francisco."

"I never heard of Miami being in the storm belt. Wouldn't some record of hurricanes be kept, if they came here?"

"Who'd keep 'em? The Seminoles? The pirates? The outlaws? This is a damned sand bar, I tell you, an' there's been nobody here, capable of keepin' a record, 'til this crazy boom came. Blow a Seminole off in the swamp an' he'll forget it, if it don't kill him, before he can tell another generation about it. The pirates an' outlaws, that are hidin' out down here, don't write in and tell about the bad weather. Maybe its been twenty-five years, maybe thirty, since the pine groves had to start all over again, but that ain't no sign the storms have quit. It means, to me, its about time to start watchin' out. Its about time for somethin' to cut aloose."

"I can't believe it," she persisted. "We... someone would have heard of it... "

"Well, what about the hurricane that destroyed Galveston, Texas, on September 8, 1900? Ever hear of it?"

"Yes, but it wasn't like that in Galveston, and there was an economic reason for it, too. That was a flood, and Galveston was reclaimed from a swamp, a sunken island. They might have expected that."

"I don't know whether God Almighty had anything to do with that one or not, but we got our entire fortune right here on a reclaimed stretch of sandy land; layin' on a dead fish foundation. An' look at them boats out there; them yachts. Hear that?"

He paused to listen to a snatch of music, floating up to where they sat.

"Their empty bottles, an' their rags, will drift in, in a few days, and hungry kids'll pick 'em up, and sell 'em for a few pennies, for bread. Millionaires, an' yachts, an' liquor an' women. This is no place to live; this is the devil's outdoor assignation house. That's all it is. It's a damn good place to play, but a damn poor one to live in."

"Is my Moman reforming? Has he turned against dissipation, and loose living? I'm startled."

"No, honey," he said earnestly, "don't misunderstand me. I got started wrong, so I've been goin' in the wrong direction all the time. I'm no hypocrite. If I'd had a little different start, I might have been somewhere else right now, but that ain't the point. I've made lots of mistakes. I've lost more money gamblin', an' I've throwed away more money on parties, an' liquor, than a lot of these tin-horn millionaires ever will, but when I got sobered up, or went broke, I went home. I've kept a thread of respectability. I never did live in no whore-house. I didn't keep my office in no gamblin' joint. I didn't sleep in jail with my crooked clients. I kept a respectable home, and went to it, most of the time. That's my point. We're livin', an' got our business, in a little part of God's earth that a bunch of tin-horns has made into an assignation house. That's the best way I can put it. When the raid comes, they'll make bond an' go home, like I've done lots of times. But us? We're stuck. We've got no place to go."

"I don't agree with you," she said, shortly. "You said yourself that the government ship channels would make this a commercial center, and that the climate would make it a healthy place for people to settle, and for capital to come in with improvements. Why, you said it was as good as the Washita Valley in the old territorial days."

"I was lyin'," he muttered. "I was lyin' and tryin' to fool myself. I was in the Silent Night last week. Charley Moreau pays me a $1,000 a month to represent him an' that joint. He's got a $100,000 invested in rugs, an' drapes, an' roulette wheels; all on a damned old scuttled gulf steamer, anchored on a pier. He's playin' the same bunch we are, an' he's makin' a hell of a lot of money, but are you goin' to tell me he'll last? He's got to fold, an' so have I. But what I'm tellin' you is, we've all got to. Values here aren't normal, an' if God don't wipe her away, a panic will. I want to sell out, an' get out."

"You've got yourself in a panic; that's the only panic I can see," she laughed. "Get a few days rest; collect a nice fee in a good case, and then try to tell me what you have tonight, all over again."

He shook his head. "Sodom and Gomorrah went down. God Almighty won't stand for such wickedness. I can feel it. Didn't old Julius Fleishmann laugh like hell when he paid Charley off what he lost on the wheel that night, an' thousands of these god-damned crackers down here went to bed hungry? An' didn't I see him fall off his horse at the polo field, dead as hell with heart failure? What does that add up to?"

"It adds up to heart failure," she answered. "Mr. Fleishmann was too fat for such exertion; his doctor's had told him that. If God Almighty, as you say, had anything to do with the case, Mr. Moreau was the one that was entitled to fall dead. That's the way I look at it."

"God Almighty's got some funny ways of workin' out His wisdom, I'm told," Pruiett chuckled. "I don't hope to understand it, so I don't question it."

"Where have we ever been so contented and so fortunate, Moman?"

she asked. "What would we do? Where should we go, and why should we leave?"

"I've got a hell of a lot of real estate down here; took most of it in for fees, an' its ten times as high as it used to be, or'll ever be again. I got that orange grove up at Stuart, all them lots in Coral Gables, Florida, an' the houses an' lots in Coconut Grove. I got two hundred acres in Jasper County that's a swamp, got alligators all over it, but I can get a $100 an acre for it now. I can get twice what I paid for this villa today, some bird in Pittsburgh, Pennsyslvania, wants to buy it so he can throw about three parties a year in it. He'll keep his gal in a flat up north the rest of the time. Honey, we can get $250,000, a quarter of a million, out of this stuff we've picked up down here, an' get out. I'm getting' old. I can't try lawsuits, like that Valiton case, all my life. I got to slow down."

"I think you're wrong about Florida," was her dogged response. "We have our health, and our peace of mind, to consider. Let's not be hasty about making a decision. Let's enjoy this bay breeze, and the sunshine while we think it over."

Then murder came by again. Pruiett undertook the defense of John Gobel, wealthy Miami real estate dealer.

"Gobel was charged with murdering Mrs. H. B. Hunt last August following the woman's death in a hospital after she had swallowed a quantity of deadly poison. She had been confined in the County Jail on a larceny charge. The charge had been preferred by the real estate dealer," reported the *Miami News* on January 15, 1923.

Norman Miller had selected the stage of an abandoned opera house for the production of his little murder. S. G. Crow had elected to start shooting at Nick Kaufman while he was being booked at the police sergeant's window, and Jim Leggett had shot Hiram Strawn to death in the Justice of the Peace Court, but it took old Gobel to surpass them all in the selection of a bizarre place, and manner, for the execution of the statute book's most serious offense. He had his victim arrested, then killed her while on a visit in the jail.

"What did you have me put in this dreadful old place, for, Daddy?" the demure little matron whined. She was talking to him in the run-around of the Dade County Jail, where prisoners could visit with callers. "I didn't think you could be so mean to me."

"I hated like hell to do it, but by god, I want that diamond back. I can't be givin' a dame a $3,000 ring. I got to have it back."

"But you gave it to me, it was my present. You can't be takin' it back now."

"I was drunk, an' you know it. You got me drunk, just to get that diamond. I suspected you, and watched you, all along, an' I know I didn't give it to you. You pulled it off of my finger. Now..."

"No, honey," she said, "you gave it to me. You said it was to be the symbol of our love."

"Love, hell," Gobel grated. "I signed the complaint against you, and by god, I'll prosecute you for that ring. I won't be hooked by no bitch. You'll go to the pen for it as sure..."

"You'll just have to appear against me, then," she sighed, mournfully. "I had it, all right, for a day after you gave it to me, but I lost it. I can't give it back."

"You pawned it," he suggested, hopefully. "Tell me where. Give me the ticket, I'll pay it out and settle up the court costs. I won't be mad; I'll get you out of here."

Mrs. Hunt shook her head. "Honest, honey, it's lost. I drank a lot myself; see how I'm shakin'? You'll never know how I've suffered in this terrible jail since you had me locked up. Terrible. But I can't get it back for you; I lost it."

"Gave it to your pimp, huh?" he glared at her balefully. "I'm the big chump; the sucker. I ought to."

Gobel checked himself, looking about apprehensively. "I didn't come here to quarrel with you, honey. I didn't mean to do that, but I got to have that god-damn diamond back. I got to, understand? Tell me where to get it now, and let's have it over with. No more fuss; no more trouble."

He was begging.

"It's gone, Daddy, gone," the little woman sighed sadly. "I wish I could give it back, but I can't. It's just gone."

The man was silent for a period, gazing at the rusty bars along the far side of the enclosure.

"Well," he mused, "if it's gone, it's gone. There's no good in pushin' you around, if I can't get my ring back. I guess I'd better tell the District Attorney to call if off, an' turn you loose."

She grasped his arm affectionately.

"I knew you would, Daddy," she said. "Let me get out, and get straightened up, and we'll have some more parties, won't we?"

"Yeah," he agreed, watching her narrowly, "how you feelin' today?"

"Just terrible," she replied, holding a hand and arm out in front of him. "See it shake? I been havin' the most terrible hang-over I ever had. Where did you get that stuff we was drinkin'?"

"It was good stuff; came in on a boat," he said, with the same strange look in his eye. "It knocked hell out of me, though, too. I went to a doctor. He gave me some stuff that was awful good for it."

"I wish I had somethin'," she said. "I sure have suffered, somethin' terrible for two or three days."

"I got some of the stuff that Doc gave me, here in my pocket." He pulled a short glass bottle from his coat. "It tastes like hell, but it'll knock the shakes out of you quicker'n anything I ever saw. Want me to fix you one?"

"What is it?" she asked, mildly curious.

"Oh, some fancy name attached to it. I can't say it or spell it either. But it's hell on the bucks. It'll straighten you up right now, an' I mean, right now."

"Just a pill?" she inquired, looking at the bottle.

"One ain't enough for a bad case," Gobel said. "I'll fix you up a dose."

A water cooler was setting on a wooden stand in the steel enclosed square. Two tin cups were setting beside it. Gobel drew a quarter of a cup of water, and shaking a half dozen of the pills from the bottle into the cup, he began to stir it with the gold head of his vest pencil.

"This way they work quicker," he said. "Dissolve 'em, then toss 'em off quick, like a bad drink, an' then it's all over. It'll fix you up."

"I need it," Mrs. Hunt advised him.

"It tastes like swamp scum, so drink it quick. I got a chaser here for you in the other cup. All at once now, and I got to go. You'll be all over the shakes by the time I have you out of here."

The prisoner followed her visitor's directions, and accepted his hurried kiss on a wry, puckered countenance. Gobel had scarcely gone from the jail before her screams began to rattle the barred windows and doors. She lived long enough to make an incriminating death-bed statement, and then she died. Gobel was given a cell fronting on the jail run-around. He was charged with murder.

"His arrest followed a visit with Mrs. Hunt in the jail. As Gobel left the institution, Mrs. Hunt summoned deputy sheriffs and told them she had been poisoned. Her dying statement, in the hospital a short time later, implicated the man who had been instrumental in her arrest. Attorneys for Gobel based their defense on the presence of poison tablets in Mrs. Hunt's cell prior to the man's visit."

That was it. Remorseful, disconsolate Mrs. Hunt had decided to put an end to herself, but why make it just an ordinary suicide? Here was a revengeful boy-friend who had played her a dirty trick, had given information against her and had her confined as a common thief, and made her suffer the horrors of breaking a bender in a dirty, noisy jail. Wouldn't it be smart? Wouldn't it be subtle? To tell the deputies and the hospital orderlies, as the lights were going out, that he had slipped her the drops? Maybe they'd cause him some trouble. Maybe he'd get some time, on the same lousy mattresses. Maybe they'd burn him. That was the answer. A trifle deep, but nevertheless, a sufficient motive, for attacking a death-bed statement.

Hadn't old Rudolph Tegeler beat the chair by claiming that Lila Meadows and husband Jim conspired against him by burying an unidentified stiff in a cornfield, and then Lila telling the cops that she helped him to murder her husband? And all the time Jim was stringing 'phone wire on the Panama Canal project, and enjoying the trouble Rudolph was having in trying to keep out of the hot seat.

There were the poison tablets, and the bottle, in her cell. They were found a day or two after she died, of course, and a day after counsel was hired, but it was a question of fact for the jury to decide how they got there and how long they had been there before they were discovered. Spooks saved George Hopkins from what looked like certain retribution; a dead cat served as a life preserver for Maggie Miller. Hokum, the Florida way, kept jelly-bean Valiton from paying the price usually exacted for the kind of liberty he took with a policeman's life. Pruiett spread the hokum on thick for John Gobel.

"John Gobel, Miami real estate dealer, was acquitted yesterday afternoon in Dade County Circuit Court of the charge of poisoning Mrs. H. B. Hunt, last August, while she was a prisoner in the County Jail. The jury returned a verdict of 'not guilty' twenty minutes after Judge Will H. Price completed his charge."

"The courthouse was crowded with spectators when the climax of one of the greatest legal battles in the annals of Dade County was

MOMAN PRUIETT SITTING ON THE BED OF HIS LAST HOME—A 50-CENTS-A-NIGHT HOTEL ROOM IN THE 200 BLOCK OF NORTHWEST 2ND STREET IN DOWNTOWN OKLAHOMA CITY. LONG GONE IS THE STRUT, THE STRIDE, AND THE LOUD PROFANITY THAT WAS SO MUCH A PART OF THE PRUIETT COURTROOM THEATRICS. COURTESY *THE DAILY OKLAHOMAN.*

reached. Many women were in the room and eagerly listened for the words which meant death or freedom for the accused. Tenseness gripped each spectator as the jury filed into the box and they watched closely as the slip of paper upon which the verdict was written was passed from the jury to Judge Price and then to Clerk Trammel. A perceptible feeling of relief swept through the room as the verdict was read."

"After Judge Price had declared court adjourned, friends and defense attorneys congratulated the man who, a few minutes before, had stood in the shadow of the electric chair. His brother, Frank Gobel, hugged him affectionately, and Attorney Moman Pruiett, of defense counsel, placed his arm around him and buried his head on his shoulder."

There was no victory celebration at the Ta-Miami or the Flamingo after the Gobel victory. There was whiskey, of course, great quantities of it, for Pruiett, but no speeches. The Pruietts were at home, sitting in the darkness and watching the rippling lights upon the bay.

"You were wonderful in your final argument to the jury, Moman," Leda told him. "Wonderful. It made me think of Rudolph Tegeler, and Agnes Gilbert, and the way you tried those cases. And it made me think of something else, of the way you used to have the bailiffs fix an easy chair inside the rail for your mother, so that she could come down and hear your closing arguments. I don't believe you've been so completely in charge of a case, since she died, until today. It was like old times."

Pruiett prolonged the silence which followed with a deep, deliberate drink.

"Funny," he mused, "how those things come up. I haven't had her on my mind much, since I was in Havana, 'til this trial started. I was tellin' myself that Betty was sittin' there, listenin', while I was goin' to that jury. That's just what I had on my mind."

"She would have been proud," Leda replied.

"Yeah?" he inquired skeptically. "Of what? Of me? Of my hokum? Those buzzards that squawked about the Valiton case were right; it's hokum, pure old unadulterated hokum. I just about got a belly full of it."

"I can't understand you, Moman," his wife said with a dubious shake of her head. "Quit drinking so much, and getting yourself into these morbid states. You're beginning to give it to me. You're back on top, selecting the cases you want and getting the fees you ask for. What more do you want?"

"There wasn't no need of him killing that old Hunt girl," Pruiett answered. "She probably liked the smell of this rotten atmosphere as well as you do, or I. Paul Ward Beck was entitled to live; Jean Day had no right to kill him. Rudolph Tegeler was as guilty as hell, and so was Red Fox, an' George Hopkins. Hokum saved 'em, ever' god damn one of 'em. Take a pencil and paper, and sit up all night some night, writin' down their names as you think of 'em. John Evans, Sam Ashton, Old Cal Stewart, Laura Reuter and Lorena Mathews. Two hundred; maybe three hundred; Doc Tyree an' Jack Lanier. There wouldn't be any end to it, and it's all hokum."

"Moman," she whispered, "is it your conscience? Are you afraid?"

"Hell, no," he answered, "my conscience is my best friend; it's the only one I got, except for you, sweetheart. I just like to tell the truth once in awhile, to keep from forgettin' how. I say Betty wouldn't be so damn proud, if she knew all the truth."

"I'm proud," she whispered again. "And Betty would be, too, for she'd understand. You've got to remember; you can't forget, now, the things that have kept you up and made you go. And you must have been right, dear. I've heard you say so much of divine retribution, I believe in it. It wouldn't have been possible to accomplish what you have, if the right wasn't on your side."

"You'll find the right, honey, where the brains are, an' the guts," he stated complacently. "The scales of justice never were tipped by a lunk-headed prosecutor, but a fast one has hung many a' innocent man. God Almighty can't see around the rail of a jury box, but I've sustained myself so long on that kind of crap, an' you've heard it so much, that we both believe it, most of the time. If some of these Florida editors would analyze it, they'd find it to be about ninety percent of that stuff we were just discussing—Hokum."

"That sounds more like you, and it sounds better to me," Leda observed. "I hate to see you strike these morbid periods."

"Sam Harris named me the black stud horse; remember?" he mused. "The black stud? Well, he'd have to take it back, if he could see how the old mane's faded. He'd have to call me the old gray mare. Why hell, Leda, I'm fifty-six. Fifty-six years, and how much of it's been in any kind of quietude, or contentment? I'd burnt up the energy I was born with when I was thirty. I fought through the thirties, an' I staggered through the forties. I gave up once, an' quit, but somethin' made me come back. That was the very first time, after twenty-five years of preachin', that I suspected that there was an underlying retribution guiding me."

"Just don't think so much, or think about things that will inflate you. Practice a little suggestion, for the sake of your health, and peace of mind."

"I want to talk to you about sellin' out an' leavin' ."

"Please don't, dear," she interrupted. "I can't think of it."

"When I was barkin' in that jury's face, and when I listened to blubberin' old John Gobel after the verdict, I knew I was getting' out of here. Did you see me put my head on his shoulder, there? I had to hide my face from the Court—to keep him from seein' me laughin'. When that jury reported, old John looked real sanctimonious, an' says 'Truth crushed to earth will rise again'. I thought I'd laugh my head off. Hypocrisy. Deceit. Fraud. Sham. That's all there is here, an' the dread of what will wreck it is getting' me. Something's goin' to happen, cause those damned bells keep ringin'. I got to go."

"We're not going." Came the flat reply.

"I hate to leave you, the way I feel about Miami, but I got to do it. I'll take about a week to get ready, and out I go. I can open up an office back in Oklahoma somewhere. I guess I can still catch a murder case once in awhile around the capitol. But I'd rather sell out here and kind of quit. I could feel real disaster while I was pleadin' for Gobel. It was somethin' tellin' me to quit this rotten business."

"You need a rest, a long one," she said. "Let's take a trip, back home, and visit our old friends. We can take a month, two months, to rest and plan, and then if you still feel the same way, if you haven't changed your mind, I'll quit holding out for Florida. I'll do whatever you say."

He patted her affectionately. "I knew you'd stay with me," he said. "It's a deal. If I can shake these bucks that are on me, we'll stay with the ease of the palmy shores. If not . . . Then we'll stick to the West. I got a good farm on the Washita, you know, an' one right near Oklahoma City. The way I been feelin', I'd like to get me a few goats an' a hoe an' a rake, and let somebody that's a little younger worry over murder for awhile."

"Make your arrangements, then," she said. "I'll pack. We'll go whenever you get ready."

"I want to spend a few days with Doc Marchman in Dallas on the way back," he mused. "There's about a half a dozen killers that owe their lives to Doc, only they don't know it. I'll surprise him, an' thank him for Hattie, and young mister Valiton."

The Pruiett villa was closed. And, as the rails of the Southern Railroad clicked a rhythmic farewell, and as the owners sped northward and westward, the chips rattled in the Silent Night, and the ball rolled. Moon-kissed bay ripples carried up empty flasks with ornamented labels and pinched sides and throats. Music and harsh laughter floated from the Ta-Miami and the Flamingo, to the dimly lighted yachts in the bay, and music and harsh laughter floated back from the drifting crafts to the resorts on the shore.

Domestic bootleg was high; the fancy-bottled imported stuff from the Indies was higher. It took money to acquire, and operate, the brass-trimmed yachts and speed boats. Jawbone alone wouldn't support parties at the Flamingo. The playboys, mindful of their good things, had a weather-eye on the status of the stock market and the welfare of the old bankroll.

Weather-eye was right: "Erratic fluctuations in cotton continued Friday, but prices moved in a narrower range, as was the case Thursday. Instead of the 40 point changes, an early improvement of less than 10 points was followed by a decline of 20 points and at the end of three hours the list was slightly under Thursday's close. The cause underlying market gyrations were more definite information regarding the progress of the tropical disturbance near Nassau, which brought storm warnings to the Florida coast," reported *The Daily Oklahoman* on September 18, 1926.

Were the bells ringing? Yes, they were. The emergency bells, and the warning sirens were screaming their excited throats raw, but no one, save the distressed, could hear. The gale which snatched up their feeble wails and carried them inland to fuse their identity with the swish of the bending pines and palms, had driven aside the telegraphic and 'phone connection with the mainland to the north. There was a hell of a disturbance going on in the Indies.

MOMAN PRUIETT AT AGE 73, JUST FIVE MONTHS BEFORE HIS DEATH ON DECEMBER 17, 1945. COURTESY *MOMAN PRUIETT: CRIMINAL LAWYER.*

"FLORIDA COAST IS SWEPT BY FIERCE TROPIC HURRICANE," the Associated Press advised its multifarious subscribers the next day, September 19, in *The Daily Oklahoman.*

"Miami Flooded, Cut Off From Rest of World, Wires Down and Trains Stopped," came the subheads. "A hundred mile wind spreads ruin over a wide area. The devastating fury of the tropical storm which swept the south Florida Coast Saturday morning has transformed Miami into a desolated Venice, with streets inundated, buildings wrecked, light and power gone and untold property damage."

Pruiett paced the floor of a hotel room in Oklahoma City, pausing long enough occasionally to stir a fresh drink with a shaking hand, or to curse an operator for her inability to get a call through to Miami, or Jacksonville. He had to have news of the situation. He feared that he was about to see his prediction come to pass. His fortune was being buried under a gale-driven chain of dunes. Why couldn't the papers get information, or come out oftener with what they had?

"500 Die In Hurricane! 38,000 Homeless in Florida! Property Damage $125,000,000!" headlined the *Daily Oklahoman* on September 20. Good God! The whole damn peninsula wasn't worth that kind of money. The works must have blowed right over west into the Gulf of Mexico. There won't be a pound of stucco left out of the villa. It's good-bye to that classy orange grove.

"A hurricane which came out of the West Indies swept over the lower east coast of Florida Friday and Saturday, causing a death list estimated at more than 500 persons, destroyed property valued at more than $125,000,000, left 38,000 people homeless and passed into the Gulf of Mexico."

"Military control was ordered in the stricken City of Miami by City Manager Frank H. Warden. More than 300 extra policemen were swore in, after looting had taken place in certain parts of Miami!"

Pruiett growled as the paper shook in his trembling hand. "The evil bastards. They brought it on themselves, an' then they steal from their own dead."

"Miami Bay front was subjected to a terrific battering as the violent windstorm struck from a more dangerous angle. The bay crept high over its accustomed level and raced like a mill pond, waist deep, from the Miami River northward toward the county causeway. Mountainous waves broke over Miami Beach hurling abandoned automobiles into the bay and destroying many homes."

When the true proportions of the tragedy became known, as the disrupted rail connections were replaced, and wire communications were resumed, President Calvin Coolidge issued a proclamation declaring a state of emergency, and urging the Nation 'to organize relief for the overwhelming disaster, according to *The Daily Oklahoman* of September 21.

"Cal had better get some relief to that white-headed bird up on the sixth floor," a wag in the lobby observed as he read the latest bulletin. "He's been up there now for five days, and the porters have to slip his meals in under their coat tails. What I mean, he's drank a barrel already."

When Pruiett finally blinked in the sunlight, he knew the worst. He had talked long distance with an associate in storm-torn Miami. The villa was down. The coast, along the Jupiter lighthouse was stripped bare, so hope for the orange grove was gone. Miami was desolate, deserted. The only activity there was the desultory plugging of the salvage and wrecking crews, and the exodus of the disillusioned. The great bonanza had played out.

"Refugees from Miami and its environs continued to move upstate to Jacksonville, where they entrained for the homes they left during the long months of the big boom in Florida. Six hundred left Palm Beach during the day and hundreds of others were preparing to get away."

Less than two months before he had known it, as surely and as terribly as he knew it then. He could have unloaded, sold out, and left the doomed strip to the wicked and the unwise. Now, he knew it, and the press was advertising the exodus to the world. Every one knew it, now. Values had dropped from the top to the bottom. The creeping scrub pine, and the alligators, and the tax collectors, could have it. He'd never go back for the salvage.

That was the end of the man who took the teeth out of the law which prohibited the wanton taking of life. He didn't die, not Pruiett. God's wrath, a breath blowing a hundred miles an hour, could scarcely bend the spirit hovering about the cold body which stalked from Rusk's dungeon. He had his farms. He had his fierce convictions, and his vicious hatreds, and he had that indomitable will which wouldn't recognize defeat.

"Hell no, I ain't goin' to quit," he growled, when Bill Maben came to town and inquired about his plans. "I may be broke, but I ain't no broker than I was when I was shinin' shoes down at Fayetteville and Fort Smith. I lack a lot of bein' through."

"You're goin' to have to be careful," Maben suggested. "Things ain't like they used to be. The old boys we used to work with are dyin' off, an' the boys we broke in are gettin' a lot of power. I notice we're gettin' a' intergrated bar, with a disciplinary committee an' a enforcement board for keepin' our ethics straight."

"They got that to guard their own crookedness," Pruiett stormed. "All the short cuts the little fellers like us took in a lifetime wouldn't average up to the corruption of one of these big corporation lawsuits. The white collar bastards ain't gettin' rich fast enough, so they throw up some ethics smoke to hide the robbin' and riflin' they got planned to do."

"You got some new ideas on the subject, ain't you?" Maben inquired.

"Just got a new way of expressin' 'em," Pruiett answered. "Did you ever see a big utility swindle, or a municipal graft, that wasn't engineered by high priced corporation counsel? Why, hell no! They got to have their big law firms back of 'em, an' they split the swag in what they call payin' counsel fees. You show me a' apprehended swindler, or a tax-dodger, an' I'll show you a guy with a corporation lawyer's philosophy that's paid out half of what he's been stealin' to fast lawyers."

"It ain't illegal to represent your client," Maben said.

"Not if you're in with the right bunch—the ones with the white collars and plush bottoms," Pruiett agreed. "But, let'em catch one of my cat-tail witnesses with one foot off the base, tryin' to save some poverty-stricken devil from livin' death in the penitentiary, an' what do they do? They take after me. They take after you. They take after that poor unfortunate guy they call the criminal lawyer, and they start to give him some discipline. Ain't that right?"

"I guess subornation of perjury is the same in a murder case as it is in a land title case," Maben agreed.

"Hell yes, it is," Pruiett gritted. "They holler about me clearin' Maggie Miller. I did that for mercy; I was conscientious about gettin' her out of a heart-breakin' situation. Frank McMurray robbed a hundred thousand ignorant Indians. Made over a million dollars in one fee, an' he didn't have any purpose in mind but fillin' his own big greasy gut. Selfishness! Lustful robbery! An' the public's forgot about that. All they can holler is Maggie Miller, an' George Hopkins an' John Gobel."

"You've got by with a lot, Moman," Maben reminded.

"Sure I have," Pruiett agreed. "I started out with a purpose, an' I accomplished it. I made a lot of money, but I never turned down a criminal defense 'cause the accused didn't have the money to pay me. Maybe I have cocked a witness or two. Maybe I been a hypocrite, in some of the acts I've put on before juries, but let me tell you this. All the crookedness I ever poured into all the lawsuits I ever tried wouldn't amount to a tenth of what any of these big railroads or oil companies has crammed into a single case, just to cheat honest landholders out of their just rights. I can look 'em in the eye an' tell 'em to go to hell. I done mine for mercy. They done theirs for greedy gold.

So the black stud ambled on. He grazed in the shade of the side streets. When the weather was fair and affairs were right, he charged up the busy avenues, lived on oats, and his coat was curried and sleek. But, in the off season, he browsed, and his coat was shaggy.

There were flashes of the old Washita fight. There were recurrences of St. Mary and Valiton brilliance. But, with each fat fee collected, there was a recess with the bottle; and, when he came back to the bar, another notch of stamina and brilliance was missing. He was up and he was down. He was cited for contempt according to the *Oklahoma City Times* on May 9, 1928. Coming to court in a drunken state wasn't to be tolerated by the more refined judiciary. The papers played up the infraction, and he lost more names from his already sparse clientele list. The committee on the enforcements of ethics objected to his manner of handling an alienation of affection suit—it smacked of extortion—they claimed, and lawyer Pruiett, an old man, was disbarred following the decision in the *L. E. Roberts vs. Moman Pruiett* heard by the State Bar of Oklahoma. In the case Pruiett had offered to drop Robert's as a defendant in a civil action in exchange for $5,000. Rather than pay, Robert's filed a complaint with the Bar Association, which after an investigation disbarred Pruiett.

He fought it through the appellate court and filed a Petition for Review with the Clerk of the Oklahoma Supreme Court. Hell's fire! Was he goin' to let a bunch of white-collared young pups railroad him without a battle, even if he was old and broke? Not the old stud. "I can't get a fair trial in that damn Supreme Court," he bawled. "There's old Doc

Threlkeld's son-in-law, settin' as one of the Associate Justices, an' that family's still sore at me for drillin' holes through the old drunk."

The conviction was affirmed; but, the punishment was modified. Disbarment was changed to a years suspension from practice as reported by the *Oklahoma City Times* on July 2, 1935.

"Ain't that hell?" Pruiett swore. "What if they was to catch me with kin-folks on my jury? Wouldn't they scream? An' here these ethics-watchers censor me—convict me—with the son-in-law of a guy I shot settin' on the Court. What did I tell you about 'em coverin' up their own corruption with a big stink over the little feller's ethics?"

The black mane had turned to a soft white. The strut, the stride, the loud profanity, the color that was Pruiett, was gone. The rumble of the black stud's charge was but an echo—a memory.

An old man with bushy hair dozed in a courtroom pew. It was Pruiett. A close eye would detect a resemblance, notwithstanding the changes of age. Lint from cottonwoods on the lawn drifted through the open window, and in the Spring haze, the purple of the Washita woods could be seen dim on the horizon. A young lawyer in stylish clothes and with a Greek-letter pin on his vest was storming and raging in a languid jury's face.

"That boy's a bear, ain't he?" a man in overalls whispered, nudging the old man with his elbow.

"How's that?" Pruiett inquired, opening his eyes. He had been asleep.

"That boy's a bear," the man repeated. "He's a regular Moman Pruiett."

"He's a what?" Pruiett repeated.

"Pruiett! I say he's a regular Moman Pruiett. He's good."

"Who was Pruiett?" Pruiett inquired.

The farmer gave him a withering look. "You never hear of Moman Pruiett, the CRIMINAL lawyer?"

Pruiett shook his head, sadly.

"He was the greatest lawyer that ever banged a table," the man whispered. "I heard him try cases in this very courtroom, an' win 'em, when he was defendin' blood-guilty murderers. He made a million dollars an' went down to Florida, an' died down there, I guess. We kind of lost track of him. He tried a murder case ever' week, an' he never lost a one of 'em."

The old man with the white hair and round shoulders rose wearily and thumped his cane toward the exit.

"No use tryin' to explain anything to a' old bastard like that," the farmer muttered. "Never heard of Moman Pruiett, the criminal lawyer. Jesus Christ!"

Pruiett roared across the horizon of the last frontier like a fiery meteor, he fell, ultimately, a charred coal—burned out by the sudden brilliance of his own glory. He had the power to justify obvious outrages in the eyes of men and laws; the power to save men and women from the retribution of their own viciousness and folly, yet he lacked the capacity to save himself from the folly and viciousness of his nature.

He was moved to impulses and paradoxical, as divergent and conflicting, as the very elements of his own character. He was kind and considerate, yet at the same time brutal, almost depraved. He was reverent, cherishing and repeating the creed of his godly mother, yet as cunning and duplicitous, even wicked, as few men ever become. He committed gross evil in the name of tender mercy, and succeeded, without great effort, in convincing not only those who watched and listened, enthralled, but even himself embraced iniquity; he expounded the doctrines of peace on earth and good will, as devoutly as the Nazarene, while he championed hate, greed and avarice, and lent his sublime gifts to their rank spread. And his every depredation was committed in the name of law and justice, after a sincere prayer had been offered to heaven for its ultimate success.

Pruiett did not know fear and, unfortunately as his life story discloses, was not too well acquainted with integrity; but, he was so determined to have the appearance of integrity that he would rant, and fight and attempt to kill when insinuations were made against him. He would fight at the drop of a hat. He usually carried a gun. He killed a man, and shot several others, who survived. He was a hard drinker, and a heavy gambler. To call him an "ex-convict" was an invitation of assault and injury.

Amongst the other strange qualities, which he possessed, was the undefinable quality called "color" and enough of it for founding a legend. He curried favor amongst the newspapermen and developed a technique for getting his name into print long before the benefits of publicity agents and press agents were accepted as practical. He could make a little case look like a big one. He could make a big case look like a huge one. He could draw a Governor's attention to a Justice of the Peace court wrangle and often have headlines, based upon his hushed whispers, suggesting international complications to purely local hassles. His prostitute clients were always misunderstood virgins. His petty thief clients were either innocent, or masterminds of crime. He never fronted for a common ordinary crook.

Some say he defended criminals for spite and because he hated law and order. Some say he tried criminal cases on the defense side because he had a big heart and wanted to befriend suffering humanity. Who knows why? After maturity, he seldom appeared without a large fee. He functioned better, when he was paid well. He liked to make money but did not care about keeping it. He was a spendthrift. He became rich. He became powerful and influential politically. He liked to throw big tips around when the eyes were on him.

He worked, played, lied, fought, fixed courts and juries, connived, tricked, prayed and toiled, until he reached the top; and, then, he quietly folded his hands across a neat small paunch, and let liquor carry him back to his native poverty, and oblivion. He was an outlaw at heart. But, strange as it may seem, he wanted to be taken and remembered as a good man. He needed money in his late years and thought he could get it from the sale of his life's story; however, he wouldn't let anyone write it as it was. He wanted to be portrayed as Sir Galahad, or a misunderstood non-sectarian evangelist—a crusader who had been framed.

Pruiett was a man of great conflicts. He could be gentle or brutal as if by whim. At times, he was all roaring wickedness. At times, he was all sympathetic kindness. Those who would say he was a bad man can produce evidence to support the point. Those who say he was good can make a pretty strong case. Some say he was a great lawyer. Some say he was a freak, sanctioned by the strange conditions of the period, and that he, and his kind, should be ignored so as to be quickly forgotten.

The Moman Pruiett legend seems to endure. It has been 60 years since he had any prominence as a lawyer. It has been fifty-five years since his death. Yet, his name, and references to his exploits, continues to crop-up in press articles, and in places where lawyers and judges meet and talk. He was always on his own, and should remain so in retrospect. He had delightful charm and effective finesse, and ability and cunning, and a quality called "color", which gave him that prominence, in his day, which was equivalent to success. Otherwise, his fame would not have spread so far, nor would his memory have been so long sustained, nor be so self-perpetuating.

Pruiett color, which was a combination of personal charm, sheer courage, shrewdness, boundless energy, and scorn for the opinion of others, permitted him to produce the witnesses that caused juries to find with him in so many strange and puzzling cases, and under such baffling circumstances. He had all of the New Testament, and much of the Old, committed to memory. Drunk or sober, he could quote scriptures like a holiness preacher, and always apropos to the plight of his suffering client. He considered himself a good and righteous man. He considered himself strictly honest, and was quick to label those who disagreed with him as "liars," or "thieves," or "crooks."

Would Pruiett have succeeded in the present day practice of law? There are those who remember him with scorn and hatred, and, although recognizing the effectiveness of his advocacy, would never acknowledge that it amounted to success. Would he win cases—acquit clients—so as to become recognized as an advocate, and be remembered correspondingly, fifteen years later, or thirty years later?

It is suggested that the innovations of the pretrial, discovery procedure, and the videotape recorder, and the absolutism of modern judges, both State and Federal, would prevent the reoccurrence of a Pruiett. Pruiett was the master of surprise with his "cat-tail" witnesses. Pruiett witnesses, regardless of their bizarre disclosures, were seldom discredited. If they were not believed, they served their purpose of whiling the jury's attention from the prosecution plan, and leaving the field open for the application of Pruiett's hypnotic charm. The human intellect is probably as tractable, and gullible, and receptive, as it was before air-conditioned courtrooms and sound amplifiers for the benefit of the jury. If another character like Pruiett ever came along, he would confound and confuse the prosecutors again, just like old Moman did.

Following his suspension from the practice of law by the Oklahoma State Supreme Court in 1936, Pruiett returned to the courtroom; however, he never regained his previous prominence. His dependence on alcohol became more apparent and he often appeared in court impaired incurring the wrath of both judges and clients. His involvement with the Congress Club, an infamous gambling and liquor joint on the Oklahoma-Canadian County line, damaged his professional reputation, as did his arraignment on gambling charges. Eventually, his clientele drifted away; and, when he rose to defend the owner of a Communist bookstore in an unpopular 1940 case, his popularity plummeted as did his finances.

In the early 1940s his wife of four decades, Leda, was stricken with cancer. With her husband broke and penniless, she spent much of her time with her sister, Madora Patterson, the ex-wife of Pruiett's one-time law partner Orban, at her home at 2133 Northeast Twenty-first Street in Oklahoma City. As her illness progressed and her husband moved from one dingy hotel room to another, Leda was admitted to a private nursing home where she died on March 15, 1944.

By 1945, Pruiett, who had earned and squandered a million dollars or more in legal fees and who was known for his fancy dress and extravagant lifestyle, was living in a 50-cent-per-night flophouse located above a cleaning shop in what he affectionately referred to as the "bat cave" in the 200 block of Northwest Second Street in downtown Oklahoma City.

His one room walk-up apartment had a single, wrought iron bed in one corner and a table, phone, and file cabinet in the other. Over the time-worn linoleum floor hung a bare light bulb, swinging from a frayed electrical cord. The walls were covered with fading and pealing wallpaper. His main source of income was a $40 per month old-age-pension check that he had been drawing for nearly four years. Although he dreamed of his former glory and longed to return to his wooded cabin near Choctaw, his health prevented it.

In early December of 1945, Pruiett fell ill with pneumonia and was admitted to Oklahoma City's General Hospital. There five days later, as he lay in bed he turned to his daughter and asked for his hat, coat, and cane saying "I'm going to try to die like I lived." Leon Hatfield, noted newspaper reporter and former editor of *The Daily Oklahoman* later remarked that "in his mind he must have been dressing his soul for his last great adventure, for hardly had he made the request when he died." It was 5:05 a.m. December 12, 1945.

SOURCES

BOOKS

Monroe Lee Billington. *Thomas P. Gore: The Blind Senator from Oklahoma.* Lawrence: University of Kansas Press, 1967.

Lyle H. Boren and Dale Boren. *Who Is Who In Oklahoma.* Guthrie, Oklahoma: The Co-Operative Publishing Company, 1935.

Art Burton. *Black, Red and Deadly.* Texas: Eakin Press, 1991.

Bob Burke and Angela Monson. *Roscoe Dunjee: Champion of Civil Rights.* Edmond, Oklahoma: University of Central Oklahoma, 1998.

Ken Butler. *Oklahoma Renegades, Their Deeds and Misdeeds.* Gretna, Louisiana: Pelican Publishing Company, 1997.

Orban J. Casey. *And Justice For All: The Legal Profession in Oklahoma, 1821-1989.* Oklahoma: Western Heritage Books, Incorporated, 1989.

O. A. Cargill. *My First 80 Years.* Oklahoma City, Oklahoma: Banner Book Company, 1965.

Chickasaw Historical Society. *Indian Territory and Carter County Pioneers.* Privately printed, 1983.

Columbia Universtiy. *The Columbia Encyclopedia.* New York: P.F. Collier and Son, multiple years.

Jack T. Conn. *One Man In His Time.* Oklahoma: Western Heritage Books, Incorporated, 1979.

Homer Croy. Trigger Marshal: *The Story of Chris Madsen.* New York: Duell, Sloane and Pierce, 1958.

C. B. Douglas. *History of Tulsa, Oklahoma.* 3 vols. Chicago: S. J. Clark Publishing Company, 1921.

Jim Edwards and Hal Ottaway. *The Vanished Spendor.* Oklahoma City: Abalache Book Shop Publishing Company, 1982.

D. C. Gideon. *Indian Territory.* New York: The Lewis Publishing Company, 1901.

Henry Woodfin Grady. *The New South.* New York: R. Bonner's and Son, 1890.

Ernestine Gravley. *Judges of the Place of Fire.* Missouri: Walsworth Publishing Company, 1980.

Laurence Greene. *The Era of Wonderful Nonsense.* New York: The Bobbs-Merrill Company, 1939.

Rex Harlow. *Makers of Government In Oklahoma.* Oklahoma City, Oklahoma: Harlow Publishing Company, 1930.

Mrs. Josiah Brantley Harrell. *Oklahoma and Oklahomans.* (Self-published and printed), October 1922.

Walter M. Harrison. *Me And My Big Mouth.* Oklahoma City, Oklahoma: Britton Publishing Company, 1954.

Luther B. Hill. *History of the State of Oklahoma.* 2 vols., Chicago: Lewis Historical Publishing Company, 1909.

Welborn Hope. *Four Men Hanging: The End of the Old West.* Oklahoma City, Oklahoma: Century Press, 1974.

Irvin Hurst. *The 46th Star: A History of Oklahoma's Constitutional Convention and Early Statehood.* Oklahoma City, Oklahoma: Semco Color Press, 1957.

Edward T. James, Janet Wilson James and Paul S. Boyer. *Notable American Women.* Cambridge, Massachusetts: Belknap Press of Harvard University, 1971.

Roy M. Johnson. *Oklahoma History, South of the Canadian.* Chicago: The S. J. Clarke Publishing Company, 1925.

G. Louis Joughin and Edmund M. Morgan. *The Legacy of Sacco and Vanzetti.* New York: Harcourt, Brace and Company, 1948.

W. F. Kerr and Ina Gainer. *The Story of Oklahoma City*, 3 vols. Chicago: The S. J. Clarke Publishing Company, 1922.

Bernice Jackson, Jewel Carlisle and Iris Colwell. *Man and the Oklahoma Panhandle.* Kansas: Mennonite Press, Incorporated, 1982.

Marquis James. *The Raven: A Biography of Sam Houston.* New York: Blue Ribbon Books,1929.

Paul Lester. *The True Story of the Galveston Flood.* Philadelphia: American Book and Bible House, 1900.

Gaston L. Litton. *History of Oklahoma at the Golden Anniversary of Statehood*, 4 vols. New York: Lewis Historical Publishing Company, 1957.

Library of Congress. *Biographical Directory of United States Congress.* Washington: Government Printing Office, multiple years.

Men of Affairs. Tulsa: The World Publishing Company, 1916.

William H. Murray. *Memoirs of Governor Murray and True-History of Oklahoma*, 3 vols. Boston: Meador Publishing Company, 1945.

Albert McRill. *And Satan Came Also: An Inside Story of a City's Social and Political History.* Oklahoma City, Oklahoma: Britton Publishing Company, 1955.

C. W. Mooney. *Localized History of Pottawatomie County, Oklahoma to 1907.* Midwest City, Oklahoma: Agent and Distribution of Thunderbird Industries, 1971.

Jay Robert Nash. *Bloodletters and Badmen: An Encyclopedia of American Criminals.* New York: M. Evans and Company, 1973.

A. W. Neville. *Backward Glances.* 2 vols., Paris, Texas: Privately printed, 1983.

Evett Dumas Nix, as told to Gordon Hines. *Oklahombres.* St. Louis: Eden Publishing Company, 1929.

Ron Owens. *Oklahoma Justice.* Paducha, Kentucky: Turner Publishing Company, 1995.

Ron Owens. *Oklahoma Heroes.* Paducha, Kentucky: Turner Publishing Company, 2000.

Richard Patterson. *Historical Atlas of the Outlaw West.* Boulder, Colorado: Johnson Publishing Company, 1985.

Robert Polito. *Savage Art: A Biography of Jim Thompson.* New York: Alfred A. Knopf Publishing Company, 1995.

Pauls Valley Chamber of Commerce. *From Bluestem to Golden Trend: Pictorial History of Garvin County.* Pauls Valley: Pauls Valley Chamber of Commerce, 1957.

Glenn Shirley. *Shotgun for Hire.* Norman: University of Oklahoma Press, 1970.

Glenn Shirley. *Temple Houston: Lawyer With A Gun.* Norman, Oklahoma: University of Oklahoma Press, 1980.

Edwin DuBois Shurter. *Complete Orations and Speeches of Henry Woodfin Grady.* Austin, Texas: Southwest Publishing Company, 1910.

George H. Shirk. *Oklahoma Place Names.* Oklahoma: University of Oklahoma Press, 1965.

Bonnie Speer. *Portrait of a Lawman: U.S. Deputy Marshal Heck Thomas.* Norman, Oklahoma: Reliance Press, 1996.

Roy P. Stewart. *Born Grown: An Oklahoma City History.* Oklahoma City, Oklahoma: Metro Press, Incorporated, 1974.

Mack Stanely. *Hanging Judge and His Desperadoes.* Sprio, Oklahoma: (Privately printed), 1983.

Joseph B. Thoburn and Muriel H. Wright. *Oklahoma: A History of the State and Its People.* 4 vols., New York: Lewis Historical Publishing Company, 1929.

Joseph B. Thoburn. *A Standard History of Oklahoma*, 5 vols. Chicago: The American Historical Society, 1916.

ARTICLES

"Death of Justice is a Shock." *Harlow's Weekly* (May 23, 1914), p. 1.

"Fred Page Branson." *Harlow's Weekly* (January 20, 1922), p. 5.

Fred Girton. "Al Capone Tells His Side Of It." *Startling Detective Adventures* (September, 1931), Vol 7, No. 38, pp. 20-23, 68-71.

Nick B. Harris. "At Last! The Real Truth About Hickman's Crime." *Startling Detective Magazine* (November, 1931), Vol. 7, No. 40, pp. 14-19, 49-50.

E. M. Kerr. "Thomas Homer Owen." *The Chronicles of Oklahoma,* Vol. XVII, No. I (March, 1939), p. 119.

W. F. Kerr. "Thomas Pryor Gore". *Sturm's Oklahoma Magazine* (January 1910), pp. 58-62.

"Robert L. Owens: United States Senator from Oklahoma." *The Chronicles of Oklahoma,* Vol. 25, No. 3 (Autumn, 1947), pp. 178-179.

Hugh McCord. "The Civil War in the West: The Battle of Pea Ridge." *Louis L'Amour Western Magazine* (November, 1995), pp. 86-95.

Moman County." *Sturm's Oklahoma Magazine* (April, 1907), p. 29.

Burton Rascoe. "Attorney For Revenge". *True: The Man's Magazine* (April 1948), pp. 124-139.

"John Fletcher Sharp." *Harlow's Weekly* (April 25, 1914), p. 40.

Isabel Stephen. "Startling Revelations About The Hall-Mills Case". *True Detective Mysteries Magazine* (June-December 1931), 7 issues.

O. P. Sturm. "The Sage of Tishomingo." *Sturm's Oklahoma Magazine* (September 1909), pp. 18-30.

Robert L. Williams. "Judge Jesse James Dunn: 1867-1926." *The Chronicles of Oklahoma,* Vol. XVIII, No. 1 (March 1940), pp. 2-11.

NEWSPAPERS

Ada Weekly News. Ada, Oklahoma.

October 15, 1903. "The Ada Shooting"

February 16, 1905, "Col. Jake Hodges Dead."

October 8, 1908. "Byrd Hotel, Ada, OK"

March 4, 1909, "Gus Bobbitt Assassinated."

Atoka Citizen. Atoka, Oklahoma.

March 28, 1907, "Blood and Tears!"

Baltimore Sun. Baltimore, Maryland.

February 20, 1914, Editorial, Senator Gore case.

Bartlesville Morning Examiner. Bartlesville, Oklahoma.

September 27, 1913. "Plot Is Unfolding Around Mrs. Laura Reuter."

Bartlesville Record. Bartlesville, Oklahoma.

May 21, 1950, "Judge R. H. Hudson Services Tomorrow."

Blackwell Sun. Blackwell, Oklahoma.

December 30, 1920, "Moman Pruiett Says the Gentle Clara is Modern Vampire."

Blackwell Times Record. Blackwell, Oklahoma.

November 7, 1912, "Mrs. Gentry Paroled."

Brighton Blade. Brighton, Colorado.

October 25, 1921. "Hill Murder Case."

October 26, 1921. "Hill Murder Case."

Capital Hill News. Oklahoma City, Oklahoma.

October 15, 1910. "Frank Gillette, Tried and True"; "Edward Oldfield"

Cherokee Advoctate. Tahlequah, Oklahoma.

September 28, 1887. "Civil War Battle at Pea Ridge"

Cherokee Republican. Cherokee, Oklahoma.

September 30, 1910, "Interesting Oklahomans: Moman Pruiett."

Cheyenne Sunbeam. Cheyenne, Oklahoma.

August 9, 1901, "A Killing on Middle Buffalo."

Chickasaw Enterprise. Pauls Valley, Oklahoma.

April 11, 1895, "A Terrible Tragedy: Judge Joe Paul Shot and Killed by Jennison McClure."

January 18, 1900. "Charlie Bias' Death Sentence Commuted to Life"

May 30, 1901, "Sam Ashton Acquitted."

November 14, 1901, "Serious shooting."

December 1, 1904, "In District Court."

December 5, 1901, "Tom Powell Case."

January 16, 1902, "George Hancock Acquitted in Killing of Marshal Charles Liddell"; "Moman Pruiett Stepping High These Days."

January 30, 1902, "Pruiett Finds Father's Lost Uncle in St. Louis While on Wade Hampton Case."

April 10, 1902, "Court Proceedings."

May 15, 1902, "Euology to Mrs. Lilly Belle Pruiett."

January 1, 1903, "A Lawyer with a Reputation."

April 23, 1903, "The Thrasher Case."

July 9, 1903, "Cupids Work."

July 16, 1903, "Stabbed to Death."

December 14, 1903, "Ashton Acquitted."

March 3, 1904, "Pruiett Receives 'Office Safe.' "; "Lawrence Walker Acquitted"

December 18, 1896, "The Stevenson Case"

Daily Advocate. Paris, Texas.

Daily Ardmoreite. Ardmore Oklahoma.

February 10, 1891, "Putty Kills Thurlow."

May 26, 1896, "Beatty Assassination."

June 24, 1896, "Desperado Arrested."

February 21, 1897," Jennison M'Clure Dead."

July 22, 1898," Murders Committed."

November 1, 1899, "Pauls Valley Court."

December 3, 1899, "Stillwell Russell of Dallas."

January 15, 1900, "Death Watch Set."

January 16, 1900, "Under the Gallows Shadow."

June 10, 1900, "At the Jail."

September 9, 1900, "This Land Our Home."

September 13, 1900, "Tired of Dodging."

September 19, 1900, "Killing at Iona."

November 3, 1899, "Banished (Jury) From Court."

January-March, 1901, "Shooting at Thackerville"; "Charles Liddell Dies"; "Liddell's Slayer Arrested"; George Hancock Charged."

April 15, 1901, "Witch Killers Acquitted."

January 27, 1901, "Shooting at Thackerville."

February 5, 1901, "Liddell Dies from Wounds."

March 4, 1901, "Liddell's Slayer Arrested."

March 11, 1901, "George Hancock Charged."

July 9, 1902, "Some Dave Putty History."

July 19, 1901, "Over Eighty Thousand Have Registered for 13,000 Homes."

January 12, 1902, "The Lawyers Speeches."

August 5, 1902, "Important Murder Case."

November 4, 1902, "Bert Casey Gets Justice."

November 5, 1902, "Grim Fate of Outlaws."

January 7, 1903, "Deadly Fight."

October 11, 1903, "The Ada Shooting."

July 6, 1902, "Resist Arrest, Killed."

November 22-December 30, 1920, "Clara Smith-Jake Hamon Shooting."

March 23, 1921, "James A. Stillman Accuses Wife of Criminal Intimacy."

March 24, 1921, "Mrs. Stillman."

March 25, 1921, "Stillman's Child."

Daily Oklahoman. Oklahoma City, Oklahoma.

June 12, 1896, "A Domestic Tragedy."

April 10, 1904, "Hamilton Bill."

June 1907 - August 1913, "Rudolph Tegeler-Jim Meadows Murder Case."

June 15, 1907, "Moman Pruiett Proves his Unswerving Party Fealty."

April 18, 1909, "Stevenson Not Guilty."

April 20, 1909, "Four Men Charged with Murder'Feared Lynching if Taken to Ada'";"Four Men Charged with Murder Lynched"; "Where to Place the Blame For Lynchings."

May 28, 1909, "Maben Guiltless of the Crime Charged."

July 8-August 8, 1909, "Cecil Mingle Trial."

July 15, 1909, "Cecil Mingle Writhes', Branded as Slayer of a Defenseless Woman.'"

December 28, 1909, "Grand Jury Returned Indictment Against Maben."

March 24, 1910, "Wife Fires Fatal Shot."

August 14, 1910, "Brawl Ends in Killing."

August 15, 1910, "Holloway is Too Fast for Sheriff.'

September 18-28, 1910, "Rudolph Tegeler-Jim Meadows Murder Case."

September 20, 1910, "Mysterious Man May be James Meadows?"; "Prosecuting Attorney Sam Harris Refers to Pruiett as the 'Great Black Stud' of the Washita."

September 29, 1910, "Judge Carney Receives Telegram from Governor Sanders of Louisiana Denies Knowing Mike O'Brien"; "Witnessess From New Orleans Say McGraw Never Worked There."

October 1, 1910, "O'Brien Calls His Parents 'That Old Canary' and 'The Old Garbage Man.'"

October 5, 1910, "Prosecuting Attorney Harris Announces that Governor Sanders of

Louisiana Denies Known Mike O'Brien"; "O'Brien/McGraw Arrested in Alley Back of the County Jail."

October 7, 1910, "Moman Pruiett's Rhetorical Assault Upon Sam Harris."

October 10, 1910, "Testimony of Mrs. McGraw in Tegeler Trial."

January 4, 1911, "Hardest Fought."

September 12, 1911, "Woodward Jury Finds Mrs. Miller is 'Not Guilty.'"

November 24, 1911, "Catherine Rogers Sues Lawyer for $100,000 Alimony."

March 26, 1915, "Death of Ellis Girl Announced."

June 15-June 25, 1915. "D. V. Monroe Trial."

June 25, 1915, "Monroe Weeps at News of Freedom."

November 30, 1915, "Divorce Asked by Common Law Wife."

March 17, 1912, "Mrs. Gentry to Fight to Finish."

September 21, 1913, "Lorena Mathews Acquitted."

November 28, 1915, "Fatal Shooting Ends Card Game."'

November 29, 1915, "John Knight in Custody."

November 30, 1915, "Murder Motive Still a Mystery."

December 3, 1915, "Minister to Aid Accused Sons."

April 21, 1916, "Jess Knight is at Last in Jail."

February 20, 1917, "Joe Davis Trial Begins at Tucson."

February 25, 1917, "Davis-Spurlock verdict is Guilty."

March 6, 1917, "Obituary: Mrs. Elizabeth Pruiett."

March 7, 1917, "Vernon Patterson a Suicide."

May 27. 1917, "W. L. Pruiett Dies Here."

February 18-March 3, 1918, "Orban C. Patterson's Murder Trial."

March 3, 1918, "Jury Finds Patterson 'Not Guilty.'"

March 17-March 26, 1919. "Lottie Baker Murder Case."

June 9-June 16, 1919. "Lottie Baker Tried, Acquitted."

June 15, 1919, "Lottie Baker Freed by Jury After 7 Hours."

November 22-December 30, 1920, "Clara Smith-Jake Hamon Shooting."

March 8, 1921, "Ardmore Trial Brings Crowd."

March 9, 1921, "Court Surprised as Haines Admits Guilt."

March 18, 1921, "Clara Smith Acquitted!"

March 28-April 15, 1921, "Annabelle Edwards' Shooting."

October 10, 1921, "Pruiett Held on Charge of Killing Negro."

October 12, 1921, "Coroners Jury Frees Pruiett."

October 4, 1922, "K. K. K. Rally in Oklahoma City."

October 5, 1922, "20,000 Crowd Watches Klan Initiate 400."

November 9-19, 1921, "Annabelle Edwards Murder Trial."

April 9, 1922, "Jury Clears Day."

October 11, 1923, "State is Defeated in Fight to Pin Lash Guilt on Klan Chief."

November 19, 1923, "Walton Impeached."

November 26, 1923, "Evidence in the Walton Case."

August 9-18, 1926."W. T. Maness Double-Murder Case."

September 18, 1926, "Cotton Prices Steadied by Gulf Hurricane Menace."

September 19, 1926, "Florida Coast is Swept by Hurricane."

September 20, 1926, "500 Die in Hurricane"; "38,000 Homeless Property Damage is $125,000,000."

September 21, 1926, "President Sounds Call for Aid to Florida."

November 24-December 6, 1926, "W. T. Maness Murder Trial."

December 12, 1927, "Thomas P. Gore Letter to Moman Pruiett."

July 8, 1933, "John Jay, Dope Ring General, Is Due Parole."

December 27, 1936, "Hail and Farewell to Politics."

April 23, 1939. "City Named for Settler."

October 4, 1936. "Civil War Battle of Pea Ridge."

January 25, 1960, "Illness is Fatal to Cheatwood, Member of Bar."

January 24, 1973, "George Short Services Set."

Daily Pointer. Oklahoma City, Oklahoma.

June 6, 1907, "Rudolph Tegeler-Jim Meadows Murder Case."

July 21, 1907, "Injunction Filed Against the Florida Bar Manager."

December 2, 1907, "Florida Bar Converted to Nickelodeon."

February 14, 1908, "Ardmore Chief Given Freedom On Murder Charge."

Daily Press. Stillwater, Oklahoma.

June 4, 1913. "Jim Chapman Testifies in Mathews Trial."

Daily Times-Journal. Oklahoma City

March 15, 1906, "Jim Peters Shot by Chief of Police."

November 20, 1906, "W. H. Murray Elected Presiding Officer of the Oklahoma Constitutional Convention."

Dallas News. Dallas, Texas, "Moman Pruiett Says the Gentle Clara is Modern Vampire."

December 29, 1920.

Democrat Record. Idabel, Oklahoma.

July 8, 1915, "Hiram C. Strawn Killed."

July 15, 1915, "To My Clients."

September 2, 1915, "On Account of Illness, J. M. Leggett was Removed from the County Jail to the Home."

September 9, 1915, "Leggett Released After $15,000 Bond."

October 7, 1915, "J. M. Leggett Acquitted."

April 20, 1916, "Attorney Leggett Killed."

Denver Daily News. Denver, Colorado.

December 12, 1912. "Negro Trails Woman 4,000 Miles."

June 13, 1913. "Lauren Mathews Defended by Moman Pruiett."

Denver Post. Denver, Colorado.

October 24, 1921.

Duncan Eagle. Duncan, Oklahoma.

April 29, 1948, "Eulogy to Cham Jones Praises His Work as Leader."

Edmonton Daily Capital. Edmonton, Ontario, Canada.

May 17, 1913 "Mathews Murder Case."

May 19, 1913. "Mathews Murder Case."

Enid Daily Eagle. Enid, Oklahoma.

September 26, 1915, "Pruiett Said Lawyer Had a Gun for Him."

March 8, 1921, "Attorney Surprises Court."

Evening Star. Washington, D. C.

February 25, 1939, feature article by Lemuel F. Parton

Fayetteville Daily. Fayetteville, Arkansas.

August 27, 1909, "Most Shocking Murder."

August 28, 1909, "Gus Sartain Committs Suicide in California Jail."

April 28, 1911. "Red Fox Murder Case."

May 5, 1911. "Red Fox Murder Trial."

May 22, 1911. "Red Fox Released."

Fort Worth Star Telegram. Fort Worth, Texas.

July 17, 1923, "Pruiett is Held at Ft. Worth."

Galveston Daily News. Galveston, Texas.

July 19, 1921. "Woman Tarred and Feathered."

Garvin County Herald. Pauls Valley, Oklahoma.

April 23, 1909, "The Stevenson Case."

Guthrie Daily Leader. Guthrie, Oklahoma.

November 20,1906, "W. H. Murray elected Presiding Officer over the Oklahoma Constitutional Convention."

December 29, 1911, "Jailer Searched Pruiett."

Guthrie Daily Ledger. Guthrie, Oklahoma.

August 24, 1893. "John Stevenson Shot and Killed Deputy Joe Gaines."

Guthrie State Capitol. Guthrie, Oklahoma.

November 8, 1902, "Hoteme, The Witch Killer."

April 18, 1907, "Haskell has Moman County Name Changed to Creek County."

Hobart Republican. Hobart, Oklahoma.

January 24, 1902, "Two Officers Killed."

Hobart Weekly Chief. Hobart, Oklahoma.

September 3, 1903, "The Week in Court.'

Holdenville Times. Holdenville, Oklahoma.

November 19,1909, "Jury Returns Verdict of Death."

Indian Chieftain. Vinita, Oklahoma.

October 27, 1887. "A Deplorable and Terrible Affair."

December 18, 1890. "Sam Paul Shoots His Son, Joe Paul."

December 24, 1891, "Joe Paul Shoots and Kills Sam Paul."

Kansas City Journal. Kansas City, Missouri.

March 9, 1907, "Charges of Graft, $5,000 Offered."

February 7, 1914, "Sen. Gore's Past."

Kansas City Post. Kansas City, Missouri.

February 16, 1914. "Senator Gore Takes the Witness Stand."

Kansas City Star. Kansas City, Missouri.

February 19, 1914. "The Lawyer for the Defense. . . "

February 19, 1914, "Editorial on Thomas P. Gore Case."

February 18, 1914, "Editorial."

October 18, 1931, "The Prayers of Friends."

Kansas City Times. Kansas City, Missouri.

February 18, 1914. "Pruiett Speaks for Gore."

Kiefer Searchlight. Kiefer, Oklahoma.

July 7, 1911, "Good Man Gone"; "The Washerwoman's Song."

Lawton News. Lawton, Oklahoma.

November 9, 1915, "A. T. Hopkins Brutally Murdered at His Livery Barn Sunday Night."

March 23, 1916, "Introduces Evidence to Corroborate Coley."

March 26, 1916, "Famous Hopkins Case now In Jury's Hands."

March 28, 1916, "George Hopkins Found 'Not Guilty' By Jury."

Lindsey News. Lindsey, Oklahoma.

June 15-July 2, 1915, "D. V. Monroe Trial."

Long Beach Sun. Long Beach, California.

November 8, 1931.

Los Angeles Examiner. Los Angeles, California.

April 9, 1922. "Day–Beck Murder Case."

Marietta Monitor. Marietta, Oklahoma.

August 17, 1906, "Kills His Brother."

June 16, 1911, "George Hancock Killed."

June 30, 1911, "C. J. Liddell Acquitted."

Miami Herald. Miami, Florida.

December 11, 1924, "Pruiett Outlined the Freckleton Defense."

December 13, 1924. "All's Well on the Potomac!"

March 19, 1925. "Give Her Liberty Or Give Her Death"' "Valiton Murder Trial."

March 30, 1925. "Pruiett Wires Fla. Gov. For a Change of Venue."

March 31, 1925. "All Jurors Challenged."

April 2, 1925. "Sheriff Spirits Prisoners Away in Garbage Cans."

May 14, 1925. "Third Day of Testimony in Valiton's Murder Trial."

May 16, 1925. "Testimony in Valiton's Murder Trial."

May 20, 1925. "The Jeptha Story Revisited."

Miami Life. Miami, Florida.

May 23, 1925. "Sell the Electric Chair."

Miami News. Miami, Florida.

January 15, 1923, "John Gobel Case."

August 15, 1923, "Pruiett's Evaluation of Florida's Growth Potential and Pleasant Climate."

August 17, 1923, "Pruiett and Patterson at Miami-Hialeah Gun Club."

March 28, 1925. "No Clarence Darrow 'Stuff' In This Case."

March 30, 1925. "Martin Pledges Troops to Guard Miami Slayers."

March 31, 1925. "Harlan Miller Reports on Valiton Case."

April 2, 1925. "Deputy Sheriff Talbot Testifies."

April 26, 1925, feature article by Harlan Miller.

May 14, 1925. "Jury Selected in Valiton Trial."

May 17, 1925. "Is There No God in Florida?"

May 18, 1925. "Valiton Testifies in His Own Defense."

December 14, 1924. "Pruiett Defends Hattie Freckleton in Miami, Fla."

Miami Tribune. Miami, Florida.

October 13, 1924, "(Mr.) Freckleton Shot. . . Wife Says, 'Oh, I Did It' ."

April 1, 1925, "Lack of Jurymen May Delay Trial of Murder Pair."

Muskogee Phoenix. Muskogee, Oklahoma.

April 19, 1907, "Editorial."

March 1, 1916, "McDarment Shot Me; Hole in Shirt a Mystery."

June 18, 1916, "McDarment Freed: Found 'Not Guilty.'"

New York Sun. New York, New York.

October 31, 1931, "An Oklahoma Lawyer."

New York Times. New York, New York.

October, 1920.

New York World. New York, New York.

February 19, 1914. "Senator Ashurst of Arizona Debates Tariff Bill."

Norman Transcript. Norman, Oklahoma.

January 25, 1900, "Ardmoreites are Mad."

May 2, 1912, "Morris Weightman Gets Five Years."

August 24-August 28, 1917, "Fulkerson Killed."

September 7, 1933, "Pence Jury Hopelesly Split."

December 13, 1921. "Lee Sharp Shot and Killed Sid Pence."

Nowata Daily Star. Nowata, Oklahoma.

July 15, 1957, "Judge Springer Succumbs at 84."

Nowata Star. Nowata, Oklahoma.

August 22, 1918, "Moman Pruiett Draws Big Fine."

Daily Pointer. Oklahoma City, Oklahoma.

September 22, 1907, "Coroners Jury Blames Railroad."

November 27, 1907, "Suit for $10,000 Filed By Widow Against Santa Fe Railroad Company/"

Oklahoma City Times. Oklahoma City, Oklahoma.

June 6, 1907, "Rudolph Tegeler-Jim Meadows Murder Case."

July 8-August 8, 1909, "Cecil Mingle Trial."

August 20, 1910, "Patrolman Crow's Wife is About to Have Her Baby."

January 6, 1911, "Expert on the Stand in Crow's Murder Hearing."

January 8, 1911, "'Not Guilty' is the Verdict in the Crow Murder Trial."

January 16, 1910, "Woman Fires Fatal Shots."

March 13, 1910, "Woman is Free on Promise to Pay the Costs."

March 25, 1910, "Woman to be Accused of Murder."

November 24, 1911, "Aims to be Common Law Wife of Attorney Rogers."

October 29, 1912, "Mrs. Gentry Out on Parole."

February 15, 1917, "Sam St. Mary Held in Jail Under Charge."

June 6, 1917, "Defendant Held Not Guilty on Murder Charge."

July 7, 1917, "St. Mary is Released: Alienists Pronounce Slayer of Henry as of Sound Mind."

September 28, 1917, "Purcell Banker Slain in Feud."

March 17-March 26, 1919

June 5-June 25, 1919.

June 6-June 9, 1919.

May 3, 1921, "Stillman Resigns Bank Presidency."

November 16, 1921, "Edward Widow Says Gamblers 'Fixed' Officials"; "Walton Named in Testimony."

November 19, 1921, "Annabelle Edwards Collapses as Jury Verdict Frees Her."

November 22-December 30, 1920, "Clara Smith-Jake Hamon Shooting."

November 19, 1921. "Annabelle Edwards Collapses as Jury Verdict Frees Her."

April 7, 1922, "Here's Hughes' Formal Statement on Beck Case."

April 8, 1922, "Blood on Mrs. Day's Face."

April 10, 1922, "Lt.. Beck Seeks to Clear Father's Name."

June 6, 1922, "Mrs. Day Tells Probers Story of Beck Death."

November 8, 1923, "Mrs. Stillman's Confession is Filed in Court."

November 26, 1923, "Martha Jones's Testimony About Her Contract with Moman Pruiett for Her Son's Pardon."

November 27, 1923, "Where Xenophon Belongs."

August 9-18, 1926.

November 19, 1926, "What the Screech Owl's Call Means."

November 9, 1933. "Alva Boy Who Made Good."

December 28, 1935, "Former City Pastor to Take Old Pulpit."

January 8, 1937, "Fist Fightin' Lawyer Will Ride Herd on State Supreme Court."

May 9, 1928, "Pruiett Fails to Appear."

May 11, 1928, "Federal Writ for Attorney is Unserved."

May 12, 1928, "Court Annuls Pruiett Case."

July 2, 1935, "Moman Pruiett is Suspended in Faked City Love Balm Suit."

Oklahoma City Times-Journal. Oklahoma City, Oklahoma.

September 21, 1907, "S. P. Adams Killed by the Santa Fe."

Oklahoma News. Oklahoma City, Oklahoma.

June 1907-August 1913, "Rudolph Tegeler-Jim Meadows Murder Case."

May 20, 1909, "Virgil R. Biggers Suspended County Attorney, to be State Witness."

July 8-August 8, 1909, "Cecil Mingle Trial."

January 16, 1910. "Katherine Snodgrass Freed."

September 11, 1911, "Miller Gets Life Sentence."

December 10, 1911. "Rogers v. Rogers."

January 9, 1912, "Gentry Murder Case."

January 10, 1912, "Gentry Trial."

January 11, 1912, "Confessions Coerced."

January 13, 1915, "Moman Questions Dying Girl."

June 15-25, 1915, "D. V. Monroe Trial."

April 15, 1916, "Taken In Mountain Feud."

April 20, 1916, "Jess Knight, Slayer, Gives Himself Up."

March 7, 1917, "Girl Suicide to be Buried at Purcell."

February 18-March 3, 1918, "Patterson Murder Trial."

March 17-March 26, 1919.

November 22-December 30, 1920, "Clara Smith-Jake Hamon Shooting."

March 28-April 15, 1921, "Annabelle Edwards' Shooting."

October 10, 1921, "Pruiett Death Plot is Seen."

October 12, 1921, "Pruiett in New Gun Affray."

November 9-19, 1921, "Annabelle Edwards' Murder Trial."

November 14, 1921, "Near Brawl in Murder Hearing."

November 18, 1921, "Giddings Got Cold Feet."

January 14, 1922.

April 6, 1922, "Impossible' Day's Reply."

August 22-August 29, 1922, "W. A. Joslyn Case."

September 12, 1922, "Threatened by Mob, Says Governor."

October 31, 1922, "Local Klan Chief in Kansas 'War.'"

December 14, 1922, "Slayer Takes Own Life."

March 22, 1923, "X. Jones Sentenced to 25 Years."

July 17, 1923, "Pruiett is Held at Ft. Worth."

October 8, 1923, "Moman Pruiett Leaving State."

October 12, 1923, "Hung Jury." (W. A. Joslyn Trial.)

August 9-18, 1926. "W. T. Maness Double-Murder Case."

November 24-December 6, 1926, "Maness Trial."

Oklahoma Post. Oklahoma City, Oklahoma.

June 15, 1907, "'Governor' is Liberated."
Oklahoma Weekly State Capitol. Guthrie, Oklahoma.

November 8, 1902, "Bert Casey Identified."

Okemah Ledger. Okemah, Oklahoma.

November 18, 1909, "Peter Thompson Must Die."

Paris Tribune. Paris, Texas.

May 4, 1896, "Moman Pruiett–Lilly Belle Thrasher Wed."

Pauls Valley Democrat. Pauls Valley, Oklahoma.

November 2, 1916, "Dr. Patterson Killed."

Pauls Valley Enterprise. Pauls Valley, Oklahoma.

June 30, 1904, "C. J. Grant's Condition Not Improved."

October 6, 1904, "Criminal Docket—District Court."

November 24, 1904, "In District Court."

December 8, 1904, "Masterly Address."

March 23, 1905, "Court Proceedings;" "Calvin J. Grant Obituary."

May 11, 1905, "Santa Fe Excursions."

June 22, 1905, "Court Proceedings."

June 29, 1905, "B. F. Driggers Gets Life."

July 20, 1905, "Garvins and Pruietts Take Vacation."

August 24, 1905, "Garvins and Pruietts Return from Vacation."

November 9, 1905, "Moman Pruiett to Oklahoma City for Democratic Executive Committee Meeting."

December 7, 1905, "Moman Pruiett Receives Telegram."

January 11, 1906, "Hamilton Bill."

February 15, 1906, "Attention Democrats."

August 6, 1906, "Killed at Maysville."

January 24, 1907, "Only One County Has Republican Name."

March 21, 1907. "Sam Garvin."

November 7, 1907, "Marshal R. W. Cathey Assassinated."

April 30, 1908, "New Trial."

June 4, 1908, "Killing at Stratford."

July 23, 1908, "Samuel J. Garvin Dead."

December 31, 1908, "John Stevenson Is Killed."

January 11, 1917, "Wade Williams 'Not Guilty.'"

Pauls Valley Sentinal. Pauls Valley, Oklahoma.

April 28, 1904, "Morehead-McMinneman Case."

May 5, 1904, "Seven to Five for Conviction."

November 24, 1904, "Tom Powell's Conviction;" "Izora Alexander Acquittal."

December 1, 1904, "The Tyree Case."

February 22, 1906. "Noted Murder Case."

Pauls Valley Tribune. Pauls Valley, Oklahoma.

Philadelphia Press. Philadelphia, Pennsylvania.

February 20, 1914. "Senator Gore Bore Himself with Great Dignity."

Ponca City News. Ponca City, Oklahoma.

March 30, 1920, "To Try Indian For Wife Murder."

October 12, 1921, "Alleged Slayer Goes to Trial."

October 13, 1921, "Indian Guilty of Manslaughter Fined $1,000."

Purcell Register. Purcell, Oklahoma.

December 1, 1899, "Not Guilty: The Verdict at Last Reached in the Douglas Case."

September 21, 1900, "Mr. A. C. Cruce Here Today."

December 15, 1921, "Lee Sharp Kills Sid Pence."

Quinlan Mirror. Quinlan, Oklahoma.

April 25, 1907, "Haskell Gets 'Even' with Moman Pruiett by Renaming Moman County to Creek County."

Renfrews Record. Alva, Oklahoma.

September 15, 1911, "The Murder of Mabel Oakes is Avenged."

Rocky Mountain News. Denver, Colorado.

July 25, 1921, "William and Thelma Hill Case."

October 30, 1921. "Hill Murder Trial Ends."

St. Louis Globe Democrat. St. Louis, Missouri.

April 18, 1907.

February 17, 1914, "Gore, on Stand, Denies Attack, Calls Suit Plot."

St. Louis Post-Dispatch. St. Louis, Missouri.

February 18, 1914, "Gore Case."

Sapulpa Evening Light. Sapulpa, Oklahoma.

July 19, 1911, "Ooley Seeks His Liberty.'

Sapulpa Light. Sapulpa, Oklahoma.

June 12, 1909, "Hold-up Men Bound Over."

August 2, 1909, "Alleged Hold-up Men on Trial."

August 3, 1909, "Hold-up Case Nearing Close."

August 4, 1909, "Hold-up Men are Acquitted."

Seattle Post Intelligencer. Seattle, Washington.

June 8, 1913, "Arrest of Lorena Mathews."

Seattle Star. Seattle, Washington.

June 9, 1913. "Mrs. Lorena Mathews Guest at Seattle Hotel."

Shawnee News. Shawnee, Oklahoma.

May 15, 1909, "Says He Got the Boodle."

May 26, 1909, "Mrs. Howell's Letter to Reverend Bulgin"; "Pruiett's Attack on West."

Stillwater Advance-Democrat. Stillwater, Oklahoma.

January 16, 1913, "Mathews-Chapman Case."

June 12, 1913, "Let the Accused Have a Fair and Impartial Trial."

Tahlequah Telegraph. Tahlequah, Oklahoma.

October 28, 1887. "A True Account of the Killing of B. H. Stone."

Times-Democrat. Atlus, Oklahoma.

May 2, 1918, "Okla. Lawyers Lugging Booze."

Times. El Dorado, Kansas.

May 22, 1922, "Roberts-Rickey Bank Robbers."

Tulsa World. Tulsa, Oklahoma.

September 27, 1913, "Mrs. Reuter and MacKenzie the Brains, Baker and Ballew, Tools."

September 28, 1913, "Quid Pro Quo"; "Detectives Foil Plot of Hired Gunmen to Assassinate Bellew."

January 10-February 1, 1914, "Laura Reuter Trial."

June 1-June 10, 1921, "Tulsa Race Riot."

Tuscon Citizen. Tucson, Arizona.

February 24, 1917, "Golden State Train Robbery Case."

Washington Post. Washington, D. C.

February 20, 1914, Editorial. (Senator Gore Case)

April 9, 1922, "Day–Beck Murder Case."

Washington Times-Herald. Washington, D.C.

January 1, 1900. "Moman Pruiett Admitted to Practice Before U.S. Supreme Court."

Januray 18, 1900. "Charlie Bias' Death Sentence Commuted to 'Life'."

January 20, 1905. "Pruiett Lobbies U.S. Congress for Oklahoma Statehood."

Waurika News-Democrat. Waurika, Oklahoma.

April 12, 1918, "Two jurists are Relieved of Snake Bit Cure"

May 3, 1918, "Pruiett and Maben to Face Liquor Charge."

Wichita Eagle. Wichita, Kansas.

April 3, 1907, "Haskell Ejected from Democratic Executive Committee Meeting in Tulsa."

Willburton, News, Wilburton, Oklahoma.

January 18, 1907, "Moman Pruiett Seems to be Cutting a High Dash."

Woodward News Bulletin. Woodward, Oklahoma.

August-September, 1911, "Maggie Miller Murder Case."

September 15, 1911, "Miller Gets Life Sentence."

Archives and Collections

Archives and Records Division. Oklahoma Historical Society. Oklahoma City, Oklahoma. Among its records are those of the federal court at Ardmore, where Pruiett was admitted to practice.

Howard K. Berry Collection. Oklahoma City, Oklahoma. Much of the original research for this work was compiled by Howard K. Berry in the late 1930s. This collection contains a number of pieces of correspondence, legal records, newspaper clippings, and other material relating to the life of Moman Pruiett. There are many personal recollections concerning Pruiett that were collected during the research for this book as well as Pruiett's office records. It also contains the judicial records of the District Court of Sebastian County, Arkansas, as relating to Pruiett's forgery trial; the District Court of Lamar County, Texas, as relating to Pruiett's robbery trial; and the Survey and Title Records, County Clerk's Office, Benton County, Arkansas. Records for the Federal Court for the Western District of Arkansas and the Eastern District of Texas, and Wise County, Texas, also are included, as are the official transcripts of many of Pruiett's cases.

Carter County, Oklahoma, District Court Records. Carter County Court Clerk Office. Ardmore, Oklahoma. Many of the records for Pruiett's cases, both in territorial and state courts, can be found among these records as well as information on prominent lawyers and judges.

Biographical Files. Library. Oklahoma Historical Society. Oklahoma City, Oklahoma. This contains numerous biographical entries for prominent people in Oklahoma Territory, Indian Territory, and the State of Oklahoma.

Cleveland County, Oklahoma, District Court. Cleveland County Court Clerk Office. Norman, Oklahoma. Many of the records for Pruiett's cases, both in territorial and state courts, can be found among these records including the case of *State of Oklahoma vs. Callie Pence* and *State of Oklahoma vs. John Jay.*

Gale Hamilton Johnson Collection. Oklahoma City, Oklahoma. Among the most valuable material is a "scrapbook" containing a myriad of entried pertaining to the life and career of Moman Pruiett.

Garvin County, Oklahoma, Land Records. Garvin County Clerk Office. Pauls Valley, Oklahoma. Copies of deeds and titles to property paid by clients to Pruiett are found in these records.

Garvin County, Oklahoma, District Court. Garvin County Court Clerk Office. Pauls Valley, Oklahoma. Many of the records involving Pruiett's cases can be found among these records including *Town of Pauls Valley vs. Moman Pruiett, United States vs. Moman Pruiett.*

Kay County, Oklahoma, District Court. Kay County Court Clerk Office. Ponca City, Oklahoma. The records of Pruiett's Kay County cases, including *State of Oklahoma vs. Napoleon Buffalohead,* are in this collection.

Love County, Oklahoma, District Court. Love County Court Clerk Office. Marietta, Oklahoma. Records of Pruiett's cases including State of Oklahoma vs. Cal Stewart. McClain County, Oklahoma, District Court. McClain County Court Clerk Office. Purcell, Oklahoma. Many of the records for Pruiett's cases, both in territorial and state courts, can be found among these records including the case of State of Oklahoma vs. Lee Sharp.

Oklahoma County, Oklahoma, District Court. Oklahoma County Court Clerk Office. Oklahoma City, Oklahoma. Many of the records for Pruiett's cases, both in territorial and state courts, can be found among these records including the cases of Territory of Oklahoma vs. Buck Garrett, State of Oklahoma vs. Lottie Baker, State of Oklahoma vs. D. V. Monroe, State of Oklahoma vs. W. T. Maness, and State of Oklahoma vs. W. A. Joslyn.

Oklahoma County, Oklahoma, Probate Court. Oklahoma County Court Clerk Office. Oklahoma City, Oklahoma. These records contain the information on Sam St. Mary's Insanity hearing.

Oklahoma Criminal Court of Appeals. Oklahoma City, Oklahoma. These records contain Pruiett's arguments filed before the appeals court on behalf of his clients including *State of Oklahoma vs. Agnes Gilbert.*

Oklahoma State Bar Association. Oklahoma City, Oklahoma. Much biographical information on pioneer lawyers and law offices in Oklahoma Territory, Indian Territory, and the State of Oklahoma can be found in these records as well as the case *L. E. Roberts vs. Moman Pruiett* which led to Pruiett's disbarment.

Oklahoma Supreme Court. Supreme Court Clerk Office. Oklahoma City, Oklahoma. These files contain the information relating to Pruiett's cases before the Oklahoma Supreme Court and Pruiett's appeal of his disbarment.

Phillips Collection. Library. University of Oklahoma. Norman, Oklahoma. Among its vast holdings on the American West, the Phillips Collection contains several items relating to the life and career of Pruiett.

Pittsburg County, Oklahoma, District Court. Pittsburg County Court Clerk

Office. McAlester, Oklahoma. Many of the records involving Pruiett's cases can be found among these records.

Records of the Federal Courts. Dallas Federal Building. Dallas, Texas. This collection contains most of the records for the Eastern District of Texas and the Northern District of Texas, including Pruiett being sworn in to practice law and other cases handled by him.

Rusk County, Texas District Court Records. Rusk County Court Clerk Office. Henderson, Texas. Among these records is the case of *State of Texas vs. Moorman Pruiett* in which Pruiett was tried and convicted of robbery.

Sebastian County, Arkansas, District Court. Sebastian County Court Clerk Office. Greenwood, Arkansas. Among these records is Pruiett's conviction and sentence for forgery on January 6, 1888.

United States District Court for the Eastern District of Oklahoma. Court Clerk Office. Muskogee, Oklahoma. Among these records is *United States vs. Moman Pruiett.*

United States District Court for the Western District of Oklahoma. Court Clerk Office. Oklahoma City, Oklahoma. Among these records are *United States vs. Joseph H. Goldstein* and *United States vs. John Jay.*

United States District Court for the Western District of Missouri. Court Clerk Office. Kansas City, Missouri. Records of Pruiett's motions, appeals, and cases before the federal court for the Western District of Missouri.

Washington County, Arkansas, Court Records. Washington County Court Clerk Office. Fayetteville, Arkansas. These contain the indictment and trial records for Pruiett's cases in Washington County, Arkansas.

Wise County, Texas District Court Records. Wise County Court Clerk Office. Decatur, Texas. Among these records is the case of *State of Texas vs. Dorsey Wilson.*